SUPERMAN

VOL. 4 MYTHOLOGICAL

SUPERMAN

VOL. 4 MYTHOLOGICAL

BRIAN MICHAEL BENDIS
writer

IVAN REIS | KEVIN MAGUIRE | JOHN TIMMS
pencillers

DANNY MIKI | KEVIN MAGUIRE | JOHN TIMMS | JOE PRADO
OCLAIR ALBERT | JULIO FERREIRA
inkers

ALEX SINCLAIR
colorist

DAVE SHARPE
letterer

IVAN REIS | JOE PRADO | ALEX SINCLAIR
collection cover artists

SUPERMAN created by **JERRY SIEGEL** and **JOE SHUSTER**
SUPERBOY created by **JERRY SIEGEL**
SUPERGIRL based on characters created by **JERRY SIEGEL**
By special arrangement with the **JERRY SIEGEL** family

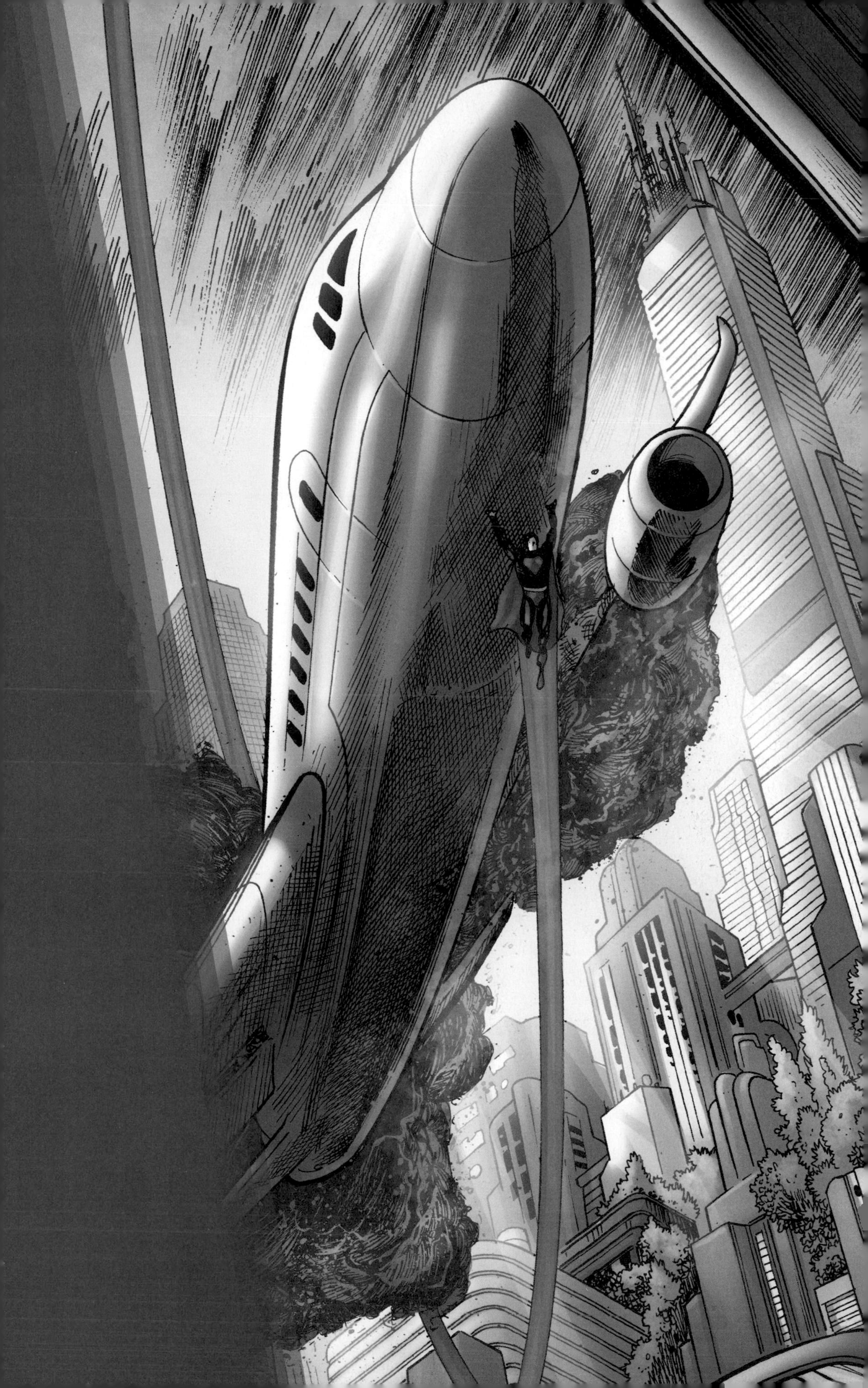

JAMIE S. RICH Editor – Original Series & Collected Edition
BRITTANY HOLZHERR Associate Editor – Original Series
BIXIE MATHIEU Assistant Editor – Original Series
STEVE COOK Design Director – Books
MONIQUE NARBONETA Publication Design
ERIN VANOVER Publication Production

MARIE JAVINS Editor-in-Chief, DC Comics

DANIEL CHERRY III Senior VP – General Manager
JIM LEE Publisher & Chief Creative Officer
DON FALLETTI VP – Manufacturing Operations & Workflow Management
LAWRENCE GANEM VP – Talent Services
ALISON GILL Senior VP – Manufacturing & Operations
NICK J. NAPOLITANO VP – Manufacturing Administration & Design
NANCY SPEARS VP – Revenue
MICHELE R. WELLS VP & Executive Editor, Young Reader

SUPERMAN VOL. 4: MYTHOLOGICAL

DC Comics, 2900 West Alameda Ave., Burbank, CA 91505
Printed by Solisco Printers, Scott, QC, Canada. 4/16/21. First Printing.
ISBN: 978-1-77950-572-9

Library of Congress Cataloging-in-Publication Data is available.

PEFC Certified

This product is from
sustainably managed
forests and controlled
sources

PEFC/26-31-02   www.pefc.org

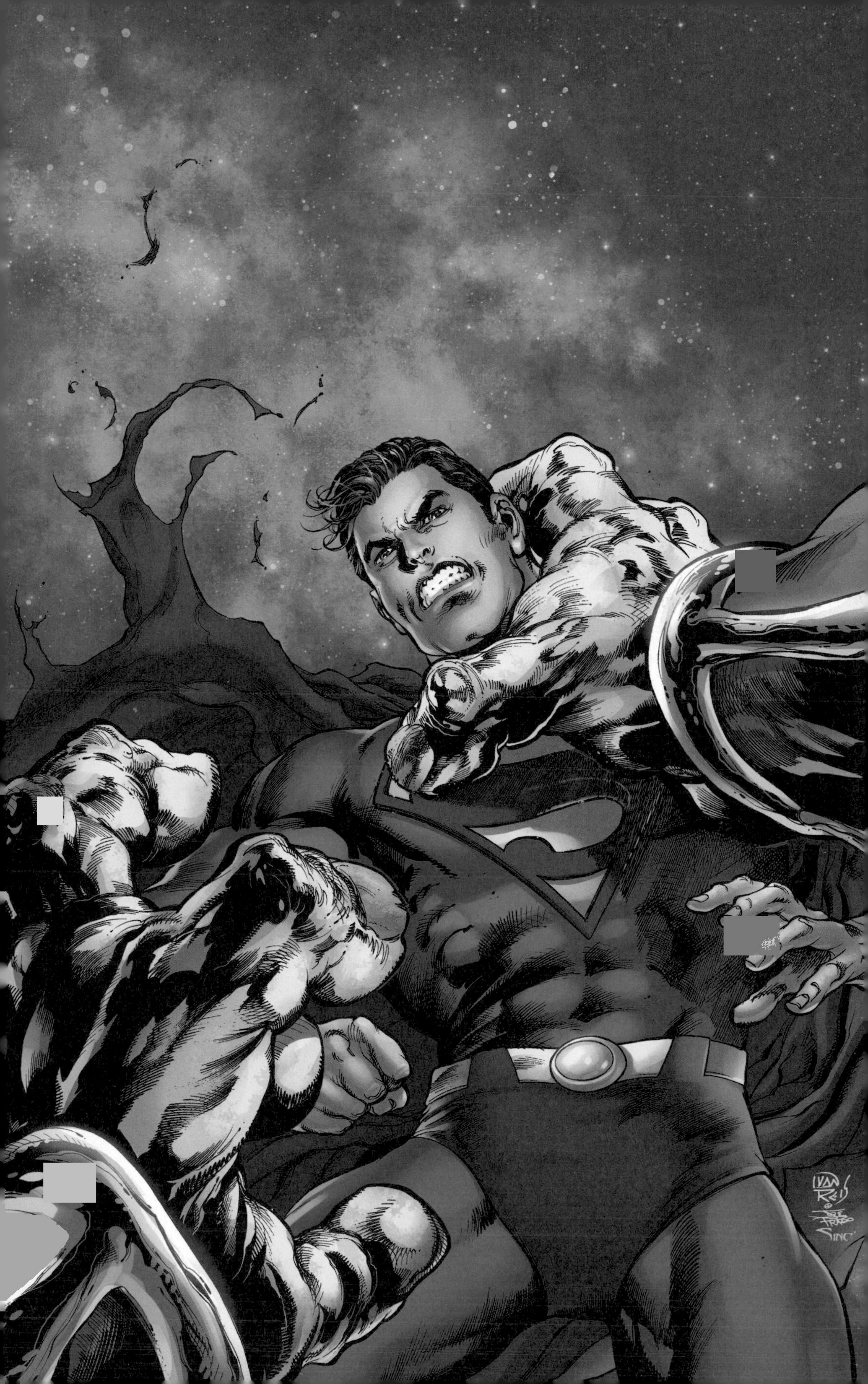

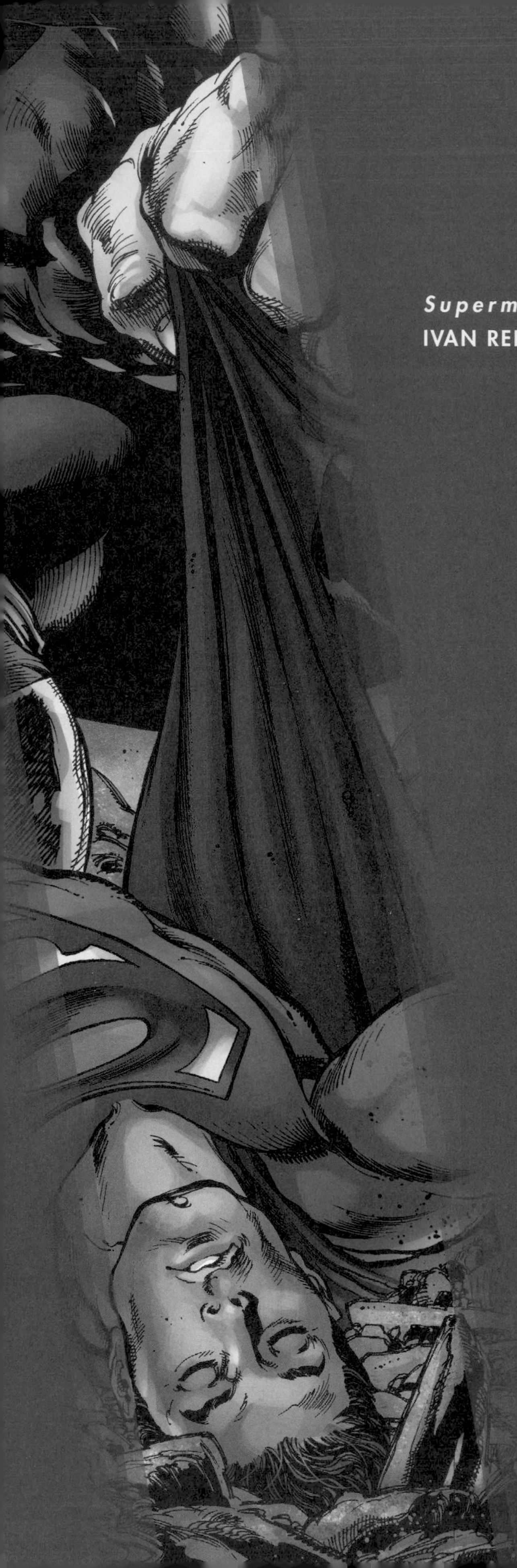

Superman #20 main cover by
IVAN REIS | JOE PRADO | ALEX SINCLAIR

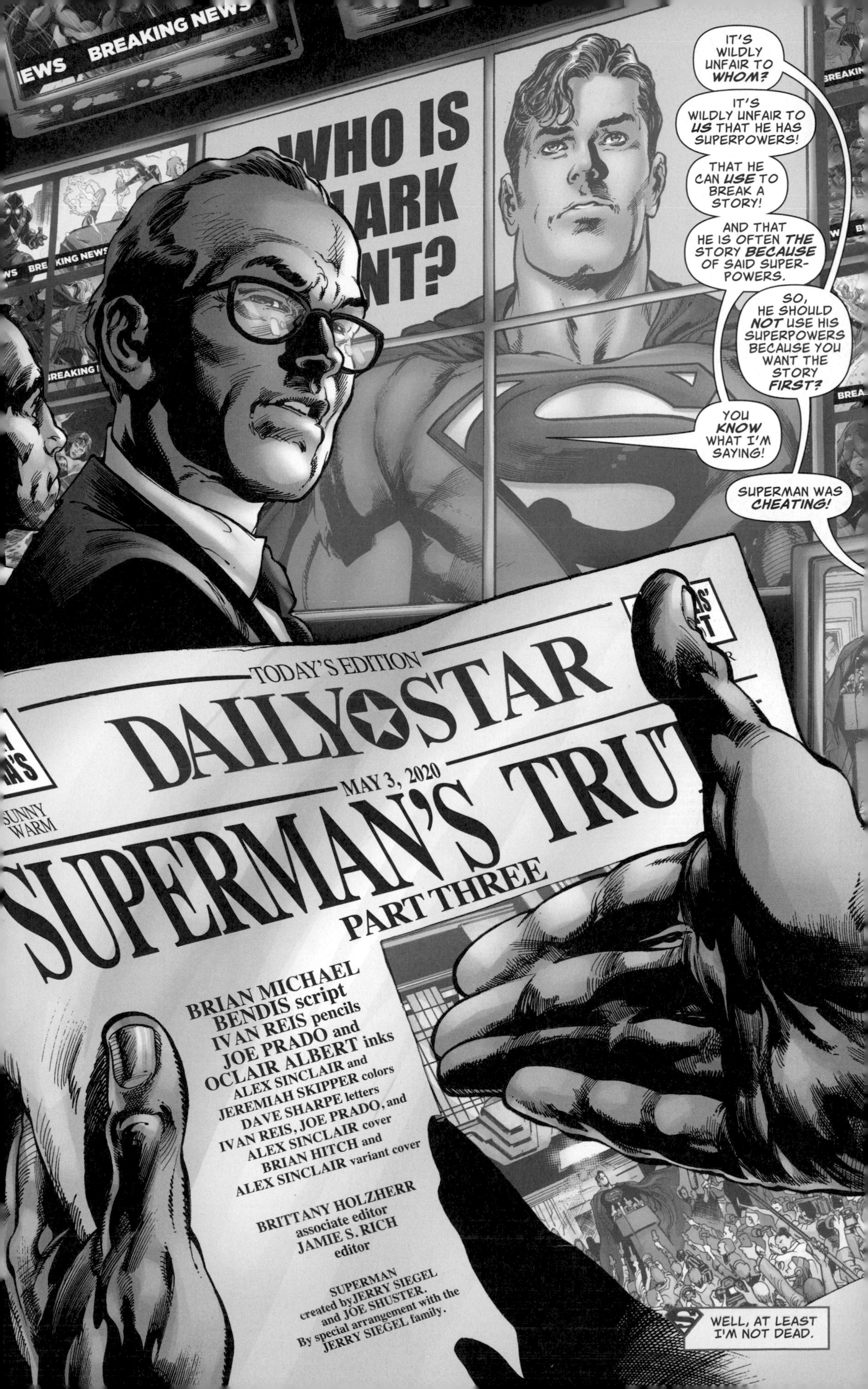
BREAKING NEWS
WHO IS
IT'S WILDLY UNFAIR TO *WHOM?*
IT'S WILDLY UNFAIR TO *US* THAT HE HAS SUPERPOWERS!
THAT HE CAN *USE* TO BREAK A STORY!
AND THAT HE IS OFTEN *THE* STORY *BECAUSE* OF SAID SUPER-POWERS.
SO, HE SHOULD *NOT* USE HIS SUPERPOWERS BECAUSE YOU WANT THE STORY *FIRST?*
YOU *KNOW* WHAT I'M SAYING!
SUPERMAN WAS *CHEATING!*
TODAY'S EDITION
DAILY STAR
MAY 3, 2020
SUNNY WARM
SUPERMAN'S TRU
PART THREE
BRIAN MICHAEL BENDIS script
IVAN REIS pencils
JOE PRADO and OCLAIR ALBERT inks
ALEX SINCLAIR and JEREMIAH SKIPPER colors
DAVE SHARPE letters
IVAN REIS, JOE PRADO, and ALEX SINCLAIR cover
BRIAN HITCH and ALEX SINCLAIR variant cover
BRITTANY HOLZHERR associate editor
JAMIE S. RICH editor
SUPERMAN created by JERRY SIEGEL and JOE SHUSTER. By special arrangement with the JERRY SIEGEL family.
WELL, AT LEAST I'M NOT DEAD.

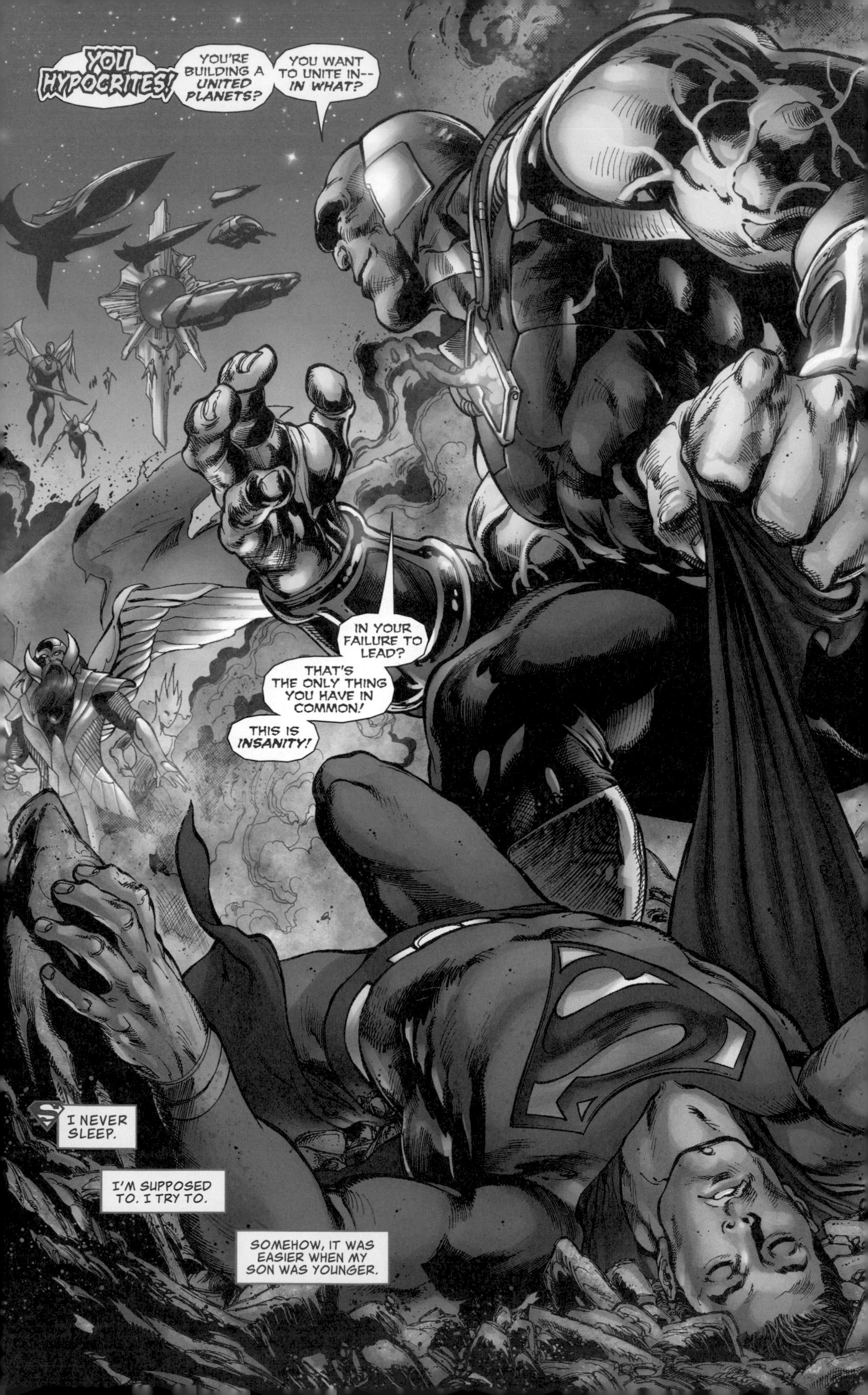
YOU HYPOCRITES!
YOU'RE BUILDING A UNITED PLANETS?
YOU WANT TO UNITE IN-- IN WHAT?
IN YOUR FAILURE TO LEAD?
THAT'S THE ONLY THING YOU HAVE IN COMMON!
THIS IS INSANITY!
I NEVER SLEEP.
I'M SUPPOSED TO. I TRY TO.
SOMEHOW, IT WAS EASIER WHEN MY SON WAS YOUNGER.

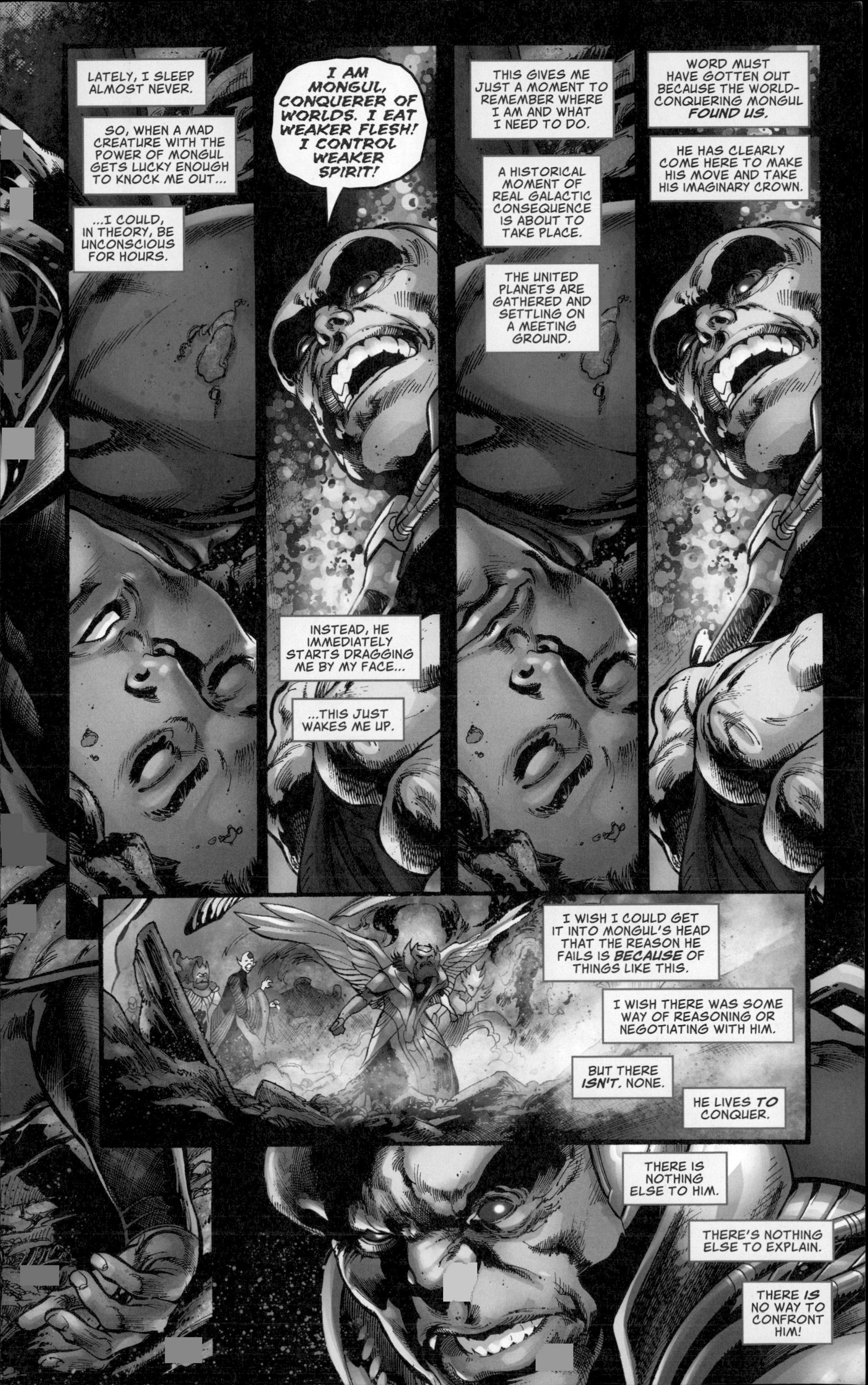
LATELY, I SLEEP ALMOST NEVER.
SO, WHEN A MAD CREATURE WITH THE POWER OF MONGUL GETS LUCKY ENOUGH TO KNOCK ME OUT...
...I COULD, IN THEORY, BE UNCONSCIOUS FOR HOURS.
I AM MONGUL, CONQUERER OF WORLDS. I EAT WEAKER FLESH! I CONTROL WEAKER SPIRIT!
INSTEAD, HE IMMEDIATELY STARTS DRAGGING ME BY MY FACE...
...THIS JUST WAKES ME UP.
THIS GIVES ME JUST A MOMENT TO REMEMBER WHERE I AM AND WHAT I NEED TO DO.
A HISTORICAL MOMENT OF REAL GALACTIC CONSEQUENCE IS ABOUT TO TAKE PLACE.
THE UNITED PLANETS ARE GATHERED AND SETTLING ON A MEETING GROUND.
WORD MUST HAVE GOTTEN OUT BECAUSE THE WORLD-CONQUERING MONGUL **FOUND US.**
HE HAS CLEARLY COME HERE TO MAKE HIS MOVE AND TAKE HIS IMAGINARY CROWN.
I WISH I COULD GET IT INTO MONGUL'S HEAD THAT THE REASON HE FAILS IS ***BECAUSE*** OF THINGS LIKE THIS.
I WISH THERE WAS SOME WAY OF REASONING OR NEGOTIATING WITH HIM.
BUT THERE ***ISN'T.*** NONE.
HE LIVES ***TO*** CONQUER.
THERE IS NOTHING ELSE TO HIM.
THERE'S NOTHING ELSE TO EXPLAIN.
THERE ***IS*** NO WAY TO CONFRONT HIM!

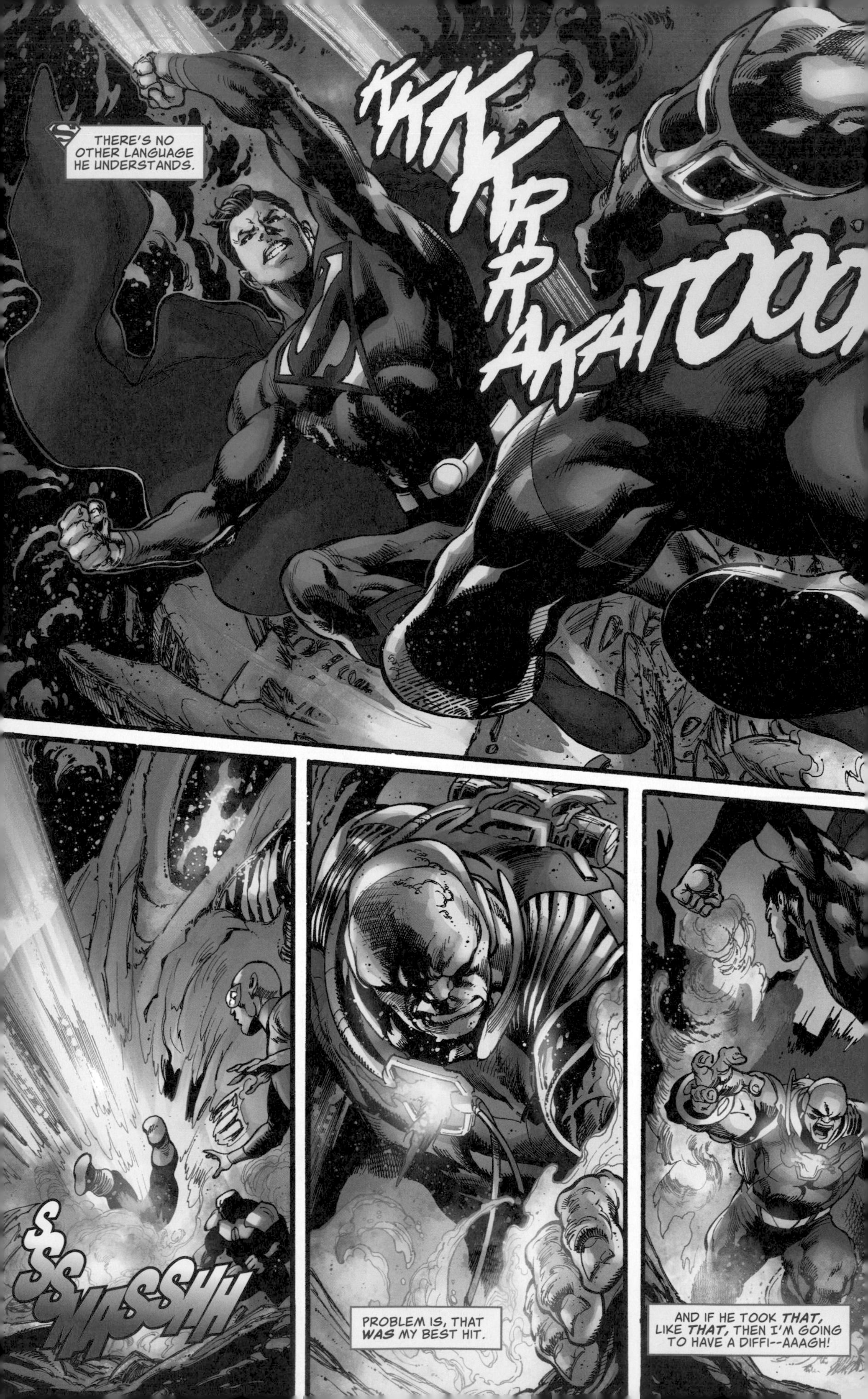
THERE'S NO OTHER LANGUAGE HE UNDERSTANDS.
SSMASSHH
PROBLEM IS, THAT **WAS** MY BEST HIT.
AND IF HE TOOK **THAT,** LIKE **THAT,** THEN I'M GOING TO HAVE A DIFFI--AAAGH!

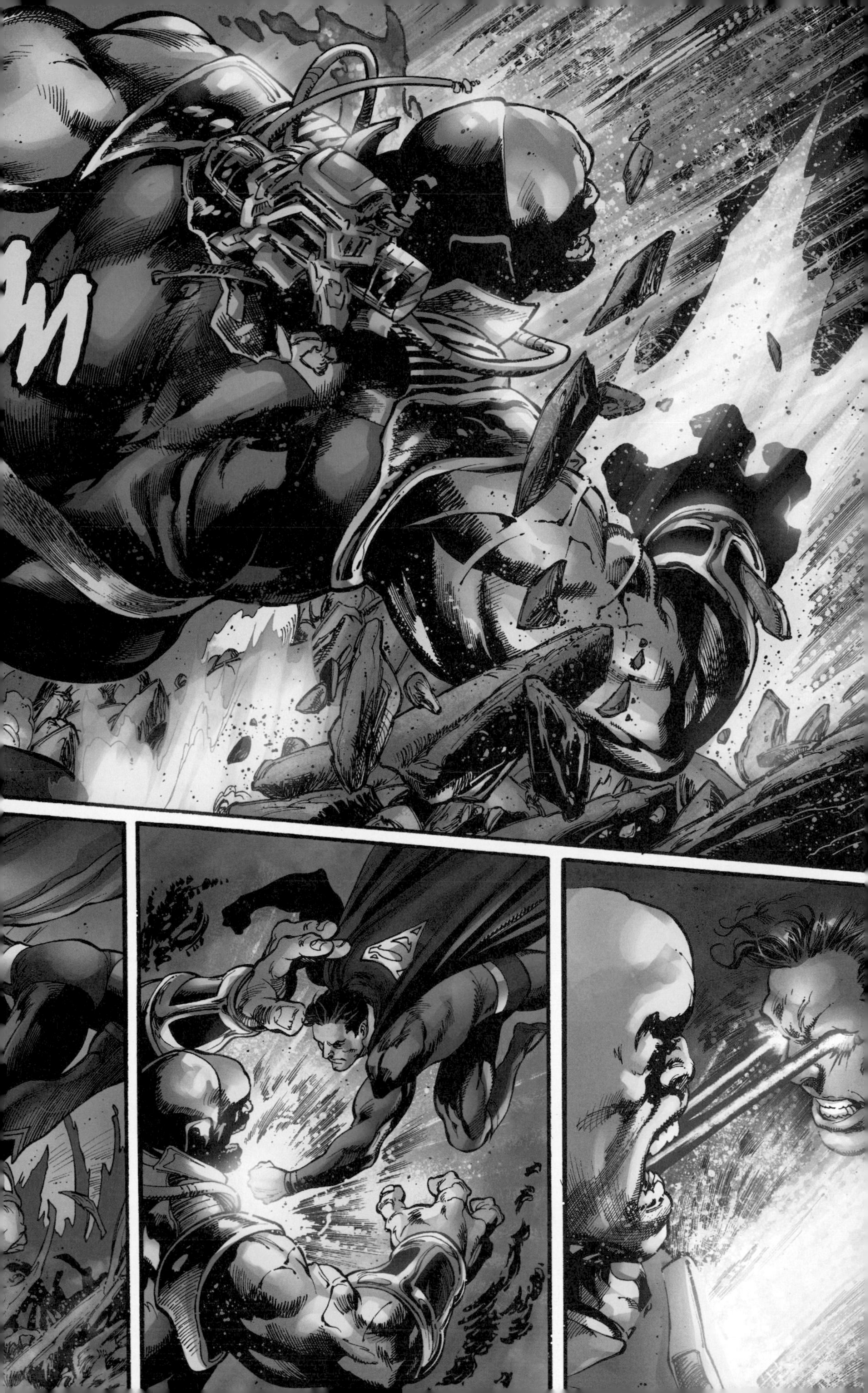

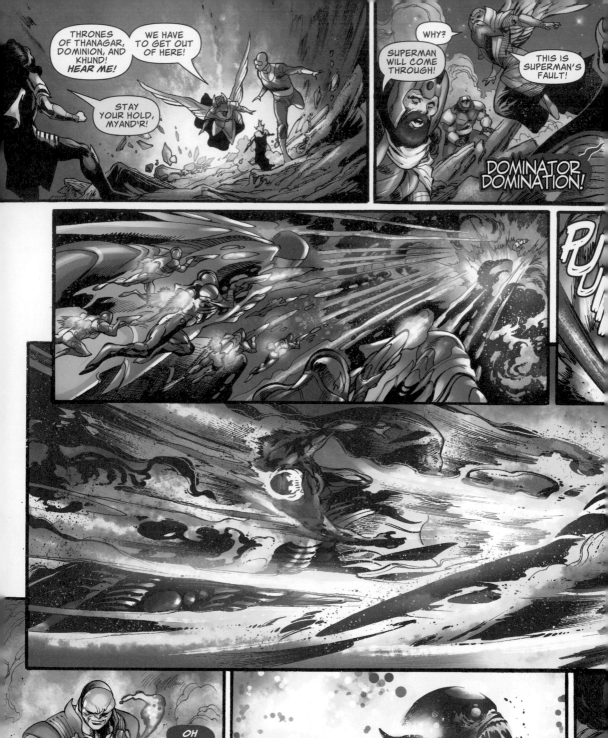

THRONES OF THANAGAR, DOMINION, AND KHUND! *HEAR ME!*

WE HAVE TO GET OUT OF HERE!

STAY YOUR HOLD, MYAND'R!

WHY? SUPERMAN WILL COME THROUGH!

THIS IS SUPERMAN'S FAULT!

DOMINATOR DOMINATION!

OH GODS!

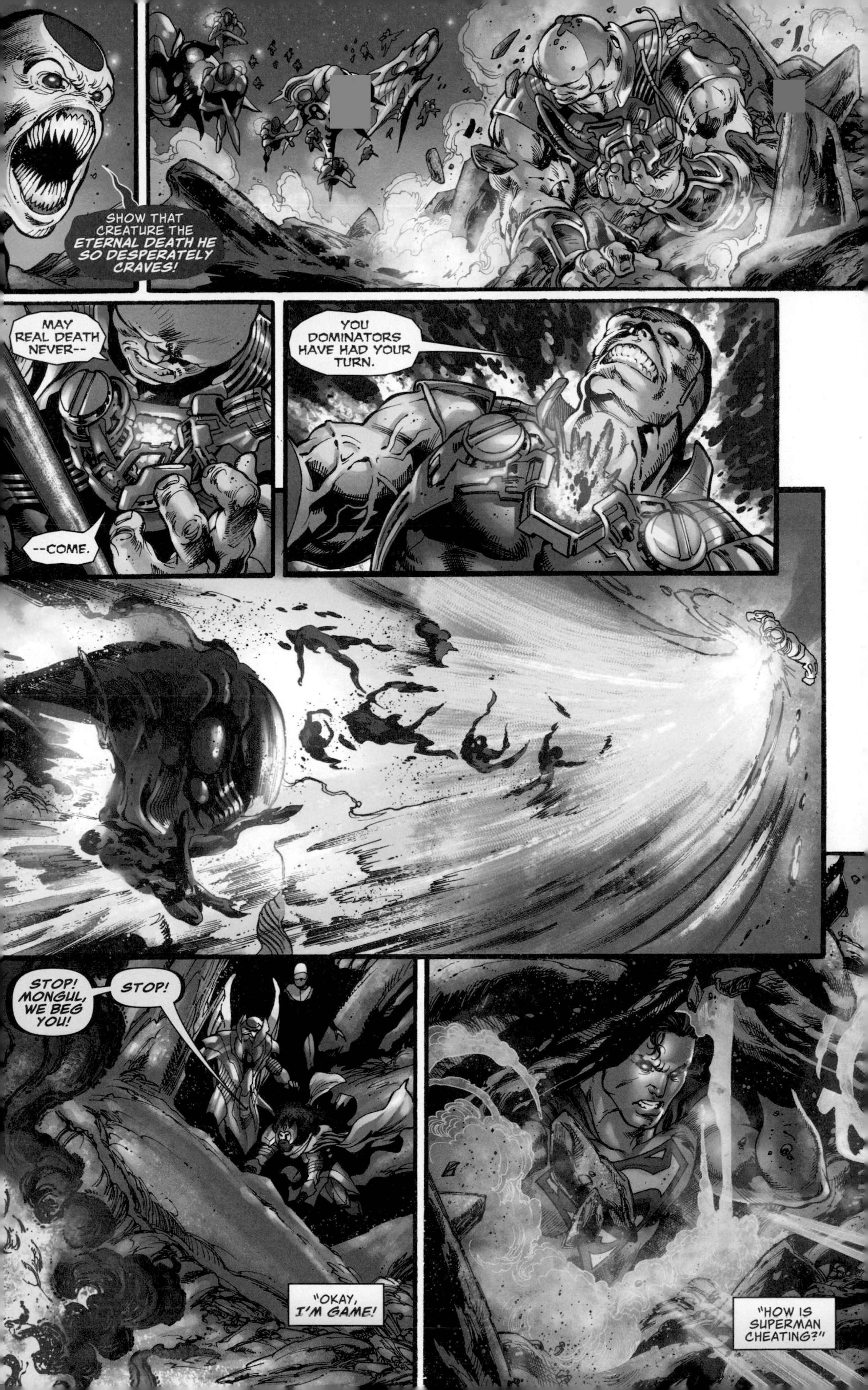
SHOW THAT CREATURE THE ETERNAL DEATH HE SO DESPERATELY CRAVES!
MAY REAL DEATH NEVER--
--COME.
YOU DOMINATORS HAVE HAD YOUR TURN.
STOP! MONGUL, WE BEG YOU!
STOP!
"OKAY, I'M GAME!
"HOW IS SUPERMAN CHEATING?"

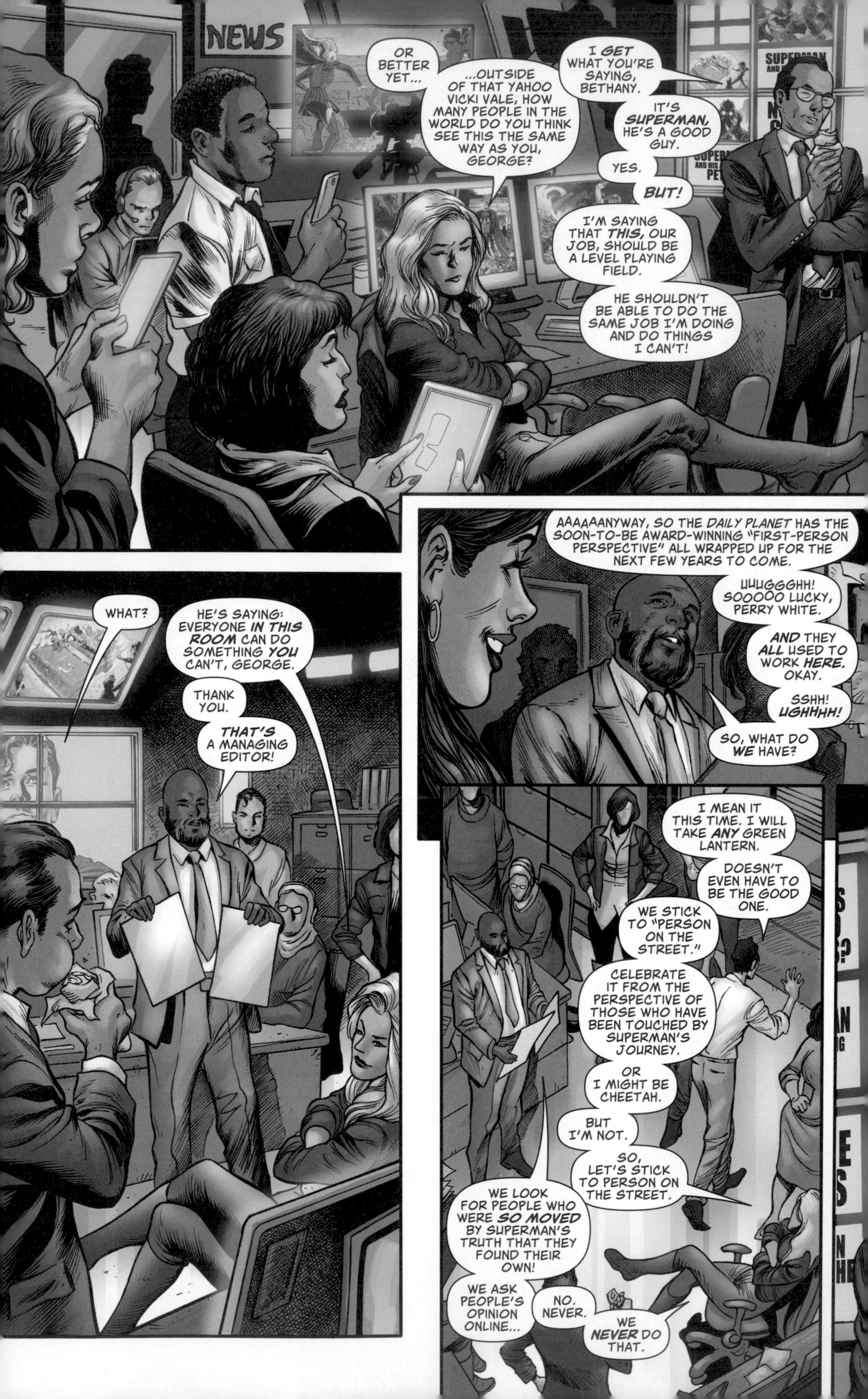
NEWS
OR BETTER YET...
...OUTSIDE OF THAT YAHOO VICKI VALE, HOW MANY PEOPLE IN THE WORLD DO YOU THINK SEE THIS THE SAME WAY AS YOU, GEORGE?
I *GET* WHAT YOU'RE SAYING, BETHANY.
IT'S *SUPERMAN,* HE'S A GOOD GUY.
YES.
BUT!
I'M SAYING THAT *THIS,* OUR JOB, SHOULD BE A LEVEL PLAYING FIELD.
HE SHOULDN'T BE ABLE TO DO THE SAME JOB I'M DOING AND DO THINGS I CAN'T!
WHAT?
HE'S SAYING: EVERYONE *IN THIS ROOM* CAN DO SOMETHING *YOU* CAN'T, GEORGE.
THANK YOU.
THAT'S A MANAGING EDITOR!
AAAAAANYWAY, SO THE *DAILY PLANET* HAS THE SOON-TO-BE AWARD-WINNING "FIRST-PERSON PERSPECTIVE" ALL WRAPPED UP FOR THE NEXT FEW YEARS TO COME.
UUUGGGHH! SOOOOO LUCKY, PERRY WHITE.
AND THEY *ALL* USED TO WORK *HERE.* OKAY.
SSHH! *UGHHHH!*
SO, WHAT DO *WE* HAVE?
I MEAN IT THIS TIME. I WILL TAKE *ANY* GREEN LANTERN.
DOESN'T EVEN HAVE TO BE THE GOOD ONE.
WE STICK TO "PERSON ON THE STREET."
CELEBRATE IT FROM THE PERSPECTIVE OF THOSE WHO HAVE BEEN TOUCHED BY SUPERMAN'S JOURNEY.
OR I MIGHT BE CHEETAH.
BUT I'M NOT.
SO, LET'S STICK TO PERSON ON THE STREET.
WE LOOK FOR PEOPLE WHO WERE *SO MOVED* BY SUPERMAN'S TRUTH THAT THEY FOUND THEIR OWN!
WE ASK PEOPLE'S OPINION ONLINE...
NO. NEVER.
WE *NEVER* DO THAT.

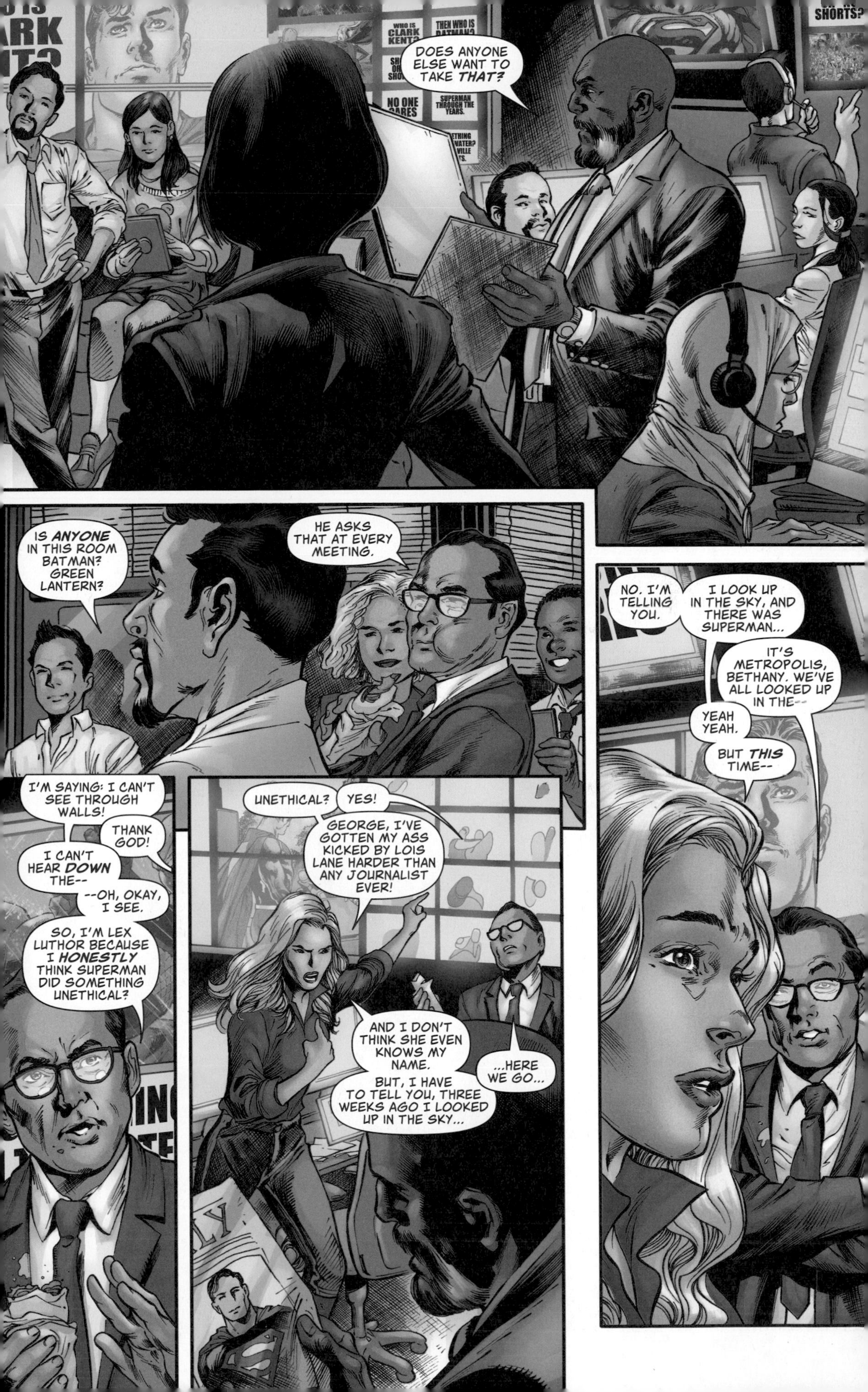
WHO IS CLARK KENT?
THEN WHO IS BATMAN?
NO ONE CARES
SUPERMAN THROUGH THE YEARS.
SHORTS?
DOES ANYONE ELSE WANT TO TAKE *THAT?*
IS *ANYONE* IN THIS ROOM BATMAN? GREEN LANTERN?
HE ASKS THAT AT EVERY MEETING.
I'M SAYING: I CAN'T SEE THROUGH WALLS!
THANK GOD!
I CAN'T HEAR *DOWN* THE--
--OH, OKAY, I SEE.
SO, I'M LEX LUTHOR BECAUSE I *HONESTLY* THINK SUPERMAN DID SOMETHING UNETHICAL?
UNETHICAL?
YES!
GEORGE, I'VE GOTTEN MY ASS KICKED BY LOIS LANE HARDER THAN ANY JOURNALIST EVER!
AND I DON'T THINK SHE EVEN KNOWS MY NAME.
BUT, I HAVE TO TELL YOU, THREE WEEKS AGO I LOOKED UP IN THE SKY...
...HERE WE GO...
NO. I'M TELLING YOU.
I LOOK UP IN THE SKY, AND THERE WAS SUPERMAN...
IT'S METROPOLIS, BETHANY. WE'VE ALL LOOKED UP IN THE--
YEAH YEAH.
BUT *THIS* TIME--

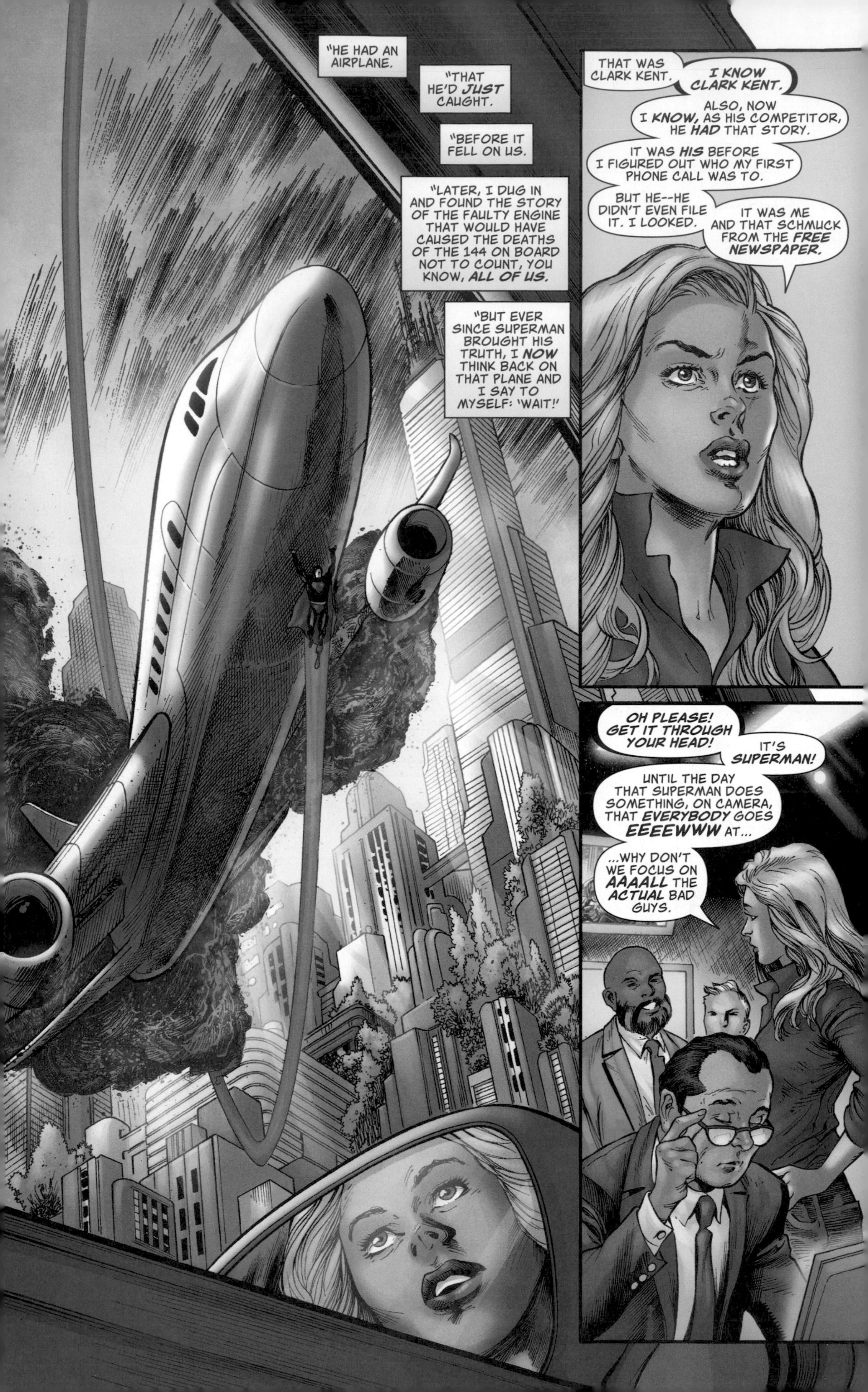

"HE HAD AN AIRPLANE.
"THAT HE'D JUST CAUGHT.
"BEFORE IT FELL ON US.
"LATER, I DUG IN AND FOUND THE STORY OF THE FAULTY ENGINE THAT WOULD HAVE CAUSED THE DEATHS OF THE 144 ON BOARD NOT TO COUNT, YOU KNOW, ALL OF US.
"BUT EVER SINCE SUPERMAN BROUGHT HIS TRUTH, I NOW THINK BACK ON THAT PLANE AND I SAY TO MYSELF: 'WAIT!'
THAT WAS CLARK KENT.
I KNOW CLARK KENT.
ALSO, NOW I KNOW, AS HIS COMPETITOR, HE HAD THAT STORY.
IT WAS HIS BEFORE I FIGURED OUT WHO MY FIRST PHONE CALL WAS TO.
BUT HE--HE DIDN'T EVEN FILE IT. I LOOKED.
IT WAS ME AND THAT SCHMUCK FROM THE FREE NEWSPAPER.
OH PLEASE! GET IT THROUGH YOUR HEAD!
IT'S SUPERMAN!
UNTIL THE DAY THAT SUPERMAN DOES SOMETHING, ON CAMERA, THAT EVERYBODY GOES EEEEWWW AT...
...WHY DON'T WE FOCUS ON AAAALL THE ACTUAL BAD GUYS.

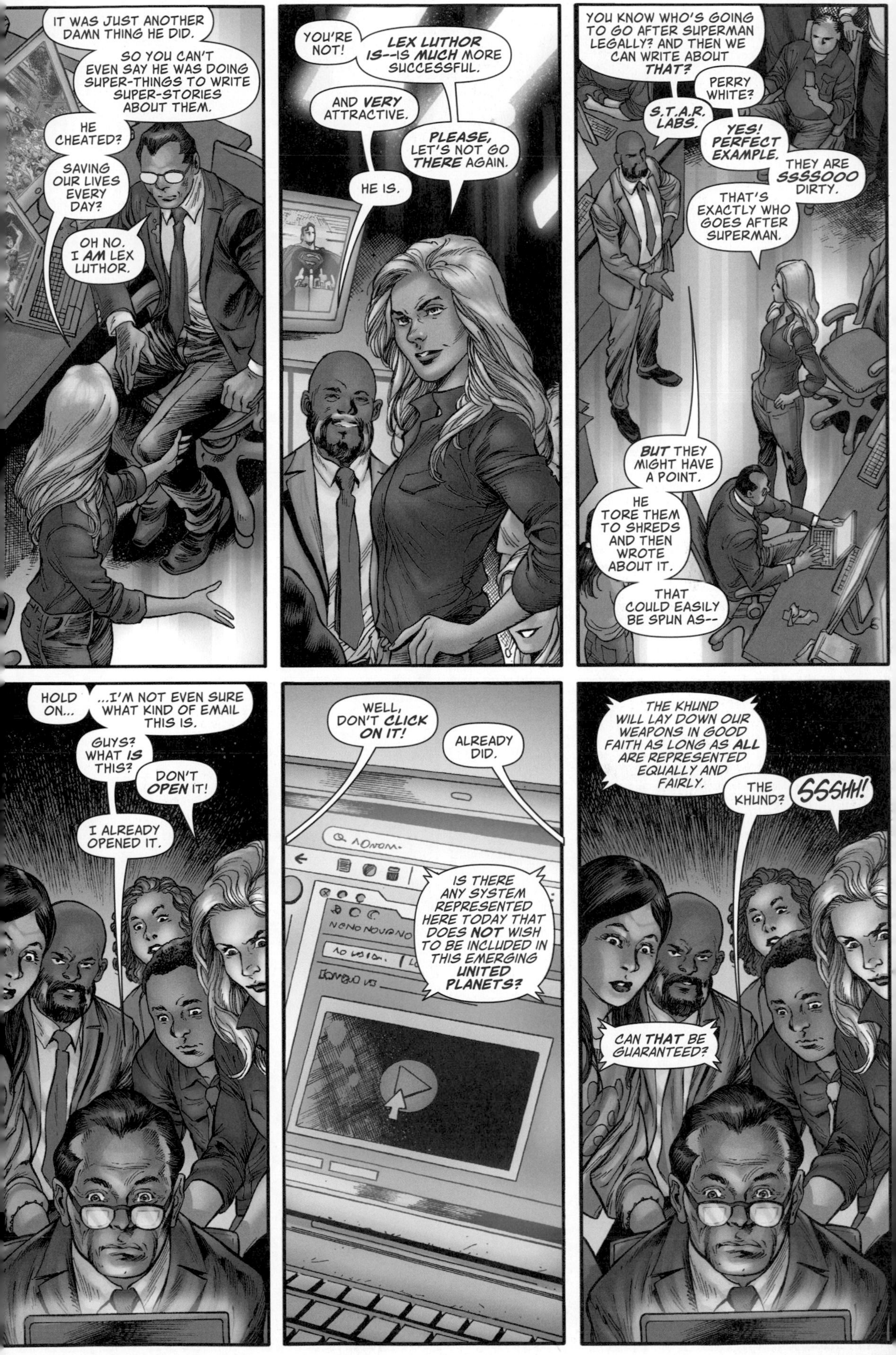
IT WAS JUST ANOTHER DAMN THING HE DID.
SO YOU CAN'T EVEN SAY HE WAS DOING SUPER-THINGS TO WRITE SUPER-STORIES ABOUT THEM.
HE CHEATED?
SAVING OUR LIVES EVERY DAY?
OH NO. I AM LEX LUTHOR.
YOU'RE NOT!
LEX LUTHOR IS--IS MUCH MORE SUCCESSFUL.
AND VERY ATTRACTIVE.
PLEASE, LET'S NOT GO THERE AGAIN.
HE IS.
YOU KNOW WHO'S GOING TO GO AFTER SUPERMAN LEGALLY? AND THEN WE CAN WRITE ABOUT THAT?
PERRY WHITE?
S.T.A.R. LABS.
YES! PERFECT EXAMPLE.
THEY ARE SSSSOOO DIRTY.
THAT'S EXACTLY WHO GOES AFTER SUPERMAN.
BUT THEY MIGHT HAVE A POINT.
HE TORE THEM TO SHREDS AND THEN WROTE ABOUT IT.
THAT COULD EASILY BE SPUN AS--
HOLD ON...
...I'M NOT EVEN SURE WHAT KIND OF EMAIL THIS IS.
GUYS? WHAT IS THIS?
DON'T OPEN IT!
I ALREADY OPENED IT.
WELL, DON'T CLICK ON IT!
ALREADY DID.
IS THERE ANY SYSTEM REPRESENTED HERE TODAY THAT DOES NOT WISH TO BE INCLUDED IN THIS EMERGING UNITED PLANETS?
THE KHUND WILL LAY DOWN OUR WEAPONS IN GOOD FAITH AS LONG AS ALL ARE REPRESENTED EQUALLY AND FAIRLY.
THE KHUND?
SSSHH!
CAN THAT BE GUARANTEED?

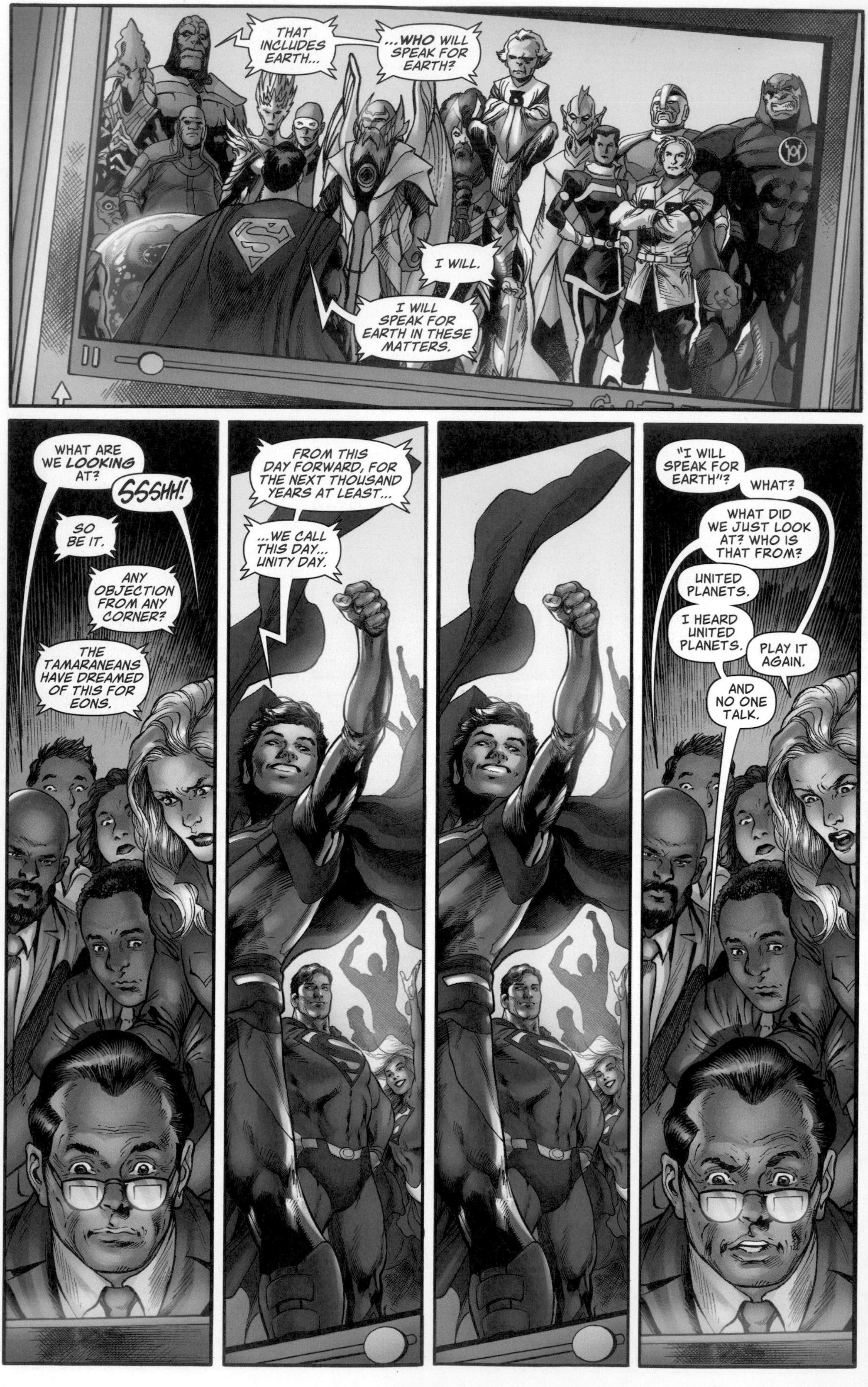
THAT INCLUDES EARTH...
...WHO WILL SPEAK FOR EARTH?
I WILL.
I WILL SPEAK FOR EARTH IN THESE MATTERS.
WHAT ARE WE LOOKING AT?
SSSHH!
SO BE IT.
ANY OBJECTION FROM ANY CORNER?
THE TAMARANEANS HAVE DREAMED OF THIS FOR EONS.
FROM THIS DAY FORWARD, FOR THE NEXT THOUSAND YEARS AT LEAST...
...WE CALL THIS DAY... UNITY DAY.
"I WILL SPEAK FOR EARTH"?
WHAT?
WHAT DID WE JUST LOOK AT? WHO IS THAT FROM?
UNITED PLANETS.
I HEARD UNITED PLANETS.
PLAY IT AGAIN.
AND NO ONE TALK.

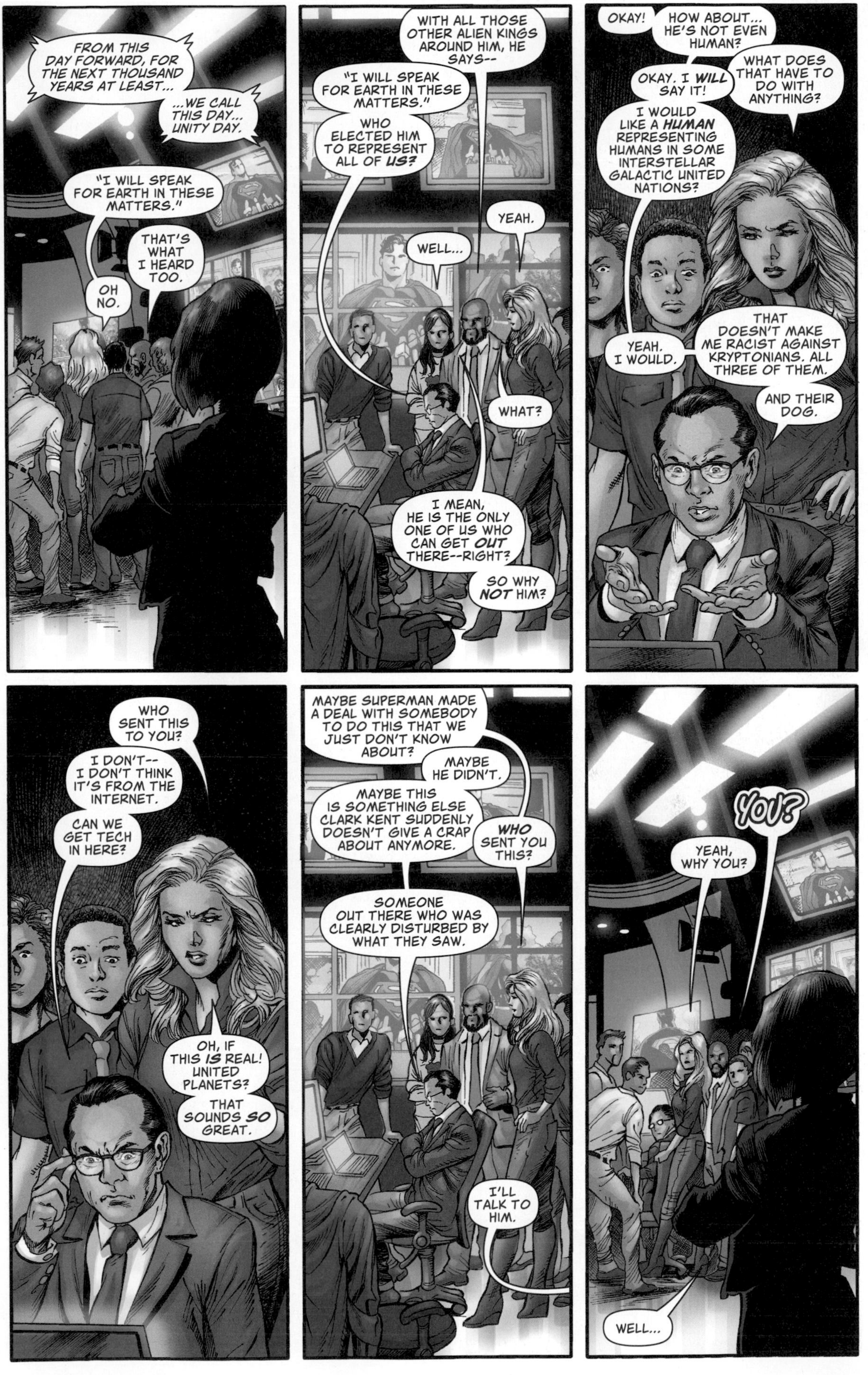
FROM THIS DAY FORWARD, FOR THE NEXT THOUSAND YEARS AT LEAST...
...WE CALL THIS DAY... UNITY DAY.
"I WILL SPEAK FOR EARTH IN THESE MATTERS."
OH NO.
THAT'S WHAT I HEARD TOO.
WITH ALL THOSE OTHER ALIEN KINGS AROUND HIM, HE SAYS--
"I WILL SPEAK FOR EARTH IN THESE MATTERS."
WHO ELECTED HIM TO REPRESENT ALL OF US?
YEAH.
WELL...
WHAT?
I MEAN, HE IS THE ONLY ONE OF US WHO CAN GET OUT THERE--RIGHT?
SO WHY NOT HIM?
OKAY!
HOW ABOUT... HE'S NOT EVEN HUMAN?
WHAT DOES THAT HAVE TO DO WITH ANYTHING?
OKAY. I WILL SAY IT!
I WOULD LIKE A HUMAN REPRESENTING HUMANS IN SOME INTERSTELLAR GALACTIC UNITED NATIONS?
YEAH. I WOULD.
THAT DOESN'T MAKE ME RACIST AGAINST KRYPTONIANS. ALL THREE OF THEM.
AND THEIR DOG.
WHO SENT THIS TO YOU?
I DON'T-- I DON'T THINK IT'S FROM THE INTERNET.
CAN WE GET TECH IN HERE?
OH, IF THIS IS REAL! UNITED PLANETS?
THAT SOUNDS SO GREAT.
MAYBE SUPERMAN MADE A DEAL WITH SOMEBODY TO DO THIS THAT WE JUST DON'T KNOW ABOUT?
MAYBE HE DIDN'T.
MAYBE THIS IS SOMETHING ELSE CLARK KENT SUDDENLY DOESN'T GIVE A CRAP ABOUT ANYMORE.
WHO SENT YOU THIS?
SOMEONE OUT THERE WHO WAS CLEARLY DISTURBED BY WHAT THEY SAW.
I'LL TALK TO HIM.
YOU?
YEAH, WHY YOU?
WELL...

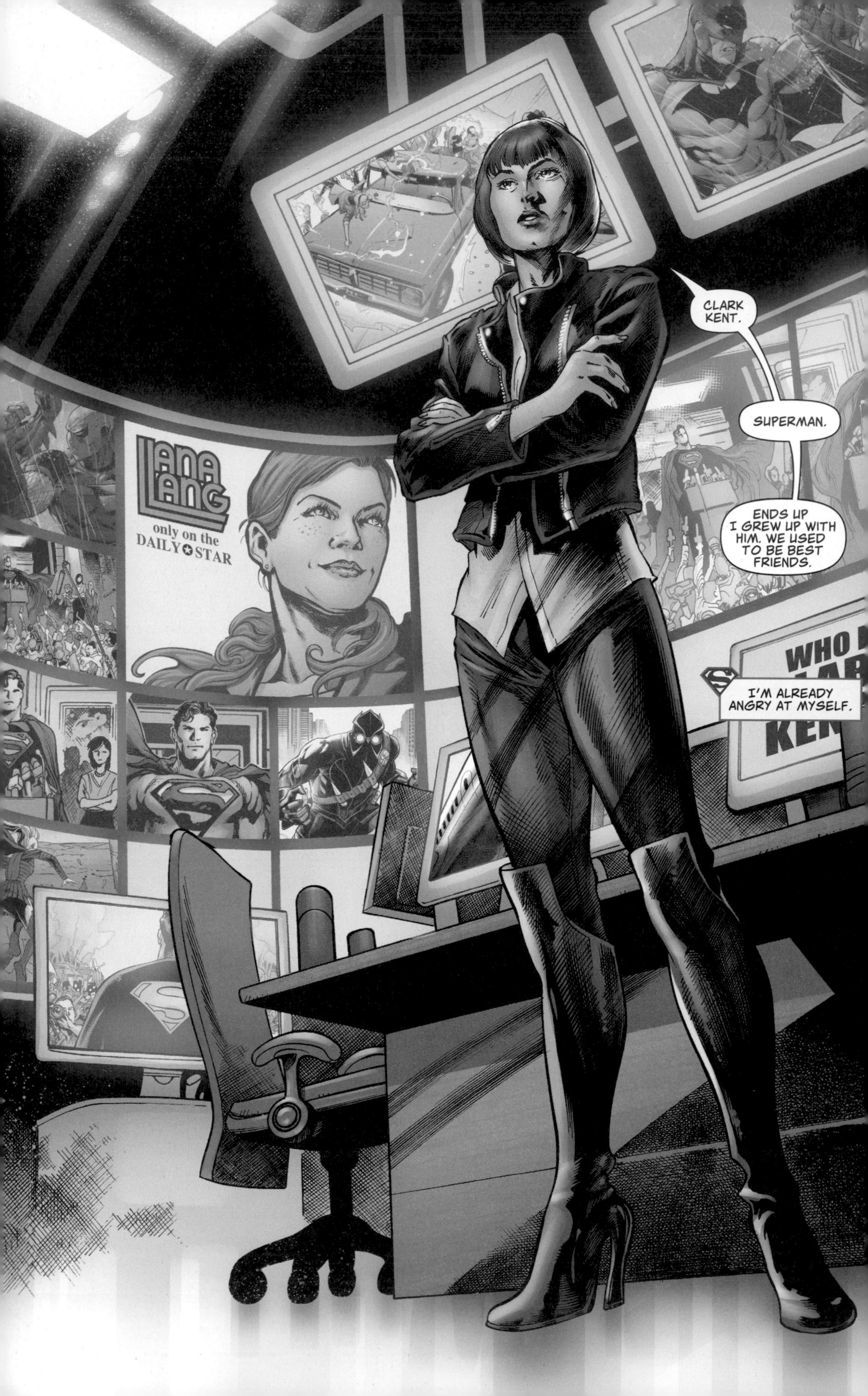
LANA LANG
only on the DAILY STAR
CLARK KENT.
SUPERMAN.
ENDS UP I GREW UP WITH HIM. WE USED TO BE BEST FRIENDS.
I'M ALREADY ANGRY AT MYSELF.

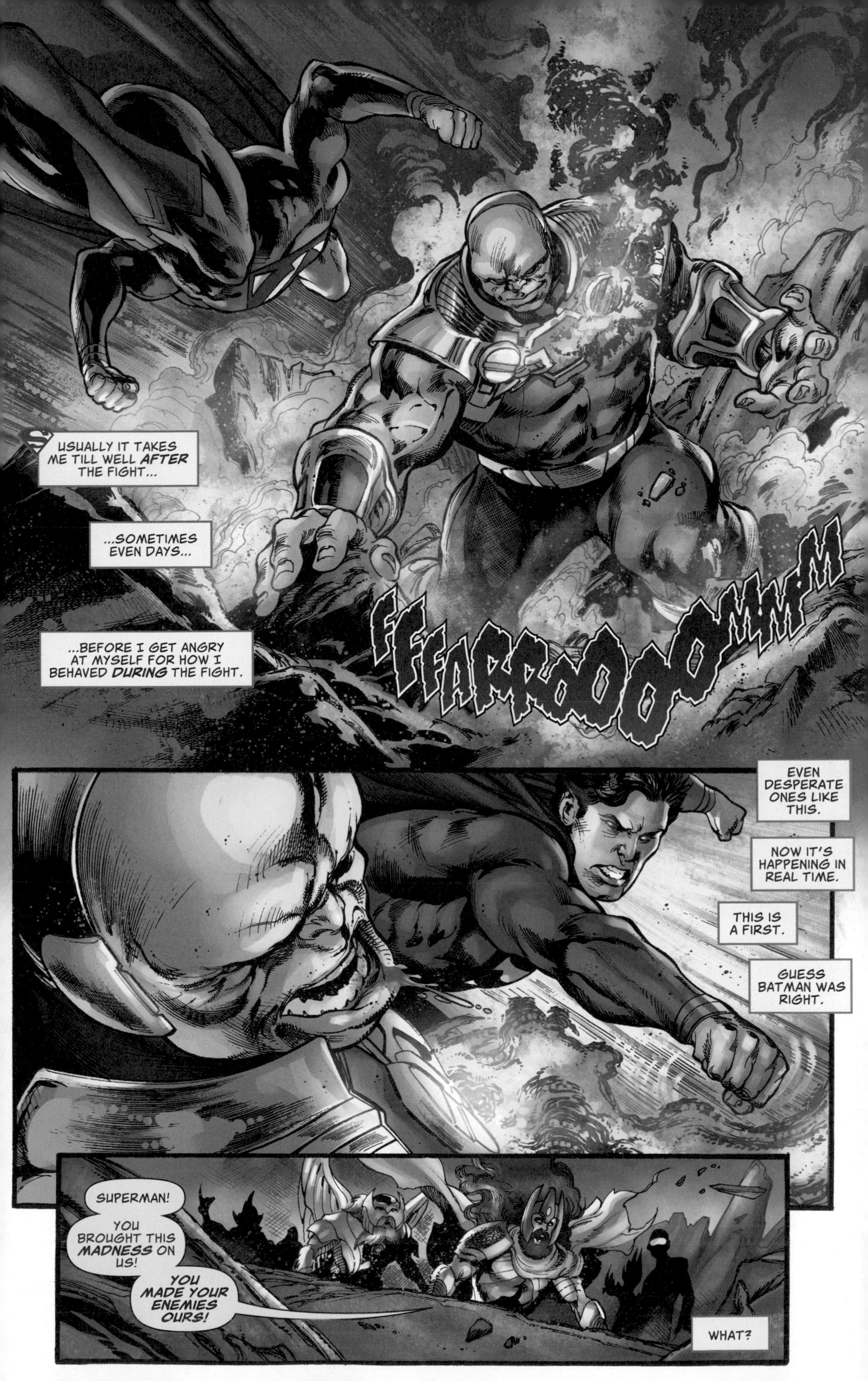
USUALLY IT TAKES ME TILL WELL AFTER THE FIGHT...
...SOMETIMES EVEN DAYS...
...BEFORE I GET ANGRY AT MYSELF FOR HOW I BEHAVED DURING THE FIGHT.
FFFARROOOOOMMMM
EVEN DESPERATE ONES LIKE THIS.
NOW IT'S HAPPENING IN REAL TIME.
THIS IS A FIRST.
GUESS BATMAN WAS RIGHT.
SUPERMAN!
YOU BROUGHT THIS MADNESS ON US!
YOU MADE YOUR ENEMIES OURS!
WHAT?

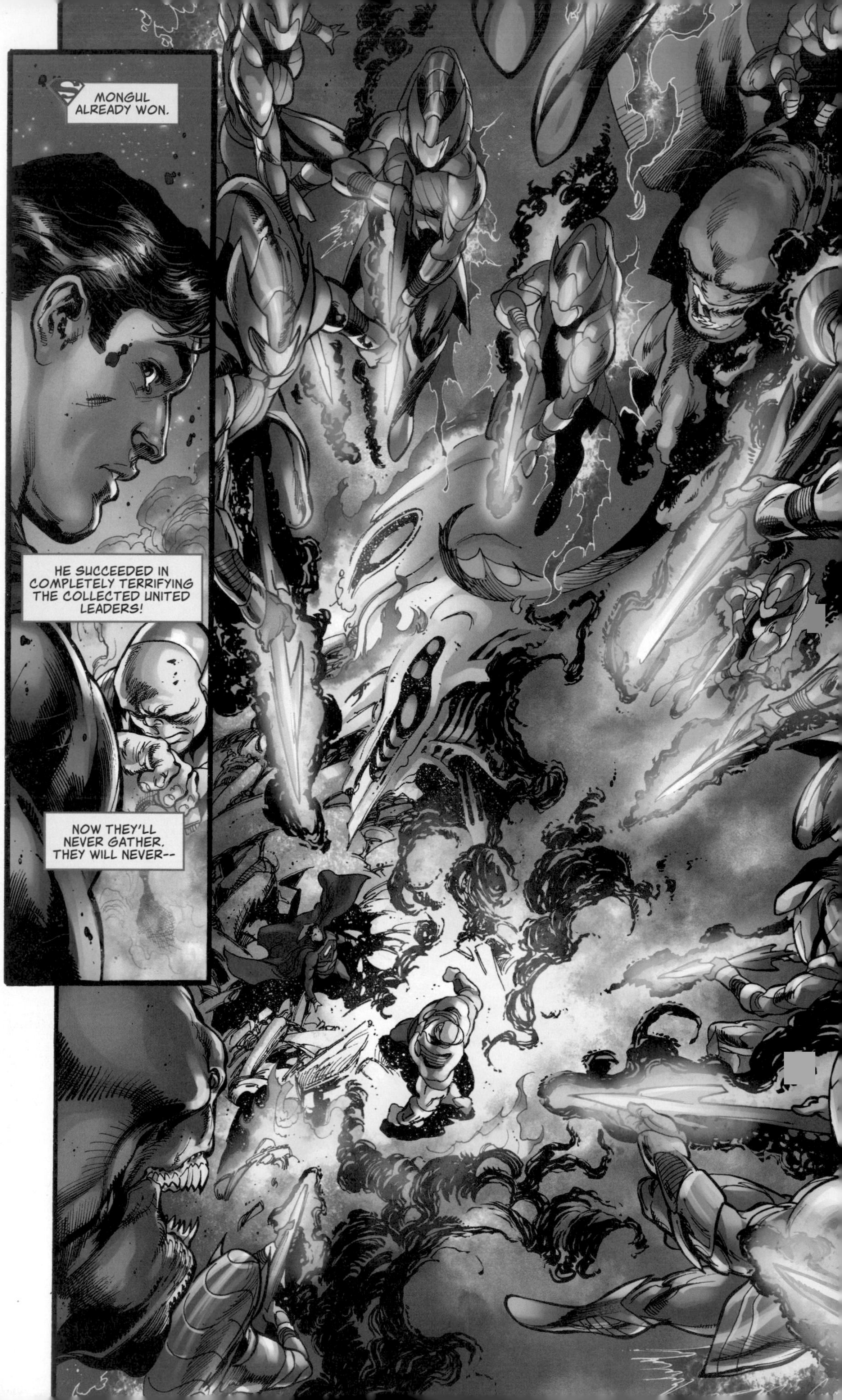
MONGUL ALREADY WON.
HE SUCCEEDED IN COMPLETELY TERRIFYING THE COLLECTED UNITED LEADERS!
NOW THEY'LL NEVER GATHER. THEY WILL NEVER--

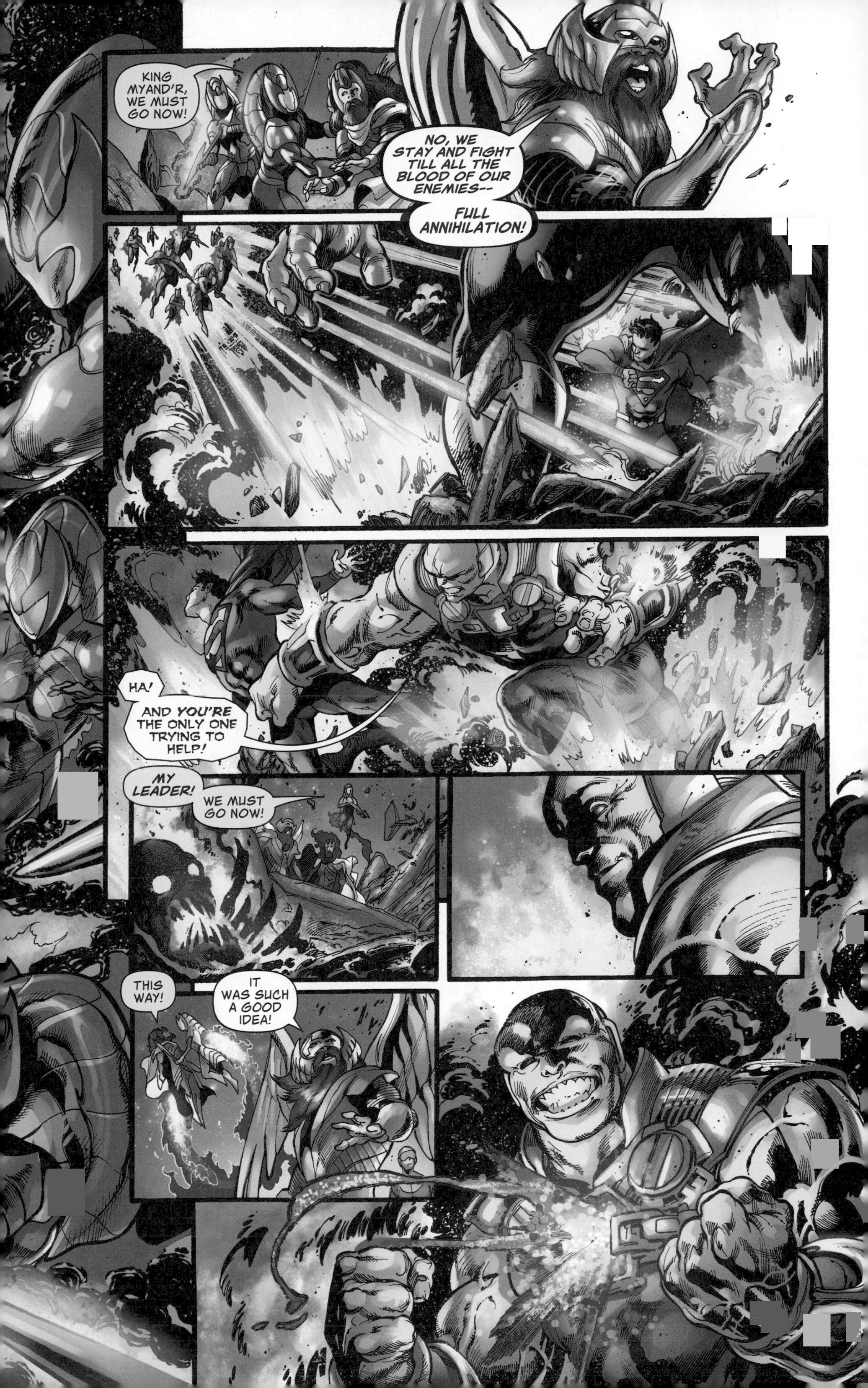
KING MYAND'R, WE MUST GO NOW!
NO, WE STAY AND FIGHT TILL ALL THE BLOOD OF OUR ENEMIES--
FULL ANNIHILATION!
HA!
AND YOU'RE THE ONLY ONE TRYING TO HELP!
MY LEADER!
WE MUST GO NOW!
THIS WAY!
IT WAS SUCH A GOOD IDEA!

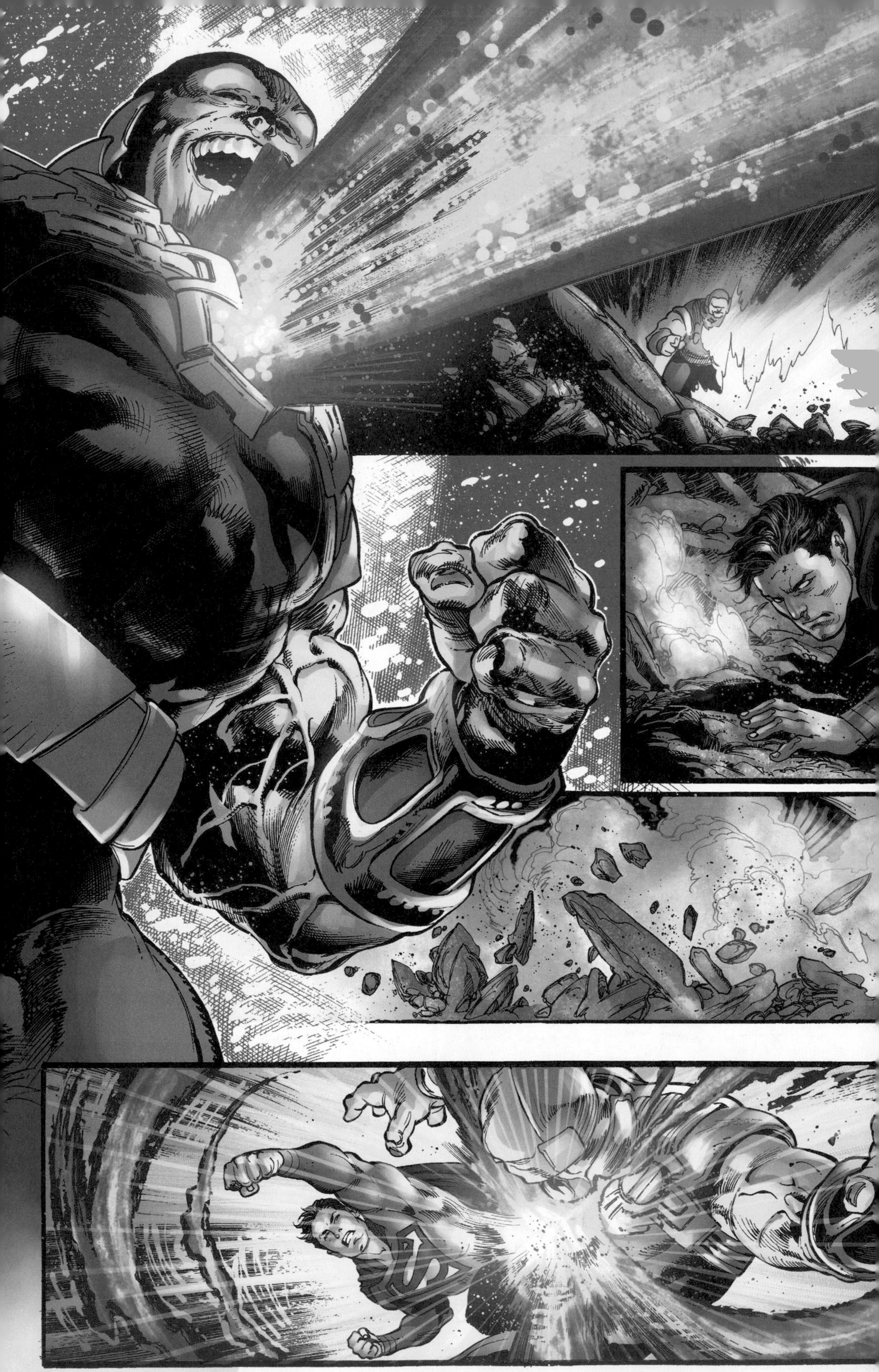

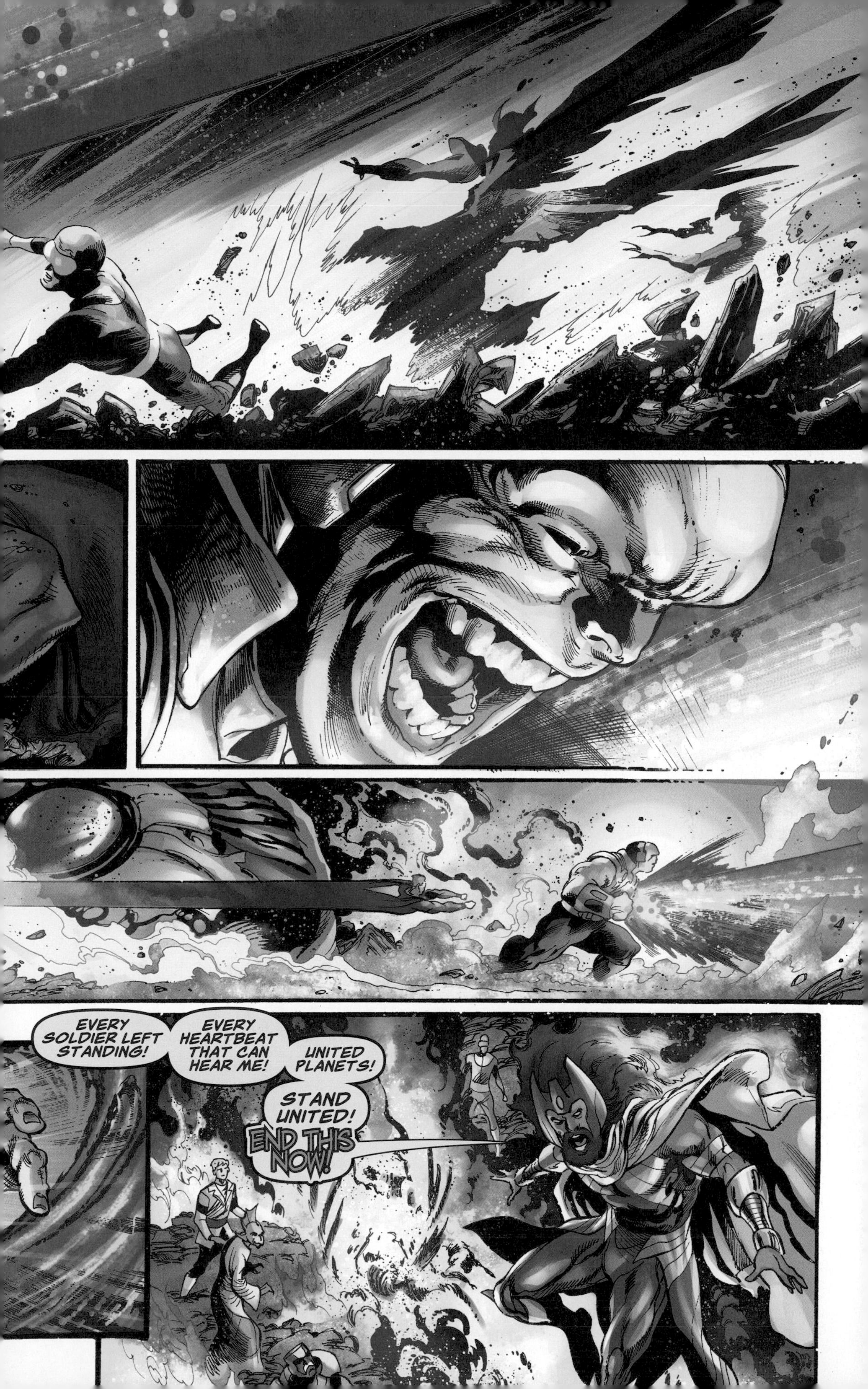
EVERY SOLDIER LEFT STANDING!
EVERY HEARTBEAT THAT CAN HEAR ME!
UNITED PLANETS!
STAND UNITED!
END THIS NOW!

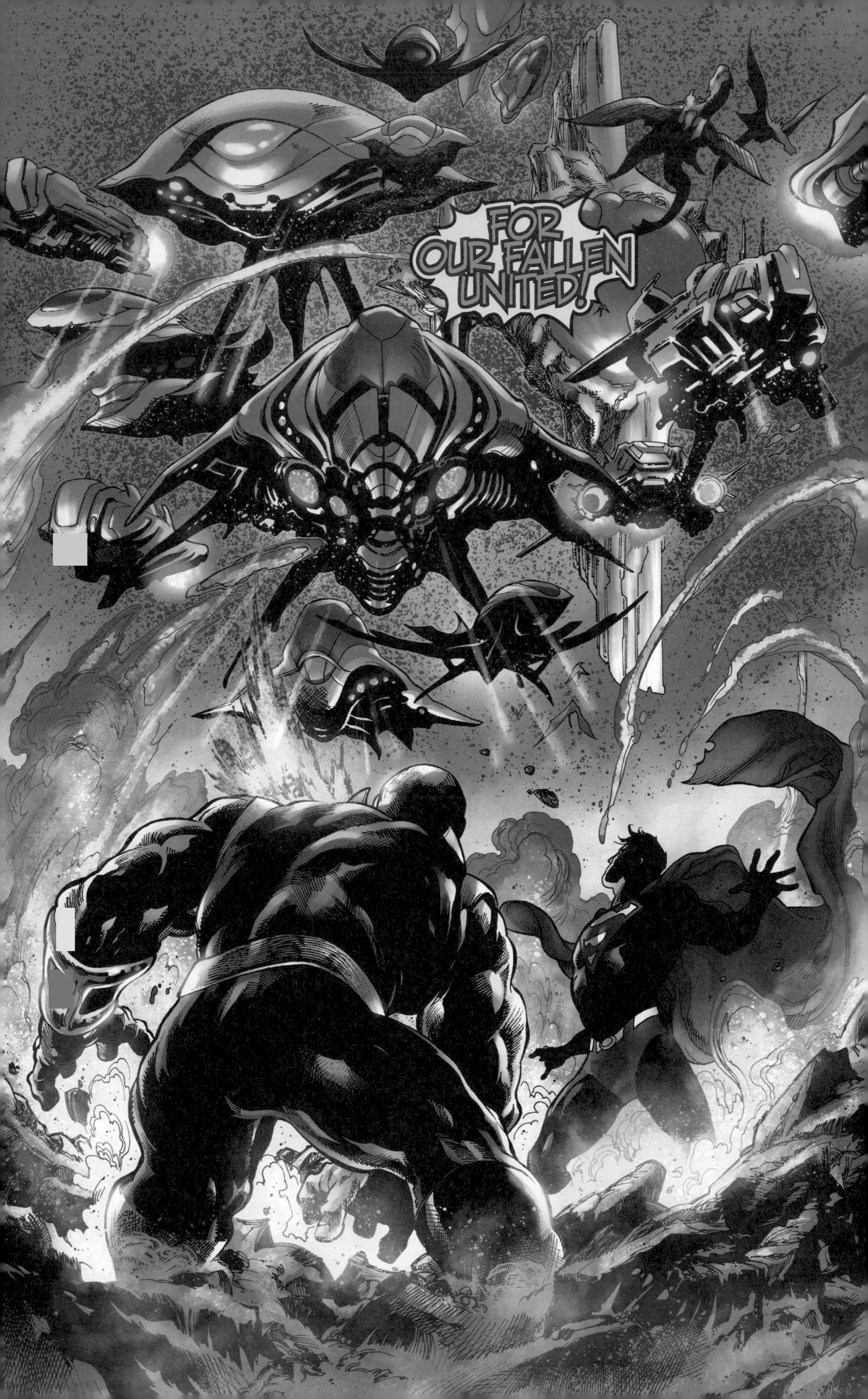
FOR OUR FALLEN UNITED!

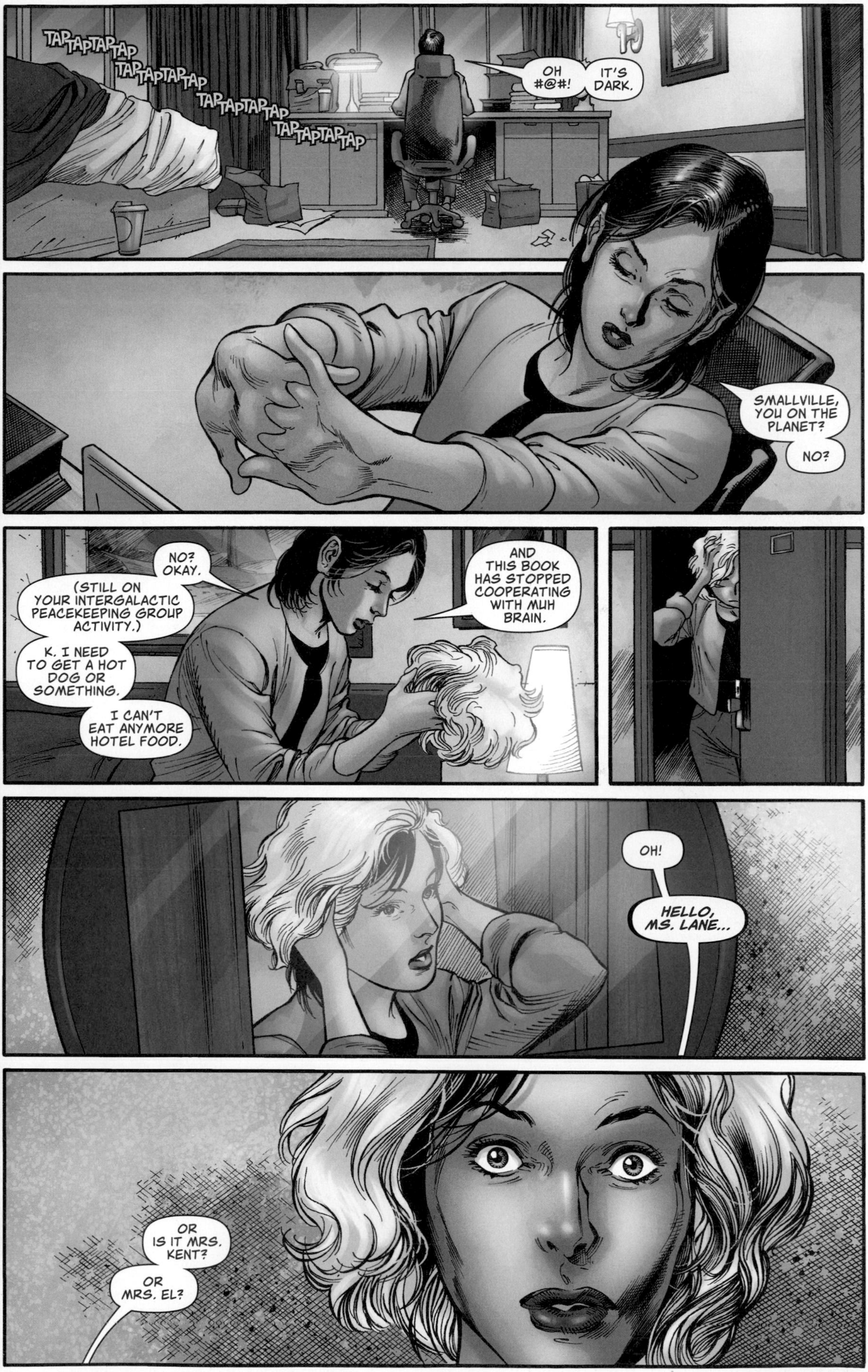
TAPTAPTAPTAP
TAPTAPTAPTAP
TAPTAPTAPTAP
TAPTAPTAPTAP
OH #@#!
IT'S DARK.
SMALLVILLE, YOU ON THE PLANET?
NO?
NO? OKAY.
(STILL ON YOUR INTERGALACTIC PEACEKEEPING GROUP ACTIVITY.)
K. I NEED TO GET A HOT DOG OR SOMETHING.
I CAN'T EAT ANYMORE HOTEL FOOD.
AND THIS BOOK HAS STOPPED COOPERATING WITH MUH BRAIN.
OH!
HELLO, MS. LANE...
OR IS IT MRS. KENT?
OR MRS. EL?

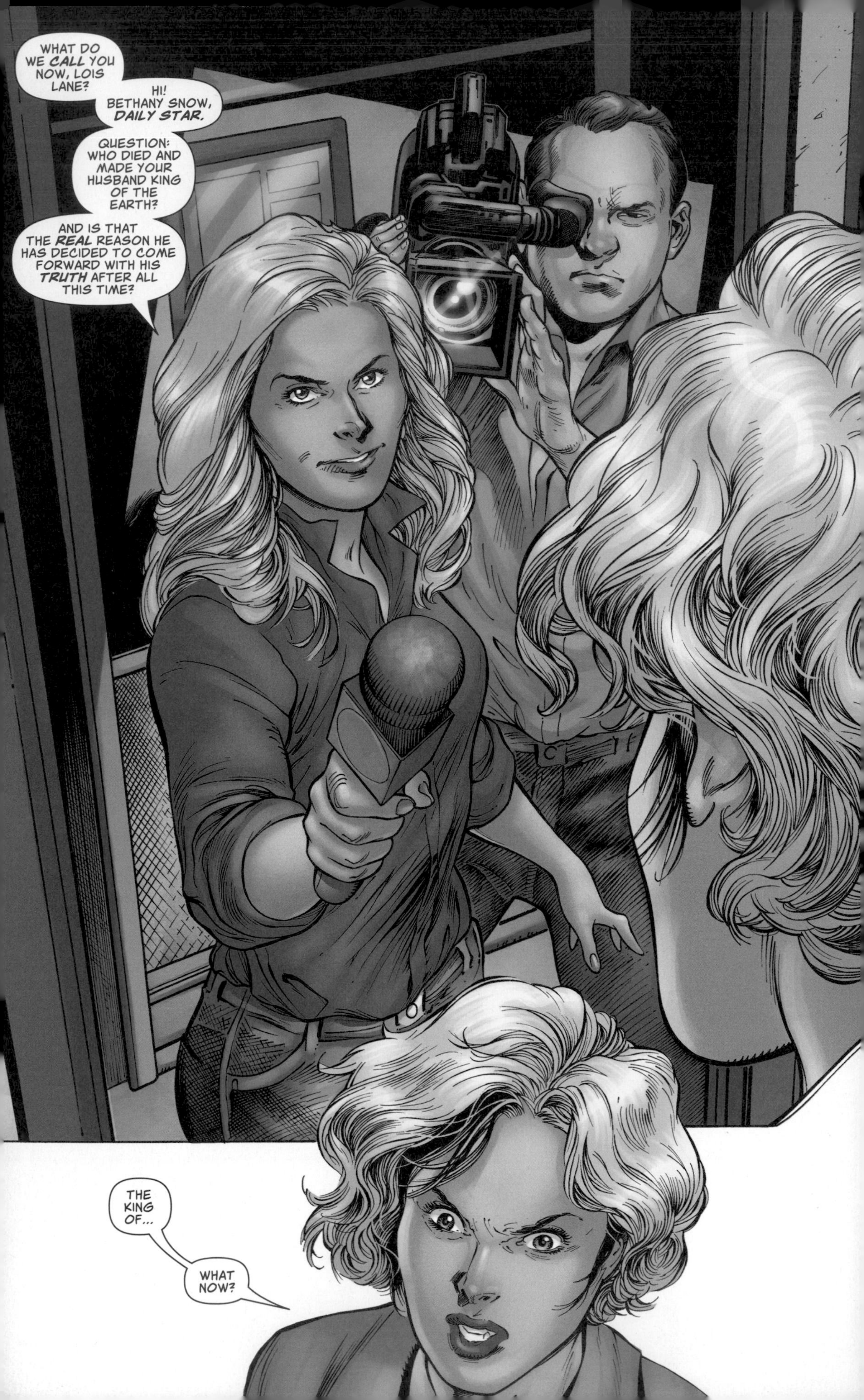
WHAT DO WE CALL YOU NOW, LOIS LANE?
HI! BETHANY SNOW, DAILY STAR.
QUESTION: WHO DIED AND MADE YOUR HUSBAND KING OF THE EARTH?
AND IS THAT THE REAL REASON HE HAS DECIDED TO COME FORWARD WITH HIS TRUTH AFTER ALL THIS TIME?
THE KING OF...
WHAT NOW?

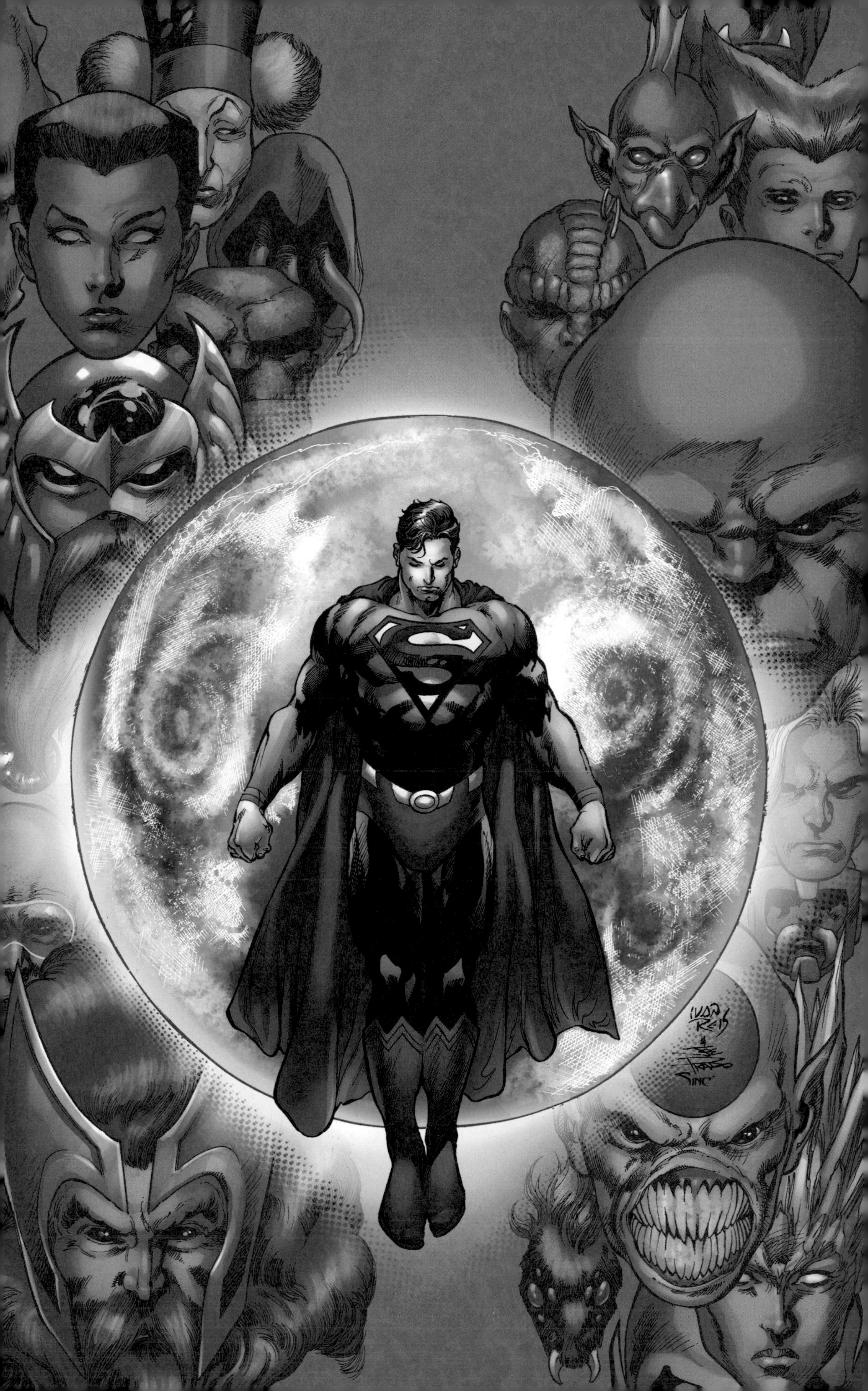

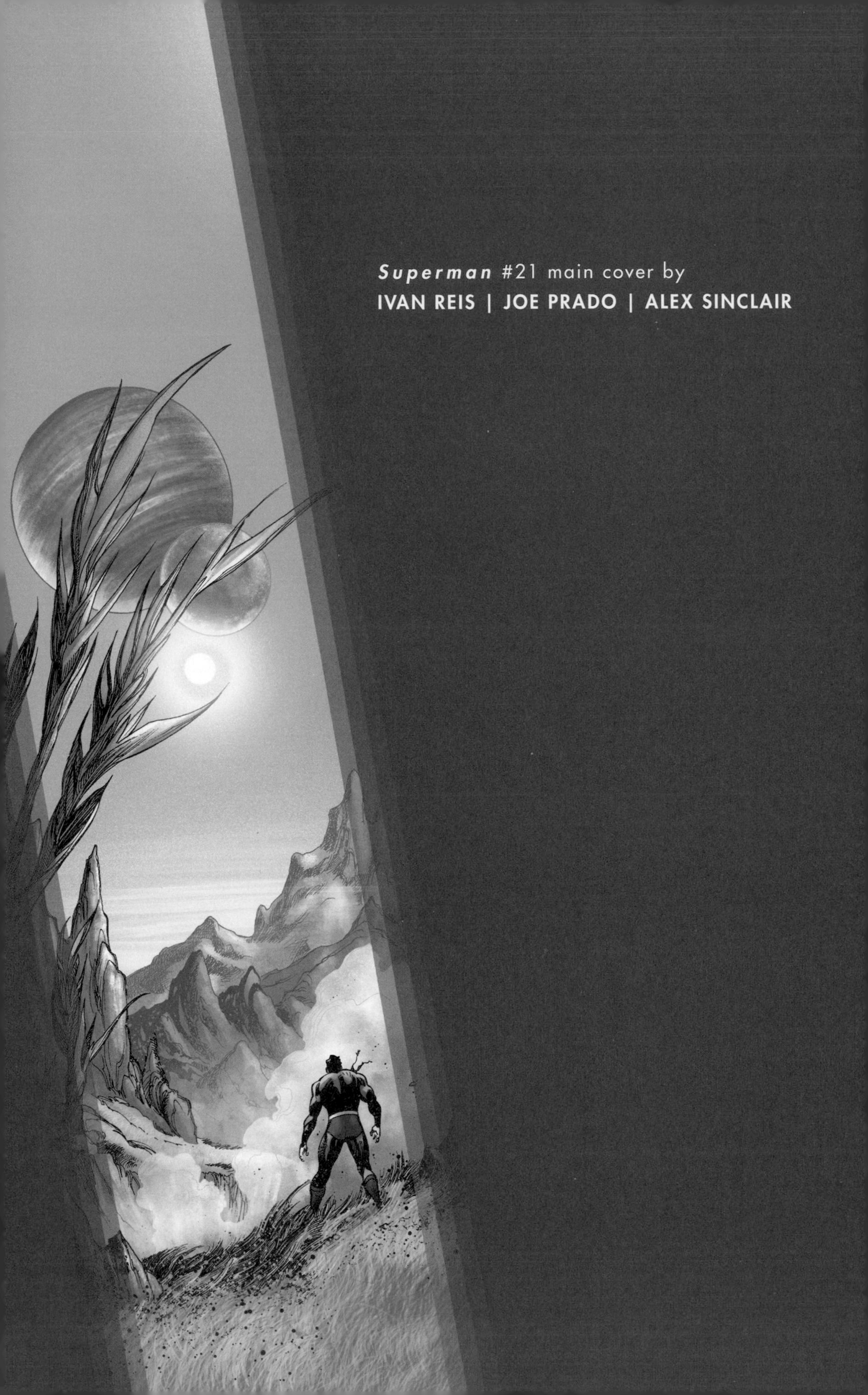

Superman #21 main cover by

IVAN REIS | JOE PRADO | ALEX SINCLAIR

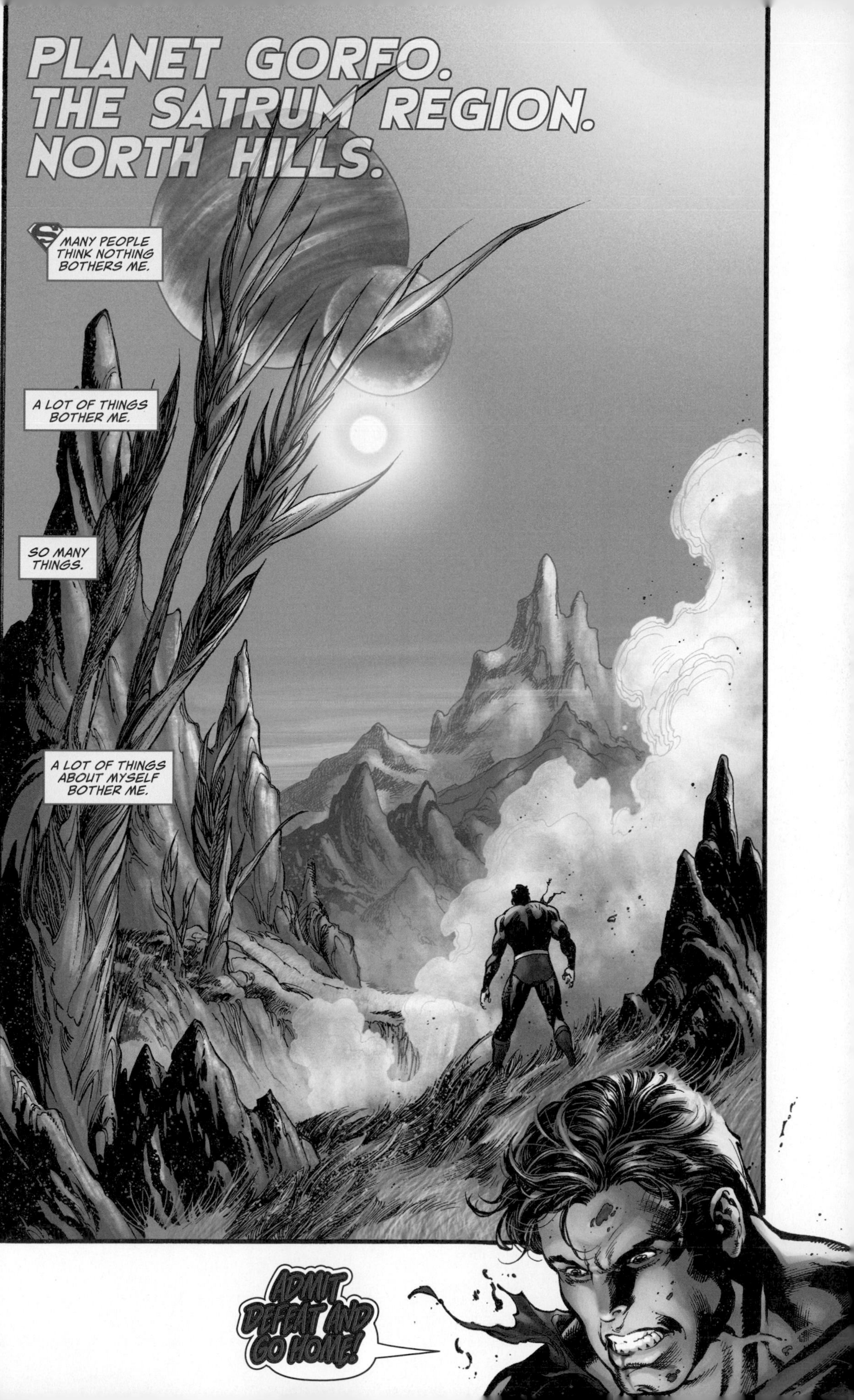
PLANET GORFO. THE SATRUM REGION. NORTH HILLS.
MANY PEOPLE THINK NOTHING BOTHERS ME.
A LOT OF THINGS BOTHER ME.
SO MANY THINGS.
A LOT OF THINGS ABOUT MYSELF BOTHER ME.
ADMIT DEFEAT AND GO HOME!

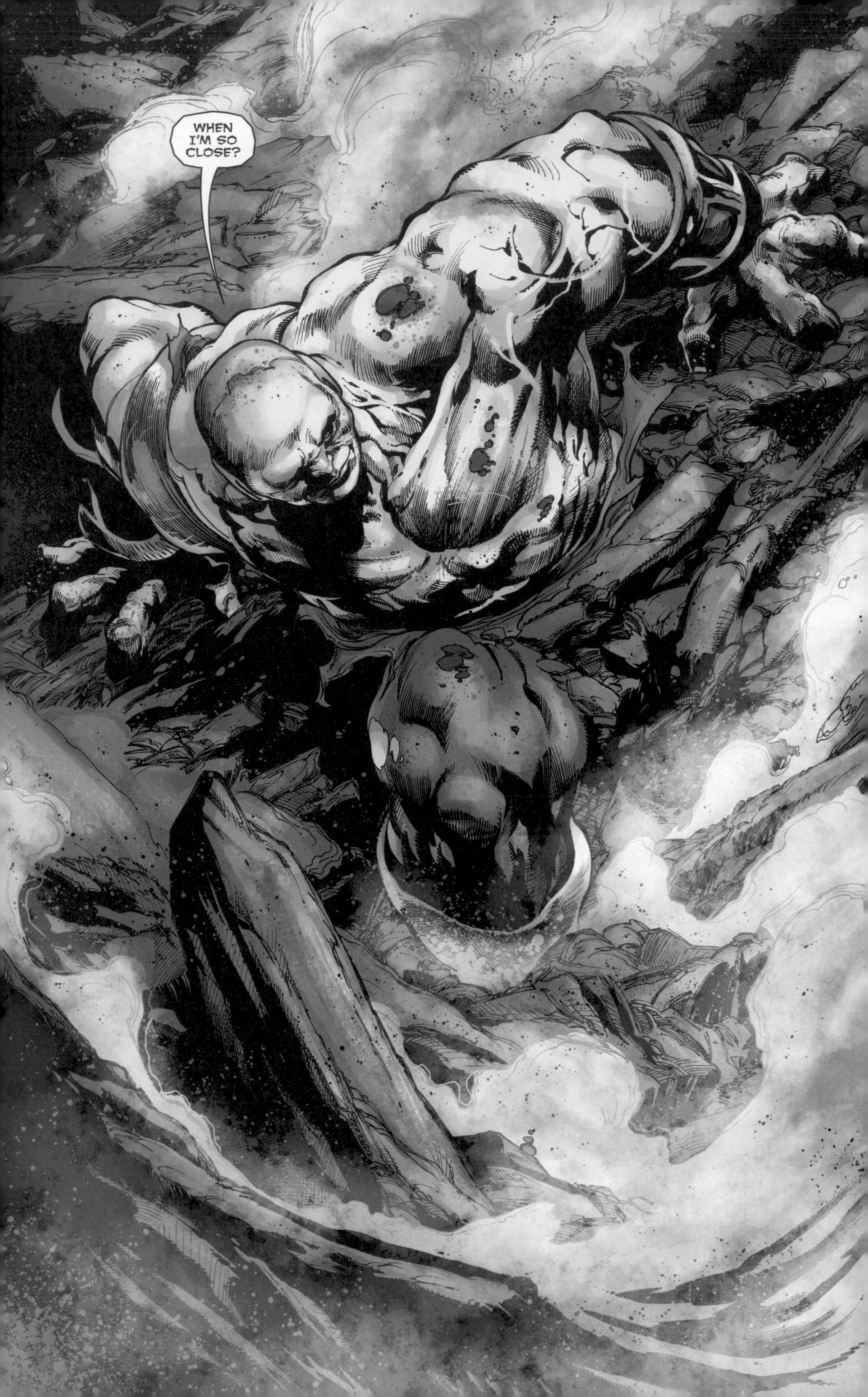
WHEN I'M SO CLOSE?

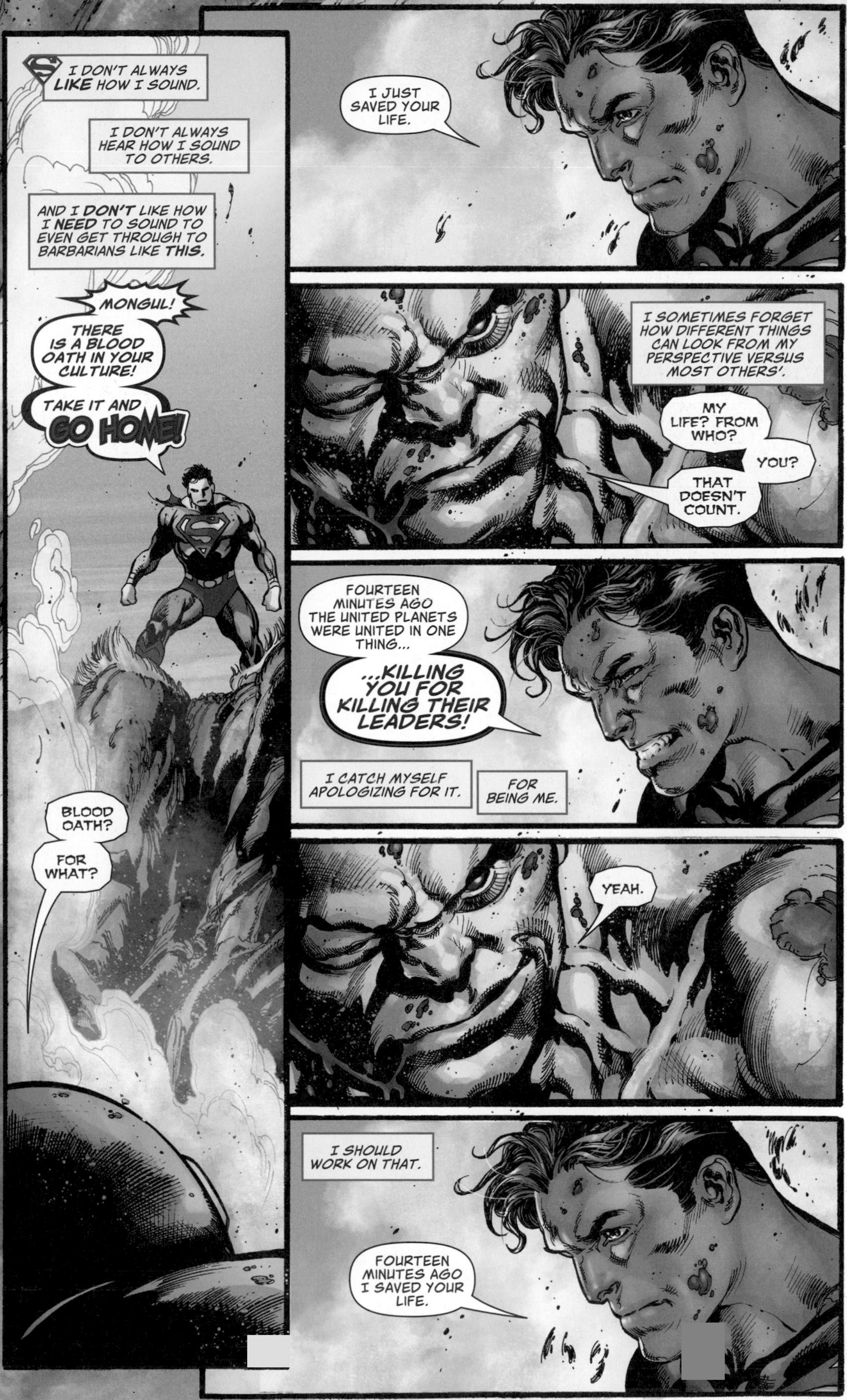
I DON'T ALWAYS LIKE HOW I SOUND.
I JUST SAVED YOUR LIFE.
I DON'T ALWAYS HEAR HOW I SOUND TO OTHERS.
AND I DON'T LIKE HOW I NEED TO SOUND TO EVEN GET THROUGH TO BARBARIANS LIKE THIS.
I SOMETIMES FORGET HOW DIFFERENT THINGS CAN LOOK FROM MY PERSPECTIVE VERSUS MOST OTHERS'.
MY LIFE? FROM WHO?
YOU?
THAT DOESN'T COUNT.
MONGUL!
THERE IS A BLOOD OATH IN YOUR CULTURE!
TAKE IT AND GO HOME!
FOURTEEN MINUTES AGO THE UNITED PLANETS WERE UNITED IN ONE THING...
...KILLING YOU FOR KILLING THEIR LEADERS!
I CATCH MYSELF APOLOGIZING FOR IT.
FOR BEING ME.
BLOOD OATH?
FOR WHAT?
YEAH.
I SHOULD WORK ON THAT.
FOURTEEN MINUTES AGO I SAVED YOUR LIFE.

FOURTEEN MINUTES AGO.
DC COMICS PROUDLY PRESENTS
SUPERMAN IN THE TRUTH
PART FOUR

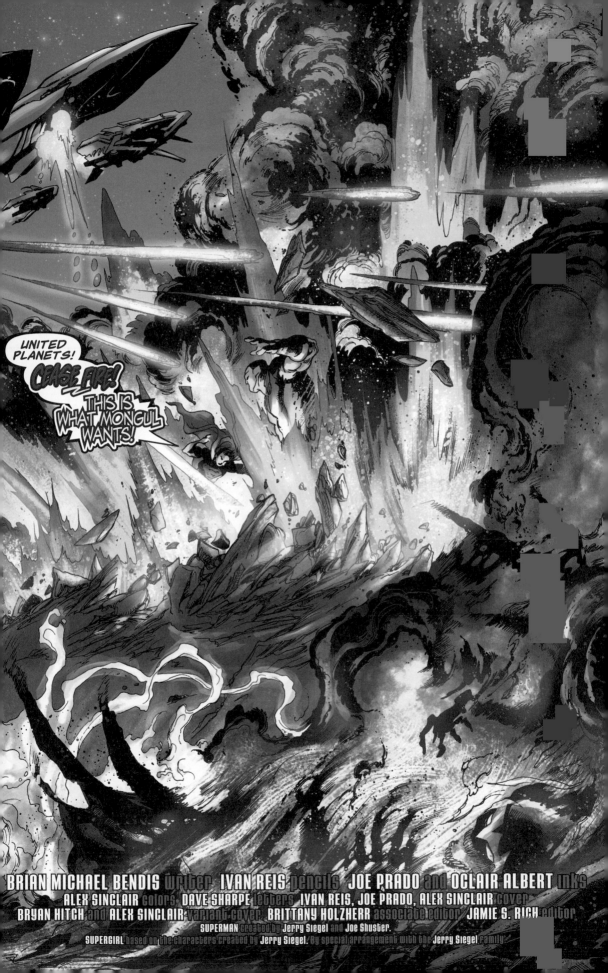

UNITED PLANETS! **CEASE FIRE!** THIS IS WHAT MONGUL WANTS!

BRIAN MICHAEL BENDIS writer IVAN REIS pencils JOE PRADO and OCLAIR ALBERT inks
ALEX SINCLAIR colors DAVE SHARPE letters IVAN REIS, JOE PRADO, ALEX SINCLAIR cover
BRYAN HITCH and ALEX SINCLAIR variant cover BRITTANY HOLZHERR associate editor JAMIE S. RICH editor
SUPERMAN created by Jerry Siegel and Joe Shuster.
SUPERGIRL based on the characters created by Jerry Siegel. By special arrangement with the Jerry Siegel family.

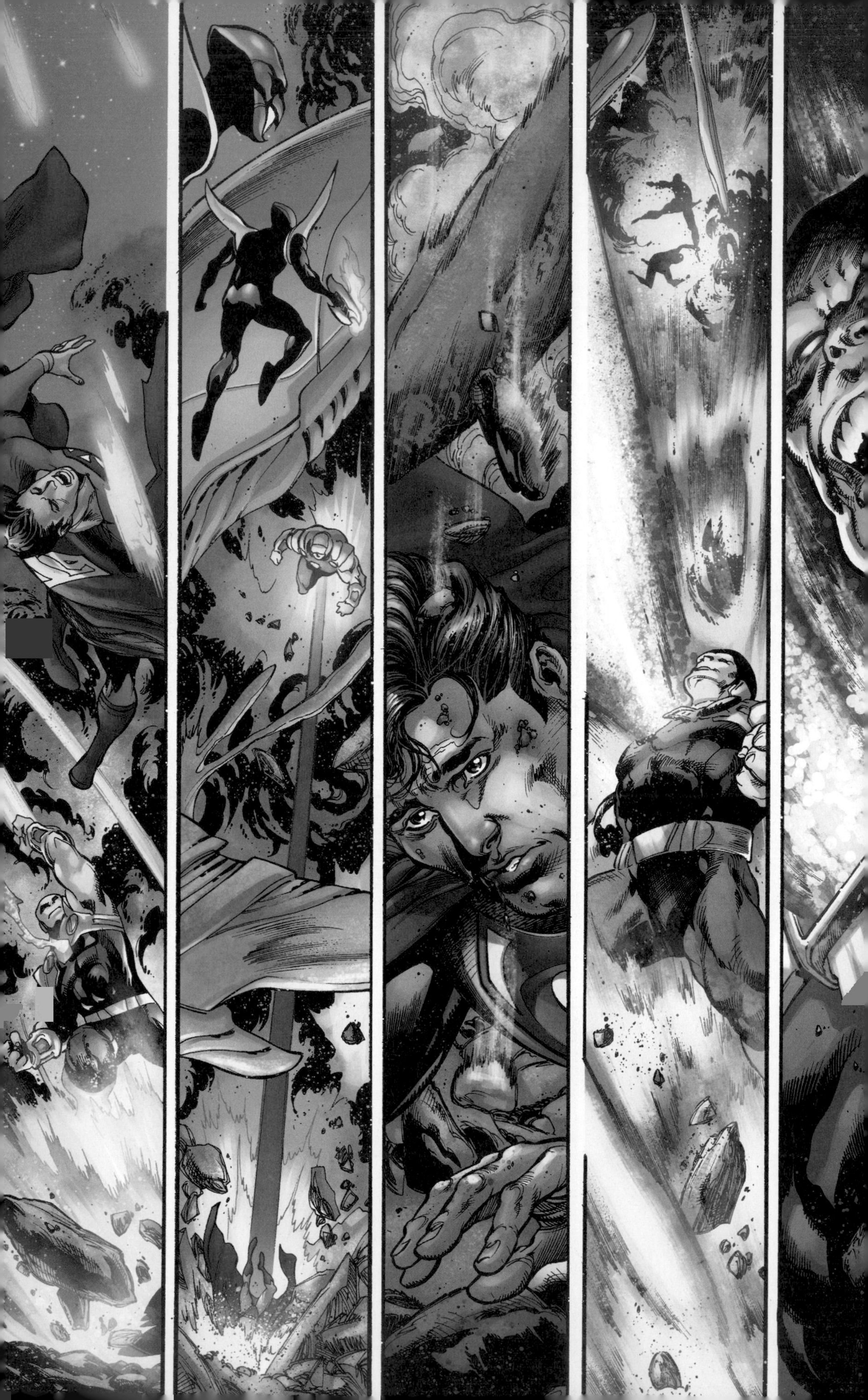

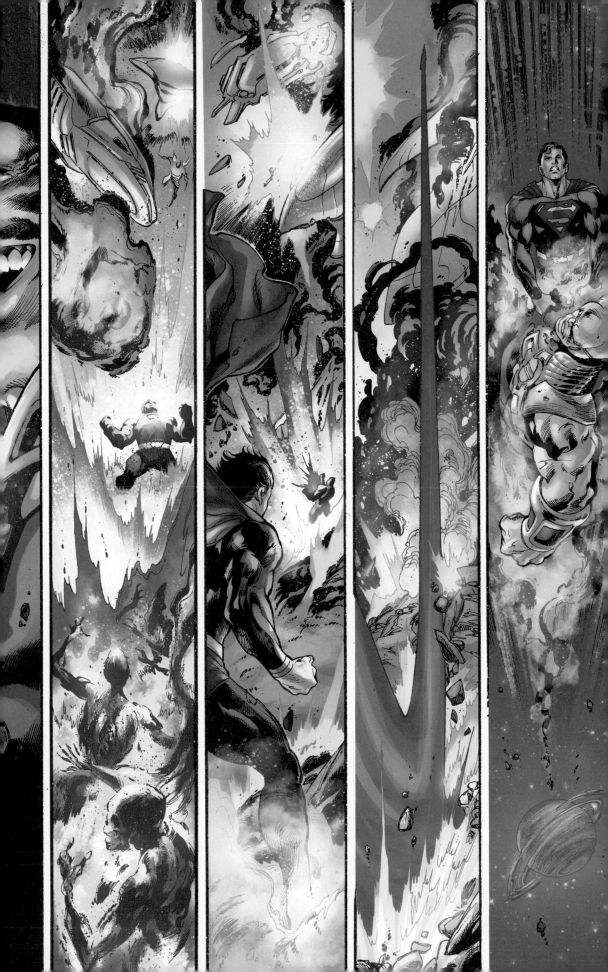

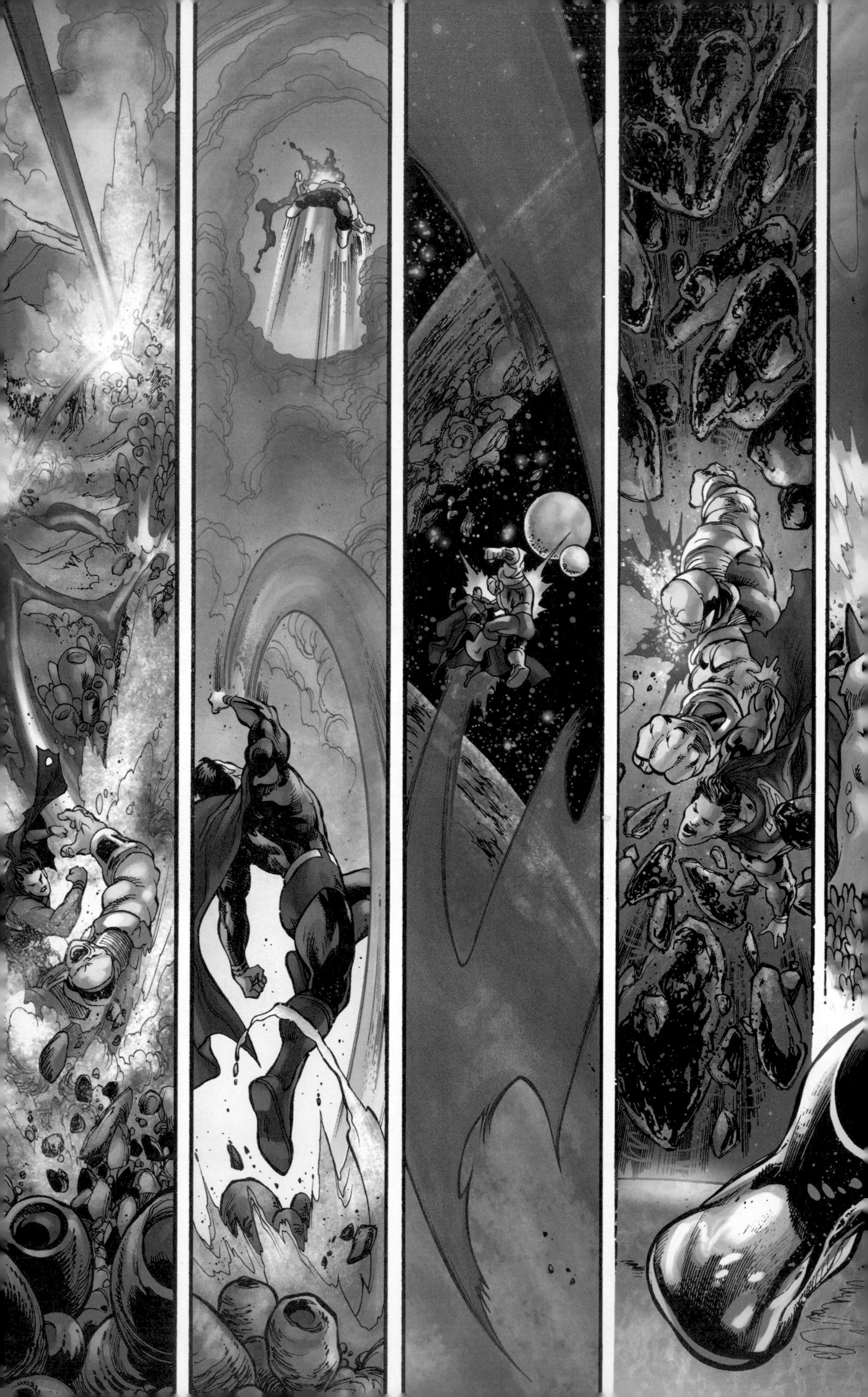

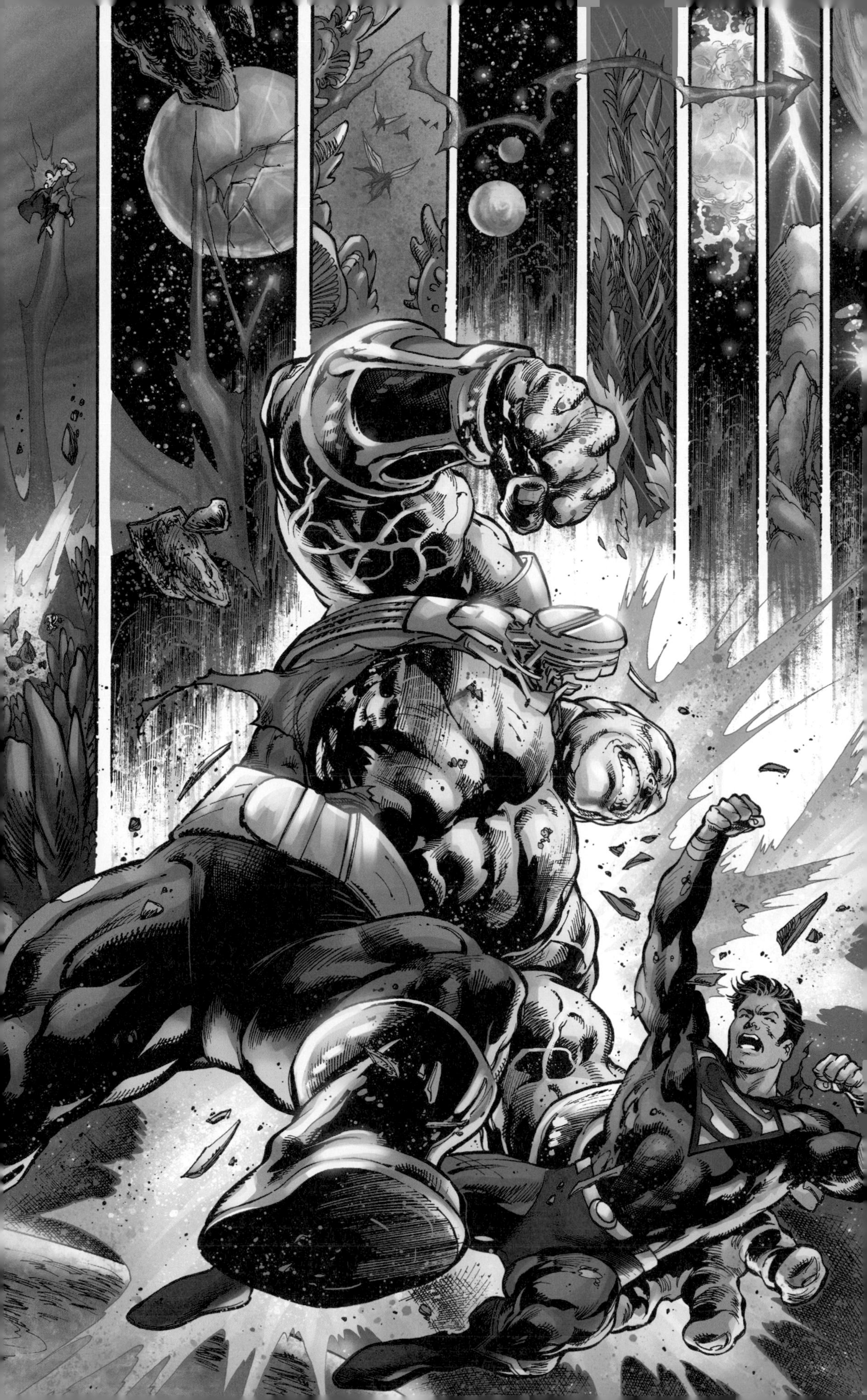

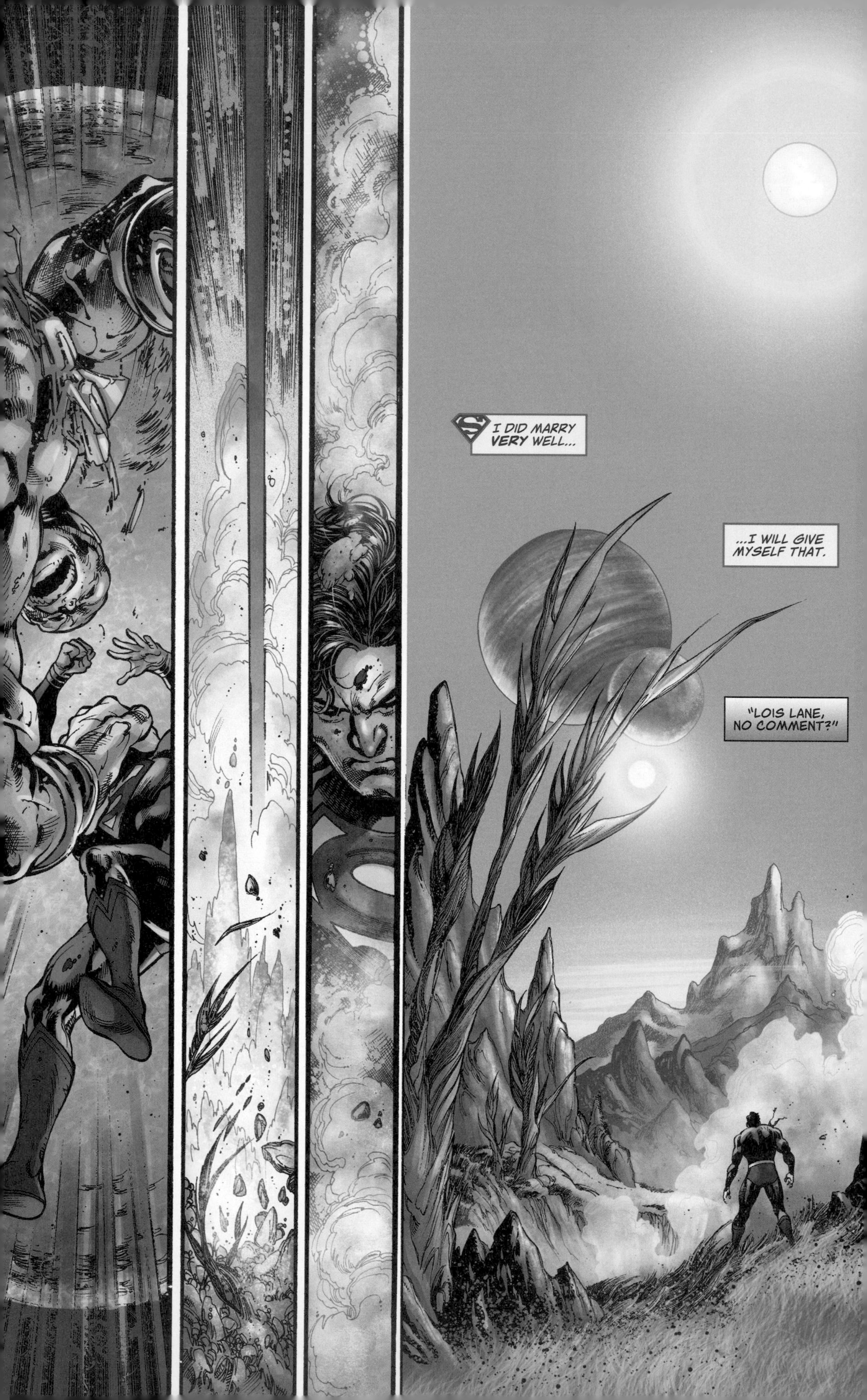
I DID MARRY VERY WELL...
...I WILL GIVE MYSELF THAT.
"LOIS LANE, NO COMMENT?"

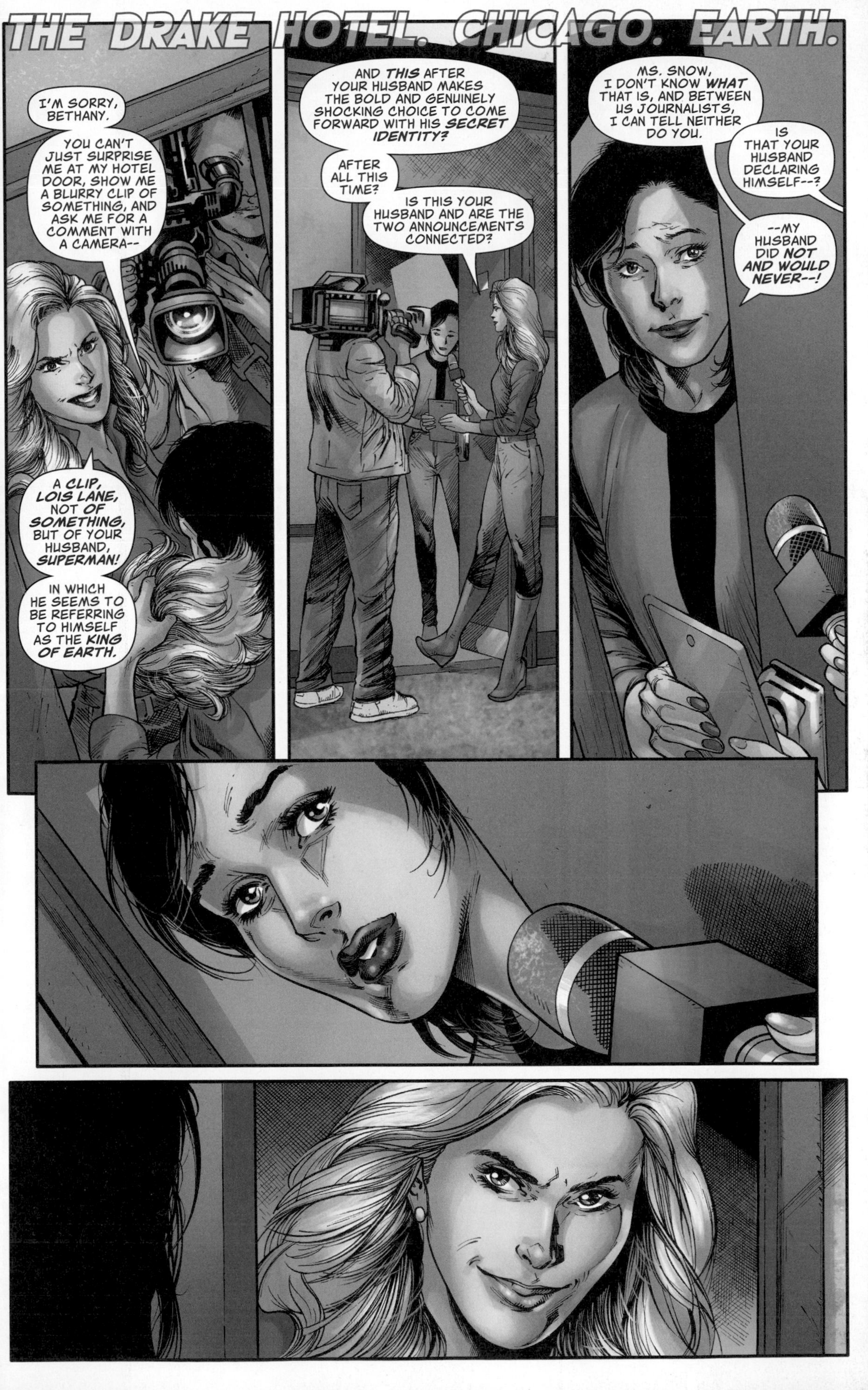
THE DRAKE HOTEL. CHICAGO. EARTH.
I'M SORRY, BETHANY.
YOU CAN'T JUST SURPRISE ME AT MY HOTEL DOOR, SHOW ME A BLURRY CLIP OF SOMETHING, AND ASK ME FOR A COMMENT WITH A CAMERA--
A CLIP, LOIS LANE, NOT OF SOMETHING, BUT OF YOUR HUSBAND, SUPERMAN!
IN WHICH HE SEEMS TO BE REFERRING TO HIMSELF AS THE KING OF EARTH.
AND THIS AFTER YOUR HUSBAND MAKES THE BOLD AND GENUINELY SHOCKING CHOICE TO COME FORWARD WITH HIS SECRET IDENTITY?
AFTER ALL THIS TIME?
IS THIS YOUR HUSBAND AND ARE THE TWO ANNOUNCEMENTS CONNECTED?
MS. SNOW, I DON'T KNOW WHAT THAT IS, AND BETWEEN US JOURNALISTS, I CAN TELL NEITHER DO YOU.
IS THAT YOUR HUSBAND DECLARING HIMSELF--?
--MY HUSBAND DID NOT AND WOULD NEVER--!

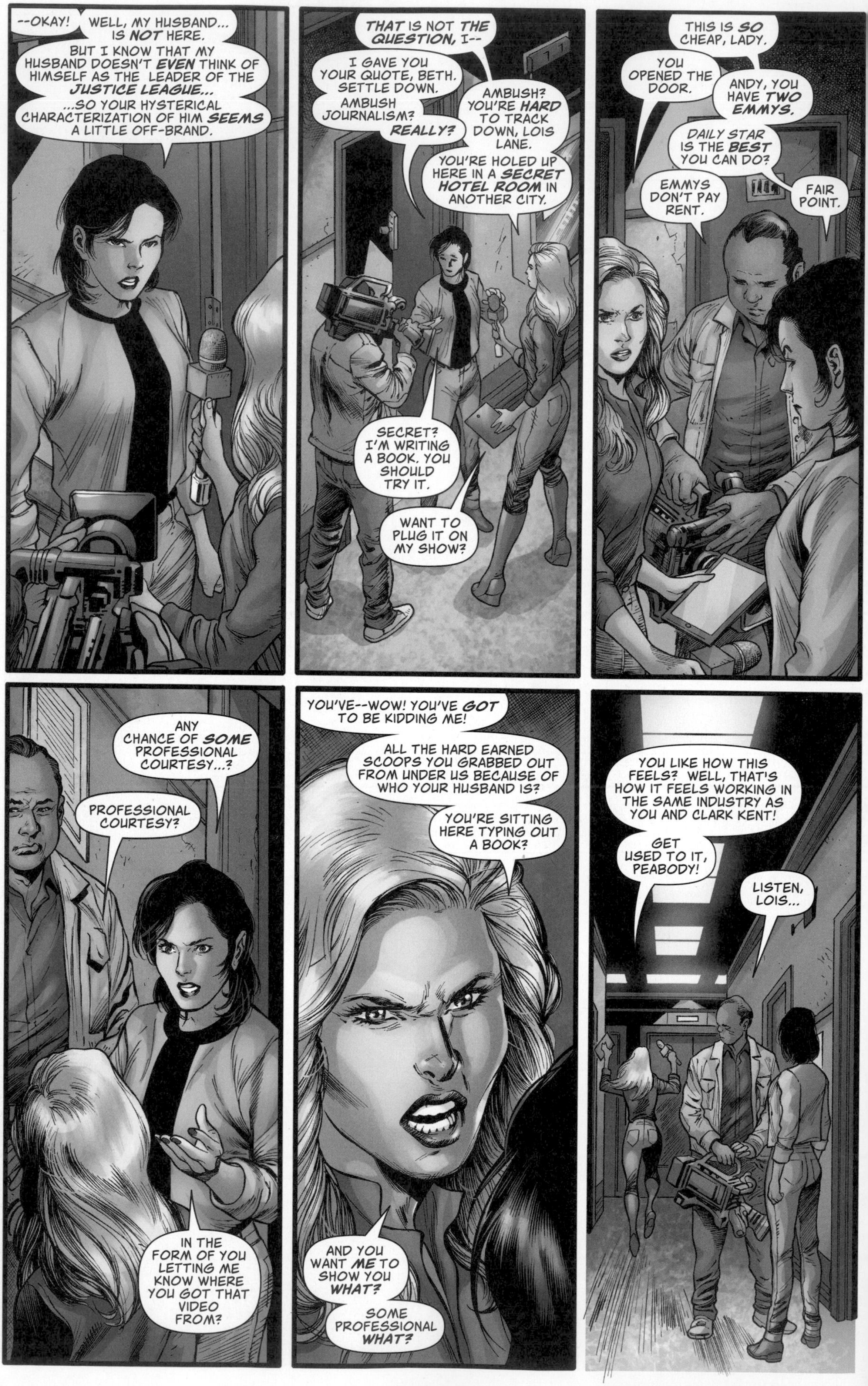
--OKAY!
WELL, MY HUSBAND... IS NOT HERE.
BUT I KNOW THAT MY HUSBAND DOESN'T EVEN THINK OF HIMSELF AS THE LEADER OF THE JUSTICE LEAGUE...
...SO YOUR HYSTERICAL CHARACTERIZATION OF HIM SEEMS A LITTLE OFF-BRAND.
THAT IS NOT THE QUESTION, I--
I GAVE YOU YOUR QUOTE, BETH. SETTLE DOWN.
AMBUSH JOURNALISM? REALLY?
AMBUSH? YOU'RE HARD TO TRACK DOWN, LOIS LANE.
YOU'RE HOLED UP HERE IN A SECRET HOTEL ROOM IN ANOTHER CITY.
SECRET? I'M WRITING A BOOK. YOU SHOULD TRY IT.
WANT TO PLUG IT ON MY SHOW?
THIS IS SO CHEAP, LADY.
YOU OPENED THE DOOR.
ANDY, YOU HAVE TWO EMMYS.
DAILY STAR IS THE BEST YOU CAN DO?
EMMYS DON'T PAY RENT.
FAIR POINT.
ANY CHANCE OF SOME PROFESSIONAL COURTESY...?
PROFESSIONAL COURTESY?
IN THE FORM OF YOU LETTING ME KNOW WHERE YOU GOT THAT VIDEO FROM?
YOU'VE--WOW! YOU'VE GOT TO BE KIDDING ME!
ALL THE HARD EARNED SCOOPS YOU GRABBED OUT FROM UNDER US BECAUSE OF WHO YOUR HUSBAND IS?
YOU'RE SITTING HERE TYPING OUT A BOOK?
AND YOU WANT ME TO SHOW YOU WHAT?
SOME PROFESSIONAL WHAT?
YOU LIKE HOW THIS FEELS? WELL, THAT'S HOW IT FEELS WORKING IN THE SAME INDUSTRY AS YOU AND CLARK KENT!
GET USED TO IT, PEABODY!
LISTEN, LOIS...

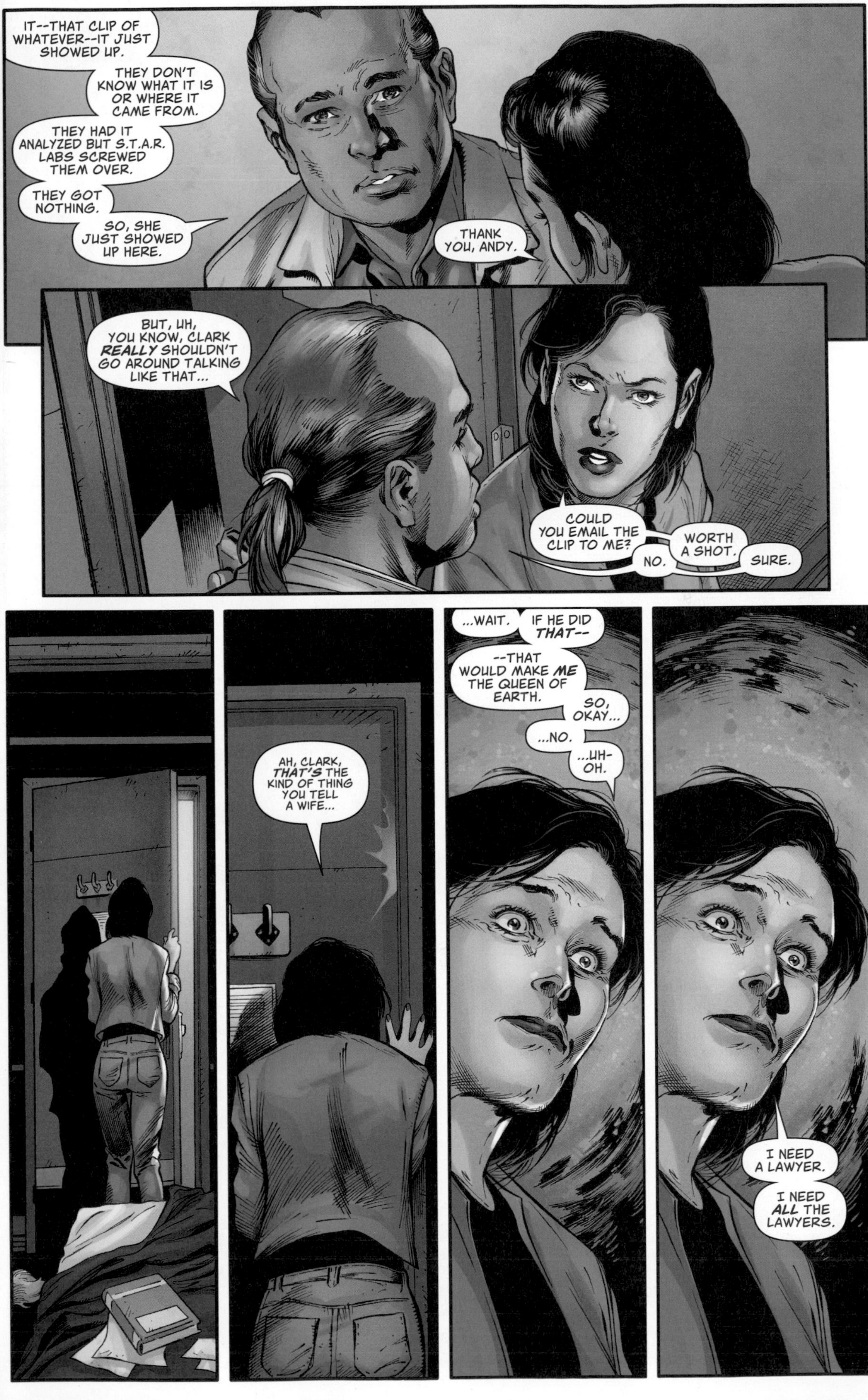
IT--THAT CLIP OF WHATEVER--IT JUST SHOWED UP.
THEY DON'T KNOW WHAT IT IS OR WHERE IT CAME FROM.
THEY HAD IT ANALYZED BUT S.T.A.R. LABS SCREWED THEM OVER.
THEY GOT NOTHING.
SO, SHE JUST SHOWED UP HERE.
THANK YOU, ANDY.
BUT, UH, YOU KNOW, CLARK REALLY SHOULDN'T GO AROUND TALKING LIKE THAT...
COULD YOU EMAIL THE CLIP TO ME?
NO.
WORTH A SHOT.
SURE.
AH, CLARK, THAT'S THE KIND OF THING YOU TELL A WIFE...
...WAIT.
IF HE DID THAT--
--THAT WOULD MAKE ME THE QUEEN OF EARTH.
SO, OKAY...
...NO.
...UH-OH.
I NEED A LAWYER.
I NEED ALL THE LAWYERS.

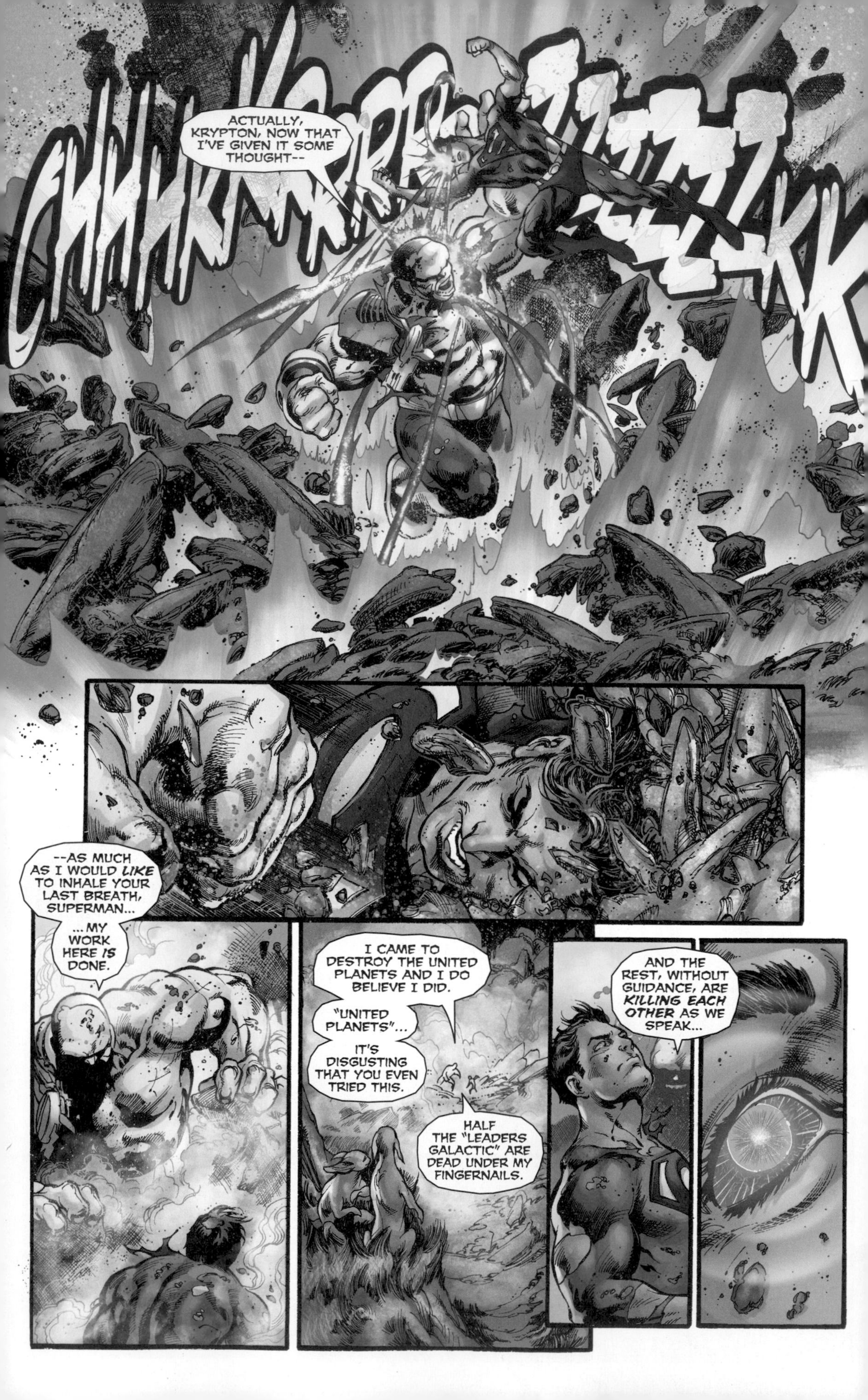
ACTUALLY, KRYPTON, NOW THAT I'VE GIVEN IT SOME THOUGHT--
--AS MUCH AS I WOULD *LIKE* TO INHALE YOUR LAST BREATH, SUPERMAN...
...MY WORK HERE *IS* DONE.
I CAME TO DESTROY THE UNITED PLANETS AND I DO BELIEVE I DID.
"UNITED PLANETS"...
IT'S DISGUSTING THAT YOU EVEN TRIED THIS.
HALF THE "LEADERS GALACTIC" ARE DEAD UNDER MY FINGERNAILS.
AND THE REST, WITHOUT GUIDANCE, ARE *KILLING EACH OTHER* AS WE SPEAK...

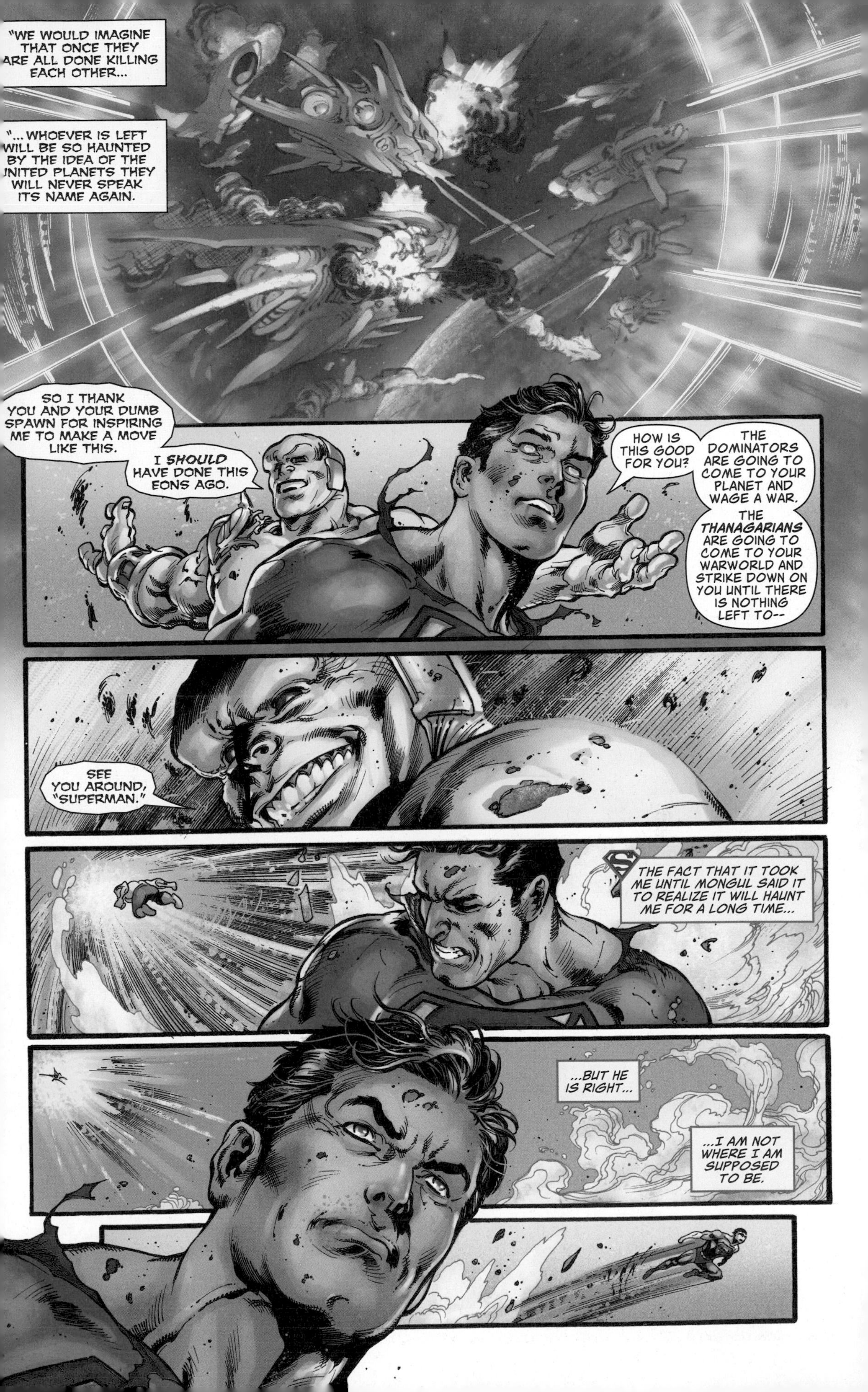
"WE WOULD IMAGINE THAT ONCE THEY ARE ALL DONE KILLING EACH OTHER...
"...WHOEVER IS LEFT WILL BE SO HAUNTED BY THE IDEA OF THE UNITED PLANETS THEY WILL NEVER SPEAK ITS NAME AGAIN.
SO I THANK YOU AND YOUR DUMB SPAWN FOR INSPIRING ME TO MAKE A MOVE LIKE THIS.
I SHOULD HAVE DONE THIS EONS AGO.
HOW IS THIS GOOD FOR YOU?
THE DOMINATORS ARE GOING TO COME TO YOUR PLANET AND WAGE A WAR.
THE THANAGARIANS ARE GOING TO COME TO YOUR WARWORLD AND STRIKE DOWN ON YOU UNTIL THERE IS NOTHING LEFT TO--
SEE YOU AROUND, "SUPERMAN."
THE FACT THAT IT TOOK ME UNTIL MONGUL SAID IT TO REALIZE IT WILL HAUNT ME FOR A LONG TIME...
...BUT HE IS RIGHT...
...I AM NOT WHERE I AM SUPPOSED TO BE.

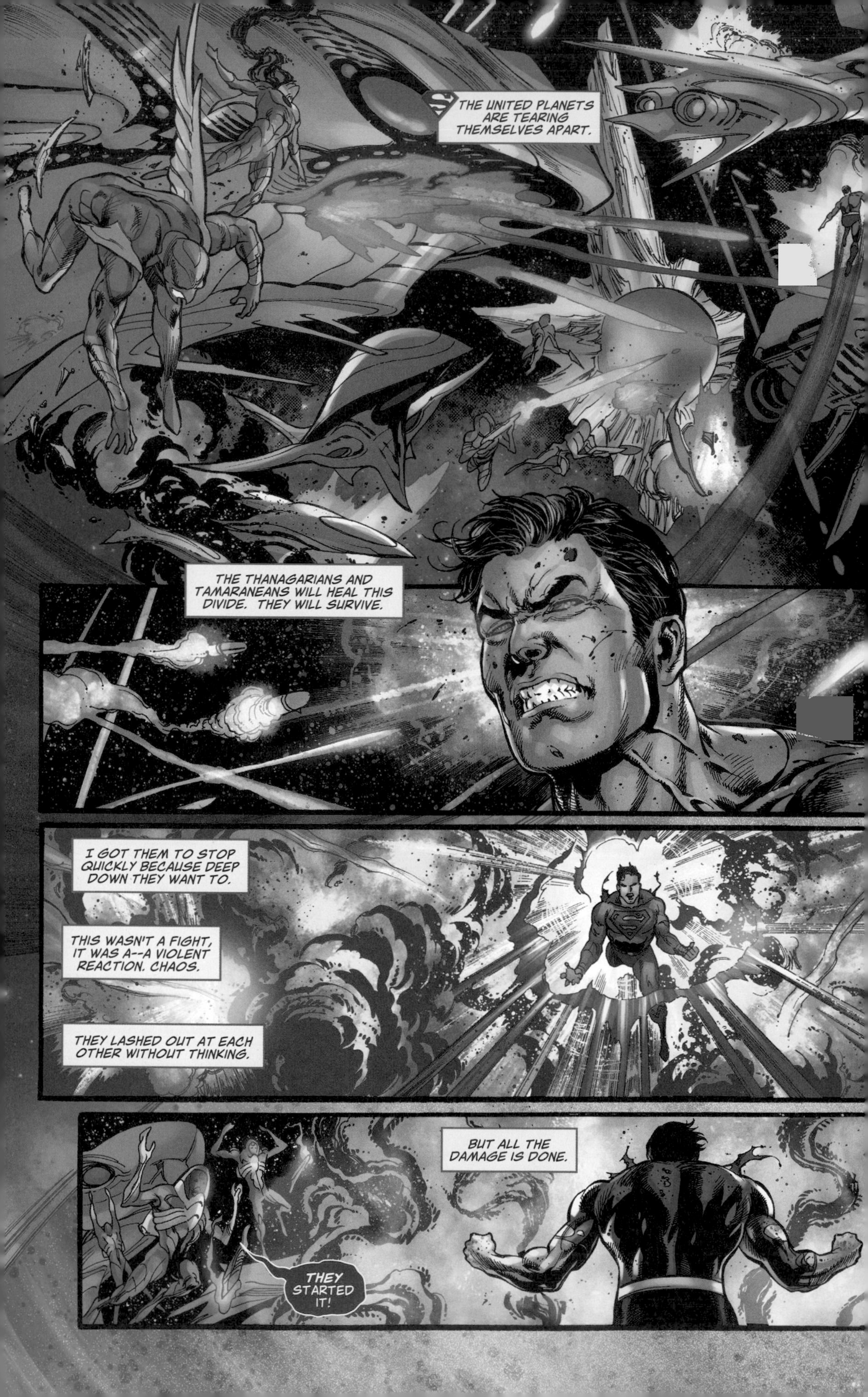
THE UNITED PLANETS ARE TEARING THEMSELVES APART.
THE THANAGARIANS AND TAMARANEANS WILL HEAL THIS DIVIDE. THEY WILL SURVIVE.
I GOT THEM TO STOP QUICKLY BECAUSE DEEP DOWN THEY WANT TO.
THIS WASN'T A FIGHT, IT WAS A--A VIOLENT REACTION. CHAOS.
THEY LASHED OUT AT EACH OTHER WITHOUT THINKING.
BUT ALL THE DAMAGE IS DONE.
THEY STARTED IT!

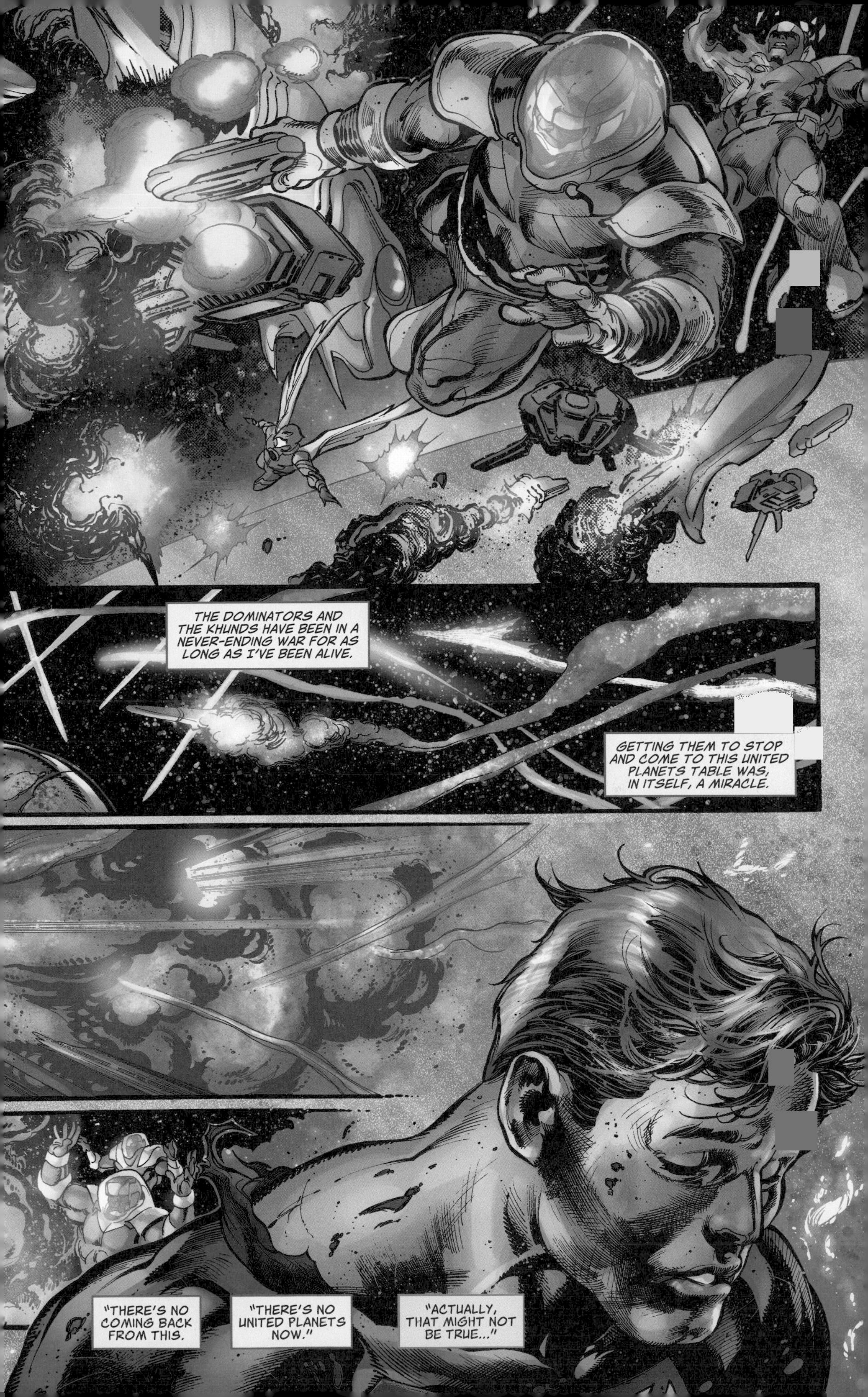
THE DOMINATORS AND THE KHUNDS HAVE BEEN IN A NEVER-ENDING WAR FOR AS LONG AS I'VE BEEN ALIVE.
GETTING THEM TO STOP AND COME TO THIS UNITED PLANETS TABLE WAS, IN ITSELF, A MIRACLE.
"THERE'S NO COMING BACK FROM THIS.
"THERE'S NO UNITED PLANETS NOW."
"ACTUALLY, THAT MIGHT NOT BE TRUE..."

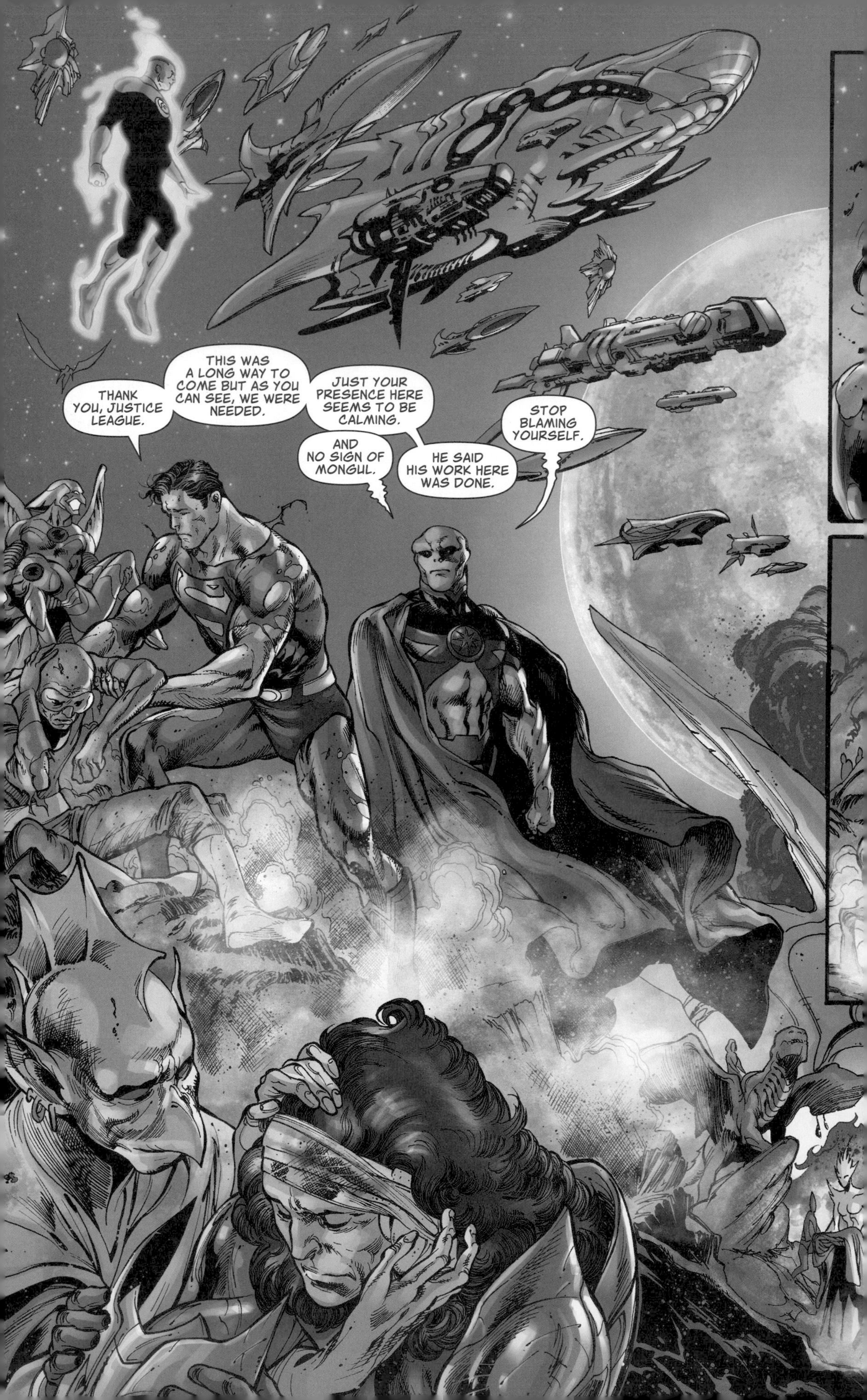
THANK YOU, JUSTICE LEAGUE.
THIS WAS A LONG WAY TO COME BUT AS YOU CAN SEE, WE WERE NEEDED.
JUST YOUR PRESENCE HERE SEEMS TO BE CALMING.
AND NO SIGN OF MONGUL.
HE SAID HIS WORK HERE WAS DONE.
STOP BLAMING YOURSELF.

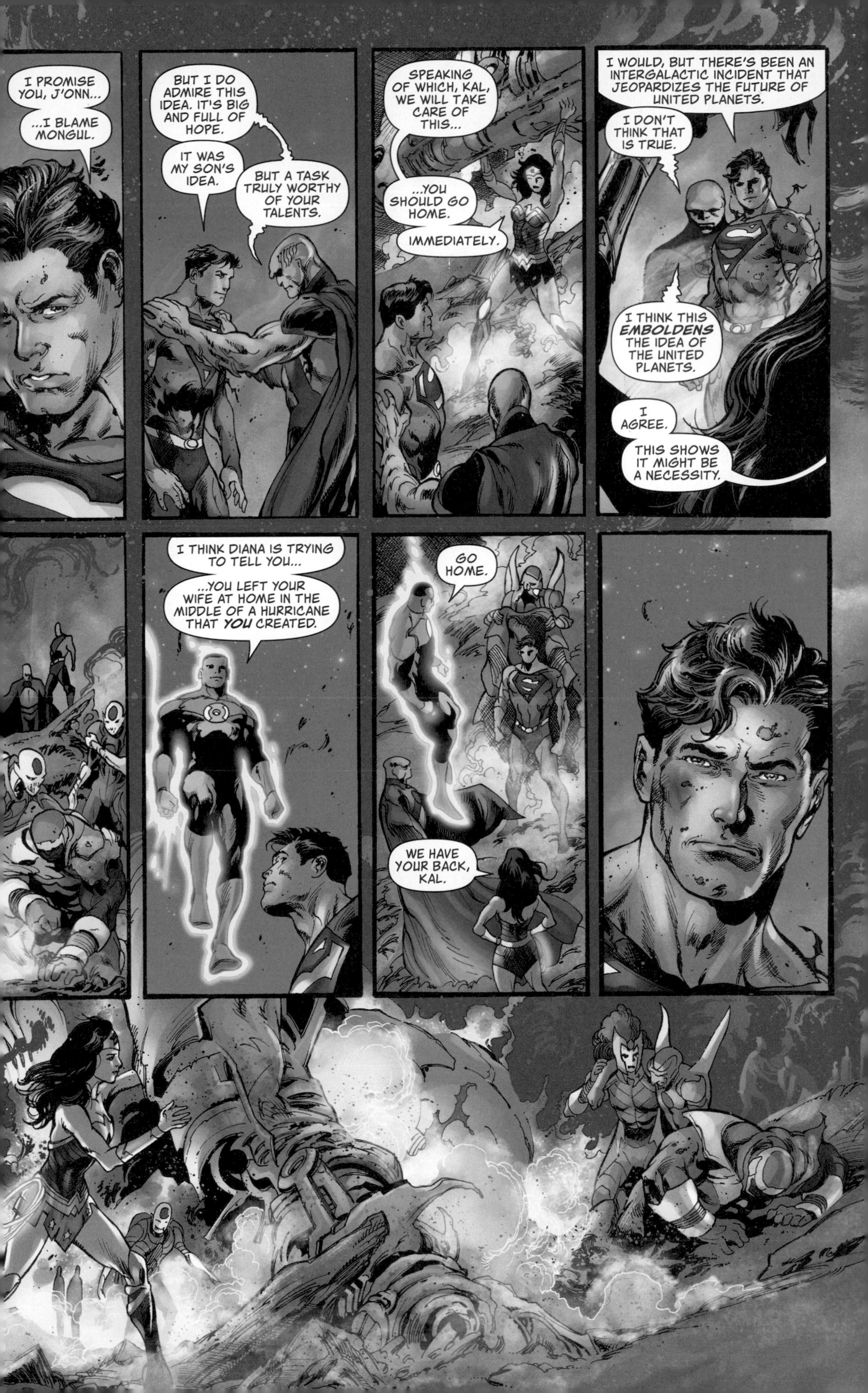

I PROMISE YOU, J'ONN...
...I BLAME MONGUL.
BUT I DO ADMIRE THIS IDEA. IT'S BIG AND FULL OF HOPE.
IT WAS MY SON'S IDEA.
BUT A TASK TRULY WORTHY OF YOUR TALENTS.
SPEAKING OF WHICH, KAL, WE WILL TAKE CARE OF THIS...
...YOU SHOULD GO HOME.
IMMEDIATELY.
I WOULD, BUT THERE'S BEEN AN INTERGALACTIC INCIDENT THAT JEOPARDIZES THE FUTURE OF UNITED PLANETS.
I DON'T THINK THAT IS TRUE.
I THINK THIS *EMBOLDENS* THE IDEA OF THE UNITED PLANETS.
I AGREE.
THIS SHOWS IT MIGHT BE A NECESSITY.
I THINK DIANA IS TRYING TO TELL YOU...
...YOU LEFT YOUR WIFE AT HOME IN THE MIDDLE OF A HURRICANE THAT *YOU* CREATED.
GO HOME.
WE HAVE YOUR BACK, KAL.

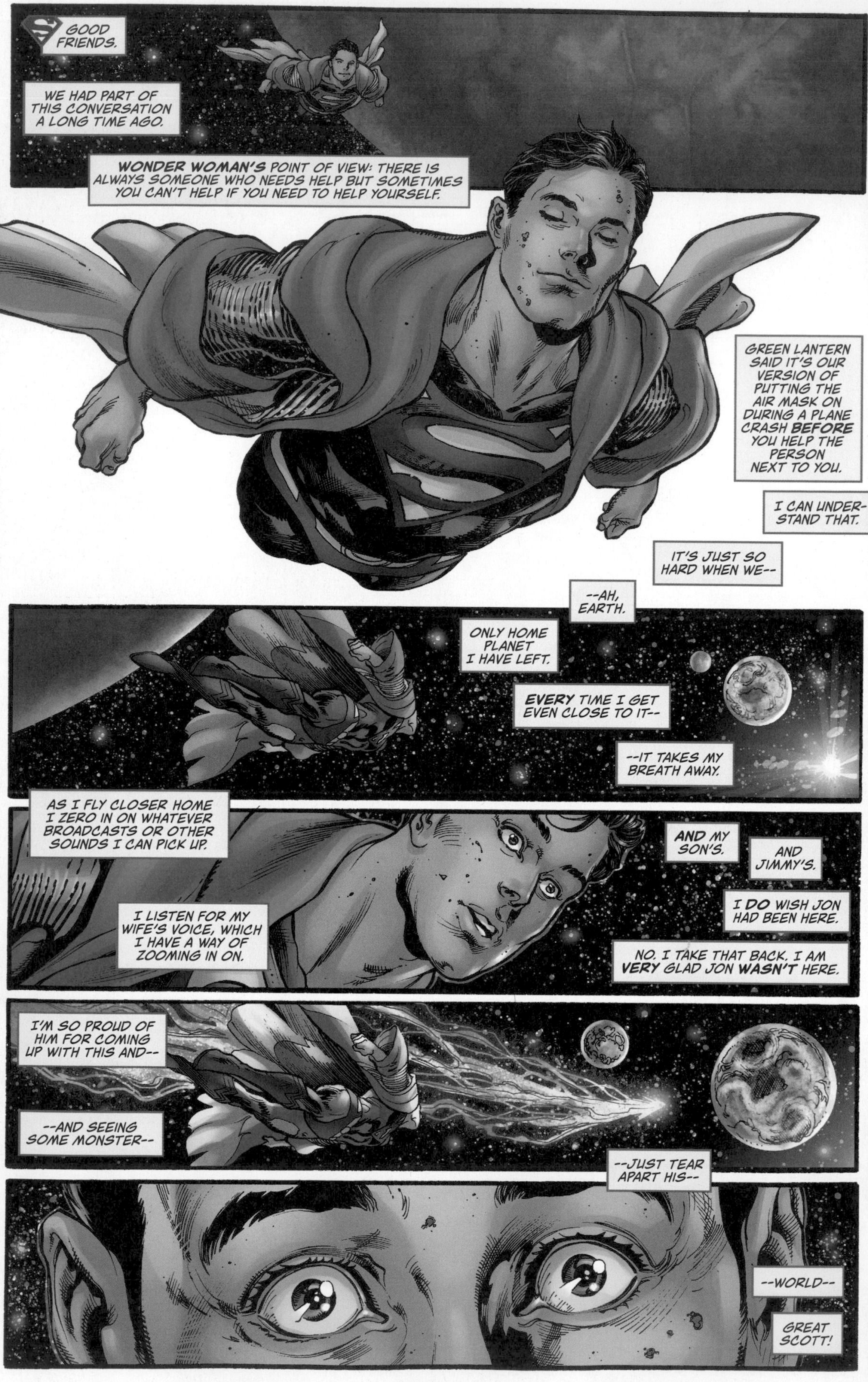
GOOD FRIENDS.
WE HAD PART OF THIS CONVERSATION A LONG TIME AGO.
WONDER WOMAN'S POINT OF VIEW: THERE IS ALWAYS SOMEONE WHO NEEDS HELP BUT SOMETIMES YOU CAN'T HELP IF YOU NEED TO HELP YOURSELF.
GREEN LANTERN SAID IT'S OUR VERSION OF PUTTING THE AIR MASK ON DURING A PLANE CRASH BEFORE YOU HELP THE PERSON NEXT TO YOU.
I CAN UNDER-STAND THAT.
IT'S JUST SO HARD WHEN WE--
--AH, EARTH.
ONLY HOME PLANET I HAVE LEFT.
EVERY TIME I GET EVEN CLOSE TO IT--
--IT TAKES MY BREATH AWAY.
AS I FLY CLOSER HOME I ZERO IN ON WHATEVER BROADCASTS OR OTHER SOUNDS I CAN PICK UP.
I LISTEN FOR MY WIFE'S VOICE, WHICH I HAVE A WAY OF ZOOMING IN ON.
AND MY SON'S.
AND JIMMY'S.
I DO WISH JON HAD BEEN HERE.
NO. I TAKE THAT BACK. I AM VERY GLAD JON WASN'T HERE.
I'M SO PROUD OF HIM FOR COMING UP WITH THIS AND--
--AND SEEING SOME MONSTER--
--JUST TEAR APART HIS--
--WORLD--
GREAT SCOTT!

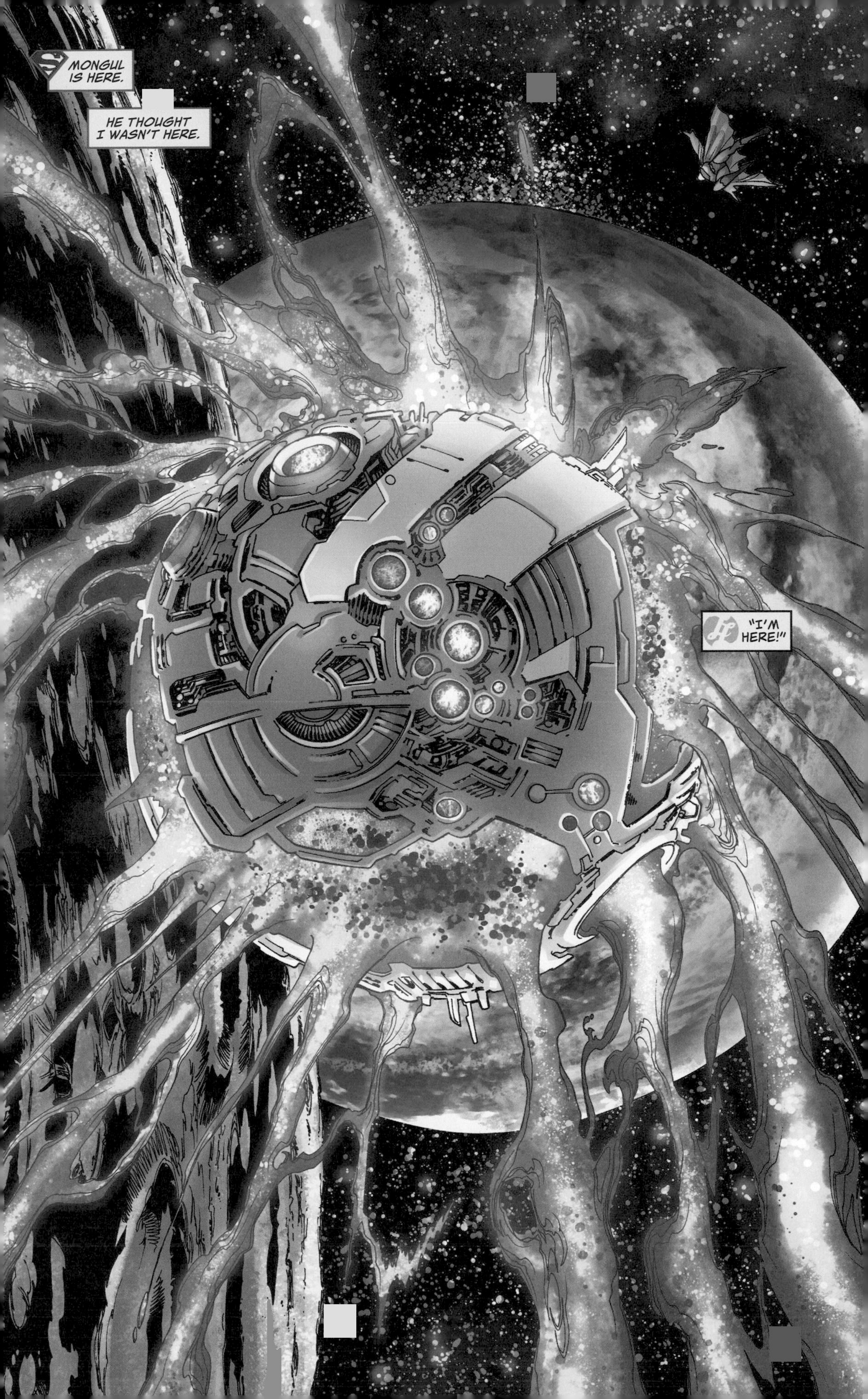
MONGUL IS HERE.
HE THOUGHT I WASN'T HERE.
"I'M HERE!"

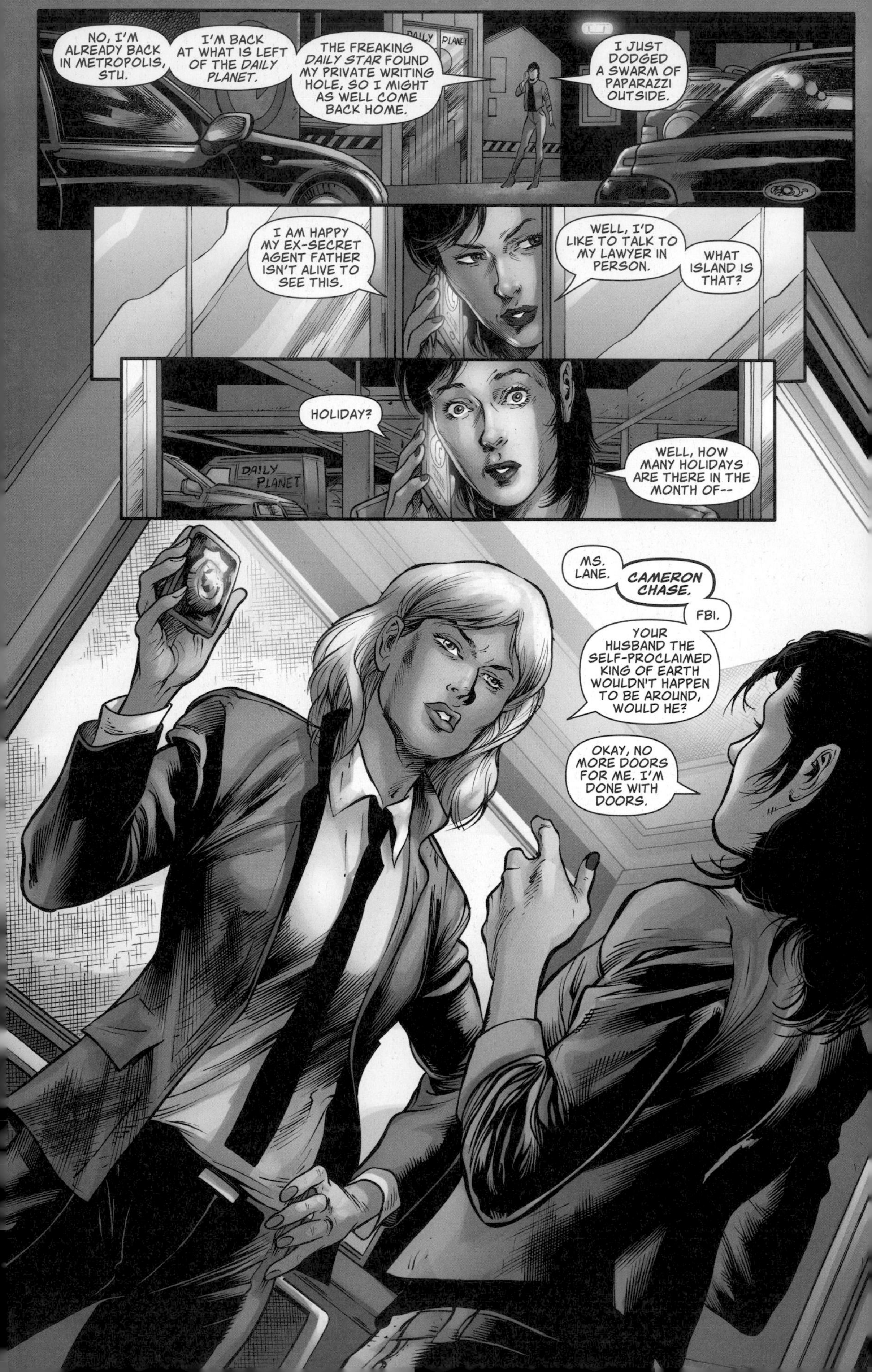
NO, I'M ALREADY BACK IN METROPOLIS, STU.
I'M BACK AT WHAT IS LEFT OF THE DAILY PLANET.
THE FREAKING DAILY STAR FOUND MY PRIVATE WRITING HOLE, SO I MIGHT AS WELL COME BACK HOME.
I JUST DODGED A SWARM OF PAPARAZZI OUTSIDE.
DAILY PLANET
I AM HAPPY MY EX-SECRET AGENT FATHER ISN'T ALIVE TO SEE THIS.
WELL, I'D LIKE TO TALK TO MY LAWYER IN PERSON.
WHAT ISLAND IS THAT?
HOLIDAY?
DAILY PLANET
WELL, HOW MANY HOLIDAYS ARE THERE IN THE MONTH OF--
MS. LANE.
CAMERON CHASE.
FBI.
YOUR HUSBAND THE SELF-PROCLAIMED KING OF EARTH WOULDN'T HAPPEN TO BE AROUND, WOULD HE?
OKAY, NO MORE DOORS FOR ME. I'M DONE WITH DOORS.

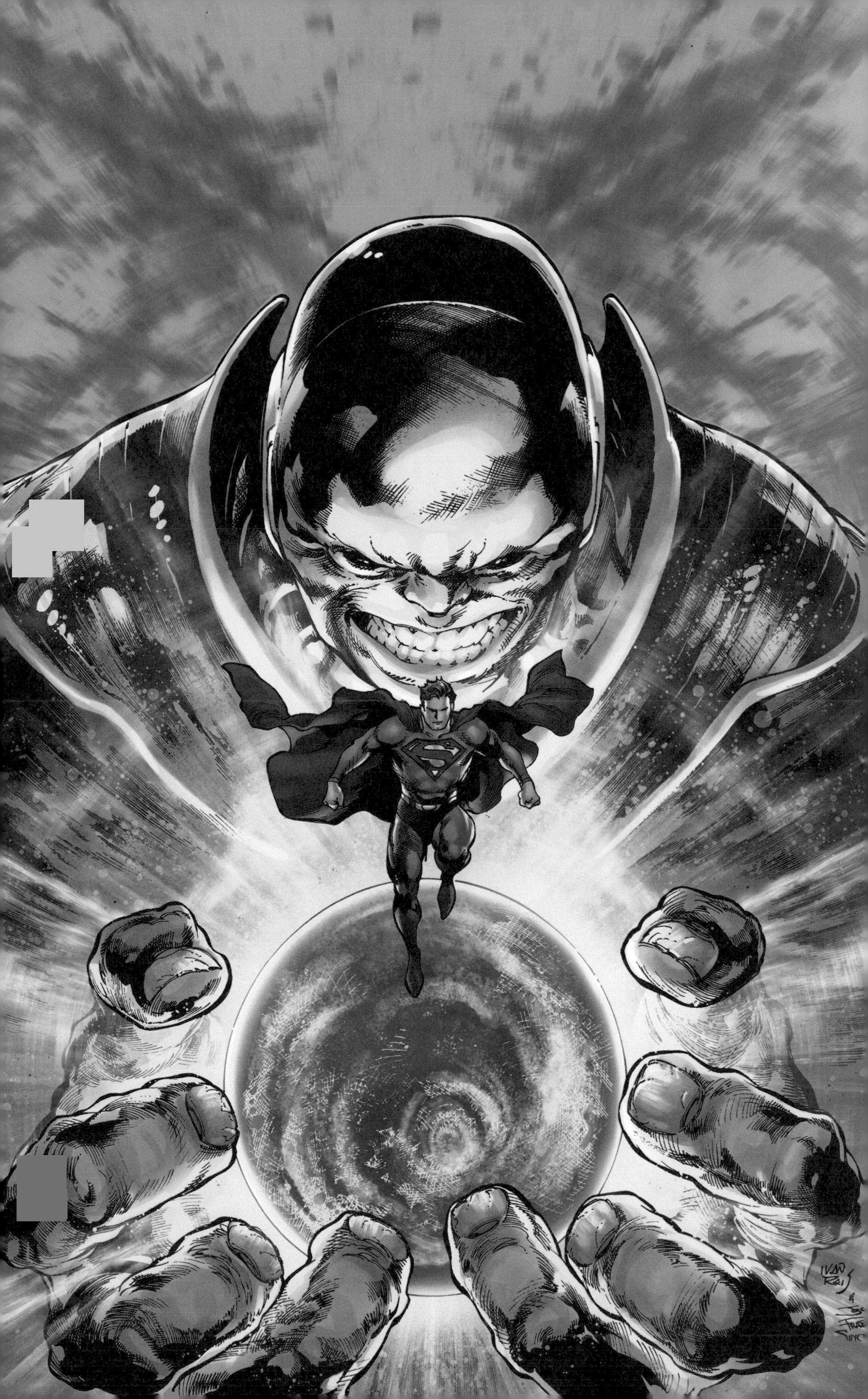

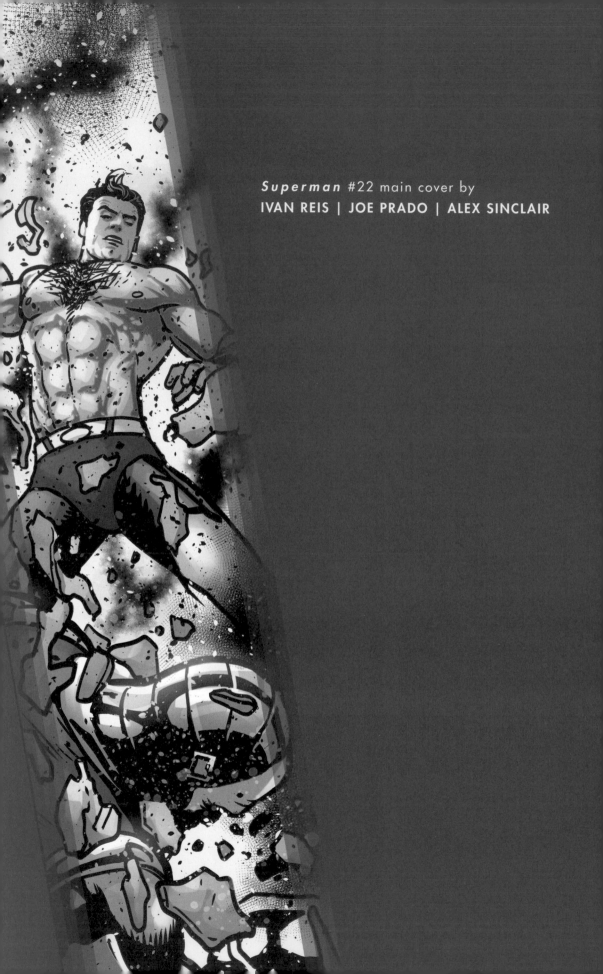

Superman #22 main cover by

IVAN REIS | JOE PRADO | ALEX SINCLAIR

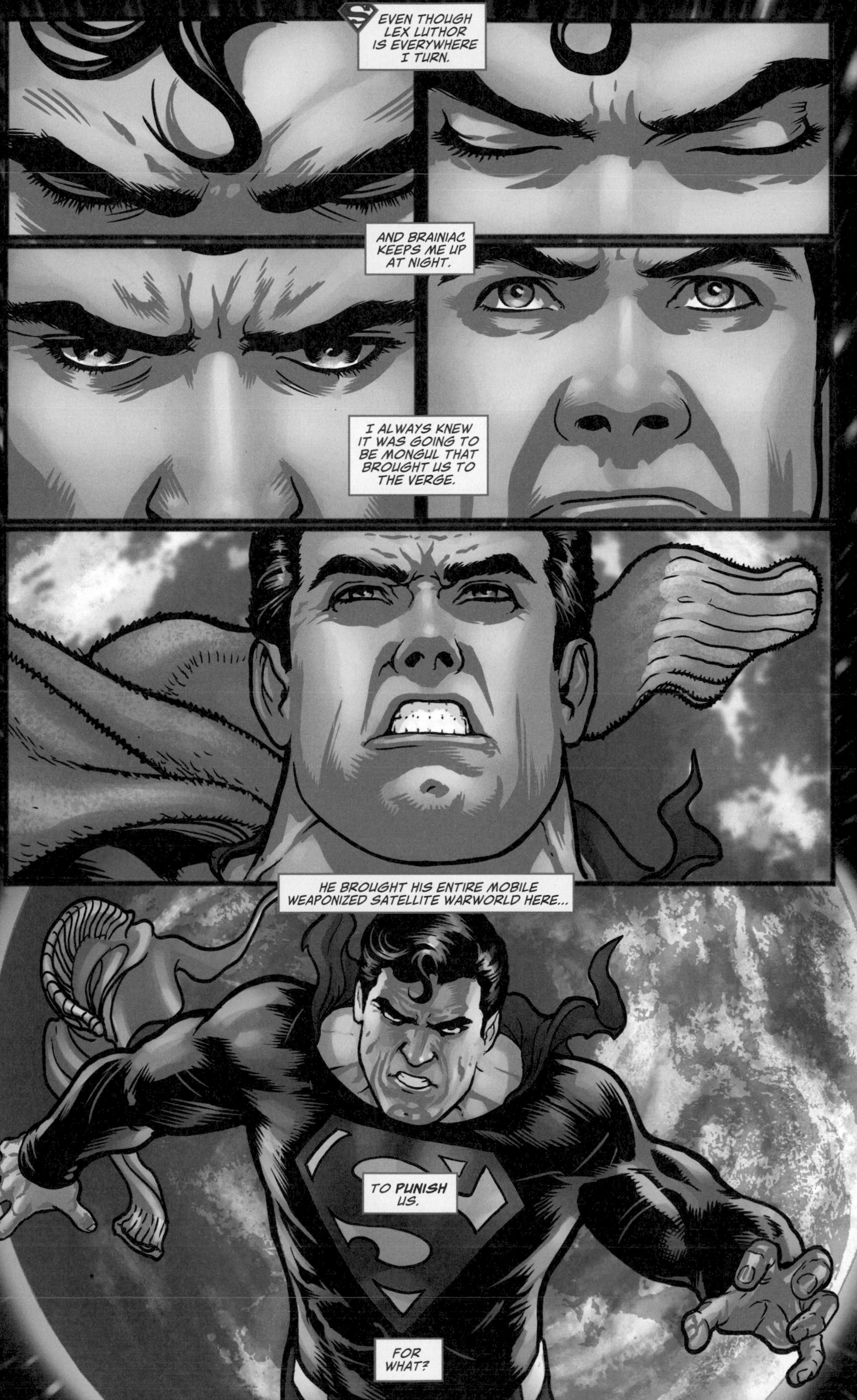
EVEN THOUGH LEX LUTHOR IS EVERYWHERE I TURN.
AND BRAINIAC KEEPS ME UP AT NIGHT.
I ALWAYS KNEW IT WAS GOING TO BE MONGUL THAT BROUGHT US TO THE VERGE.
HE BROUGHT HIS ENTIRE MOBILE WEAPONIZED SATELLITE WARWORLD HERE...
TO **PUNISH** US.
FOR WHAT?

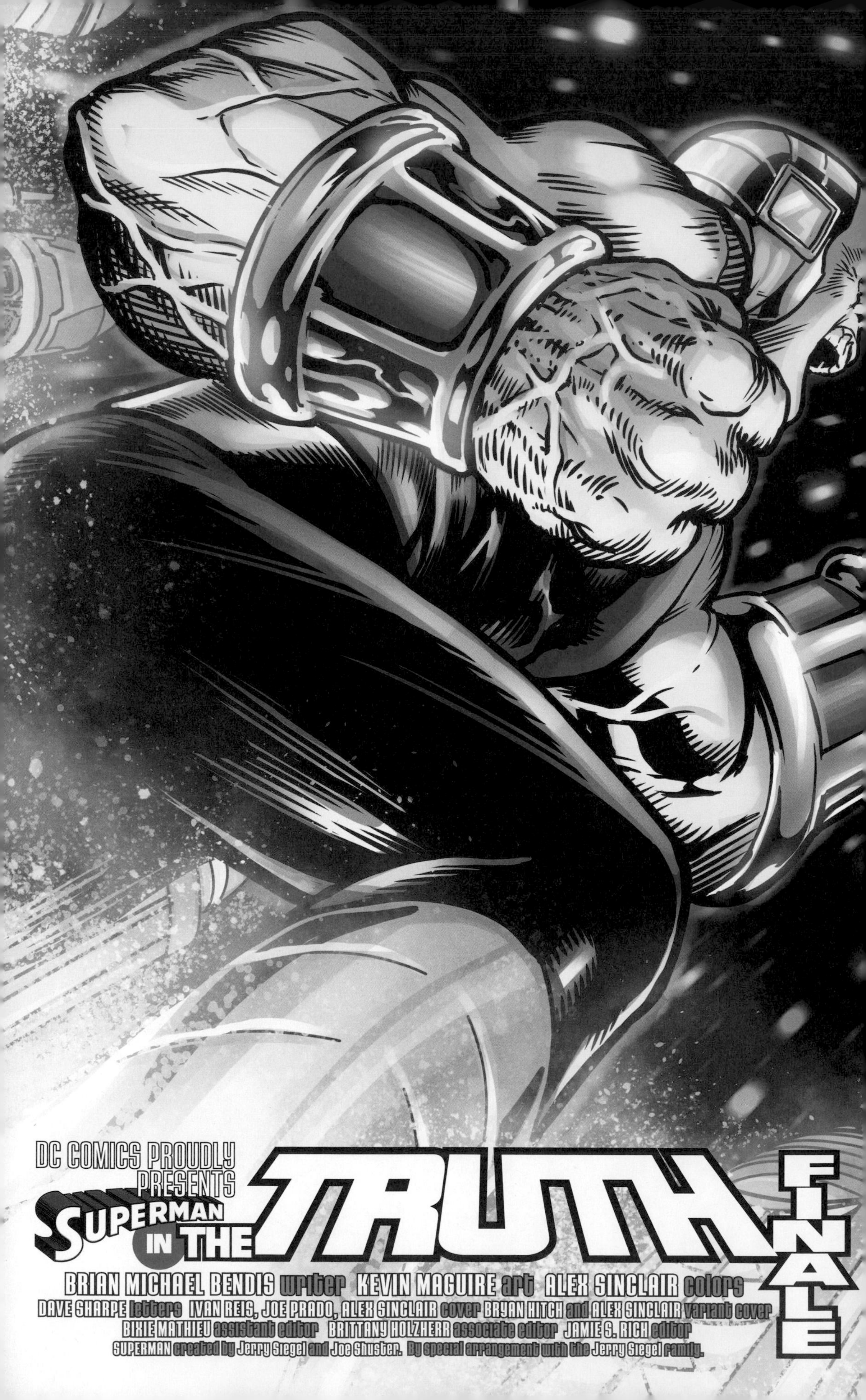
DC COMICS PROUDLY PRESENTS
SUPERMAN IN THE TRUTH
FINALE
BRIAN MICHAEL BENDIS writer KEVIN MAGUIRE art ALEX SINCLAIR colors
DAVE SHARPE letters IVAN REIS, JOE PRADO, ALEX SINCLAIR cover BRYAN HITCH and ALEX SINCLAIR variant cover
BIXIE MATHIEU assistant editor BRITTANY HOLZHERR associate editor JAMIE S. RICH editor
SUPERMAN created by Jerry Siegel and Joe Shuster. By special arrangement with the Jerry Siegel family.

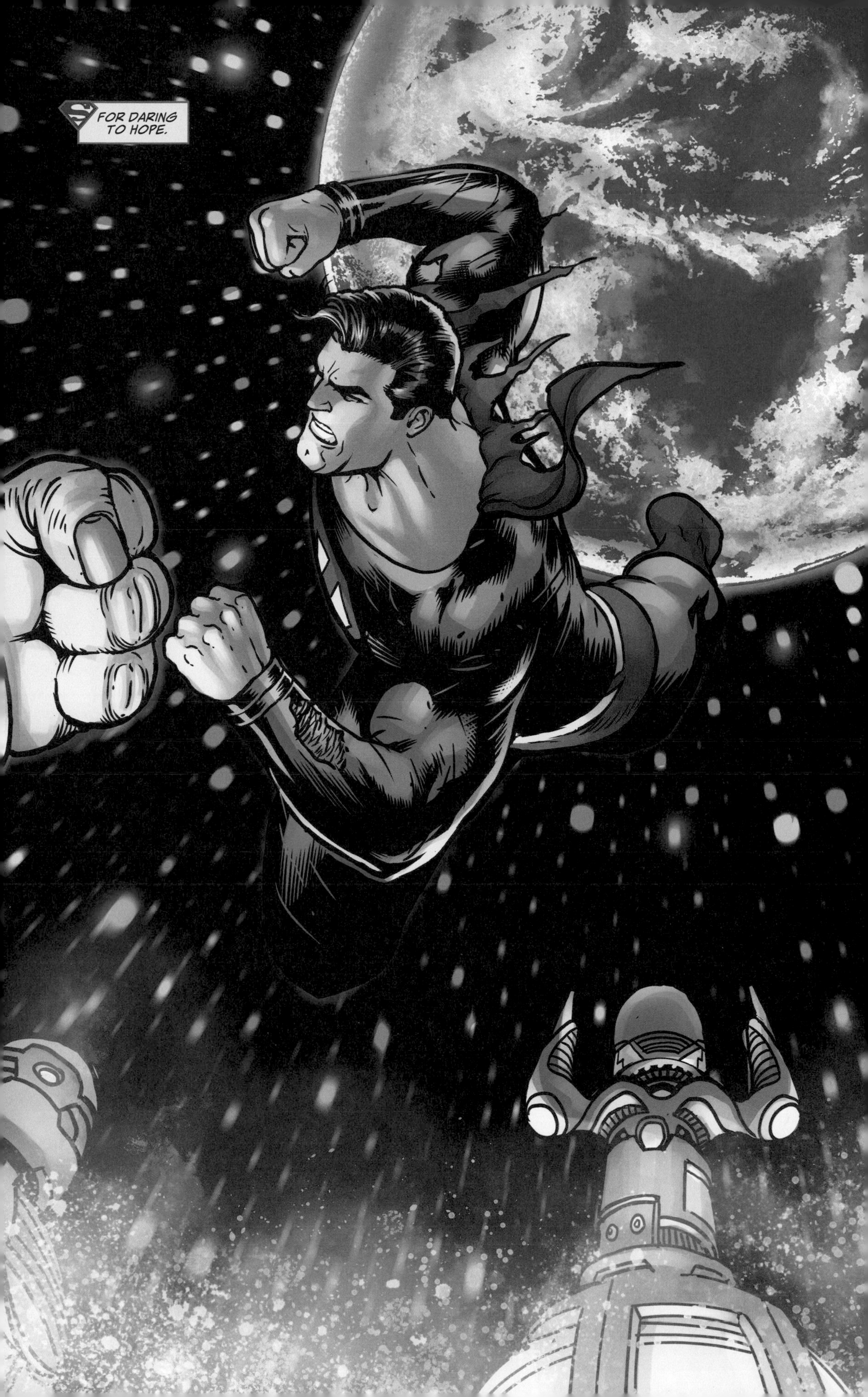
FOR DARING TO HOPE.

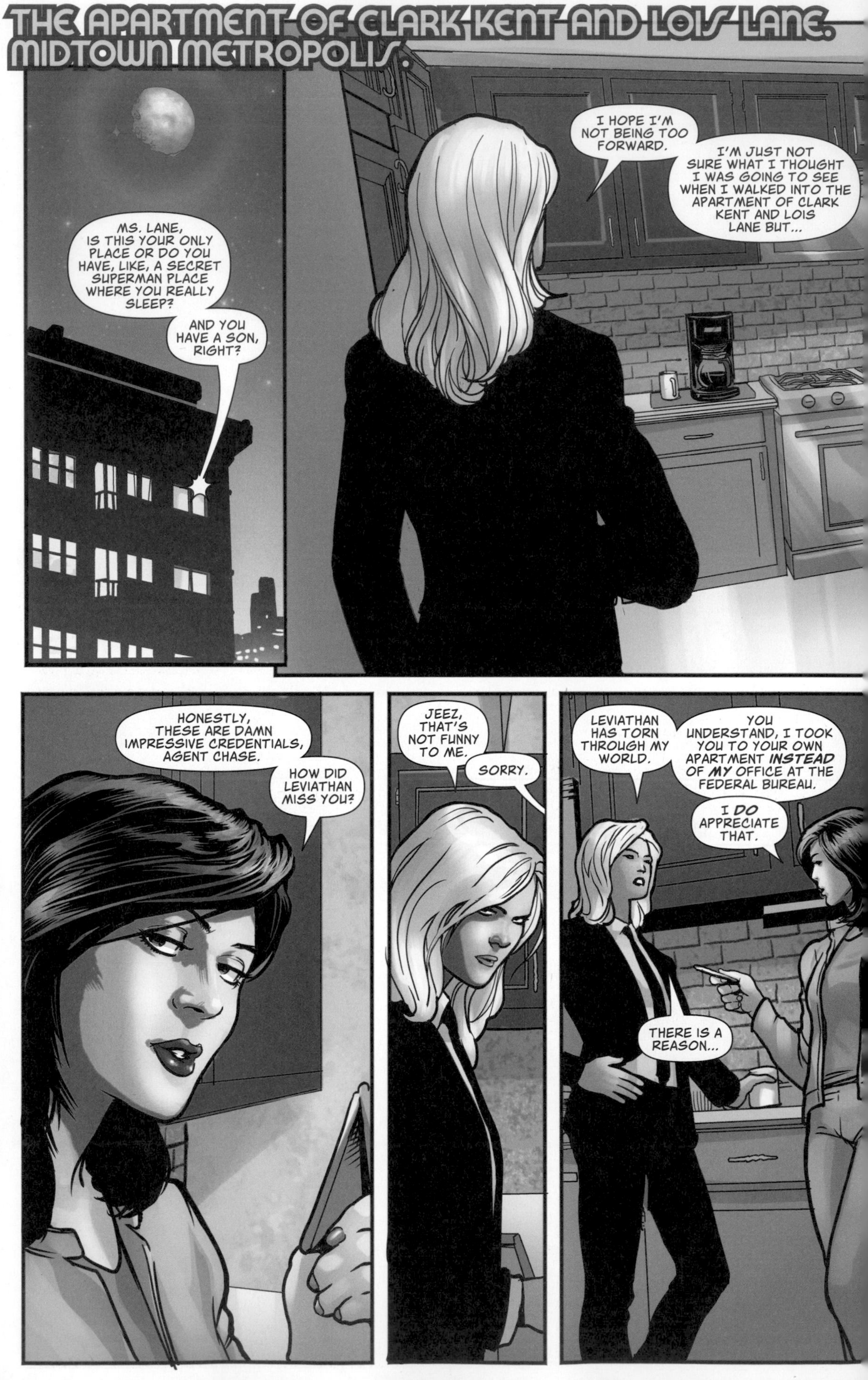
THE APARTMENT OF CLARK KENT AND LOIS LANE. MIDTOWN METROPOLIS.
MS. LANE, IS THIS YOUR ONLY PLACE OR DO YOU HAVE, LIKE, A SECRET SUPERMAN PLACE WHERE YOU REALLY SLEEP?
AND YOU HAVE A SON, RIGHT?
I HOPE I'M NOT BEING TOO FORWARD.
I'M JUST NOT SURE WHAT I THOUGHT I WAS GOING TO SEE WHEN I WALKED INTO THE APARTMENT OF CLARK KENT AND LOIS LANE BUT...
HONESTLY, THESE ARE DAMN IMPRESSIVE CREDENTIALS, AGENT CHASE.
HOW DID LEVIATHAN MISS YOU?
JEEZ, THAT'S NOT FUNNY TO ME.
SORRY.
LEVIATHAN HAS TORN THROUGH MY WORLD.
YOU UNDERSTAND, I TOOK YOU TO YOUR OWN APARTMENT *INSTEAD* OF *MY* OFFICE AT THE FEDERAL BUREAU.
I *DO* APPRECIATE THAT.
THERE IS A REASON...

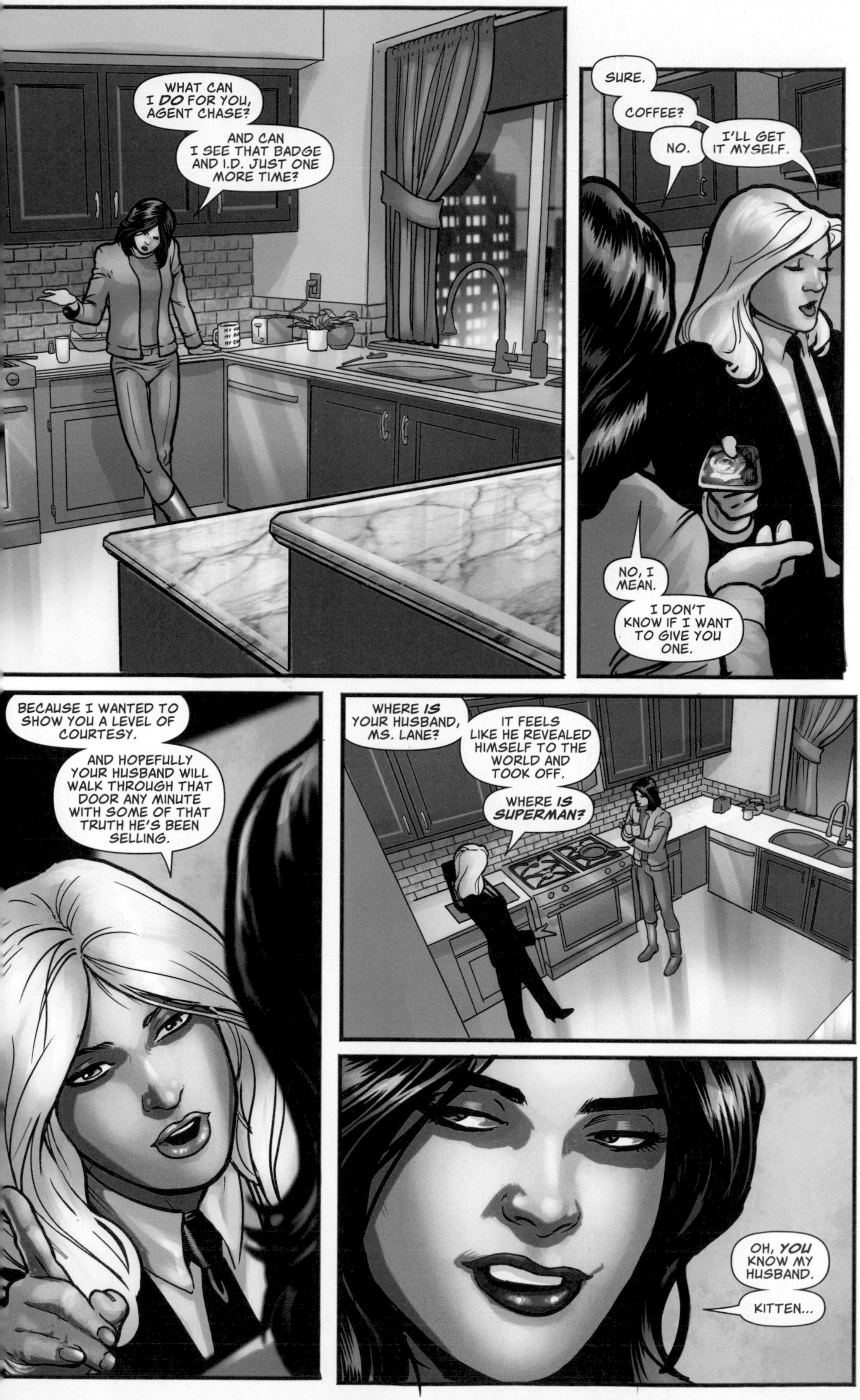
WHAT CAN I *DO* FOR YOU, AGENT CHASE?
AND CAN I SEE THAT BADGE AND I.D. JUST ONE MORE TIME?
SURE.
COFFEE?
NO.
I'LL GET IT MYSELF.
NO, I MEAN.
I DON'T KNOW IF I WANT TO GIVE YOU ONE.
BECAUSE I WANTED TO SHOW YOU A LEVEL OF COURTESY.
AND HOPEFULLY YOUR HUSBAND WILL WALK THROUGH THAT DOOR ANY MINUTE WITH SOME OF THAT TRUTH HE'S BEEN SELLING.
WHERE *IS* YOUR HUSBAND, MS. LANE?
IT FEELS LIKE HE REVEALED HIMSELF TO THE WORLD AND TOOK OFF.
WHERE *IS SUPERMAN?*
OH, *YOU* KNOW MY HUSBAND.
KITTEN...

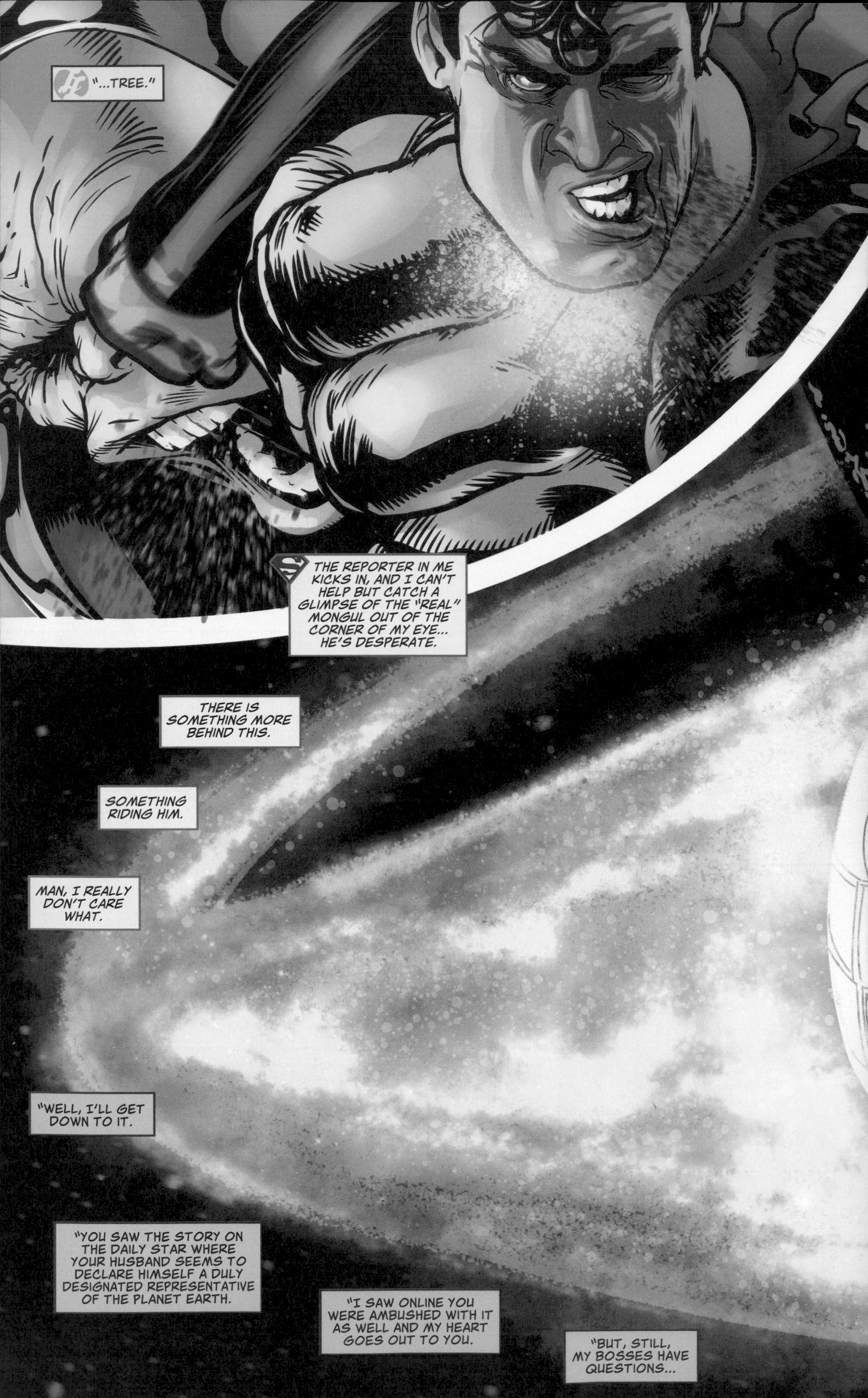
"...TREE."
THE REPORTER IN ME KICKS IN, AND I CAN'T HELP BUT CATCH A GLIMPSE OF THE "REAL" MONGUL OUT OF THE CORNER OF MY EYE... HE'S DESPERATE.
THERE IS SOMETHING MORE BEHIND THIS.
SOMETHING RIDING HIM.
MAN, I REALLY DON'T CARE WHAT.
"WELL, I'LL GET DOWN TO IT.
"YOU SAW THE STORY ON THE DAILY STAR WHERE YOUR HUSBAND SEEMS TO DECLARE HIMSELF A DULY DESIGNATED REPRESENTATIVE OF THE PLANET EARTH.
"I SAW ONLINE YOU WERE AMBUSHED WITH IT AS WELL AND MY HEART GOES OUT TO YOU.
"BUT, STILL, MY BOSSES HAVE QUESTIONS...

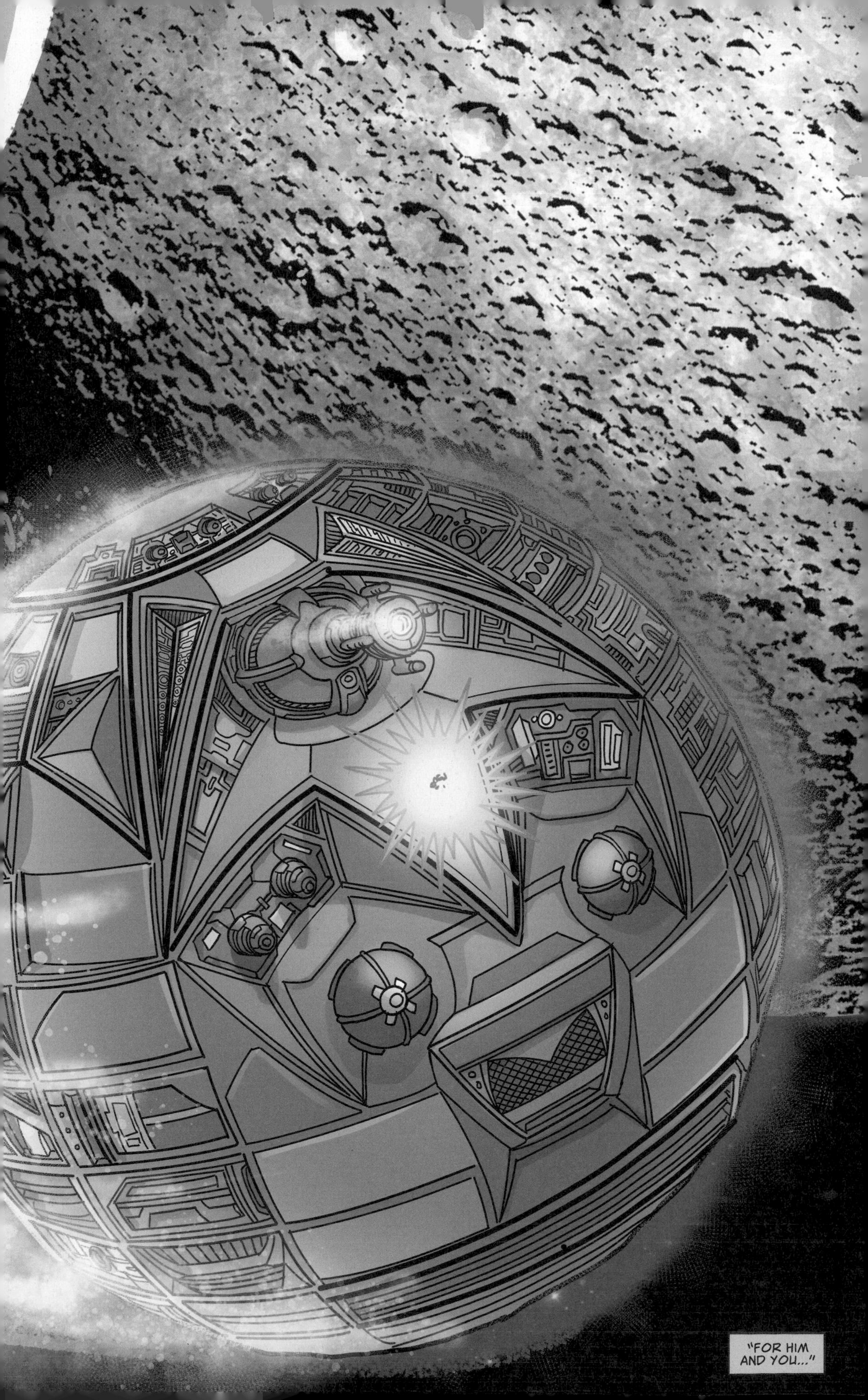
"FOR HIM
AND YOU..."

WHY TAKE OUT ALL YOUR FRUSTRATIONS ABOUT THE UNITED PLANETS ON THIS LITTLE PLANET?

WHY? WHY EARTH?

A MILLION LITTLE PLANETS IN A MILLION LITTLE CORNERS OF THE GALAXY...

WHY DOES ALL OF THIS COME TO OUR FRONT DOOR?

I AM SO DESPERATE TO END THIS. I START SCROLLING THROUGH MY HEAD.

ALL OF OUR PAST BATTLES AND FIGHTS WITH MONGUL THAT--

KARA.

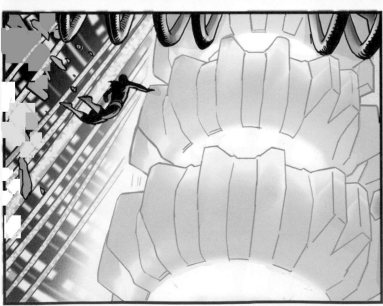

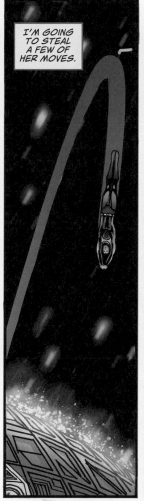

I'M GOING TO STEAL A FEW OF HER MOVES.

SHE WON'T MIND.

IT'S REALLY A COMPLIMENT.

NOT TOO LONG AGO, MY COUSIN REALLY NAILED A MOMENT WITH MONGUL.

I WAS, AT THAT MOMENT, PROFESSIONALLY JEALOUS.

THAT'S HOW GOOD.

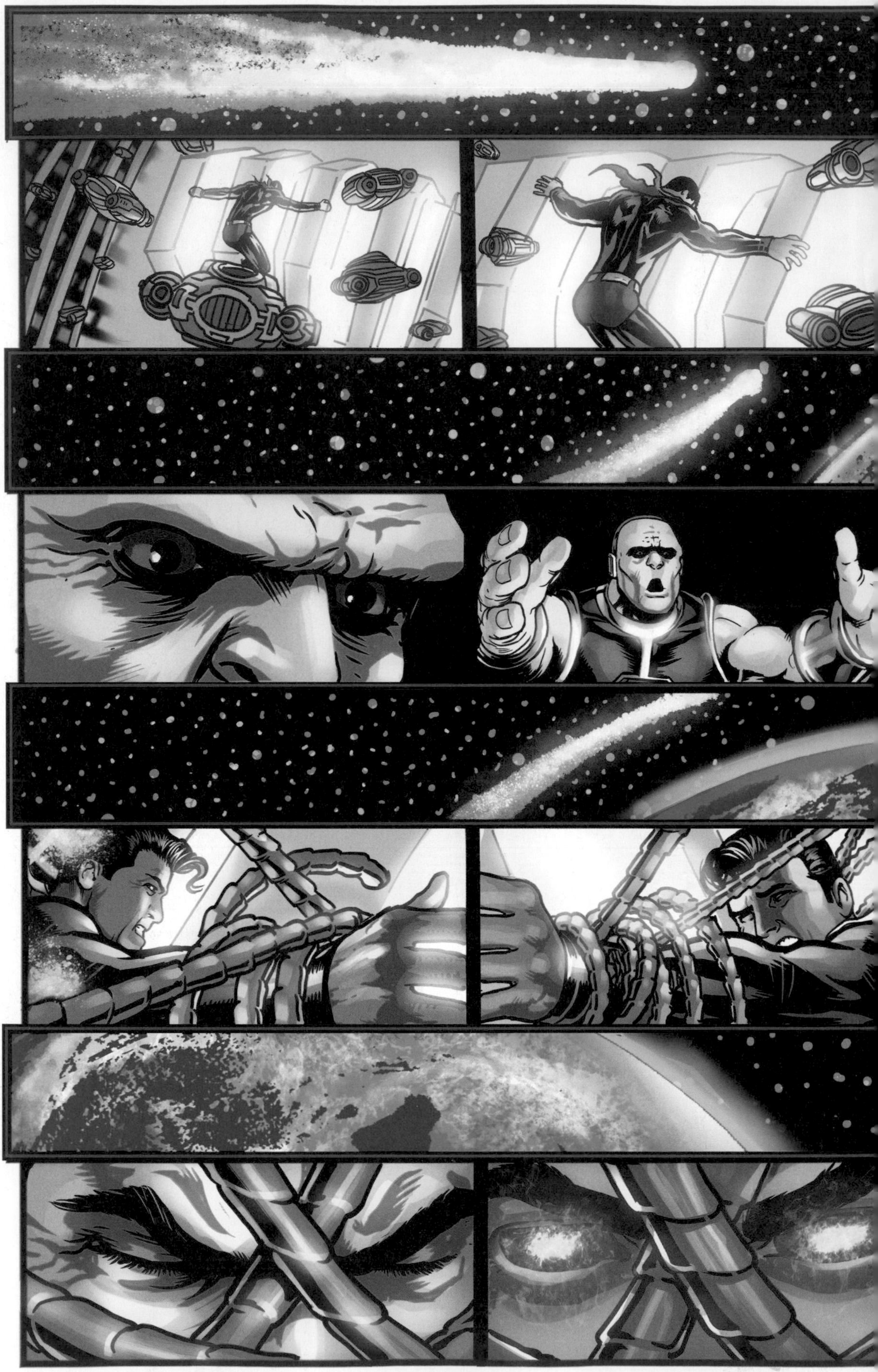

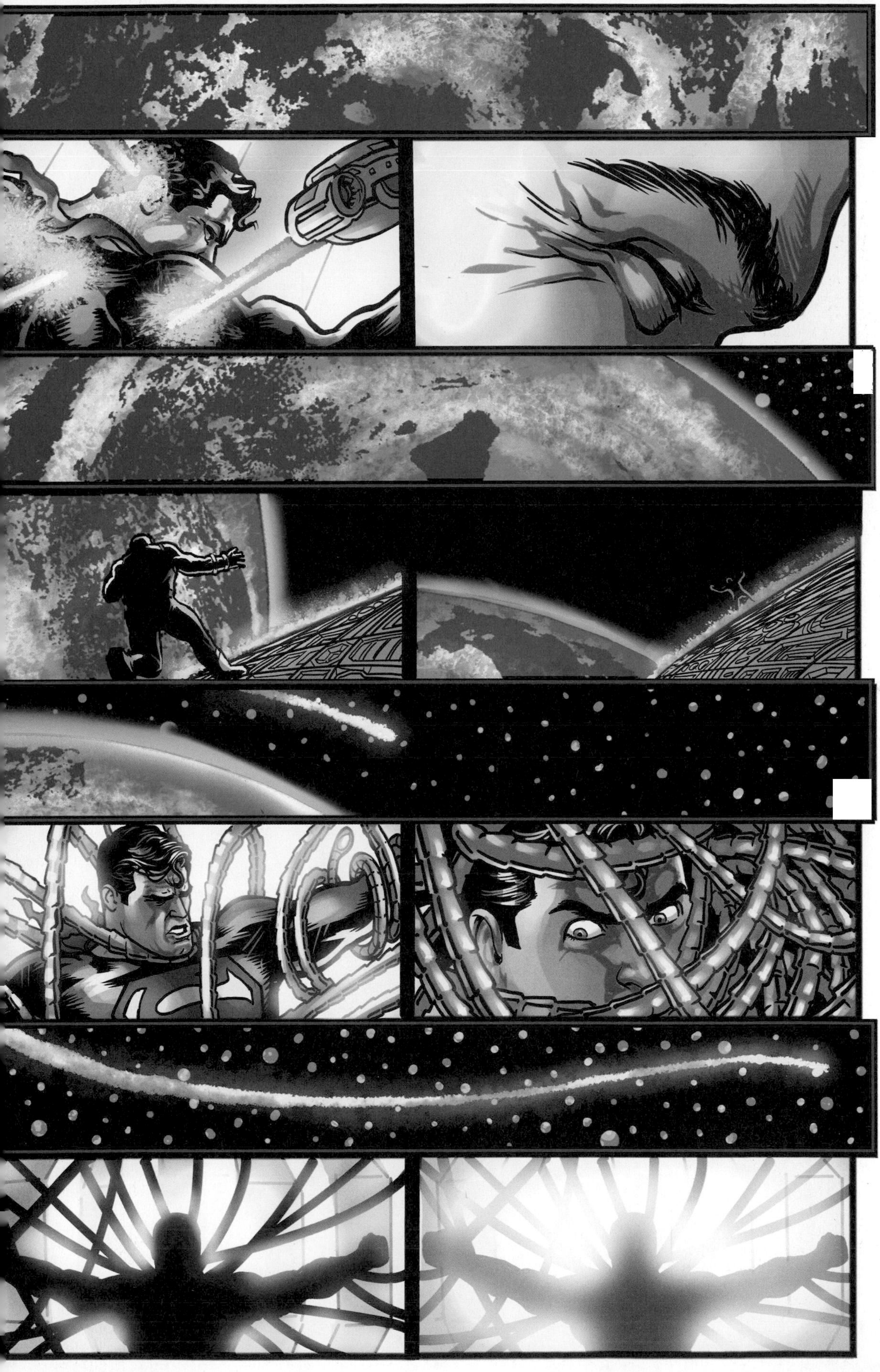

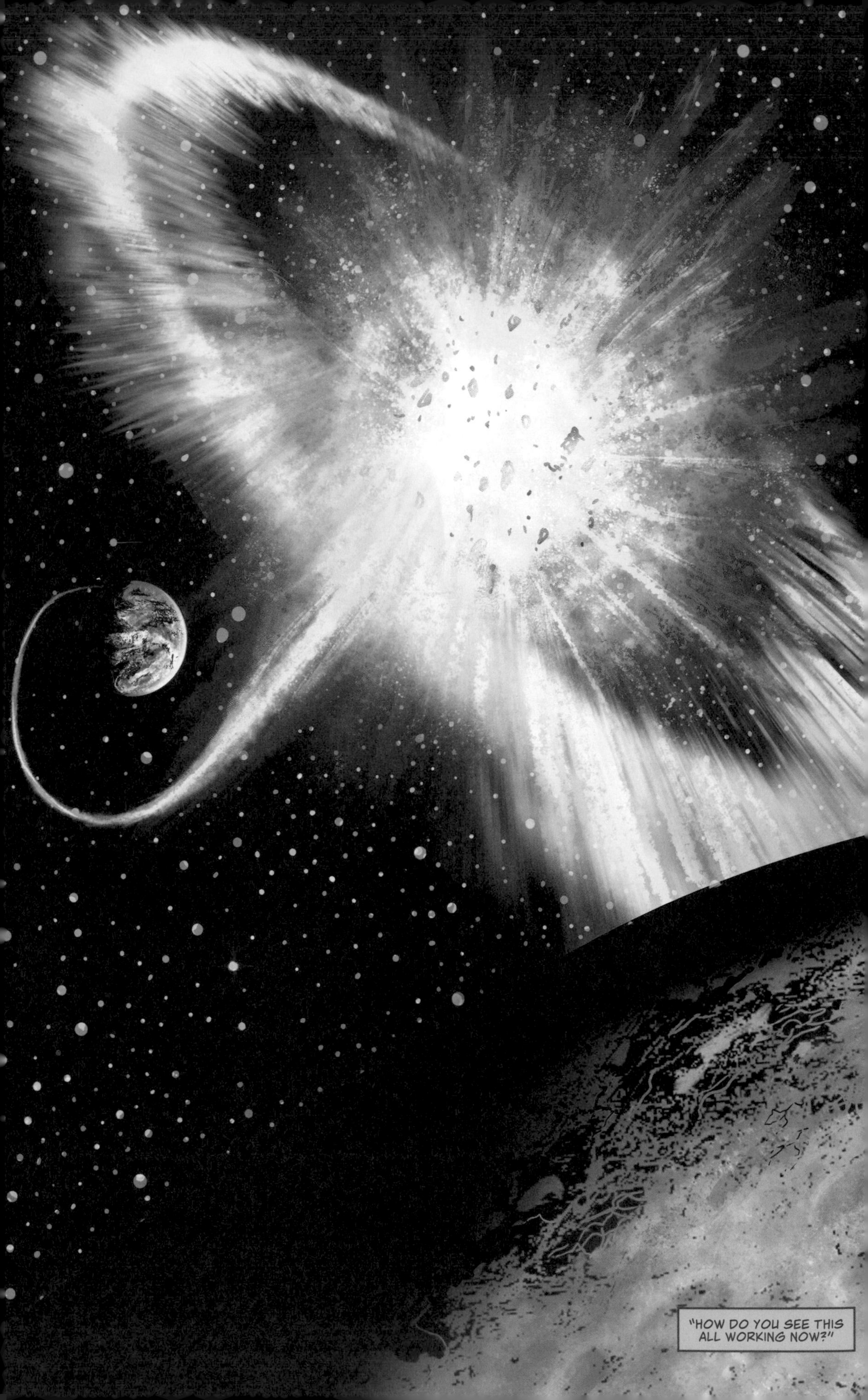
"HOW DO YOU SEE THIS ALL WORKING NOW?"

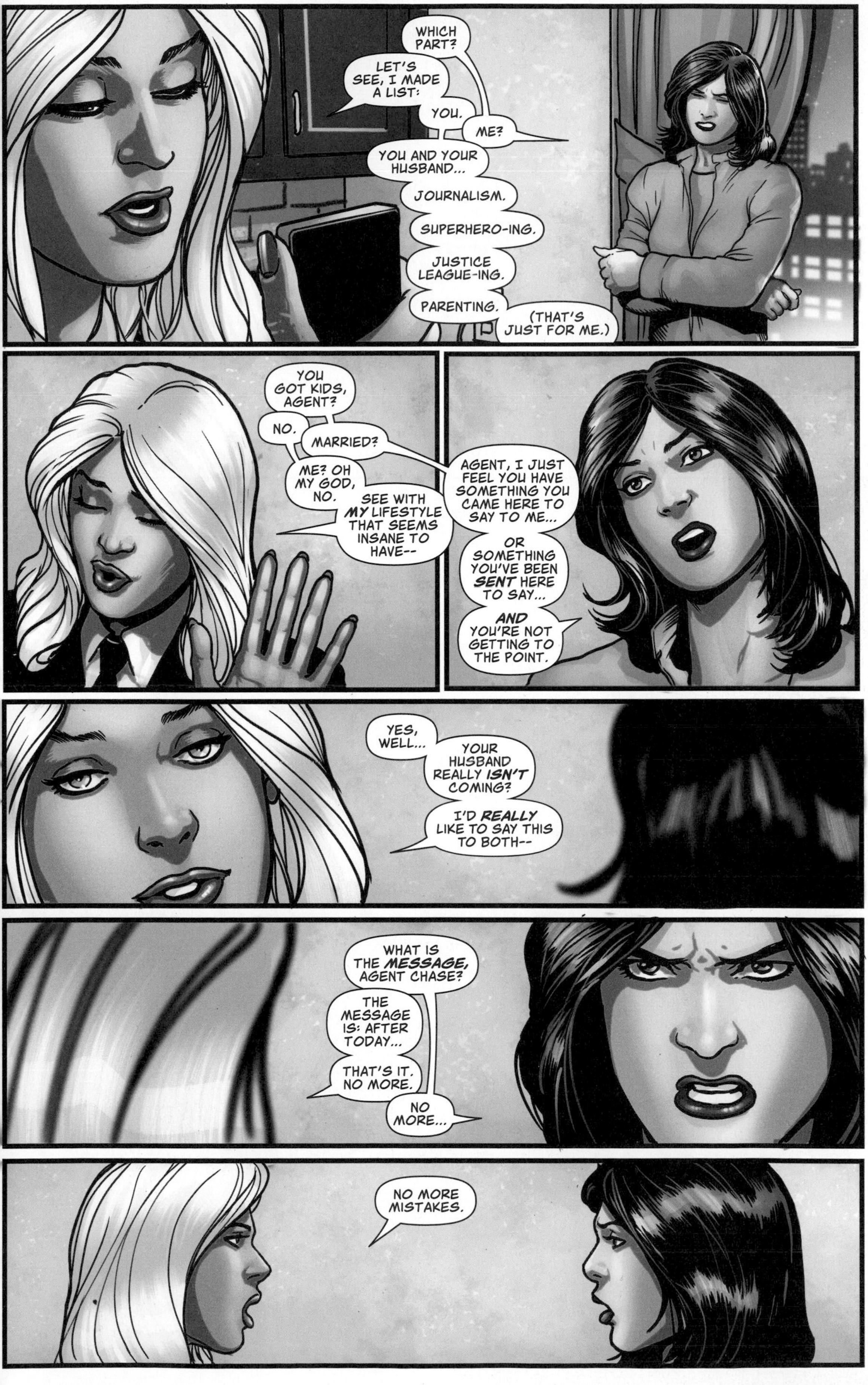
WHICH PART?
LET'S SEE, I MADE A LIST:
YOU.
ME?
YOU AND YOUR HUSBAND...
JOURNALISM.
SUPERHERO-ING.
JUSTICE LEAGUE-ING.
PARENTING.
(THAT'S JUST FOR ME.)
YOU GOT KIDS, AGENT?
NO.
MARRIED?
ME? OH MY GOD, NO.
SEE WITH MY LIFESTYLE THAT SEEMS INSANE TO HAVE--
AGENT, I JUST FEEL YOU HAVE SOMETHING YOU CAME HERE TO SAY TO ME...
OR SOMETHING YOU'VE BEEN SENT HERE TO SAY...
AND YOU'RE NOT GETTING TO THE POINT.
YES, WELL...
YOUR HUSBAND REALLY ISN'T COMING?
I'D REALLY LIKE TO SAY THIS TO BOTH--
WHAT IS THE MESSAGE, AGENT CHASE?
THE MESSAGE IS: AFTER TODAY...
THAT'S IT. NO MORE.
NO MORE...
NO MORE MISTAKES.

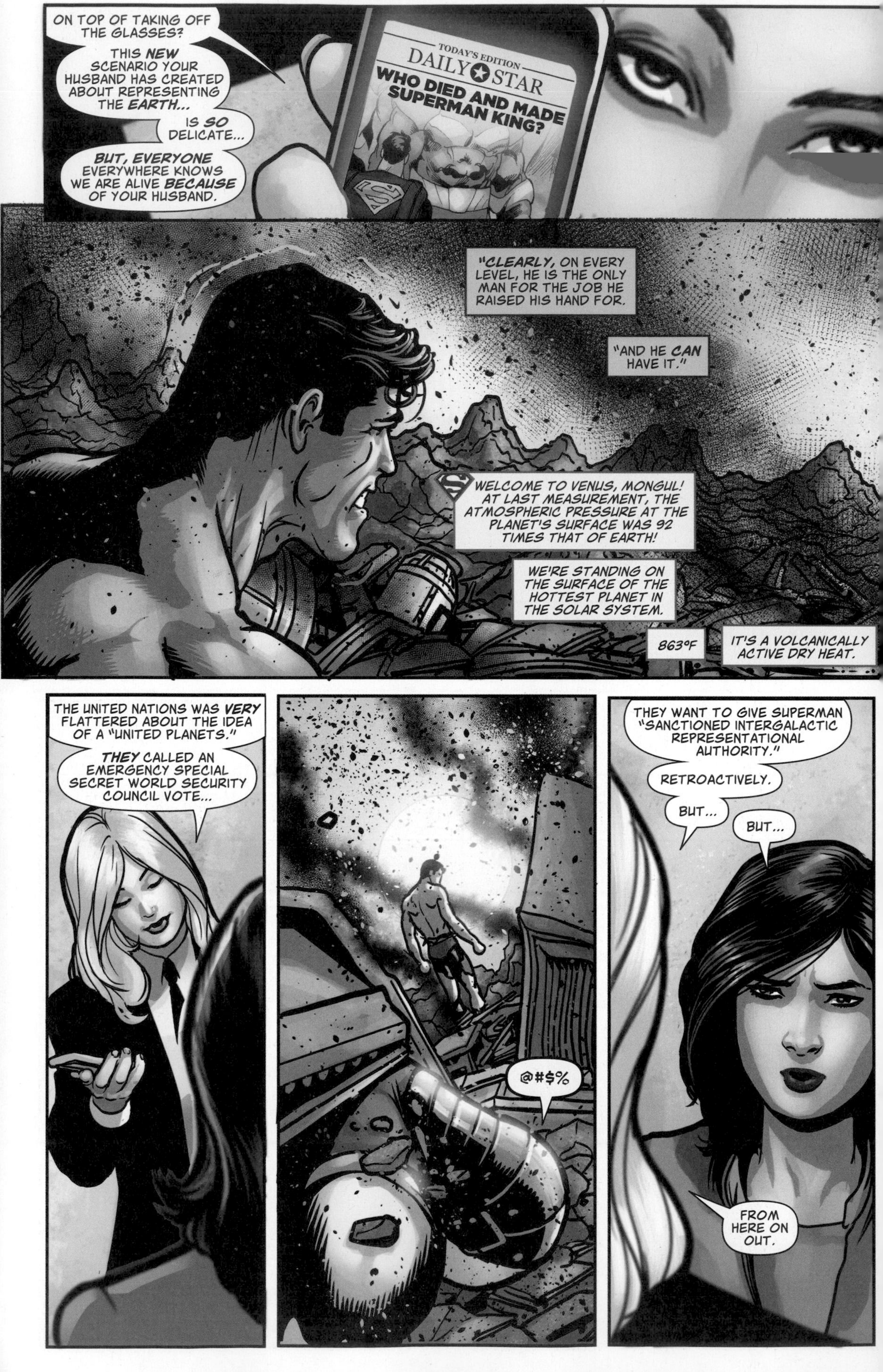

ON TOP OF TAKING OFF THE GLASSES?
THIS NEW SCENARIO YOUR HUSBAND HAS CREATED ABOUT REPRESENTING THE EARTH...
IS SO DELICATE...
BUT, EVERYONE EVERYWHERE KNOWS WE ARE ALIVE BECAUSE OF YOUR HUSBAND.
TODAY'S EDITION
DAILY STAR
WHO DIED AND MADE SUPERMAN KING?
"CLEARLY, ON EVERY LEVEL, HE IS THE ONLY MAN FOR THE JOB HE RAISED HIS HAND FOR.
"AND HE CAN HAVE IT."
WELCOME TO VENUS, MONGUL! AT LAST MEASUREMENT, THE ATMOSPHERIC PRESSURE AT THE PLANET'S SURFACE WAS 92 TIMES THAT OF EARTH!
WE'RE STANDING ON THE SURFACE OF THE HOTTEST PLANET IN THE SOLAR SYSTEM.
863°F
IT'S A VOLCANICALLY ACTIVE DRY HEAT.
THE UNITED NATIONS WAS VERY FLATTERED ABOUT THE IDEA OF A "UNITED PLANETS."
THEY CALLED AN EMERGENCY SPECIAL SECRET WORLD SECURITY COUNCIL VOTE...
@#$%
THEY WANT TO GIVE SUPERMAN "SANCTIONED INTERGALACTIC REPRESENTATIONAL AUTHORITY."
RETROACTIVELY.
BUT...
BUT...
FROM HERE ON OUT.

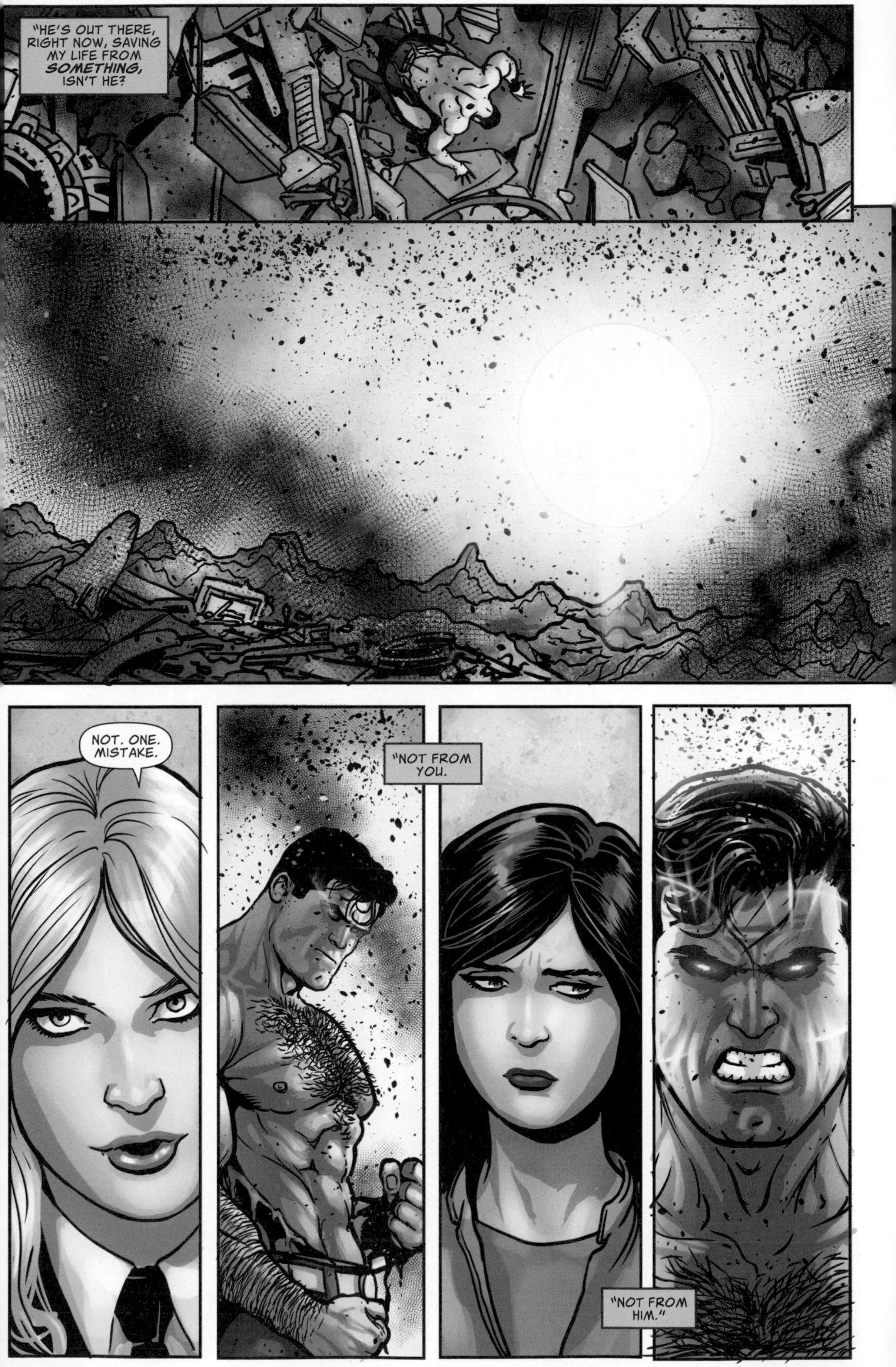
"HE'S OUT THERE, RIGHT NOW, SAVING MY LIFE FROM SOMETHING, ISN'T HE?
NOT. ONE. MISTAKE.
"NOT FROM YOU.
"NOT FROM HIM."

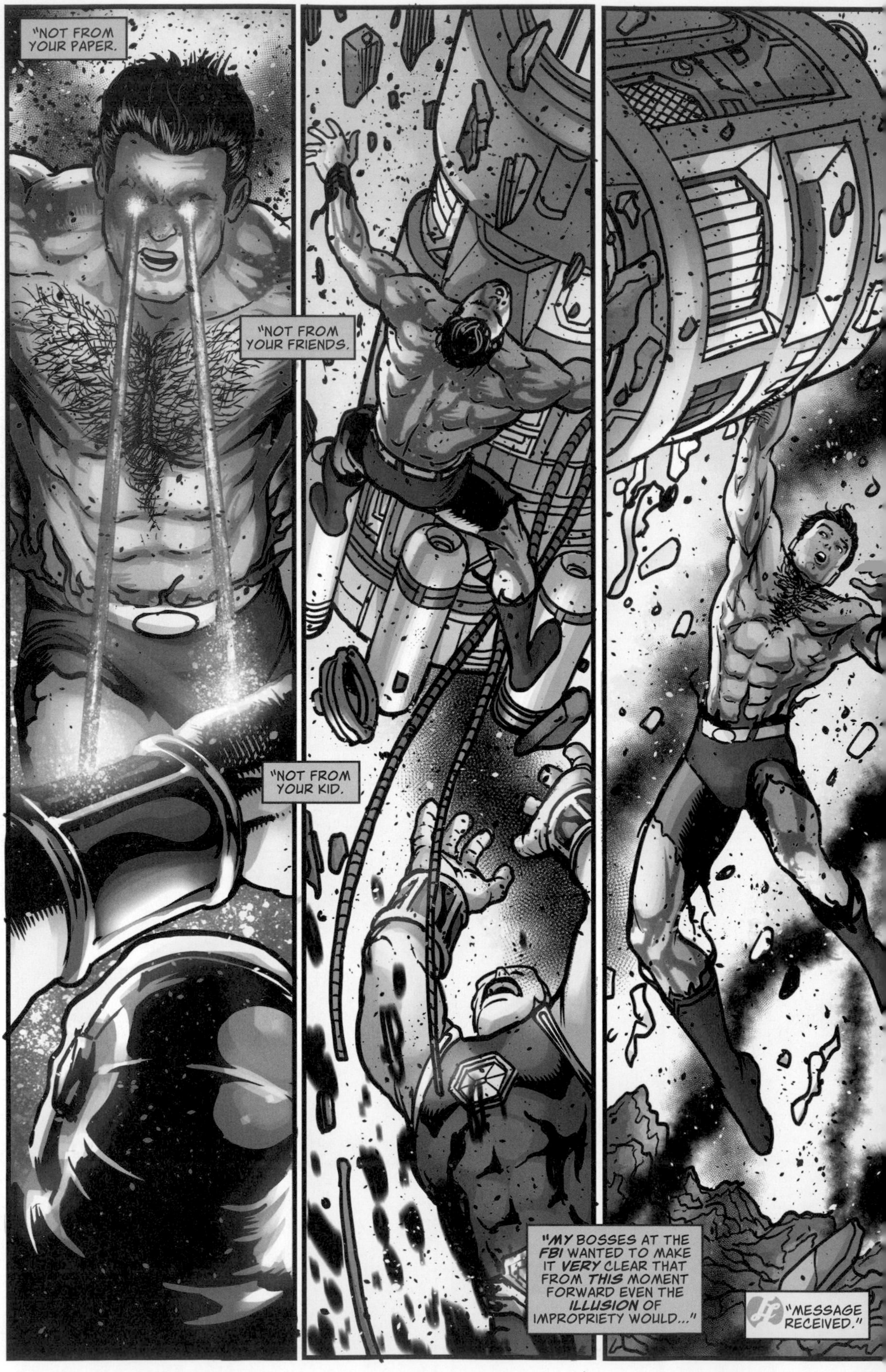
"NOT FROM YOUR PAPER.
"NOT FROM YOUR FRIENDS.
"NOT FROM YOUR KID.
"MY BOSSES AT THE FBI WANTED TO MAKE IT VERY CLEAR THAT FROM THIS MOMENT FORWARD EVEN THE ILLUSION OF IMPROPRIETY WOULD..."
"MESSAGE RECEIVED."

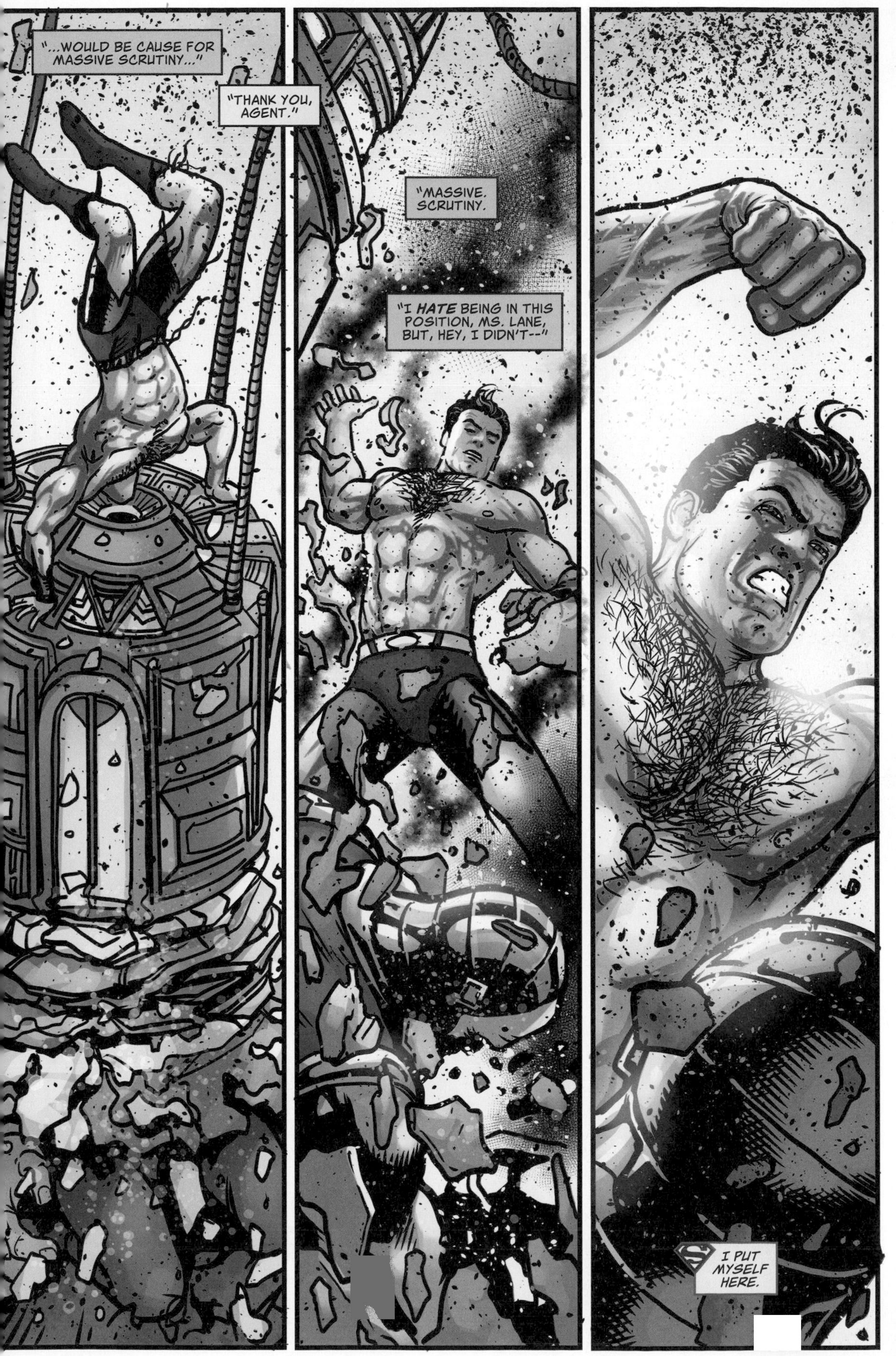
"...WOULD BE CAUSE FOR MASSIVE SCRUTINY..."
"THANK YOU, AGENT."
"MASSIVE. SCRUTINY.
"I *HATE* BEING IN THIS POSITION, MS. LANE, BUT, HEY, I DIDN'T--"
I PUT MYSELF HERE.

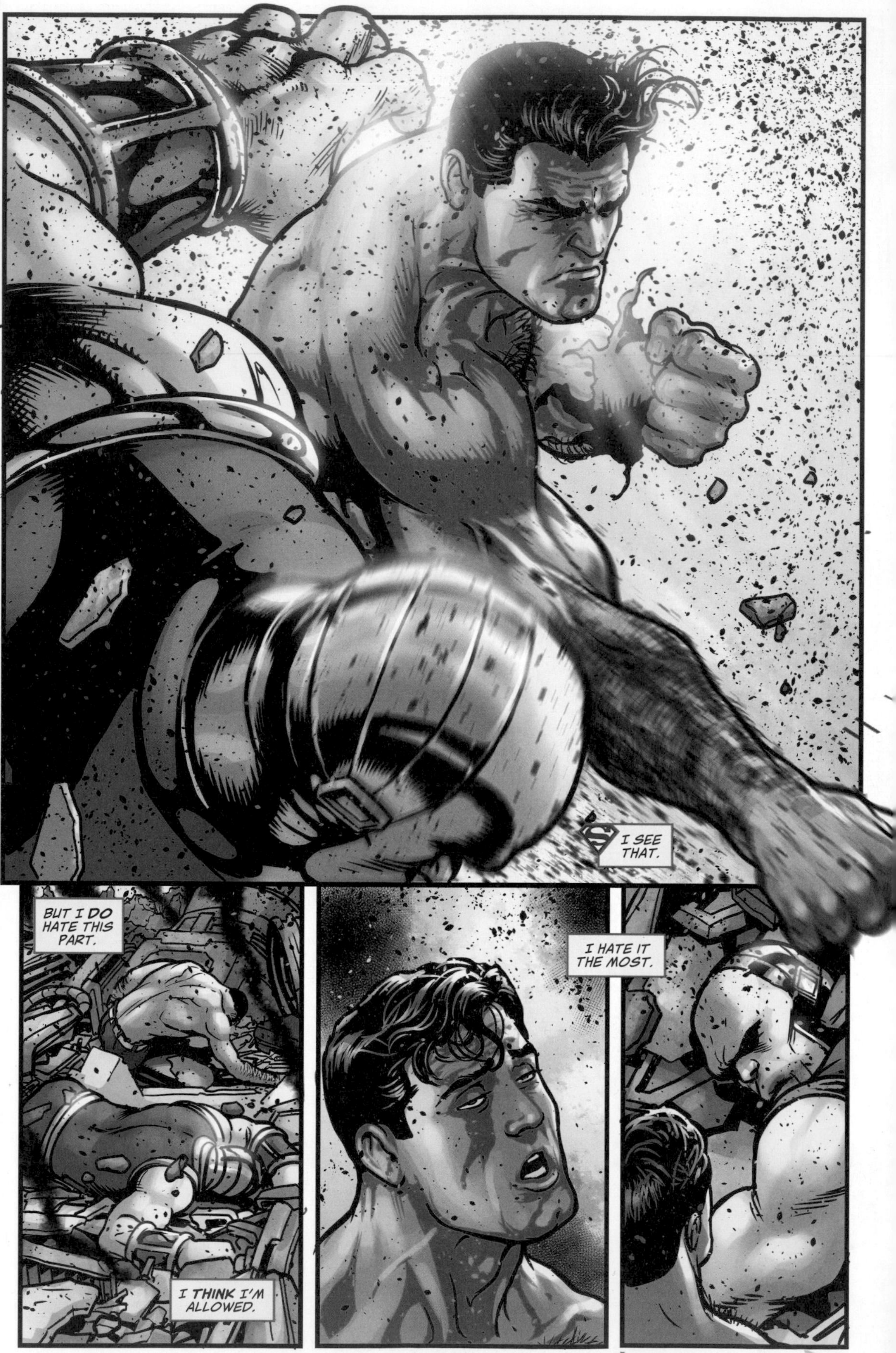
I SEE THAT.
BUT I DO HATE THIS PART.
I THINK I'M ALLOWED.
I HATE IT THE MOST.

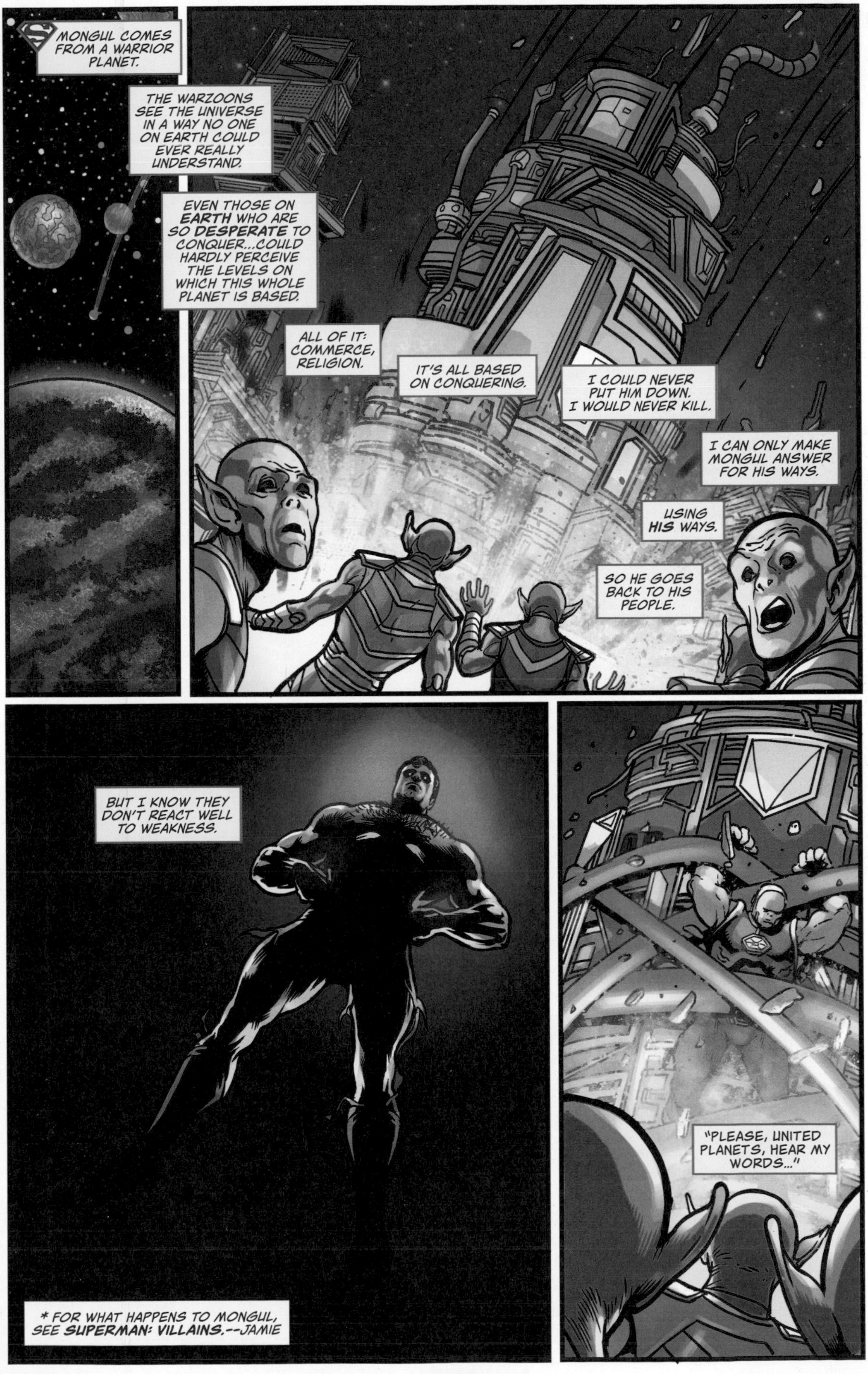

MONGUL COMES FROM A WARRIOR PLANET.
THE WARZOONS SEE THE UNIVERSE IN A WAY NO ONE ON EARTH COULD EVER REALLY UNDERSTAND.
EVEN THOSE ON **EARTH** WHO ARE SO **DESPERATE** TO CONQUER...COULD HARDLY PERCEIVE THE LEVELS ON WHICH THIS WHOLE PLANET IS BASED.
ALL OF IT: COMMERCE, RELIGION.
IT'S ALL BASED ON CONQUERING.
I COULD NEVER PUT HIM DOWN. I WOULD NEVER KILL.
I CAN ONLY MAKE MONGUL ANSWER FOR HIS WAYS.
USING **HIS** WAYS.
SO HE GOES BACK TO HIS PEOPLE.
BUT I KNOW THEY DON'T REACT WELL TO WEAKNESS.
* FOR WHAT HAPPENS TO MONGUL, SEE **SUPERMAN: VILLAINS.**--JAMIE
"PLEASE, UNITED PLANETS, HEAR MY WORDS..."

DAXAM PLANETARY.

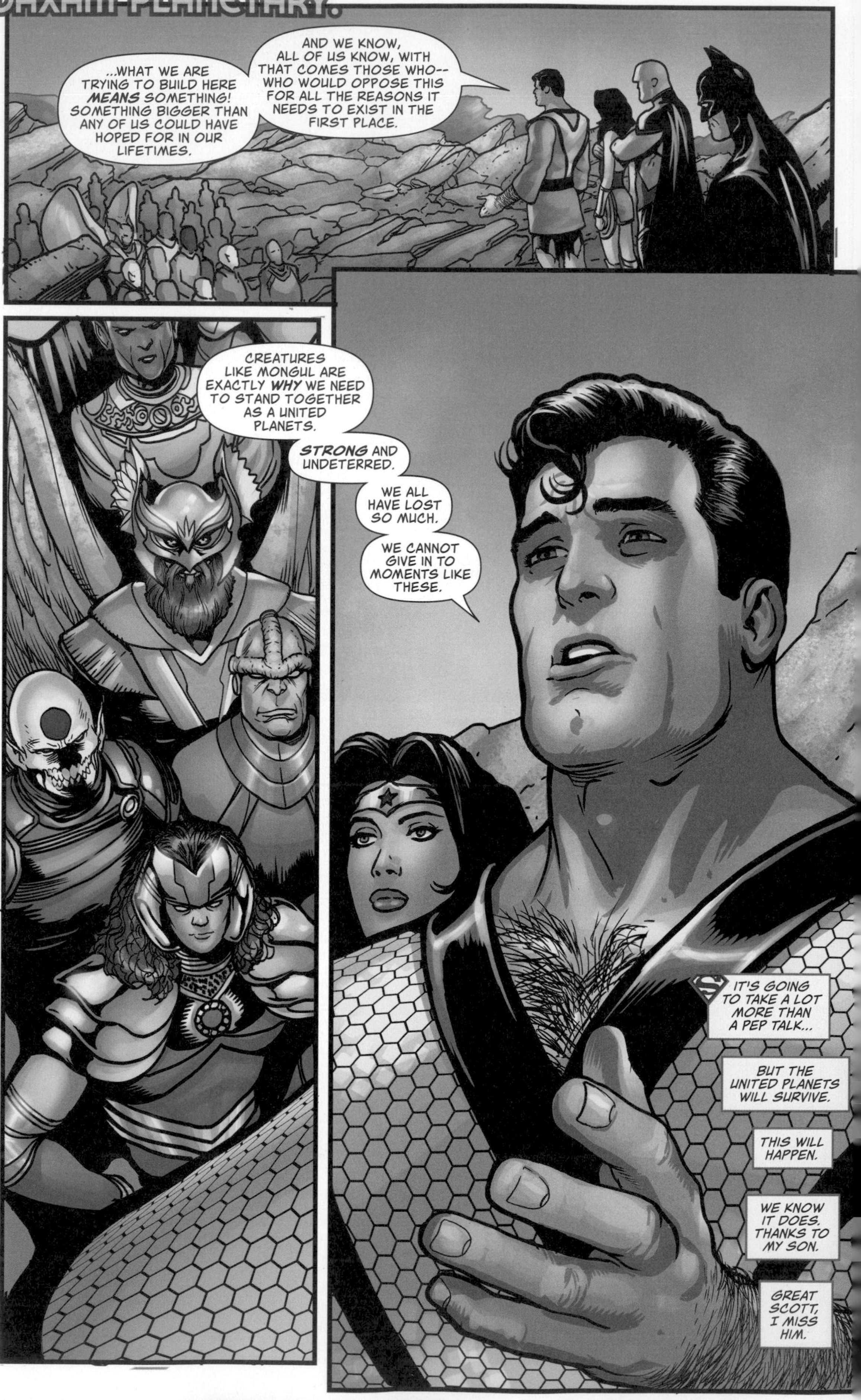
...WHAT WE ARE TRYING TO BUILD HERE MEANS SOMETHING! SOMETHING BIGGER THAN ANY OF US COULD HAVE HOPED FOR IN OUR LIFETIMES.
AND WE KNOW, ALL OF US KNOW, WITH THAT COMES THOSE WHO-- WHO WOULD OPPOSE THIS FOR ALL THE REASONS IT NEEDS TO EXIST IN THE FIRST PLACE.
CREATURES LIKE MONGUL ARE EXACTLY WHY WE NEED TO STAND TOGETHER AS A UNITED PLANETS.
STRONG AND UNDETERRED.
WE ALL HAVE LOST SO MUCH.
WE CANNOT GIVE IN TO MOMENTS LIKE THESE.
IT'S GOING TO TAKE A LOT MORE THAN A PEP TALK...
BUT THE UNITED PLANETS WILL SURVIVE.
THIS WILL HAPPEN.
WE KNOW IT DOES. THANKS TO MY SON.
GREAT SCOTT, I MISS HIM.

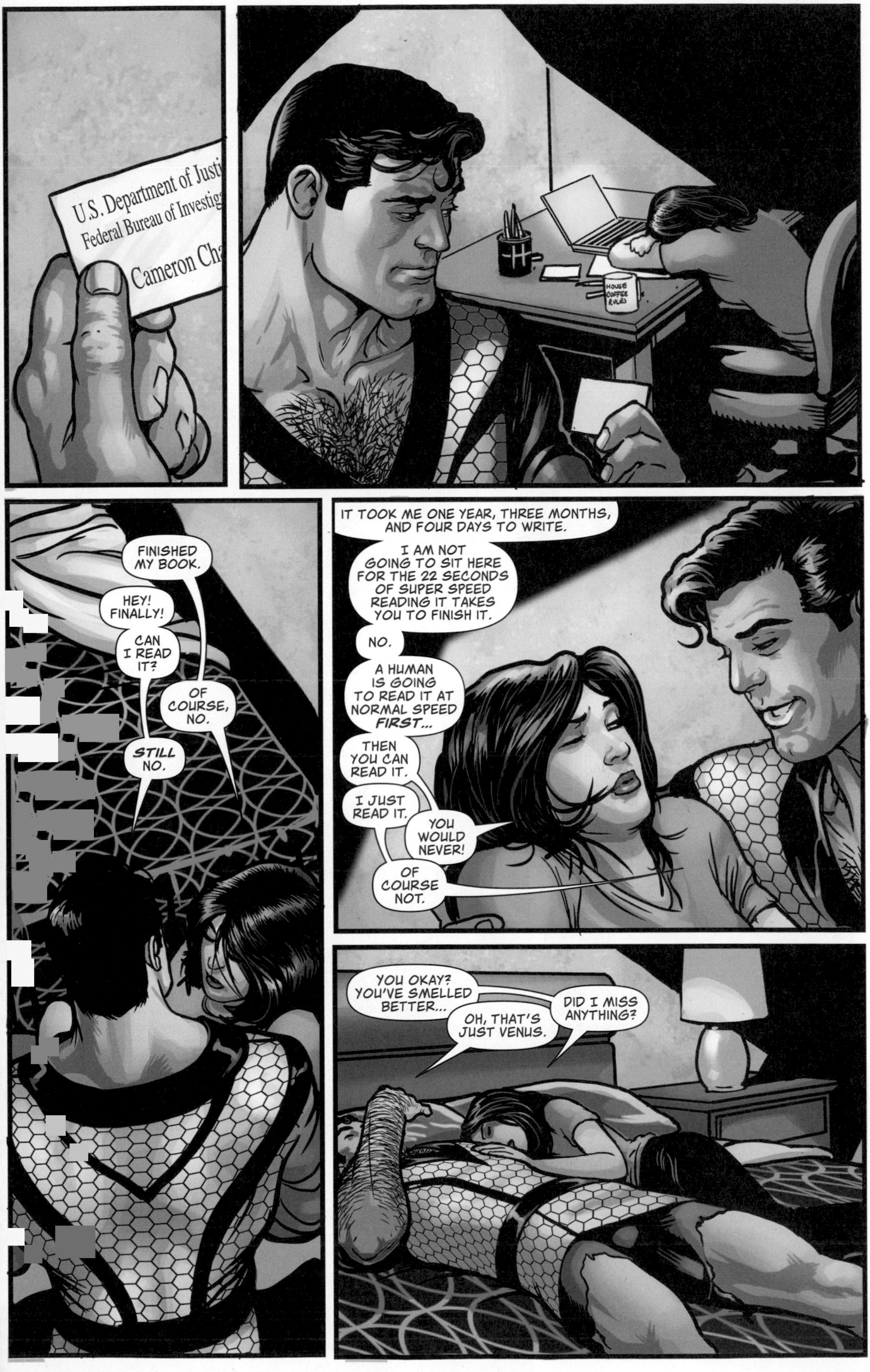
U.S. Department of Justi
Federal Bureau of Investig
Cameron Cha
HOUSE COFFEE RULES
FINISHED MY BOOK.
HEY! FINALLY!
CAN I READ IT?
OF COURSE, NO.
STILL NO.
IT TOOK ME ONE YEAR, THREE MONTHS, AND FOUR DAYS TO WRITE.
I AM NOT GOING TO SIT HERE FOR THE 22 SECONDS OF SUPER SPEED READING IT TAKES YOU TO FINISH IT.
NO.
A HUMAN IS GOING TO READ IT AT NORMAL SPEED FIRST...
THEN YOU CAN READ IT.
I JUST READ IT.
YOU WOULD NEVER!
OF COURSE NOT.
YOU OKAY? YOU'VE SMELLED BETTER...
OH, THAT'S JUST VENUS.
DID I MISS ANYTHING?

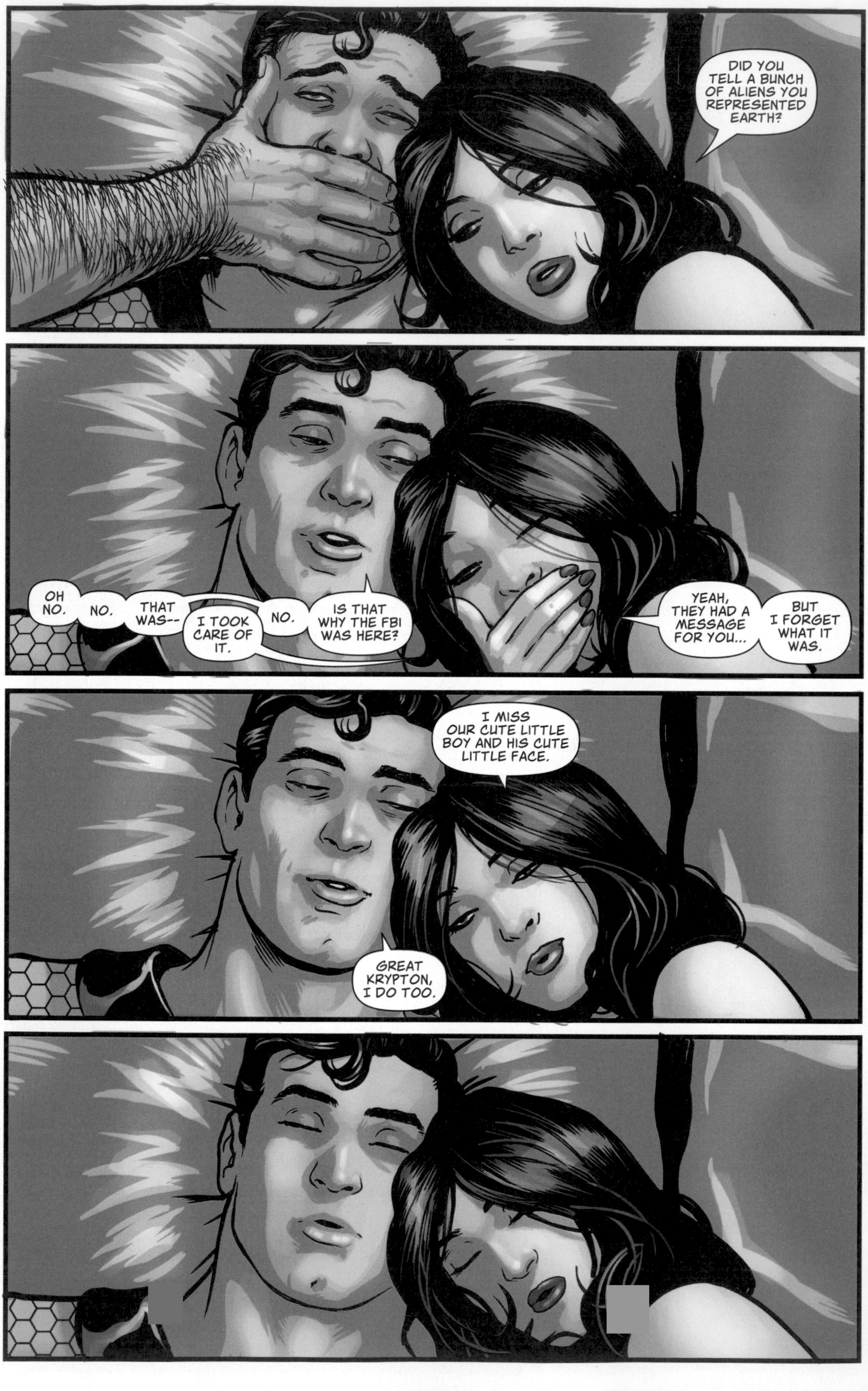
DID YOU TELL A BUNCH OF ALIENS YOU REPRESENTED EARTH?
OH NO.
NO.
THAT WAS--
I TOOK CARE OF IT.
NO.
IS THAT WHY THE FBI WAS HERE?
YEAH, THEY HAD A MESSAGE FOR YOU...
BUT I FORGET WHAT IT WAS.
I MISS OUR CUTE LITTLE BOY AND HIS CUTE LITTLE FACE.
GREAT KRYPTON, I DO TOO.

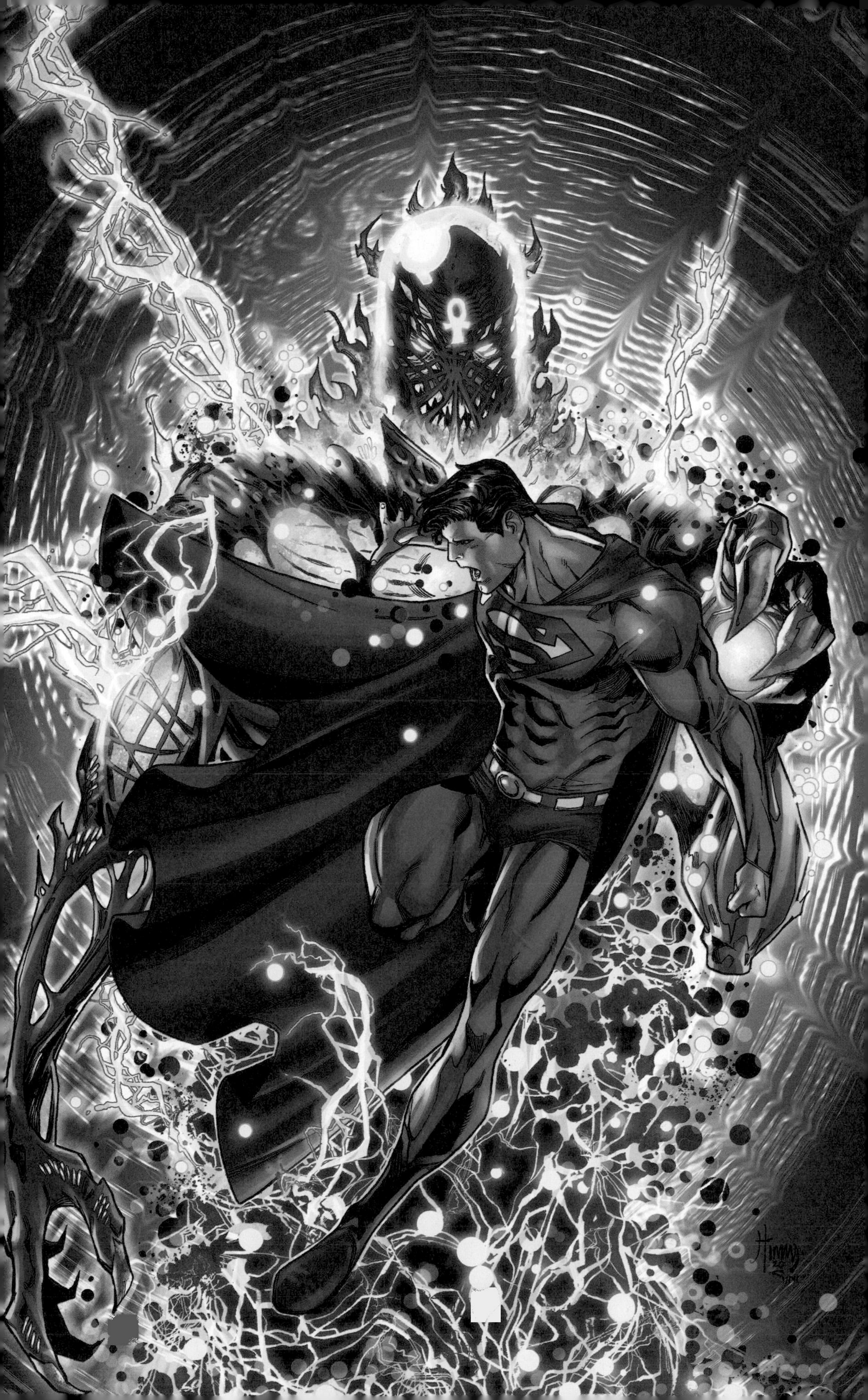

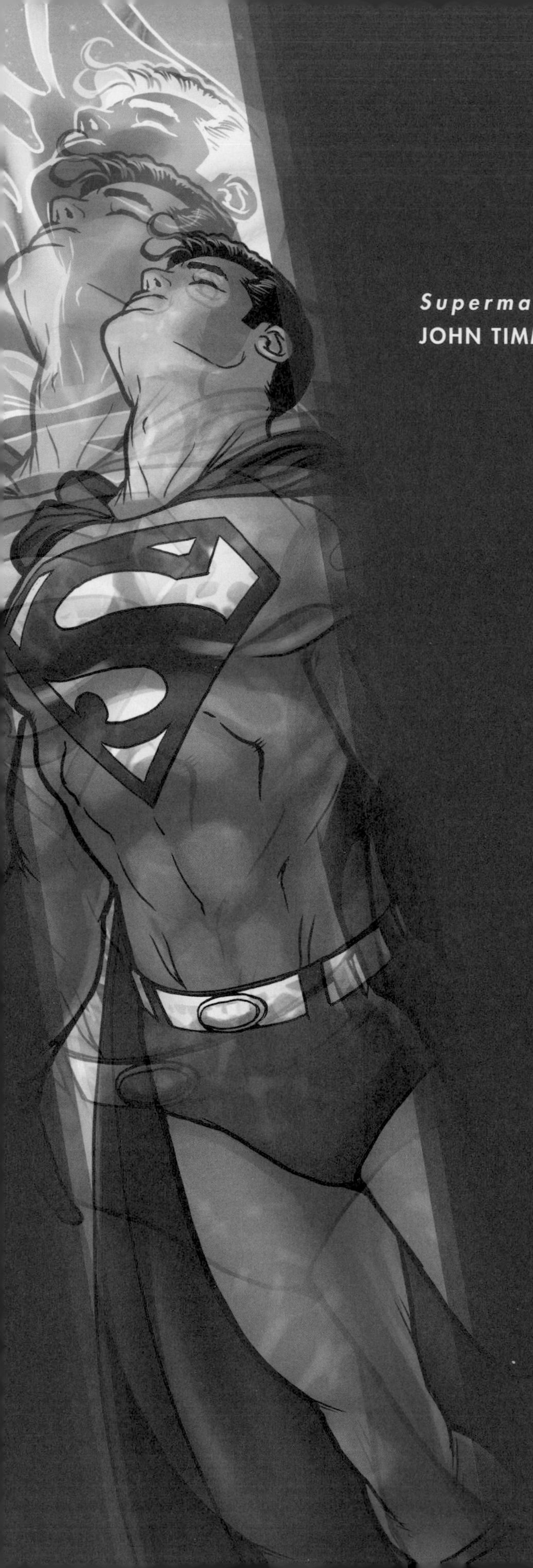

Superman #23 main cover by
JOHN TIMMS | ALEX SINCLAIR

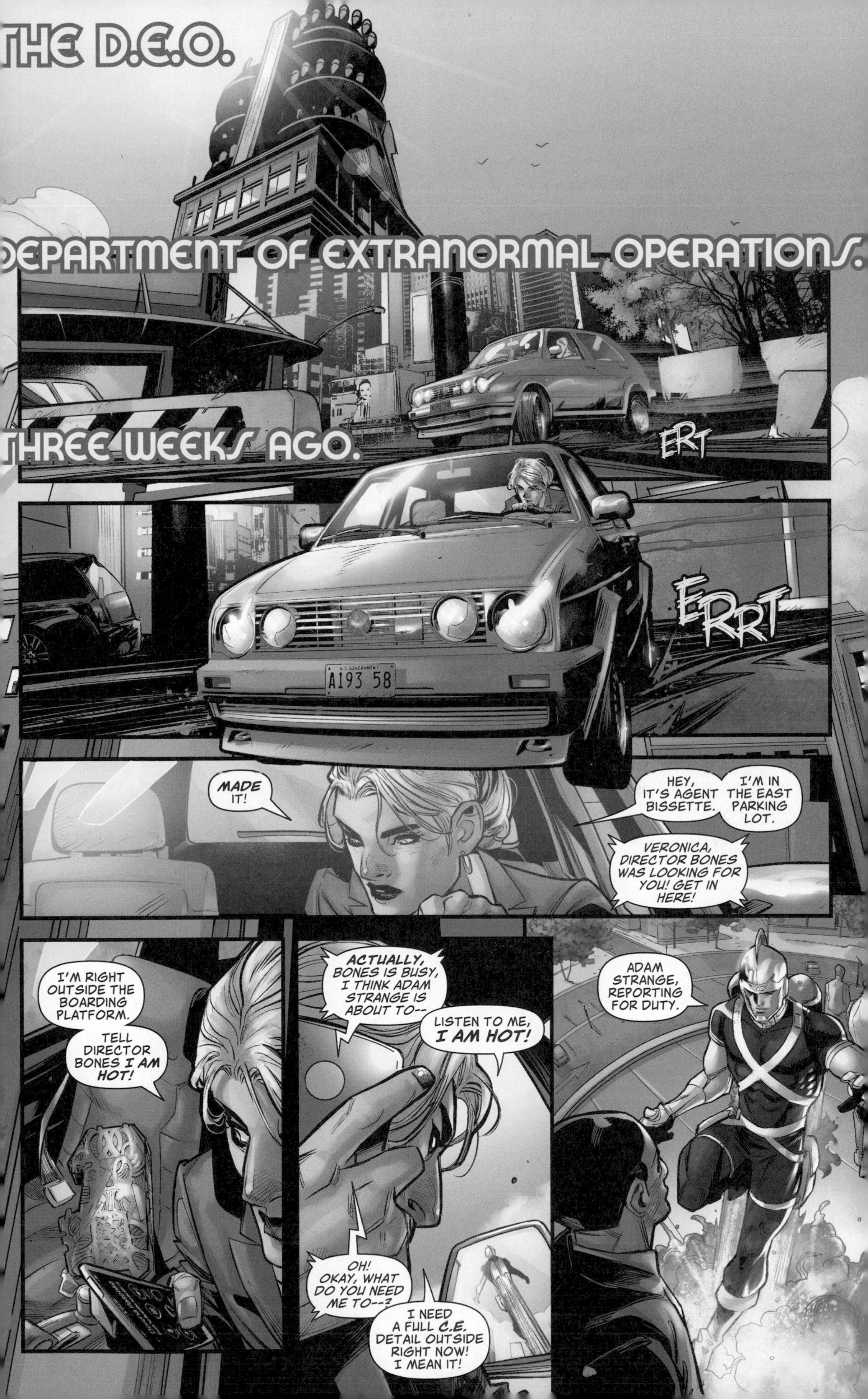
THE D.E.O.
DEPARTMENT OF EXTRANORMAL OPERATIONS.
THREE WEEKS AGO.
ERT
ERRT
MADE IT!
HEY, IT'S AGENT BISSETTE.
I'M IN THE EAST PARKING LOT.
VERONICA, DIRECTOR BONES WAS LOOKING FOR YOU! GET IN HERE!
I'M RIGHT OUTSIDE THE BOARDING PLATFORM.
TELL DIRECTOR BONES I AM HOT!
ACTUALLY, BONES IS BUSY, I THINK ADAM STRANGE IS ABOUT TO--
LISTEN TO ME, I AM HOT!
OH! OKAY, WHAT DO YOU NEED ME TO--?
I NEED A FULL C.E. DETAIL OUTSIDE RIGHT NOW! I MEAN IT!
ADAM STRANGE, REPORTING FOR DUTY.

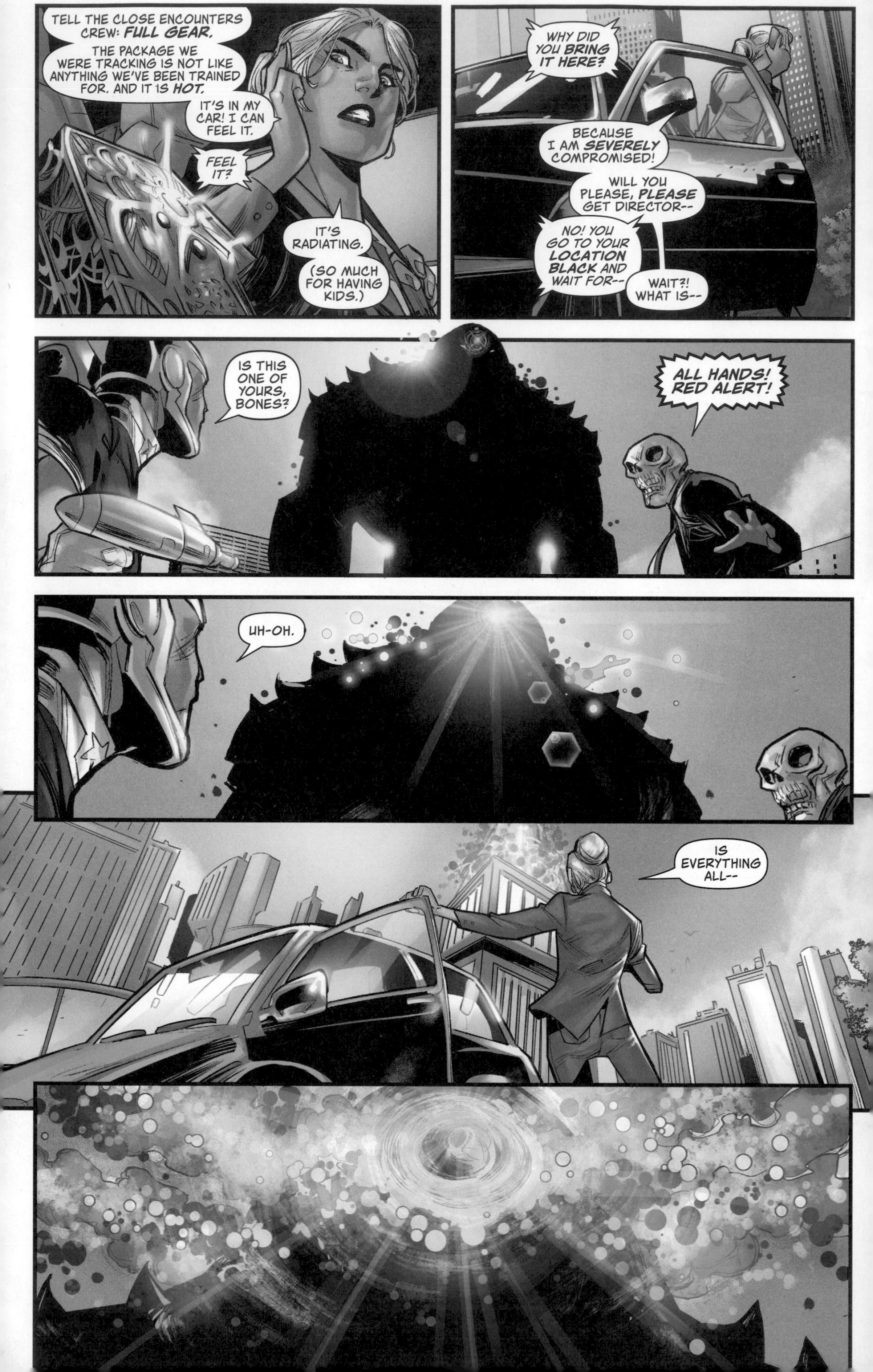
TELL THE CLOSE ENCOUNTERS CREW: FULL GEAR.
THE PACKAGE WE WERE TRACKING IS NOT LIKE ANYTHING WE'VE BEEN TRAINED FOR. AND IT IS HOT.
IT'S IN MY CAR! I CAN FEEL IT.
FEEL IT?
IT'S RADIATING.
(SO MUCH FOR HAVING KIDS.)
WHY DID YOU BRING IT HERE?
BECAUSE I AM SEVERELY COMPROMISED!
WILL YOU PLEASE, PLEASE GET DIRECTOR--
NO! YOU GO TO YOUR LOCATION BLACK AND WAIT FOR--
WAIT?! WHAT IS--
IS THIS ONE OF YOURS, BONES?
ALL HANDS! RED ALERT!
UH-OH.
IS EVERYTHING ALL--

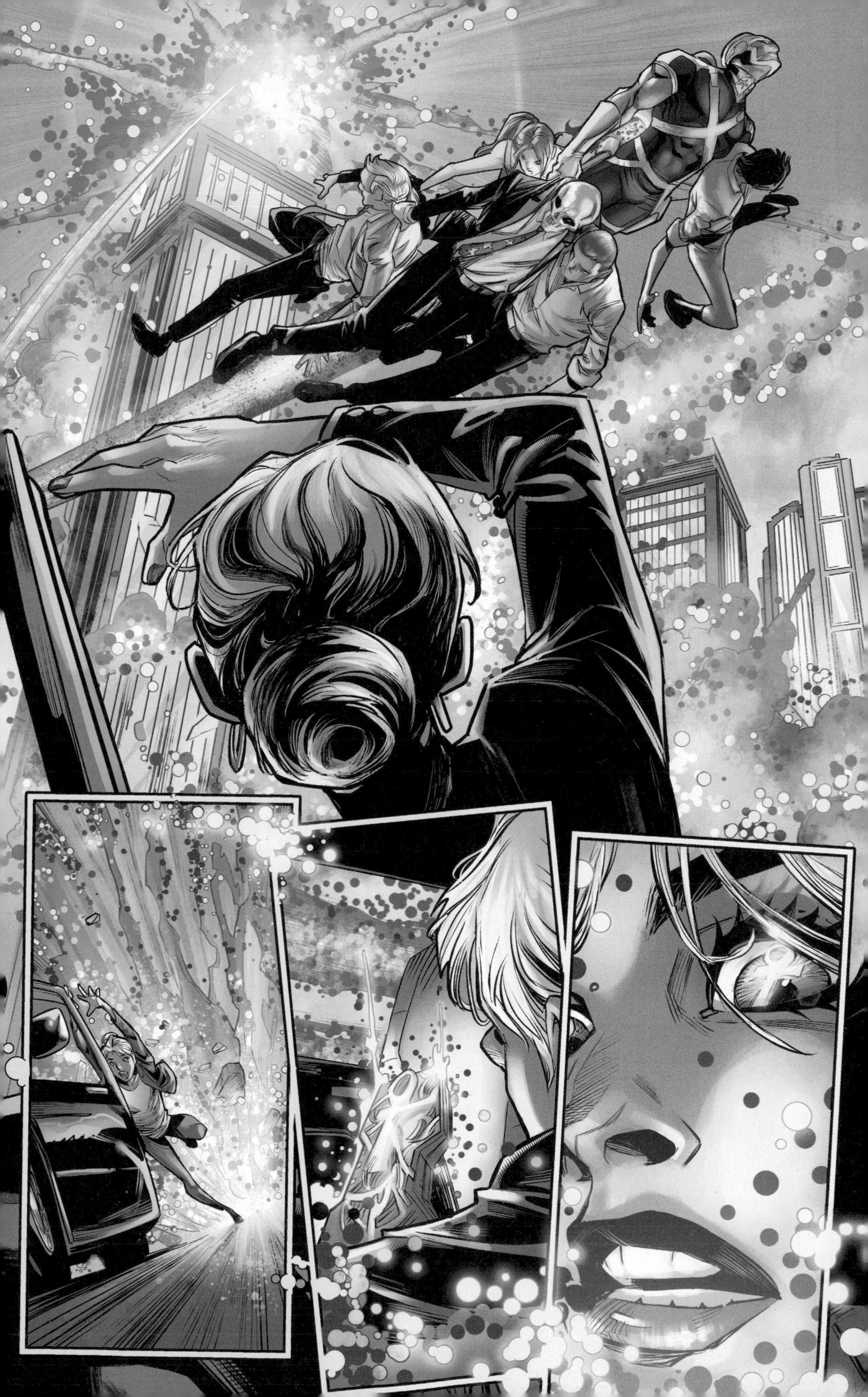

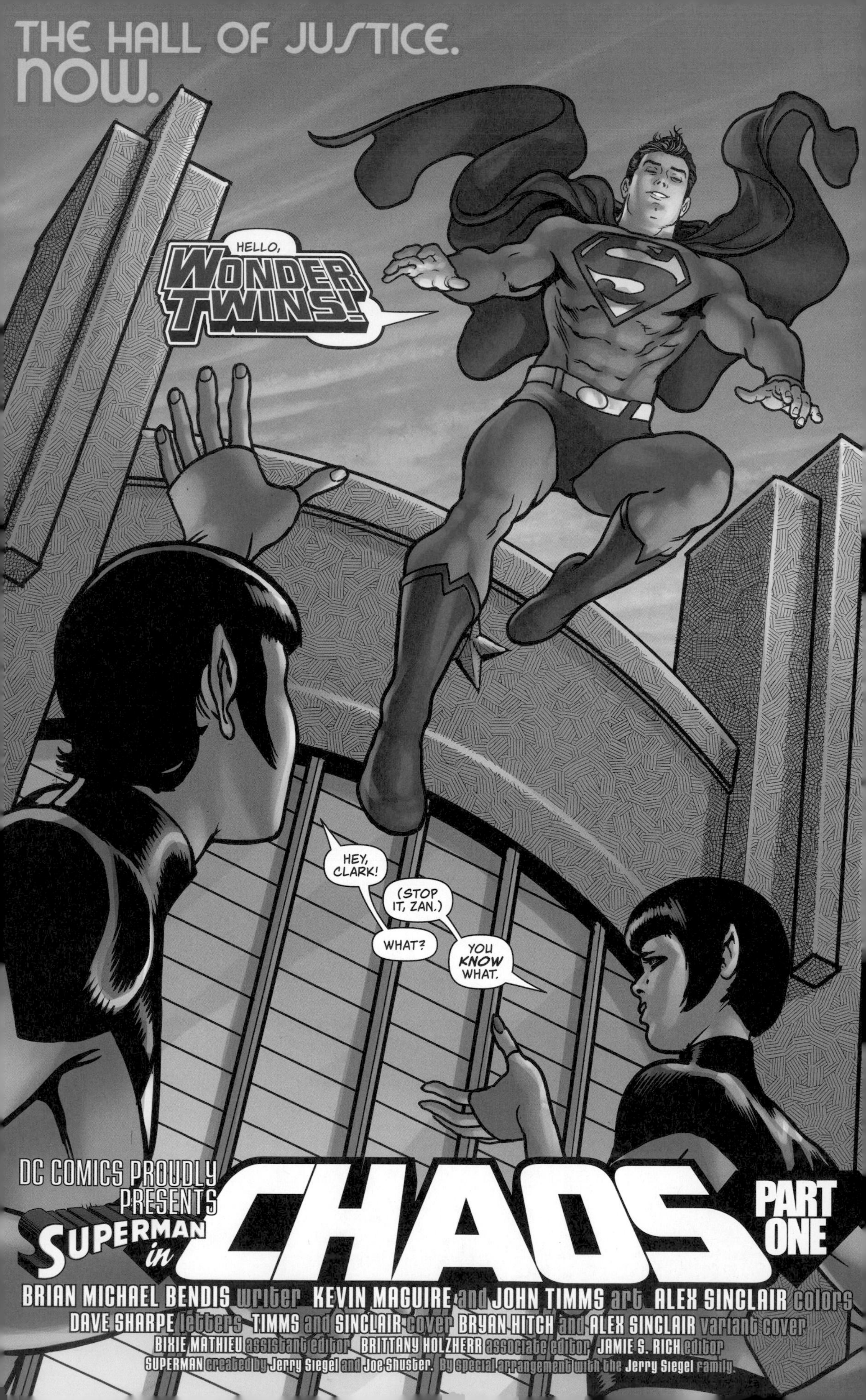
THE HALL OF JUSTICE.
NOW.
HELLO, WONDER TWINS!
HEY, CLARK!
(STOP IT, ZAN.)
WHAT?
YOU KNOW WHAT.
DC COMICS PROUDLY PRESENTS
SUPERMAN in CHAOS PART ONE
BRIAN MICHAEL BENDIS writer KEVIN MAGUIRE and JOHN TIMMS art ALEX SINCLAIR colors
DAVE SHARPE letters TIMMS and SINCLAIR cover BRYAN HITCH and ALEX SINCLAIR variant cover
BIXIE MATHIEU assistant editor BRITTANY HOLZHERR associate editor JAMIE S. RICH editor
SUPERMAN created by Jerry Siegel and Joe Shuster. By special arrangement with the Jerry Siegel family.

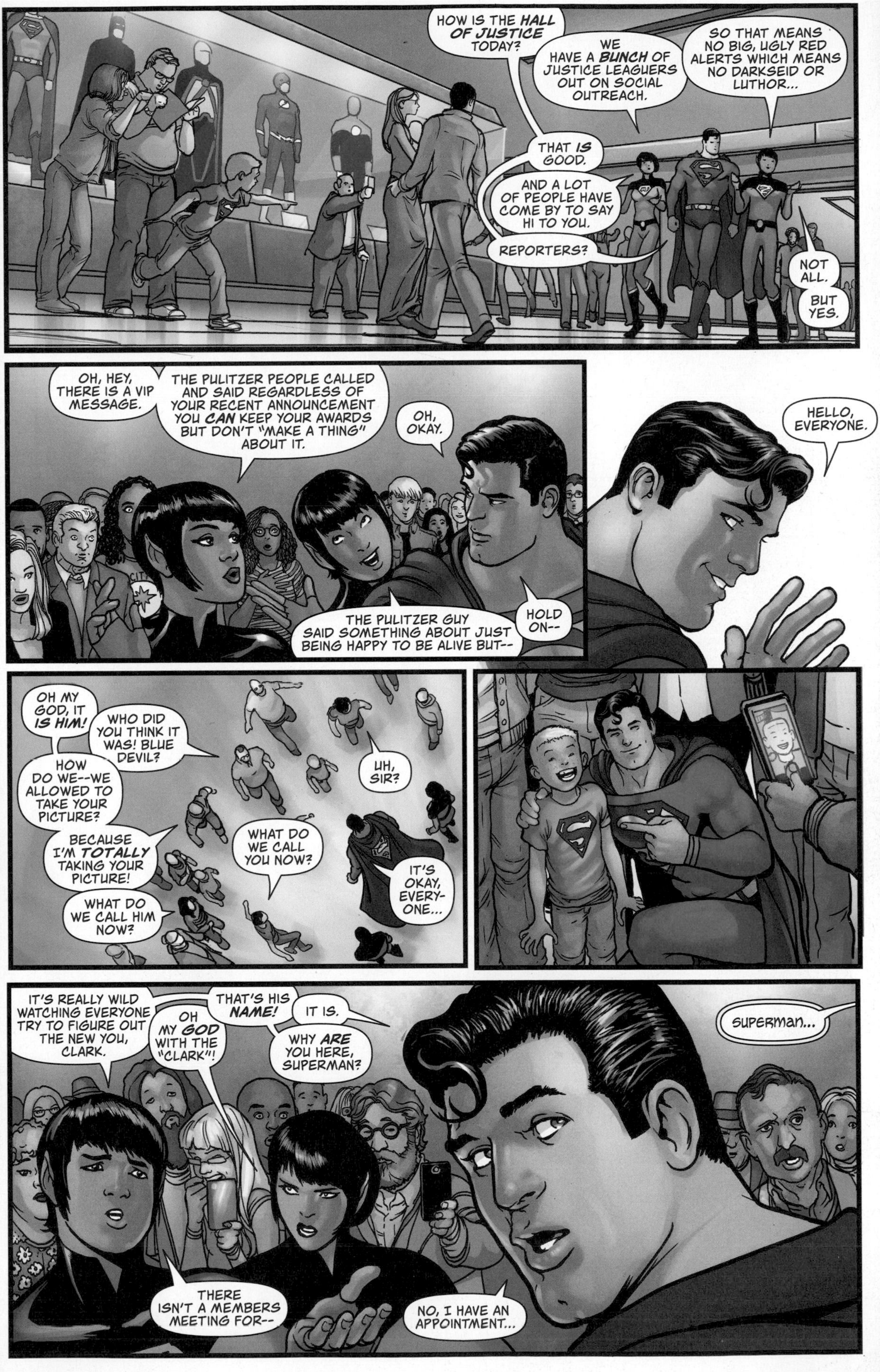
HOW IS THE HALL OF JUSTICE TODAY?
WE HAVE A BUNCH OF JUSTICE LEAGUERS OUT ON SOCIAL OUTREACH.
SO THAT MEANS NO BIG, UGLY RED ALERTS WHICH MEANS NO DARKSEID OR LUTHOR...
THAT IS GOOD.
AND A LOT OF PEOPLE HAVE COME BY TO SAY HI TO YOU.
REPORTERS?
NOT ALL.
BUT YES.
OH, HEY, THERE IS A VIP MESSAGE.
THE PULITZER PEOPLE CALLED AND SAID REGARDLESS OF YOUR RECENT ANNOUNCEMENT YOU CAN KEEP YOUR AWARDS BUT DON'T "MAKE A THING" ABOUT IT.
OH, OKAY.
THE PULITZER GUY SAID SOMETHING ABOUT JUST BEING HAPPY TO BE ALIVE BUT--
HOLD ON--
HELLO, EVERYONE.
OH MY GOD, IT IS HIM!
WHO DID YOU THINK IT WAS! BLUE DEVIL?
HOW DO WE--WE ALLOWED TO TAKE YOUR PICTURE?
BECAUSE I'M TOTALLY TAKING YOUR PICTURE!
WHAT DO WE CALL HIM NOW?
WHAT DO WE CALL YOU NOW?
UH, SIR?
IT'S OKAY, EVERY-ONE...
IT'S REALLY WILD WATCHING EVERYONE TRY TO FIGURE OUT THE NEW YOU, CLARK.
OH MY GOD WITH THE "CLARK"!
THAT'S HIS NAME!
IT IS.
WHY ARE YOU HERE, SUPERMAN?
SUPERMAN...
THERE ISN'T A MEMBERS MEETING FOR--
NO, I HAVE AN APPOINTMENT...

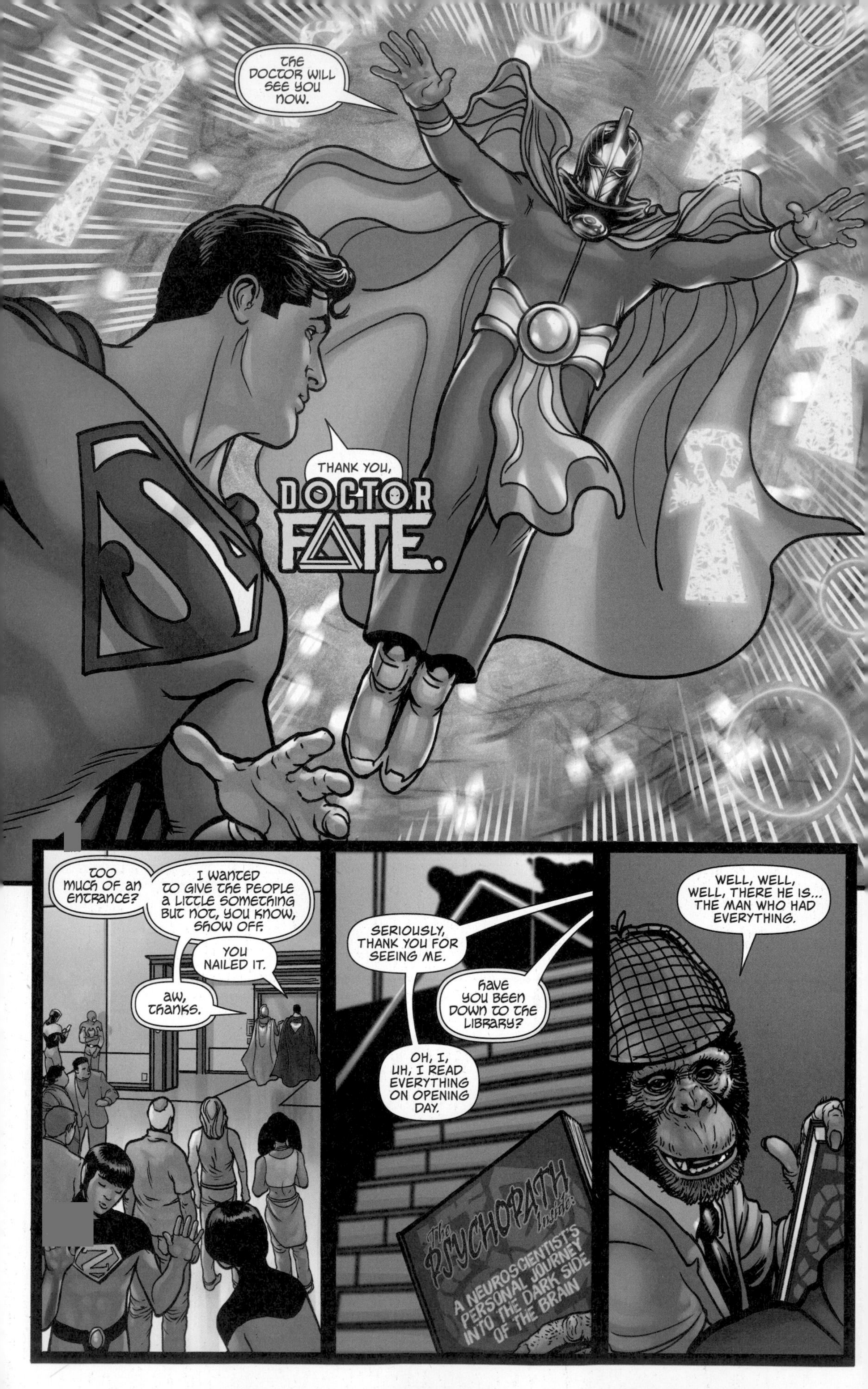

THE DOCTOR WILL SEE YOU NOW.
THANK YOU,
DOCTOR FATE.
TOO MUCH OF AN ENTRANCE?
I WANTED TO GIVE THE PEOPLE A LITTLE SOMETHING BUT NOT, YOU KNOW, SHOW OFF.
YOU NAILED IT.
AW, THANKS.
SERIOUSLY, THANK YOU FOR SEEING ME.
HAVE YOU BEEN DOWN TO THE LIBRARY?
OH, I, UH, I READ EVERYTHING ON OPENING DAY.
The PSYCHOPATH Inside:
A NEUROSCIENTIST'S PERSONAL JOURNEY INTO THE DARK SIDE OF THE BRAIN
WELL, WELL, WELL, THERE HE IS... THE MAN WHO HAD EVERYTHING.

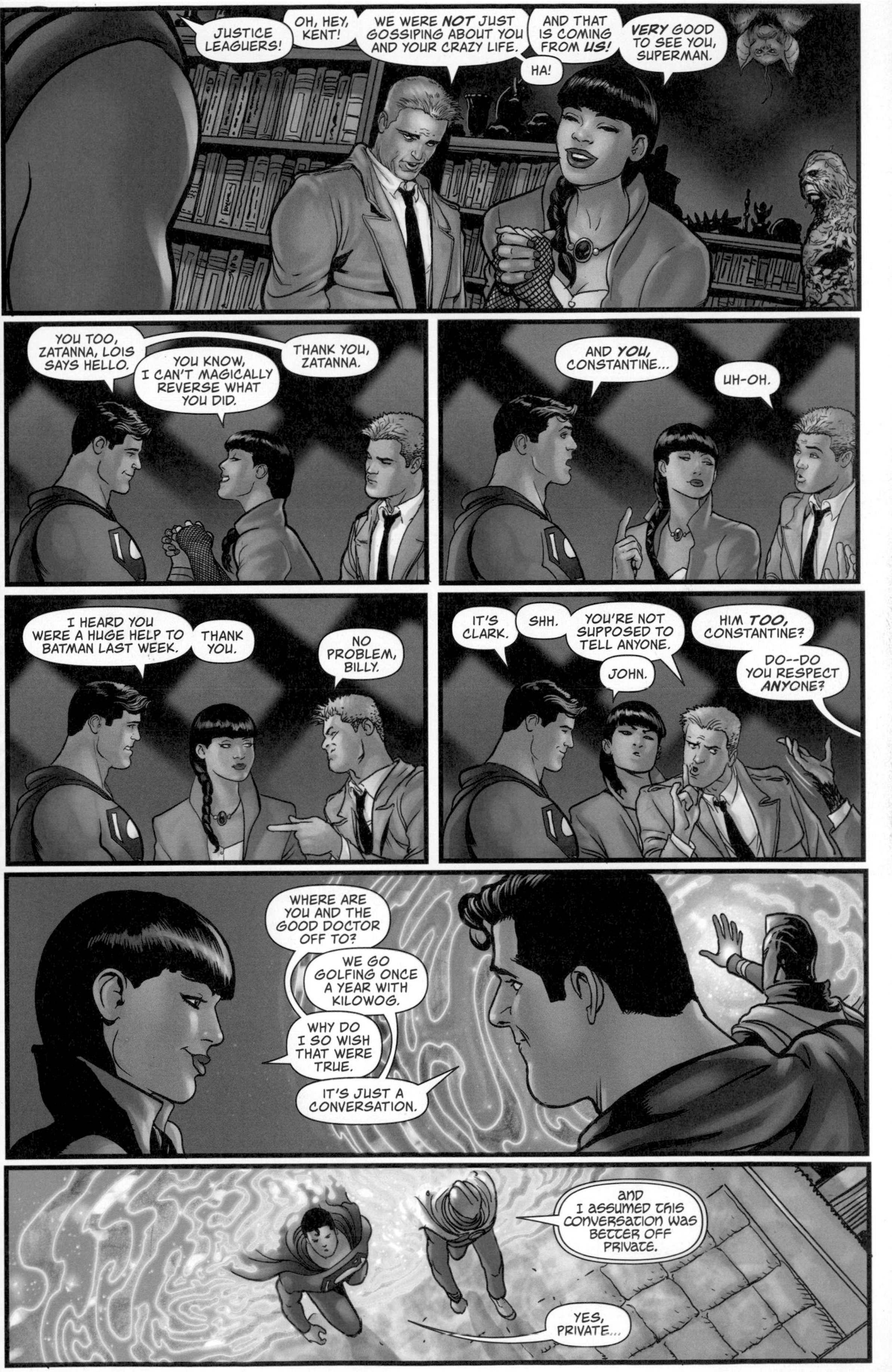
JUSTICE LEAGUERS!
OH, HEY, KENT!
WE WERE NOT JUST GOSSIPING ABOUT YOU AND YOUR CRAZY LIFE.
HA!
AND THAT IS COMING FROM US!
VERY GOOD TO SEE YOU, SUPERMAN.
YOU TOO, ZATANNA, LOIS SAYS HELLO.
THANK YOU, ZATANNA.
YOU KNOW, I CAN'T MAGICALLY REVERSE WHAT YOU DID.
AND YOU, CONSTANTINE...
UH-OH.
I HEARD YOU WERE A HUGE HELP TO BATMAN LAST WEEK.
THANK YOU.
NO PROBLEM, BILLY.
IT'S CLARK.
SHH.
YOU'RE NOT SUPPOSED TO TELL ANYONE.
JOHN.
HIM TOO, CONSTANTINE?
DO--DO YOU RESPECT ANYONE?
WHERE ARE YOU AND THE GOOD DOCTOR OFF TO?
WE GO GOLFING ONCE A YEAR WITH KILOWOG.
WHY DO I SO WISH THAT WERE TRUE.
IT'S JUST A CONVERSATION.
and I assumed this conversation was better off private.
YES, PRIVATE...

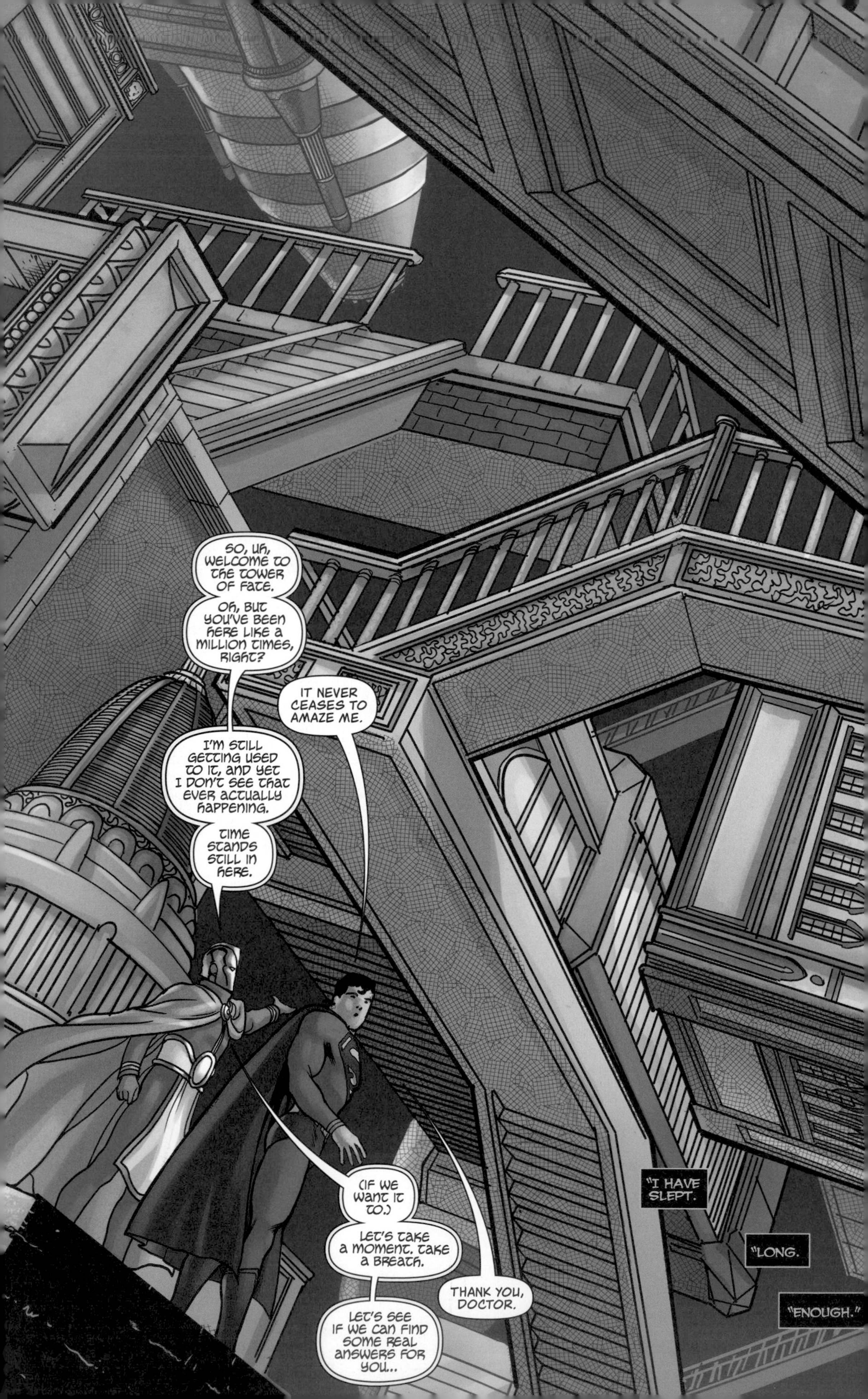
SO, UH, WELCOME TO THE TOWER OF FATE.
OH, BUT YOU'VE BEEN HERE LIKE A MILLION TIMES, RIGHT?
IT NEVER CEASES TO AMAZE ME.
I'M STILL GETTING USED TO IT, AND YET I DON'T SEE THAT EVER ACTUALLY HAPPENING.
TIME STANDS STILL IN HERE.
(IF WE WANT IT TO.)
LET'S TAKE A MOMENT. TAKE A BREATH.
LET'S SEE IF WE CAN FIND SOME REAL ANSWERS FOR YOU...
THANK YOU, DOCTOR.
"I HAVE SLEPT.
"LONG.
"ENOUGH."

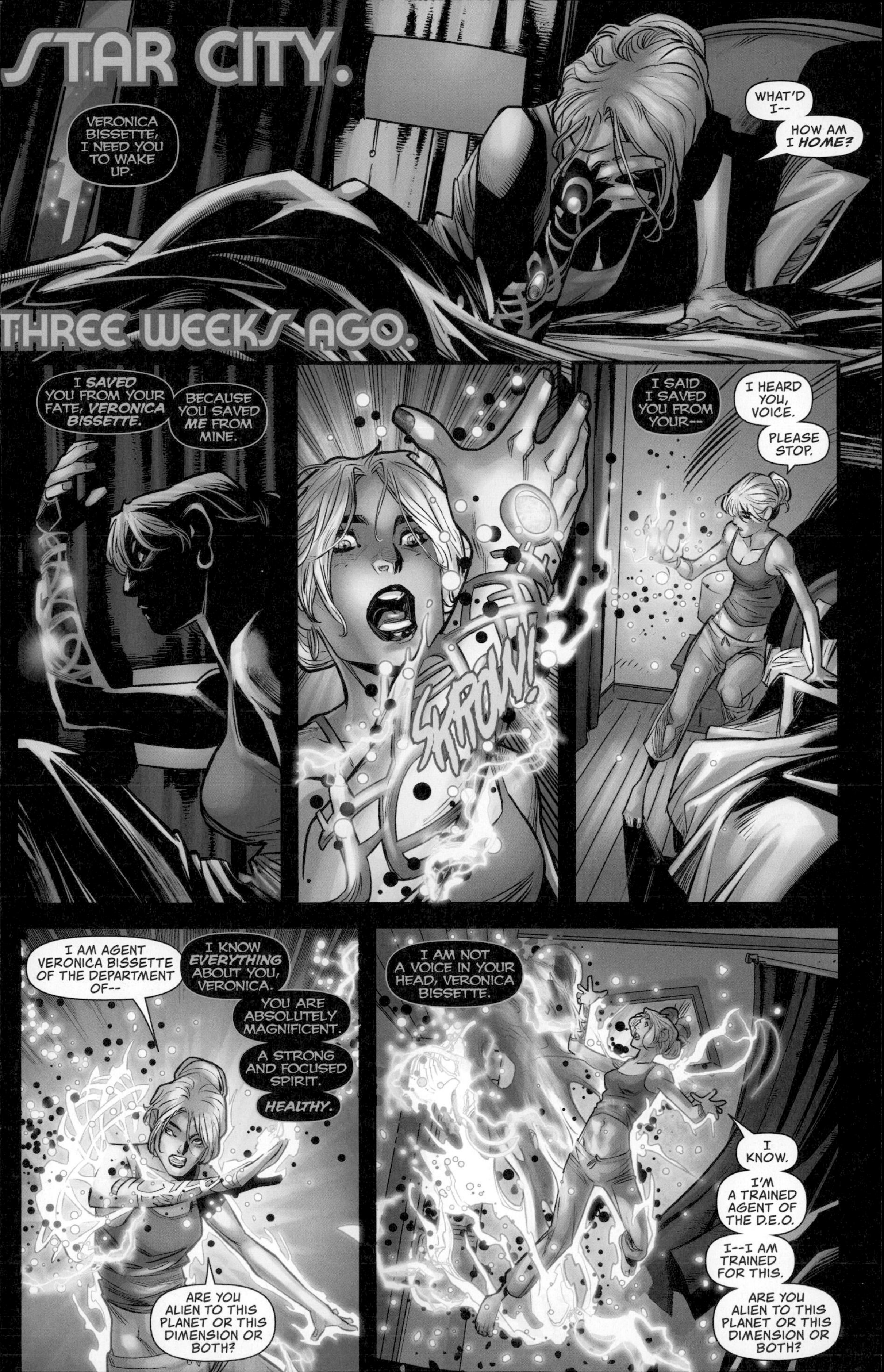
STAR CITY.
VERONICA BISSETTE, I NEED YOU TO WAKE UP.
WHAT'D I--
HOW AM I HOME?
THREE WEEKS AGO.
I SAVED YOU FROM YOUR FATE, VERONICA BISSETTE.
BECAUSE YOU SAVED ME FROM MINE.
SKRAOW!
I SAID I SAVED YOU FROM YOUR--
I HEARD YOU, VOICE.
PLEASE STOP.
I AM AGENT VERONICA BISSETTE OF THE DEPARTMENT OF--
I KNOW EVERYTHING ABOUT YOU, VERONICA.
YOU ARE ABSOLUTELY MAGNIFICENT.
A STRONG AND FOCUSED SPIRIT.
HEALTHY.
ARE YOU ALIEN TO THIS PLANET OR THIS DIMENSION OR BOTH?
I AM NOT A VOICE IN YOUR HEAD, VERONICA BISSETTE.
I KNOW.
I'M A TRAINED AGENT OF THE D.E.O.
I--I AM TRAINED FOR THIS.
ARE YOU ALIEN TO THIS PLANET OR THIS DIMENSION OR BOTH?

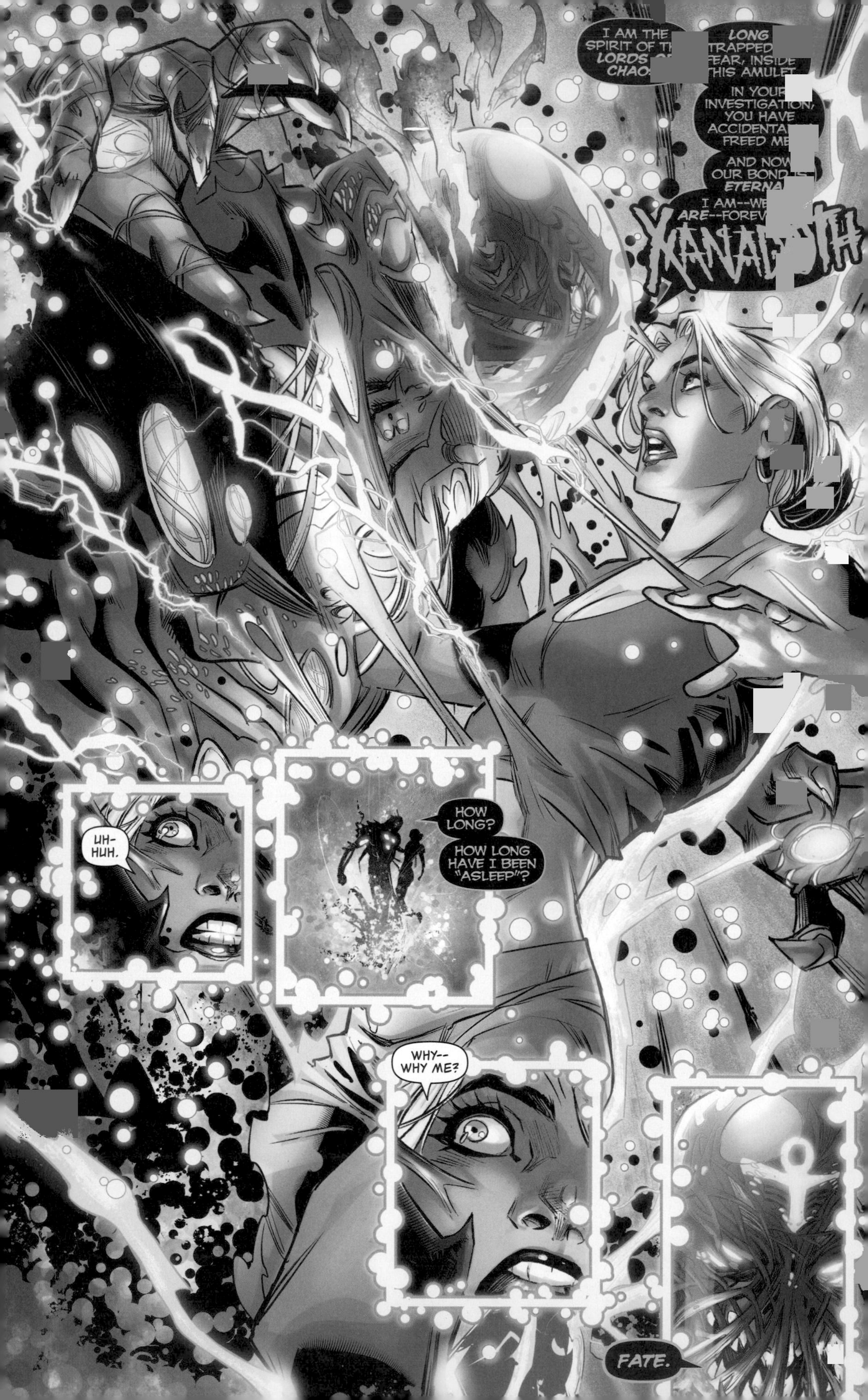
I AM THE SPIRIT OF LORDS CHAOS
LONG TRAPPED FEAR, INSIDE THIS AMULET.
IN YOUR INVESTIGATION, YOU HAVE FREED ME.
AND NOW OUR BOND
I AM--WE ARE--
UH-HUH.
HOW LONG?
HOW LONG HAVE I BEEN "ASLEEP"?
WHY-- WHY ME?
FATE.

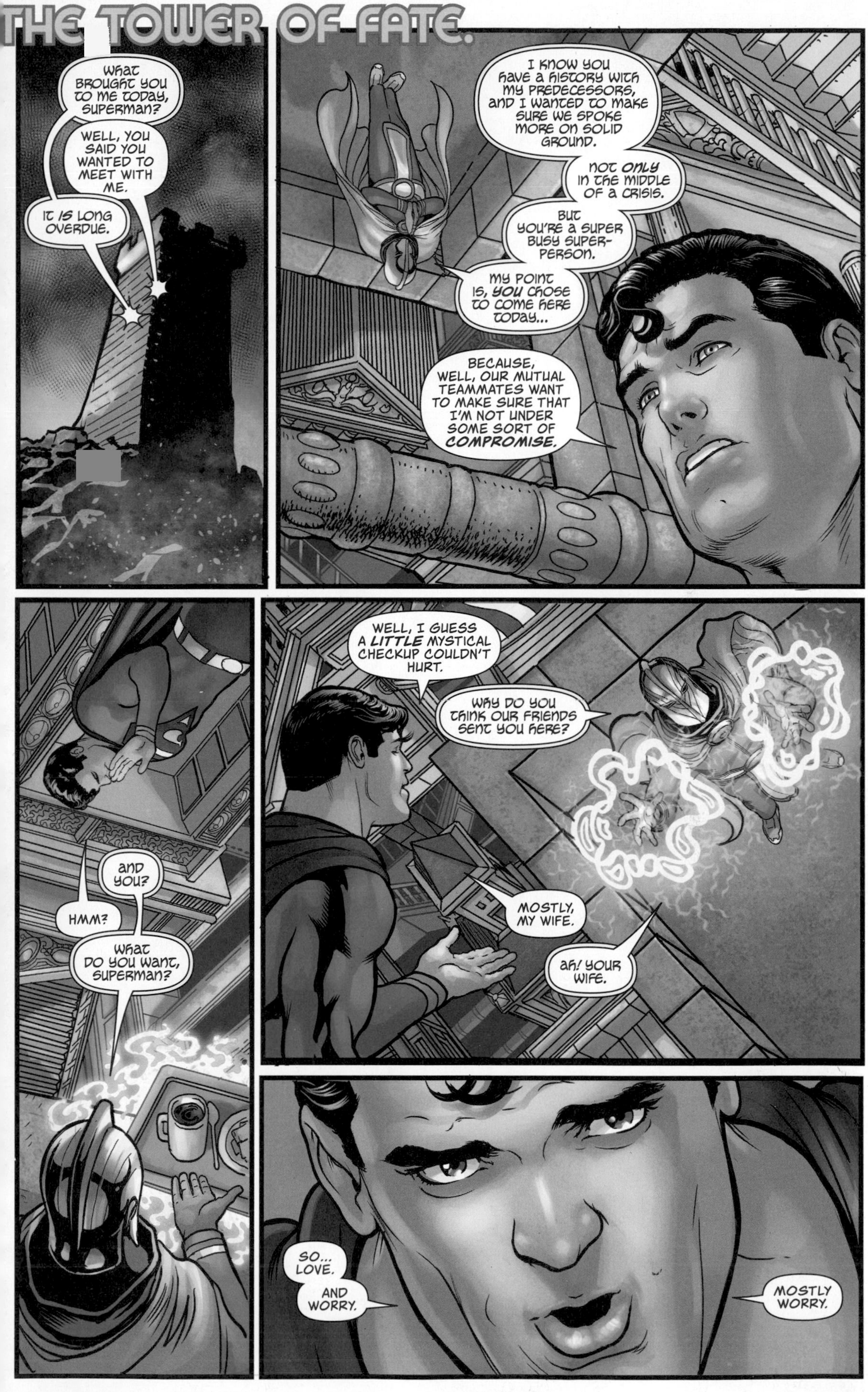
THE TOWER OF FATE.
WHAT BROUGHT YOU TO ME TODAY, SUPERMAN?
WELL, YOU SAID YOU WANTED TO MEET WITH ME.
IT IS LONG OVERDUE.
I KNOW YOU HAVE A HISTORY WITH MY PREDECESSORS, AND I WANTED TO MAKE SURE WE SPOKE MORE ON SOLID GROUND.
NOT ONLY IN THE MIDDLE OF A CRISIS.
BUT YOU'RE A SUPER BUSY SUPER-PERSON.
MY POINT IS, YOU CHOSE TO COME HERE TODAY...
BECAUSE, WELL, OUR MUTUAL TEAMMATES WANT TO MAKE SURE THAT I'M NOT UNDER SOME SORT OF COMPROMISE.
WELL, I GUESS A LITTLE MYSTICAL CHECKUP COULDN'T HURT.
WHY DO YOU THINK OUR FRIENDS SENT YOU HERE?
AND YOU?
HMM?
WHAT DO YOU WANT, SUPERMAN?
MOSTLY, MY WIFE.
AH! YOUR WIFE.
SO... LOVE.
AND WORRY.
MOSTLY WORRY.

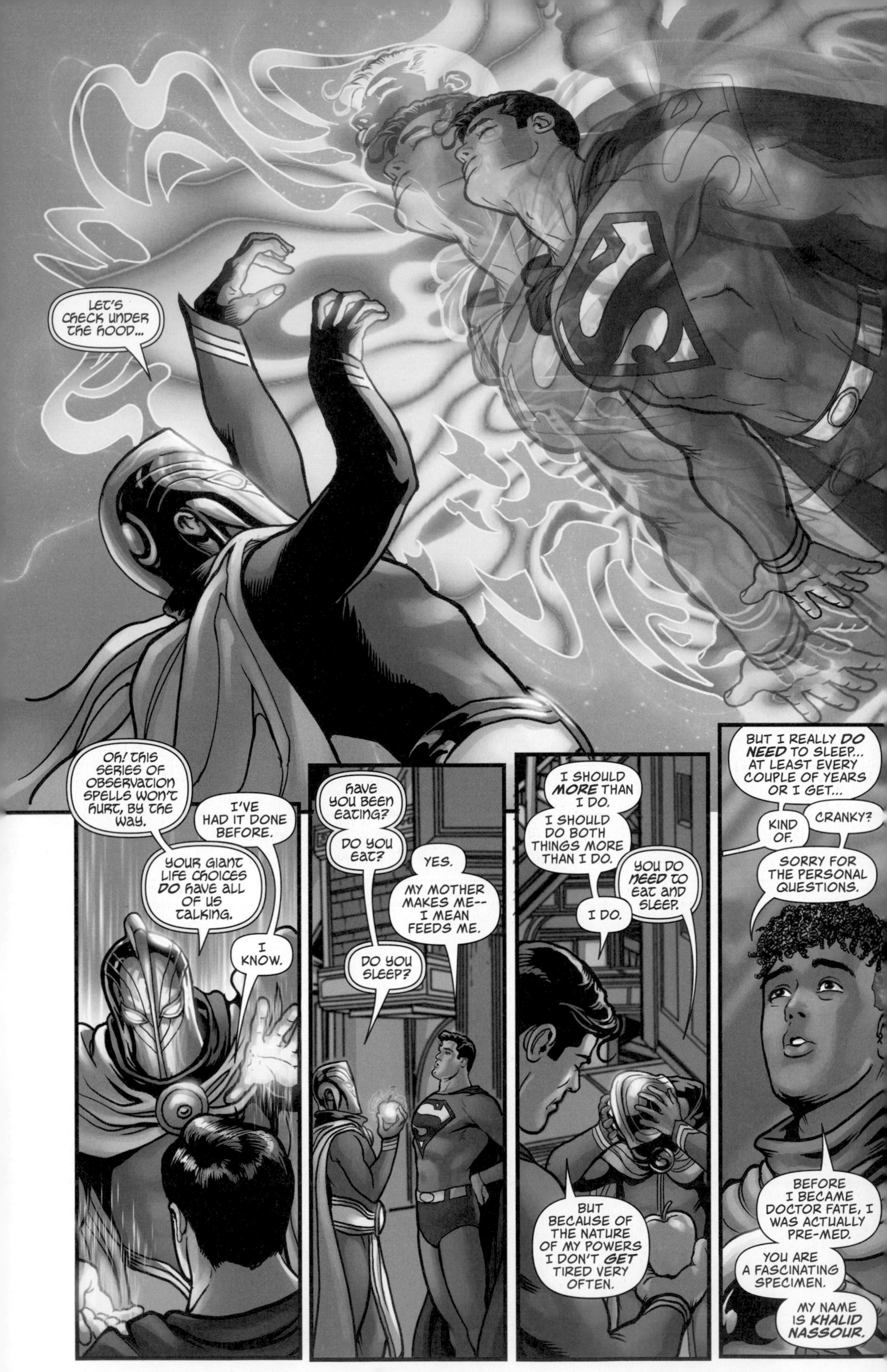

LET'S CHECK UNDER THE HOOD...
OH! THIS SERIES OF OBSERVATION SPELLS WON'T HURT, BY THE WAY.
I'VE HAD IT DONE BEFORE.
YOUR GIANT LIFE CHOICES DO HAVE ALL OF US TALKING.
I KNOW.
HAVE YOU BEEN EATING?
DO YOU EAT?
YES.
MY MOTHER MAKES ME-- I MEAN FEEDS ME.
DO YOU SLEEP?
I SHOULD MORE THAN I DO.
I SHOULD DO BOTH THINGS MORE THAN I DO.
YOU DO NEED TO EAT AND SLEEP.
I DO.
BUT BECAUSE OF THE NATURE OF MY POWERS I DON'T GET TIRED VERY OFTEN.
BUT I REALLY DO NEED TO SLEEP... AT LEAST EVERY COUPLE OF YEARS OR I GET...
KIND OF.
CRANKY?
SORRY FOR THE PERSONAL QUESTIONS.
BEFORE I BECAME DOCTOR FATE, I WAS ACTUALLY PRE-MED.
YOU ARE A FASCINATING SPECIMEN.
MY NAME IS KHALID NASSOUR.

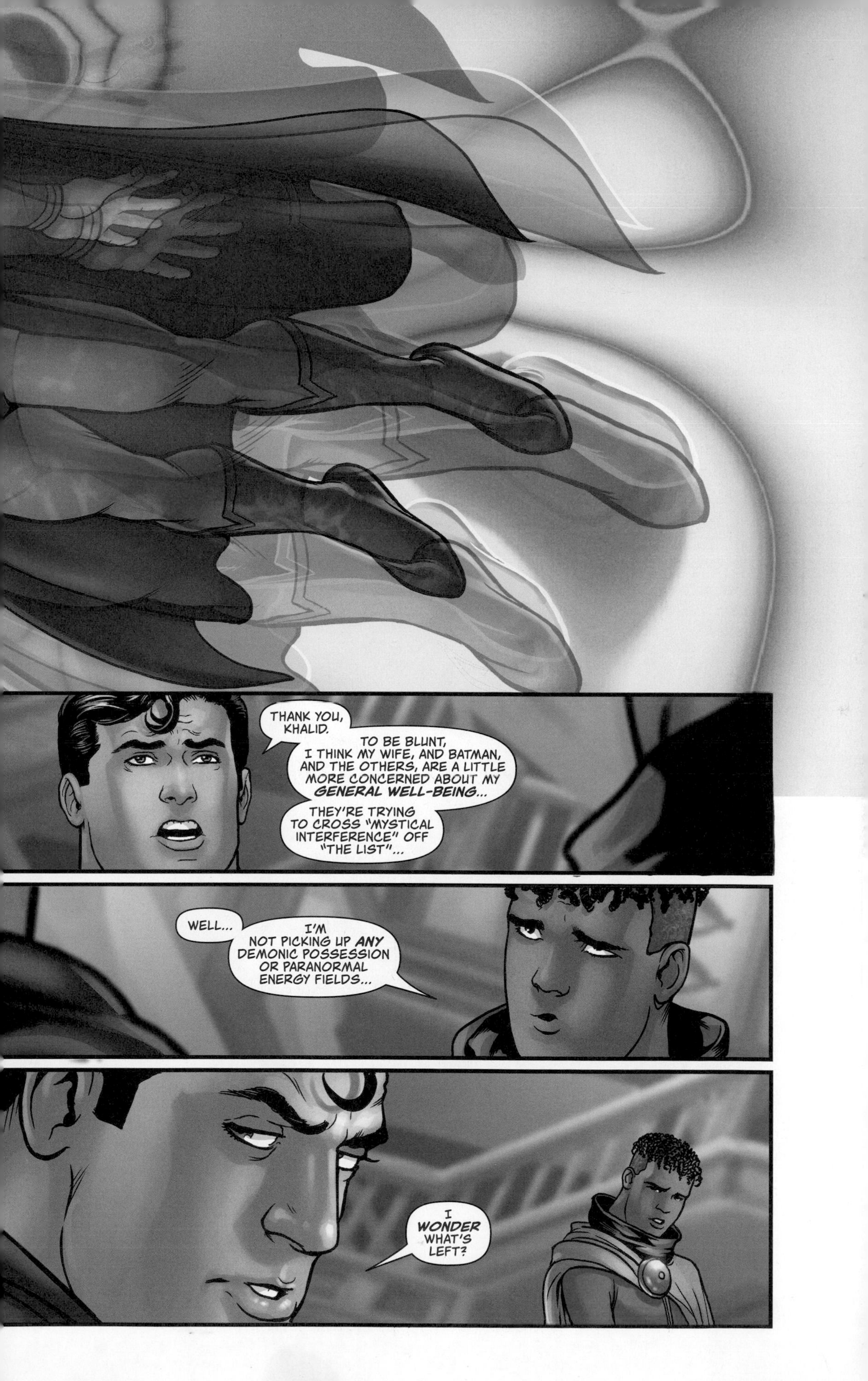
THANK YOU, KHALID.
TO BE BLUNT, I THINK MY WIFE, AND BATMAN, AND THE OTHERS, ARE A LITTLE MORE CONCERNED ABOUT MY GENERAL WELL-BEING...
THEY'RE TRYING TO CROSS "MYSTICAL INTERFERENCE" OFF "THE LIST"...
WELL...
I'M NOT PICKING UP ANY DEMONIC POSSESSION OR PARANORMAL ENERGY FIELDS...
I WONDER WHAT'S LEFT?

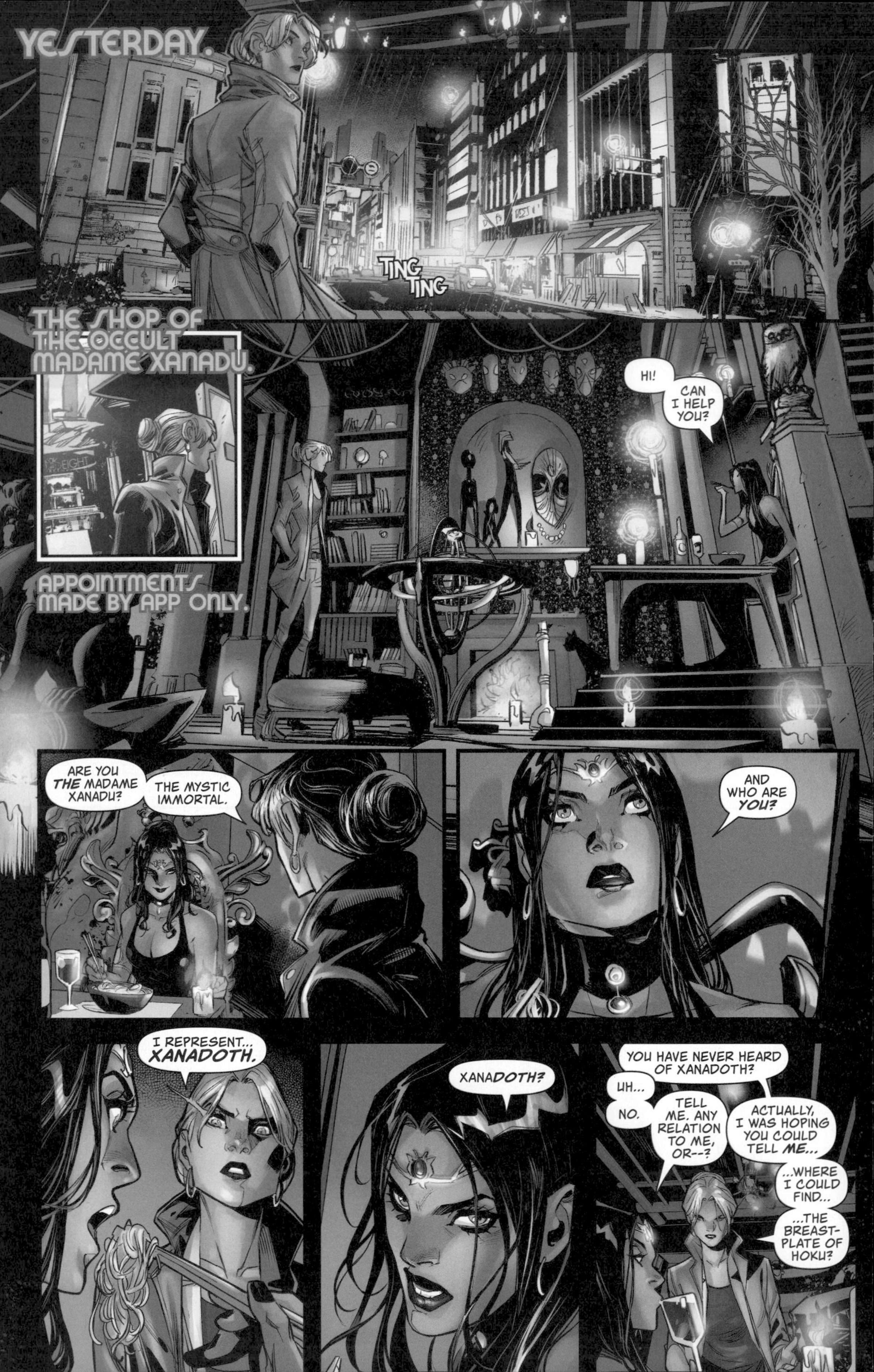
YESTERDAY.
TING TING
THE SHOP OF THE OCCULT MADAME XANADU.
APPOINTMENTS MADE BY APP ONLY.
HI!
CAN I HELP YOU?
ARE YOU THE MADAME XANADU?
THE MYSTIC IMMORTAL.
AND WHO ARE YOU?
I REPRESENT... XANADOTH.
XANADOTH?
YOU HAVE NEVER HEARD OF XANADOTH?
UH...
NO.
TELL ME. ANY RELATION TO ME, OR--?
ACTUALLY, I WAS HOPING YOU COULD TELL ME...
...WHERE I COULD FIND...
...THE BREAST-PLATE OF HOKU?

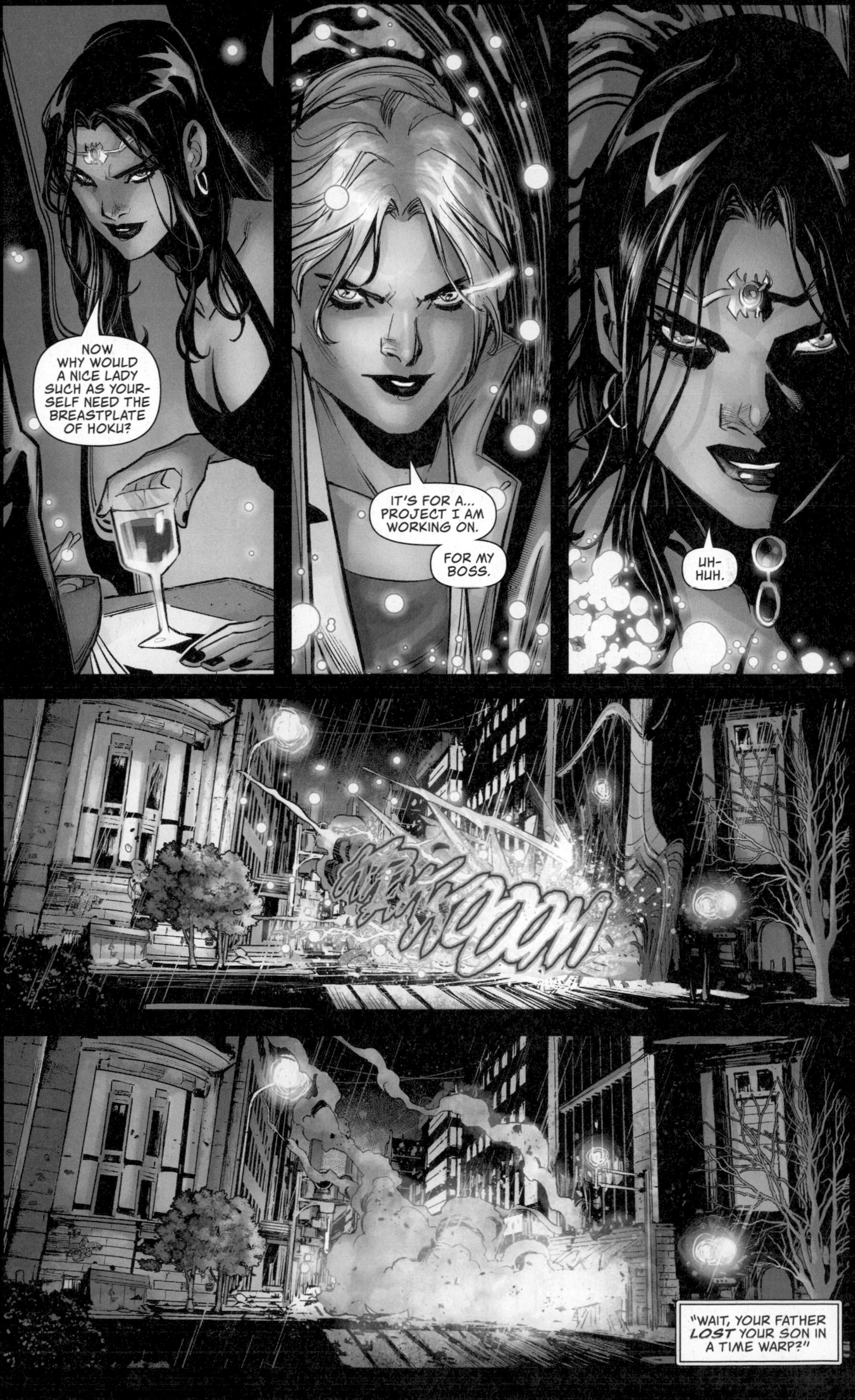
NOW WHY WOULD A NICE LADY SUCH AS YOURSELF NEED THE BREASTPLATE OF HOKU?
IT'S FOR A... PROJECT I AM WORKING ON.
FOR MY BOSS.
UH-HUH.
"WAIT, YOUR FATHER LOST YOUR SON IN A TIME WARP?"

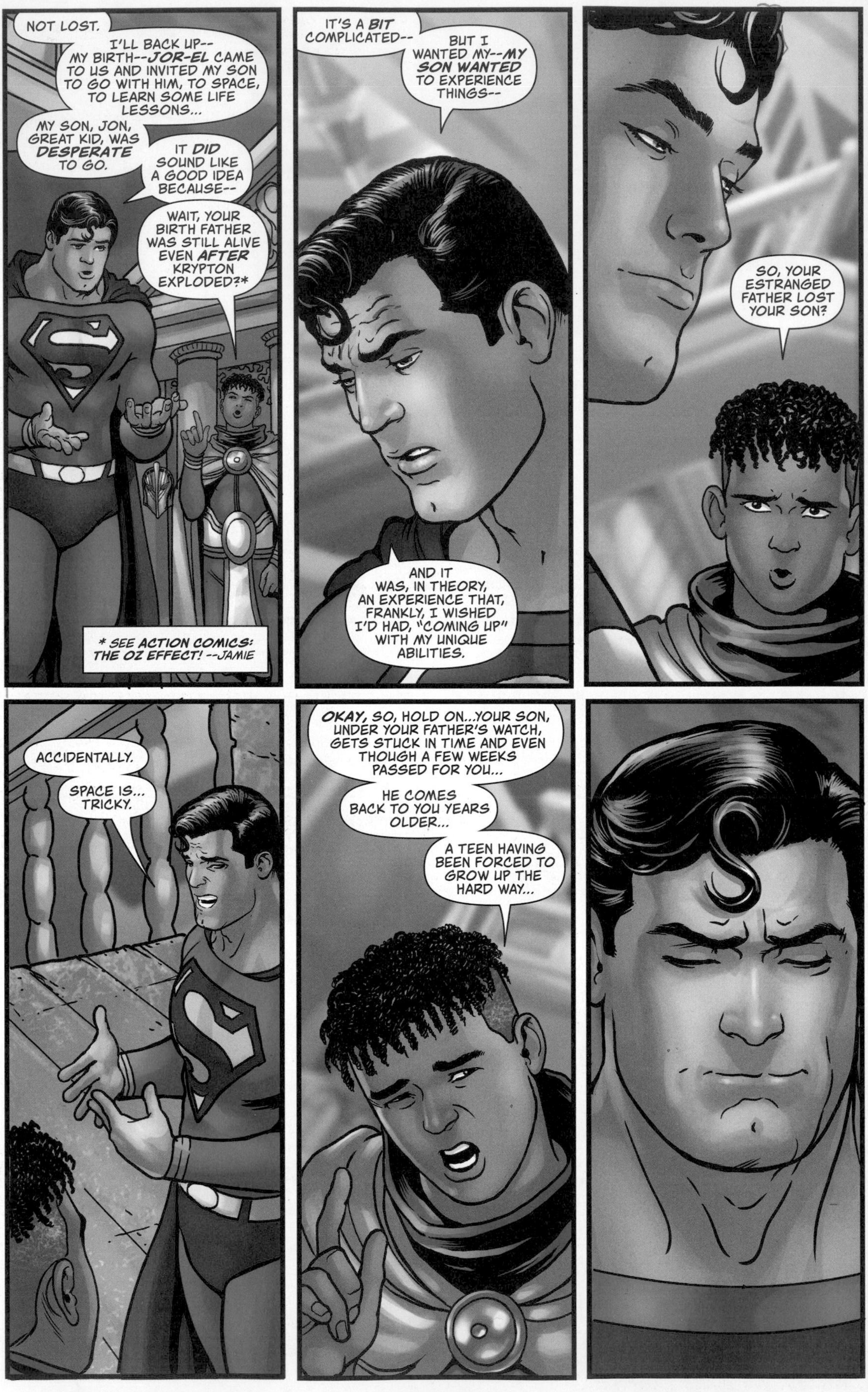
NOT LOST.
I'LL BACK UP-- MY BIRTH--JOR-EL CAME TO US AND INVITED MY SON TO GO WITH HIM, TO SPACE, TO LEARN SOME LIFE LESSONS...
MY SON, JON, GREAT KID, WAS DESPERATE TO GO.
IT DID SOUND LIKE A GOOD IDEA BECAUSE--
WAIT, YOUR BIRTH FATHER WAS STILL ALIVE EVEN AFTER KRYPTON EXPLODED?*
* SEE ACTION COMICS: THE OZ EFFECT! --JAMIE
IT'S A BIT COMPLICATED--
BUT I WANTED MY--MY SON WANTED TO EXPERIENCE THINGS--
AND IT WAS, IN THEORY, AN EXPERIENCE THAT, FRANKLY, I WISHED I'D HAD, "COMING UP" WITH MY UNIQUE ABILITIES.
SO, YOUR ESTRANGED FATHER LOST YOUR SON?
ACCIDENTALLY.
SPACE IS... TRICKY.
OKAY, SO, HOLD ON...YOUR SON, UNDER YOUR FATHER'S WATCH, GETS STUCK IN TIME AND EVEN THOUGH A FEW WEEKS PASSED FOR YOU...
HE COMES BACK TO YOU YEARS OLDER...
A TEEN HAVING BEEN FORCED TO GROW UP THE HARD WAY...

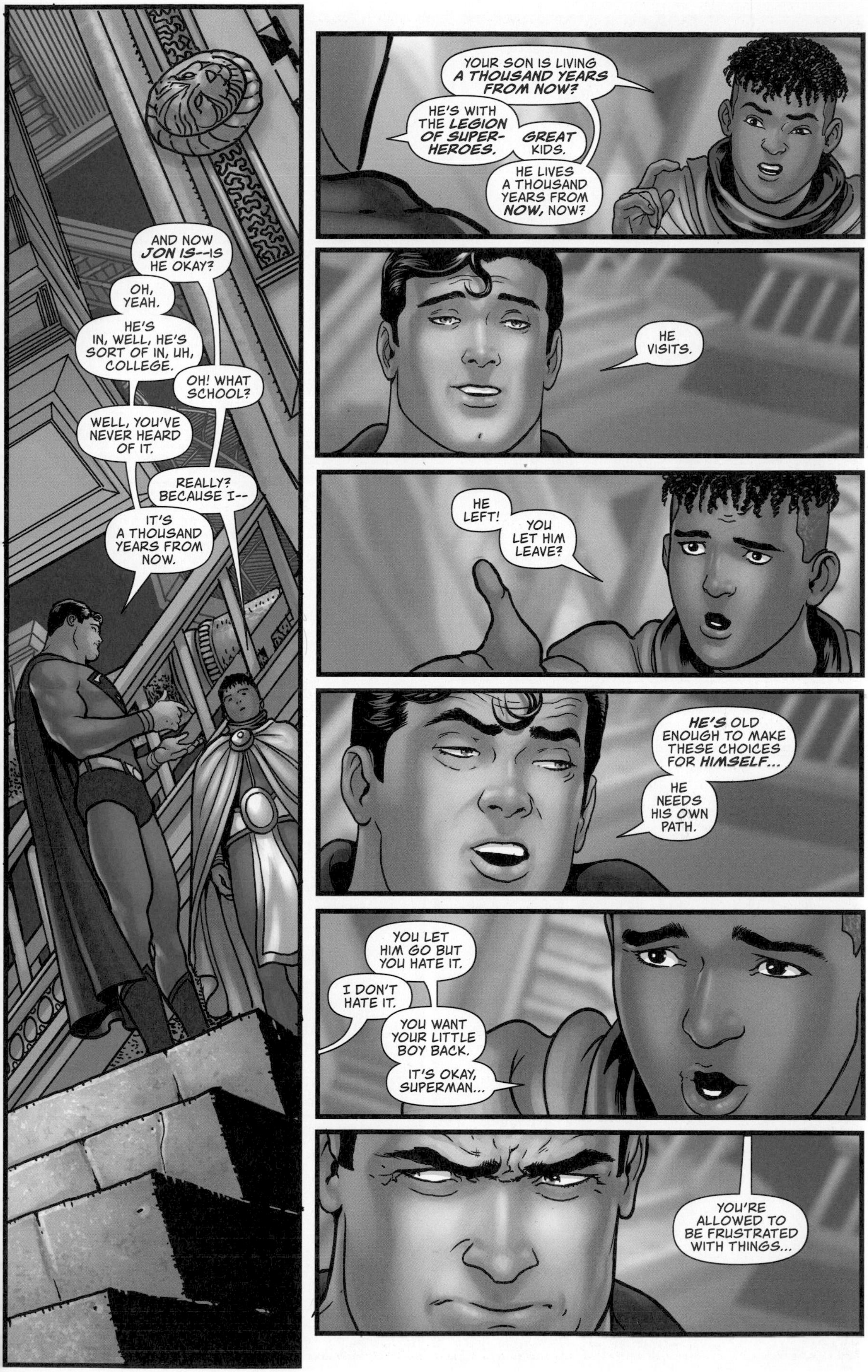
AND NOW JON IS--IS HE OKAY?
OH, YEAH.
HE'S IN, WELL, HE'S SORT OF IN, UH, COLLEGE.
OH! WHAT SCHOOL?
WELL, YOU'VE NEVER HEARD OF IT.
REALLY? BECAUSE I--
IT'S A THOUSAND YEARS FROM NOW.
YOUR SON IS LIVING A THOUSAND YEARS FROM NOW?
HE'S WITH THE LEGION OF SUPER-HEROES.
GREAT KIDS.
HE LIVES A THOUSAND YEARS FROM NOW, NOW?
HE VISITS.
HE LEFT!
YOU LET HIM LEAVE?
HE'S OLD ENOUGH TO MAKE THESE CHOICES FOR HIMSELF...
HE NEEDS HIS OWN PATH.
YOU LET HIM GO BUT YOU HATE IT.
I DON'T HATE IT.
YOU WANT YOUR LITTLE BOY BACK.
IT'S OKAY, SUPERMAN...
YOU'RE ALLOWED TO BE FRUSTRATED WITH THINGS...

AND THAT WAS TAKEN FROM YOU...

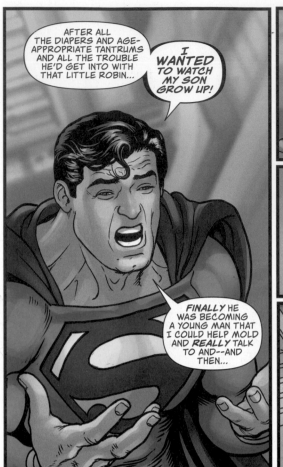
AFTER ALL THE DIAPERS AND AGE-APPROPRIATE TANTRUMS AND ALL THE TROUBLE HE'D GET INTO WITH THAT LITTLE ROBIN...

I WANTED TO WATCH MY SON GROW UP!

FINALLY HE WAS BECOMING A YOUNG MAN THAT I COULD HELP MOLD AND REALLY TALK TO AND--AND THEN...

IT WAS.

BY YOUR FATHER.

I DON'T BLAME JOR-EL.

YOU DON'T NEED TO BLAME. YOU CAN JUST BE MAD.

NO. I CAN'T.

WHAT DOES YOUR WIFE SAY?

OH, LOIS'S FATHER PASSED AWAY VERY RECENTLY. IN HER ARMS.

IT WAS SO MESSY.

AND THEY, THE TWO OF THEM, HAD UNRESOLVED ISSUES.

DEEP ISSUES.

WAIT, HER FATHER JUST DIED?

AND YOUR FATHER IS ALIVE?

WELL, NO.

NO?

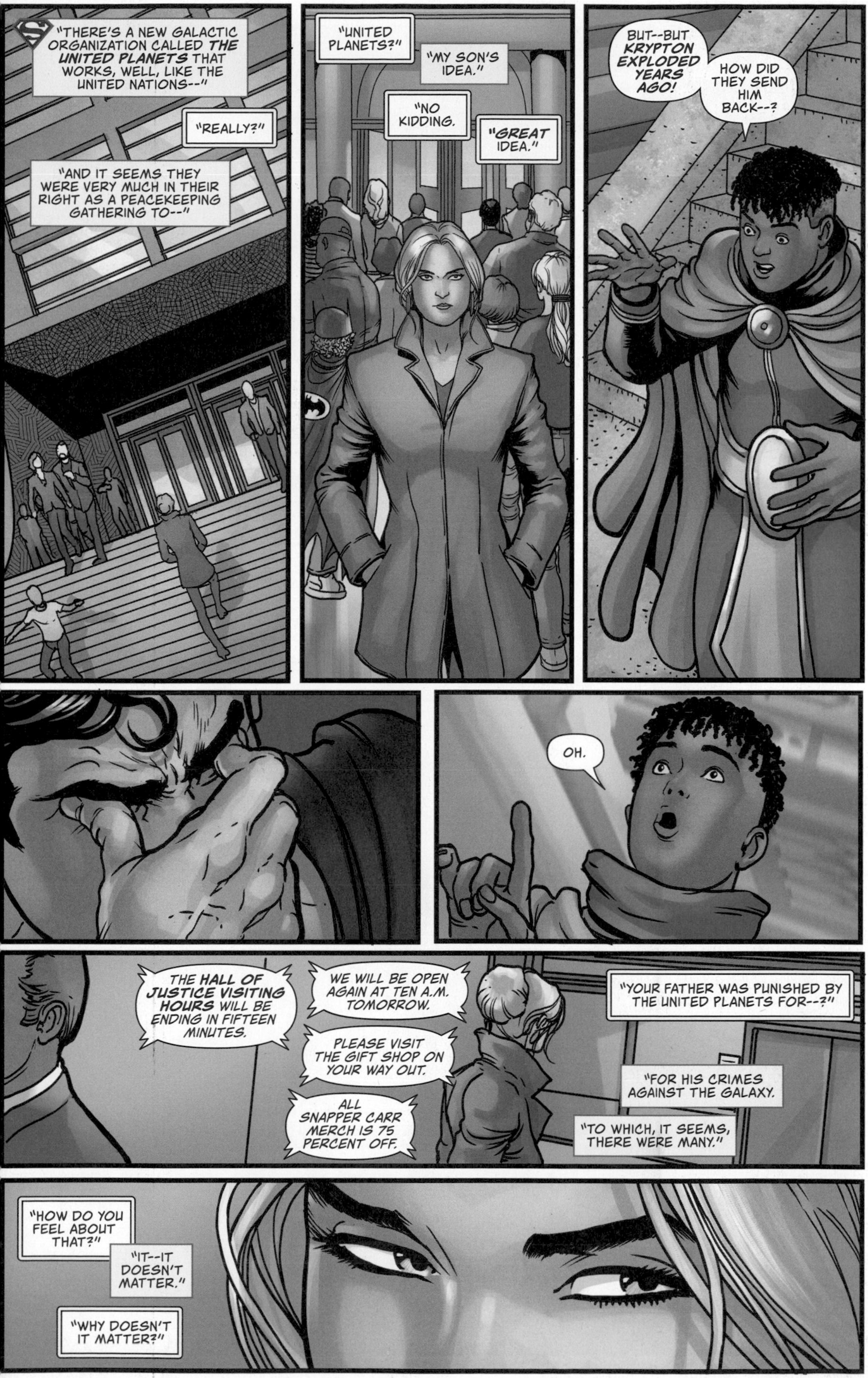
"THERE'S A NEW GALACTIC ORGANIZATION CALLED THE UNITED PLANETS THAT WORKS, WELL, LIKE THE UNITED NATIONS--"
"REALLY?"
"AND IT SEEMS THEY WERE VERY MUCH IN THEIR RIGHT AS A PEACEKEEPING GATHERING TO--"
"UNITED PLANETS?"
"MY SON'S IDEA."
"NO KIDDING.
"GREAT IDEA."
BUT--BUT KRYPTON EXPLODED YEARS AGO!
HOW DID THEY SEND HIM BACK--?
OH.
THE HALL OF JUSTICE VISITING HOURS WILL BE ENDING IN FIFTEEN MINUTES.
WE WILL BE OPEN AGAIN AT TEN A.M. TOMORROW.
PLEASE VISIT THE GIFT SHOP ON YOUR WAY OUT.
ALL SNAPPER CARR MERCH IS 75 PERCENT OFF.
"YOUR FATHER WAS PUNISHED BY THE UNITED PLANETS FOR--?"
"FOR HIS CRIMES AGAINST THE GALAXY.
"TO WHICH, IT SEEMS, THERE WERE MANY."
"HOW DO YOU FEEL ABOUT THAT?"
"IT--IT DOESN'T MATTER."
"WHY DOESN'T IT MATTER?"

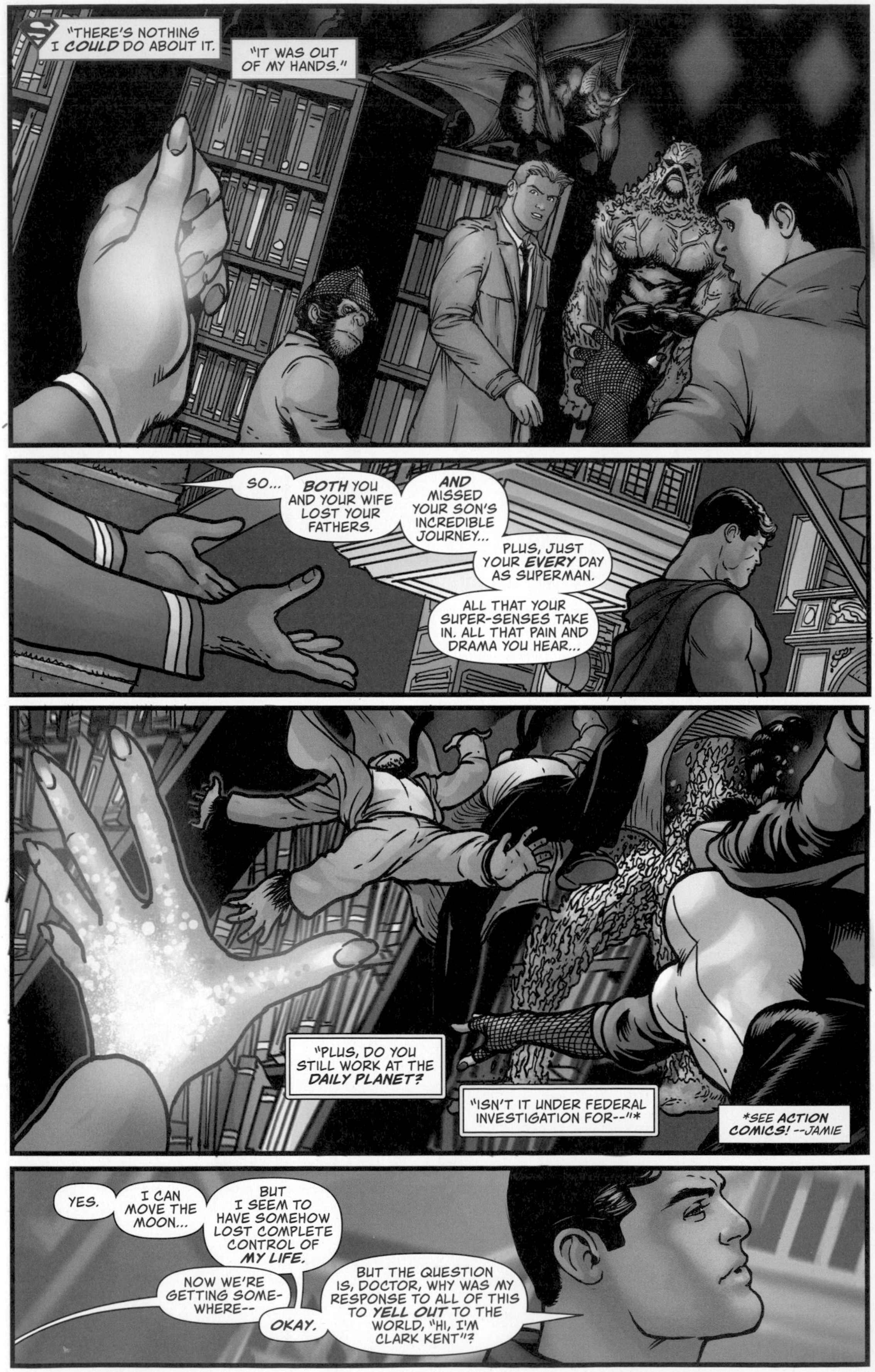
"THERE'S NOTHING I COULD DO ABOUT IT.
"IT WAS OUT OF MY HANDS."
SO...
BOTH YOU AND YOUR WIFE LOST YOUR FATHERS.
AND MISSED YOUR SON'S INCREDIBLE JOURNEY...
PLUS, JUST YOUR EVERY DAY AS SUPERMAN.
ALL THAT YOUR SUPER-SENSES TAKE IN. ALL THAT PAIN AND DRAMA YOU HEAR...
"PLUS, DO YOU STILL WORK AT THE DAILY PLANET?
"ISN'T IT UNDER FEDERAL INVESTIGATION FOR--"*
*SEE ACTION COMICS! --JAMIE
YES.
I CAN MOVE THE MOON...
BUT I SEEM TO HAVE SOMEHOW LOST COMPLETE CONTROL OF MY LIFE.
NOW WE'RE GETTING SOME-WHERE--
OKAY.
BUT THE QUESTION IS, DOCTOR, WHY WAS MY RESPONSE TO ALL OF THIS TO YELL OUT TO THE WORLD, "HI, I'M CLARK KENT"?

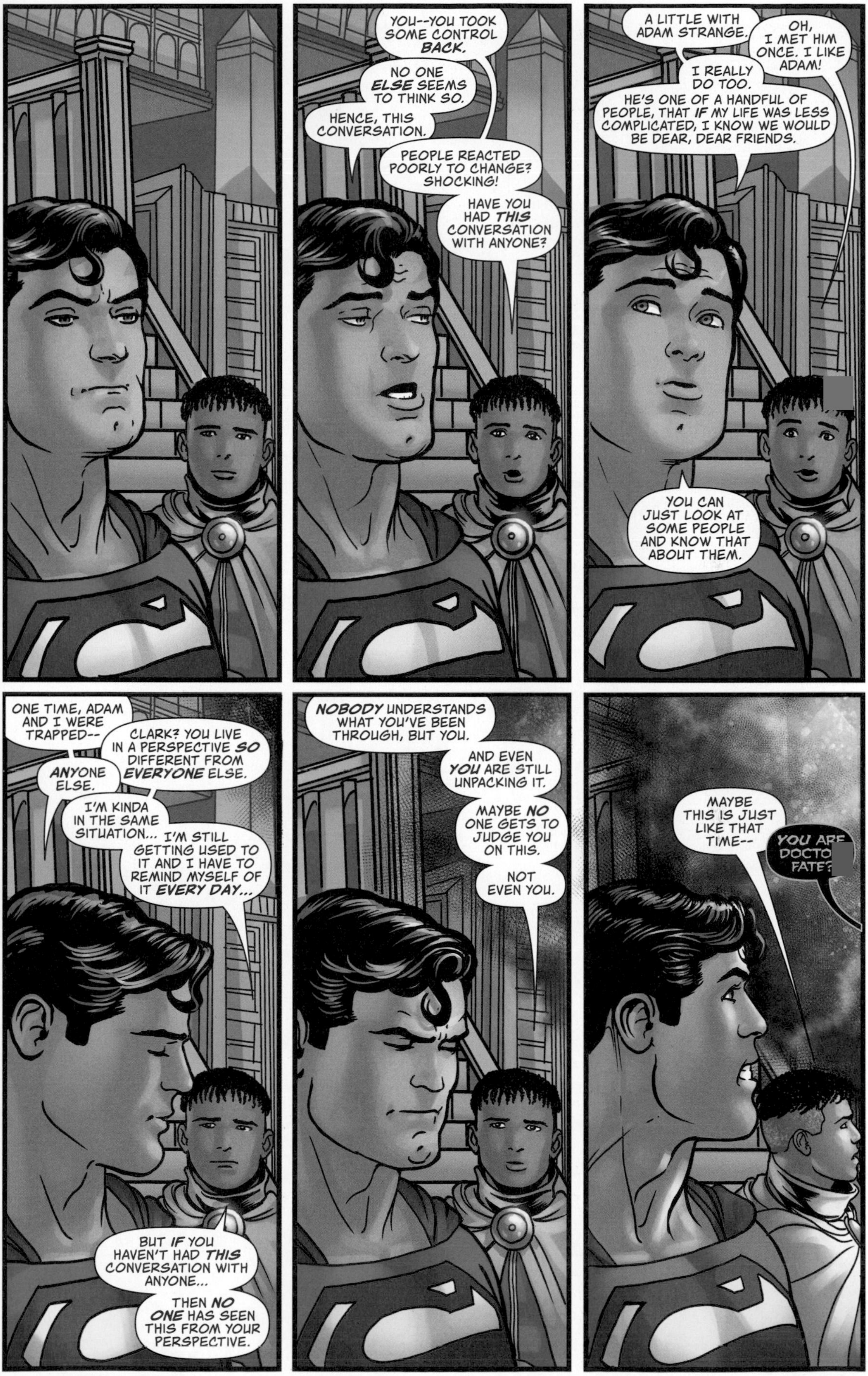

YOU--YOU TOOK SOME CONTROL BACK.
NO ONE ELSE SEEMS TO THINK SO.
HENCE, THIS CONVERSATION.
PEOPLE REACTED POORLY TO CHANGE? SHOCKING!
HAVE YOU HAD THIS CONVERSATION WITH ANYONE?
A LITTLE WITH ADAM STRANGE.
OH, I MET HIM ONCE. I LIKE ADAM!
I REALLY DO TOO.
HE'S ONE OF A HANDFUL OF PEOPLE, THAT IF MY LIFE WAS LESS COMPLICATED, I KNOW WE WOULD BE DEAR, DEAR FRIENDS.
YOU CAN JUST LOOK AT SOME PEOPLE AND KNOW THAT ABOUT THEM.
ONE TIME, ADAM AND I WERE TRAPPED--
CLARK? YOU LIVE IN A PERSPECTIVE SO DIFFERENT FROM EVERYONE ELSE.
ANYONE ELSE.
I'M KINDA IN THE SAME SITUATION...
I'M STILL GETTING USED TO IT AND I HAVE TO REMIND MYSELF OF IT EVERY DAY...
BUT IF YOU HAVEN'T HAD THIS CONVERSATION WITH ANYONE...
THEN NO ONE HAS SEEN THIS FROM YOUR PERSPECTIVE.
NOBODY UNDERSTANDS WHAT YOU'VE BEEN THROUGH, BUT YOU.
AND EVEN YOU ARE STILL UNPACKING IT.
MAYBE NO ONE GETS TO JUDGE YOU ON THIS.
NOT EVEN YOU.
MAYBE THIS IS JUST LIKE THAT TIME--
YOU ARE DOCTO FATE?

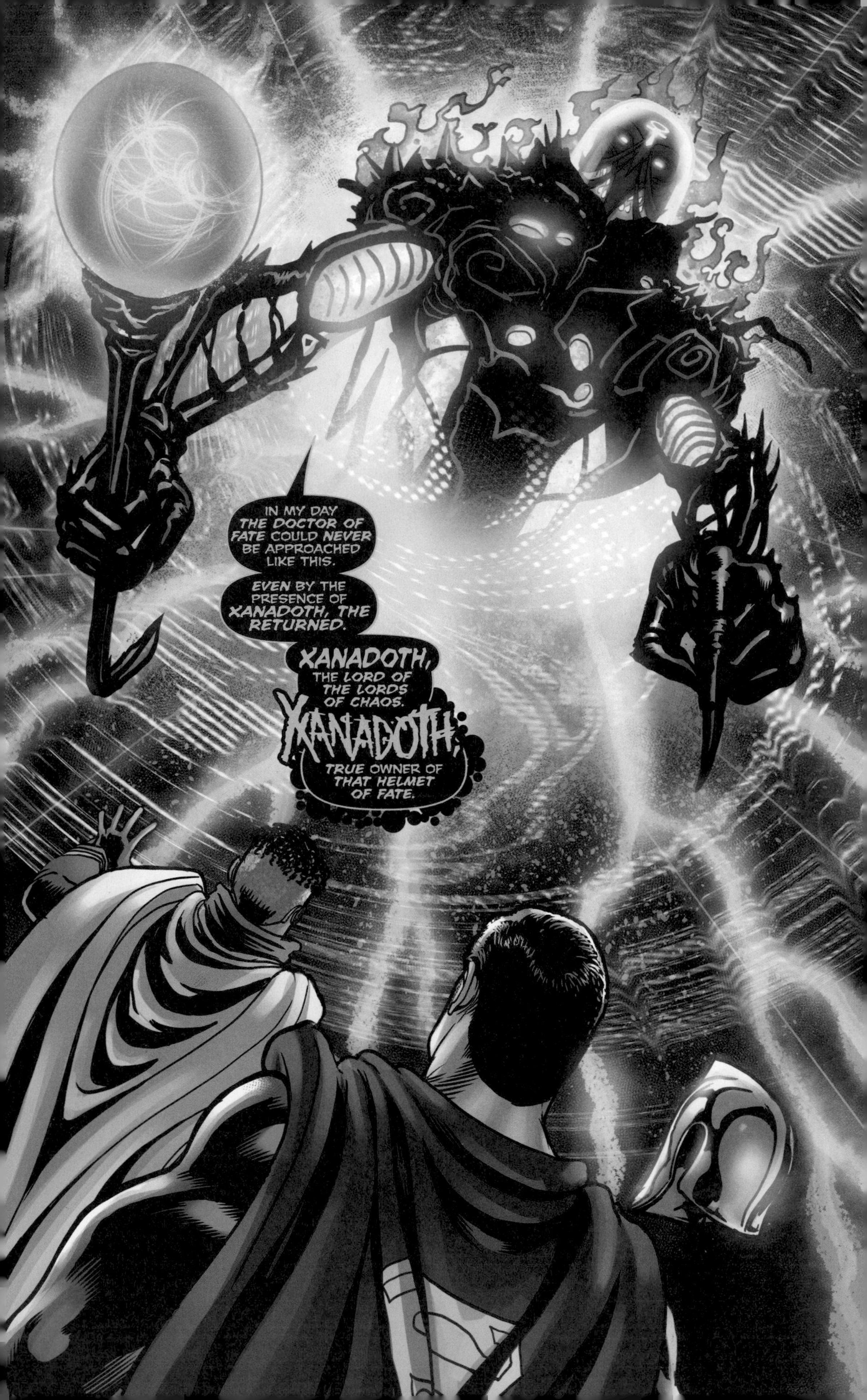
IN MY DAY THE DOCTOR OF FATE COULD NEVER BE APPROACHED LIKE THIS.
EVEN BY THE PRESENCE OF XANADOTH, THE RETURNED.
XANADOTH, THE LORD OF THE LORDS OF CHAOS.
XANADOTH, TRUE OWNER OF THAT HELMET OF FATE.

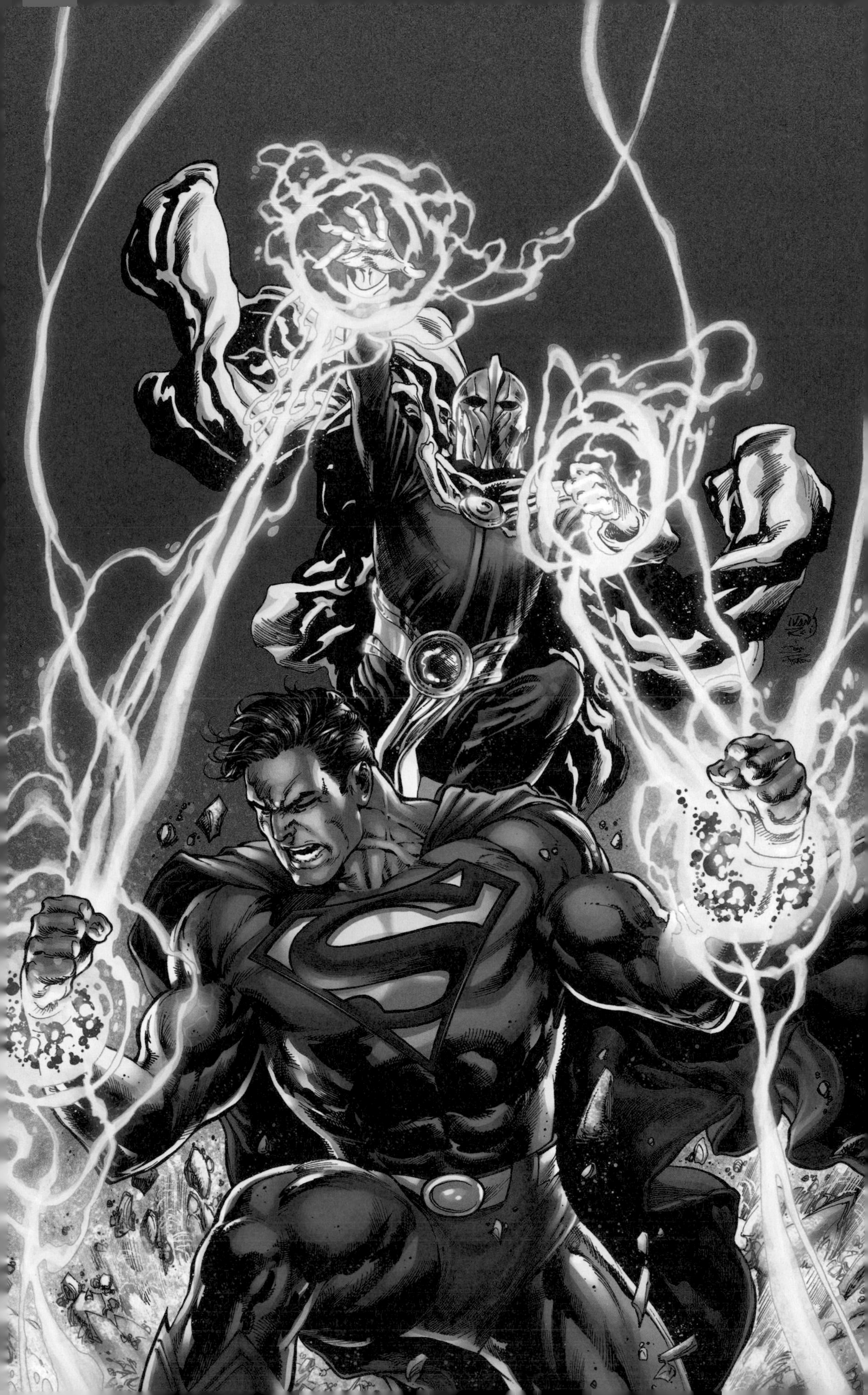

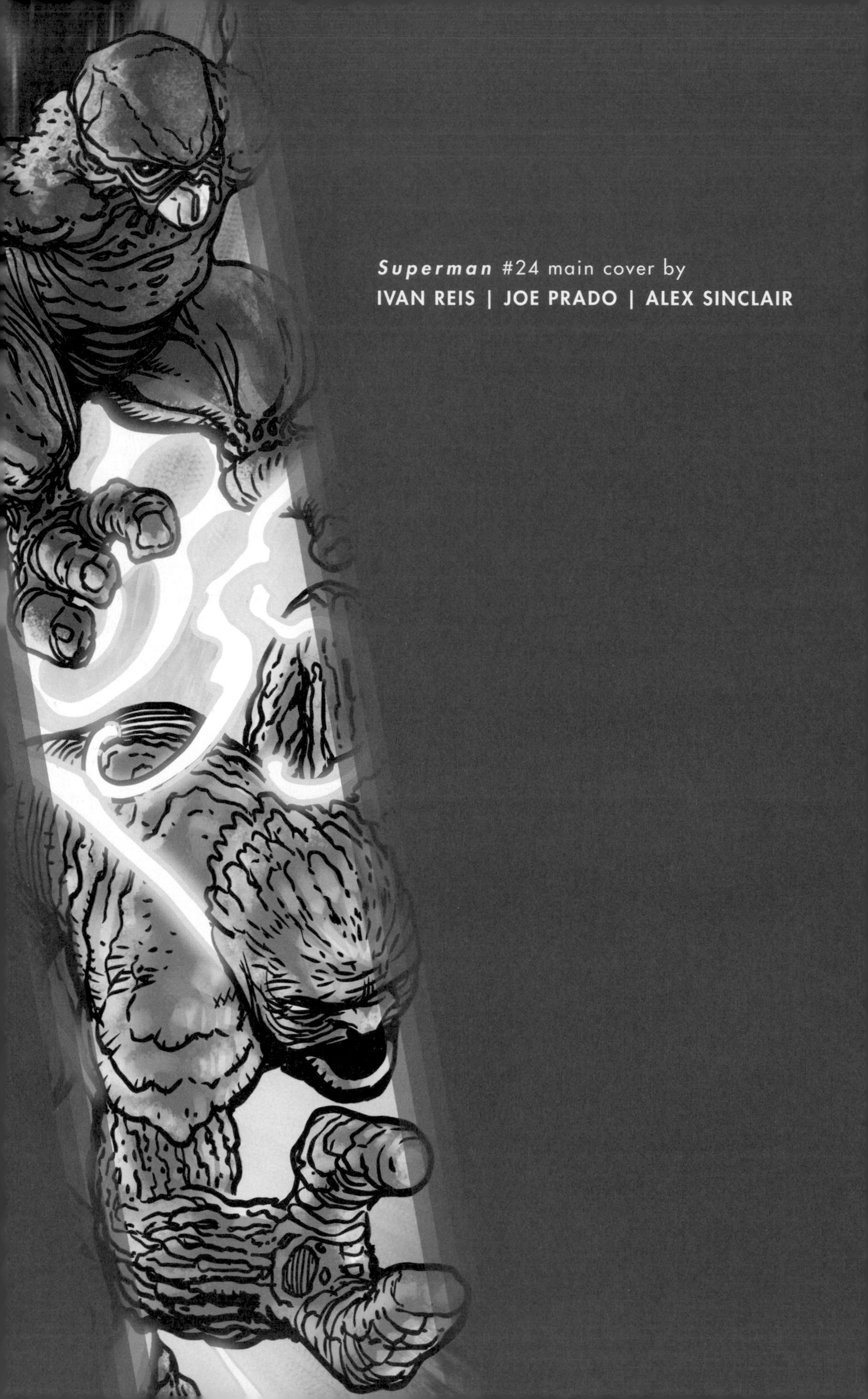

Superman #24 main cover by
IVAN REIS | JOE PRADO | ALEX SINCLAIR

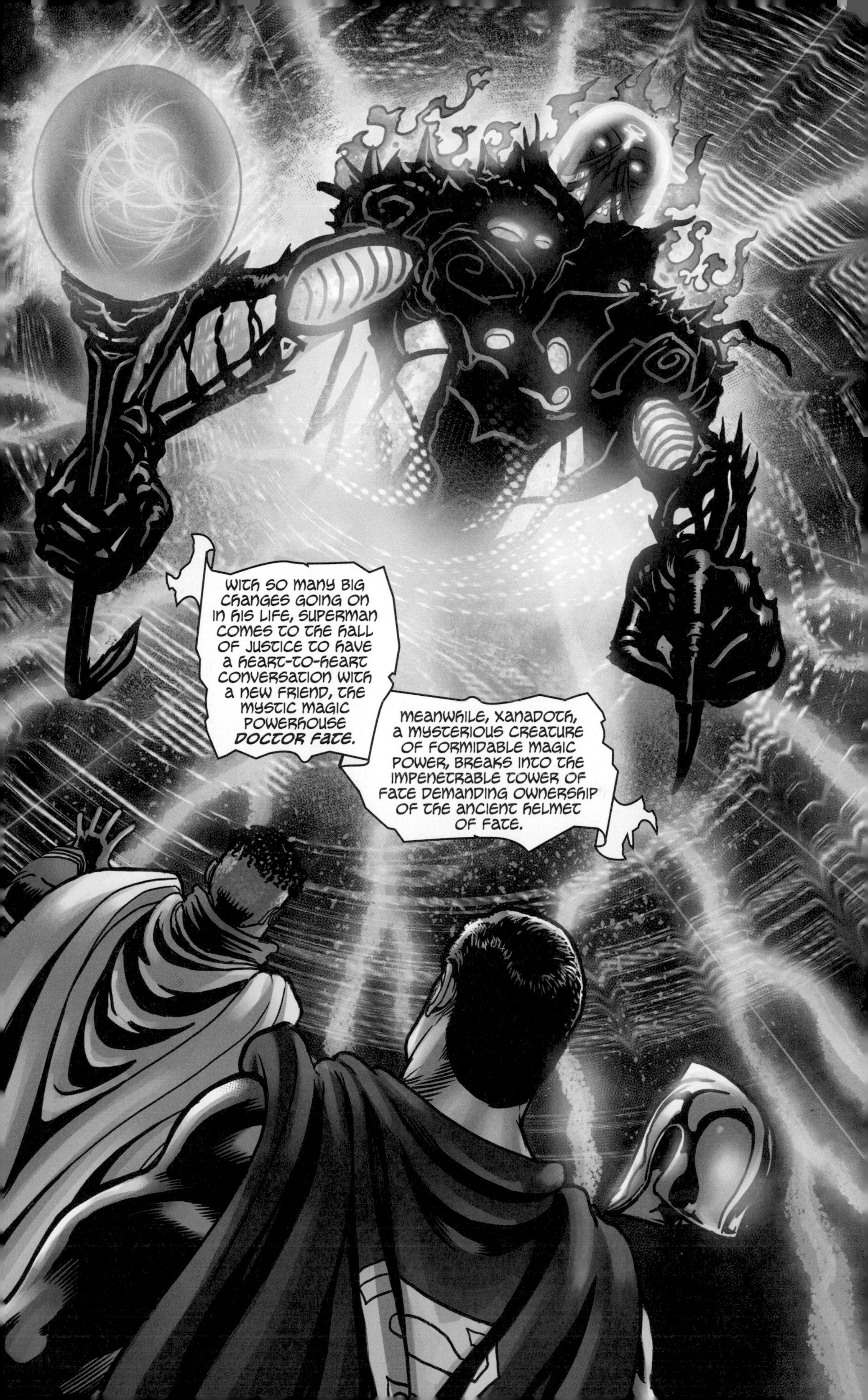
WITH SO MANY BIG CHANGES GOING ON IN HIS LIFE, SUPERMAN COMES TO THE HALL OF JUSTICE TO HAVE A HEART-TO-HEART CONVERSATION WITH A NEW FRIEND, THE MYSTIC MAGIC POWERHOUSE DOCTOR FATE.
MEANWHILE, XANADOTH, A MYSTERIOUS CREATURE OF FORMIDABLE MAGIC POWER, BREAKS INTO THE IMPENETRABLE TOWER OF FATE DEMANDING OWNERSHIP OF THE ANCIENT HELMET OF FATE.

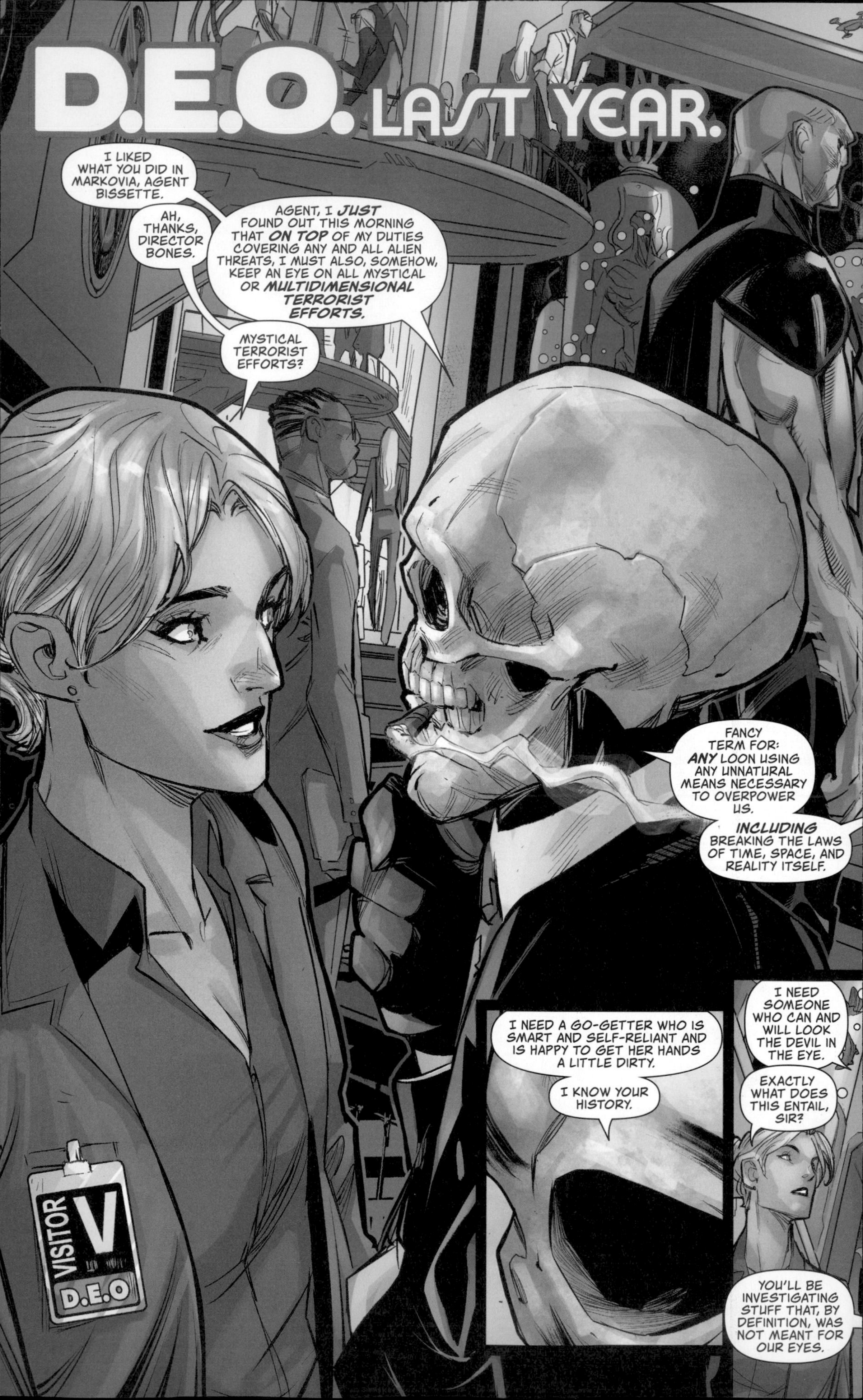
D.E.O. LAST YEAR.
I LIKED WHAT YOU DID IN MARKOVIA, AGENT BISSETTE.
AH, THANKS, DIRECTOR BONES.
AGENT, I JUST FOUND OUT THIS MORNING THAT ON TOP OF MY DUTIES COVERING ANY AND ALL ALIEN THREATS, I MUST ALSO, SOMEHOW, KEEP AN EYE ON ALL MYSTICAL OR MULTIDIMENSIONAL TERRORIST EFFORTS.
MYSTICAL TERRORIST EFFORTS?
FANCY TERM FOR: ANY LOON USING ANY UNNATURAL MEANS NECESSARY TO OVERPOWER US.
INCLUDING BREAKING THE LAWS OF TIME, SPACE, AND REALITY ITSELF.
VISITOR V D.E.O
I NEED A GO-GETTER WHO IS SMART AND SELF-RELIANT AND IS HAPPY TO GET HER HANDS A LITTLE DIRTY.
I KNOW YOUR HISTORY.
I NEED SOMEONE WHO CAN AND WILL LOOK THE DEVIL IN THE EYE.
EXACTLY WHAT DOES THIS ENTAIL, SIR?
YOU'LL BE INVESTIGATING STUFF THAT, BY DEFINITION, WAS NOT MEANT FOR OUR EYES.

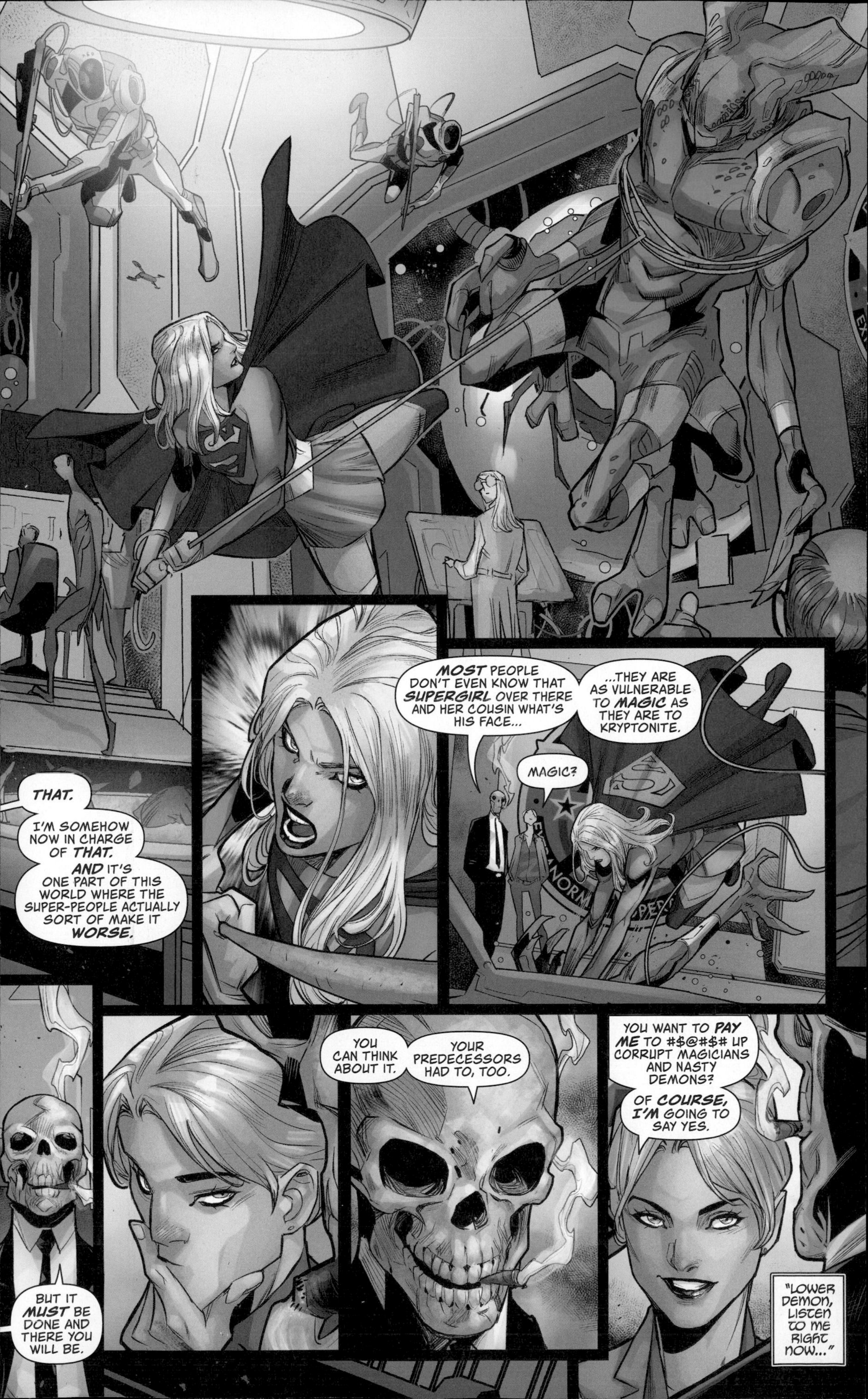

THAT.
I'M SOMEHOW NOW IN CHARGE OF THAT.
AND IT'S ONE PART OF THIS WORLD WHERE THE SUPER-PEOPLE ACTUALLY SORT OF MAKE IT WORSE.
MOST PEOPLE DON'T EVEN KNOW THAT SUPERGIRL OVER THERE AND HER COUSIN WHAT'S HIS FACE...
...THEY ARE AS VULNERABLE TO MAGIC AS THEY ARE TO KRYPTONITE.
MAGIC?
BUT IT MUST BE DONE AND THERE YOU WILL BE.
YOU CAN THINK ABOUT IT.
YOUR PREDECESSORS HAD TO, TOO.
YOU WANT TO PAY ME TO #$@#$# UP CORRUPT MAGICIANS AND NASTY DEMONS?
OF COURSE, I'M GOING TO SAY YES.
"LOWER DEMON, LISTEN TO ME RIGHT NOW..."

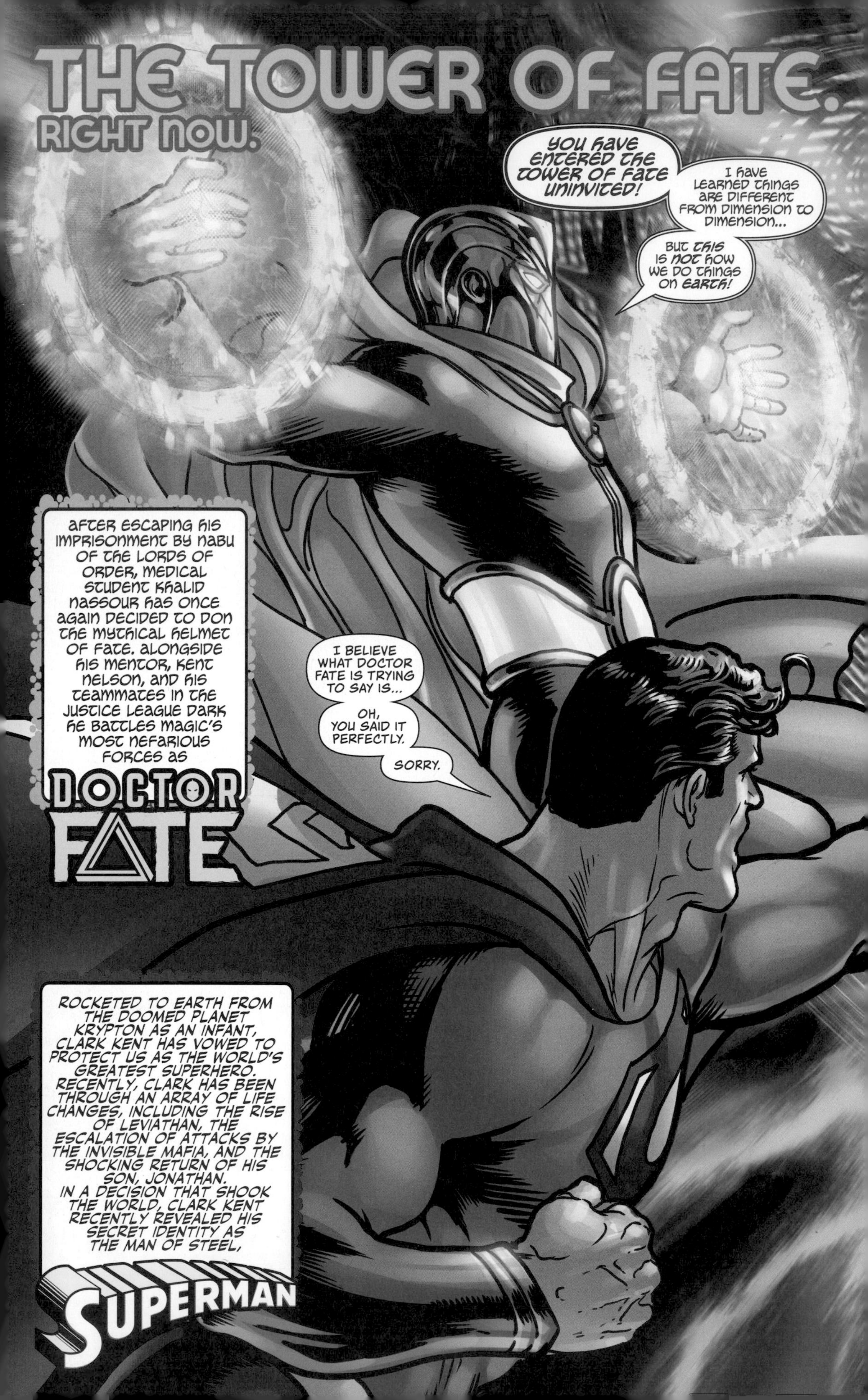
THE TOWER OF FATE.
RIGHT NOW.
YOU HAVE ENTERED THE TOWER OF FATE UNINVITED!
I HAVE LEARNED THINGS ARE DIFFERENT FROM DIMENSION TO DIMENSION...
BUT THIS IS NOT HOW WE DO THINGS ON EARTH!
AFTER ESCAPING HIS IMPRISONMENT BY NABU OF THE LORDS OF ORDER, MEDICAL STUDENT KHALID NASSOUR HAS ONCE AGAIN DECIDED TO DON THE MYTHICAL HELMET OF FATE. ALONGSIDE HIS MENTOR, KENT NELSON, AND HIS TEAMMATES IN THE JUSTICE LEAGUE DARK HE BATTLES MAGIC'S MOST NEFARIOUS FORCES AS
DOCTOR FATE
I BELIEVE WHAT DOCTOR FATE IS TRYING TO SAY IS...
OH, YOU SAID IT PERFECTLY.
SORRY.
ROCKETED TO EARTH FROM THE DOOMED PLANET KRYPTON AS AN INFANT, CLARK KENT HAS VOWED TO PROTECT US AS THE WORLD'S GREATEST SUPERHERO. RECENTLY, CLARK HAS BEEN THROUGH AN ARRAY OF LIFE CHANGES, INCLUDING THE RISE OF LEVIATHAN, THE ESCALATION OF ATTACKS BY THE INVISIBLE MAFIA, AND THE SHOCKING RETURN OF HIS SON, JONATHAN. IN A DECISION THAT SHOOK THE WORLD, CLARK KENT RECENTLY REVEALED HIS SECRET IDENTITY AS THE MAN OF STEEL,
SUPERMAN

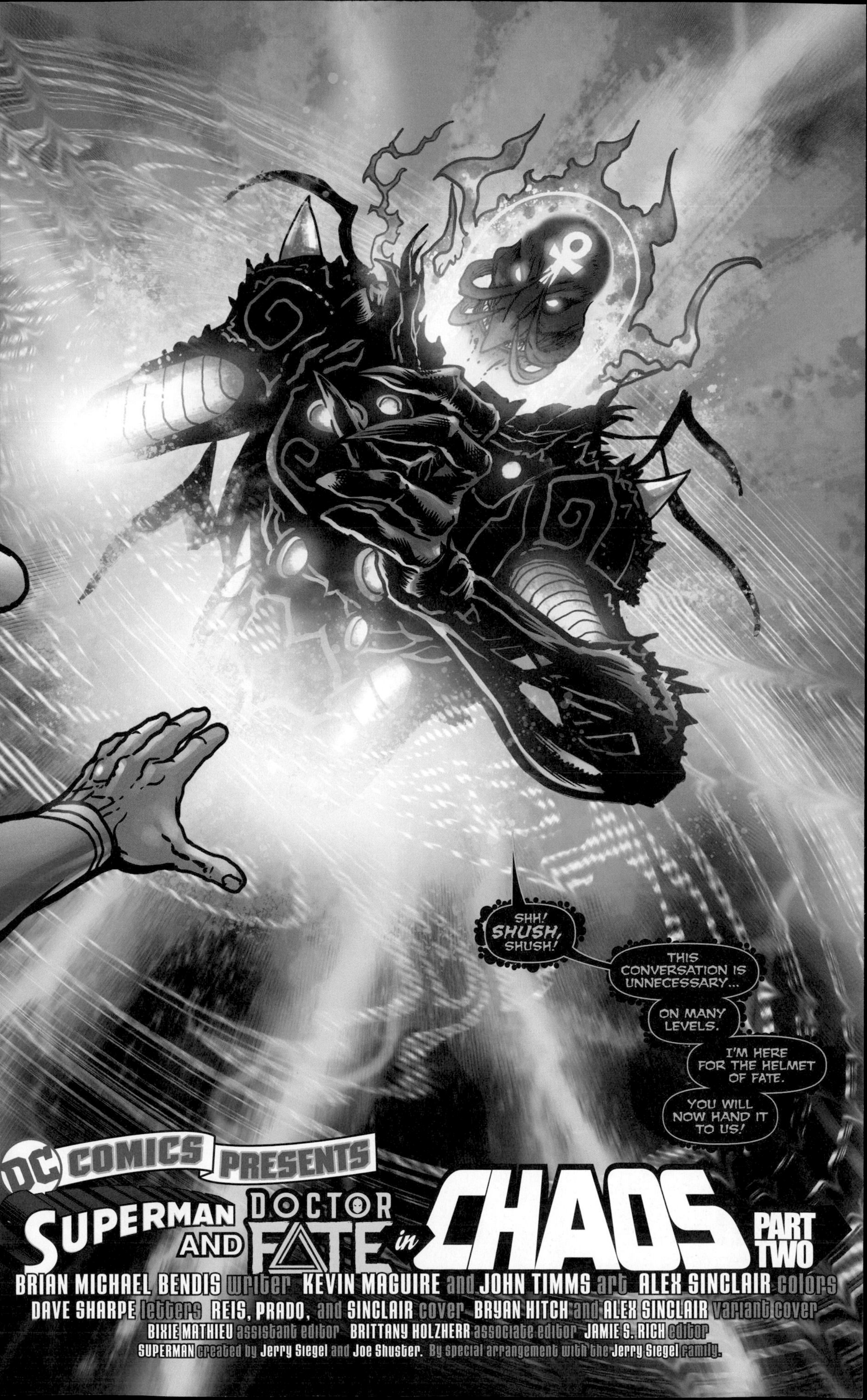
SHH! SHUSH, SHUSH!
THIS CONVERSATION IS UNNECESSARY...
ON MANY LEVELS.
I'M HERE FOR THE HELMET OF FATE.
YOU WILL NOW HAND IT TO US!
DC COMICS PRESENTS
SUPERMAN AND DOCTOR FATE in CHAOS PART TWO
BRIAN MICHAEL BENDIS writer KEVIN MAGUIRE and JOHN TIMMS art ALEX SINCLAIR colors
DAVE SHARPE letters REIS, PRADO, and SINCLAIR cover BRYAN HITCH and ALEX SINCLAIR variant cover
BIXIE MATHIEU assistant editor BRITTANY HOLZHERR associate editor JAMIE S. RICH editor
SUPERMAN created by Jerry Siegel and Joe Shuster. By special arrangement with the Jerry Siegel family.

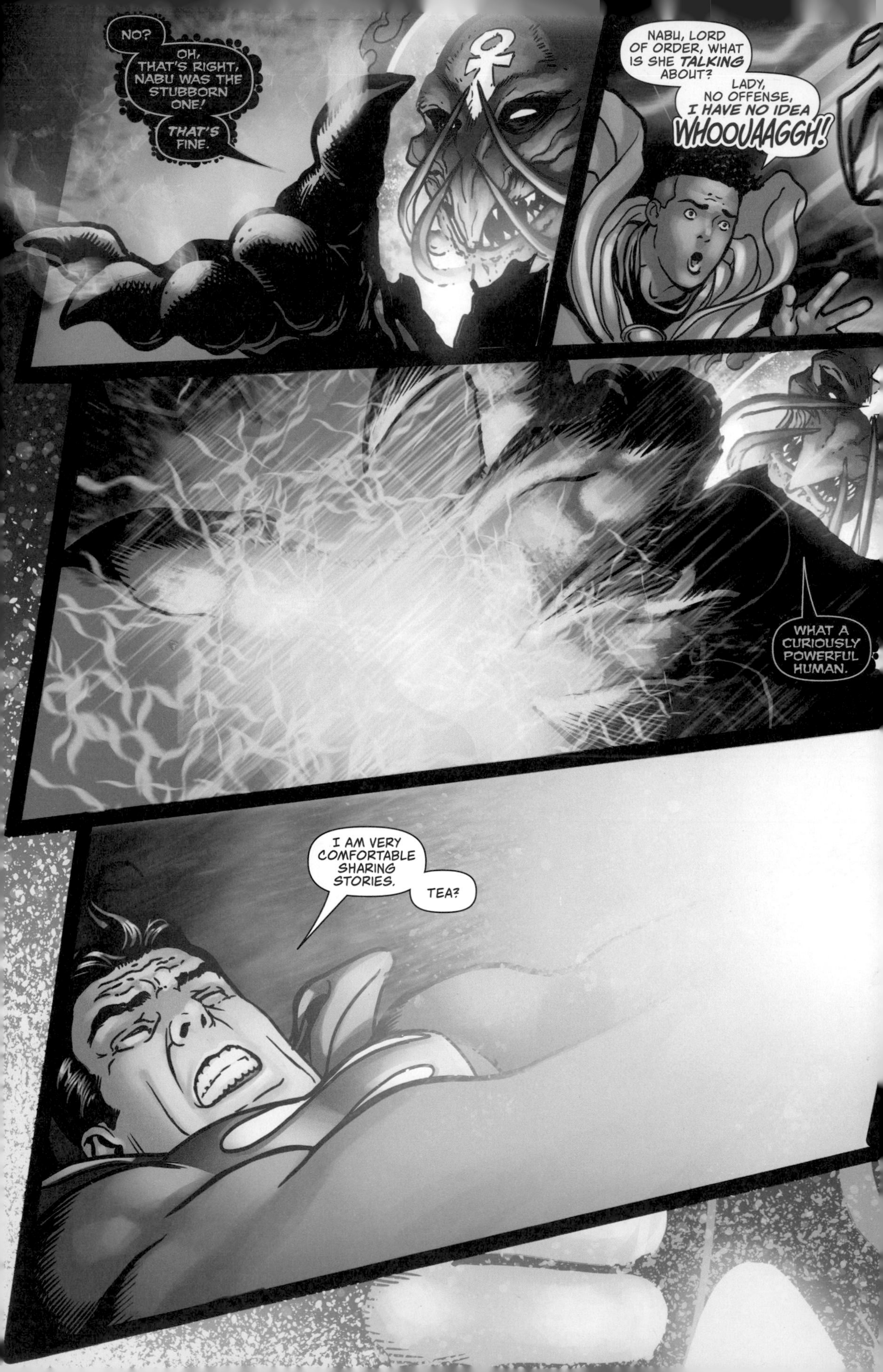
NO?
OH, THAT'S RIGHT, NABU WAS THE STUBBORN ONE!
THAT'S FINE.
NABU, LORD OF ORDER, WHAT IS SHE TALKING ABOUT?
LADY, NO OFFENSE, I HAVE NO IDEA WHOOUAAGGH!
WHAT A CURIOUSLY POWERFUL HUMAN.
I AM VERY COMFORTABLE SHARING STORIES.
TEA?

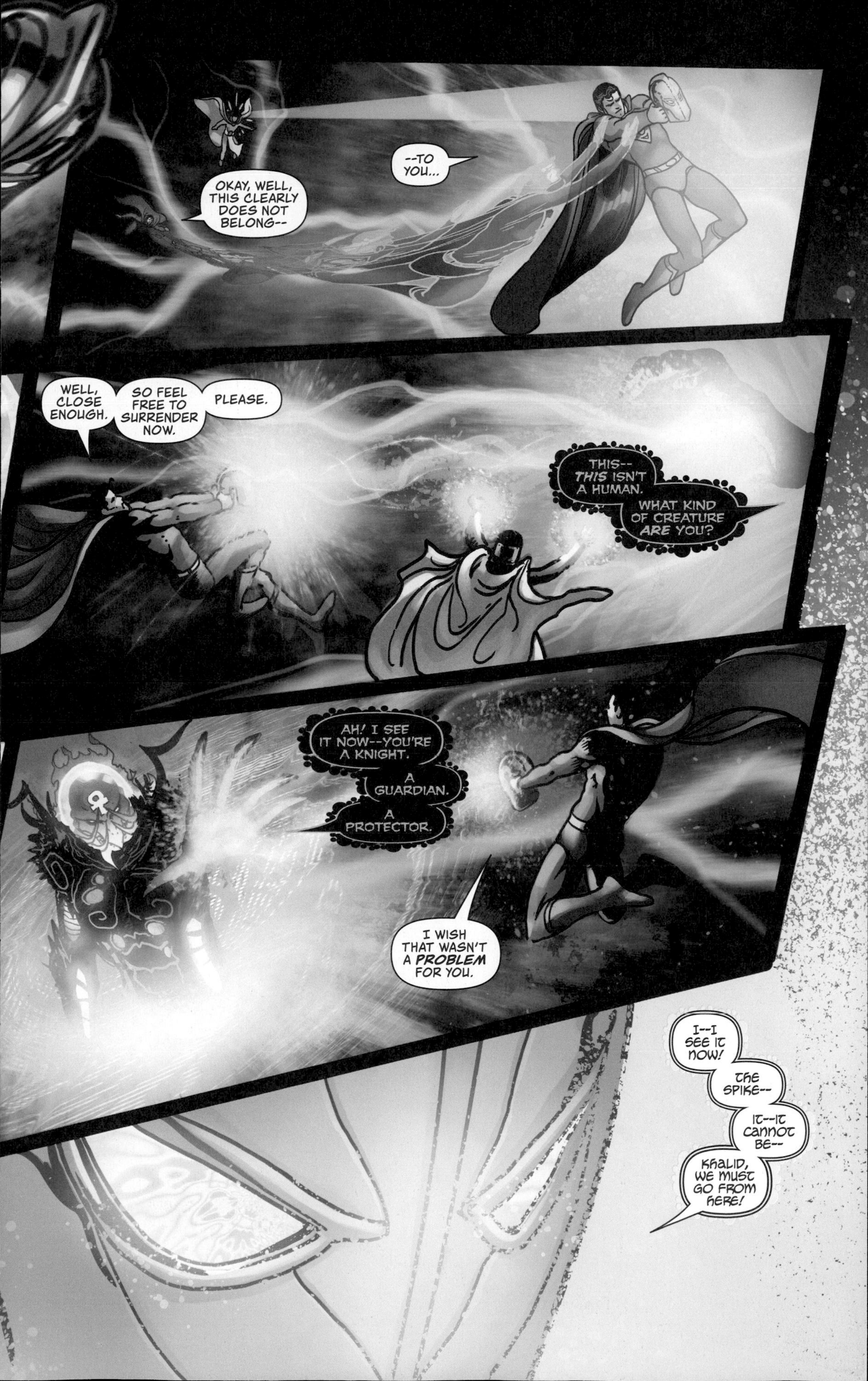
OKAY, WELL, THIS CLEARLY DOES NOT BELONG--
--TO YOU...
WELL, CLOSE ENOUGH.
SO FEEL FREE TO SURRENDER NOW.
PLEASE.
THIS-- THIS ISN'T A HUMAN.
WHAT KIND OF CREATURE ARE YOU?
AH! I SEE IT NOW--YOU'RE A KNIGHT.
A GUARDIAN.
A PROTECTOR.
I WISH THAT WASN'T A PROBLEM FOR YOU.
I--I SEE IT NOW!
THE SPIKE--
IT--IT CANNOT BE--
KHALID, WE MUST GO FROM HERE!

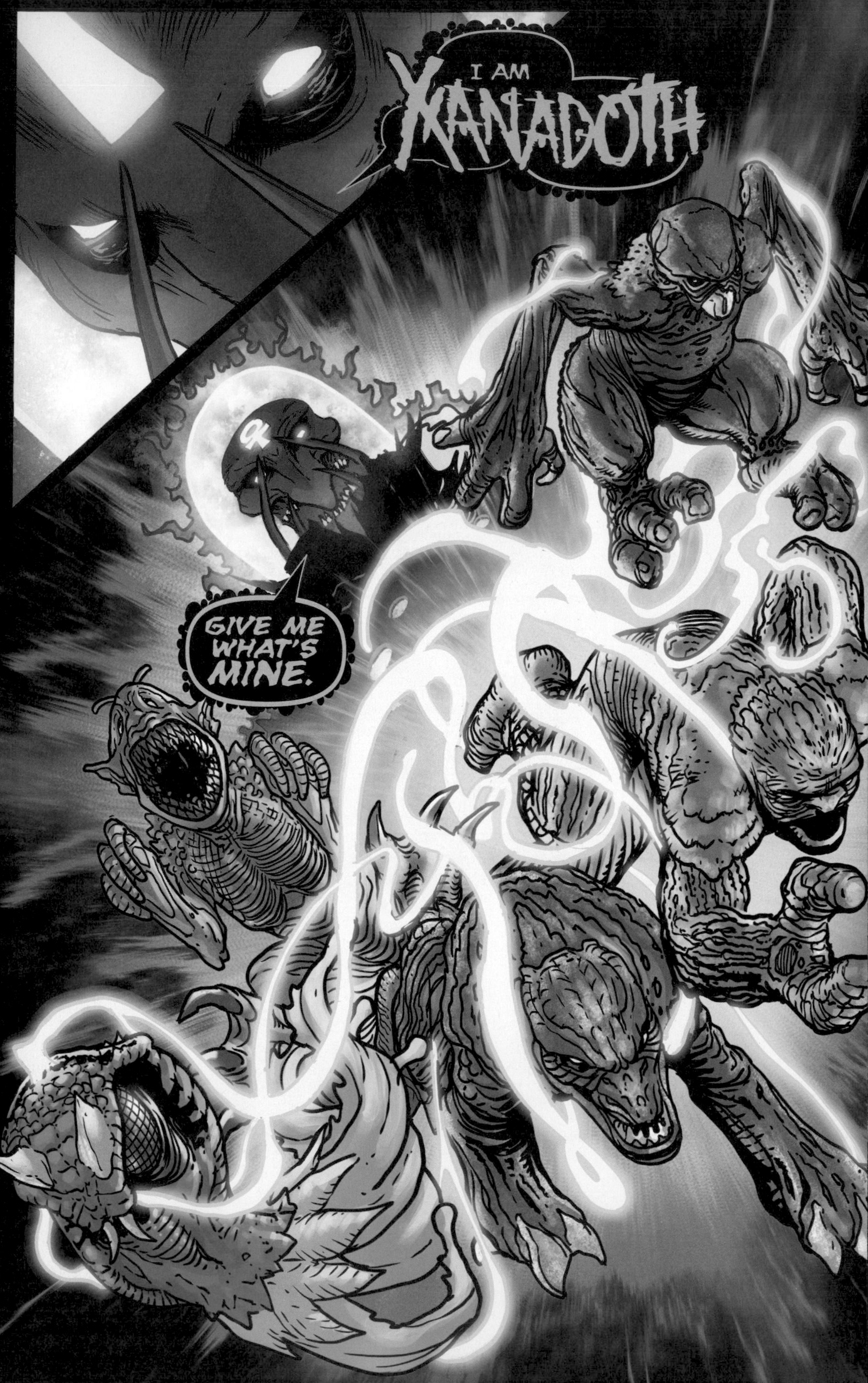
I AM XANADOTH
GIVE ME WHAT'S MINE.

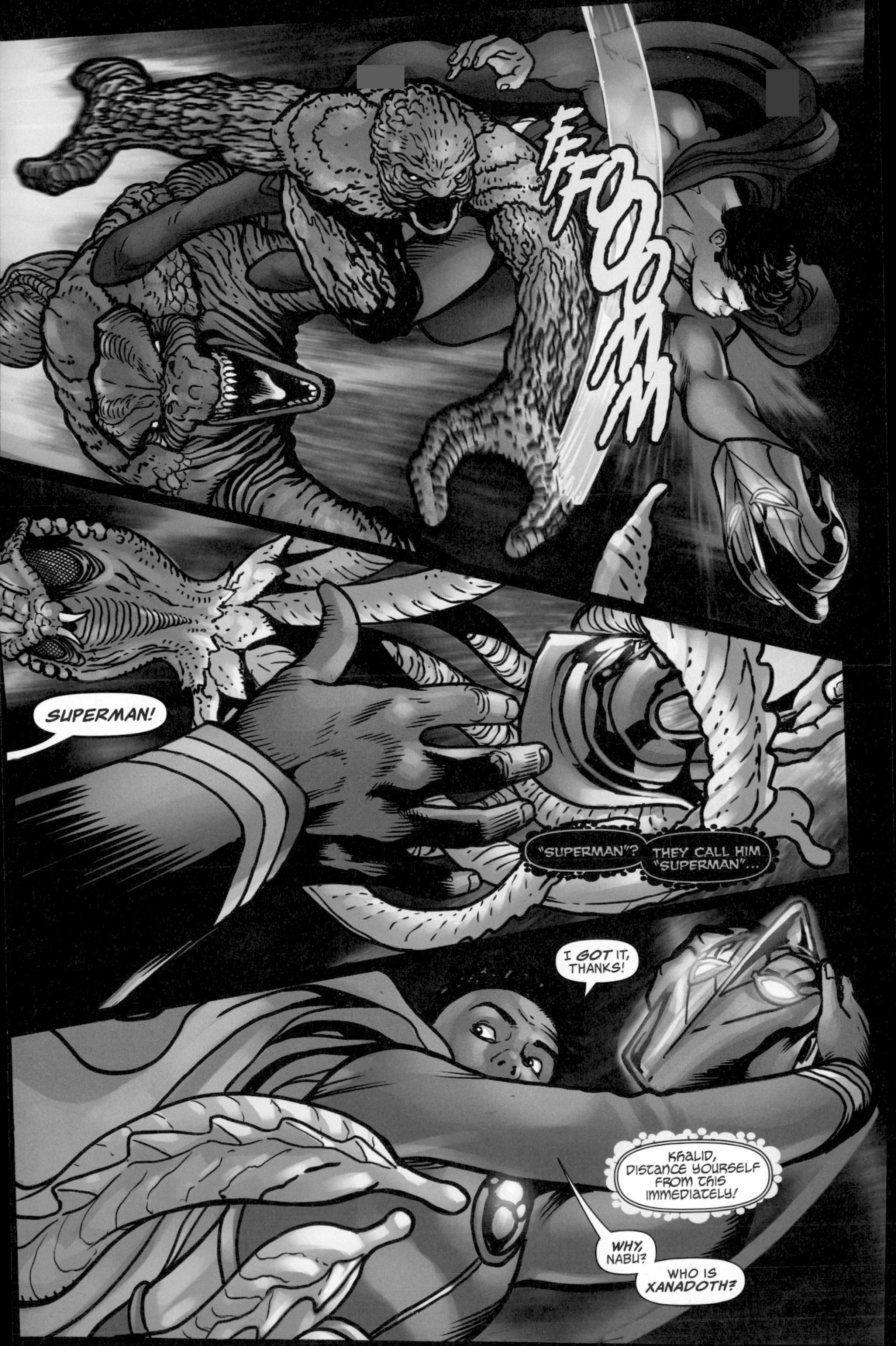
EFFOOOMM
SUPERMAN!
"SUPERMAN"? THEY CALL HIM "SUPERMAN"...
I GOT IT, THANKS!
KHALID, DISTANCE YOURSELF FROM THIS IMMEDIATELY!
WHY, NABU?
WHO IS XANADOTH?

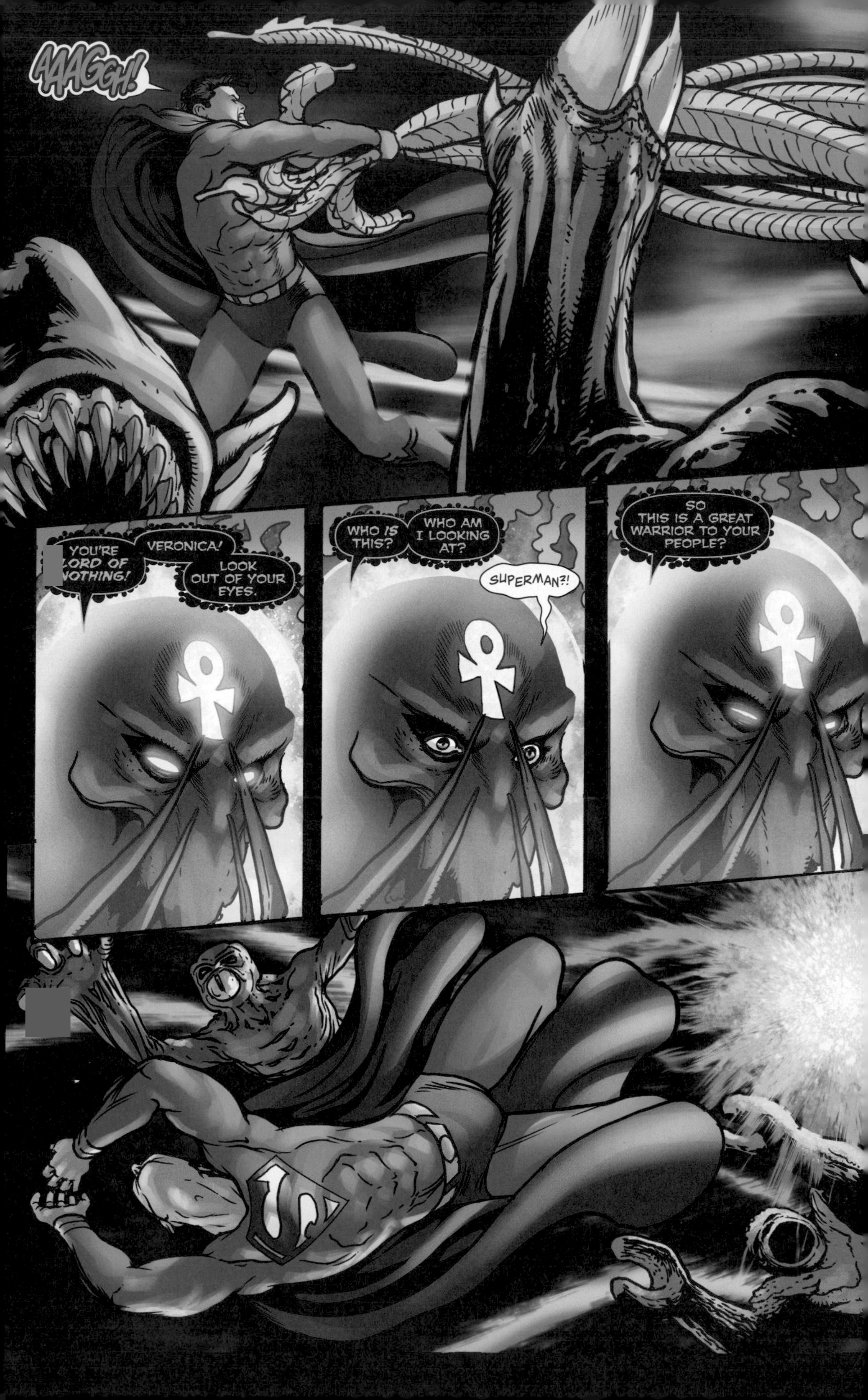
AAAGGH!
YOU'RE LORD OF NOTHING!
VERONICA!
LOOK OUT OF YOUR EYES.
WHO IS THIS?
WHO AM I LOOKING AT?
SUPERMAN?!
SO THIS IS A GREAT WARRIOR TO YOUR PEOPLE?

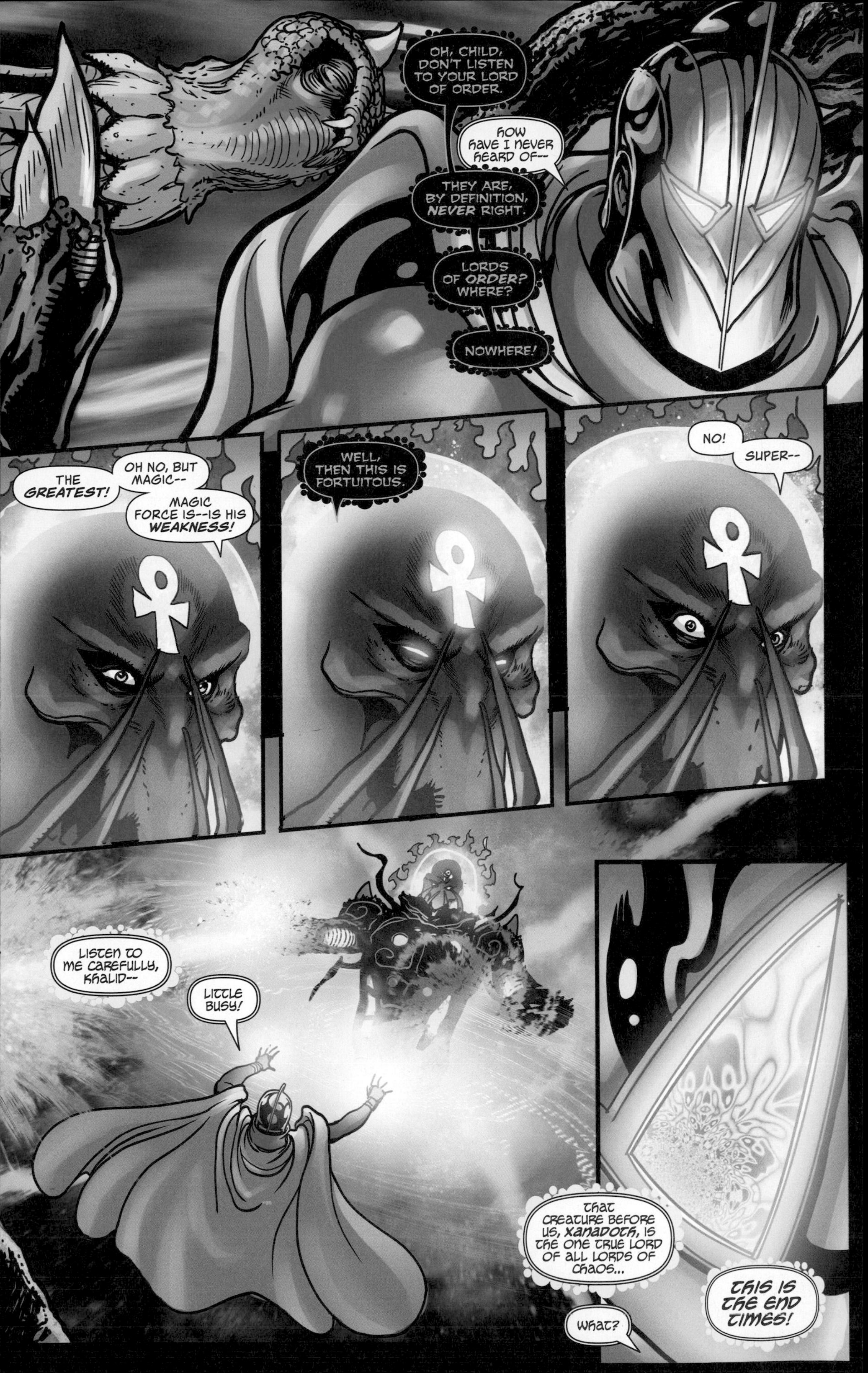
OH, CHILD, DON'T LISTEN TO YOUR LORD OF ORDER.
HOW HAVE I NEVER HEARD OF--
THEY ARE, BY DEFINITION, NEVER RIGHT.
LORDS OF ORDER? WHERE?
NOWHERE!
THE GREATEST!
OH NO, BUT MAGIC--
MAGIC FORCE IS--IS HIS WEAKNESS!
WELL, THEN THIS IS FORTUITOUS.
NO!
SUPER--
LISTEN TO ME CAREFULLY, KHALID--
LITTLE BUSY!
THAT CREATURE BEFORE US, XANADOTH, IS THE ONE TRUE LORD OF ALL LORDS OF CHAOS...
WHAT?
THIS IS THE END TIMES!

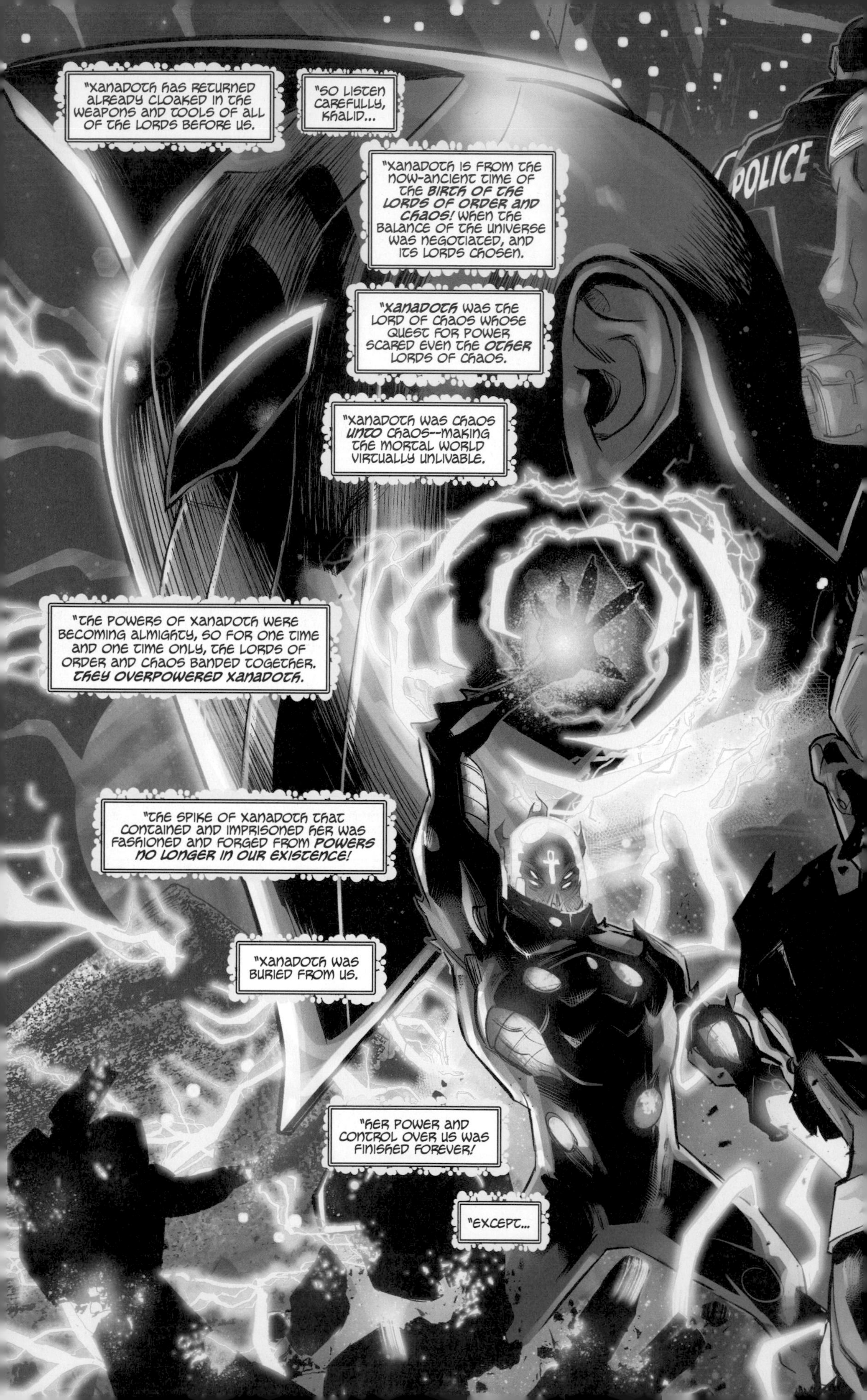
"XANADOTH HAS RETURNED ALREADY CLOAKED IN THE WEAPONS AND TOOLS OF ALL OF THE LORDS BEFORE US.
"SO LISTEN CAREFULLY, KHALID...
"XANADOTH IS FROM THE NOW-ANCIENT TIME OF THE BIRTH OF THE LORDS OF ORDER AND CHAOS! WHEN THE BALANCE OF THE UNIVERSE WAS NEGOTIATED, AND ITS LORDS CHOSEN.
"XANADOTH WAS THE LORD OF CHAOS WHOSE QUEST FOR POWER SCARED EVEN THE OTHER LORDS OF CHAOS.
"XANADOTH WAS CHAOS UNTO CHAOS--MAKING THE MORTAL WORLD VIRTUALLY UNLIVABLE.
POLICE
"THE POWERS OF XANADOTH WERE BECOMING ALMIGHTY, SO FOR ONE TIME AND ONE TIME ONLY, THE LORDS OF ORDER AND CHAOS BANDED TOGETHER. THEY OVERPOWERED XANADOTH.
"THE SPIKE OF XANADOTH THAT CONTAINED AND IMPRISONED HER WAS FASHIONED AND FORGED FROM POWERS NO LONGER IN OUR EXISTENCE!
"XANADOTH WAS BURIED FROM US.
"HER POWER AND CONTROL OVER US WAS FINISHED FOREVER!
"EXCEPT...

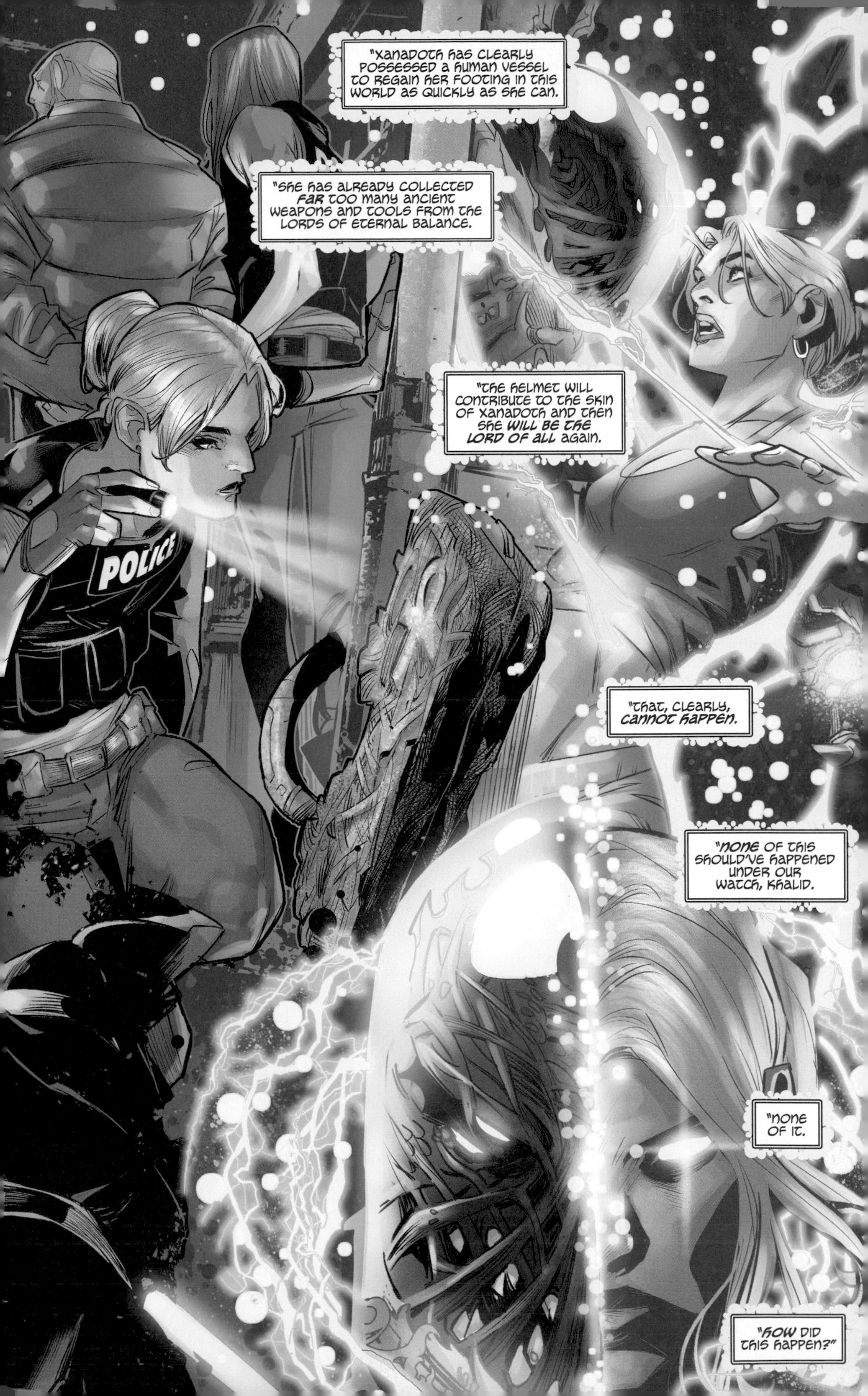
"XANADOTH HAS CLEARLY POSSESSED A HUMAN VESSEL TO REGAIN HER FOOTING IN THIS WORLD AS QUICKLY AS SHE CAN.
"SHE HAS ALREADY COLLECTED FAR TOO MANY ANCIENT WEAPONS AND TOOLS FROM THE LORDS OF ETERNAL BALANCE.
"THE HELMET WILL CONTRIBUTE TO THE SKIN OF XANADOTH AND THEN SHE WILL BE THE LORD OF ALL AGAIN.
POLICE
"THAT, CLEARLY, CANNOT HAPPEN.
"NONE OF THIS SHOULD'VE HAPPENED UNDER OUR WATCH, KHALID.
"NONE OF IT.
"HOW DID THIS HAPPEN?"

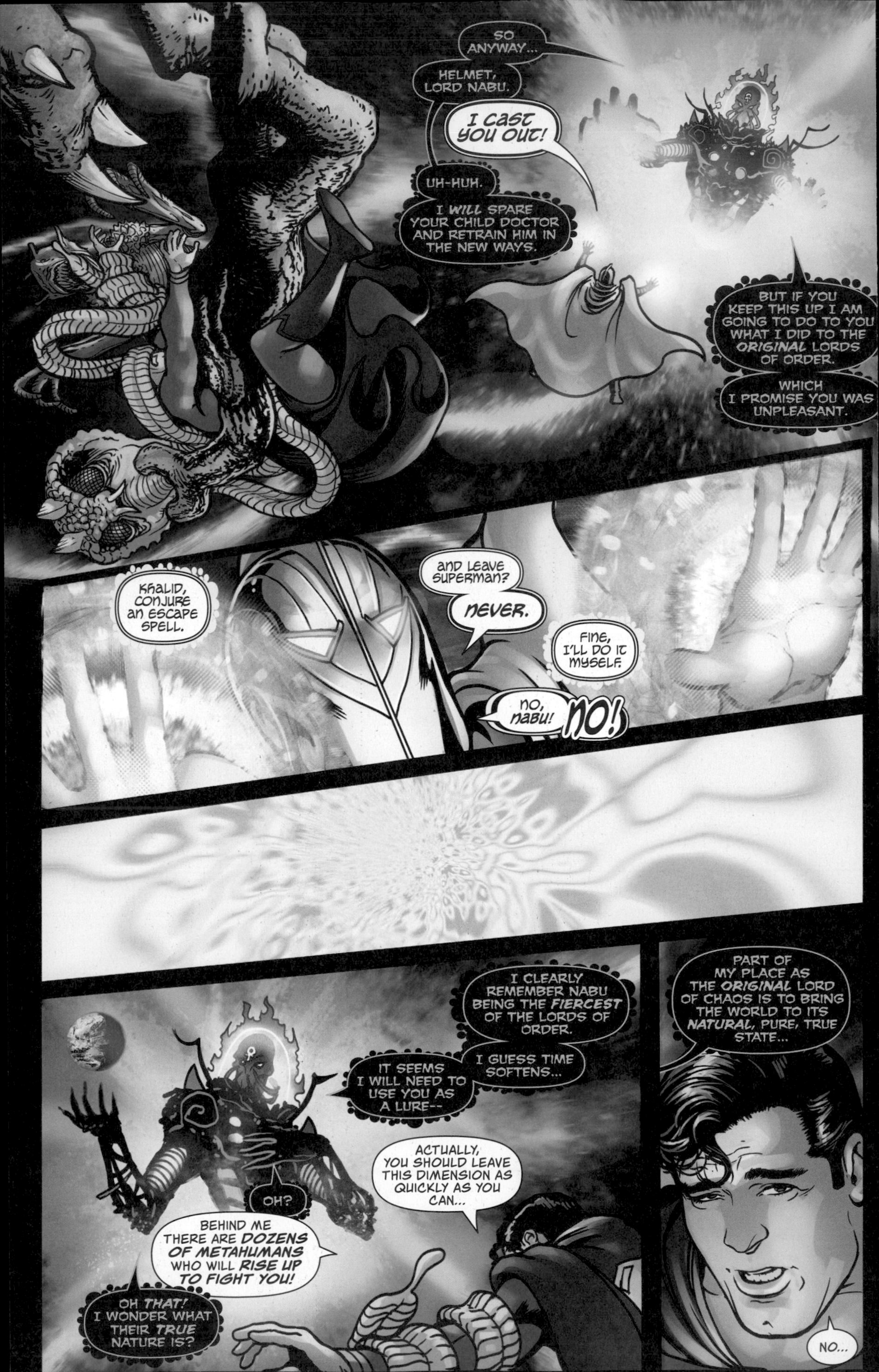
SO ANYWAY...
HELMET, LORD NABU.
I CAST YOU OUT!
UH-HUH.
I WILL SPARE YOUR CHILD DOCTOR AND RETRAIN HIM IN THE NEW WAYS.
BUT IF YOU KEEP THIS UP I AM GOING TO DO TO YOU WHAT I DID TO THE ORIGINAL LORDS OF ORDER.
WHICH I PROMISE YOU WAS UNPLEASANT.
KHALID, CONJURE AN ESCAPE SPELL.
AND LEAVE SUPERMAN?
NEVER.
FINE, I'LL DO IT MYSELF.
NO, NABU!
NO!
I CLEARLY REMEMBER NABU BEING THE FIERCEST OF THE LORDS OF ORDER.
I GUESS TIME SOFTENS...
IT SEEMS I WILL NEED TO USE YOU AS A LURE--
ACTUALLY, YOU SHOULD LEAVE THIS DIMENSION AS QUICKLY AS YOU CAN...
OH?
BEHIND ME THERE ARE DOZENS OF METAHUMANS WHO WILL RISE UP TO FIGHT YOU!
OH THAT! I WONDER WHAT THEIR TRUE NATURE IS?
PART OF MY PLACE AS THE ORIGINAL LORD OF CHAOS IS TO BRING THE WORLD TO ITS NATURAL, PURE, TRUE STATE...
NO...

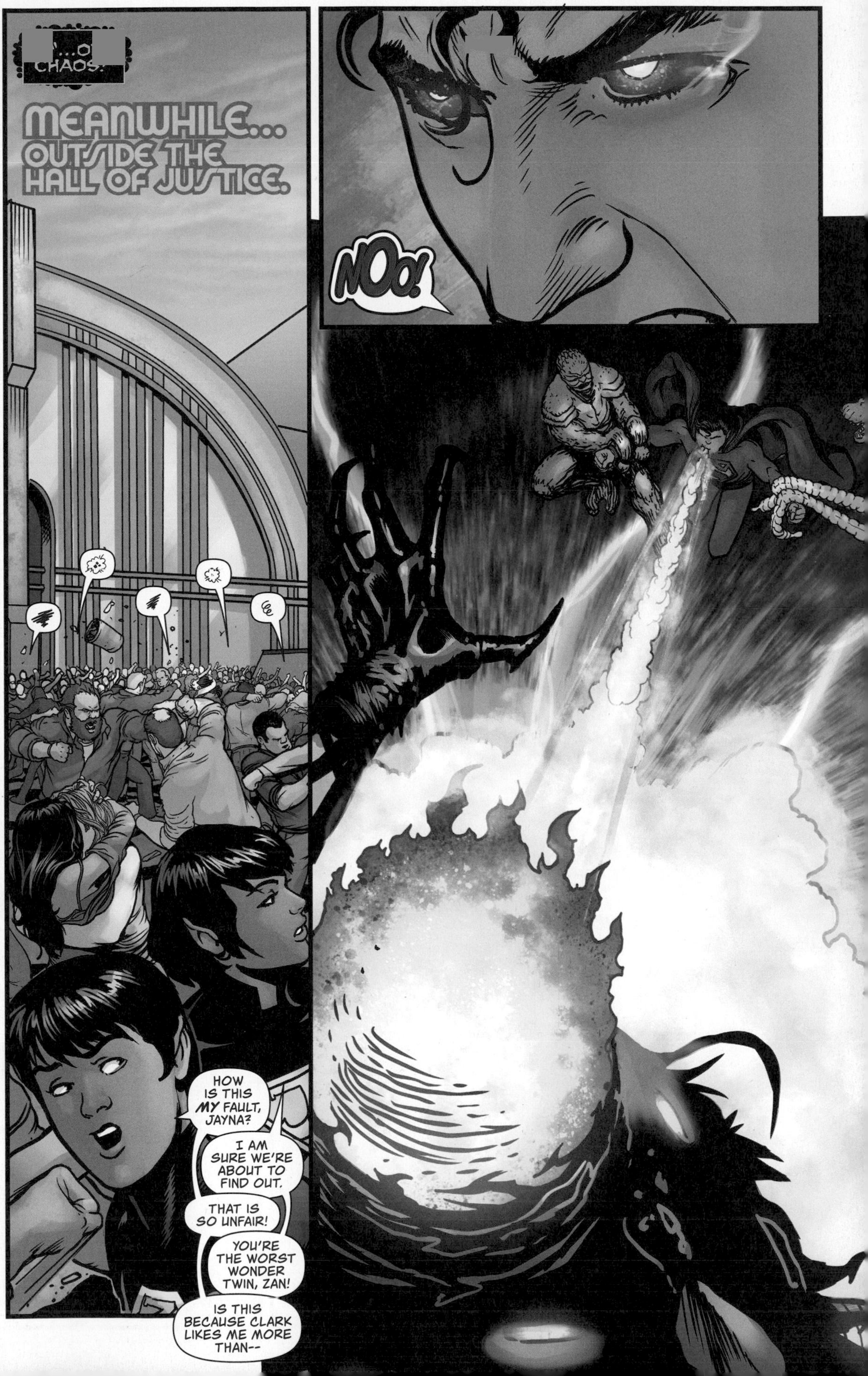
[redacted] CHAOS?
MEANWHILE... OUTSIDE THE HALL OF JUSTICE.
NOO!
HOW IS THIS MY FAULT, JAYNA?
I AM SURE WE'RE ABOUT TO FIND OUT.
THAT IS SO UNFAIR!
YOU'RE THE WORST WONDER TWIN, ZAN!
IS THIS BECAUSE CLARK LIKES ME MORE THAN--

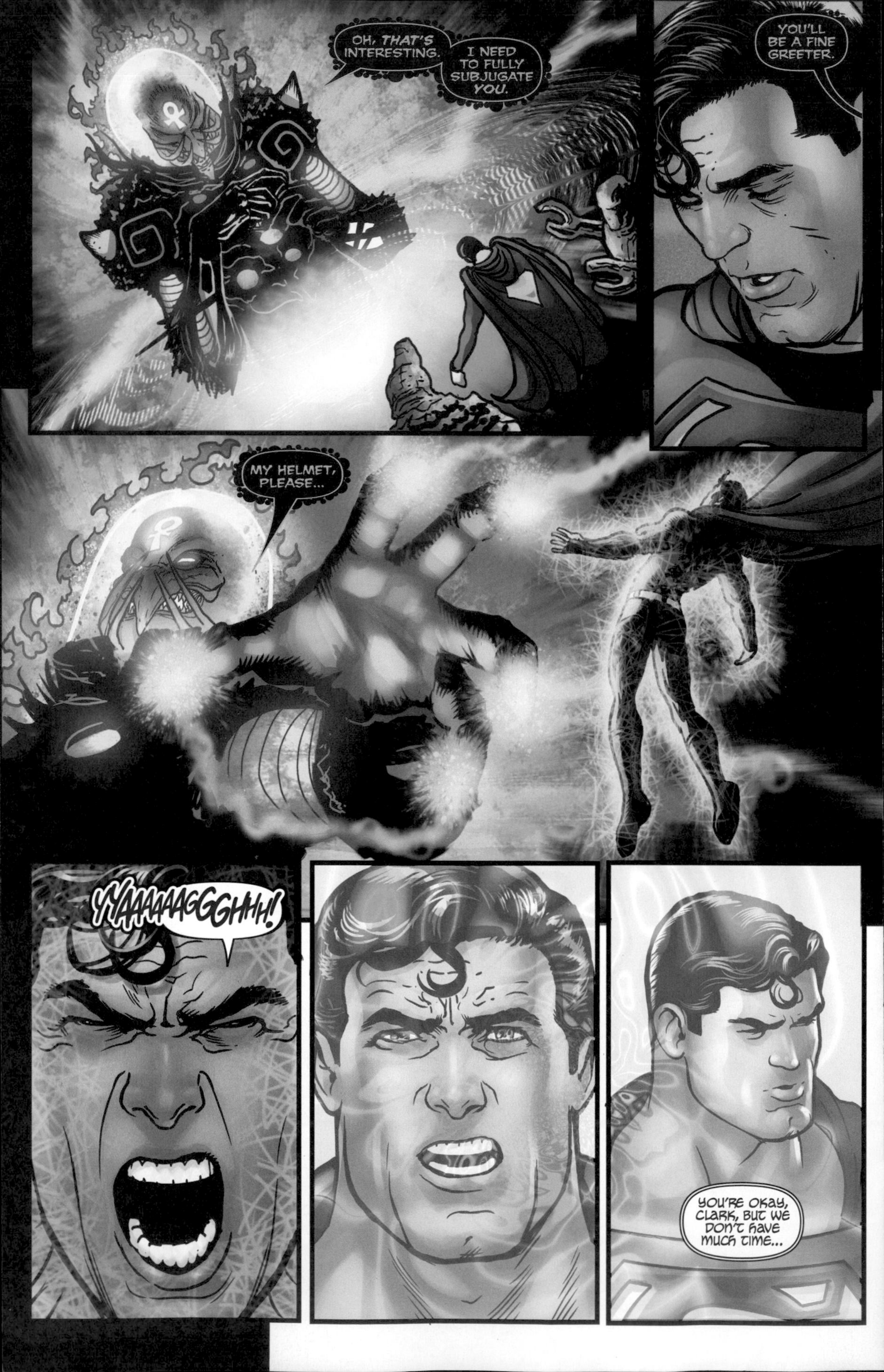
OH, THAT'S INTERESTING.
I NEED TO FULLY SUBJUGATE YOU.
YOU'LL BE A FINE GREETER.
MY HELMET, PLEASE...
YYAAAAAAGGGHHH!
YOU'RE OKAY, CLARK, BUT WE DON'T HAVE MUCH TIME...

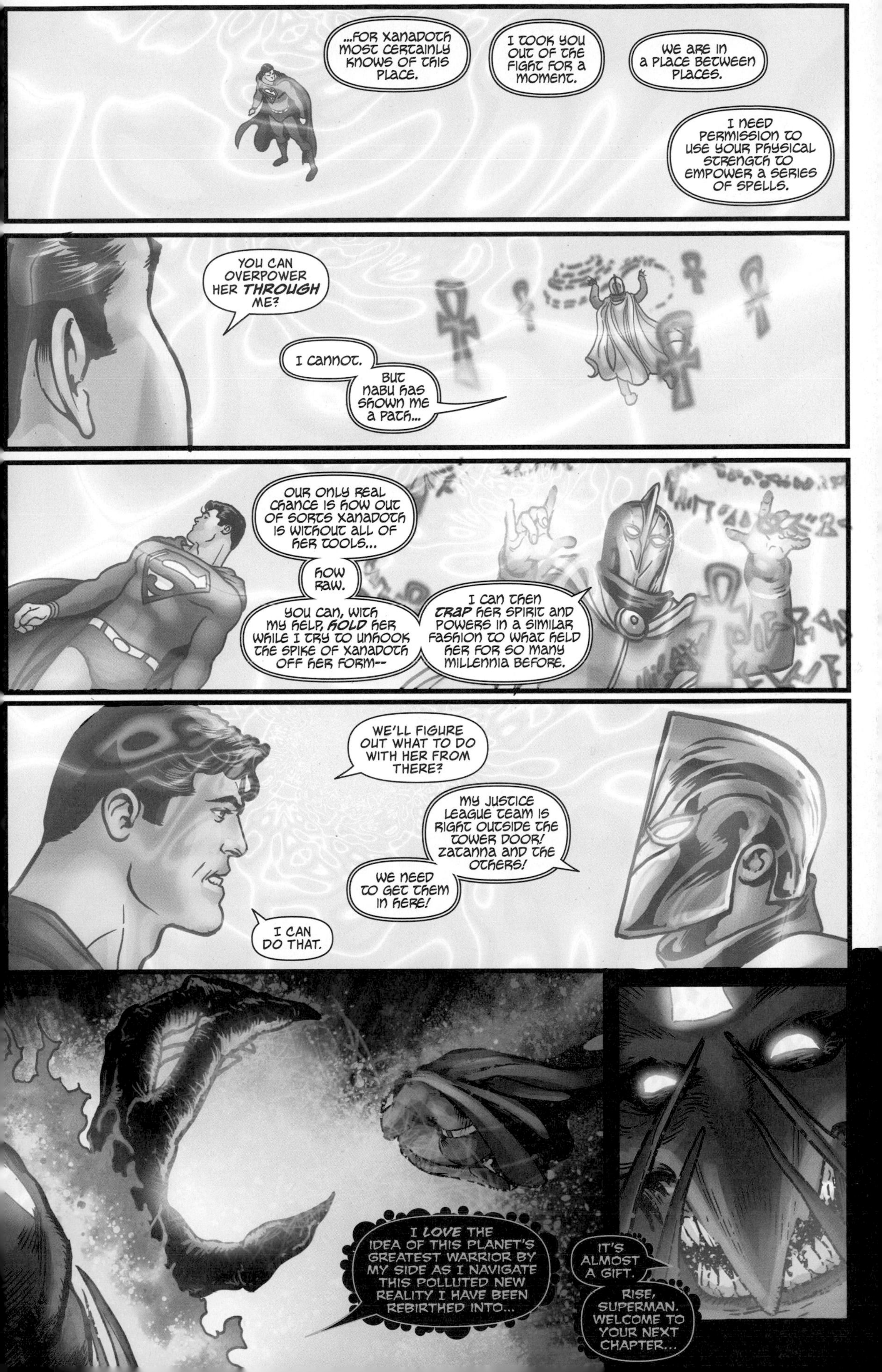
...FOR XANADOTH MOST CERTAINLY KNOWS OF THIS PLACE.
I TOOK YOU OUT OF THE FIGHT FOR A MOMENT.
WE ARE IN A PLACE BETWEEN PLACES.
I NEED PERMISSION TO USE YOUR PHYSICAL STRENGTH TO EMPOWER A SERIES OF SPELLS.
YOU CAN OVERPOWER HER THROUGH ME?
I CANNOT.
BUT NABU HAS SHOWN ME A PATH...
OUR ONLY REAL CHANCE IS HOW OUT OF SORTS XANADOTH IS WITHOUT ALL OF HER TOOLS...
HOW RAW.
YOU CAN, WITH MY HELP, HOLD HER WHILE I TRY TO UNHOOK THE SPIKE OF XANADOTH OFF HER FORM--
I CAN THEN TRAP HER SPIRIT AND POWERS IN A SIMILAR FASHION TO WHAT HELD HER FOR SO MANY MILLENNIA BEFORE.
WE'LL FIGURE OUT WHAT TO DO WITH HER FROM THERE?
MY JUSTICE LEAGUE TEAM IS RIGHT OUTSIDE THE TOWER DOOR! ZATANNA AND THE OTHERS!
WE NEED TO GET THEM IN HERE!
I CAN DO THAT.
I LOVE THE IDEA OF THIS PLANET'S GREATEST WARRIOR BY MY SIDE AS I NAVIGATE THIS POLLUTED NEW REALITY I HAVE BEEN REBIRTHED INTO...
IT'S ALMOST A GIFT.
RISE, SUPERMAN. WELCOME TO YOUR NEXT CHAPTER...

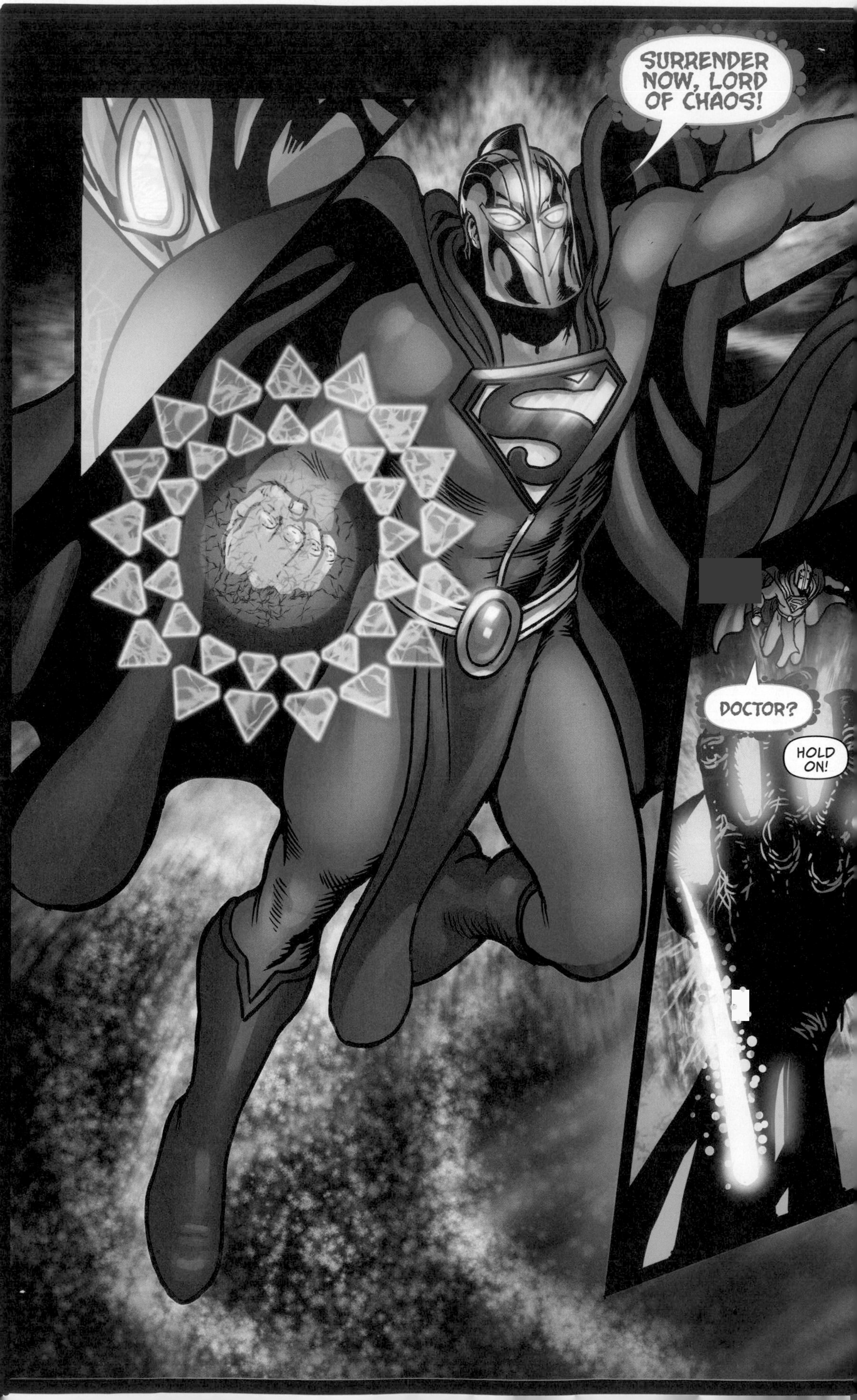
SURRENDER NOW, LORD OF CHAOS!
DOCTOR?
HOLD ON!

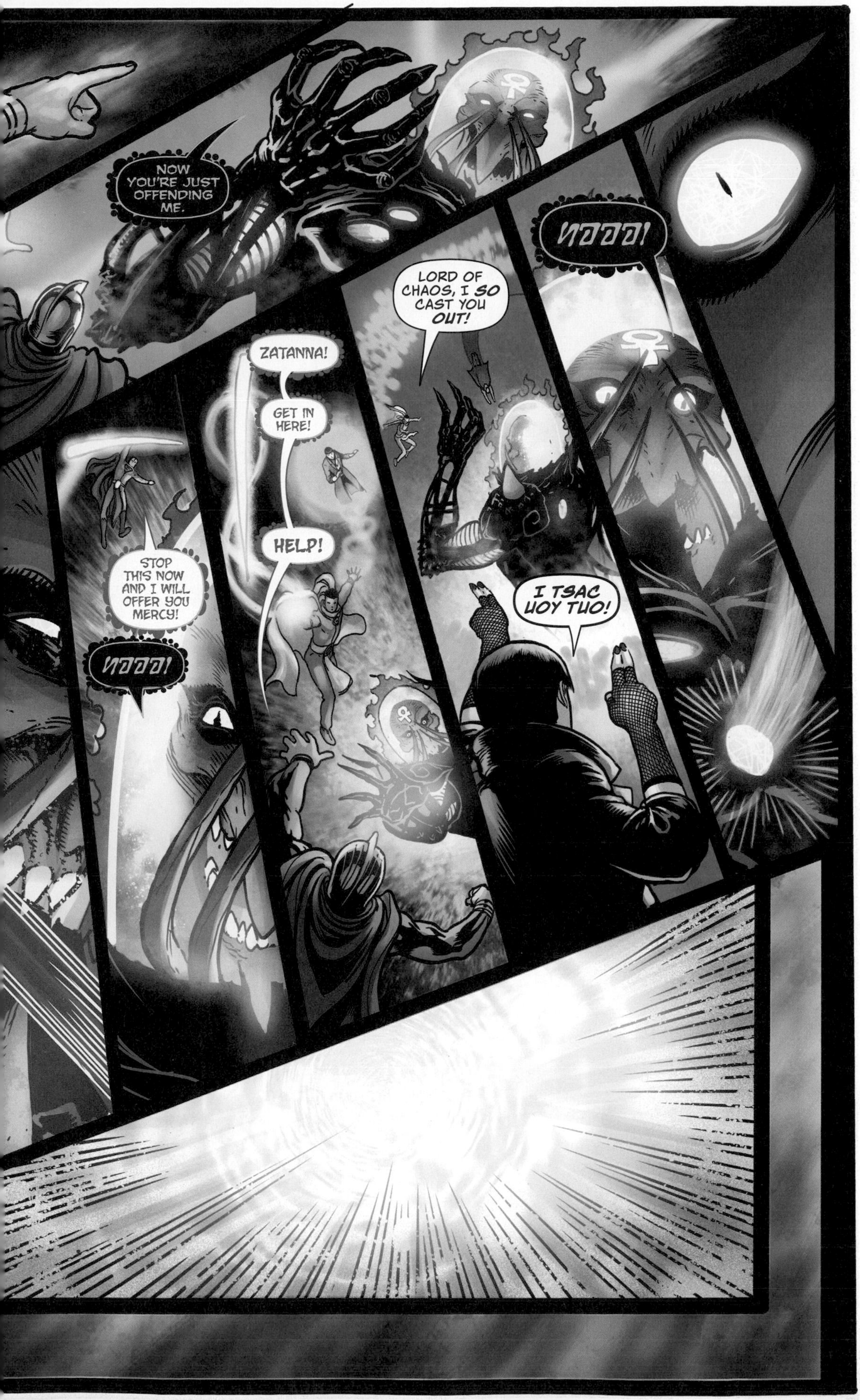
NOW YOU'RE JUST OFFENDING ME.
STOP THIS NOW AND I WILL OFFER YOU MERCY!
NOOO!
ZATANNA!
GET IN HERE!
HELP!
LORD OF CHAOS, I SO CAST YOU OUT!
I TSAC UOY TUO!
NOOO!

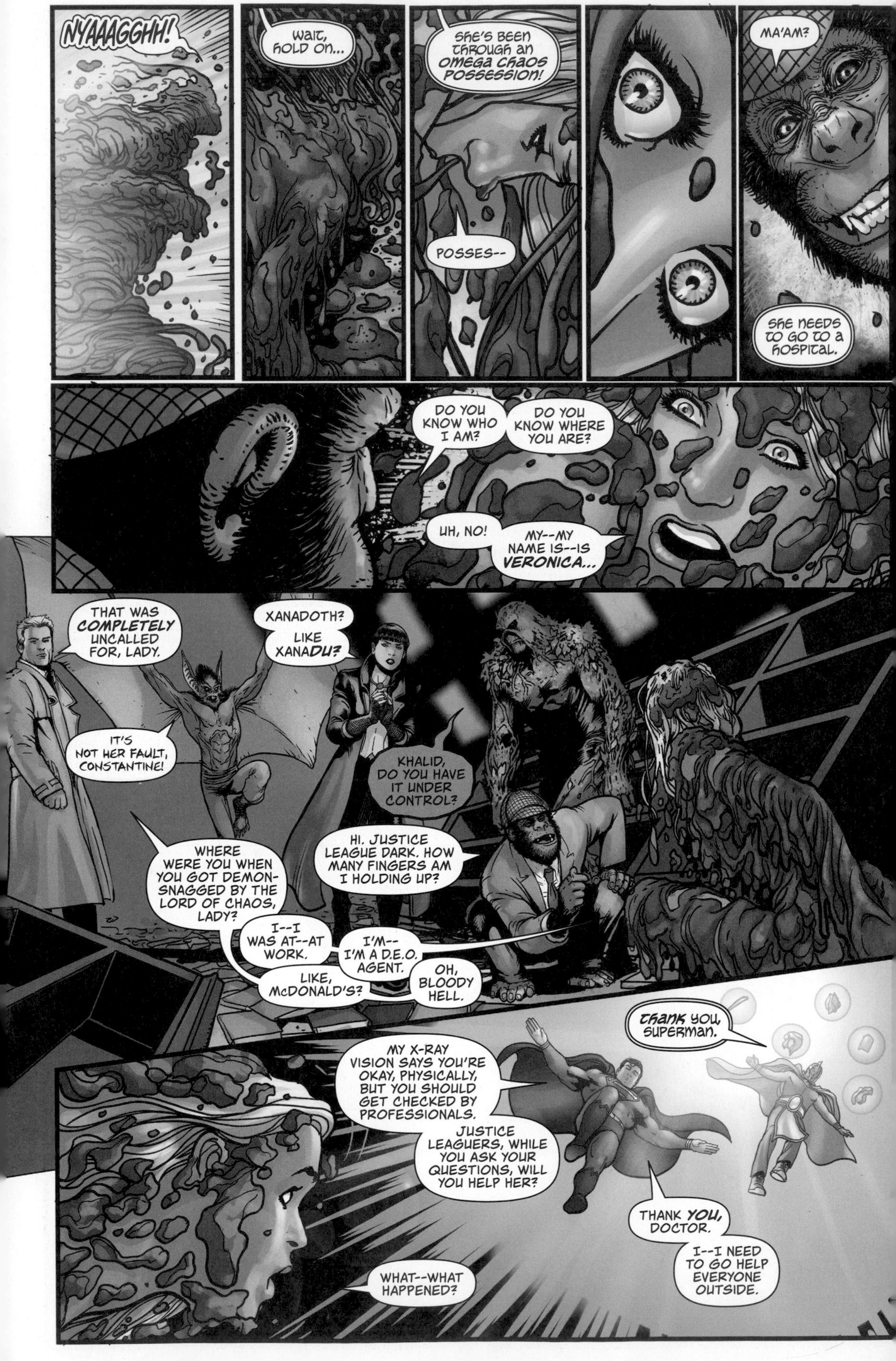
NYAAAGGHH!
WAIT, HOLD ON...
SHE'S BEEN THROUGH AN OMEGA CHAOS POSSESSION!
POSSES--
MA'AM?
SHE NEEDS TO GO TO A HOSPITAL.
DO YOU KNOW WHO I AM?
DO YOU KNOW WHERE YOU ARE?
UH, NO!
MY--MY NAME IS--IS VERONICA...
THAT WAS COMPLETELY UNCALLED FOR, LADY.
XANADOTH?
LIKE XANADU?
IT'S NOT HER FAULT, CONSTANTINE!
KHALID, DO YOU HAVE IT UNDER CONTROL?
WHERE WERE YOU WHEN YOU GOT DEMON-SNAGGED BY THE LORD OF CHAOS, LADY?
HI. JUSTICE LEAGUE DARK. HOW MANY FINGERS AM I HOLDING UP?
I--I WAS AT--AT WORK.
I'M--I'M A D.E.O. AGENT.
LIKE, McDONALD'S?
OH, BLOODY HELL.
THANK YOU, SUPERMAN.
MY X-RAY VISION SAYS YOU'RE OKAY, PHYSICALLY, BUT YOU SHOULD GET CHECKED BY PROFESSIONALS.
JUSTICE LEAGUERS, WHILE YOU ASK YOUR QUESTIONS, WILL YOU HELP HER?
THANK YOU, DOCTOR.
I--I NEED TO GO HELP EVERYONE OUTSIDE.
WHAT--WHAT HAPPENED?

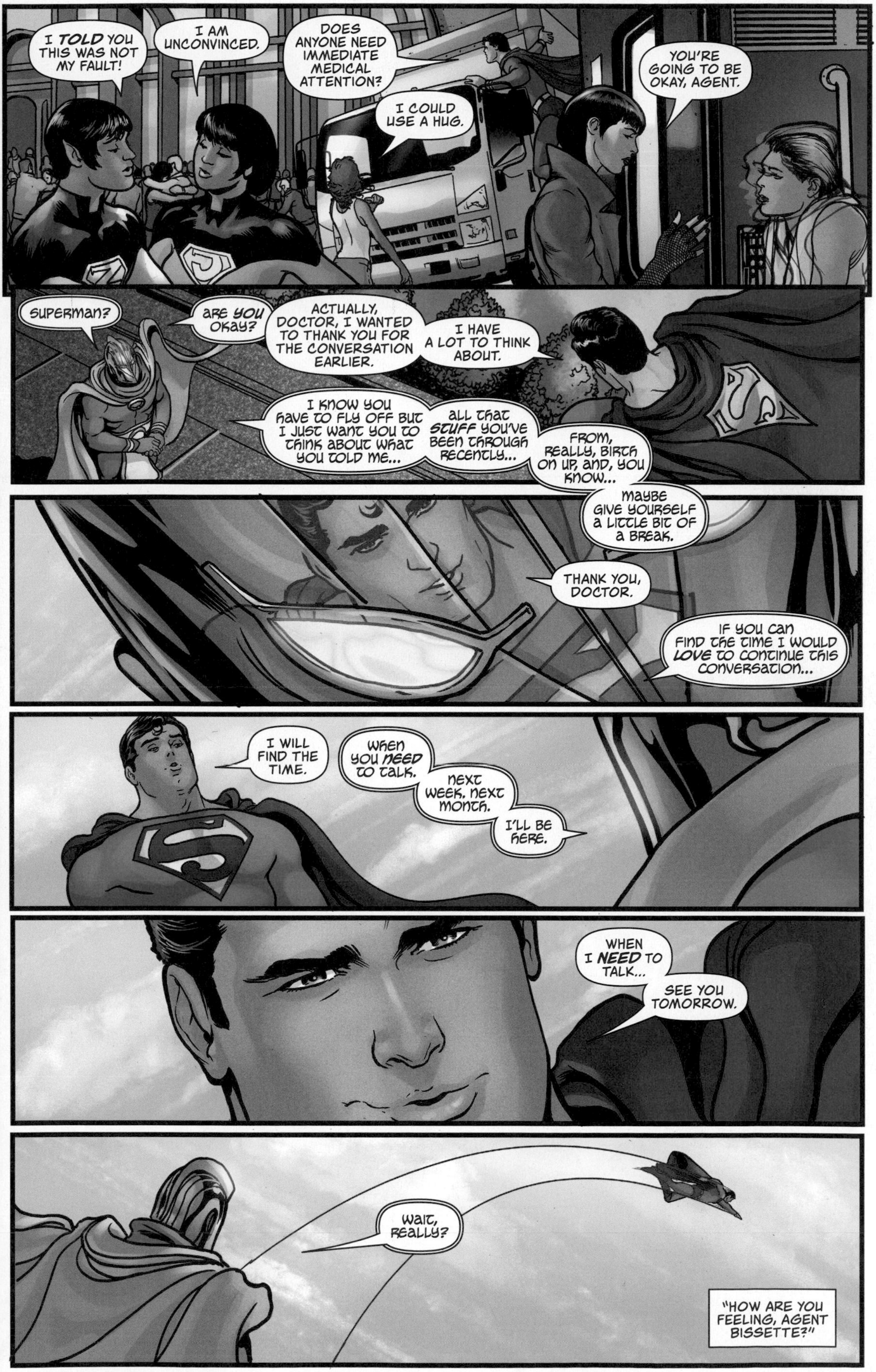
I TOLD YOU THIS WAS NOT MY FAULT!
I AM UNCONVINCED.
DOES ANYONE NEED IMMEDIATE MEDICAL ATTENTION?
I COULD USE A HUG.
YOU'RE GOING TO BE OKAY, AGENT.
SUPERMAN?
ARE YOU OKAY?
ACTUALLY, DOCTOR, I WANTED TO THANK YOU FOR THE CONVERSATION EARLIER.
I HAVE A LOT TO THINK ABOUT.
I KNOW YOU HAVE TO FLY OFF BUT I JUST WANT YOU TO THINK ABOUT WHAT YOU TOLD ME...
ALL THAT STUFF YOU'VE BEEN THROUGH RECENTLY...
FROM, REALLY, BIRTH ON UP, AND, YOU KNOW...
MAYBE GIVE YOURSELF A LITTLE BIT OF A BREAK.
THANK YOU, DOCTOR.
IF YOU CAN FIND THE TIME I WOULD LOVE TO CONTINUE THIS CONVERSATION...
I WILL FIND THE TIME.
WHEN YOU NEED TO TALK.
NEXT WEEK. NEXT MONTH.
I'LL BE HERE.
WHEN I NEED TO TALK...
SEE YOU TOMORROW.
WAIT, REALLY?
"HOW ARE YOU FEELING, AGENT BISSETTE?"

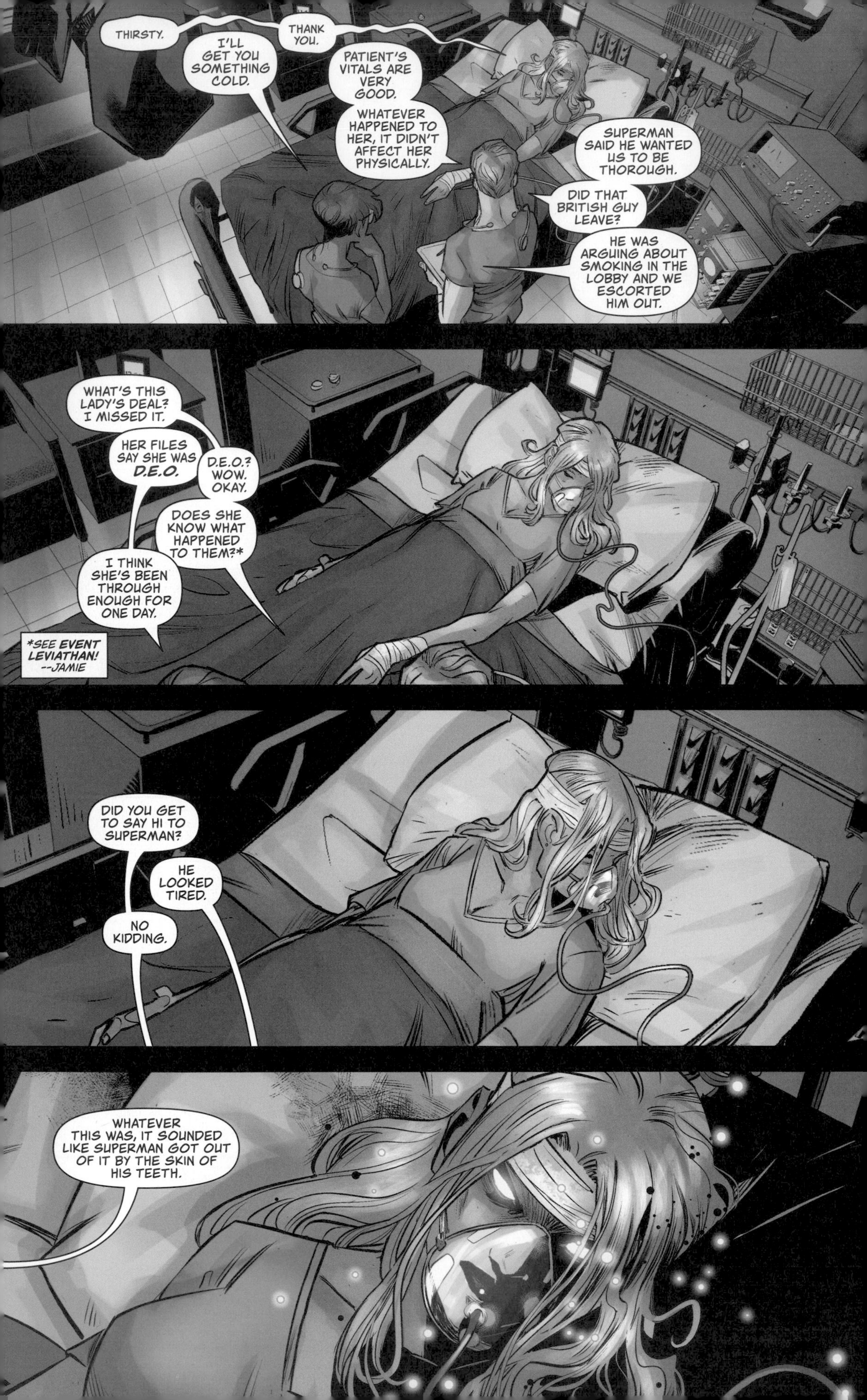
THIRSTY.
THANK YOU.
I'LL GET YOU SOMETHING COLD.
PATIENT'S VITALS ARE VERY GOOD.
WHATEVER HAPPENED TO HER, IT DIDN'T AFFECT HER PHYSICALLY.
SUPERMAN SAID HE WANTED US TO BE THOROUGH.
DID THAT BRITISH GUY LEAVE?
HE WAS ARGUING ABOUT SMOKING IN THE LOBBY AND WE ESCORTED HIM OUT.
WHAT'S THIS LADY'S DEAL? I MISSED IT.
HER FILES SAY SHE WAS D.E.O.
D.E.O.? WOW. OKAY.
DOES SHE KNOW WHAT HAPPENED TO THEM?*
I THINK SHE'S BEEN THROUGH ENOUGH FOR ONE DAY.
*SEE EVENT LEVIATHAN! --JAMIE
DID YOU GET TO SAY HI TO SUPERMAN?
HE LOOKED TIRED.
NO KIDDING.
WHATEVER THIS WAS, IT SOUNDED LIKE SUPERMAN GOT OUT OF IT BY THE SKIN OF HIS TEETH.

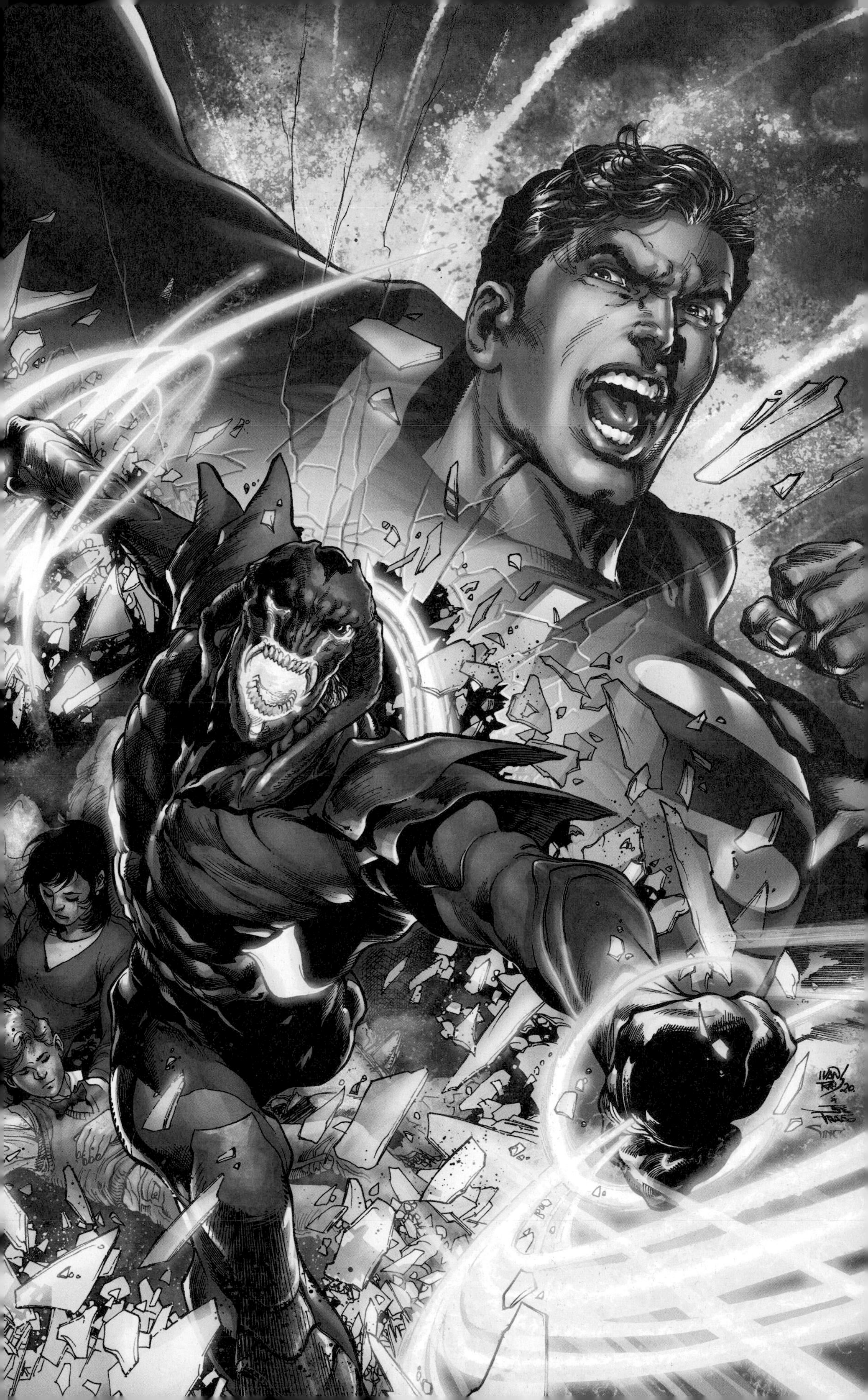

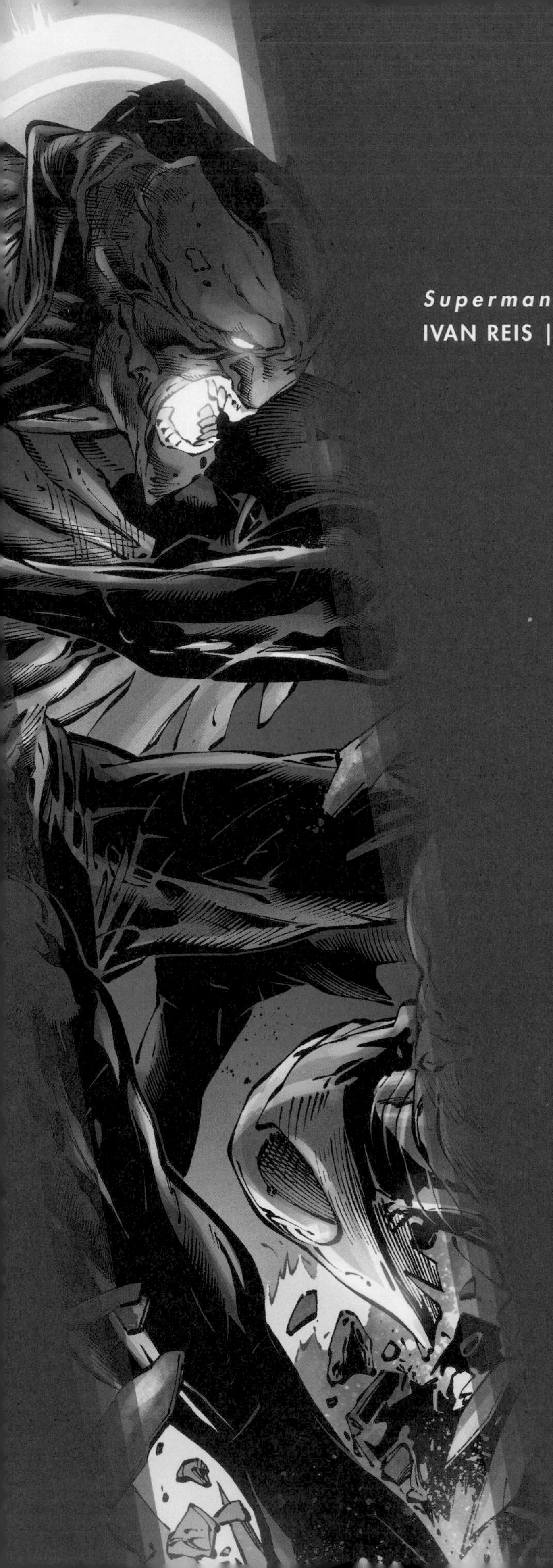

Superman #25 main cover by
IVAN REIS | JOE PRADO | ALEX SINCLAIR

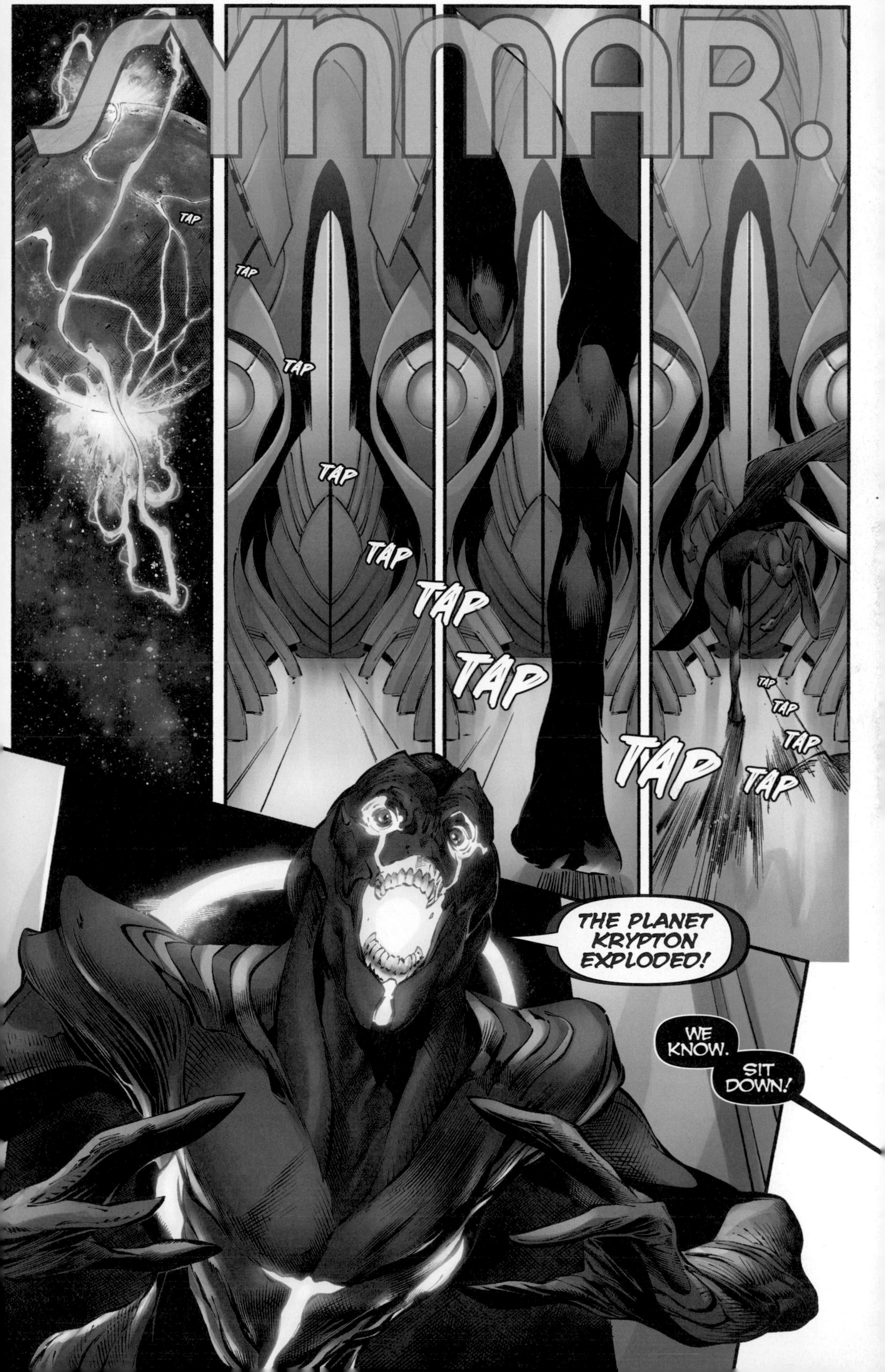
SYNMAR!
TAP
TAP
TAP
TAP
TAP
TAP
TAP
TAP
TAP
TAP
TAP
TAP
THE PLANET KRYPTON EXPLODED!
WE KNOW.
SIT DOWN!

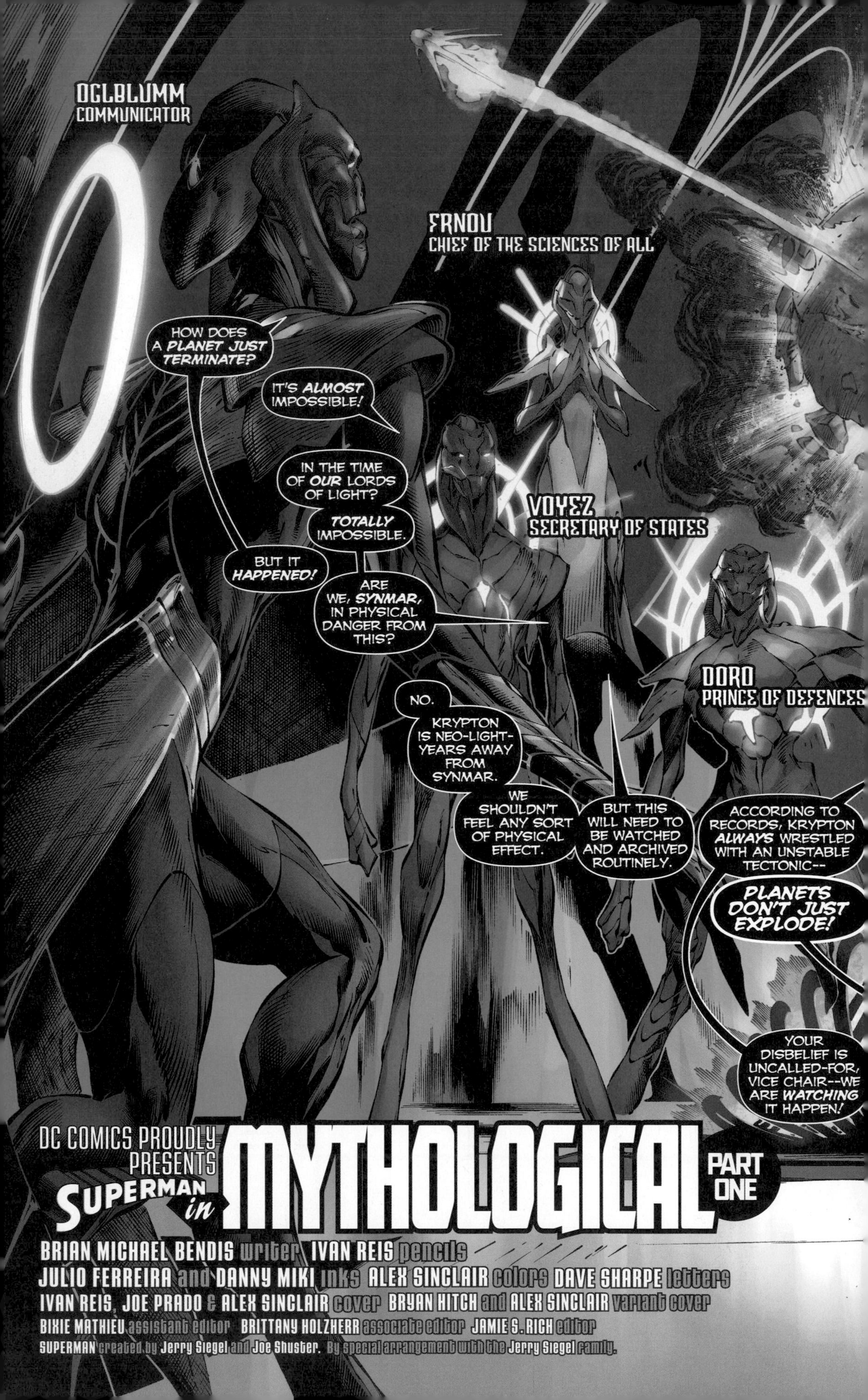
OGLBLUMM
COMMUNICATOR
FRNOU
CHIEF OF THE SCIENCES OF ALL
VOYEZ
SECRETARY OF STATES
DORO
PRINCE OF DEFENCES
HOW DOES A PLANET JUST TERMINATE?
IT'S ALMOST IMPOSSIBLE!
IN THE TIME OF OUR LORDS OF LIGHT?
TOTALLY IMPOSSIBLE.
BUT IT HAPPENED!
ARE WE, SYNMAR, IN PHYSICAL DANGER FROM THIS?
NO.
KRYPTON IS NEO-LIGHT-YEARS AWAY FROM SYNMAR.
WE SHOULDN'T FEEL ANY SORT OF PHYSICAL EFFECT.
BUT THIS WILL NEED TO BE WATCHED AND ARCHIVED ROUTINELY.
ACCORDING TO RECORDS, KRYPTON ALWAYS WRESTLED WITH AN UNSTABLE TECTONIC--
PLANETS DON'T JUST EXPLODE!
YOUR DISBELIEF IS UNCALLED-FOR, VICE CHAIR--WE ARE WATCHING IT HAPPEN!
DC COMICS PROUDLY PRESENTS
SUPERMAN in
MYTHOLOGICAL
PART ONE
BRIAN MICHAEL BENDIS writer IVAN REIS pencils
JULIO FERREIRA and DANNY MIKI inks ALEX SINCLAIR colors DAVE SHARPE letters
IVAN REIS, JOE PRADO & ALEX SINCLAIR cover BRYAN HITCH and ALEX SINCLAIR variant cover
BIXIE MATHIEU assistant editor BRITTANY HOLZHERR associate editor JAMIE S. RICH editor
SUPERMAN created by Jerry Siegel and Joe Shuster. By special arrangement with the Jerry Siegel family.

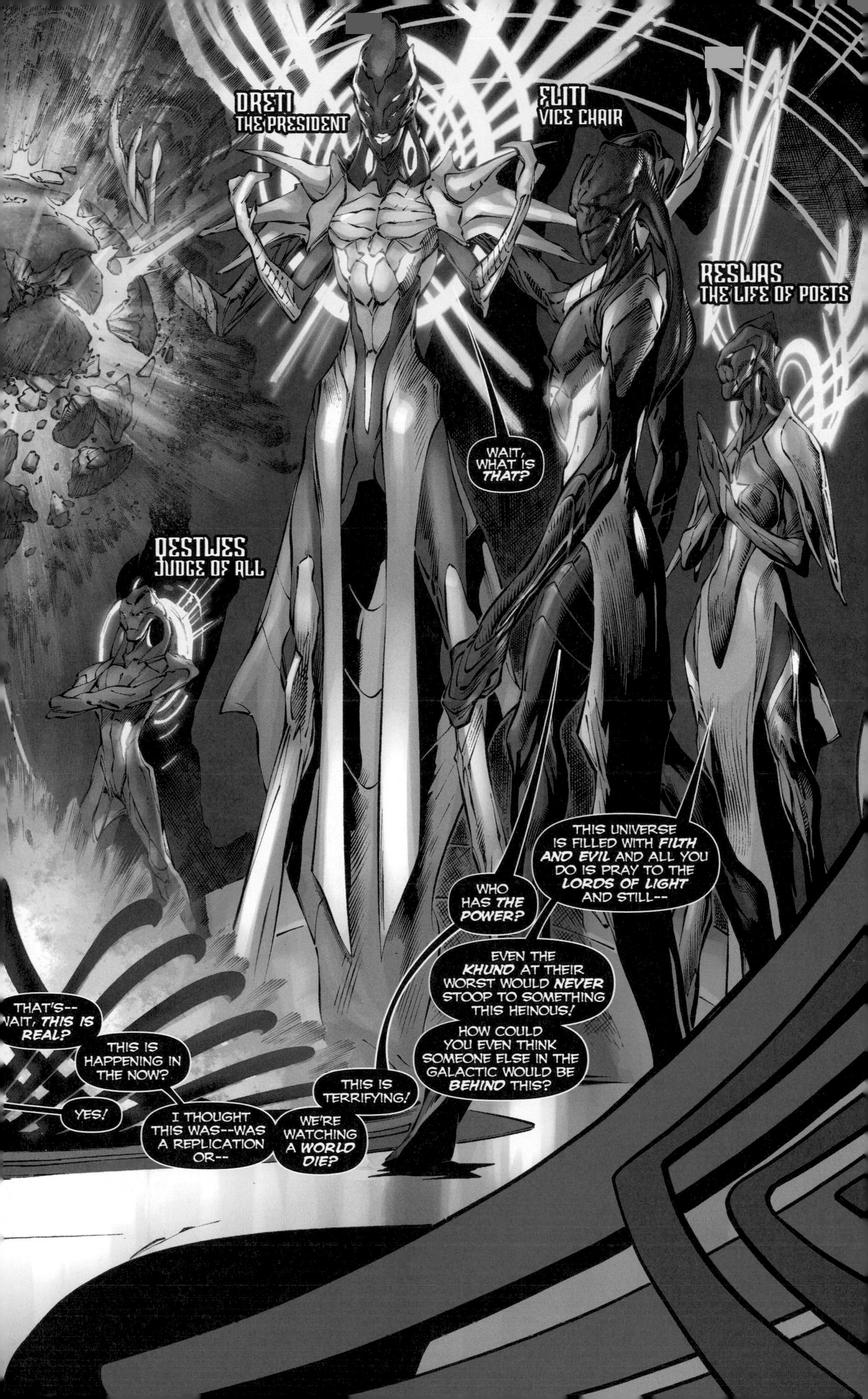
DRETI
THE PRESIDENT
ELITI
VICE CHAIR
RESWAS
THE LIFE OF POETS
WAIT, WHAT IS *THAT?*
QESTWES
JUDGE OF ALL
THIS UNIVERSE IS FILLED WITH *FILTH AND EVIL* AND ALL YOU DO IS PRAY TO THE *LORDS OF LIGHT* AND STILL--
WHO HAS *THE POWER?*
EVEN THE *KHUND* AT THEIR WORST WOULD *NEVER* STOOP TO SOMETHING THIS HEINOUS!
HOW COULD YOU EVEN THINK SOMEONE ELSE IN THE GALACTIC WOULD BE *BEHIND* THIS?
THAT'S-- AIT, *THIS IS REAL?*
THIS IS HAPPENING IN THE NOW?
YES!
I THOUGHT THIS WAS--WAS A REPLICATION OR--
THIS IS TERRIFYING!
WE'RE WATCHING A *WORLD DIE?*

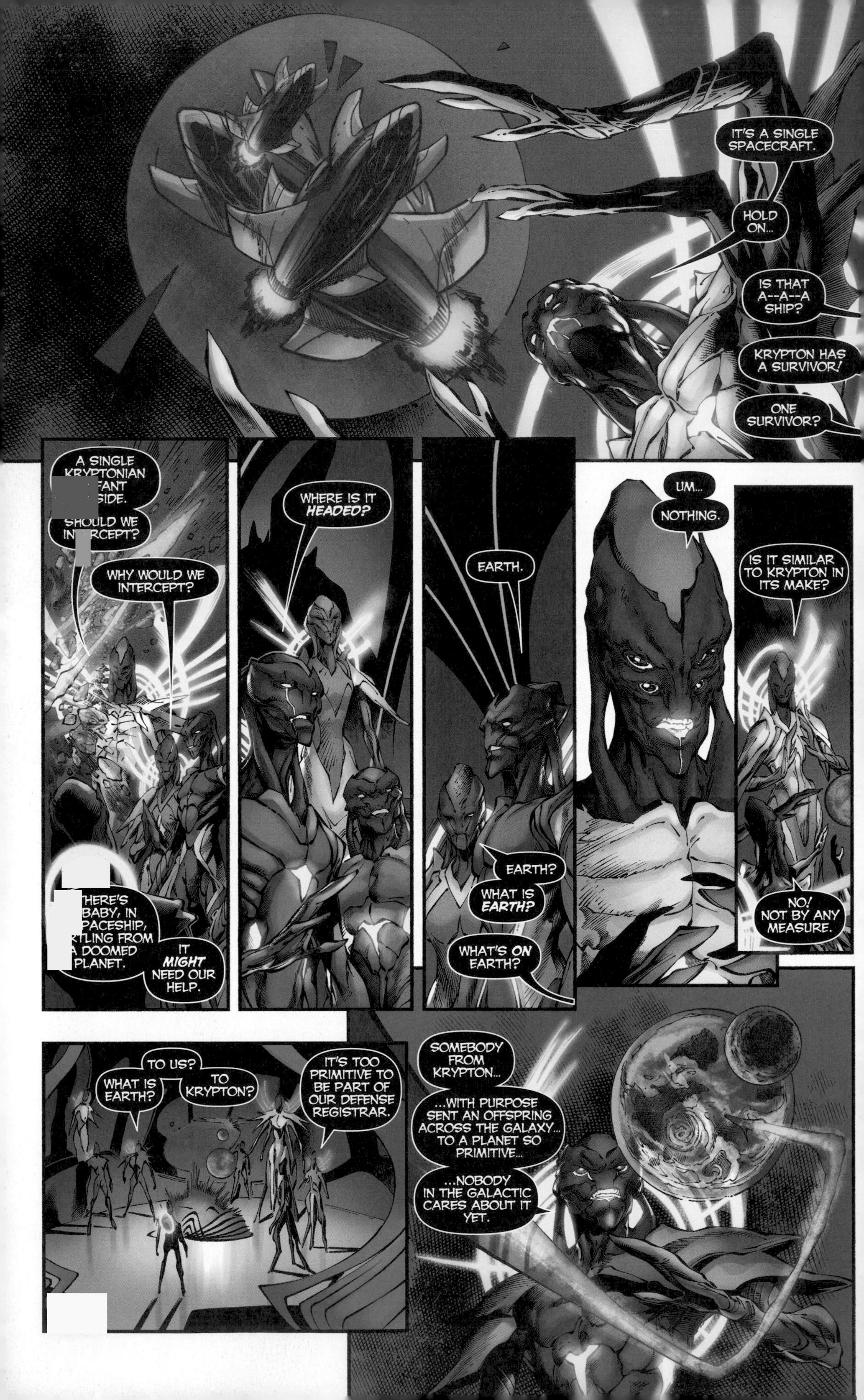

IT'S A SINGLE SPACECRAFT.
HOLD ON...
IS THAT A--A--A SHIP?
KRYPTON HAS A SURVIVOR!
ONE SURVIVOR?
A SINGLE KRYPTONIAN [redacted] SIDE.
SHOULD WE [redacted] RCEPT?
WHY WOULD WE INTERCEPT?
BABY, IN A DOOMED PLANET.
IT MIGHT NEED OUR HELP.
WHERE IS IT HEADED?
EARTH.
EARTH? WHAT IS EARTH?
WHAT'S ON EARTH?
UM... NOTHING.
IS IT SIMILAR TO KRYPTON IN ITS MAKE?
NO! NOT BY ANY MEASURE.
TO US?
WHAT IS EARTH?
TO KRYPTON?
IT'S TOO PRIMITIVE TO BE PART OF OUR DEFENSE REGISTRAR.
SOMEBODY FROM KRYPTON...
...WITH PURPOSE SENT AN OFFSPRING ACROSS THE GALAXY... TO A PLANET SO PRIMITIVE...
...NOBODY IN THE GALACTIC CARES ABOUT IT YET.

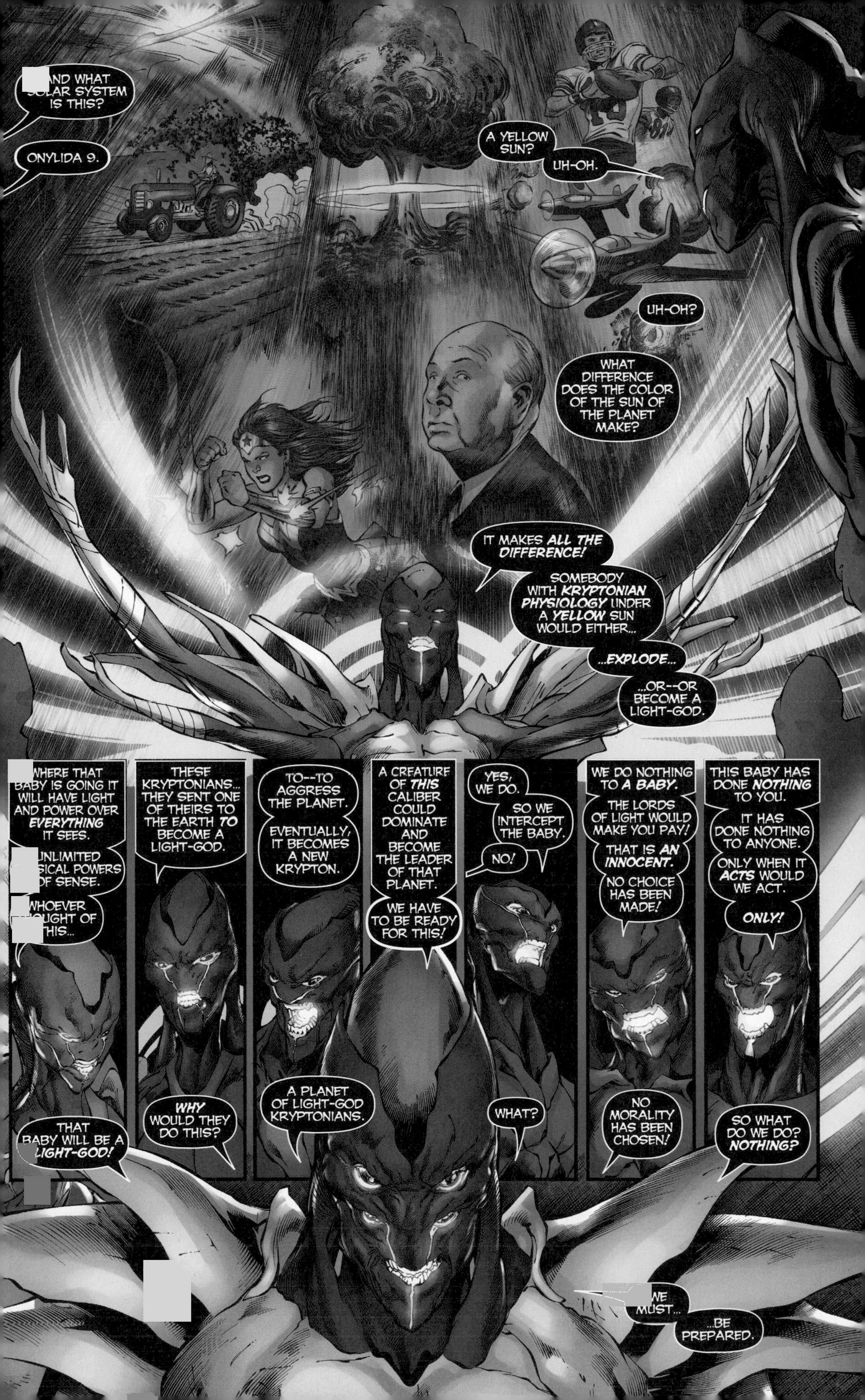
AND WHAT OLAR SYSTEM IS THIS?
ONYLIDA 9.
A YELLOW SUN?
UH-OH.
UH-OH?
WHAT DIFFERENCE DOES THE COLOR OF THE SUN OF THE PLANET MAKE?
IT MAKES ALL THE DIFFERENCE!
SOMEBODY WITH KRYPTONIAN PHYSIOLOGY UNDER A YELLOW SUN WOULD EITHER...
...EXPLODE...
...OR--OR BECOME A LIGHT-GOD.
WHERE THAT BABY IS GOING IT WILL HAVE LIGHT AND POWER OVER EVERYTHING IT SEES.
UNLIMITED SICAL POWERS OF SENSE.
WHOEVER OUGHT OF THIS...
THAT BABY WILL BE A LIGHT-GOD!
THESE KRYPTONIANS... THEY SENT ONE OF THEIRS TO THE EARTH TO BECOME A LIGHT-GOD.
WHY WOULD THEY DO THIS?
TO--TO AGGRESS THE PLANET.
EVENTUALLY, IT BECOMES A NEW KRYPTON.
A PLANET OF LIGHT-GOD KRYPTONIANS.
A CREATURE OF THIS CALIBER COULD DOMINATE AND BECOME THE LEADER OF THAT PLANET.
WE HAVE TO BE READY FOR THIS!
YES, WE DO.
SO WE INTERCEPT THE BABY.
NO!
WHAT?
WE DO NOTHING TO A BABY.
THE LORDS OF LIGHT WOULD MAKE YOU PAY!
THAT IS AN INNOCENT.
NO CHOICE HAS BEEN MADE!
NO MORALITY HAS BEEN CHOSEN!
THIS BABY HAS DONE NOTHING TO YOU.
IT HAS DONE NOTHING TO ANYONE.
ONLY WHEN IT ACTS WOULD WE ACT.
ONLY!
SO WHAT DO WE DO? NOTHING?
WE MUST...
...BE PREPARED.

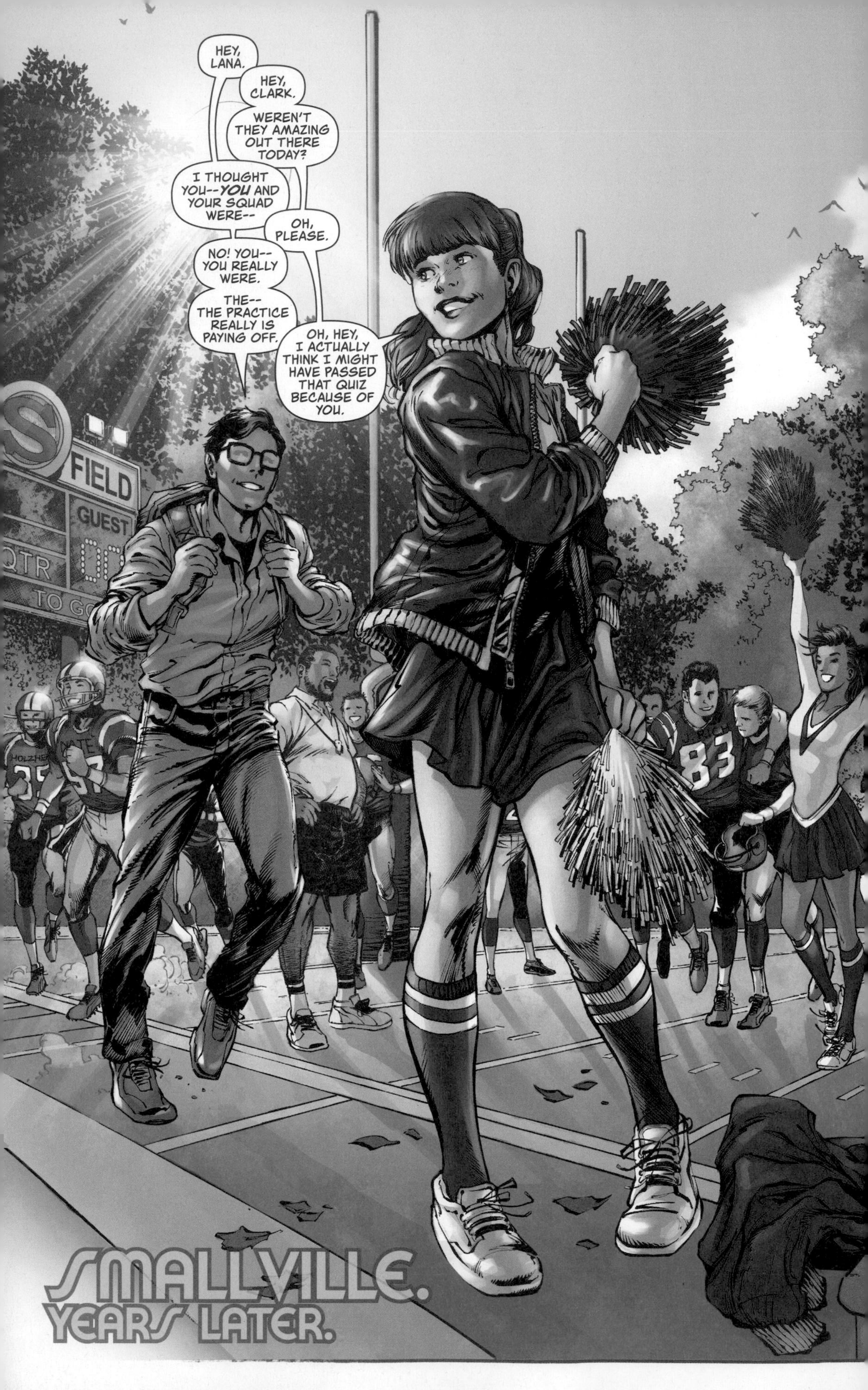
HEY, LANA.
HEY, CLARK.
WEREN'T THEY AMAZING OUT THERE TODAY?
I THOUGHT YOU--YOU AND YOUR SQUAD WERE--
OH, PLEASE.
NO! YOU-- YOU REALLY WERE.
THE-- THE PRACTICE REALLY IS PAYING OFF.
OH, HEY, I ACTUALLY THINK I MIGHT HAVE PASSED THAT QUIZ BECAUSE OF YOU.
FIELD
GUEST
QTR
83
SMALLVILLE.
YEARS LATER.

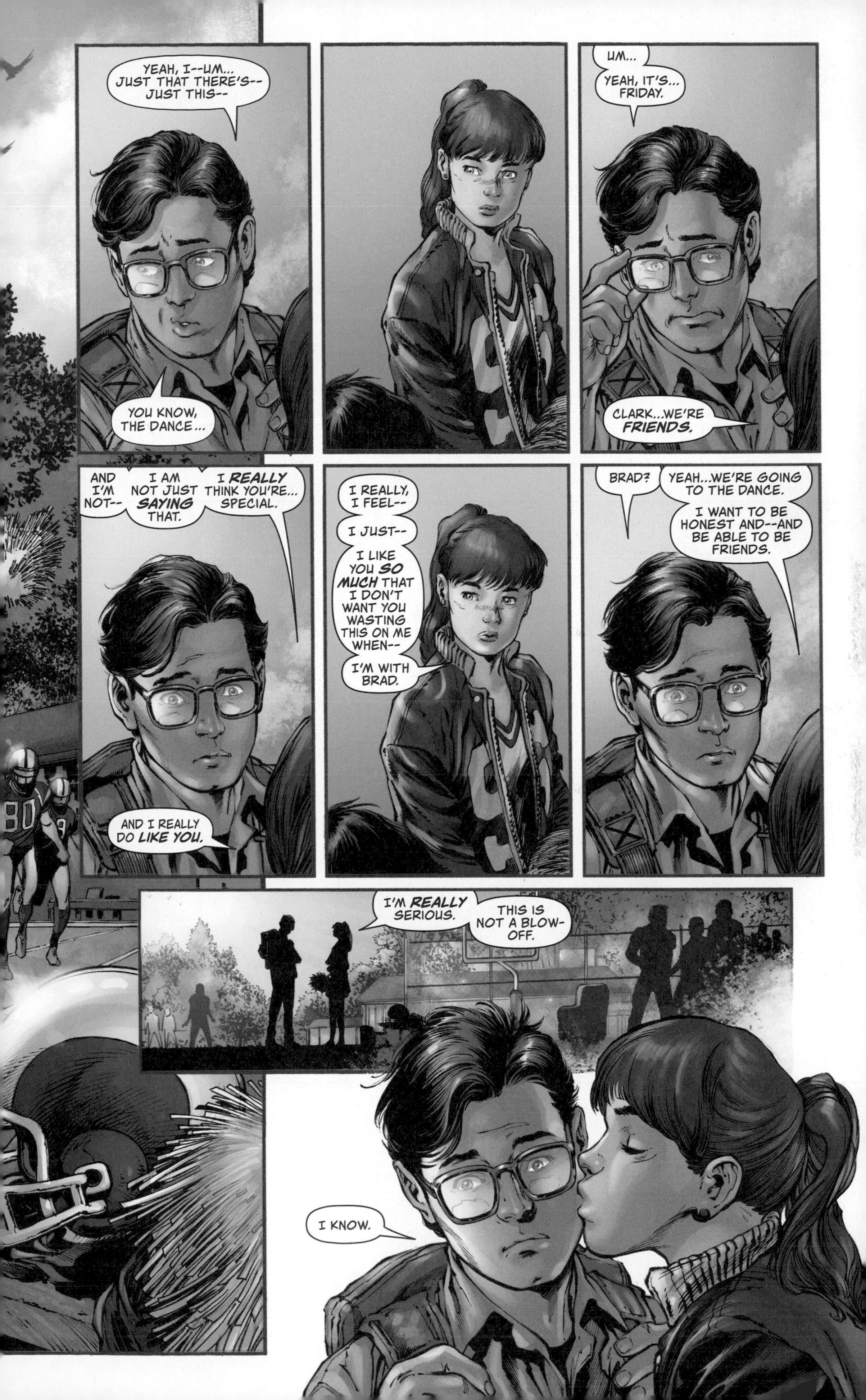
YEAH, I--UM... JUST THAT THERE'S-- JUST THIS--
YOU KNOW, THE DANCE...
UM...
YEAH, IT'S... FRIDAY.
CLARK...WE'RE FRIENDS.
AND I'M NOT--
I AM NOT JUST SAYING THAT.
I REALLY THINK YOU'RE... SPECIAL.
AND I REALLY DO LIKE YOU.
I REALLY, I FEEL--
I JUST--
I LIKE YOU SO MUCH THAT I DON'T WANT YOU WASTING THIS ON ME WHEN--
I'M WITH BRAD.
BRAD?
YEAH...WE'RE GOING TO THE DANCE.
I WANT TO BE HONEST AND--AND BE ABLE TO BE FRIENDS.
I'M REALLY SERIOUS.
THIS IS NOT A BLOW-OFF.
I KNOW.

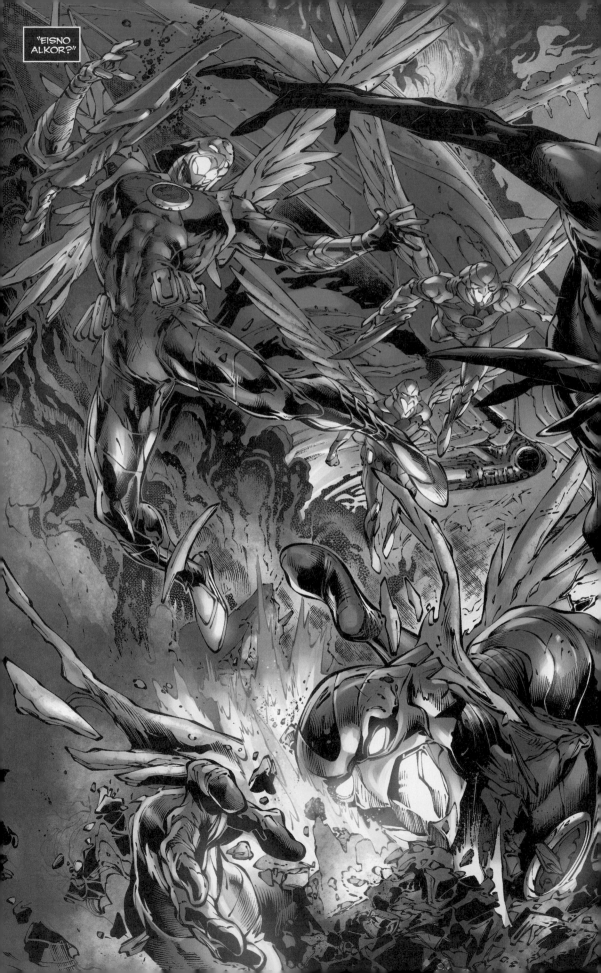

"EISNO
ALKOR?"

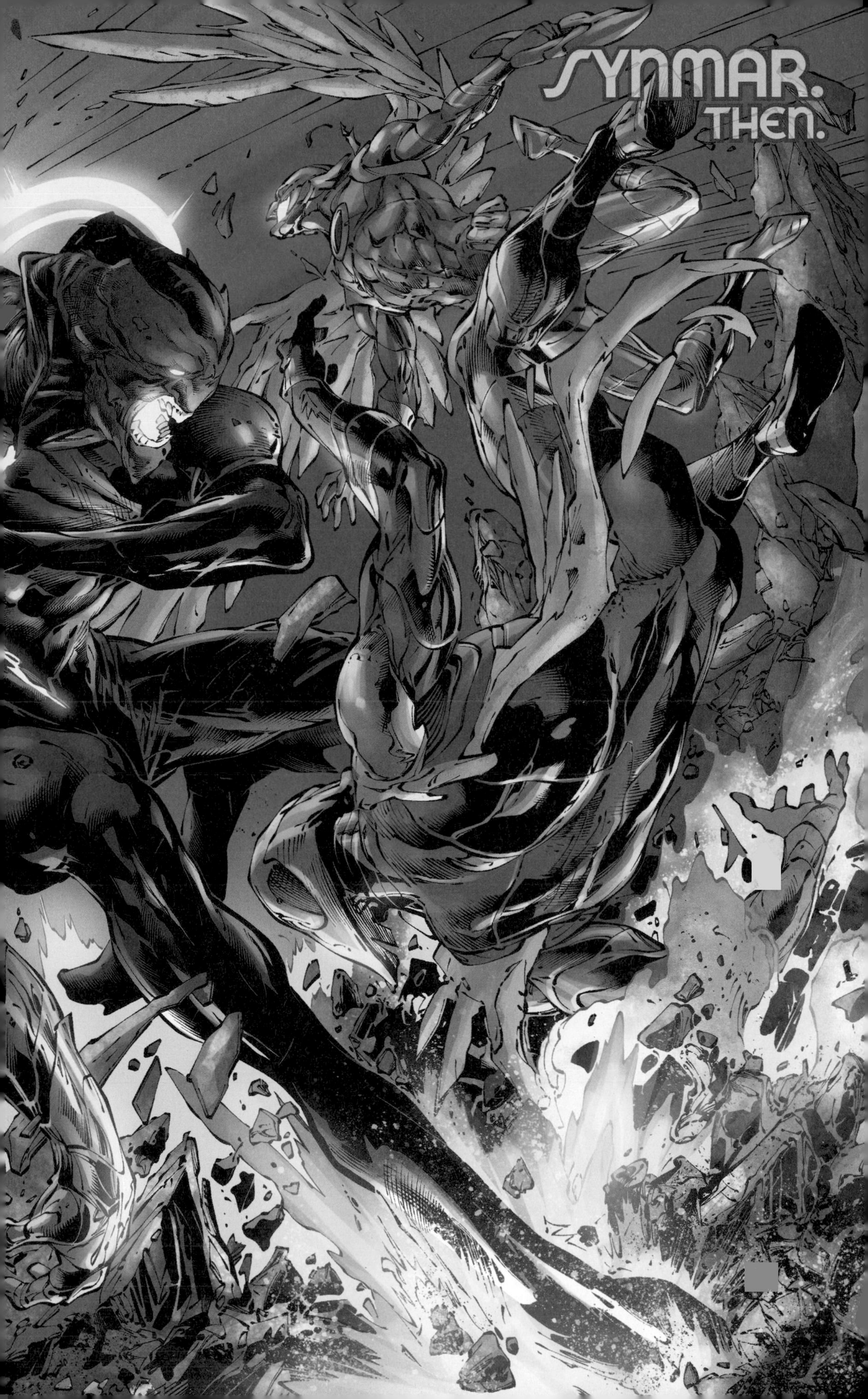
SYNMAR.
THEN.

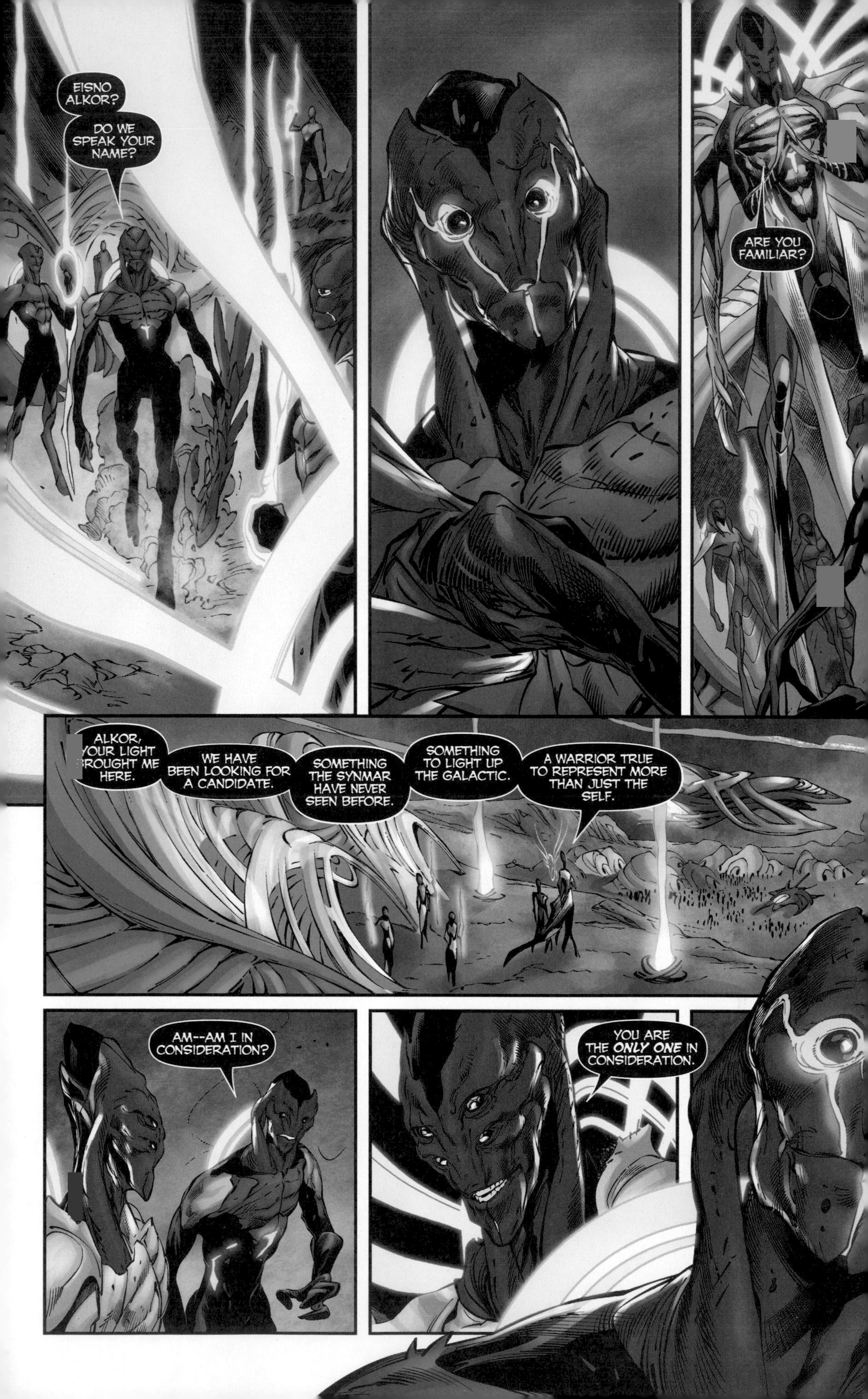
EISNO ALKOR?
DO WE SPEAK YOUR NAME?
ARE YOU FAMILIAR?
ALKOR, YOUR LIGHT BROUGHT ME HERE.
WE HAVE BEEN LOOKING FOR A CANDIDATE.
SOMETHING THE SYNMAR HAVE NEVER SEEN BEFORE.
SOMETHING TO LIGHT UP THE GALACTIC.
A WARRIOR TRUE TO REPRESENT MORE THAN JUST THE SELF.
AM--AM I IN CONSIDERATION?
YOU ARE THE ONLY ONE IN CONSIDERATION.

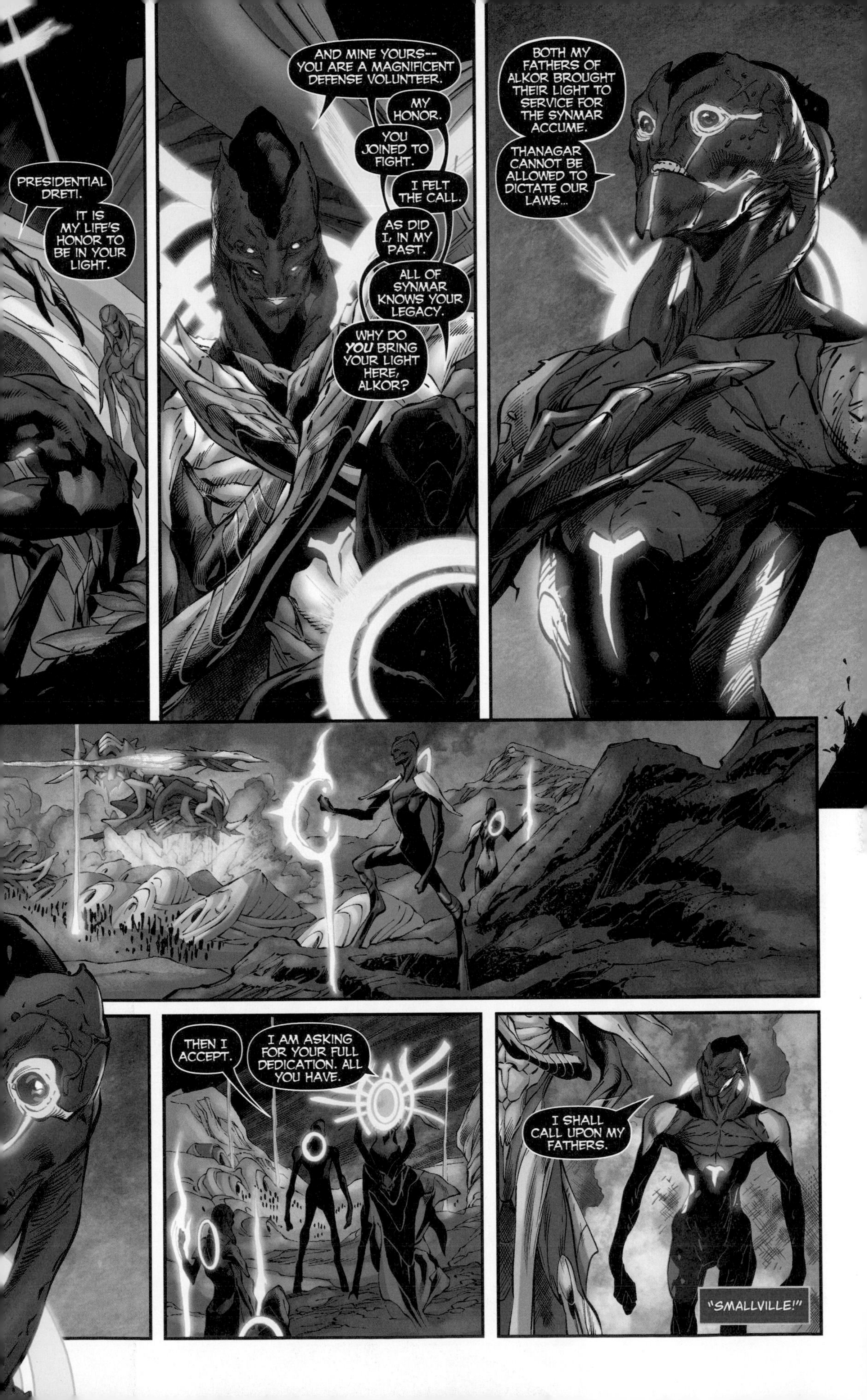
PRESIDENTIAL DRETI.
IT IS MY LIFE'S HONOR TO BE IN YOUR LIGHT.
AND MINE YOURS-- YOU ARE A MAGNIFICENT DEFENSE VOLUNTEER.
MY HONOR.
YOU JOINED TO FIGHT.
I FELT THE CALL.
AS DID I, IN MY PAST.
ALL OF SYNMAR KNOWS YOUR LEGACY.
WHY DO *YOU* BRING YOUR LIGHT HERE, ALKOR?
BOTH MY FATHERS OF ALKOR BROUGHT THEIR LIGHT TO SERVICE FOR THE SYNMAR ACCUME.
THANAGAR CANNOT BE ALLOWED TO DICTATE OUR LAWS...
I AM ASKING FOR YOUR FULL DEDICATION. ALL YOU HAVE.
THEN I ACCEPT.
I SHALL CALL UPON MY FATHERS.
"SMALLVILLE!"

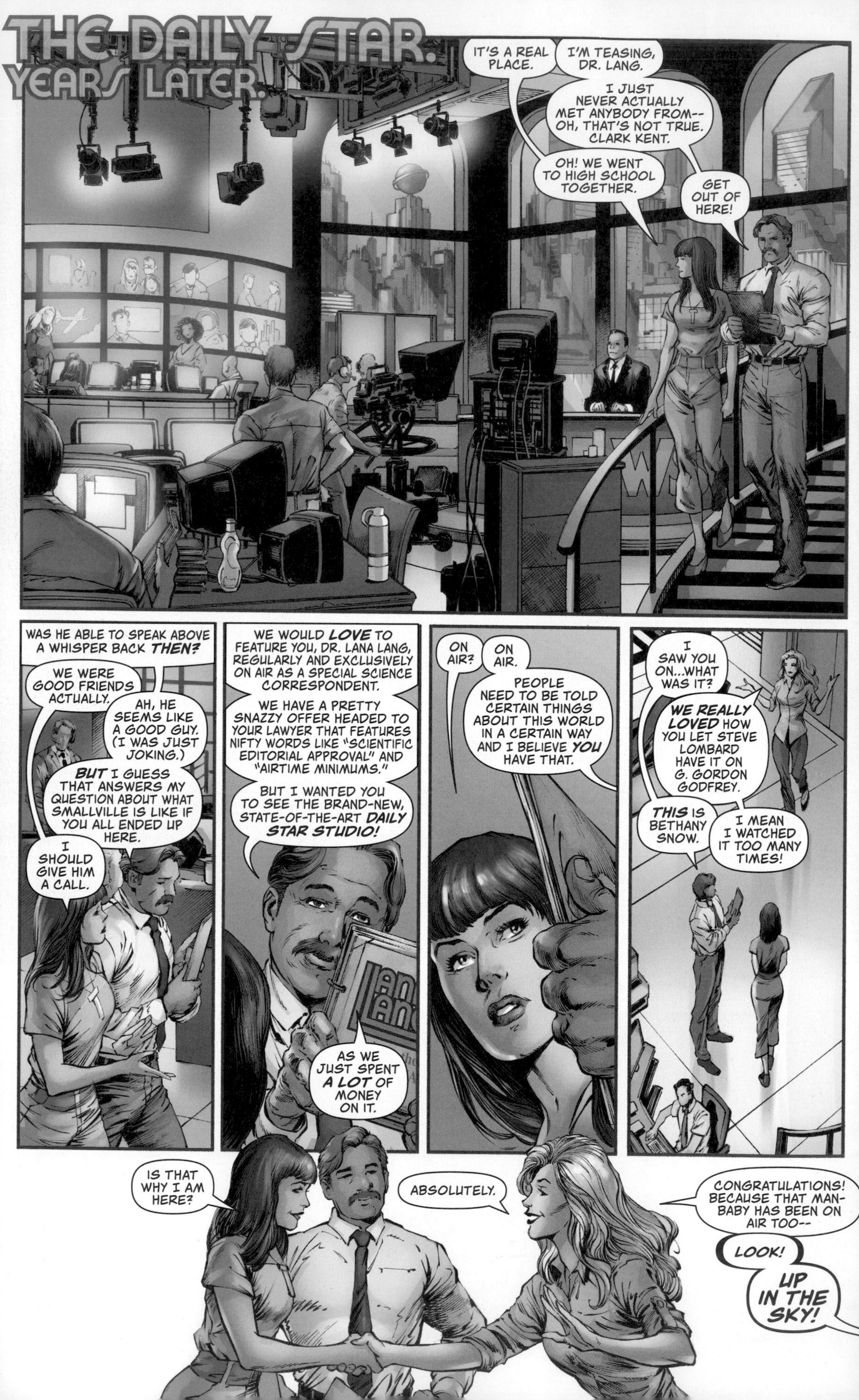
THE DAILY STAR. YEARS LATER.
IT'S A REAL PLACE.
I'M TEASING, DR. LANG.
I JUST NEVER ACTUALLY MET ANYBODY FROM-- OH, THAT'S NOT TRUE. CLARK KENT.
OH! WE WENT TO HIGH SCHOOL TOGETHER.
GET OUT OF HERE!
WAS HE ABLE TO SPEAK ABOVE A WHISPER BACK THEN?
WE WERE GOOD FRIENDS ACTUALLY.
AH, HE SEEMS LIKE A GOOD GUY. (I WAS JUST JOKING.)
BUT I GUESS THAT ANSWERS MY QUESTION ABOUT WHAT SMALLVILLE IS LIKE IF YOU ALL ENDED UP HERE.
I SHOULD GIVE HIM A CALL.
WE WOULD LOVE TO FEATURE YOU, DR. LANA LANG, REGULARLY AND EXCLUSIVELY ON AIR AS A SPECIAL SCIENCE CORRESPONDENT.
WE HAVE A PRETTY SNAZZY OFFER HEADED TO YOUR LAWYER THAT FEATURES NIFTY WORDS LIKE "SCIENTIFIC EDITORIAL APPROVAL" AND "AIRTIME MINIMUMS."
BUT I WANTED YOU TO SEE THE BRAND-NEW, STATE-OF-THE-ART DAILY STAR STUDIO!
AS WE JUST SPENT A LOT OF MONEY ON IT.
ON AIR?
ON AIR.
PEOPLE NEED TO BE TOLD CERTAIN THINGS ABOUT THIS WORLD IN A CERTAIN WAY AND I BELIEVE YOU HAVE THAT.
I SAW YOU ON...WHAT WAS IT?
WE REALLY LOVED HOW YOU LET STEVE LOMBARD HAVE IT ON G. GORDON GODFREY.
THIS IS BETHANY SNOW.
I MEAN I WATCHED IT TOO MANY TIMES!
IS THAT WHY I AM HERE?
ABSOLUTELY.
CONGRATULATIONS! BECAUSE THAT MAN-BABY HAS BEEN ON AIR TOO--
LOOK!
UP IN THE SKY!

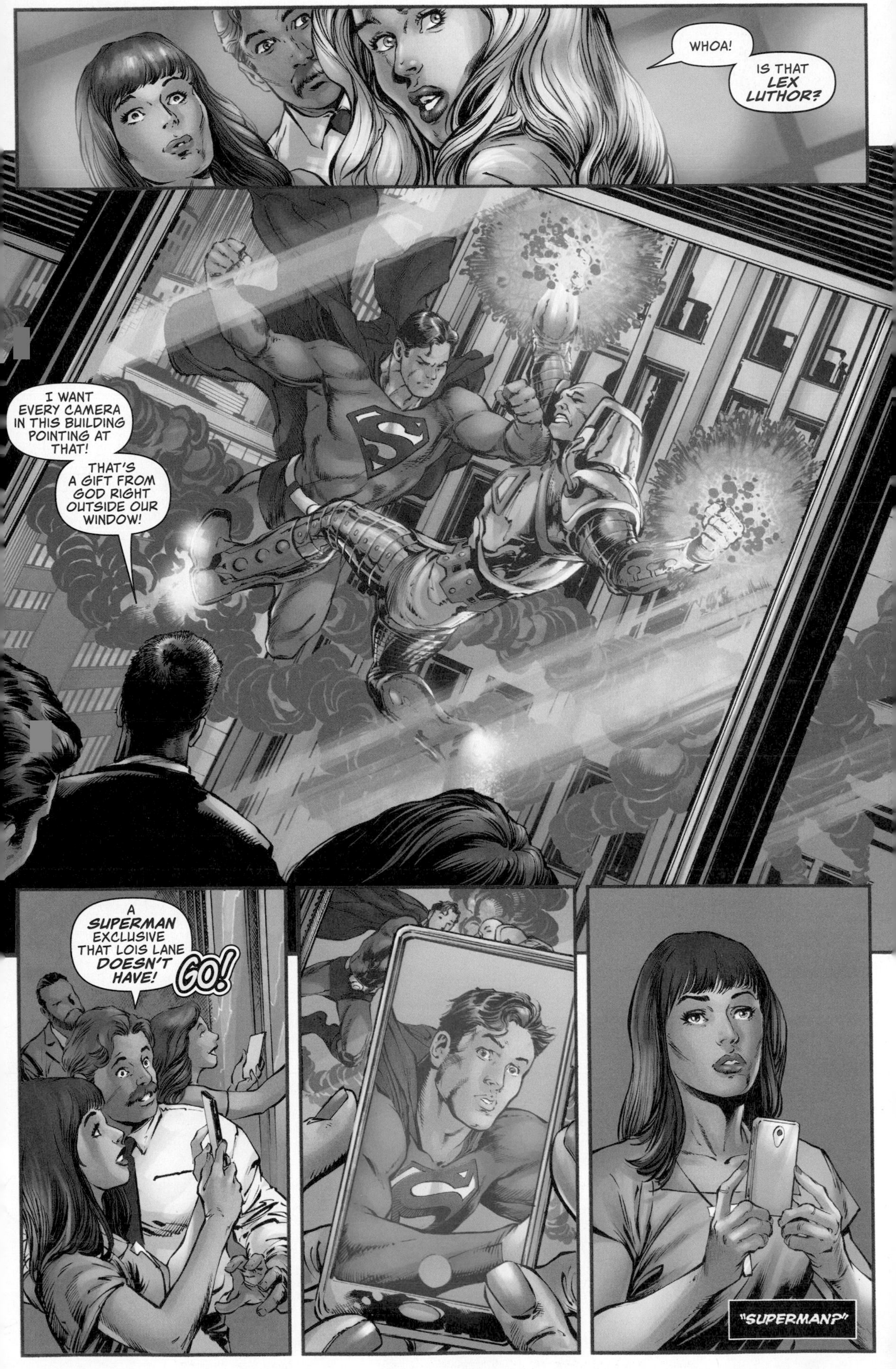

WHOA!
IS THAT LEX LUTHOR?
I WANT EVERY CAMERA IN THIS BUILDING POINTING AT THAT!
THAT'S A GIFT FROM GOD RIGHT OUTSIDE OUR WINDOW!
A SUPERMAN EXCLUSIVE THAT LOIS LANE DOESN'T HAVE!
GO!
"SUPERMAN?"

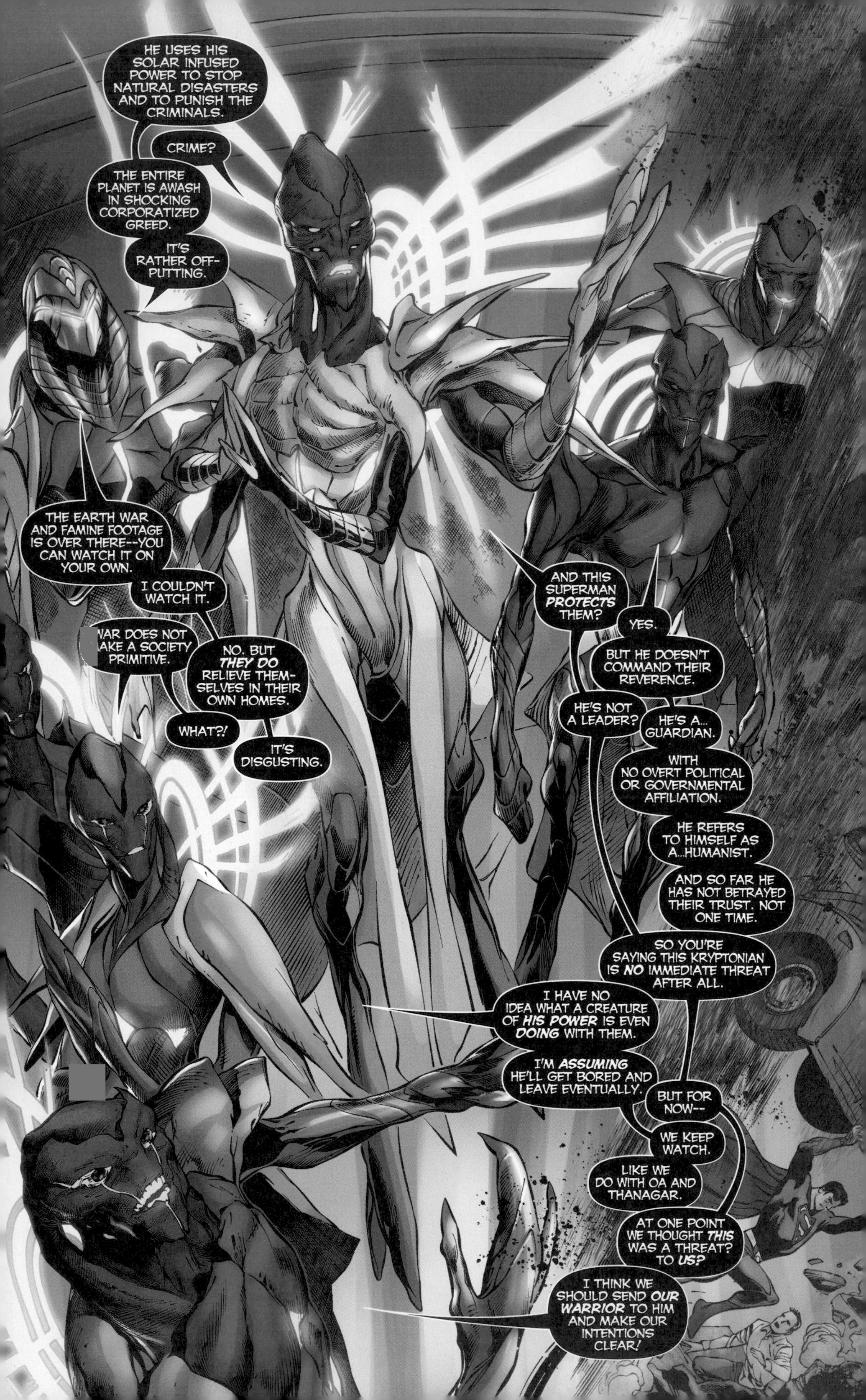

HE USES HIS SOLAR INFUSED POWER TO STOP NATURAL DISASTERS AND TO PUNISH THE CRIMINALS.
CRIME?
THE ENTIRE PLANET IS AWASH IN SHOCKING CORPORATIZED GREED.
IT'S RATHER OFF-PUTTING.
THE EARTH WAR AND FAMINE FOOTAGE IS OVER THERE--YOU CAN WATCH IT ON YOUR OWN.
I COULDN'T WATCH IT.
WAR DOES NOT AKE A SOCIETY PRIMITIVE.
NO. BUT **THEY DO** RELIEVE THEM-SELVES IN THEIR OWN HOMES.
WHAT?!
IT'S DISGUSTING.
AND THIS SUPERMAN **PROTECTS** THEM?
YES.
BUT HE DOESN'T COMMAND THEIR REVERENCE.
HE'S NOT A LEADER?
HE'S A... GUARDIAN.
WITH NO OVERT POLITICAL OR GOVERNMENTAL AFFILIATION.
HE REFERS TO HIMSELF AS A...HUMANIST.
AND SO FAR HE HAS NOT BETRAYED THEIR TRUST. NOT ONE TIME.
SO YOU'RE SAYING THIS KRYPTONIAN IS **NO** IMMEDIATE THREAT AFTER ALL.
I HAVE NO IDEA WHAT A CREATURE OF **HIS POWER** IS EVEN **DOING** WITH THEM.
I'M **ASSUMING** HE'LL GET BORED AND LEAVE EVENTUALLY.
BUT FOR NOW--
WE KEEP WATCH.
LIKE WE DO WITH OA AND THANAGAR.
AT ONE POINT WE THOUGHT **THIS** WAS A THREAT? TO **US?**
I THINK WE SHOULD SEND **OUR WARRIOR** TO HIM AND MAKE OUR INTENTIONS CLEAR!

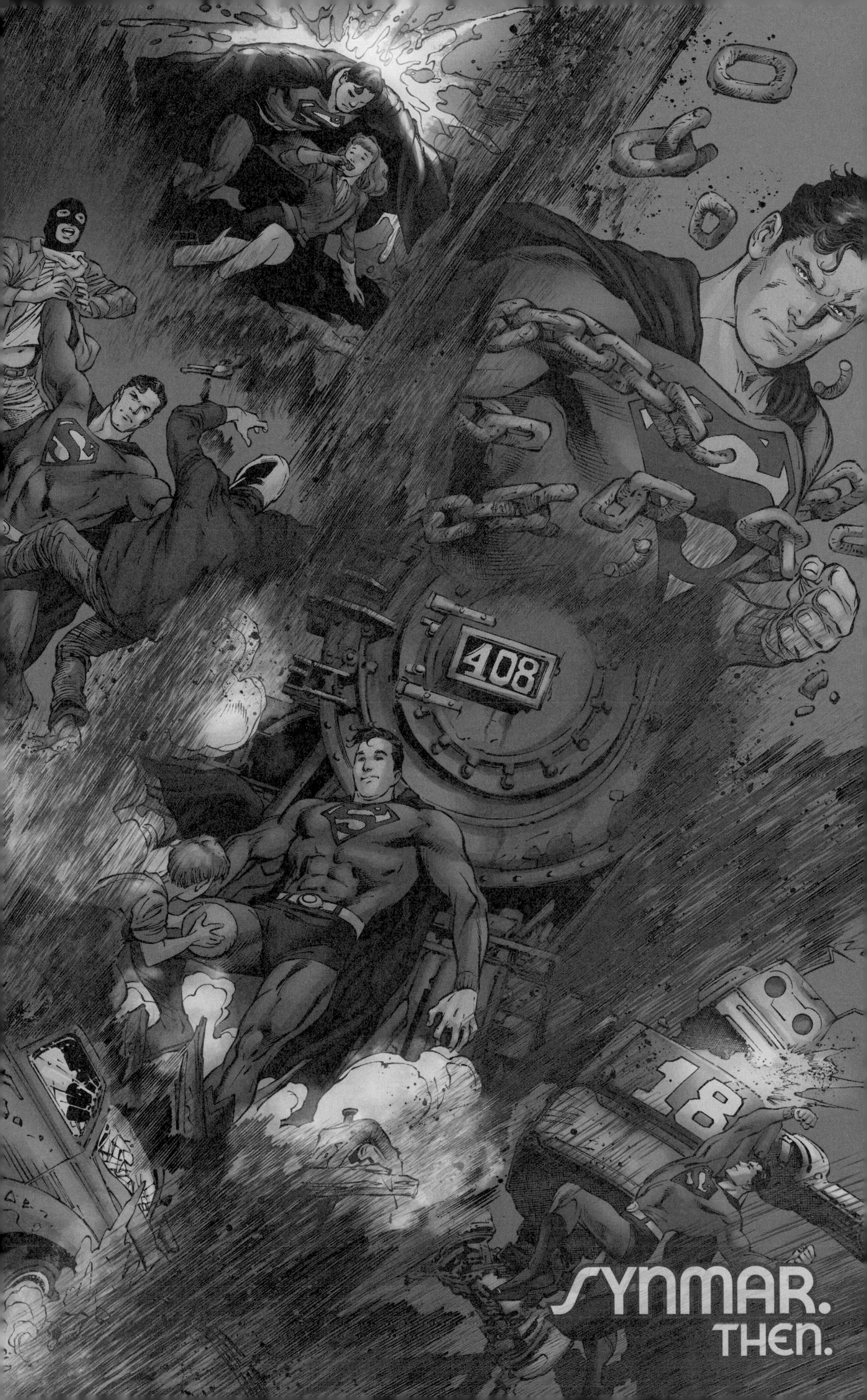
408
18
SYNMAR.
THEN.

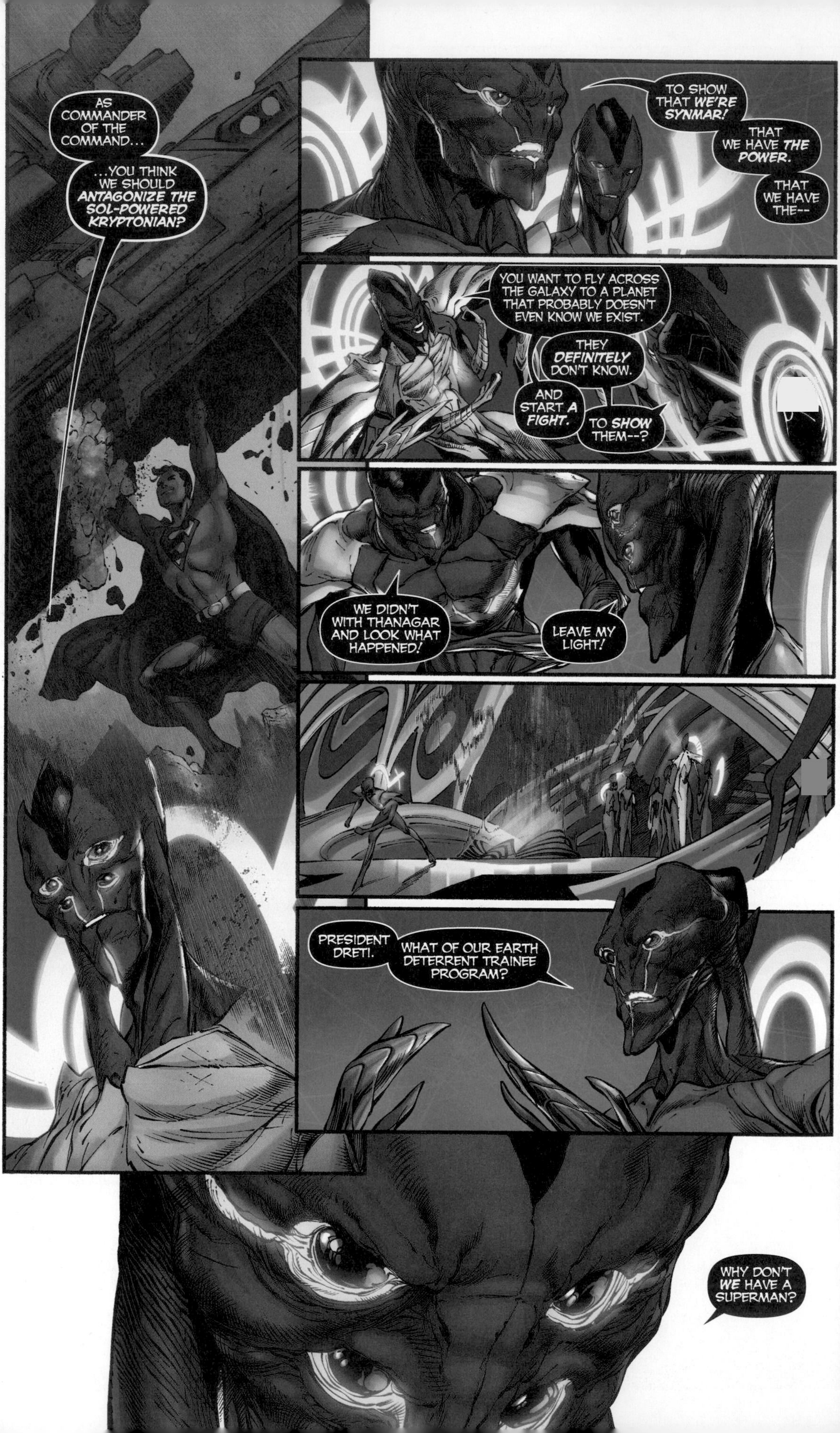
AS COMMANDER OF THE COMMAND...
...YOU THINK WE SHOULD ANTAGONIZE THE SOL-POWERED KRYPTONIAN?
TO SHOW THAT WE'RE SYNMAR!
THAT WE HAVE THE POWER.
THAT WE HAVE THE--
YOU WANT TO FLY ACROSS THE GALAXY TO A PLANET THAT PROBABLY DOESN'T EVEN KNOW WE EXIST.
THEY DEFINITELY DON'T KNOW.
AND START A FIGHT.
TO SHOW THEM--?
WE DIDN'T WITH THANAGAR AND LOOK WHAT HAPPENED!
LEAVE MY LIGHT!
PRESIDENT DRET!.
WHAT OF OUR EARTH DETERRENT TRAINEE PROGRAM?
WHY DON'T WE HAVE A SUPERMAN?

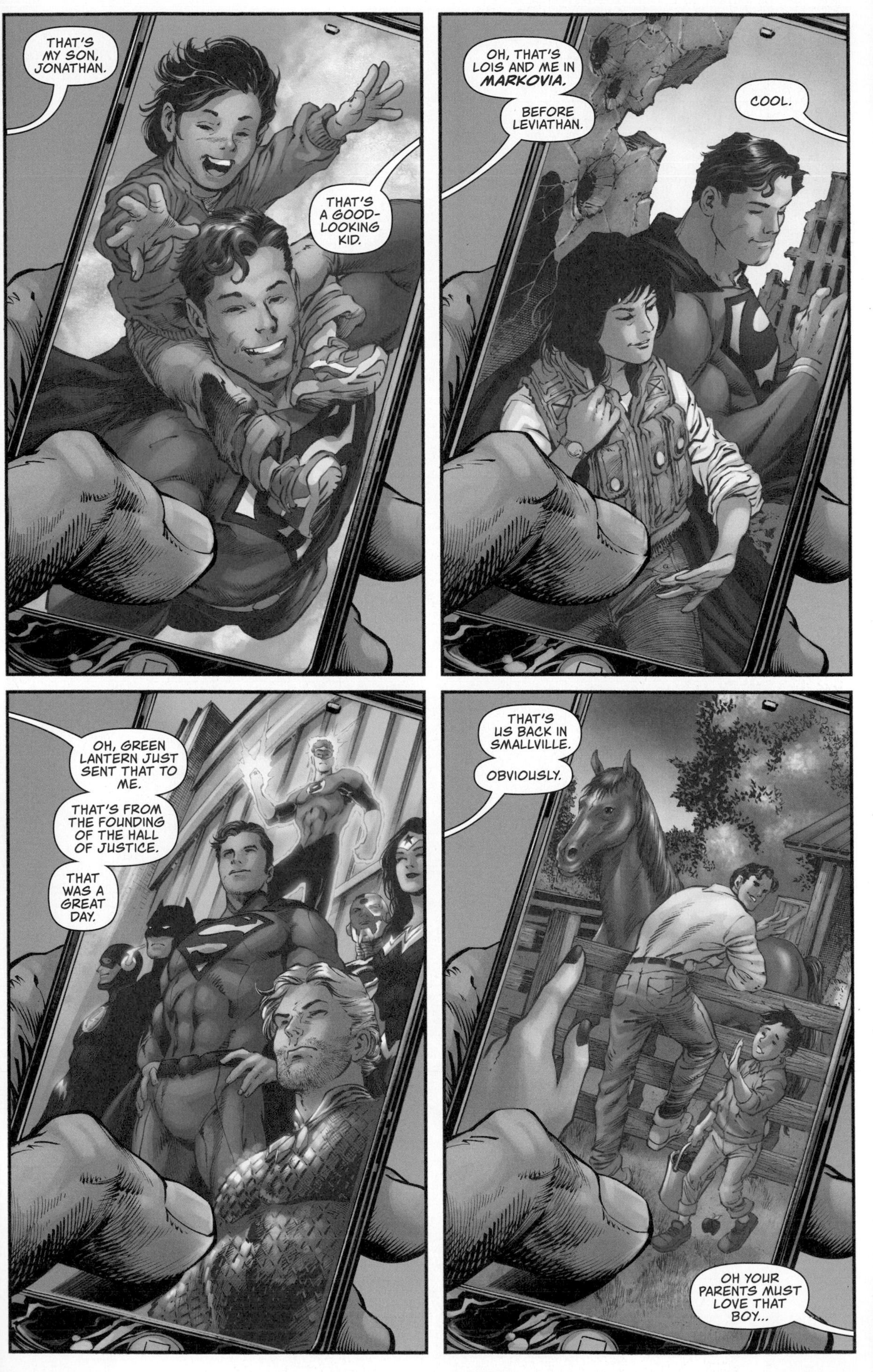
THAT'S MY SON, JONATHAN.
THAT'S A GOOD-LOOKING KID.
OH, THAT'S LOIS AND ME IN *MARKOVIA.*
BEFORE LEVIATHAN.
COOL.
OH, GREEN LANTERN JUST SENT THAT TO ME.
THAT'S FROM THE FOUNDING OF THE HALL OF JUSTICE.
THAT WAS A GREAT DAY.
THAT'S US BACK IN SMALLVILLE.
OBVIOUSLY.
OH YOUR PARENTS MUST LOVE THAT BOY...

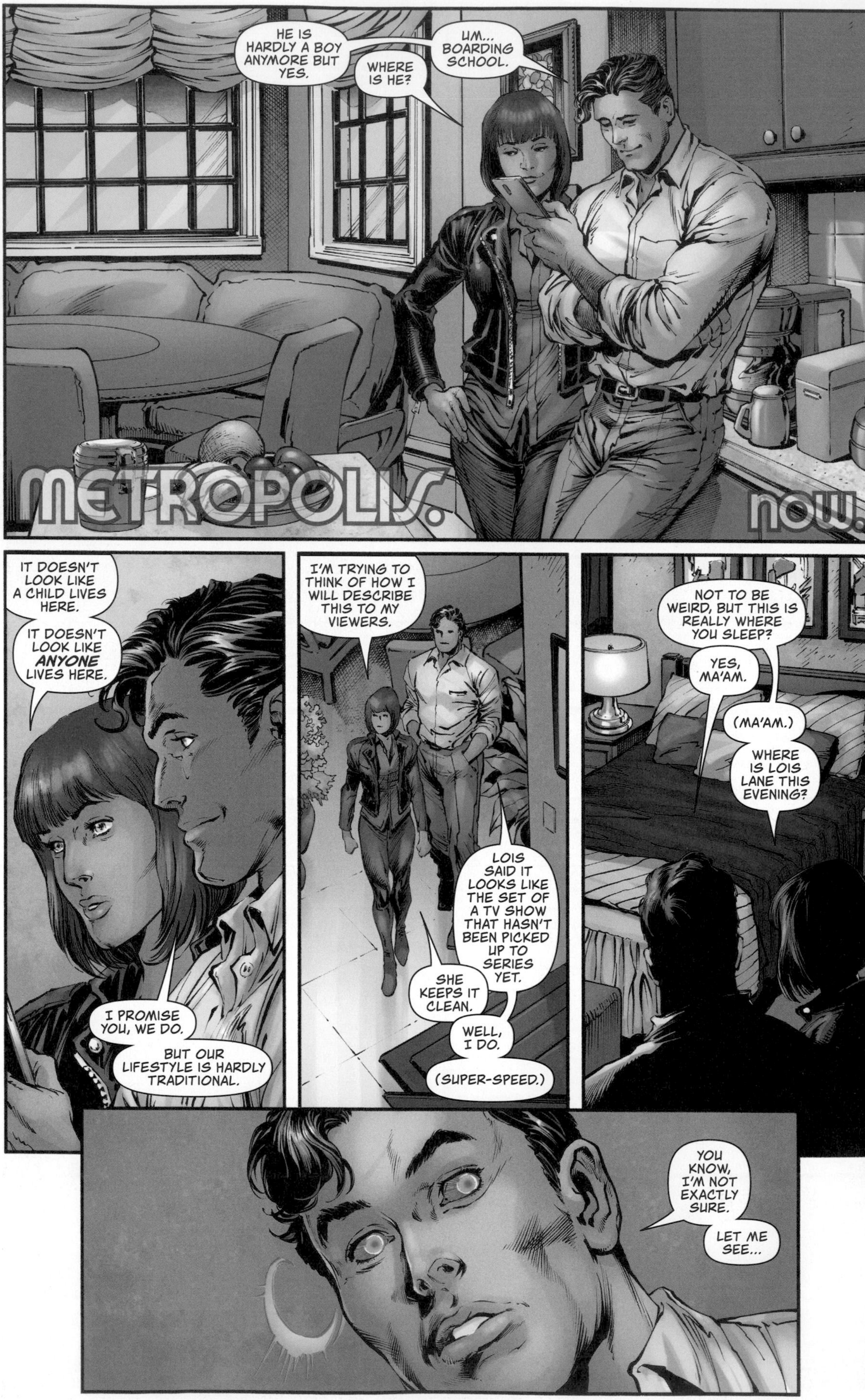
HE IS HARDLY A BOY ANYMORE BUT YES.
WHERE IS HE?
UM... BOARDING SCHOOL.
METROPOLIS.
NOW.
IT DOESN'T LOOK LIKE A CHILD LIVES HERE.
IT DOESN'T LOOK LIKE ANYONE LIVES HERE.
I PROMISE YOU, WE DO.
BUT OUR LIFESTYLE IS HARDLY TRADITIONAL.
I'M TRYING TO THINK OF HOW I WILL DESCRIBE THIS TO MY VIEWERS.
LOIS SAID IT LOOKS LIKE THE SET OF A TV SHOW THAT HASN'T BEEN PICKED UP TO SERIES YET.
SHE KEEPS IT CLEAN.
WELL, I DO.
(SUPER-SPEED.)
NOT TO BE WEIRD, BUT THIS IS REALLY WHERE YOU SLEEP?
YES, MA'AM.
(MA'AM.)
WHERE IS LOIS LANE THIS EVENING?
YOU KNOW, I'M NOT EXACTLY SURE.
LET ME SEE...

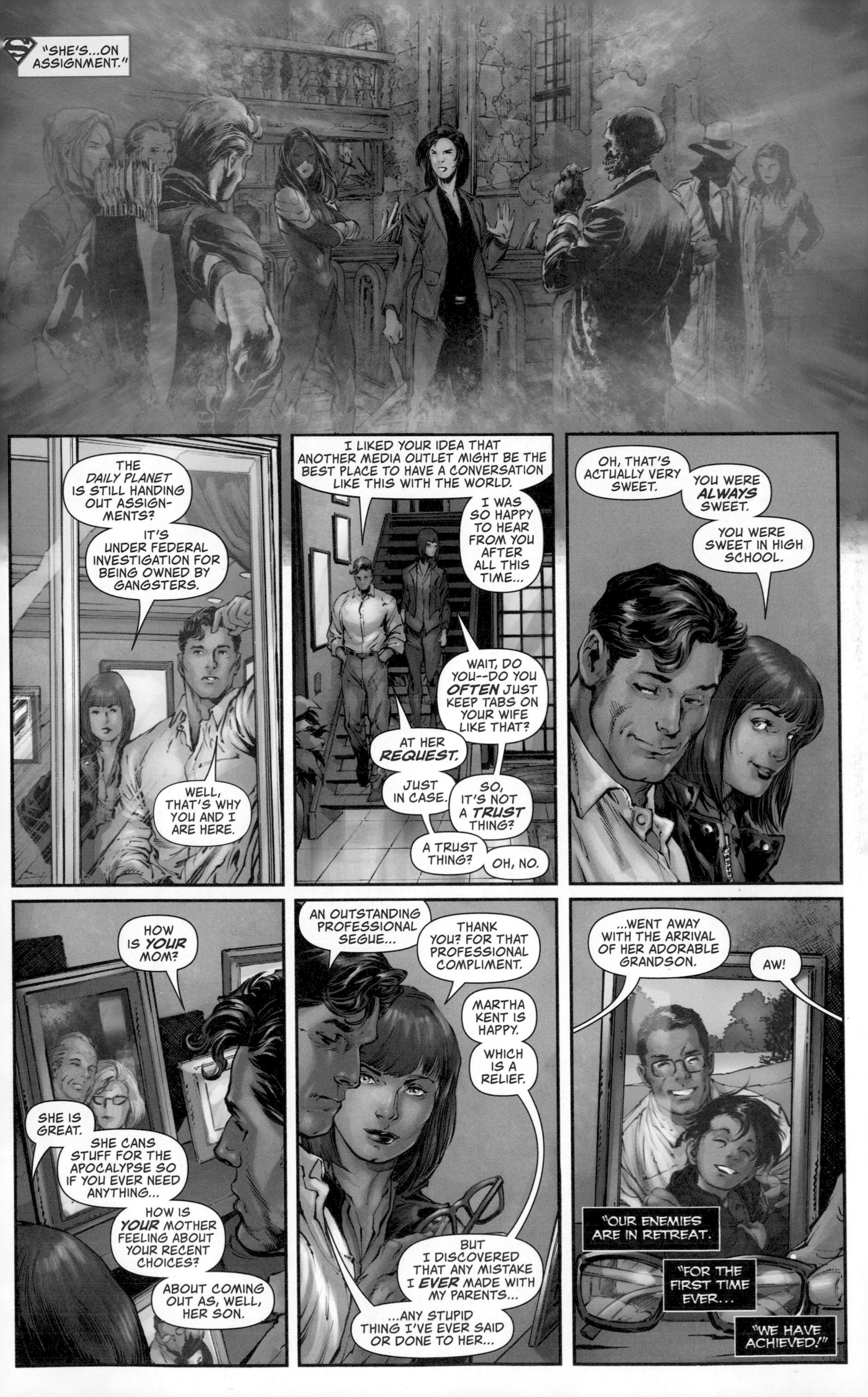
"SHE'S...ON ASSIGNMENT."
THE DAILY PLANET IS STILL HANDING OUT ASSIGN-MENTS?
IT'S UNDER FEDERAL INVESTIGATION FOR BEING OWNED BY GANGSTERS.
WELL, THAT'S WHY YOU AND I ARE HERE.
I LIKED YOUR IDEA THAT ANOTHER MEDIA OUTLET MIGHT BE THE BEST PLACE TO HAVE A CONVERSATION LIKE THIS WITH THE WORLD.
I WAS SO HAPPY TO HEAR FROM YOU AFTER ALL THIS TIME...
WAIT, DO YOU--DO YOU OFTEN JUST KEEP TABS ON YOUR WIFE LIKE THAT?
AT HER REQUEST.
JUST IN CASE.
SO, IT'S NOT A TRUST THING?
A TRUST THING?
OH, NO.
OH, THAT'S ACTUALLY VERY SWEET.
YOU WERE ALWAYS SWEET.
YOU WERE SWEET IN HIGH SCHOOL.
HOW IS YOUR MOM?
SHE IS GREAT.
SHE CANS STUFF FOR THE APOCALYPSE SO IF YOU EVER NEED ANYTHING...
HOW IS YOUR MOTHER FEELING ABOUT YOUR RECENT CHOICES?
ABOUT COMING OUT AS, WELL, HER SON.
AN OUTSTANDING PROFESSIONAL SEGUE...
THANK YOU? FOR THAT PROFESSIONAL COMPLIMENT.
MARTHA KENT IS HAPPY.
WHICH IS A RELIEF.
BUT I DISCOVERED THAT ANY MISTAKE I EVER MADE WITH MY PARENTS...
...ANY STUPID THING I'VE EVER SAID OR DONE TO HER...
...WENT AWAY WITH THE ARRIVAL OF HER ADORABLE GRANDSON.
AW!
"OUR ENEMIES ARE IN RETREAT.
"FOR THE FIRST TIME EVER...
"WE HAVE ACHIEVED!"

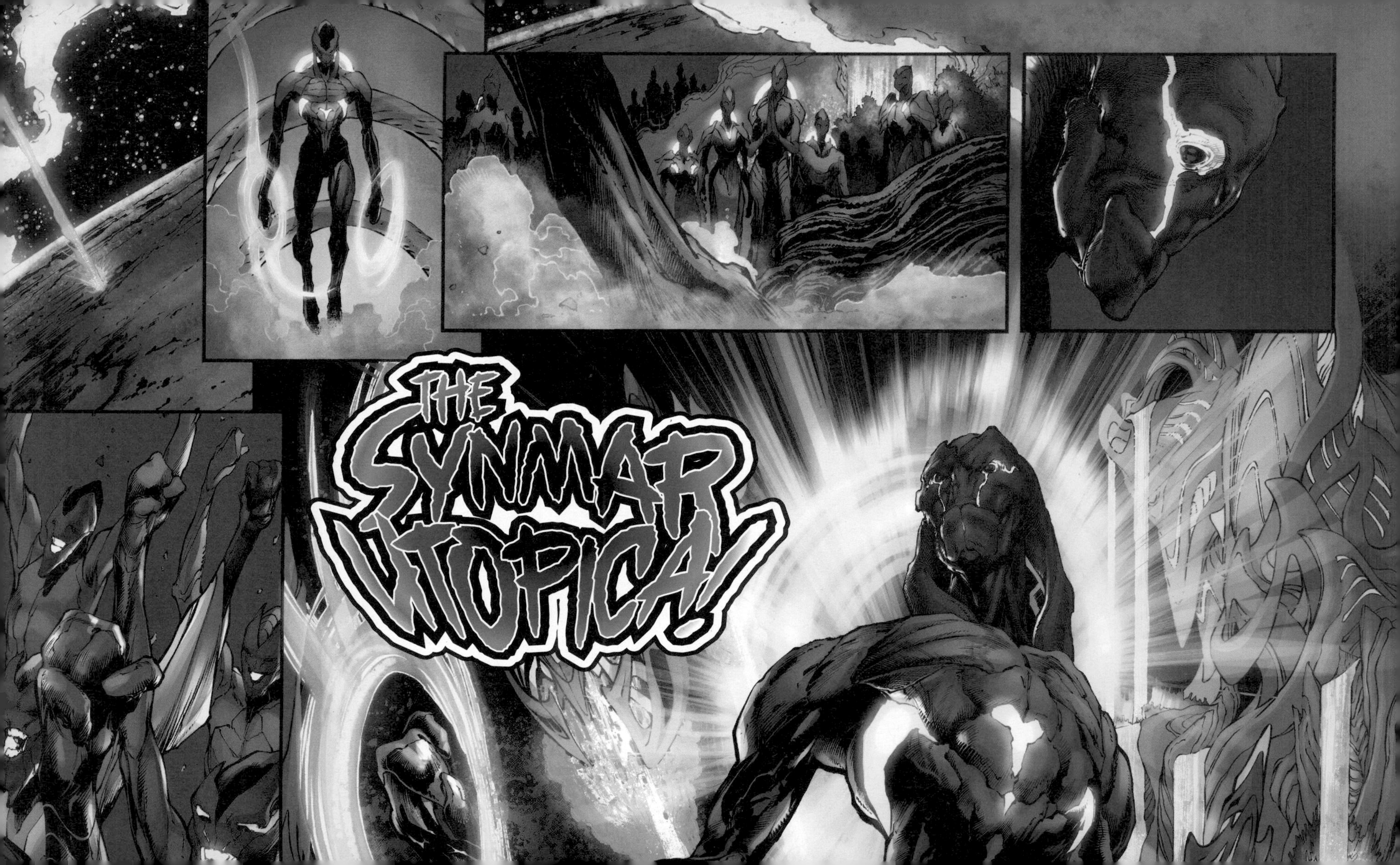
THE SYNMAR UTOPICA!

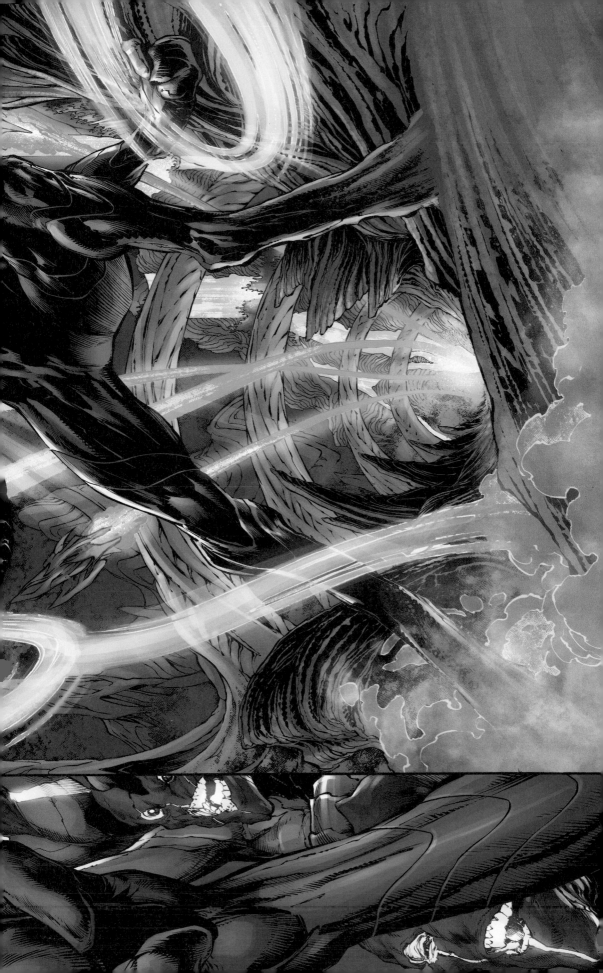

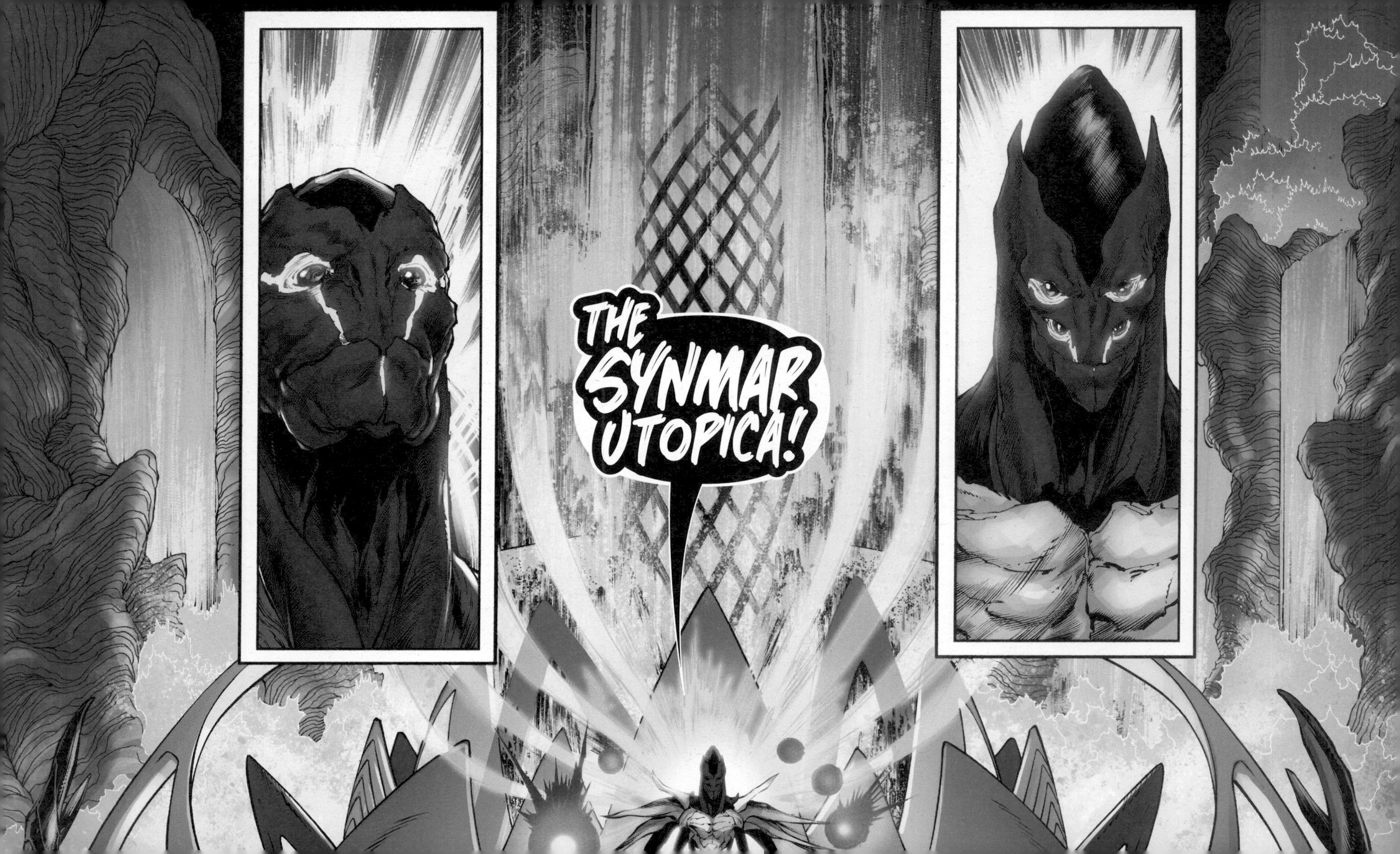
THE SYNMAR UTOPICA!

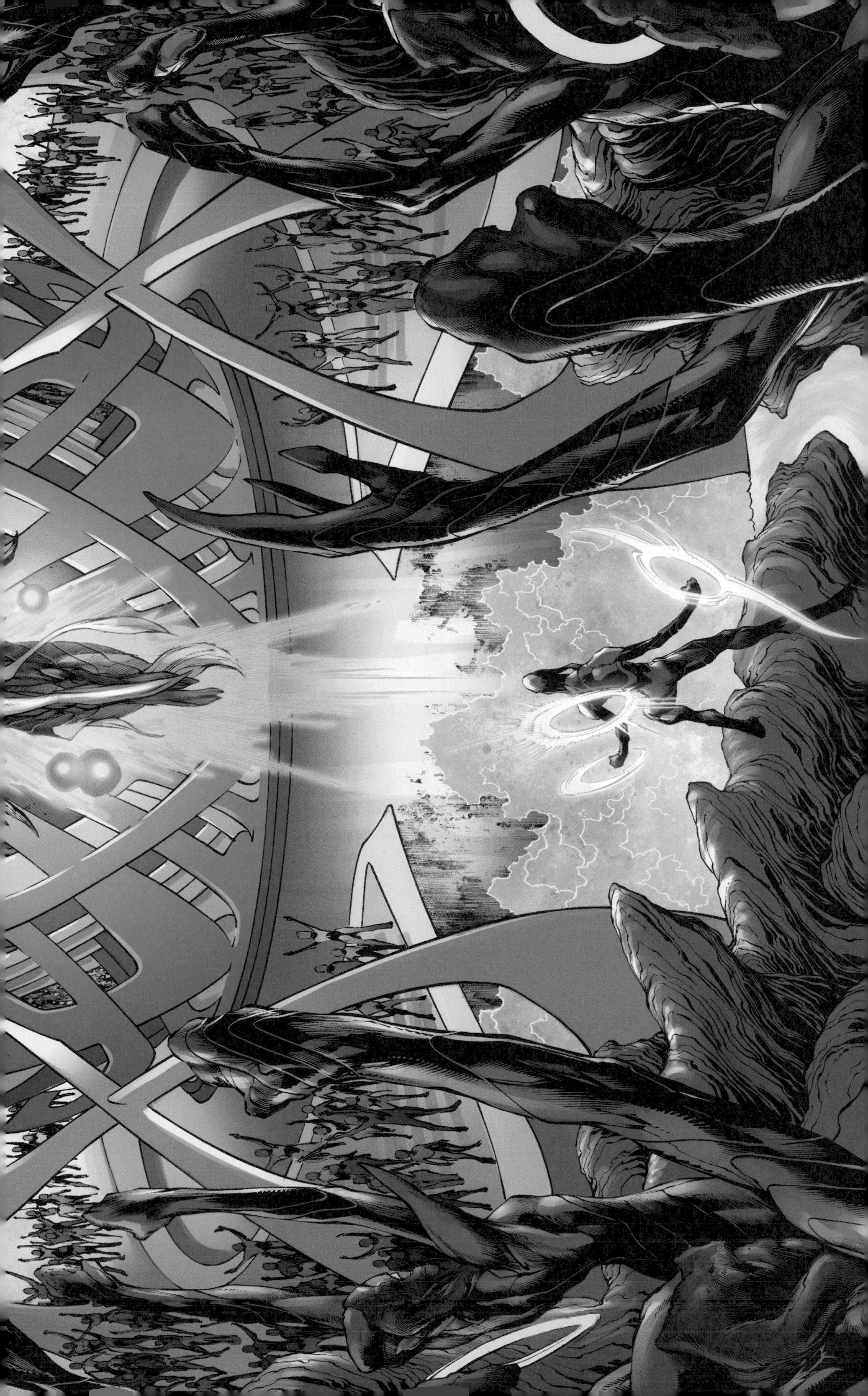

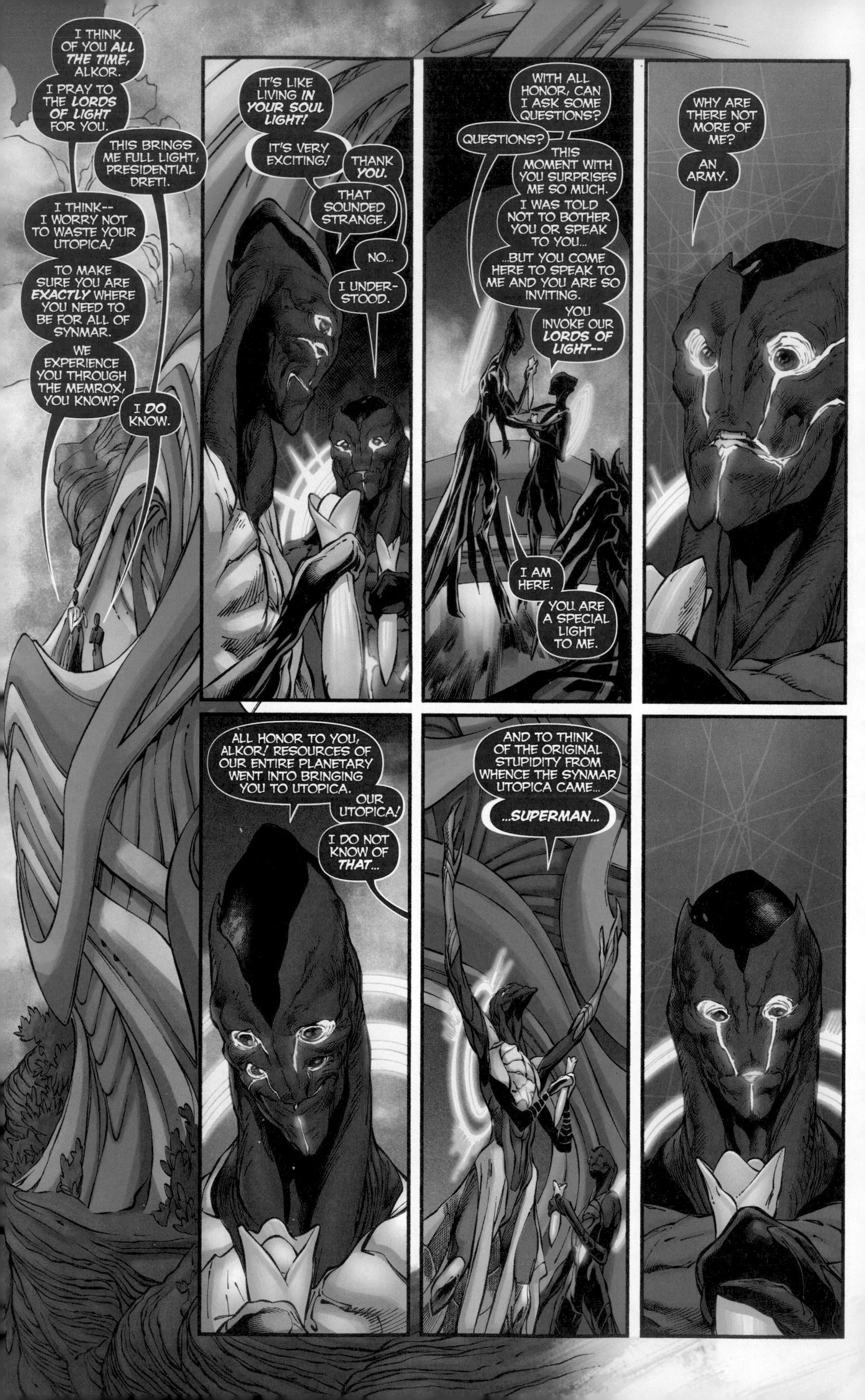

I THINK OF YOU ALL THE TIME, ALKOR.
I PRAY TO THE LORDS OF LIGHT FOR YOU.
THIS BRINGS ME FULL LIGHT, PRESIDENTIAL DRETI.
I THINK-- I WORRY NOT TO WASTE YOUR UTOPICA!
TO MAKE SURE YOU ARE EXACTLY WHERE YOU NEED TO BE FOR ALL OF SYNMAR.
WE EXPERIENCE YOU THROUGH THE MEMROX, YOU KNOW?
I DO KNOW.
IT'S LIKE LIVING IN YOUR SOUL LIGHT!
IT'S VERY EXCITING!
THANK YOU.
THAT SOUNDED STRANGE.
NO...
I UNDER-STOOD.
WITH ALL HONOR, CAN I ASK SOME QUESTIONS?
QUESTIONS?
THIS MOMENT WITH YOU SURPRISES ME SO MUCH.
I WAS TOLD NOT TO BOTHER YOU OR SPEAK TO YOU...
...BUT YOU COME HERE TO SPEAK TO ME AND YOU ARE SO INVITING.
YOU INVOKE OUR LORDS OF LIGHT--
I AM HERE.
YOU ARE A SPECIAL LIGHT TO ME.
WHY ARE THERE NOT MORE OF ME?
AN ARMY.
ALL HONOR TO YOU, ALKOR! RESOURCES OF OUR ENTIRE PLANETARY WENT INTO BRINGING YOU TO UTOPICA.
OUR UTOPICA!
I DO NOT KNOW OF THAT...
AND TO THINK OF THE ORIGINAL STUPIDITY FROM WHENCE THE SYNMAR UTOPICA CAME...
...SUPERMAN...

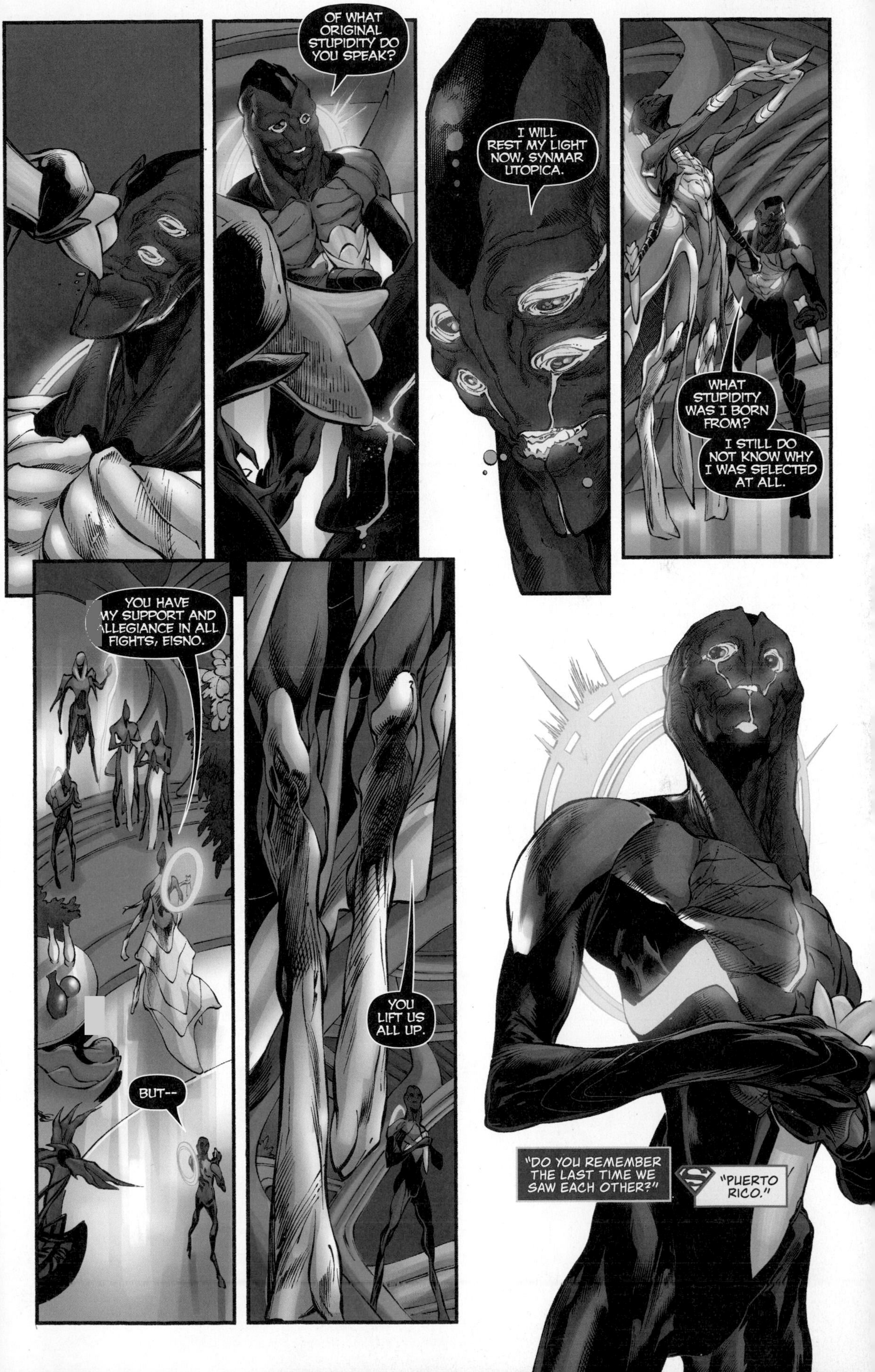
OF WHAT ORIGINAL STUPIDITY DO YOU SPEAK?
I WILL REST MY LIGHT NOW, SYNMAR UTOPICA.
WHAT STUPIDITY WAS I BORN FROM?
I STILL DO NOT KNOW WHY I WAS SELECTED AT ALL.
YOU HAVE MY SUPPORT AND ALLEGIANCE IN ALL FIGHTS, EISNO.
BUT--
YOU LIFT US ALL UP.
"DO YOU REMEMBER THE LAST TIME WE SAW EACH OTHER?"
"PUERTO RICO."

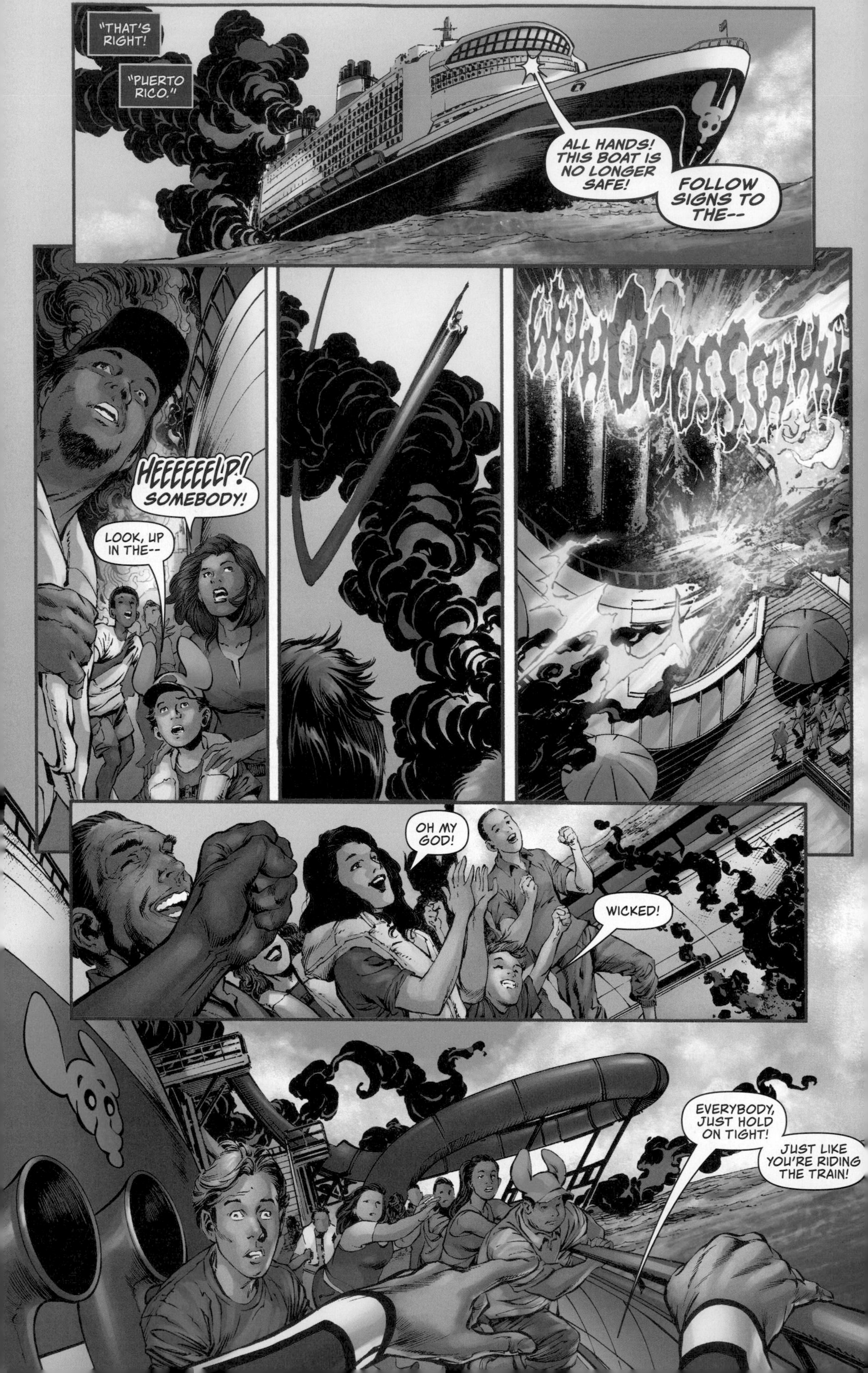
"THAT'S RIGHT!
"PUERTO RICO."
ALL HANDS! THIS BOAT IS NO LONGER SAFE!
FOLLOW SIGNS TO THE--
HEEEEEELP! SOMEBODY!
LOOK, UP IN THE--
OH MY GOD!
WICKED!
EVERYBODY, JUST HOLD ON TIGHT!
JUST LIKE YOU'RE RIDING THE TRAIN!

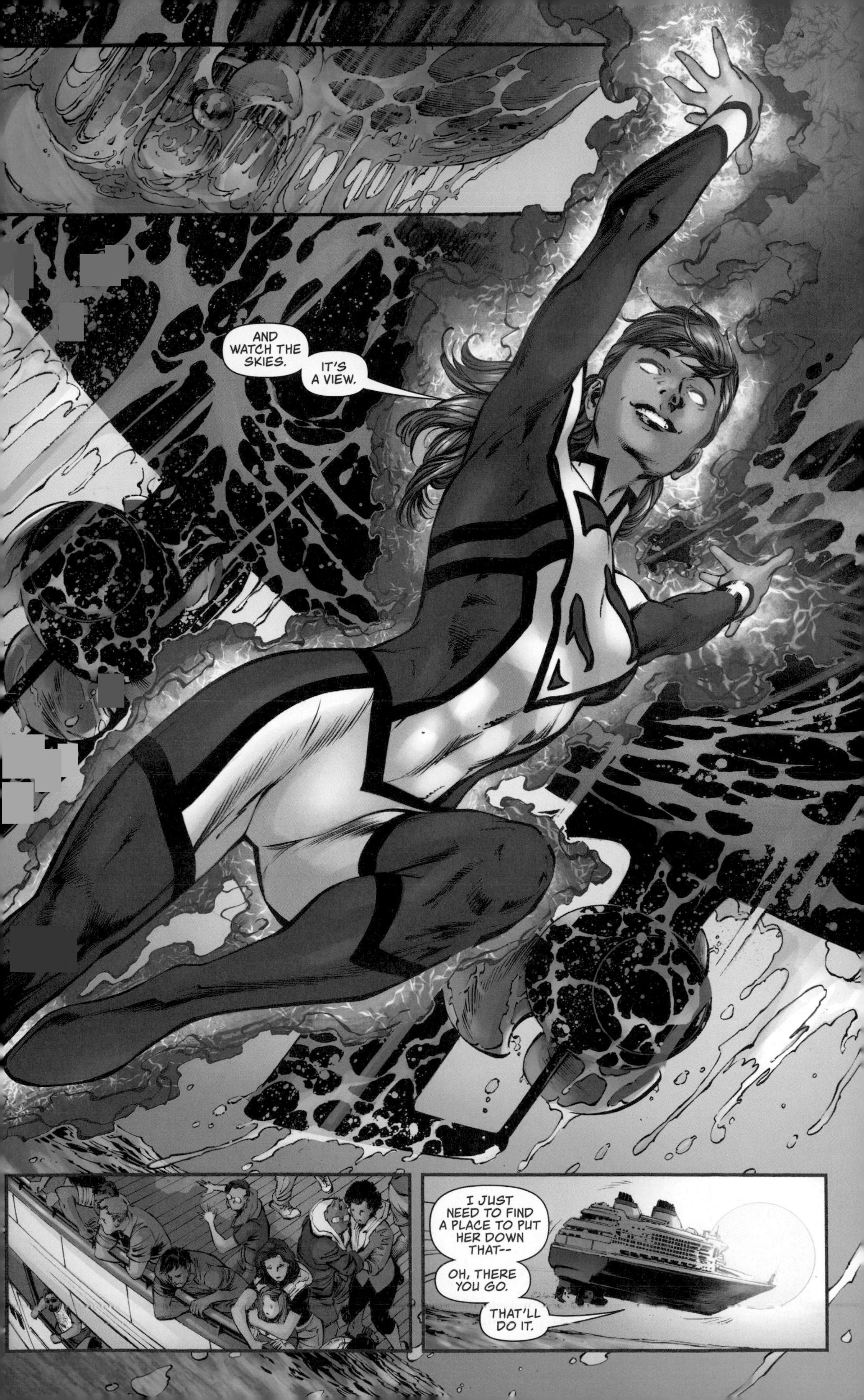
AND WATCH THE SKIES.
IT'S A VIEW.
I JUST NEED TO FIND A PLACE TO PUT HER DOWN THAT--
OH, THERE YOU GO.
THAT'LL DO IT.

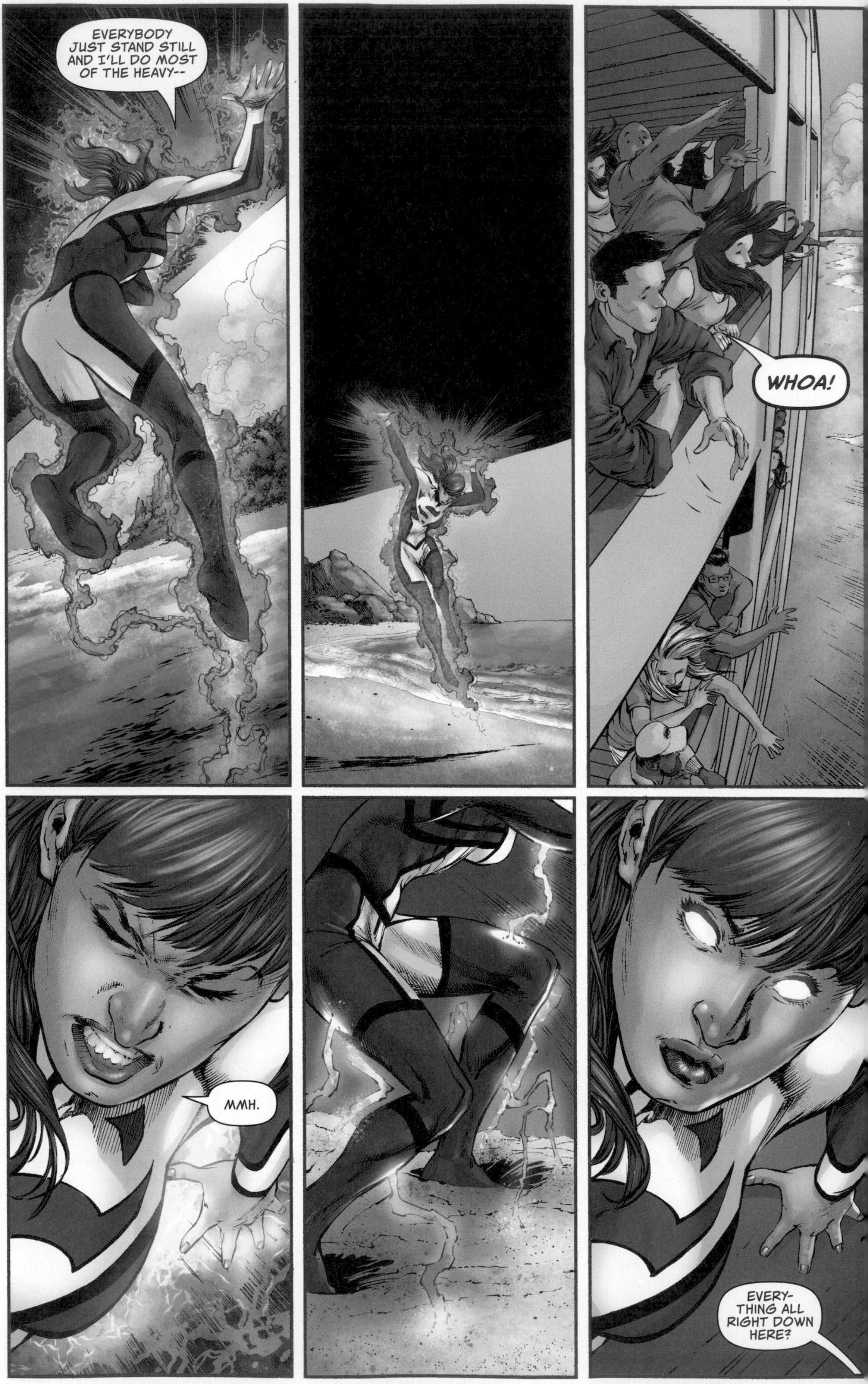
EVERYBODY JUST STAND STILL AND I'LL DO MOST OF THE HEAVY--
WHOA!
MMH.
EVERY-THING ALL RIGHT DOWN HERE?

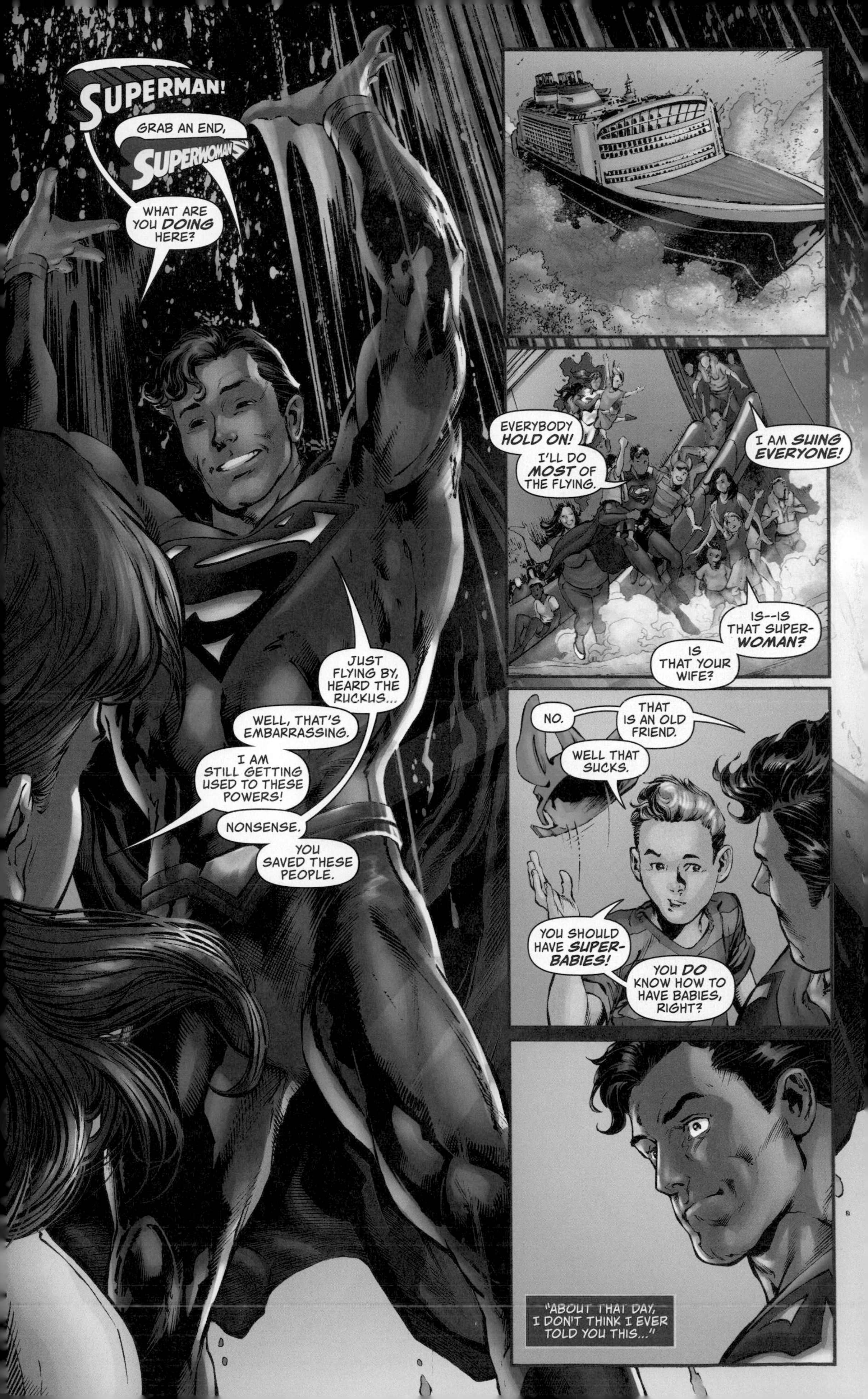
SUPERMAN!
GRAB AN END, SUPERWOMAN!
WHAT ARE YOU DOING HERE?
JUST FLYING BY, HEARD THE RUCKUS...
WELL, THAT'S EMBARRASSING.
I AM STILL GETTING USED TO THESE POWERS!
NONSENSE.
YOU SAVED THESE PEOPLE.
EVERYBODY HOLD ON!
I'LL DO MOST OF THE FLYING.
I AM SUING EVERYONE!
IS--IS THAT SUPER-WOMAN?
IS THAT YOUR WIFE?
NO.
THAT IS AN OLD FRIEND.
WELL THAT SUCKS.
YOU SHOULD HAVE SUPER-BABIES!
YOU DO KNOW HOW TO HAVE BABIES, RIGHT?
"ABOUT THAT DAY, I DON'T THINK I EVER TOLD YOU THIS..."

"*THAT* WAS THE DAY I KNEW THIS WASN'T FOR ME.

"THOSE-- THOSE POWERS--

"WHICH I GOT BY *ACCIDENT.*"

"ALMOST EVERYONE GETS THEIR POWERS BY ACCIDENT."

"ALMOST EVERYONE I *KNOW* GETS POWERS BY HANGING AROUND *YOU* TOO LONG.

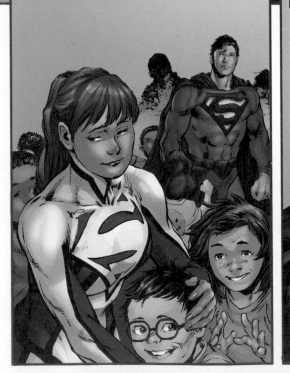

"I DON'T KNOW WHAT I WOULD'VE DONE WITHOUT YOU."

"HOW ARE YOU NOW?"

"I'M JUST A MILD-MANNERED REPORTER FOR THE *DAILY STAR* MULTIMEDIA CONGLOM."

"BUT YOU'RE FEELING ALL RIGHT?"

"IT WAS WEIRD HAVING POWERS FOR A SHORT TIME.

"I WAS *JUST* GETTING USED TO THEM AND THEN...

"BUT I MUST SAY, CLARK, IT-- IT OPENED MY EYES.

"I HAVE SUCH A UNIQUE APPRECIATION FOR YOU."

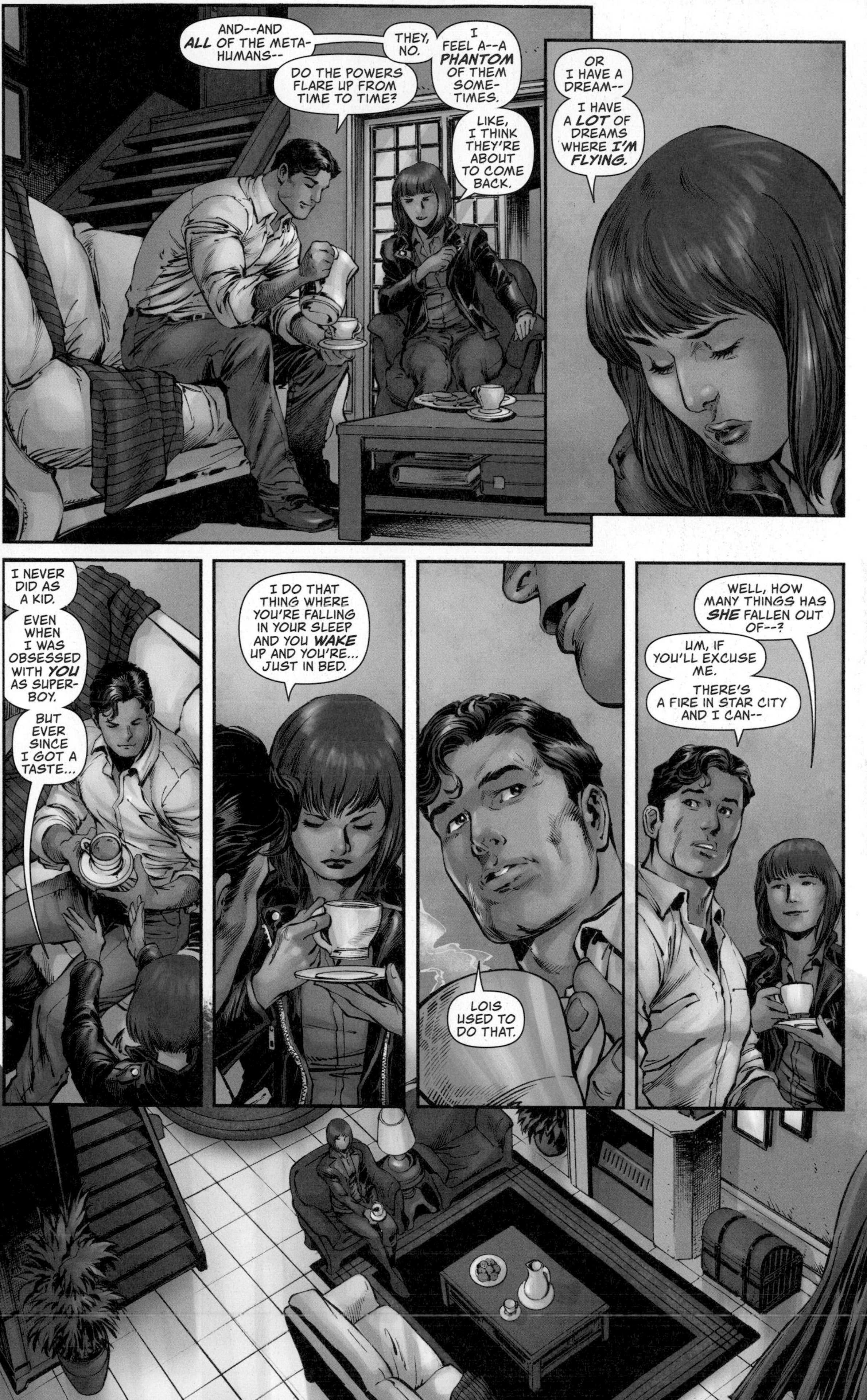

AND--AND ALL OF THE META-HUMANS--
THEY, NO.
DO THE POWERS FLARE UP FROM TIME TO TIME?
I FEEL A--A PHANTOM OF THEM SOME-TIMES.
LIKE, I THINK THEY'RE ABOUT TO COME BACK.
OR I HAVE A DREAM--
I HAVE A LOT OF DREAMS WHERE I'M FLYING.
I NEVER DID AS A KID.
EVEN WHEN I WAS OBSESSED WITH YOU AS SUPER-BOY.
BUT EVER SINCE I GOT A TASTE...
I DO THAT THING WHERE YOU'RE FALLING IN YOUR SLEEP AND YOU WAKE UP AND YOU'RE... JUST IN BED.
LOIS USED TO DO THAT.
WELL, HOW MANY THINGS HAS SHE FALLEN OUT OF--?
UM, IF YOU'LL EXCUSE ME.
THERE'S A FIRE IN STAR CITY AND I CAN--

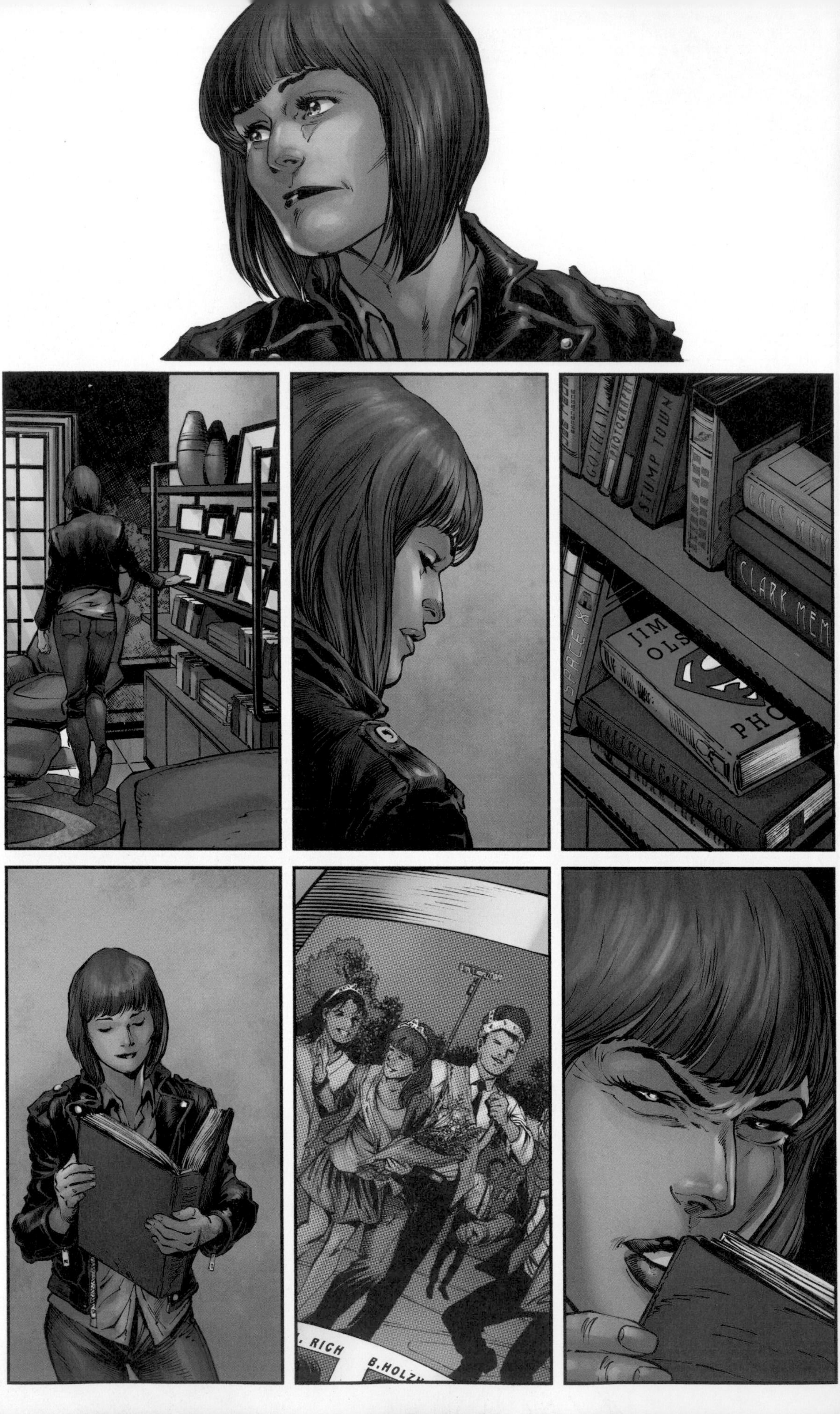
GOTHAM
PHOTOGRAPHY
STUMP TOWN
LOIS MEM
CLARK MEM
JIM
OLS
PHO
SPACE X
SMALLVILLE YEARBOOK
RICH
B.HOLZ

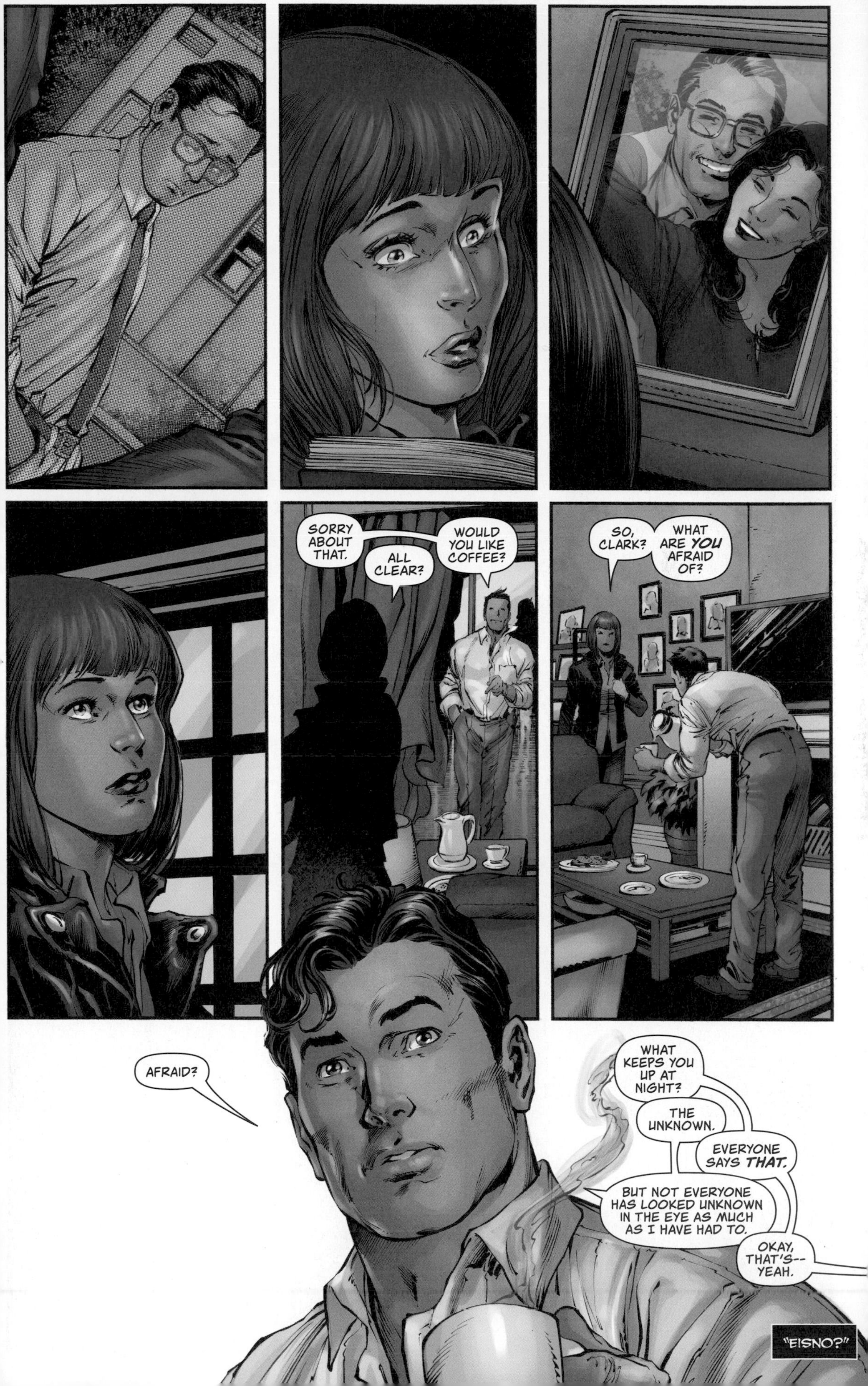

SORRY ABOUT THAT.
ALL CLEAR?
WOULD YOU LIKE COFFEE?
SO, CLARK?
WHAT ARE YOU AFRAID OF?
AFRAID?
WHAT KEEPS YOU UP AT NIGHT?
THE UNKNOWN.
EVERYONE SAYS THAT.
BUT NOT EVERYONE HAS LOOKED UNKNOWN IN THE EYE AS MUCH AS I HAVE HAD TO.
OKAY, THAT'S--YEAH.
"EISNO?"

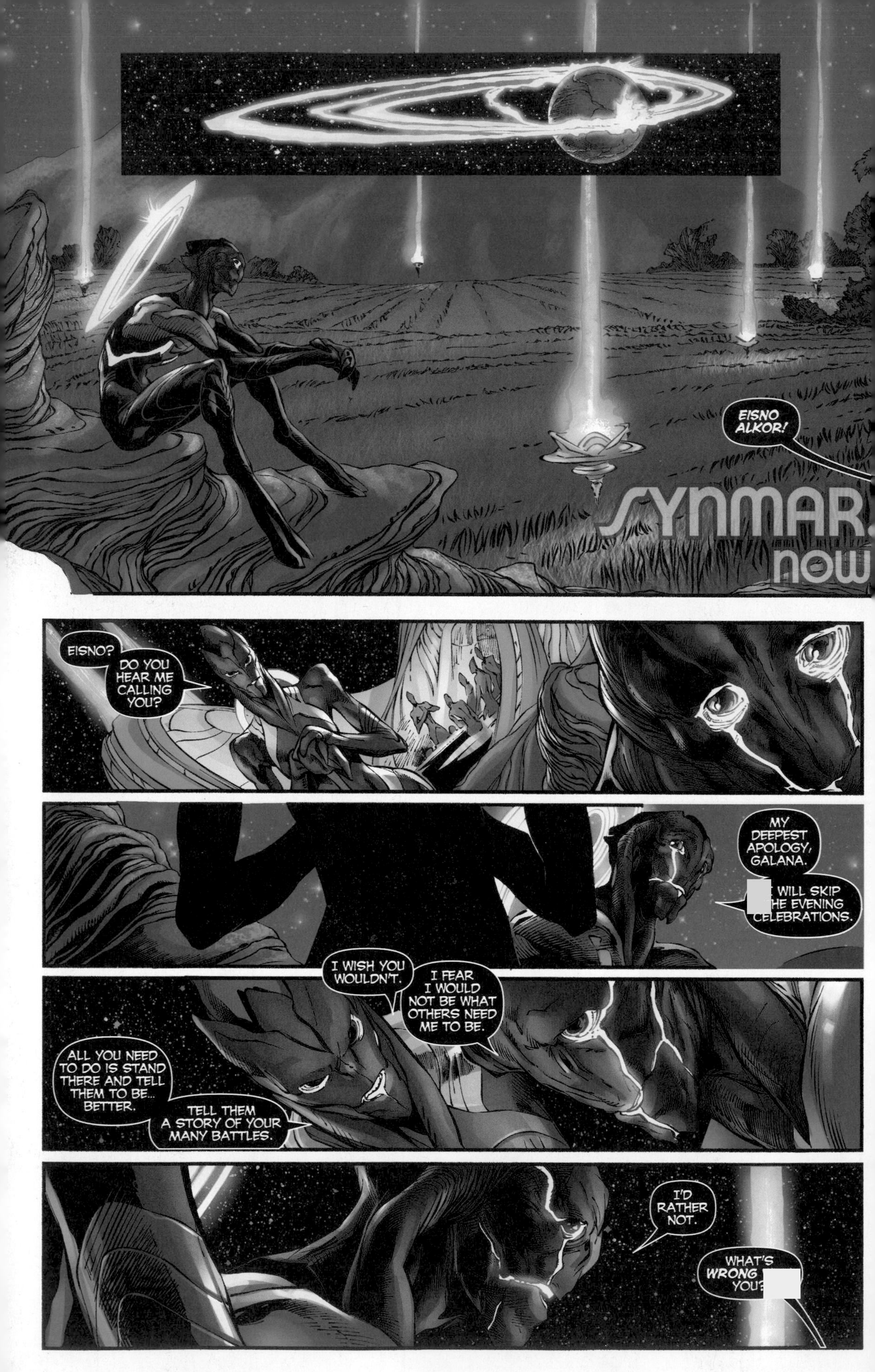
EISNO ALKOR!
SYNMAR. NOW
EISNO? DO YOU HEAR ME CALLING YOU?
MY DEEPEST APOLOGY, GALANA.
WILL SKIP HE EVENING CELEBRATIONS.
I WISH YOU WOULDN'T.
I FEAR I WOULD NOT BE WHAT OTHERS NEED ME TO BE.
ALL YOU NEED TO DO IS STAND THERE AND TELL THEM TO BE... BETTER.
TELL THEM A STORY OF YOUR MANY BATTLES.
I'D RATHER NOT.
WHAT'S *WRONG* YOU?

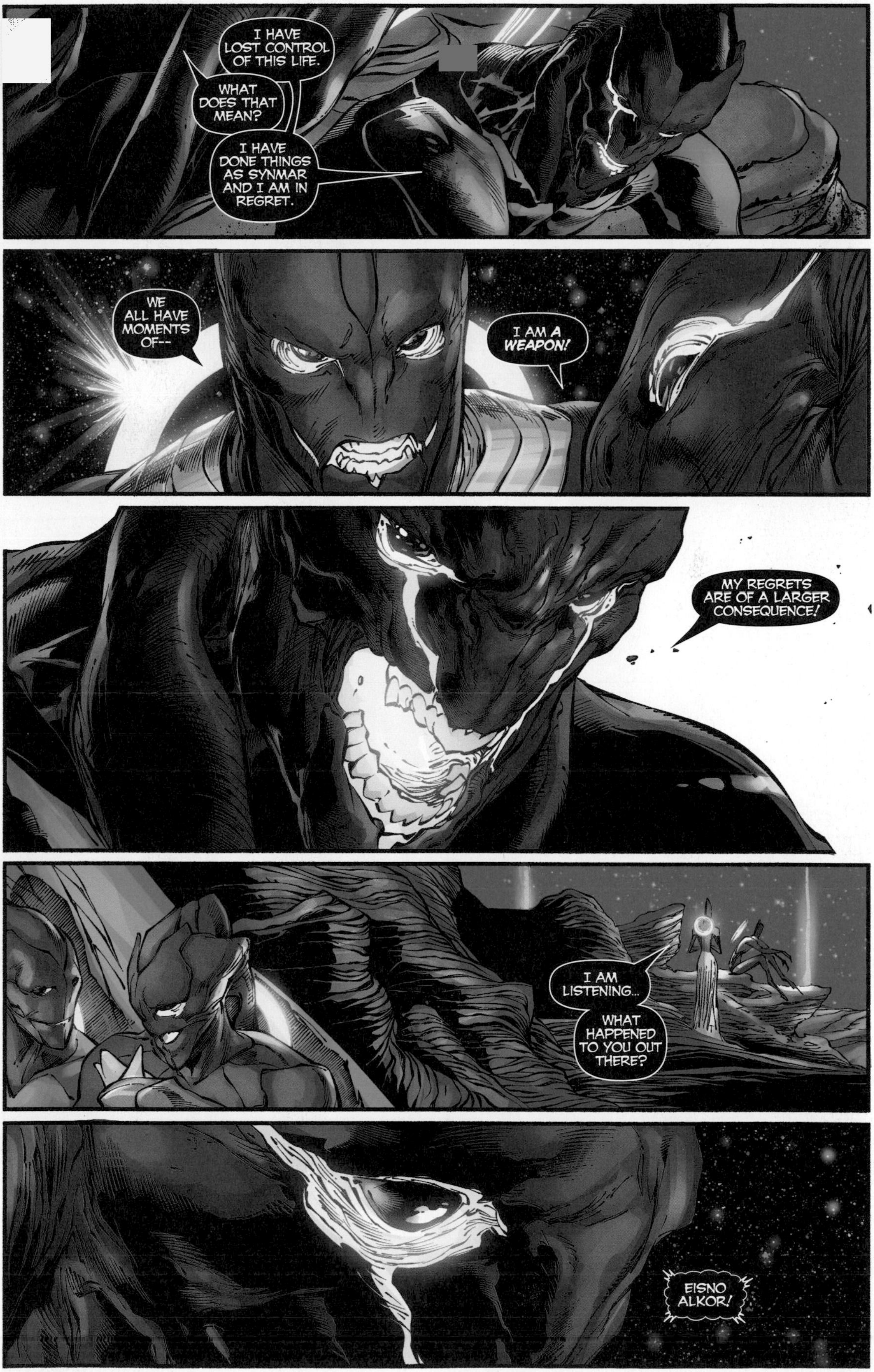
I HAVE LOST CONTROL OF THIS LIFE.
WHAT DOES THAT MEAN?
I HAVE DONE THINGS AS SYNMAR AND I AM IN REGRET.
WE ALL HAVE MOMENTS OF--
I AM A *WEAPON!*
MY REGRETS ARE OF A LARGER CONSEQUENCE!
I AM LISTENING...
WHAT HAPPENED TO YOU OUT THERE?
EISNO ALKOR!

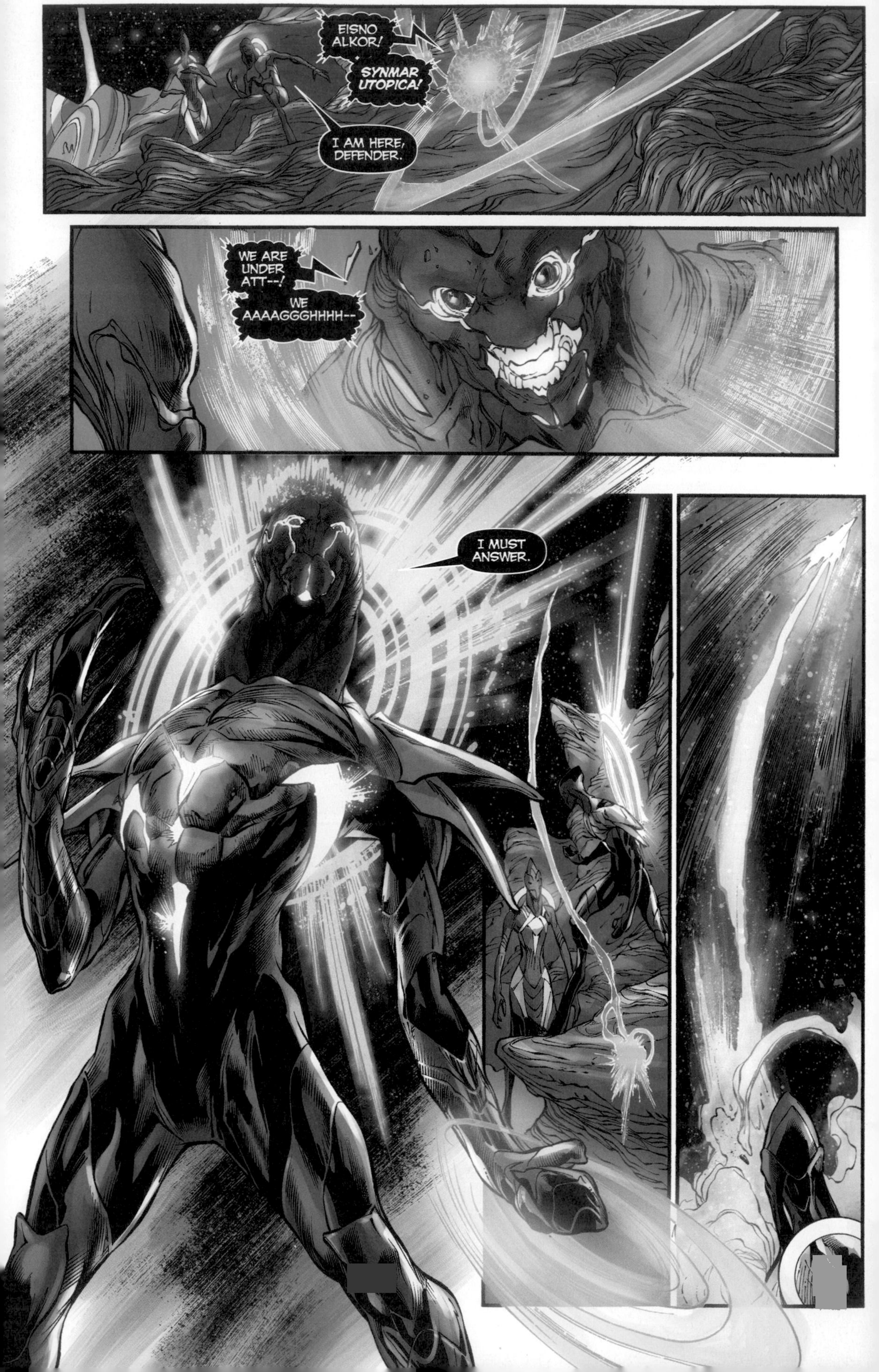

EISNO ALKOR!
SYNMAR UTOPICA!
I AM HERE, DEFENDER.
WE ARE UNDER ATT--!
WE AAAAGGGHHHH--
I MUST ANSWER.

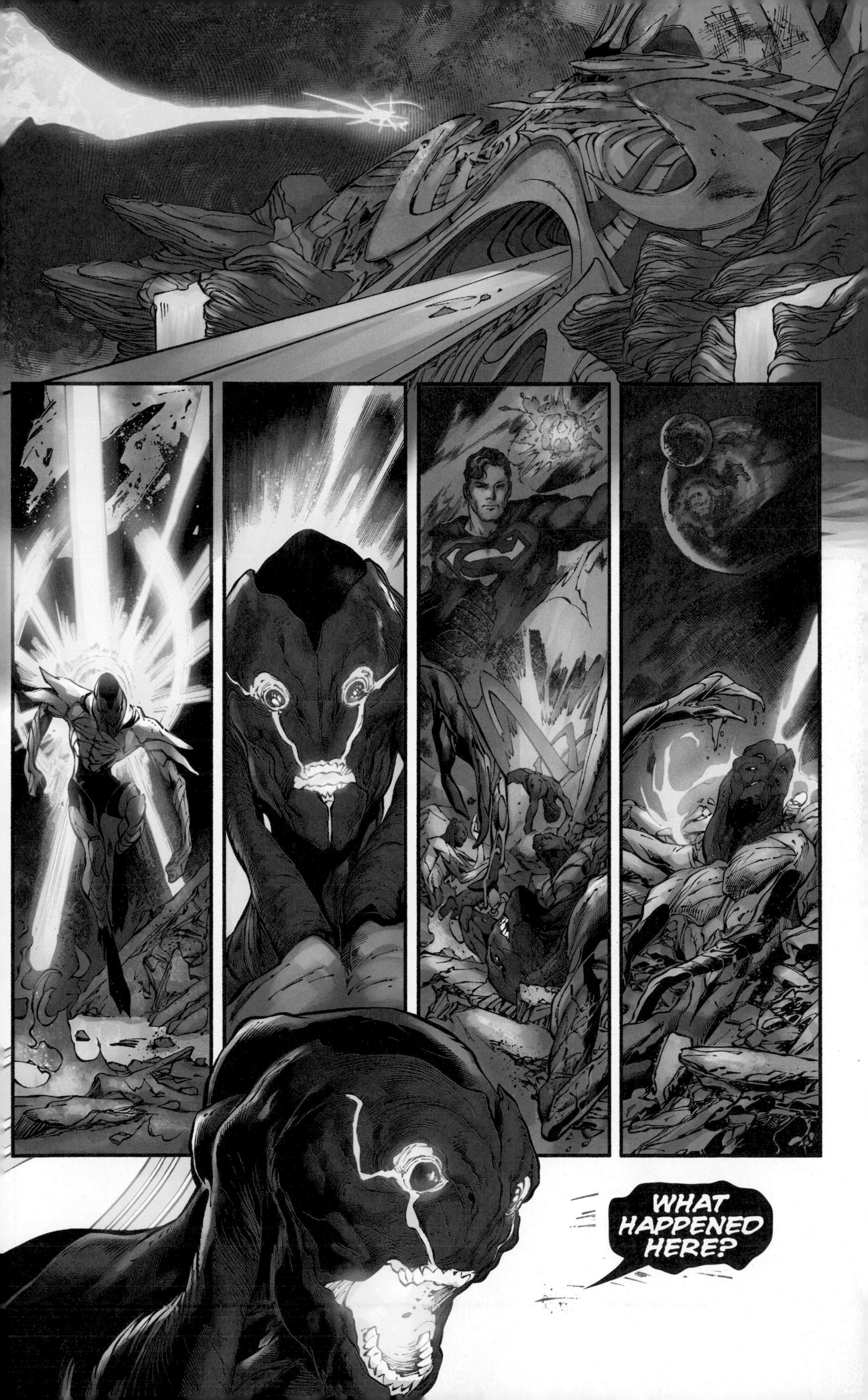
WHAT HAPPENED HERE?

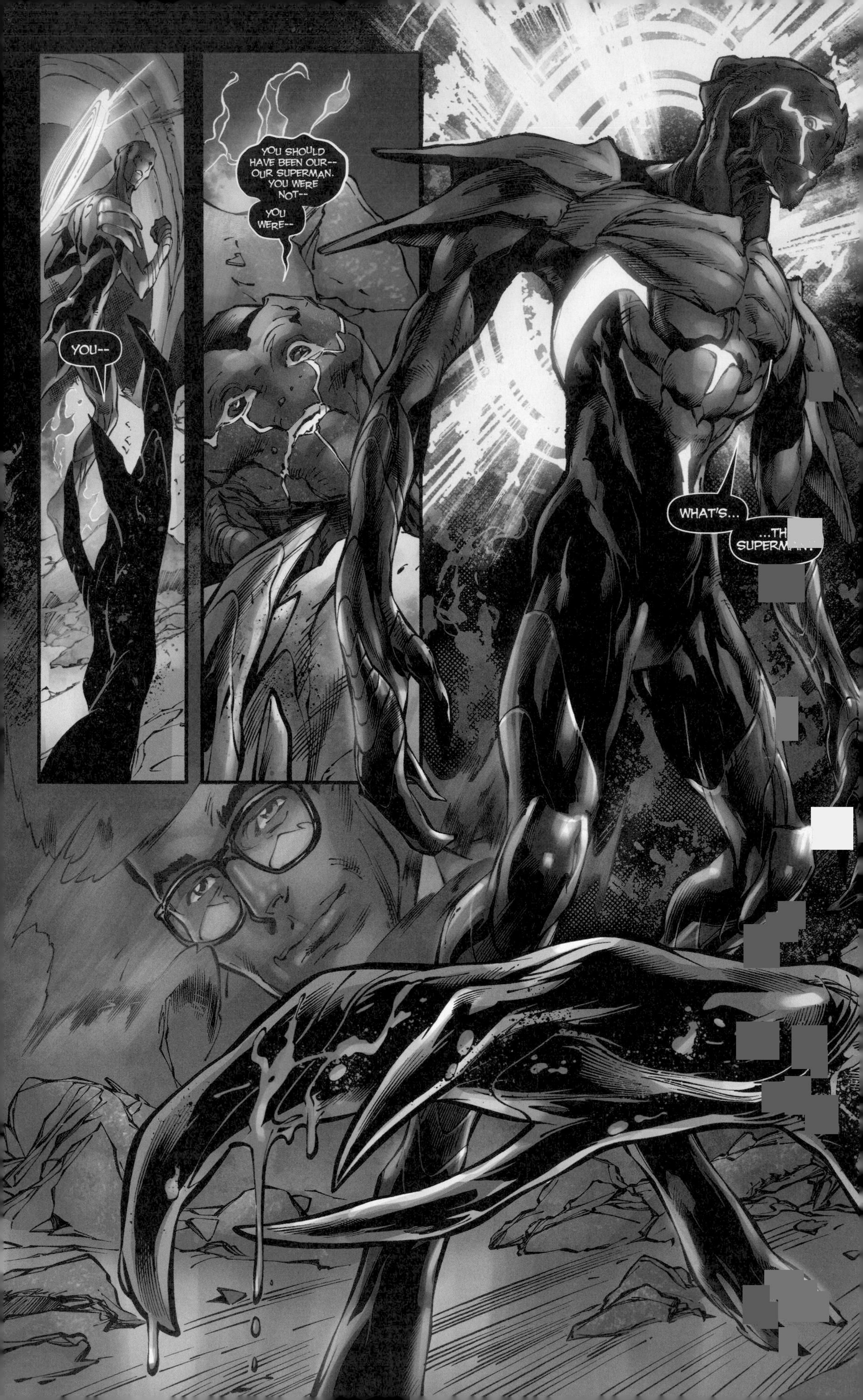
YOU--
YOU SHOULD HAVE BEEN OUR-- OUR SUPERMAN. YOU WERE NOT--
YOU WERE--
WHAT'S...
...TH
SUPERM

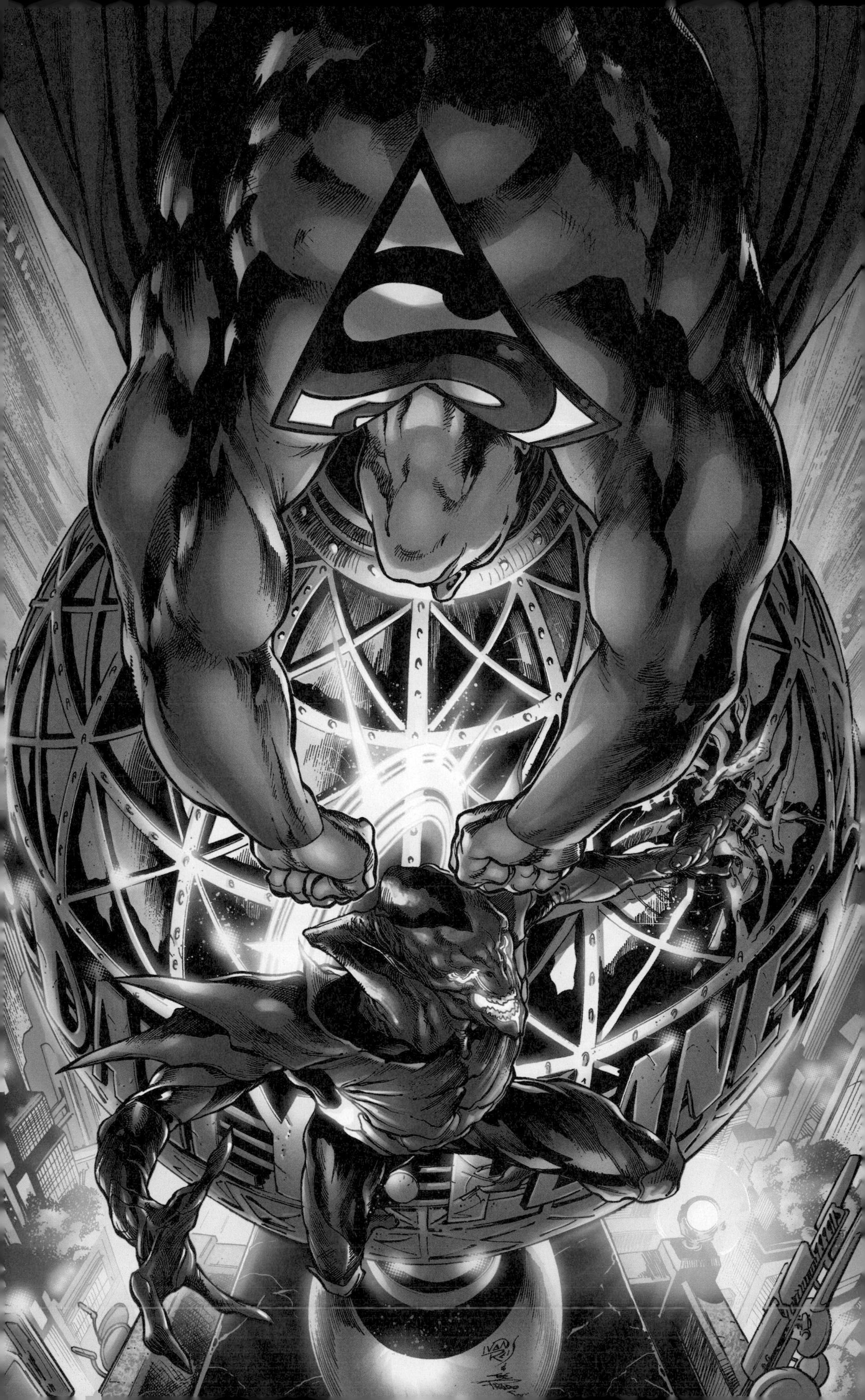

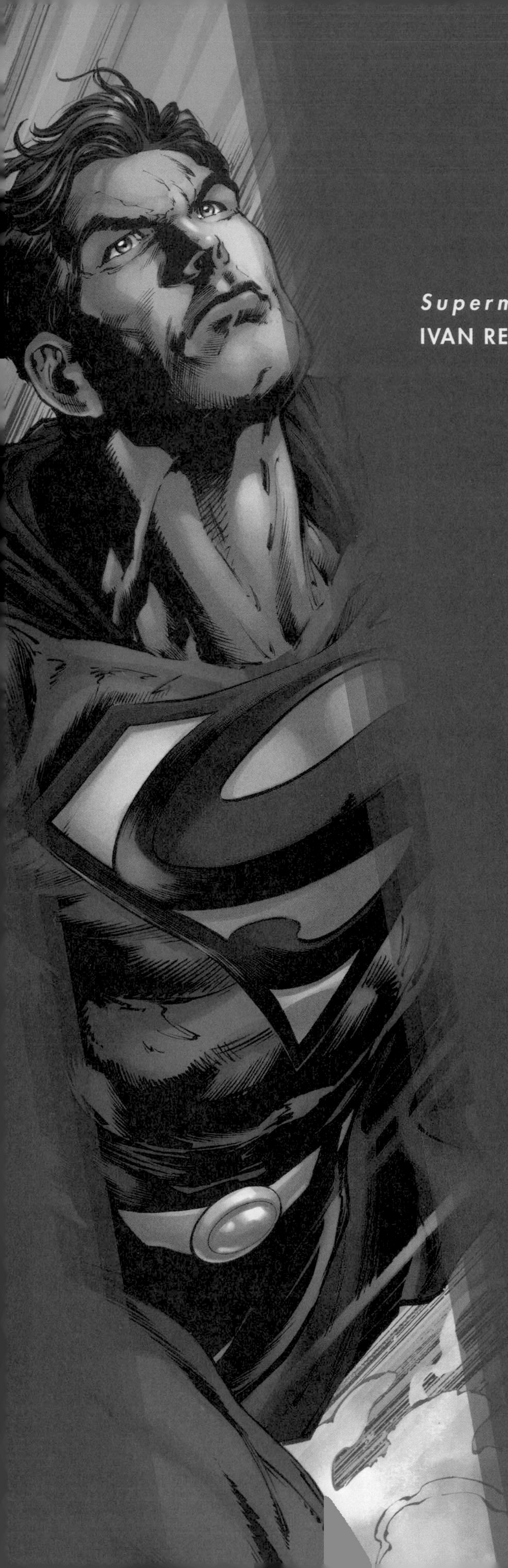

Superman #26 main cover by
IVAN REIS | JOE PRADO | ALEX SINCLAIR

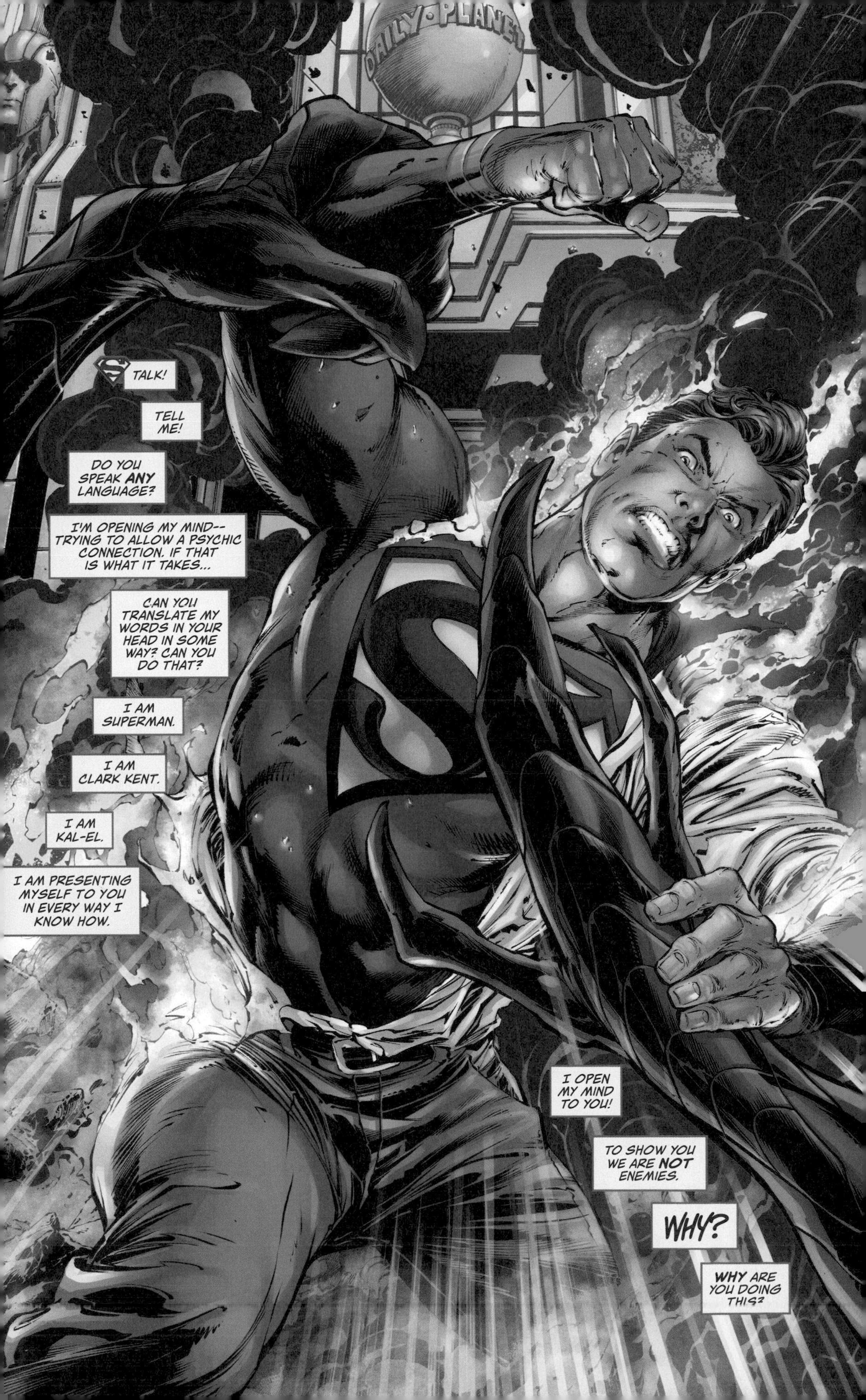
DAILY PLANET
TALK!
TELL ME!
DO YOU SPEAK ANY LANGUAGE?
I'M OPENING MY MIND-- TRYING TO ALLOW A PSYCHIC CONNECTION. IF THAT IS WHAT IT TAKES...
CAN YOU TRANSLATE MY WORDS IN YOUR HEAD IN SOME WAY? CAN YOU DO THAT?
I AM SUPERMAN.
I AM CLARK KENT.
I AM KAL-EL.
I AM PRESENTING MYSELF TO YOU IN EVERY WAY I KNOW HOW.
I OPEN MY MIND TO YOU!
TO SHOW YOU WE ARE NOT ENEMIES.
WHY?
WHY ARE YOU DOING THIS?

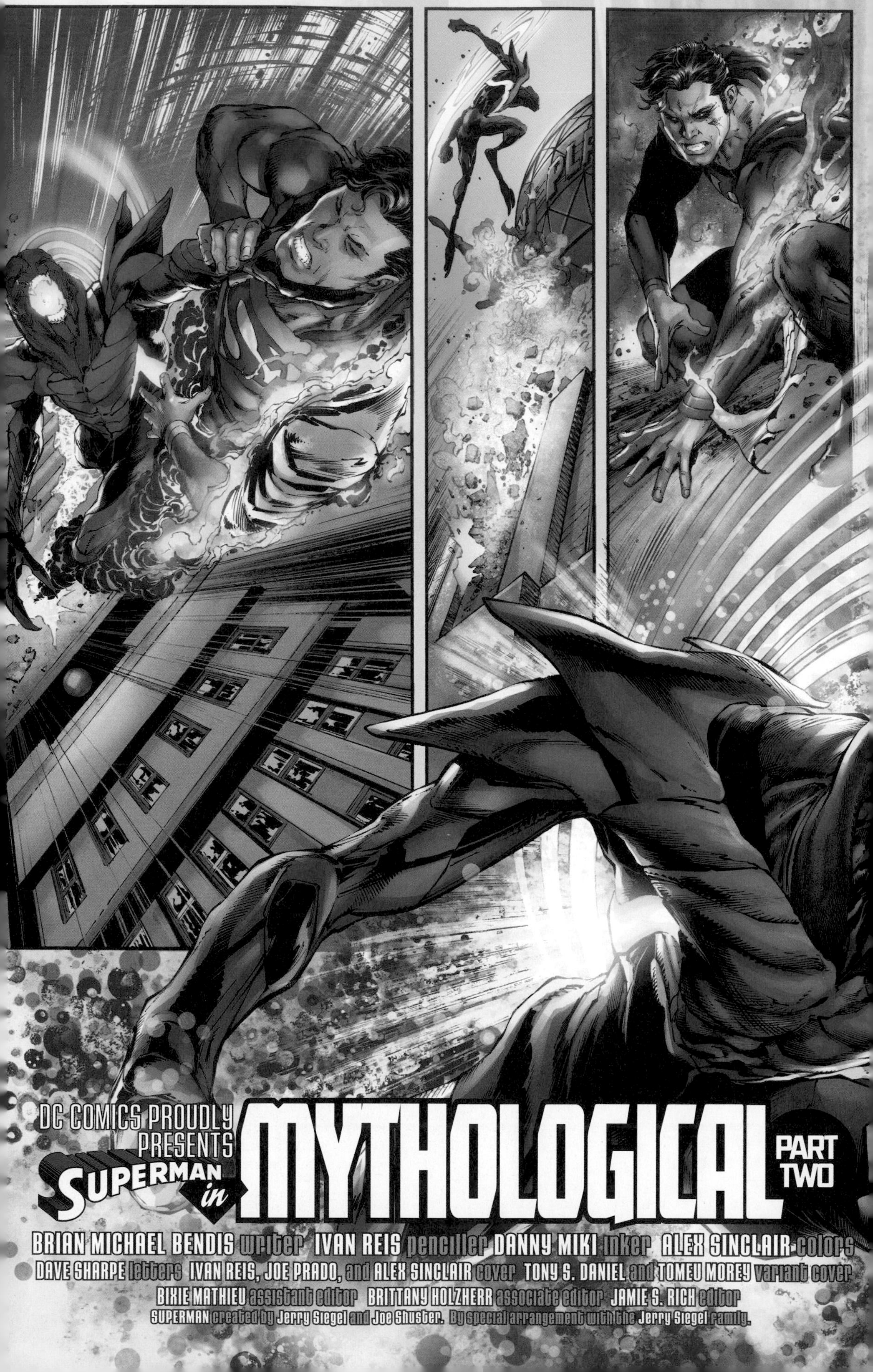
DC COMICS PROUDLY PRESENTS
SUPERMAN in
MYTHOLOGICAL
PART TWO
BRIAN MICHAEL BENDIS writer IVAN REIS penciller DANNY MIKI inker ALEX SINCLAIR colors
DAVE SHARPE letters IVAN REIS, JOE PRADO, and ALEX SINCLAIR cover TONY S. DANIEL and TOMEU MOREY variant cover
BIXIE MATHIEU assistant editor BRITTANY HOLZHERR associate editor JAMIE S. RICH editor
SUPERMAN created by Jerry Siegel and Joe Shuster. By special arrangement with the Jerry Siegel family.

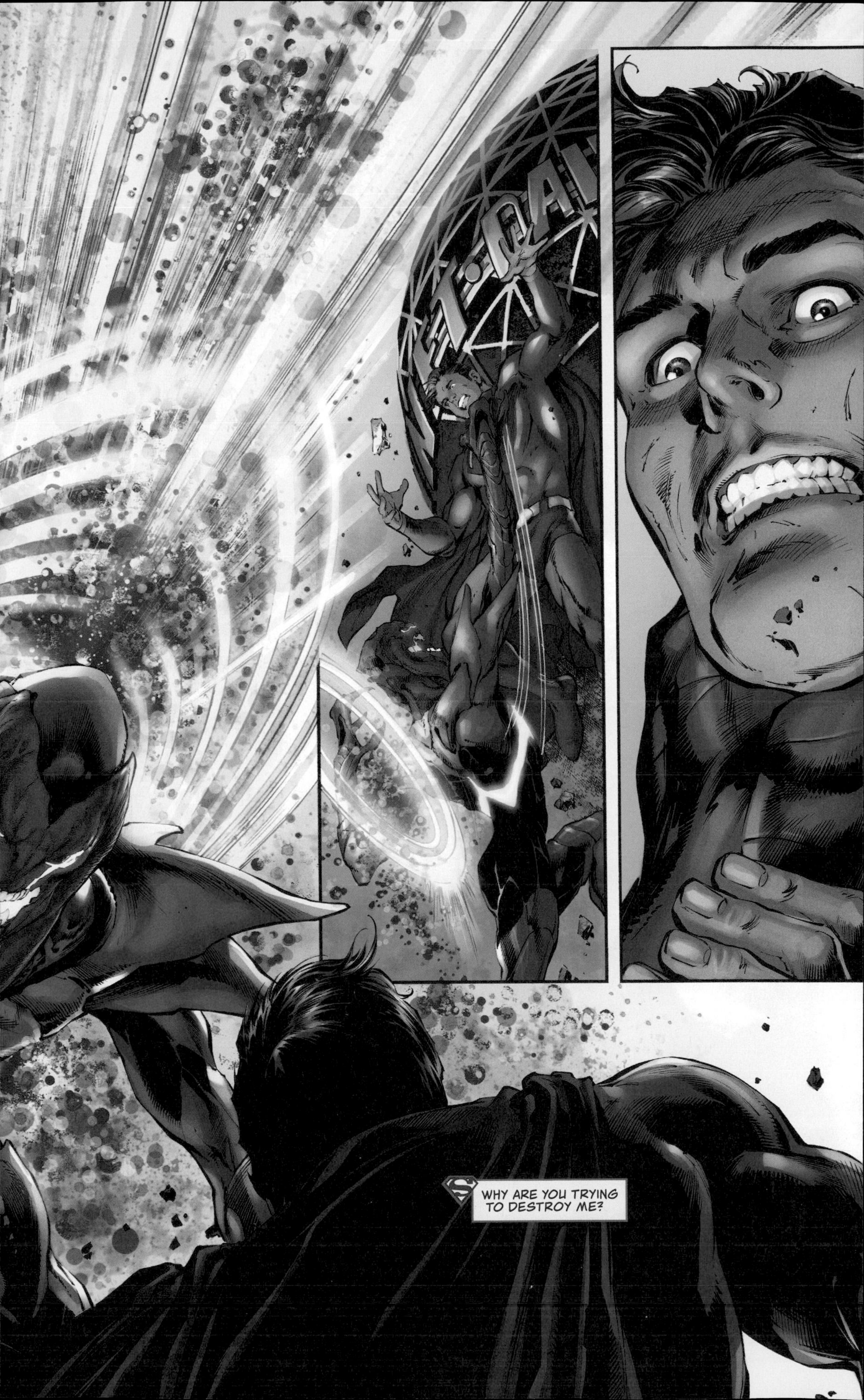
WHY ARE YOU TRYING TO DESTROY ME?

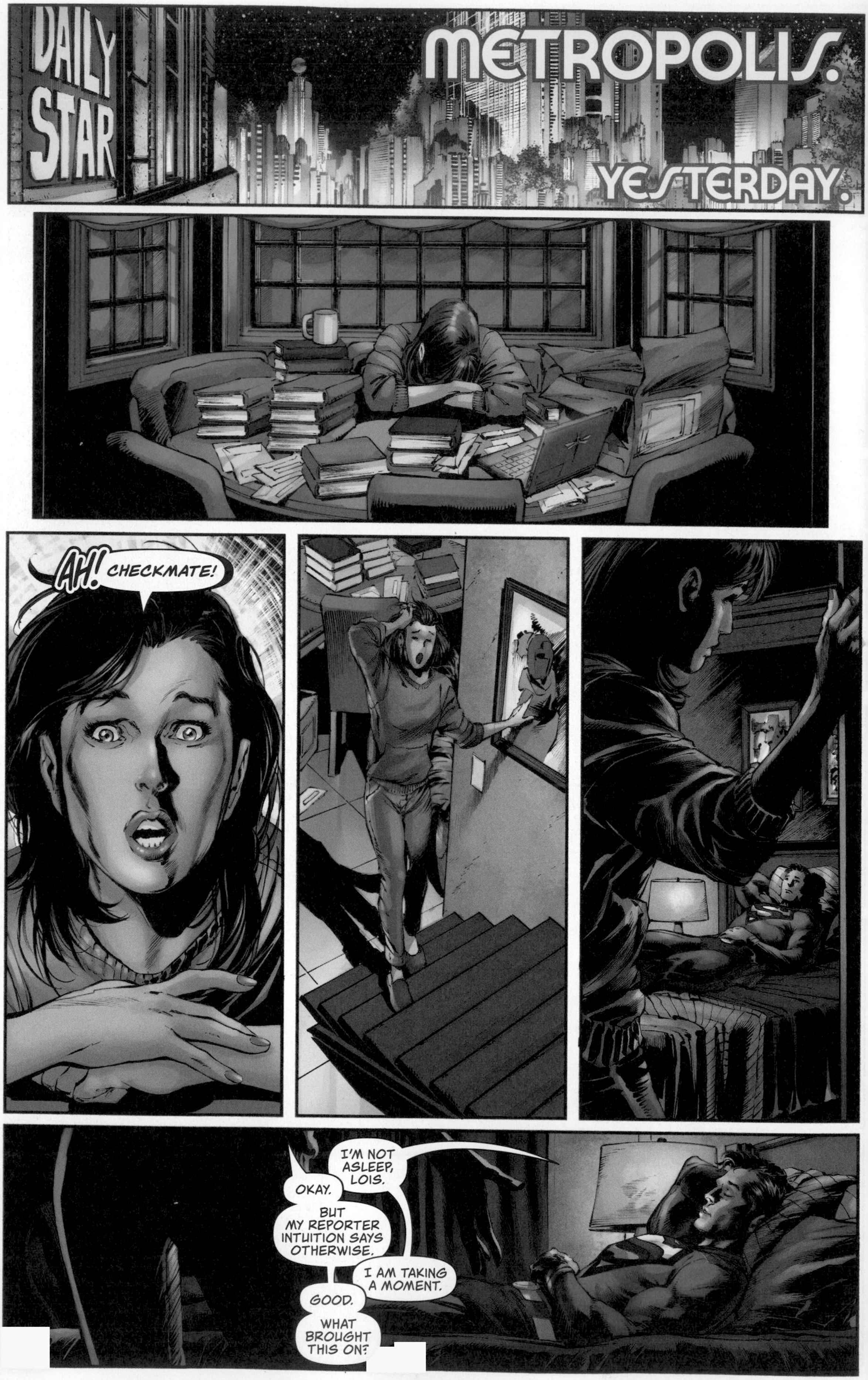
DAILY STAR
METROPOLIS.
YESTERDAY.
AH! CHECKMATE!
I'M NOT ASLEEP, LOIS.
OKAY.
BUT MY REPORTER INTUITION SAYS OTHERWISE.
I AM TAKING A MOMENT.
GOOD.
WHAT BROUGHT THIS ON?

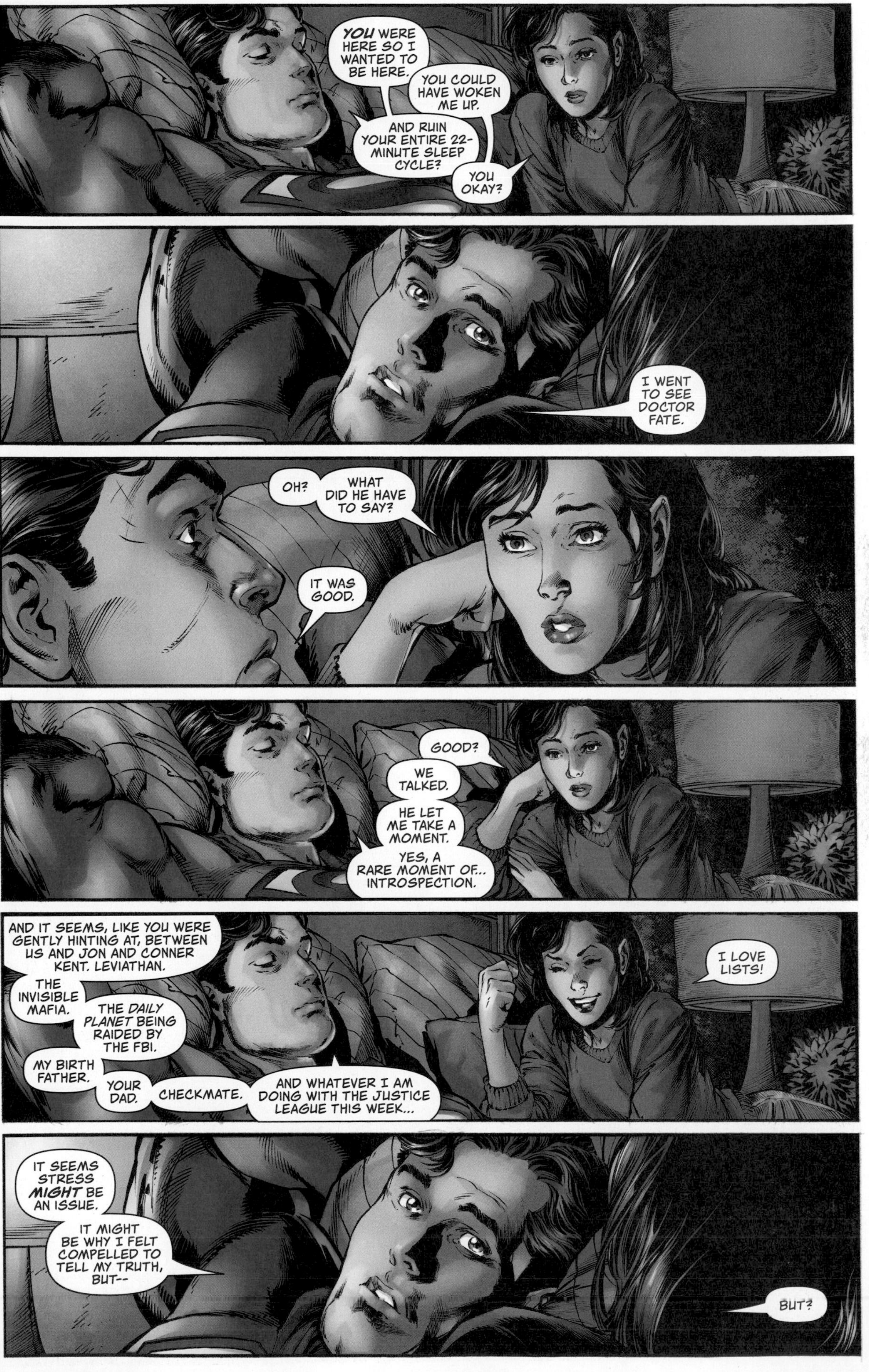
YOU WERE HERE SO I WANTED TO BE HERE.
YOU COULD HAVE WOKEN ME UP.
AND RUIN YOUR ENTIRE 22-MINUTE SLEEP CYCLE?
YOU OKAY?
I WENT TO SEE DOCTOR FATE.
OH?
WHAT DID HE HAVE TO SAY?
IT WAS GOOD.
GOOD?
WE TALKED.
HE LET ME TAKE A MOMENT.
YES, A RARE MOMENT OF... INTROSPECTION.
AND IT SEEMS, LIKE YOU WERE GENTLY HINTING AT, BETWEEN US AND JON AND CONNER KENT. LEVIATHAN.
THE INVISIBLE MAFIA.
THE *DAILY PLANET* BEING RAIDED BY THE FBI.
MY BIRTH FATHER.
YOUR DAD.
CHECKMATE.
AND WHATEVER I AM DOING WITH THE JUSTICE LEAGUE THIS WEEK...
I LOVE LISTS!
IT SEEMS STRESS **MIGHT** BE AN ISSUE.
IT MIGHT BE WHY I FELT COMPELLED TO TELL MY TRUTH, BUT--
BUT?

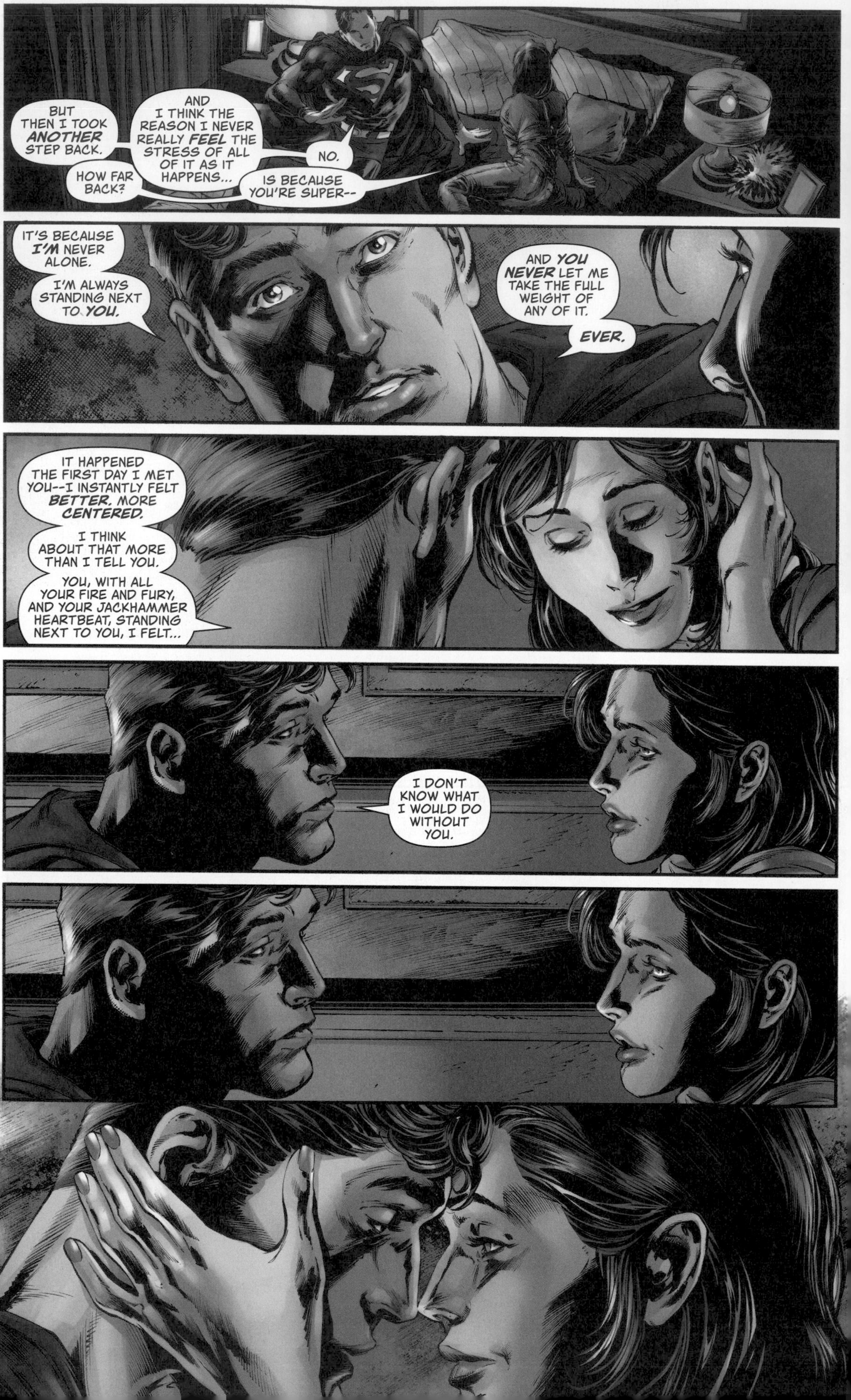

BUT THEN I TOOK ANOTHER STEP BACK.
AND I THINK THE REASON I NEVER REALLY FEEL THE STRESS OF ALL OF IT AS IT HAPPENS...
NO.
HOW FAR BACK?
IS BECAUSE YOU'RE SUPER--
IT'S BECAUSE I'M NEVER ALONE.
I'M ALWAYS STANDING NEXT TO YOU.
AND YOU NEVER LET ME TAKE THE FULL WEIGHT OF ANY OF IT.
EVER.
IT HAPPENED THE FIRST DAY I MET YOU--I INSTANTLY FELT BETTER. MORE CENTERED.
I THINK ABOUT THAT MORE THAN I TELL YOU.
YOU, WITH ALL YOUR FIRE AND FURY, AND YOUR JACKHAMMER HEARTBEAT, STANDING NEXT TO YOU, I FELT...
I DON'T KNOW WHAT I WOULD DO WITHOUT YOU.

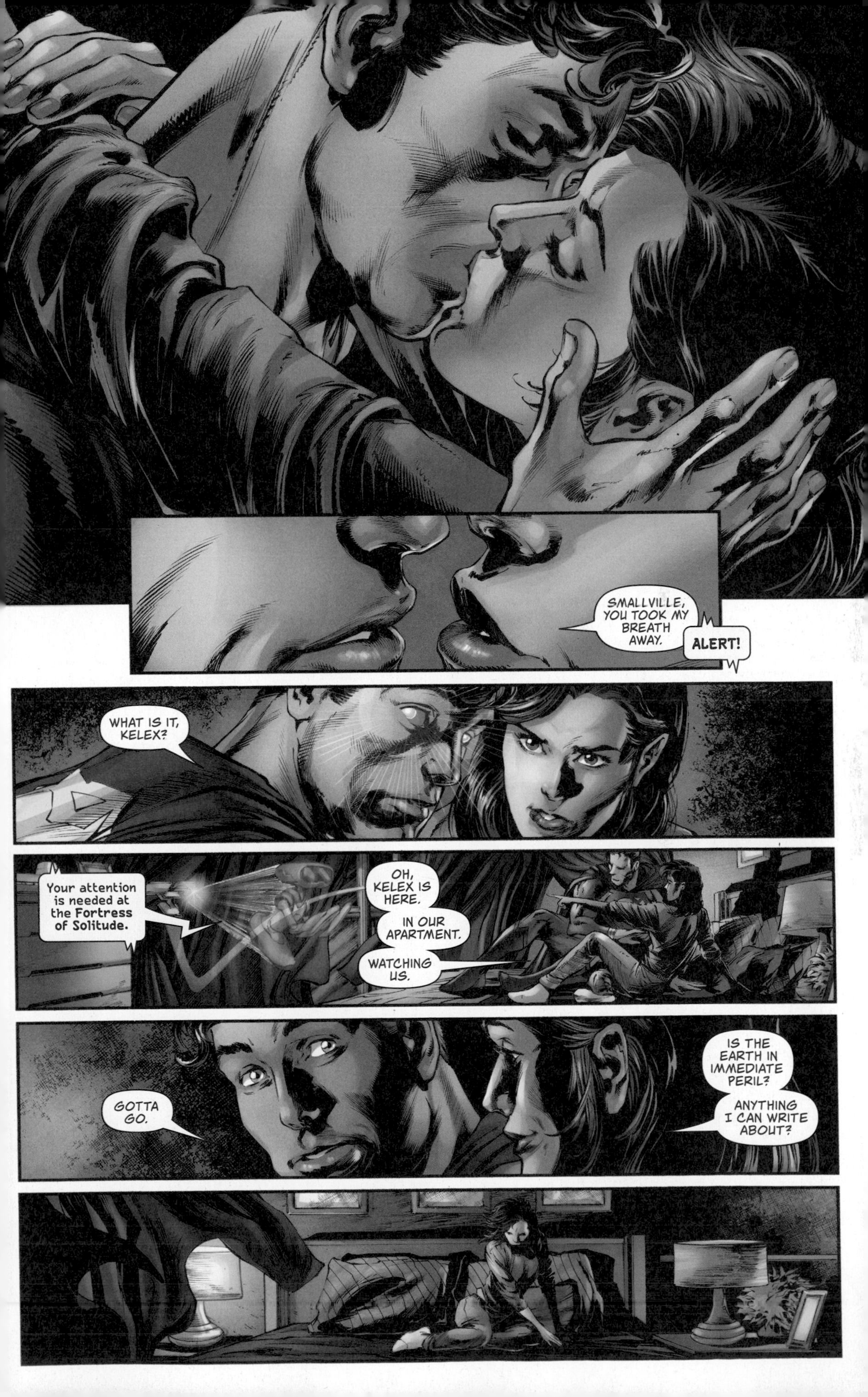
SMALLVILLE, YOU TOOK MY BREATH AWAY.
ALERT!
WHAT IS IT, KELEX?
Your attention is needed at the Fortress of Solitude.
OH, KELEX IS HERE.
IN OUR APARTMENT.
WATCHING US.
GOTTA GO.
IS THE EARTH IN IMMEDIATE PERIL?
ANYTHING I CAN WRITE ABOUT?

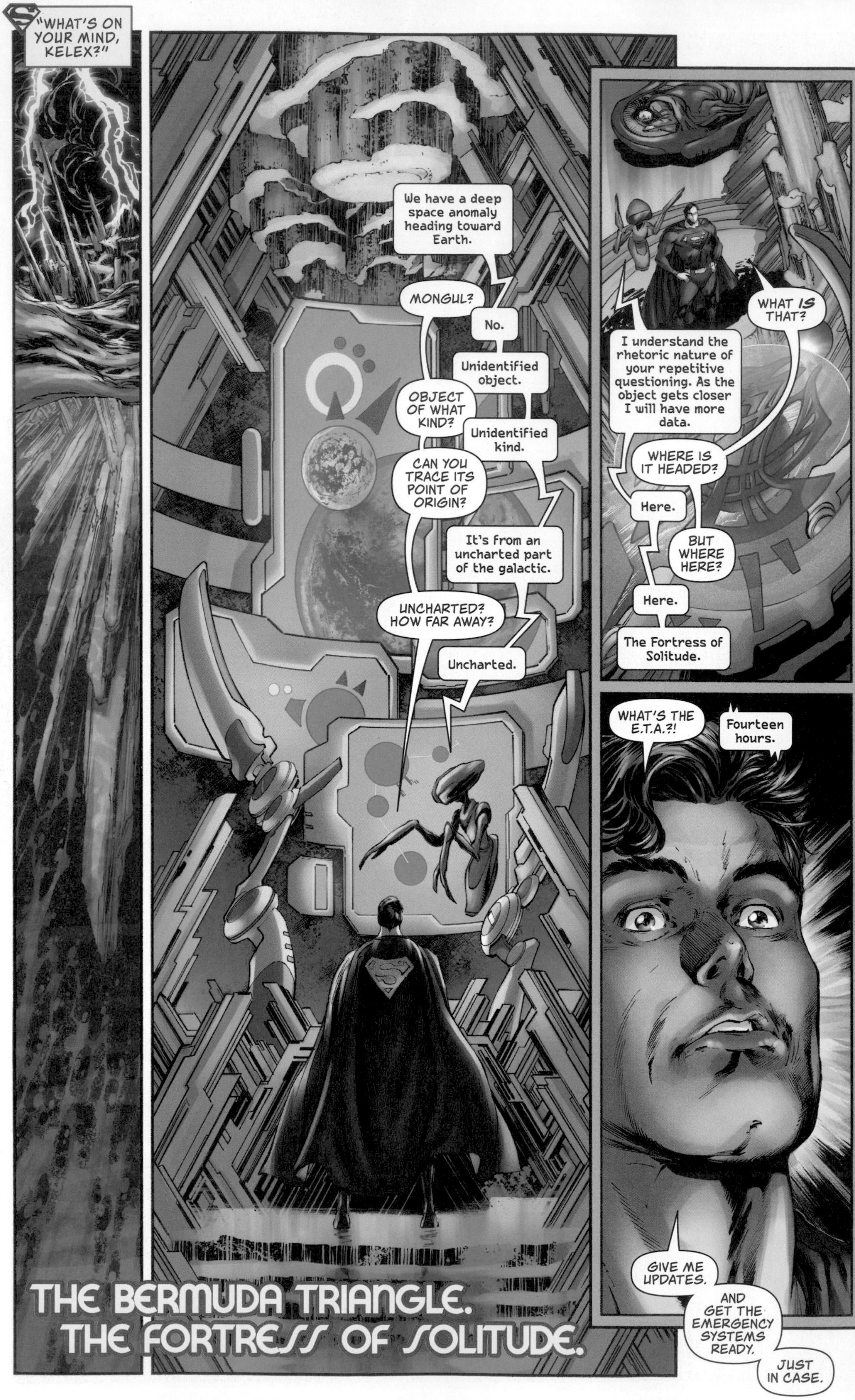
"WHAT'S ON YOUR MIND, KELEX?"
We have a deep space anomaly heading toward Earth.
MONGUL?
No.
Unidentified object.
OBJECT OF WHAT KIND?
Unidentified kind.
CAN YOU TRACE ITS POINT OF ORIGIN?
It's from an uncharted part of the galactic.
UNCHARTED? HOW FAR AWAY?
Uncharted.
THE BERMUDA TRIANGLE. THE FORTRESS OF SOLITUDE.
WHAT IS THAT?
I understand the rhetoric nature of your repetitive questioning. As the object gets closer I will have more data.
WHERE IS IT HEADED?
Here.
BUT WHERE HERE?
Here.
The Fortress of Solitude.
WHAT'S THE E.T.A.?!
Fourteen hours.
GIVE ME UPDATES.
AND GET THE EMERGENCY SYSTEMS READY.
JUST IN CASE.

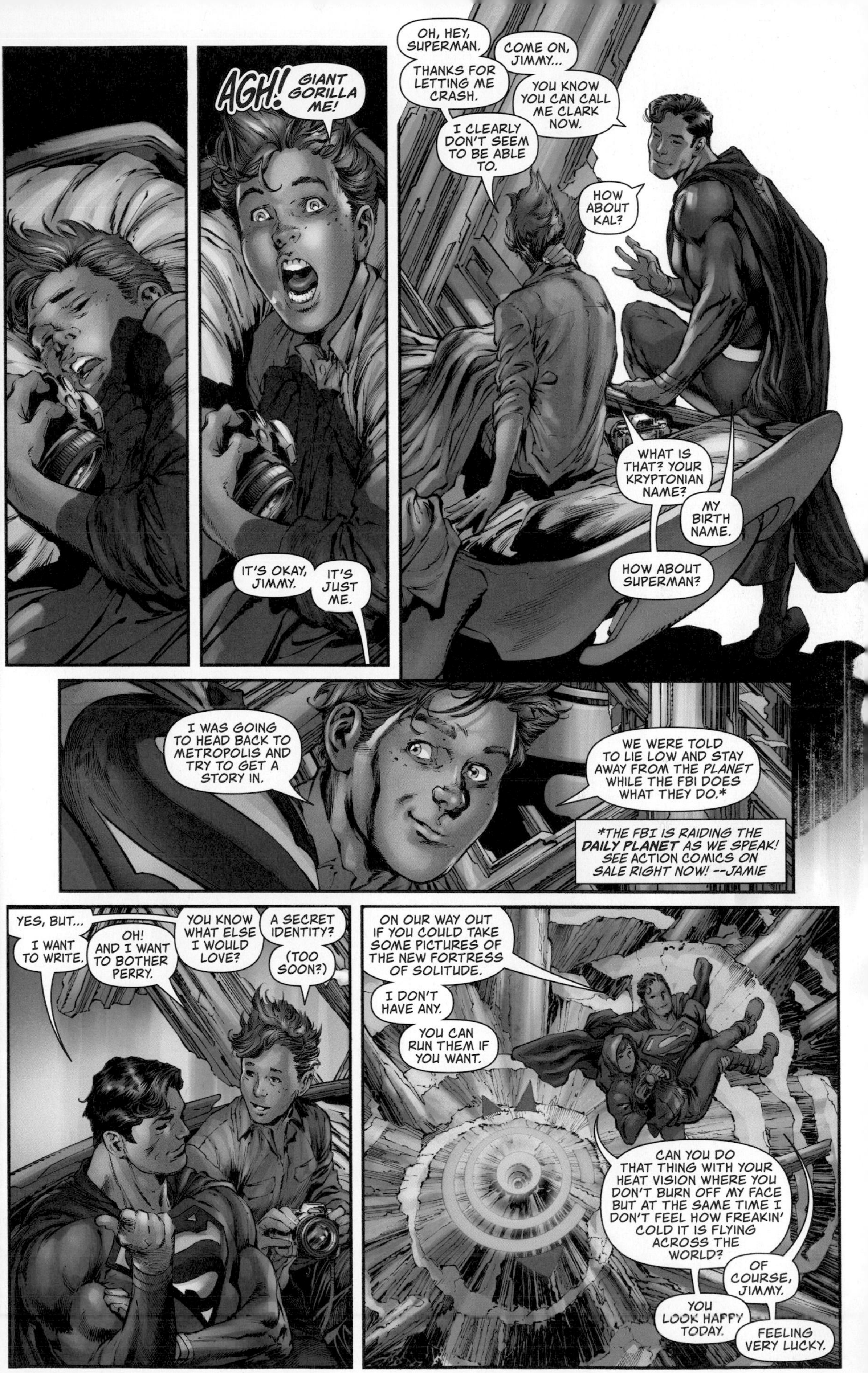
AGH! GIANT GORILLA ME!
IT'S OKAY, JIMMY.
IT'S JUST ME.
OH, HEY, SUPERMAN.
THANKS FOR LETTING ME CRASH.
I CLEARLY DON'T SEEM TO BE ABLE TO.
COME ON, JIMMY...
YOU KNOW YOU CAN CALL ME CLARK NOW.
HOW ABOUT KAL?
WHAT IS THAT? YOUR KRYPTONIAN NAME?
MY BIRTH NAME.
HOW ABOUT SUPERMAN?
I WAS GOING TO HEAD BACK TO METROPOLIS AND TRY TO GET A STORY IN.
WE WERE TOLD TO LIE LOW AND STAY AWAY FROM THE PLANET WHILE THE FBI DOES WHAT THEY DO.*
*THE FBI IS RAIDING THE DAILY PLANET AS WE SPEAK! SEE ACTION COMICS ON SALE RIGHT NOW! --JAMIE
YES, BUT...
I WANT TO WRITE.
OH! AND I WANT TO BOTHER PERRY.
YOU KNOW WHAT ELSE I WOULD LOVE?
A SECRET IDENTITY?
(TOO SOON?)
ON OUR WAY OUT IF YOU COULD TAKE SOME PICTURES OF THE NEW FORTRESS OF SOLITUDE.
I DON'T HAVE ANY.
YOU CAN RUN THEM IF YOU WANT.
CAN YOU DO THAT THING WITH YOUR HEAT VISION WHERE YOU DON'T BURN OFF MY FACE BUT AT THE SAME TIME I DON'T FEEL HOW FREAKIN' COLD IT IS FLYING ACROSS THE WORLD?
OF COURSE, JIMMY.
YOU LOOK HAPPY TODAY.
FEELING VERY LUCKY.

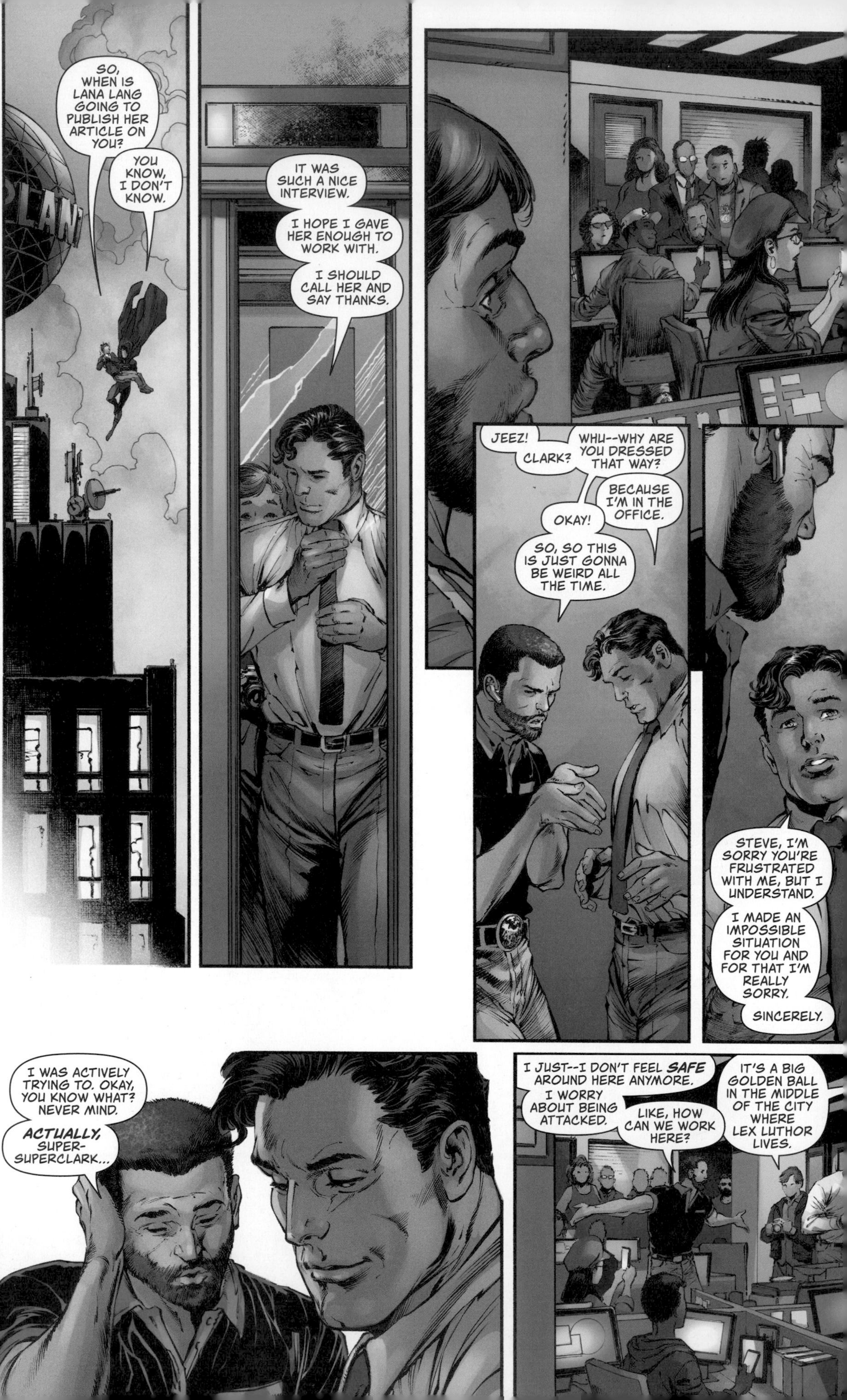
SO, WHEN IS LANA LANG GOING TO PUBLISH HER ARTICLE ON YOU?
YOU KNOW, I DON'T KNOW.
IT WAS SUCH A NICE INTERVIEW.
I HOPE I GAVE HER ENOUGH TO WORK WITH.
I SHOULD CALL HER AND SAY THANKS.
JEEZ!
CLARK?
WHU--WHY ARE YOU DRESSED THAT WAY?
BECAUSE I'M IN THE OFFICE.
OKAY!
SO, SO THIS IS JUST GONNA BE WEIRD ALL THE TIME.
STEVE, I'M SORRY YOU'RE FRUSTRATED WITH ME, BUT I UNDERSTAND.
I MADE AN IMPOSSIBLE SITUATION FOR YOU AND FOR THAT I'M REALLY SORRY.
SINCERELY.
I WAS ACTIVELY TRYING TO. OKAY, YOU KNOW WHAT? NEVER MIND.
ACTUALLY, SUPER-SUPERCLARK...
I JUST--I DON'T FEEL SAFE AROUND HERE ANYMORE.
I WORRY ABOUT BEING ATTACKED.
LIKE, HOW CAN WE WORK HERE?
IT'S A BIG GOLDEN BALL IN THE MIDDLE OF THE CITY WHERE LEX LUTHOR LIVES.

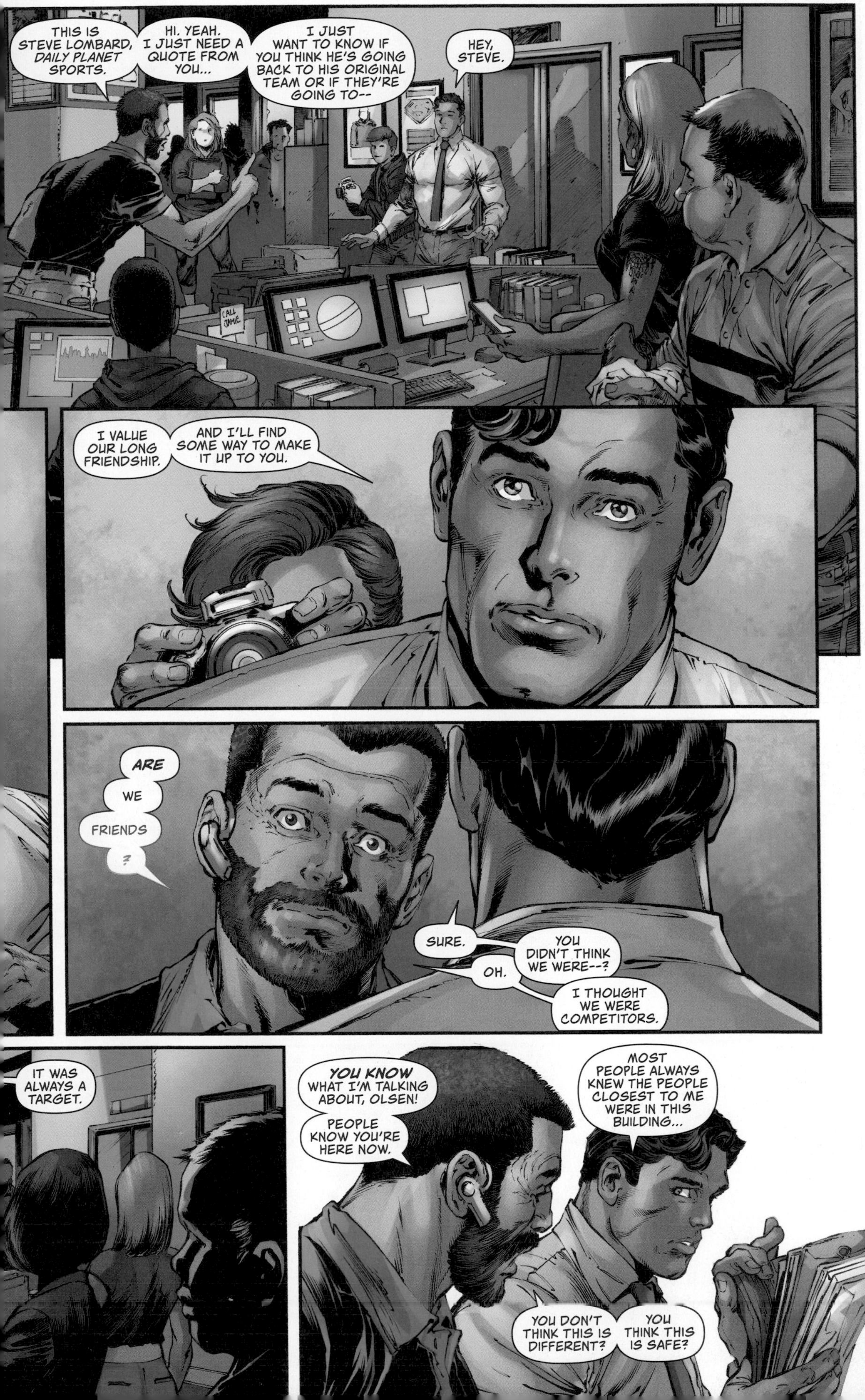
THIS IS STEVE LOMBARD, DAILY PLANET SPORTS.
HI. YEAH. I JUST NEED A QUOTE FROM YOU...
I JUST WANT TO KNOW IF YOU THINK HE'S GOING BACK TO HIS ORIGINAL TEAM OR IF THEY'RE GOING TO--
HEY, STEVE.
CALL JAMIE
I VALUE OUR LONG FRIENDSHIP.
AND I'LL FIND SOME WAY TO MAKE IT UP TO YOU.
ARE WE FRIENDS ?
SURE.
YOU DIDN'T THINK WE WERE--?
OH.
I THOUGHT WE WERE COMPETITORS.
IT WAS ALWAYS A TARGET.
YOU KNOW WHAT I'M TALKING ABOUT, OLSEN!
PEOPLE KNOW YOU'RE HERE NOW.
MOST PEOPLE ALWAYS KNEW THE PEOPLE CLOSEST TO ME WERE IN THIS BUILDING...
YOU DON'T THINK THIS IS DIFFERENT?
YOU THINK THIS IS SAFE?

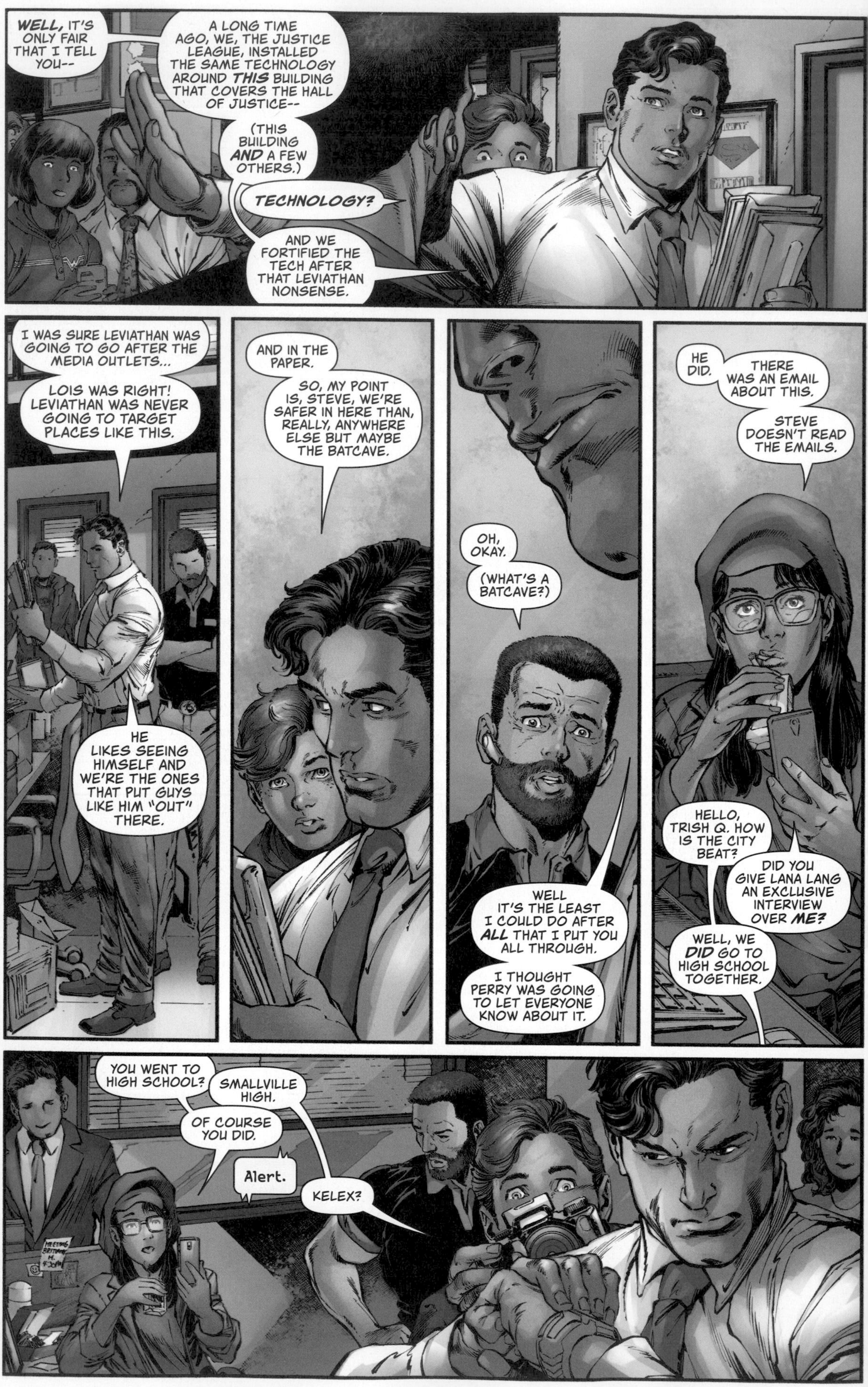
WELL, IT'S ONLY FAIR THAT I TELL YOU--
A LONG TIME AGO, WE, THE JUSTICE LEAGUE, INSTALLED THE SAME TECHNOLOGY AROUND THIS BUILDING THAT COVERS THE HALL OF JUSTICE--
(THIS BUILDING AND A FEW OTHERS.)
TECHNOLOGY?
AND WE FORTIFIED THE TECH AFTER THAT LEVIATHAN NONSENSE.
I WAS SURE LEVIATHAN WAS GOING TO GO AFTER THE MEDIA OUTLETS...
LOIS WAS RIGHT! LEVIATHAN WAS NEVER GOING TO TARGET PLACES LIKE THIS.
HE LIKES SEEING HIMSELF AND WE'RE THE ONES THAT PUT GUYS LIKE HIM "OUT" THERE.
AND IN THE PAPER.
SO, MY POINT IS, STEVE, WE'RE SAFER IN HERE THAN, REALLY, ANYWHERE ELSE BUT MAYBE THE BATCAVE.
OH, OKAY.
(WHAT'S A BATCAVE?)
WELL IT'S THE LEAST I COULD DO AFTER ALL THAT I PUT YOU ALL THROUGH.
I THOUGHT PERRY WAS GOING TO LET EVERYONE KNOW ABOUT IT.
HE DID.
THERE WAS AN EMAIL ABOUT THIS.
STEVE DOESN'T READ THE EMAILS.
HELLO, TRISH Q. HOW IS THE CITY BEAT?
DID YOU GIVE LANA LANG AN EXCLUSIVE INTERVIEW OVER ME?
WELL, WE DID GO TO HIGH SCHOOL TOGETHER.
YOU WENT TO HIGH SCHOOL?
SMALLVILLE HIGH.
OF COURSE YOU DID.
Alert.
KELEX?

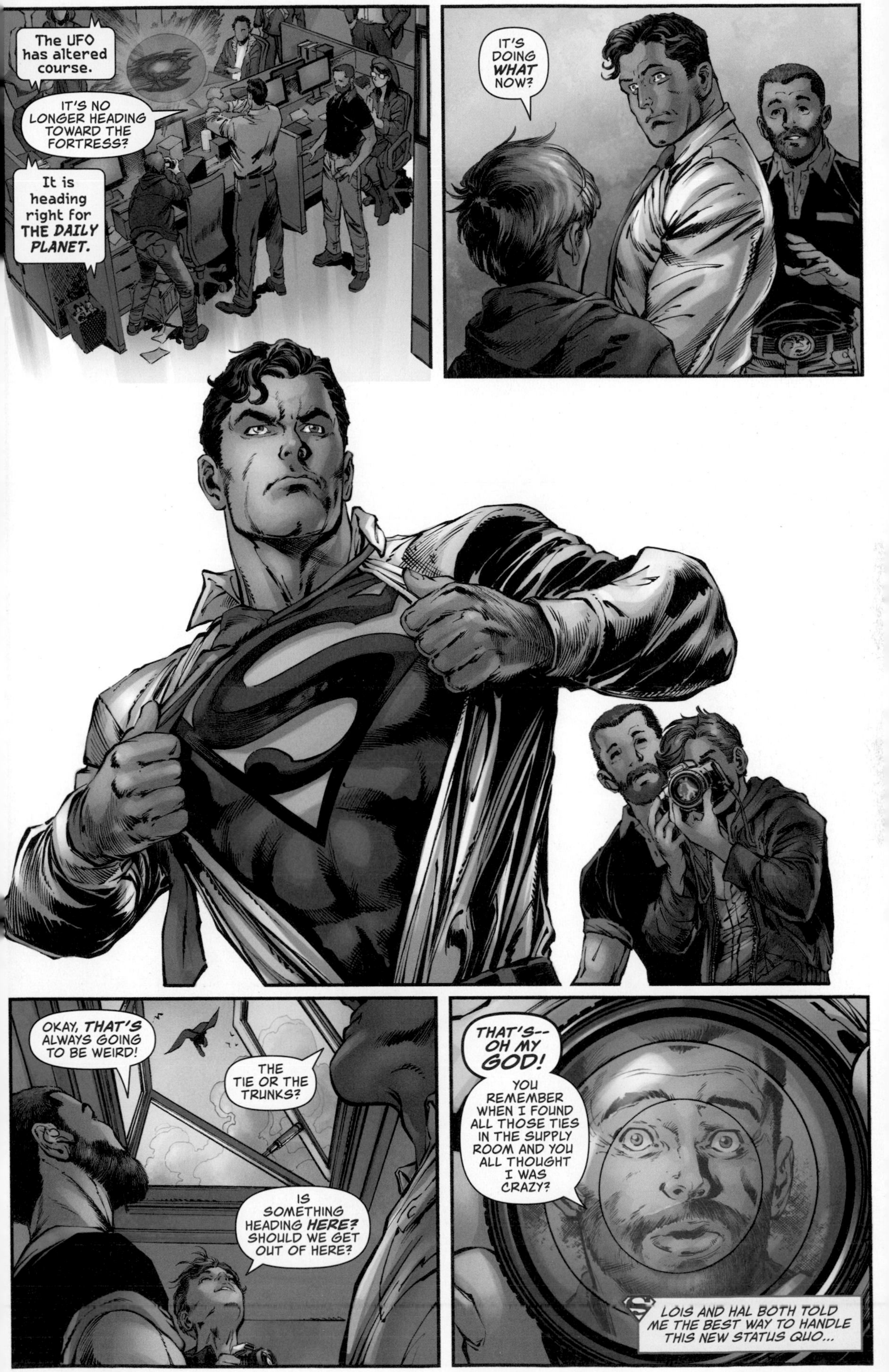
The UFO has altered course.
IT'S NO LONGER HEADING TOWARD THE FORTRESS?
It is heading right for THE DAILY PLANET.
IT'S DOING WHAT NOW?
OKAY, THAT'S ALWAYS GOING TO BE WEIRD!
THE TIE OR THE TRUNKS?
IS SOMETHING HEADING HERE? SHOULD WE GET OUT OF HERE?
THAT'S-- OH MY GOD!
YOU REMEMBER WHEN I FOUND ALL THOSE TIES IN THE SUPPLY ROOM AND YOU ALL THOUGHT I WAS CRAZY?
LOIS AND HAL BOTH TOLD ME THE BEST WAY TO HANDLE THIS NEW STATUS QUO...

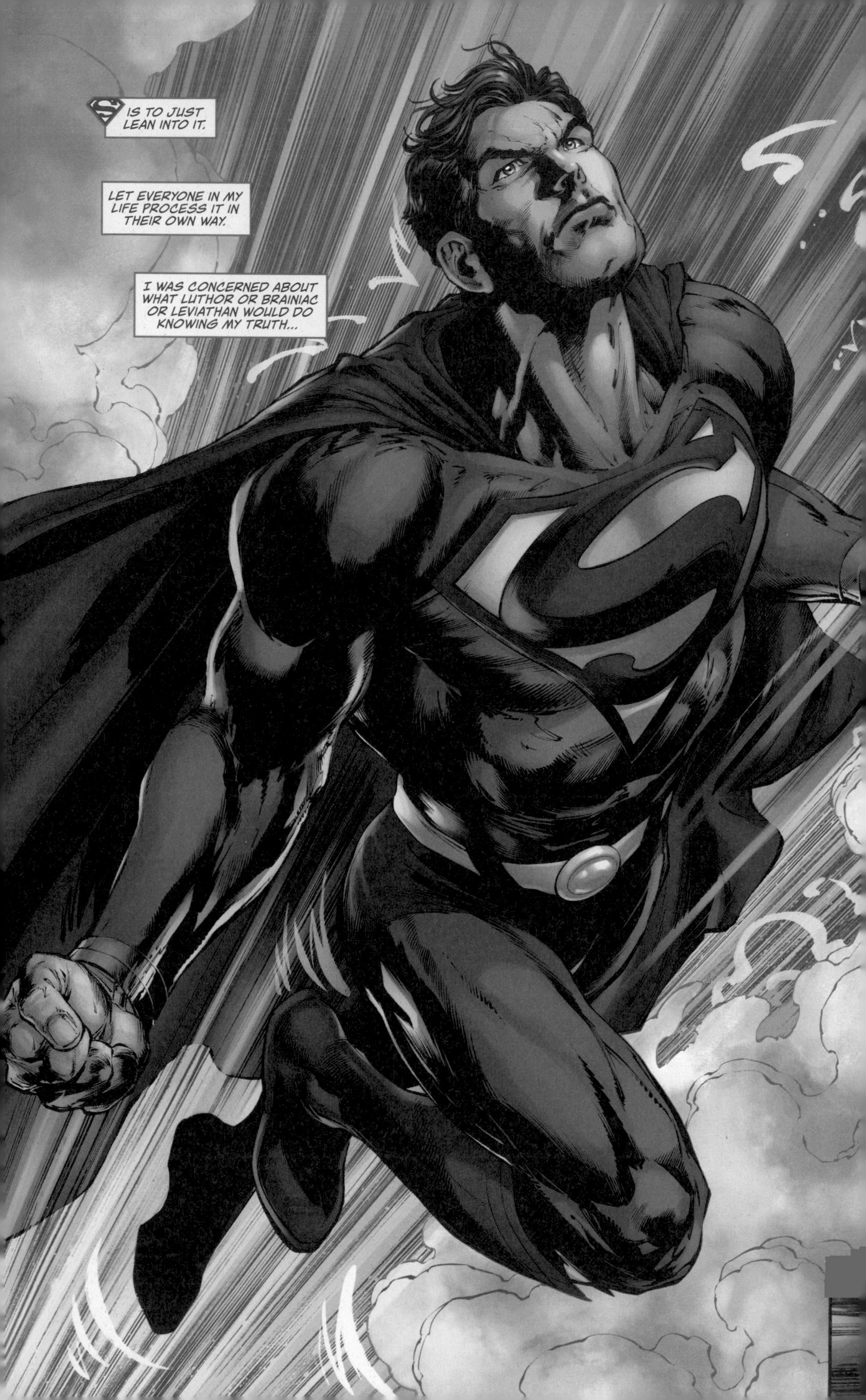
IS TO JUST LEAN INTO IT.
LET EVERYONE IN MY LIFE PROCESS IT IN THEIR OWN WAY.
I WAS CONCERNED ABOUT WHAT LUTHOR OR BRAINIAC OR LEVIATHAN WOULD DO KNOWING MY TRUTH...

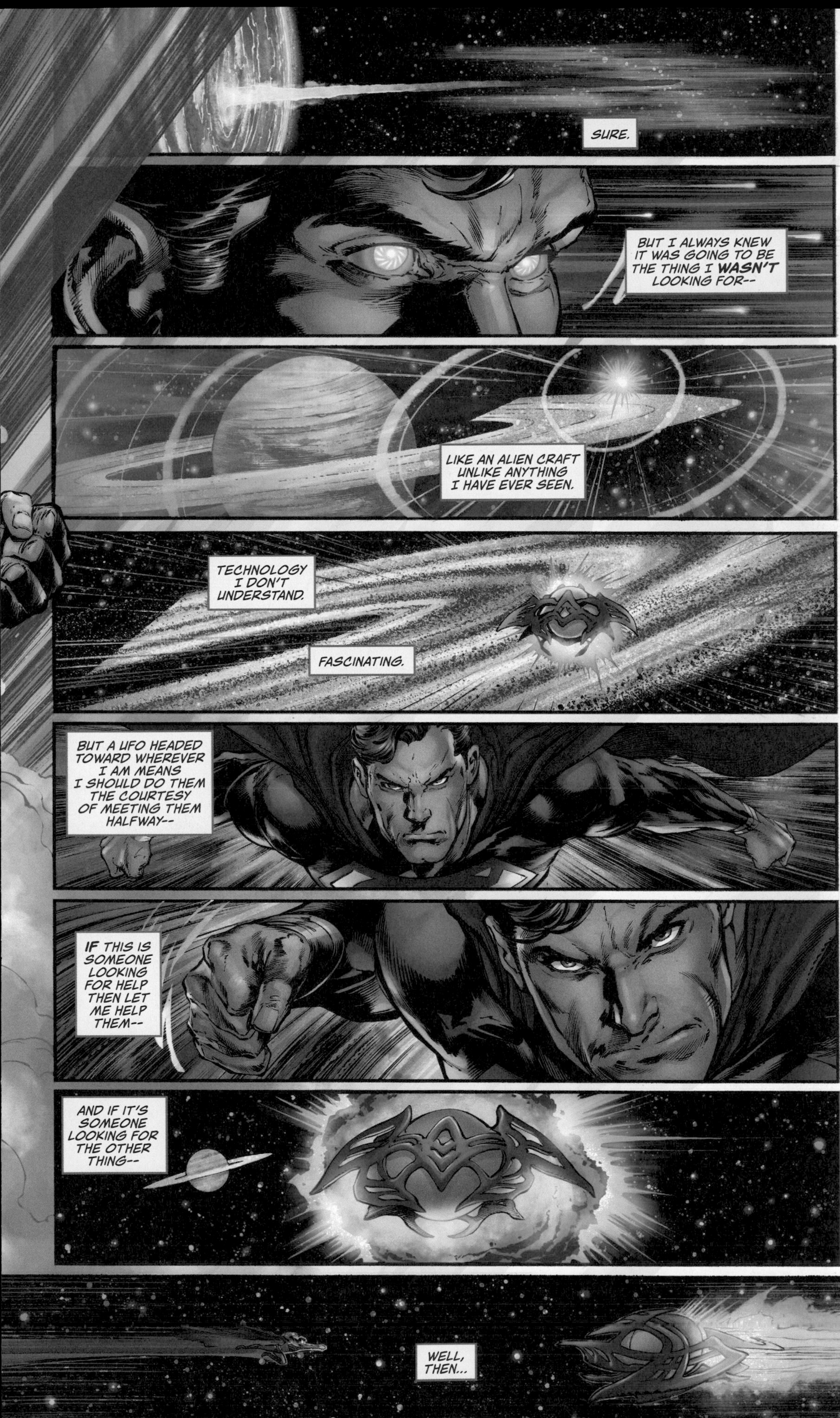
SURE.
BUT I ALWAYS KNEW IT WAS GOING TO BE THE THING I **WASN'T** LOOKING FOR--
LIKE AN ALIEN CRAFT UNLIKE ANYTHING I HAVE EVER SEEN.
TECHNOLOGY I DON'T UNDERSTAND.
FASCINATING.
BUT A UFO HEADED TOWARD WHEREVER I AM MEANS I SHOULD DO THEM THE COURTESY OF MEETING THEM HALFWAY--
IF THIS IS SOMEONE LOOKING FOR HELP THEN LET ME HELP THEM--
AND IF IT'S SOMEONE LOOKING FOR THE OTHER THING--
WELL, THEN...

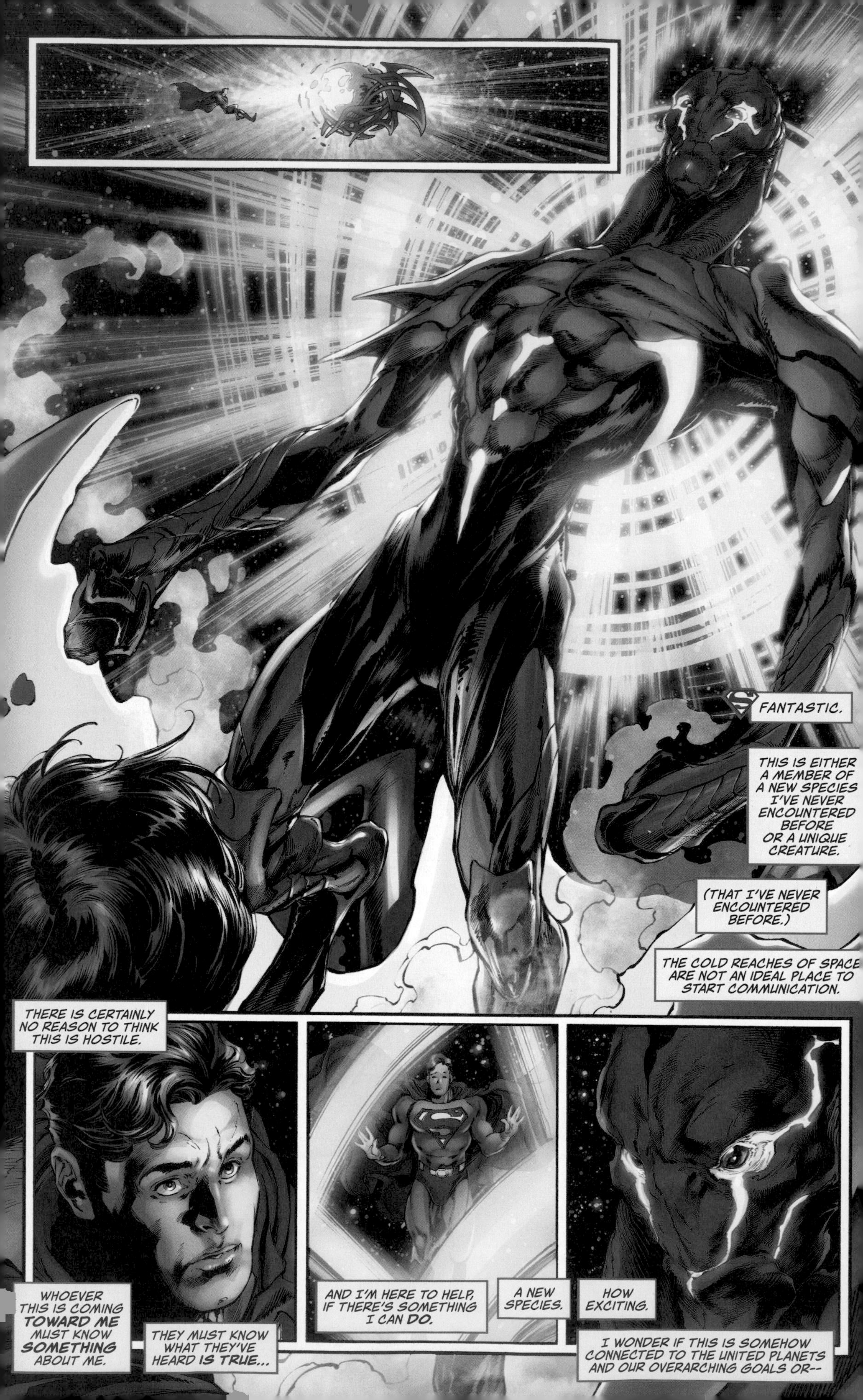
FANTASTIC.
THIS IS EITHER A MEMBER OF A NEW SPECIES I'VE NEVER ENCOUNTERED BEFORE OR A UNIQUE CREATURE.
(THAT I'VE NEVER ENCOUNTERED BEFORE.)
THE COLD REACHES OF SPACE ARE NOT AN IDEAL PLACE TO START COMMUNICATION.
THERE IS CERTAINLY NO REASON TO THINK THIS IS HOSTILE.
WHOEVER THIS IS COMING TOWARD ME MUST KNOW SOMETHING ABOUT ME.
THEY MUST KNOW WHAT THEY'VE HEARD IS TRUE...
AND I'M HERE TO HELP, IF THERE'S SOMETHING I CAN DO.
A NEW SPECIES.
HOW EXCITING.
I WONDER IF THIS IS SOMEHOW CONNECTED TO THE UNITED PLANETS AND OUR OVERARCHING GOALS OR--

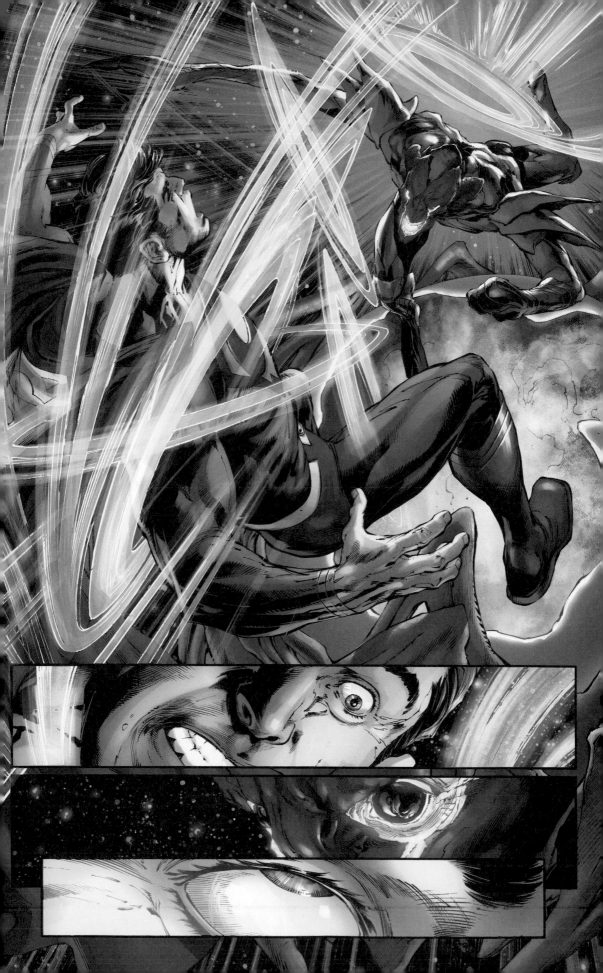

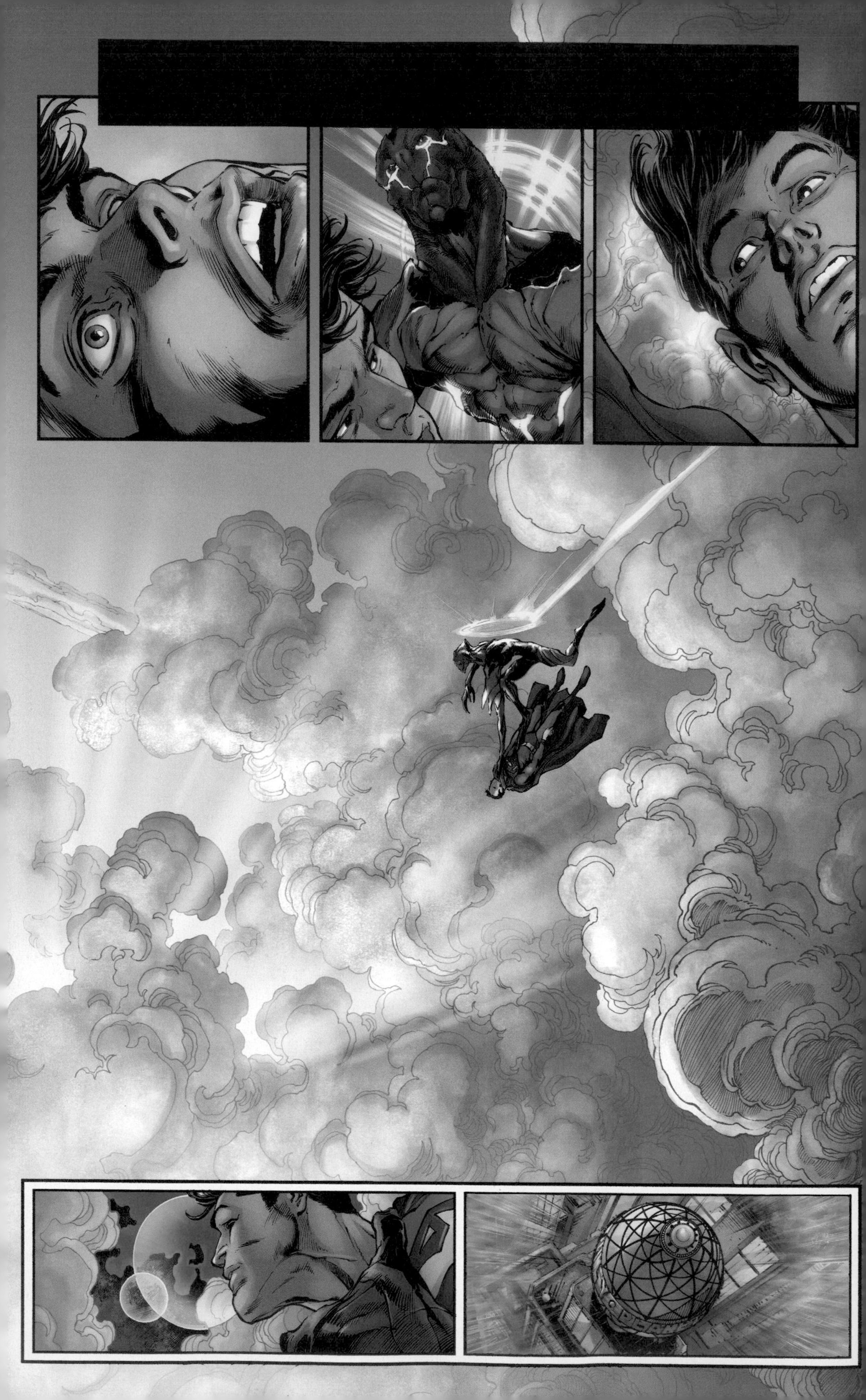
[redacted]

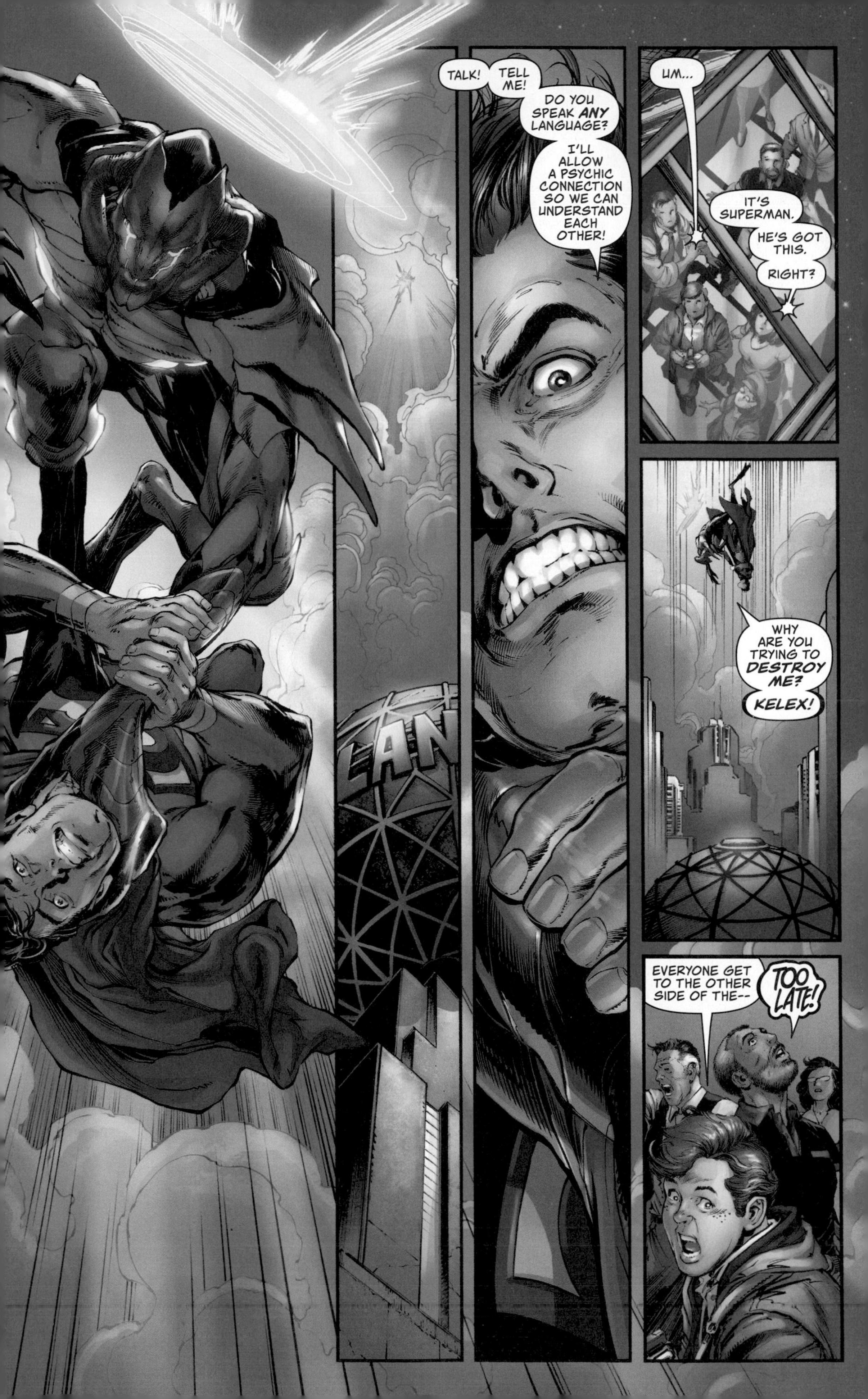
TALK!
TELL ME!
DO YOU SPEAK ANY LANGUAGE?
I'LL ALLOW A PSYCHIC CONNECTION SO WE CAN UNDERSTAND EACH OTHER!
UM...
IT'S SUPERMAN.
HE'S GOT THIS.
RIGHT?
WHY ARE YOU TRYING TO DESTROY ME?
KELEX!
EVERYONE GET TO THE OTHER SIDE OF THE--
TOO LATE!

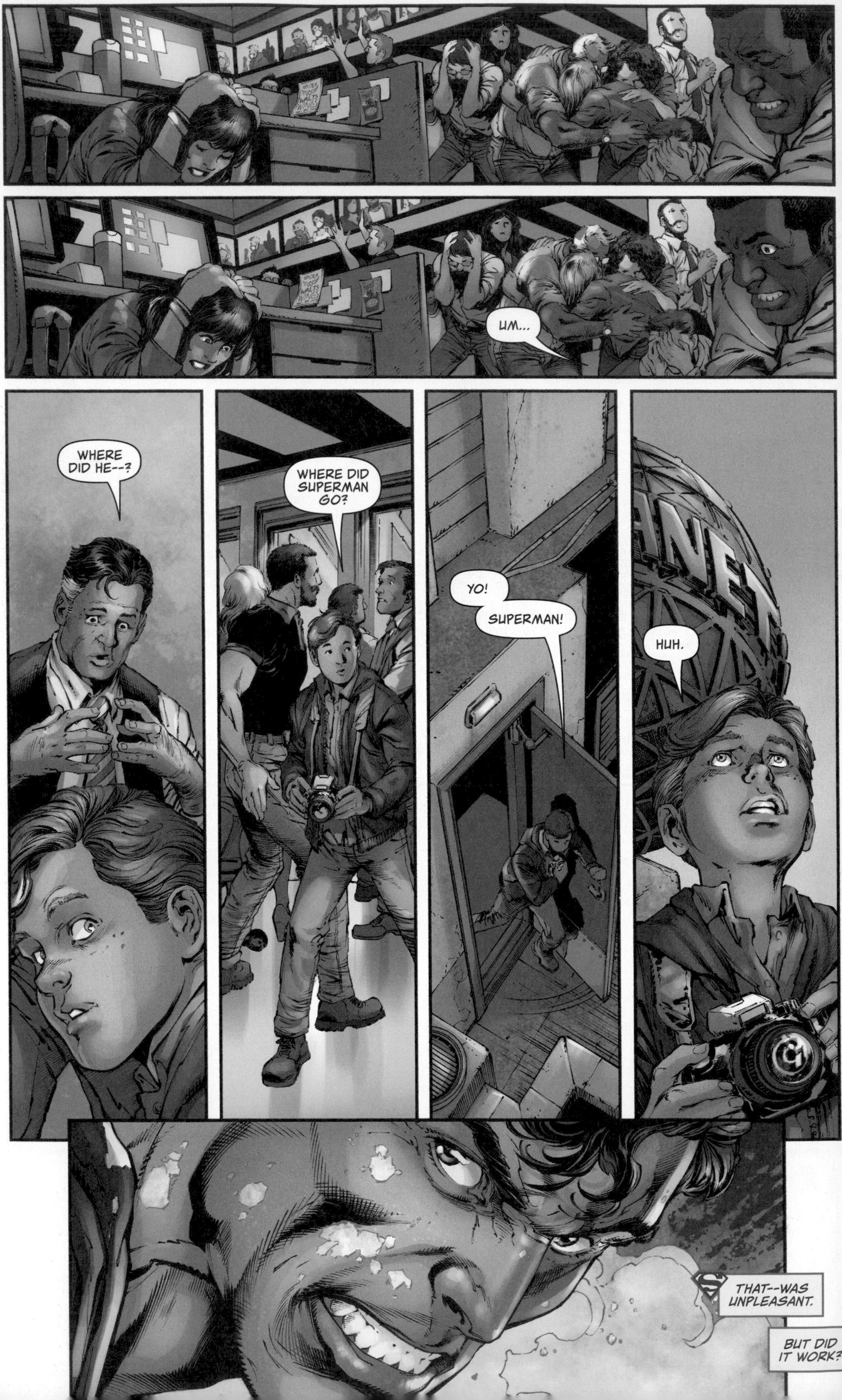

UM...
WHERE DID HE--?
WHERE DID SUPERMAN GO?
YO!
SUPERMAN!
HUH.
THAT--WAS UNPLEASANT.
BUT DID IT WORK?

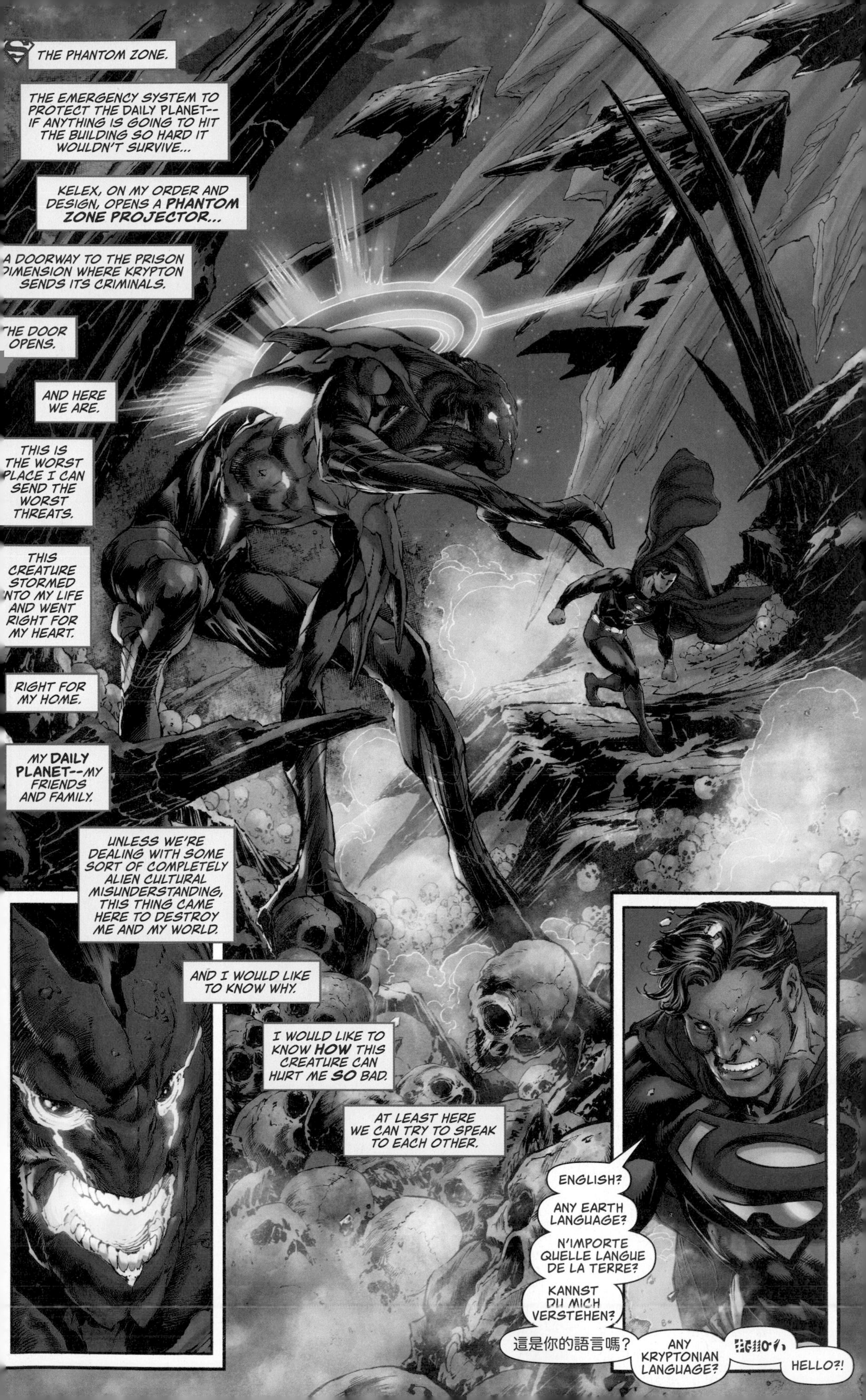
THE PHANTOM ZONE.
THE EMERGENCY SYSTEM TO PROTECT THE DAILY PLANET--IF ANYTHING IS GOING TO HIT THE BUILDING SO HARD IT WOULDN'T SURVIVE...
KELEX, ON MY ORDER AND DESIGN, OPENS A PHANTOM ZONE PROJECTOR...
A DOORWAY TO THE PRISON DIMENSION WHERE KRYPTON SENDS ITS CRIMINALS.
THE DOOR OPENS.
AND HERE WE ARE.
THIS IS THE WORST PLACE I CAN SEND THE WORST THREATS.
THIS CREATURE STORMED INTO MY LIFE AND WENT RIGHT FOR MY HEART.
RIGHT FOR MY HOME.
MY DAILY PLANET--MY FRIENDS AND FAMILY.
UNLESS WE'RE DEALING WITH SOME SORT OF COMPLETELY ALIEN CULTURAL MISUNDERSTANDING, THIS THING CAME HERE TO DESTROY ME AND MY WORLD.
AND I WOULD LIKE TO KNOW WHY.
I WOULD LIKE TO KNOW HOW THIS CREATURE CAN HURT ME SO BAD.
AT LEAST HERE WE CAN TRY TO SPEAK TO EACH OTHER.
ENGLISH?
ANY EARTH LANGUAGE?
N'IMPORTE QUELLE LANGUE DE LA TERRE?
KANNST DU MICH VERSTEHEN?
這是你的語言嗎?
ANY KRYPTONIAN LANGUAGE?
HELLO?!

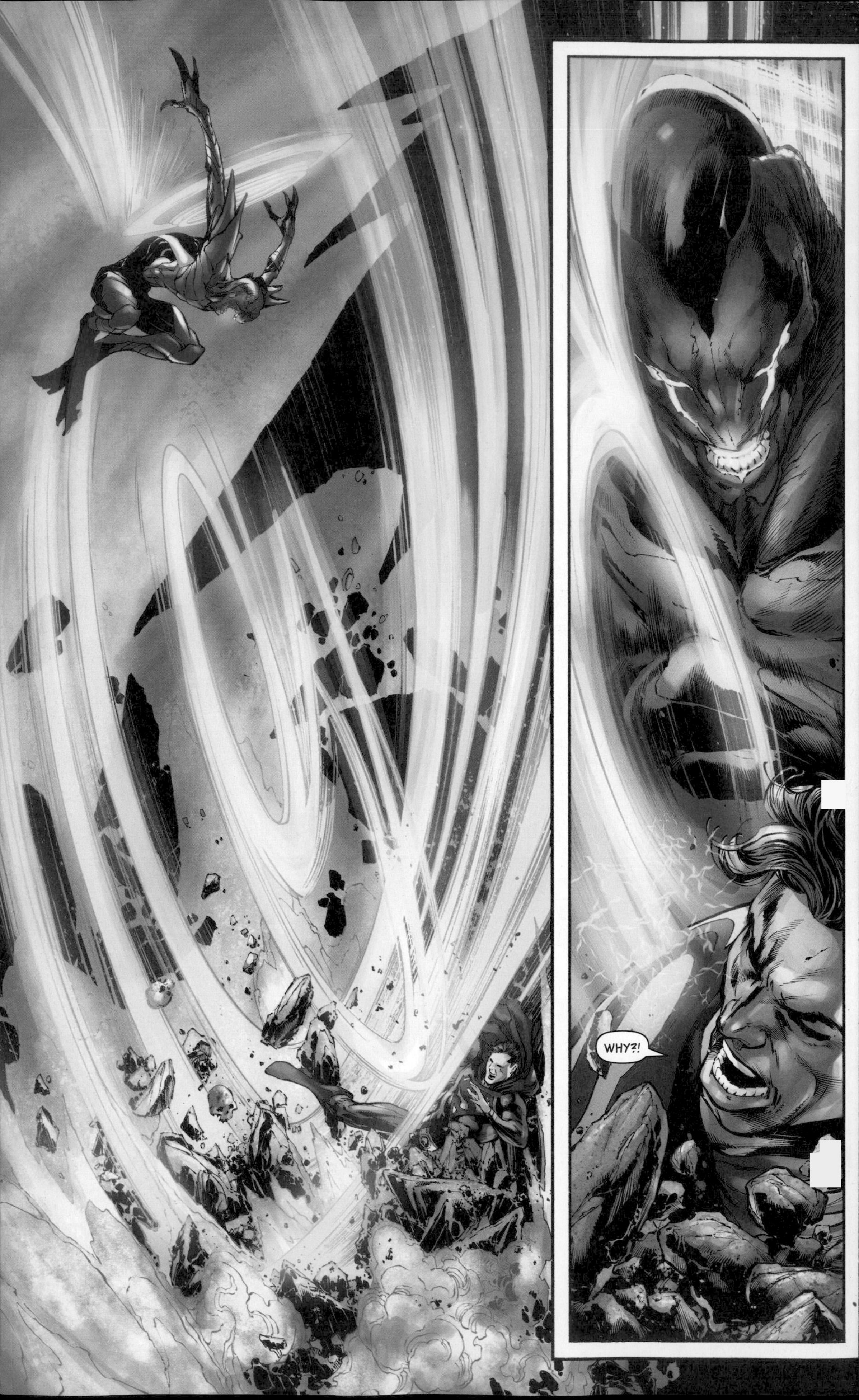
WHY?!

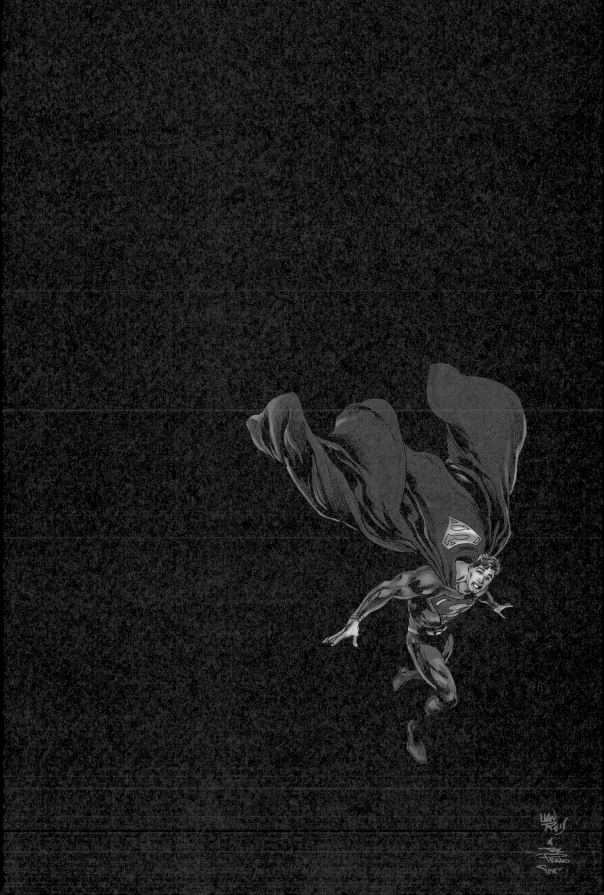

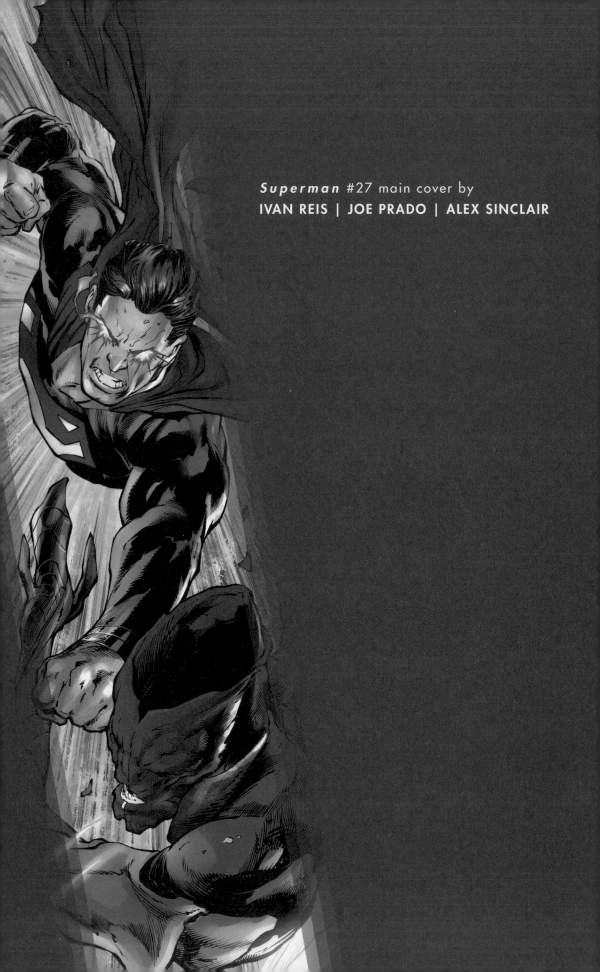

Superman #27 main cover by
IVAN REIS | JOE PRADO | ALEX SINCLAIR

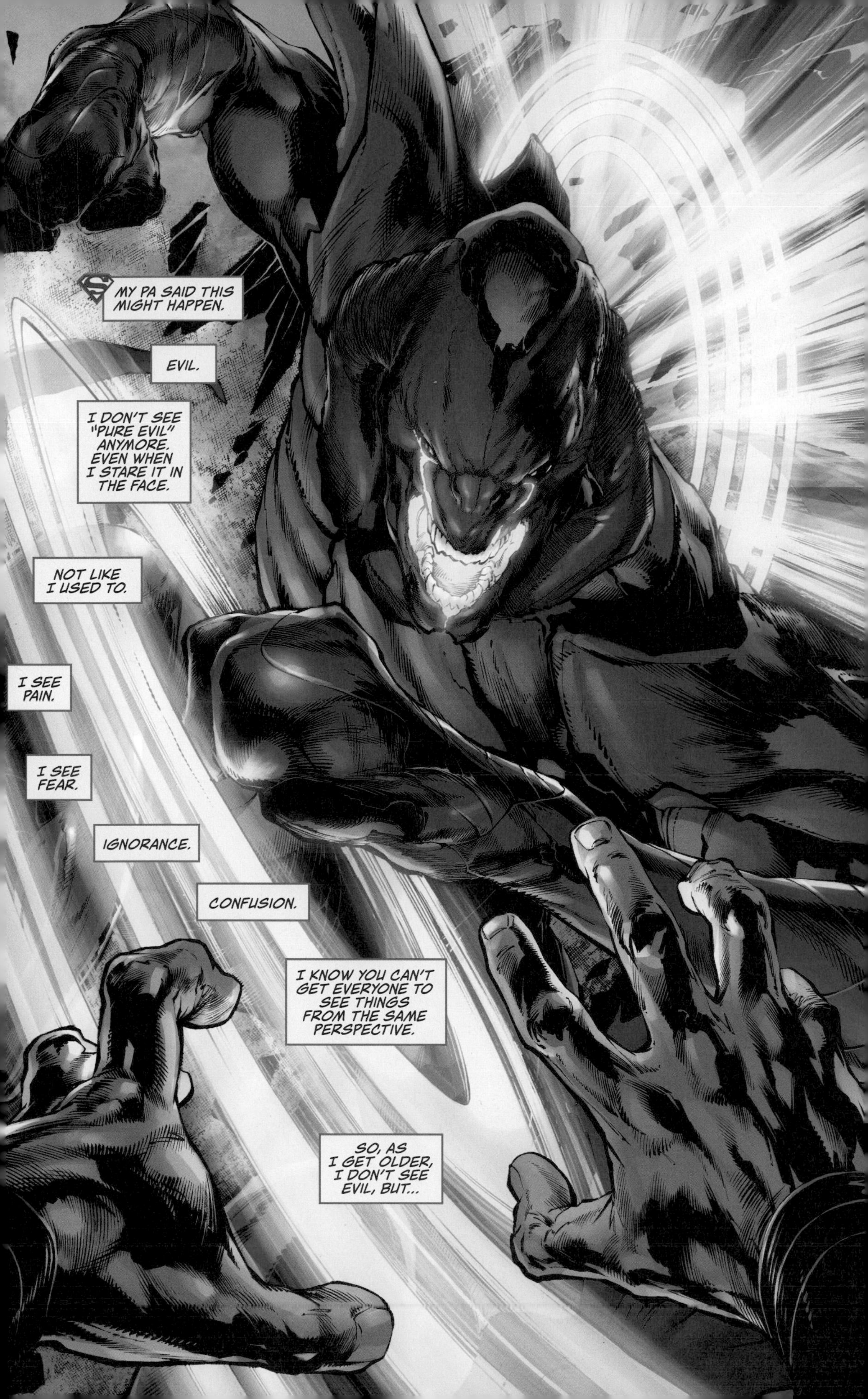
MY PA SAID THIS MIGHT HAPPEN.
EVIL.
I DON'T SEE "PURE EVIL" ANYMORE. EVEN WHEN I STARE IT IN THE FACE.
NOT LIKE I USED TO.
I SEE PAIN.
I SEE FEAR.
IGNORANCE.
CONFUSION.
I KNOW YOU CAN'T GET EVERYONE TO SEE THINGS FROM THE SAME PERSPECTIVE.
SO, AS I GET OLDER, I DON'T SEE EVIL, BUT...

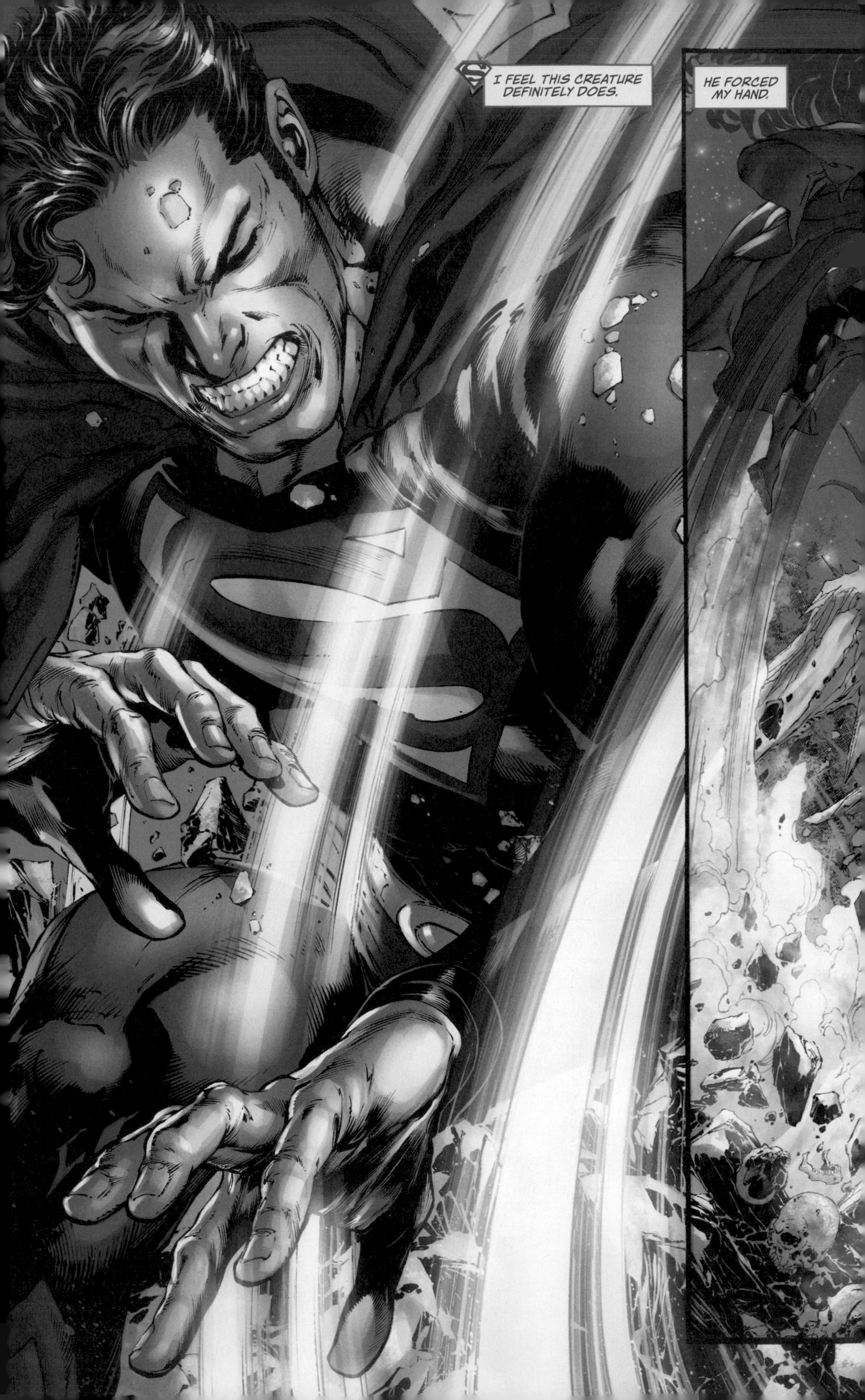
I FEEL THIS CREATURE DEFINITELY DOES.
HE FORCED MY HAND.

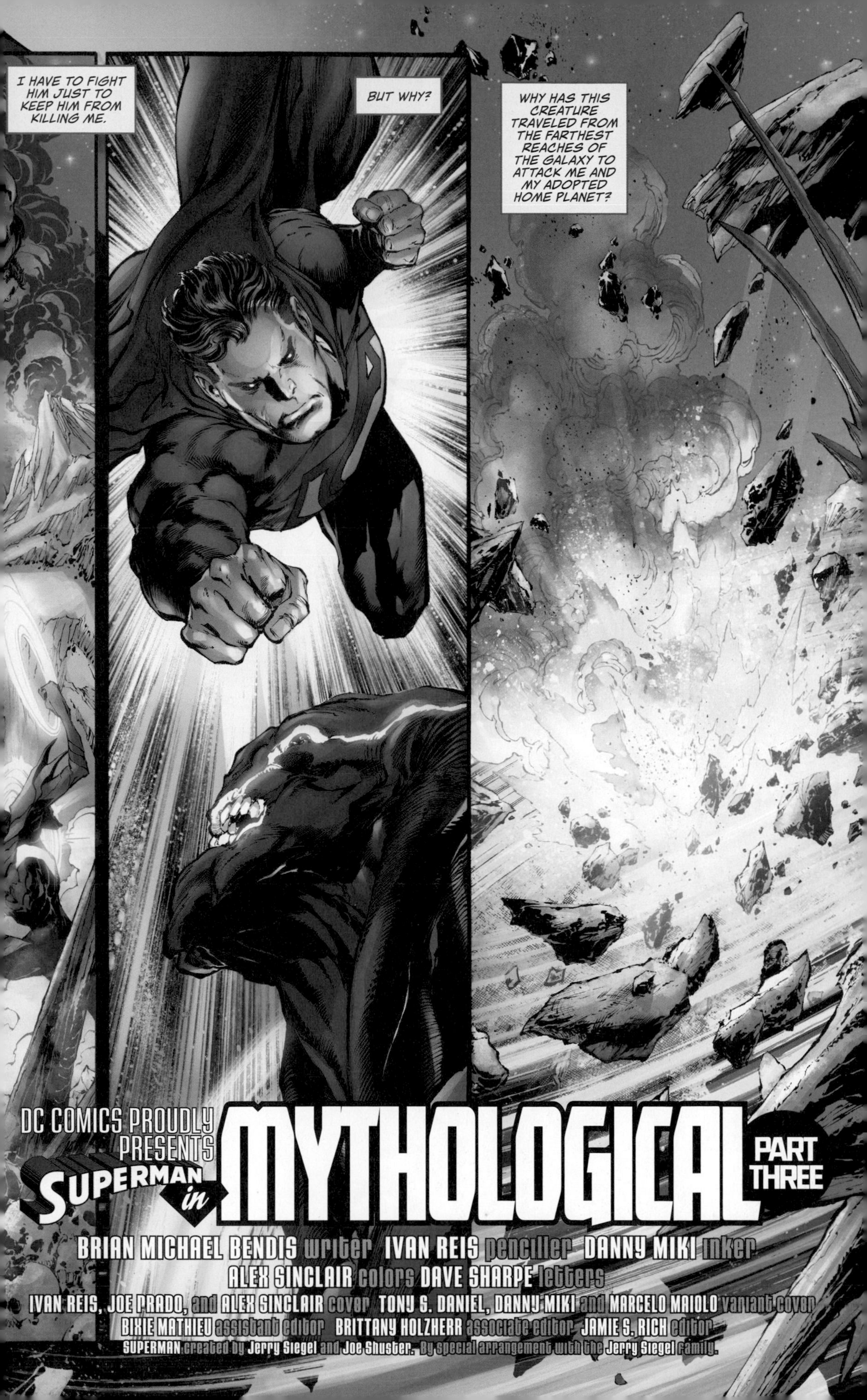
I HAVE TO FIGHT HIM JUST TO KEEP HIM FROM KILLING ME.
BUT WHY?
WHY HAS THIS CREATURE TRAVELED FROM THE FARTHEST REACHES OF THE GALAXY TO ATTACK ME AND MY ADOPTED HOME PLANET?
DC COMICS PROUDLY PRESENTS
SUPERMAN in
MYTHOLOGICAL
PART THREE
BRIAN MICHAEL BENDIS writer IVAN REIS penciller DANNY MIKI inker
ALEX SINCLAIR colors DAVE SHARPE letters
IVAN REIS, JOE PRADO, and ALEX SINCLAIR cover TONY S. DANIEL, DANNY MIKI and MARCELO MAIOLO variant cover
BIXIE MATHIEU assistant editor BRITTANY HOLZHERR associate editor JAMIE S. RICH editor
SUPERMAN created by Jerry Siegel and Joe Shuster. By special arrangement with the Jerry Siegel family.

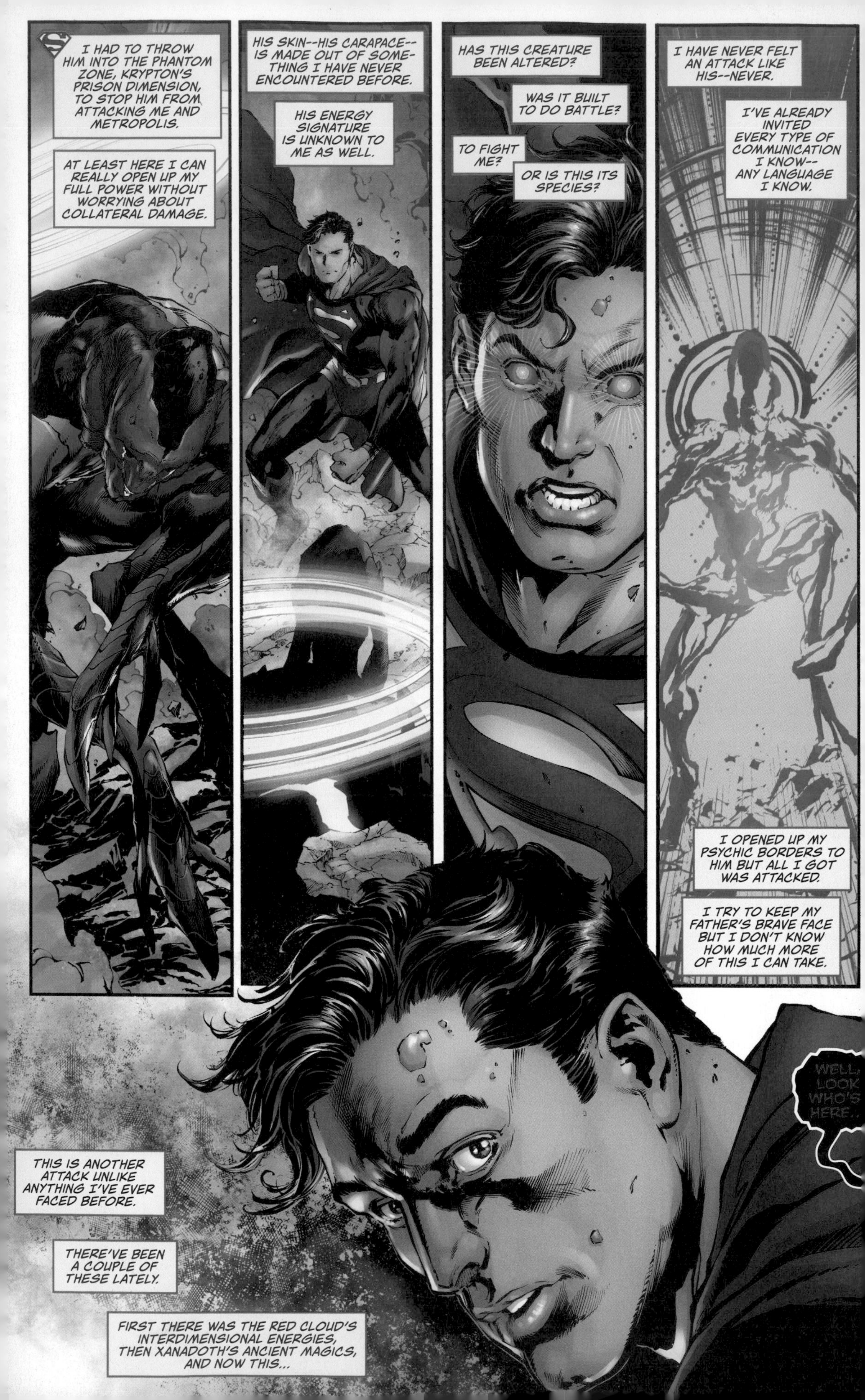

I HAD TO THROW HIM INTO THE PHANTOM ZONE, KRYPTON'S PRISON DIMENSION, TO STOP HIM FROM ATTACKING ME AND METROPOLIS.
AT LEAST HERE I CAN REALLY OPEN UP MY FULL POWER WITHOUT WORRYING ABOUT COLLATERAL DAMAGE.
HIS SKIN--HIS CARAPACE--IS MADE OUT OF SOMETHING I HAVE NEVER ENCOUNTERED BEFORE.
HIS ENERGY SIGNATURE IS UNKNOWN TO ME AS WELL.
HAS THIS CREATURE BEEN ALTERED?
WAS IT BUILT TO DO BATTLE?
TO FIGHT ME?
OR IS THIS ITS SPECIES?
I HAVE NEVER FELT AN ATTACK LIKE HIS--NEVER.
I'VE ALREADY INVITED EVERY TYPE OF COMMUNICATION I KNOW--ANY LANGUAGE I KNOW.
I OPENED UP MY PSYCHIC BORDERS TO HIM BUT ALL I GOT WAS ATTACKED.
I TRY TO KEEP MY FATHER'S BRAVE FACE BUT I DON'T KNOW HOW MUCH MORE OF THIS I CAN TAKE.
WELL, LOOK WHO'S HERE.
THIS IS ANOTHER ATTACK UNLIKE ANYTHING I'VE EVER FACED BEFORE.
THERE'VE BEEN A COUPLE OF THESE LATELY.
FIRST THERE WAS THE RED CLOUD'S INTERDIMENSIONAL ENERGIES, THEN XANADOTH'S ANCIENT MAGICS, AND NOW THIS...

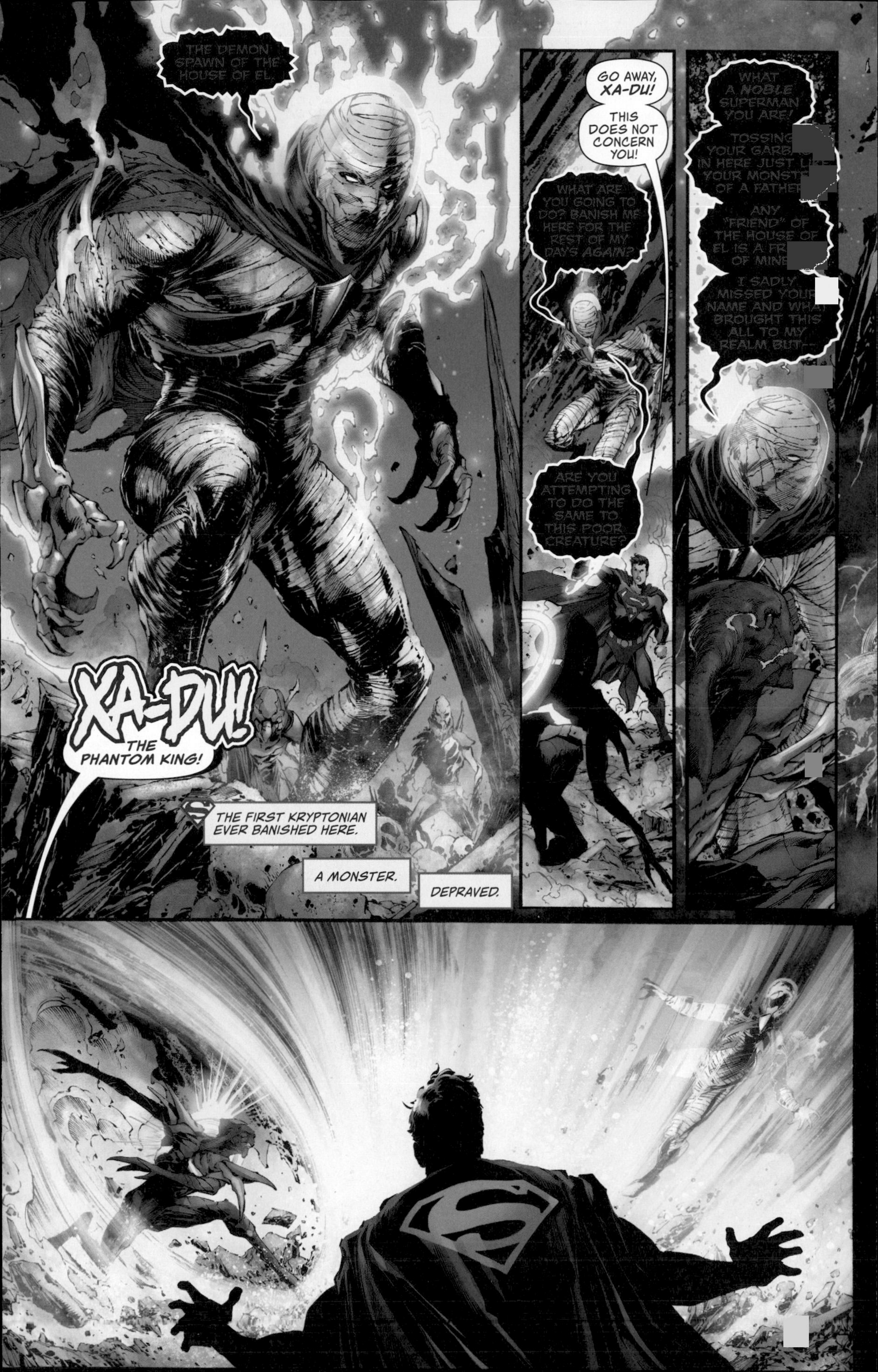
THE DEMON SPAWN OF THE HOUSE OF EL.
XA-DU! THE PHANTOM KING!
THE FIRST KRYPTONIAN EVER BANISHED HERE.
A MONSTER.
DEPRAVED.
GO AWAY, XA-DU!
THIS DOES NOT CONCERN YOU!
WHAT ARE YOU GOING TO DO? BANISH ME HERE FOR THE REST OF MY DAYS AGAIN?
ARE YOU ATTEMPTING TO DO THE SAME TO THIS POOR CREATURE?
WHAT A NOBLE SUPERMAN YOU ARE!
TOSSING [redacted] YOUR GARB[redacted] IN HERE JUST L[redacted] YOUR MONST[redacted] OF A FATHE[redacted]
ANY "FRIEND" OF THE HOUSE OF EL IS A FR[redacted] OF MINE[redacted]
I SADLY MISSED YOUR NAME AND WHA[redacted] BROUGHT THIS ALL TO MY REALM BUT--

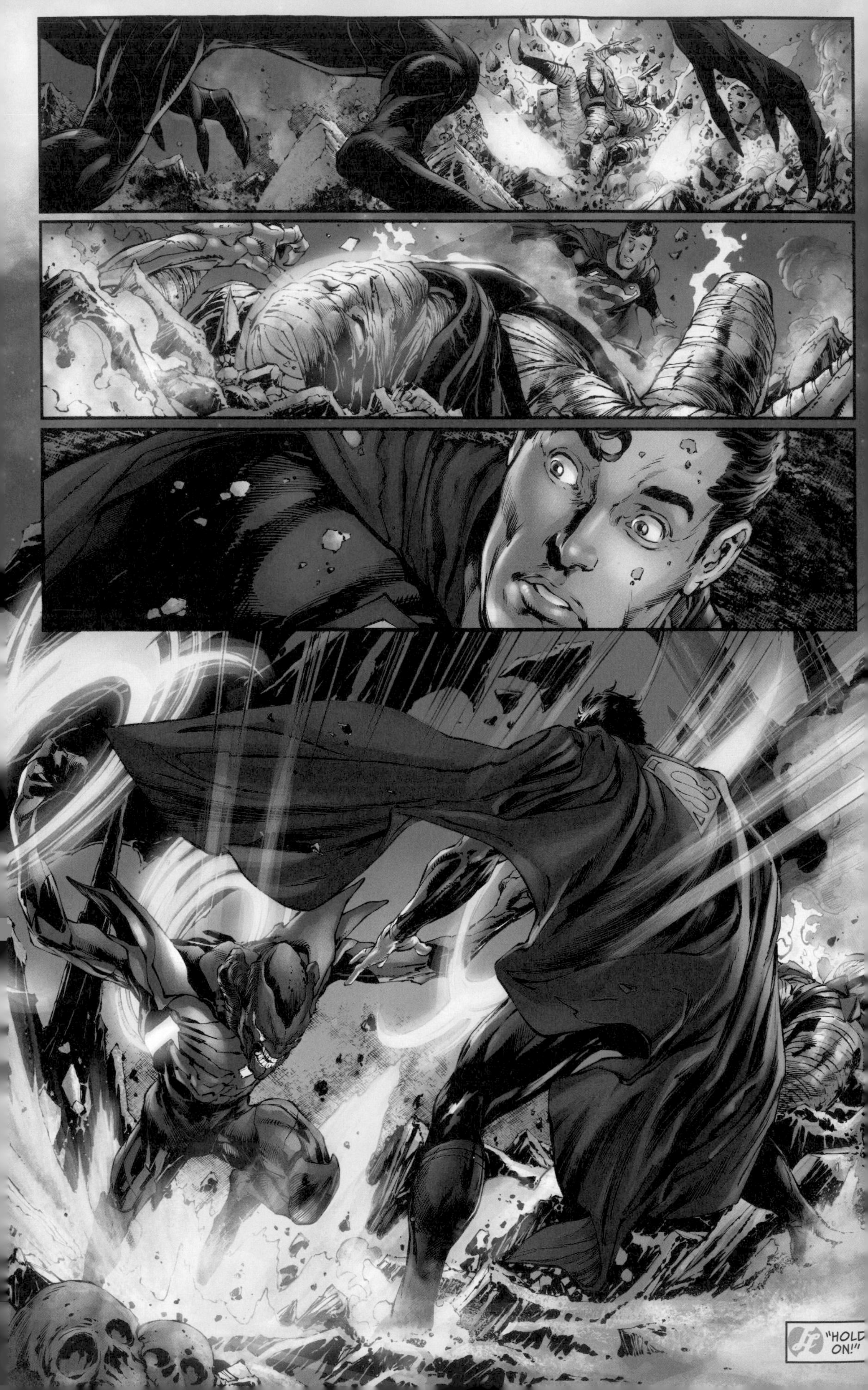
"HOLD
ON!"

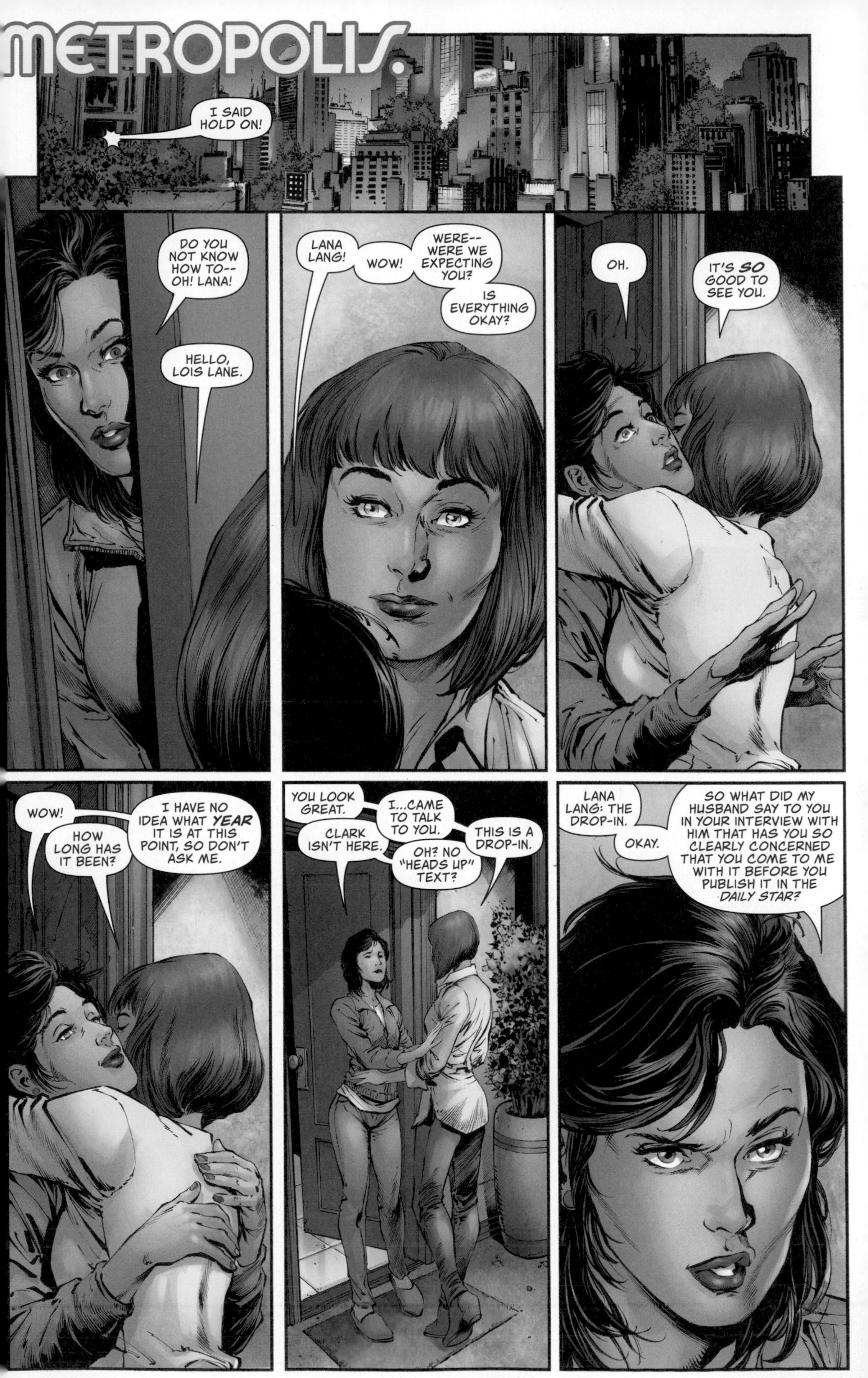
METROPOLIS.
I SAID HOLD ON!
DO YOU NOT KNOW HOW TO-- OH! LANA!
HELLO, LOIS LANE.
LANA LANG!
WOW!
WERE-- WERE WE EXPECTING YOU?
IS EVERYTHING OKAY?
OH.
IT'S SO GOOD TO SEE YOU.
WOW!
HOW LONG HAS IT BEEN?
I HAVE NO IDEA WHAT YEAR IT IS AT THIS POINT, SO DON'T ASK ME.
YOU LOOK GREAT.
CLARK ISN'T HERE.
I...CAME TO TALK TO YOU.
OH? NO "HEADS UP" TEXT?
THIS IS A DROP-IN.
LANA LANG: THE DROP-IN.
OKAY.
SO WHAT DID MY HUSBAND SAY TO YOU IN YOUR INTERVIEW WITH HIM THAT HAS YOU SO CLEARLY CONCERNED THAT YOU COME TO ME WITH IT BEFORE YOU PUBLISH IT IN THE DAILY STAR?

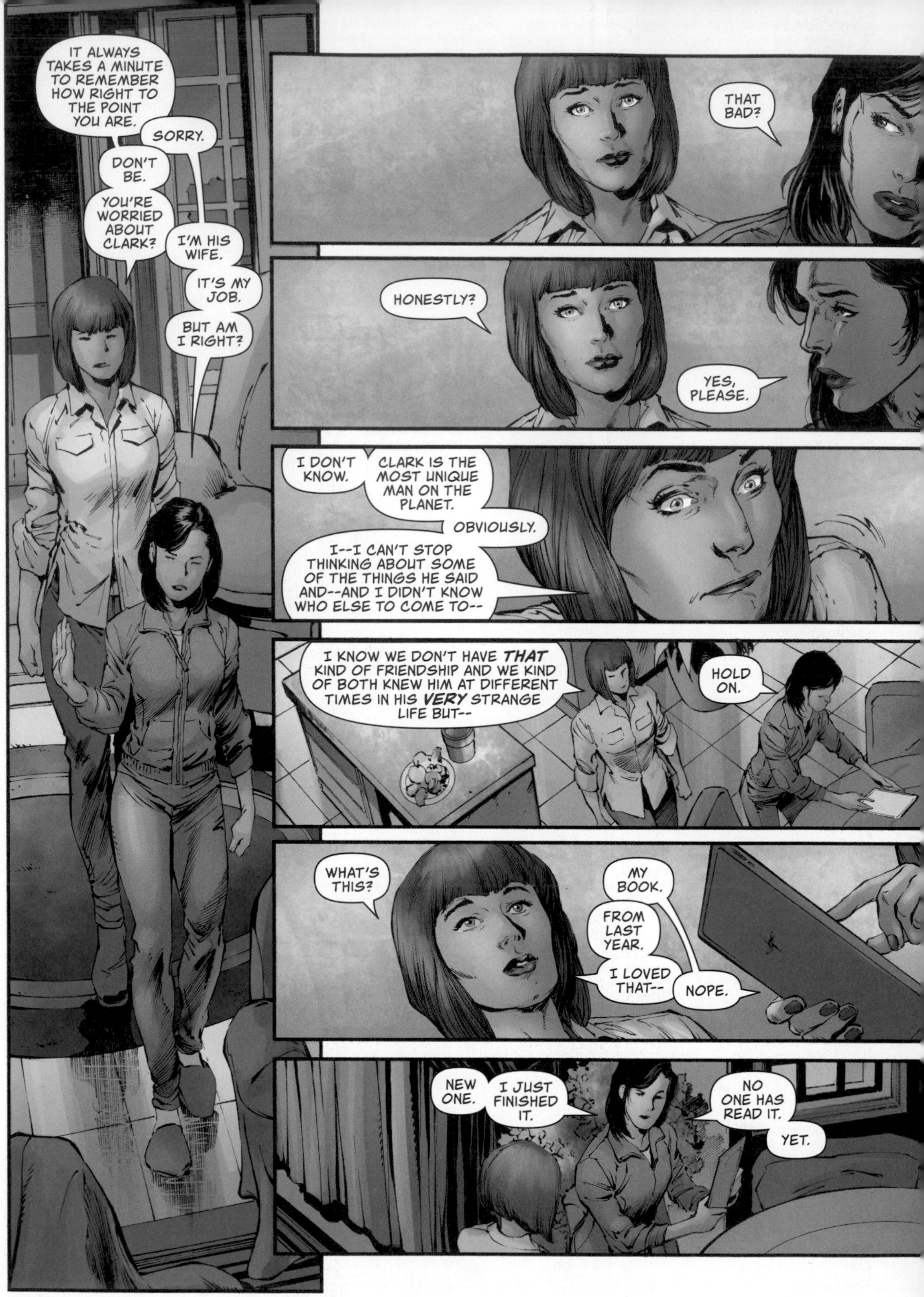
IT ALWAYS TAKES A MINUTE TO REMEMBER HOW RIGHT TO THE POINT YOU ARE.
SORRY.
DON'T BE.
YOU'RE WORRIED ABOUT CLARK?
I'M HIS WIFE.
IT'S MY JOB.
BUT AM I RIGHT?
THAT BAD?
HONESTLY?
YES, PLEASE.
I DON'T KNOW.
CLARK IS THE MOST UNIQUE MAN ON THE PLANET.
OBVIOUSLY.
I--I CAN'T STOP THINKING ABOUT SOME OF THE THINGS HE SAID AND--AND I DIDN'T KNOW WHO ELSE TO COME TO--
I KNOW WE DON'T HAVE *THAT* KIND OF FRIENDSHIP AND WE KIND OF BOTH KNEW HIM AT DIFFERENT TIMES IN HIS *VERY* STRANGE LIFE BUT--
HOLD ON.
WHAT'S THIS?
MY BOOK.
FROM LAST YEAR.
I LOVED THAT--
NOPE.
NEW ONE.
I JUST FINISHED IT.
NO ONE HAS READ IT.
YET.

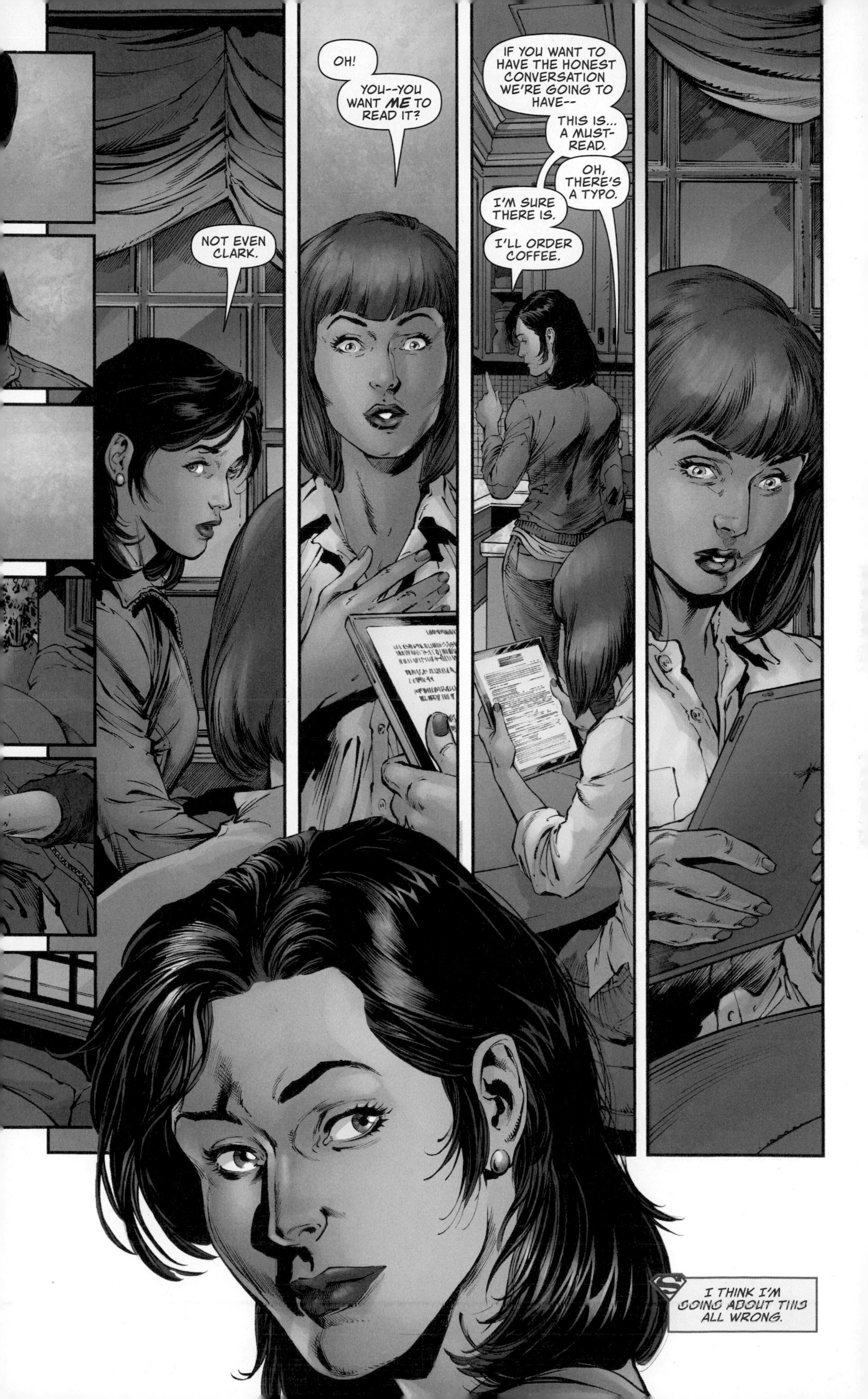
NOT EVEN CLARK.
OH!
YOU--YOU WANT ME TO READ IT?
IF YOU WANT TO HAVE THE HONEST CONVERSATION WE'RE GOING TO HAVE--
THIS IS... A MUST-READ.
I'M SURE THERE IS.
I'LL ORDER COFFEE.
OH, THERE'S A TYPO.
I THINK I'M GOING ABOUT THIS ALL WRONG.

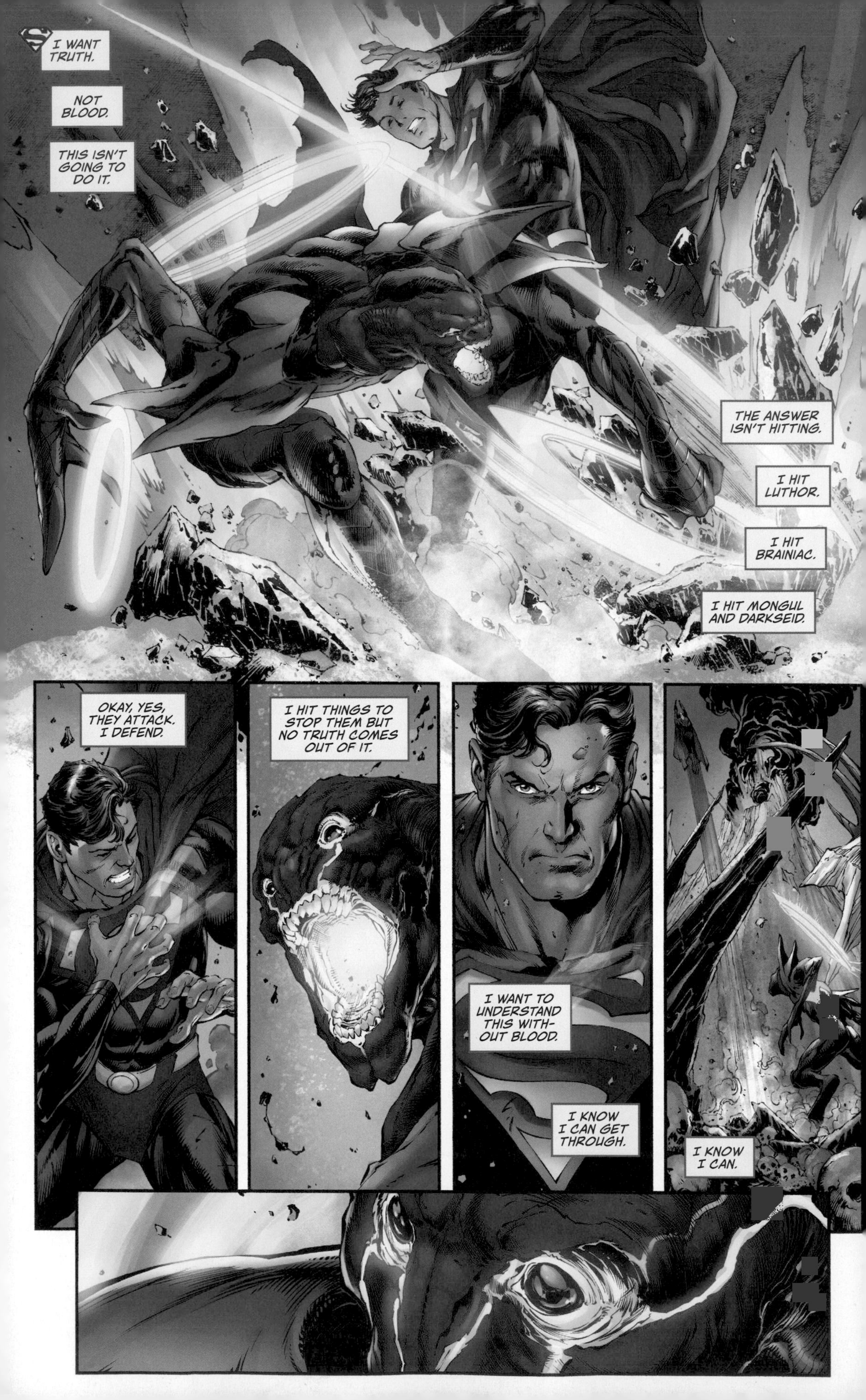
I WANT TRUTH.
NOT BLOOD.
THIS ISN'T GOING TO DO IT.
THE ANSWER ISN'T HITTING.
I HIT LUTHOR.
I HIT BRAINIAC.
I HIT MONGUL AND DARKSEID.
OKAY, YES, THEY ATTACK. I DEFEND.
I HIT THINGS TO STOP THEM BUT NO TRUTH COMES OUT OF IT.
I WANT TO UNDERSTAND THIS WITH-OUT BLOOD.
I KNOW I CAN GET THROUGH.
I KNOW I CAN.

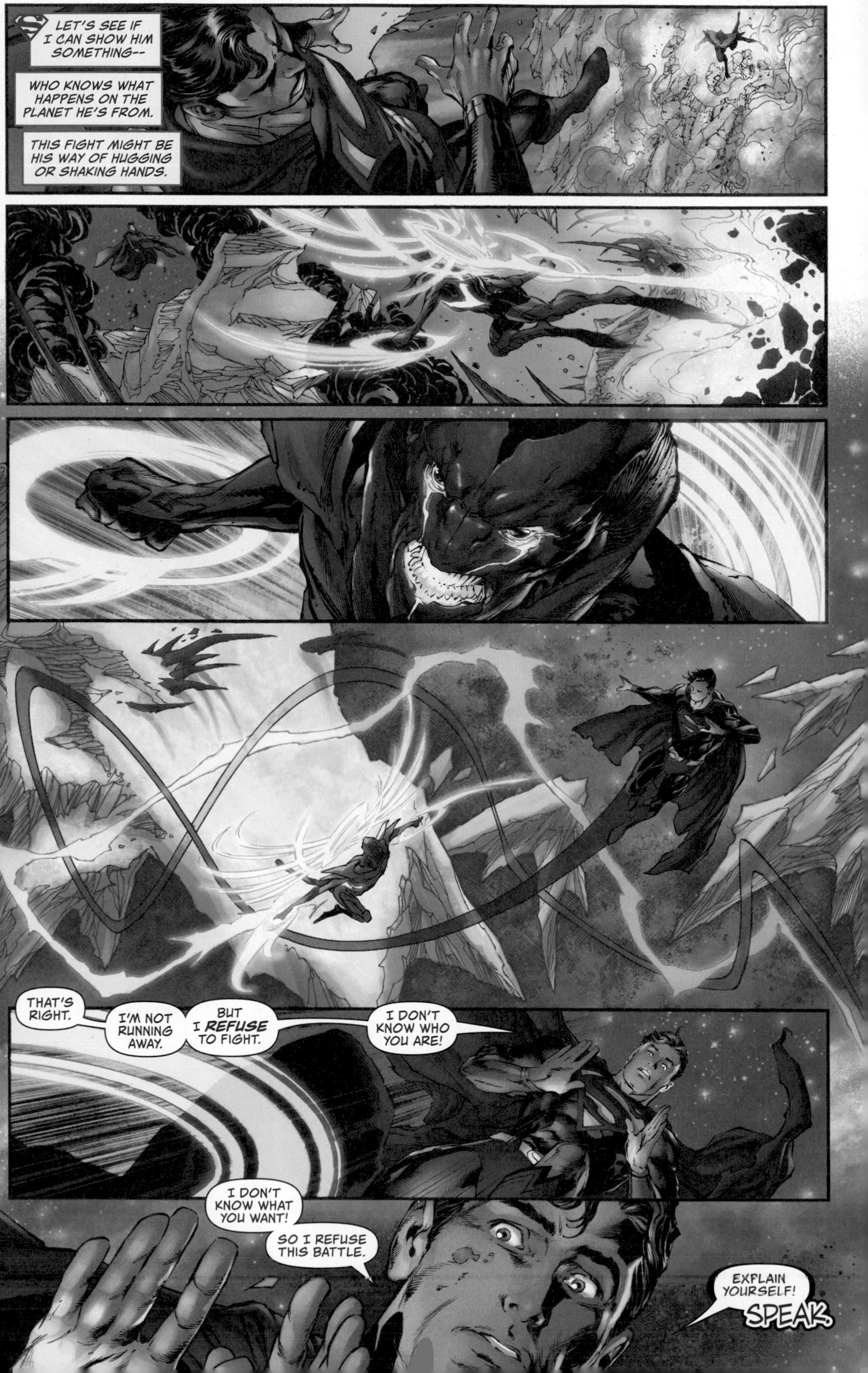
LET'S SEE IF I CAN SHOW HIM SOMETHING--
WHO KNOWS WHAT HAPPENS ON THE PLANET HE'S FROM.
THIS FIGHT MIGHT BE HIS WAY OF HUGGING OR SHAKING HANDS.
THAT'S RIGHT.
I'M NOT RUNNING AWAY.
BUT I REFUSE TO FIGHT.
I DON'T KNOW WHO YOU ARE!
I DON'T KNOW WHAT YOU WANT!
SO I REFUSE THIS BATTLE.
EXPLAIN YOURSELF!
SPEAK.

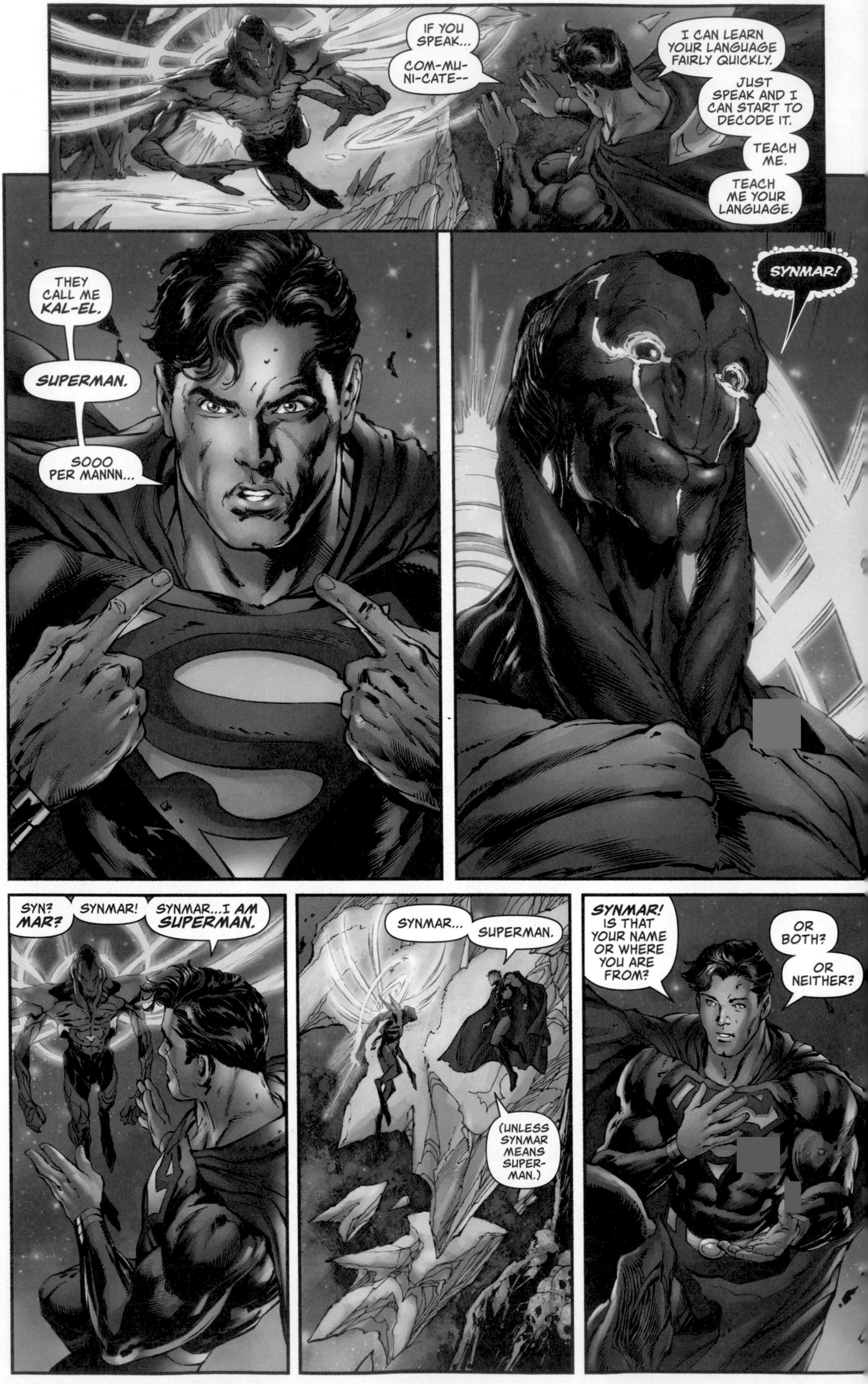

IF YOU SPEAK...
COM-MU-NI-CATE--
I CAN LEARN YOUR LANGUAGE FAIRLY QUICKLY.
JUST SPEAK AND I CAN START TO DECODE IT.
TEACH ME.
TEACH ME YOUR LANGUAGE.
THEY CALL ME KAL-EL.
SUPERMAN.
SOOO PER MANNN...
SYNMAR!
SYN? MAR?
SYNMAR!
SYNMAR...I AM SUPERMAN.
SYNMAR...
SUPERMAN.
(UNLESS SYNMAR MEANS SUPER-MAN.)
SYNMAR! IS THAT YOUR NAME OR WHERE YOU ARE FROM?
OR BOTH?
OR NEITHER?

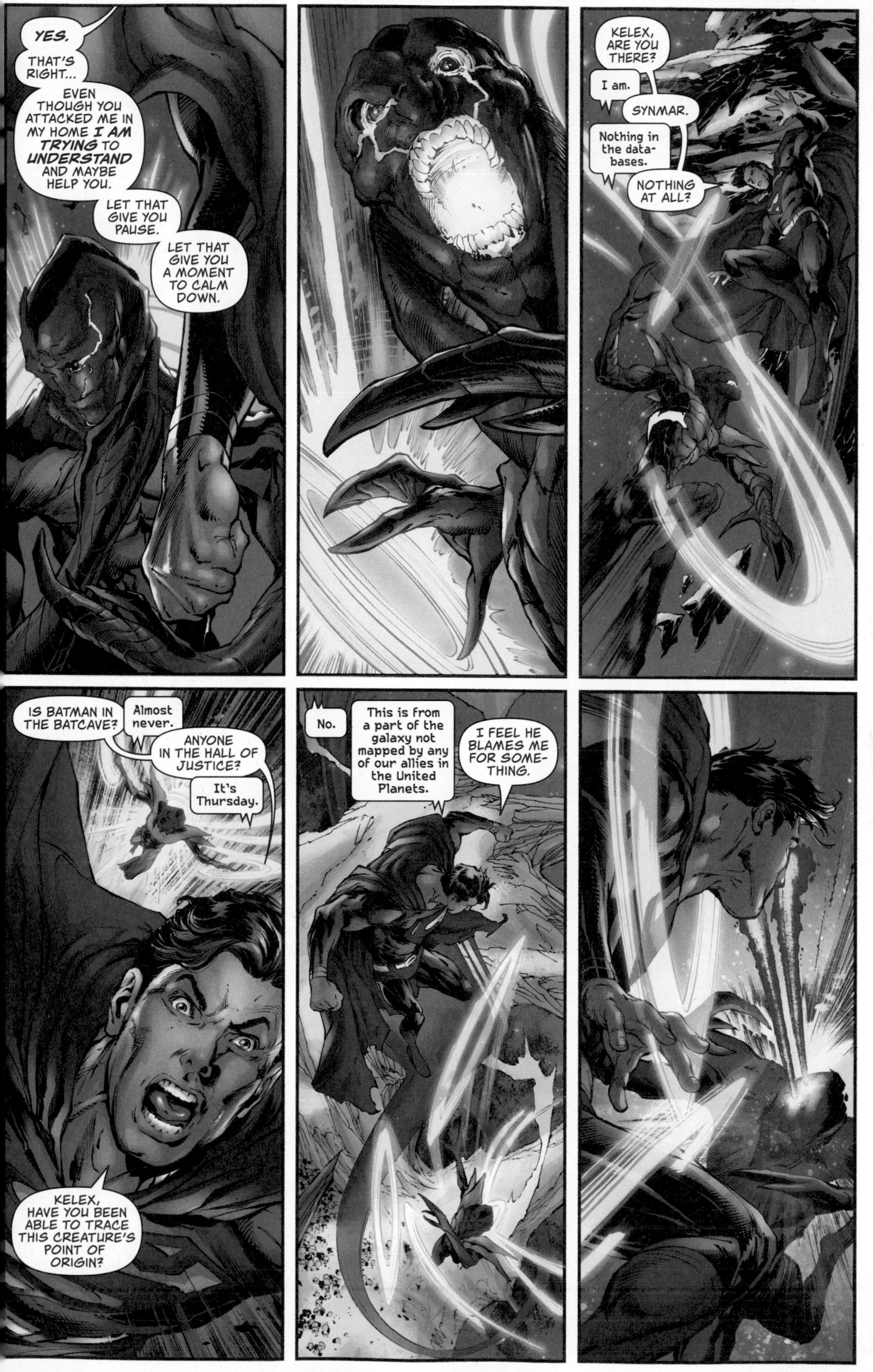

YES.
THAT'S RIGHT...
EVEN THOUGH YOU ATTACKED ME IN MY HOME I AM TRYING TO UNDERSTAND AND MAYBE HELP YOU.
LET THAT GIVE YOU PAUSE.
LET THAT GIVE YOU A MOMENT TO CALM DOWN.
KELEX, ARE YOU THERE?
I am.
SYNMAR.
Nothing in the data-bases.
NOTHING AT ALL?
IS BATMAN IN THE BATCAVE?
Almost never.
ANYONE IN THE HALL OF JUSTICE?
It's Thursday.
KELEX, HAVE YOU BEEN ABLE TO TRACE THIS CREATURE'S POINT OF ORIGIN?
No.
This is from a part of the galaxy not mapped by any of our allies in the United Planets.
I FEEL HE BLAMES ME FOR SOME-THING.

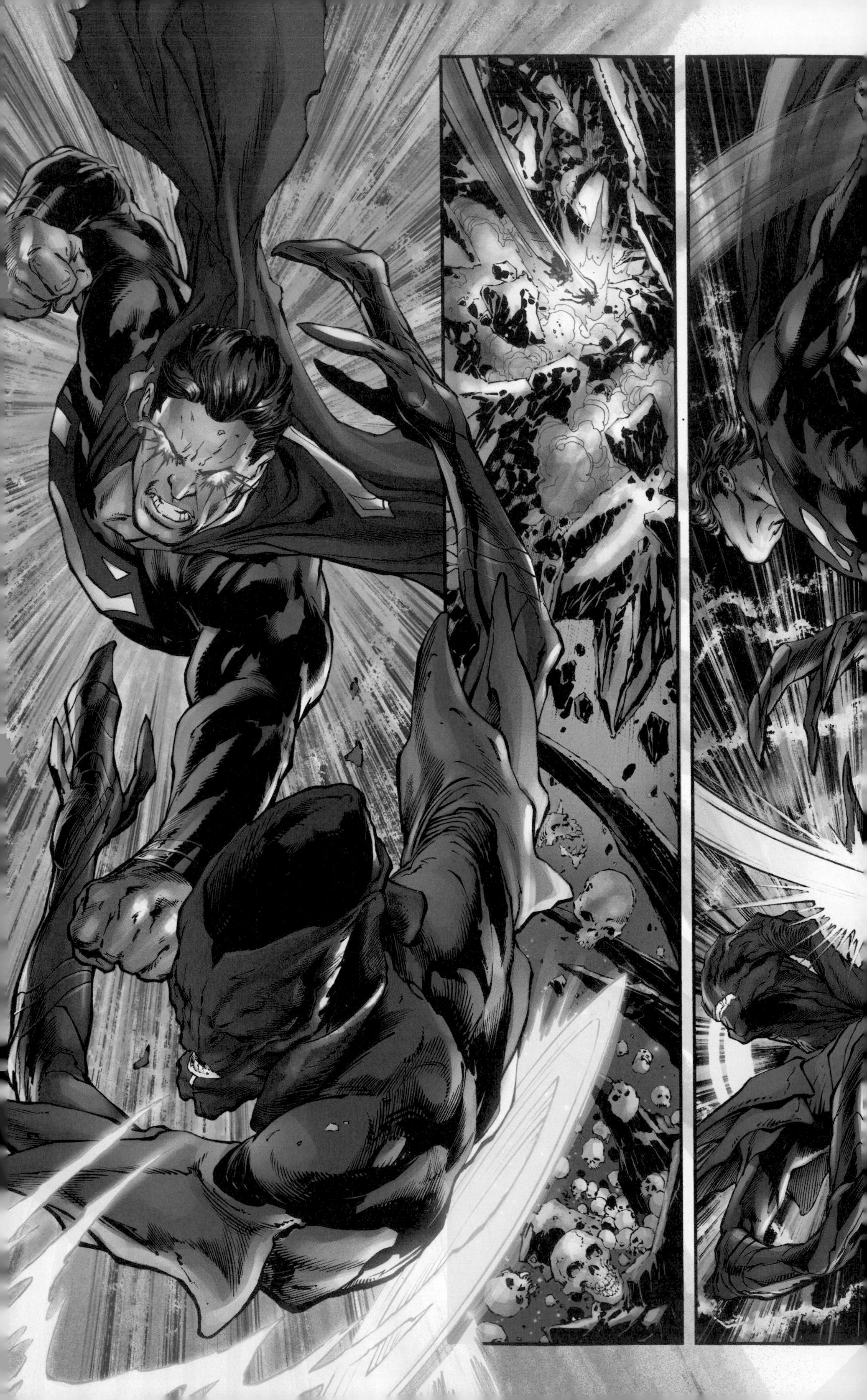

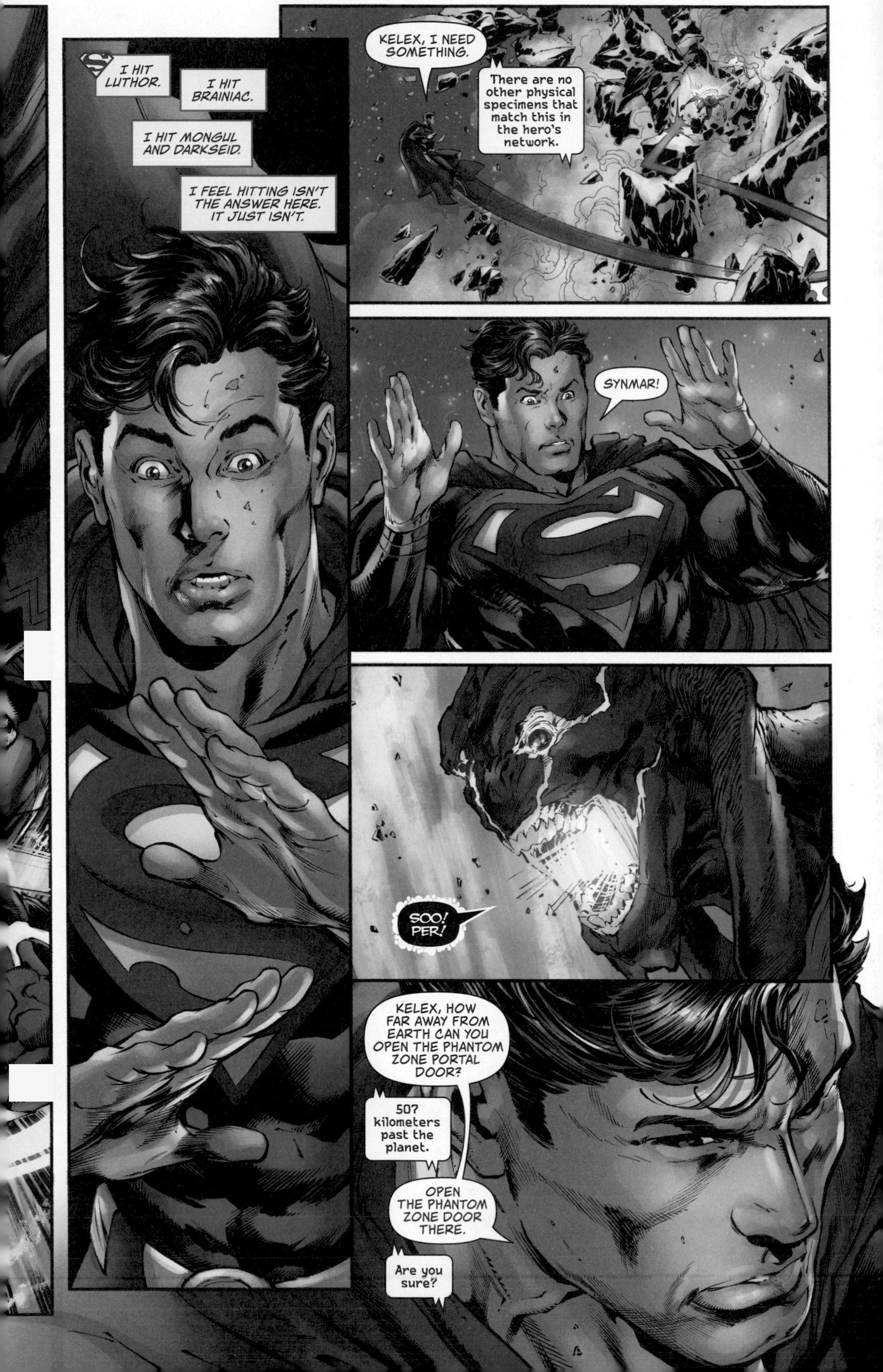
I HIT LUTHOR.
I HIT BRAINIAC.
I HIT MONGUL AND DARKSEID.
I FEEL HITTING ISN'T THE ANSWER HERE. IT JUST ISN'T.
KELEX, I NEED SOMETHING.
There are no other physical specimens that match this in the hero's network.
SYNMAR!
SOO! PER!
KELEX, HOW FAR AWAY FROM EARTH CAN YOU OPEN THE PHANTOM ZONE PORTAL DOOR?
507 kilometers past the planet.
OPEN THE PHANTOM ZONE DOOR THERE.
Are you sure?

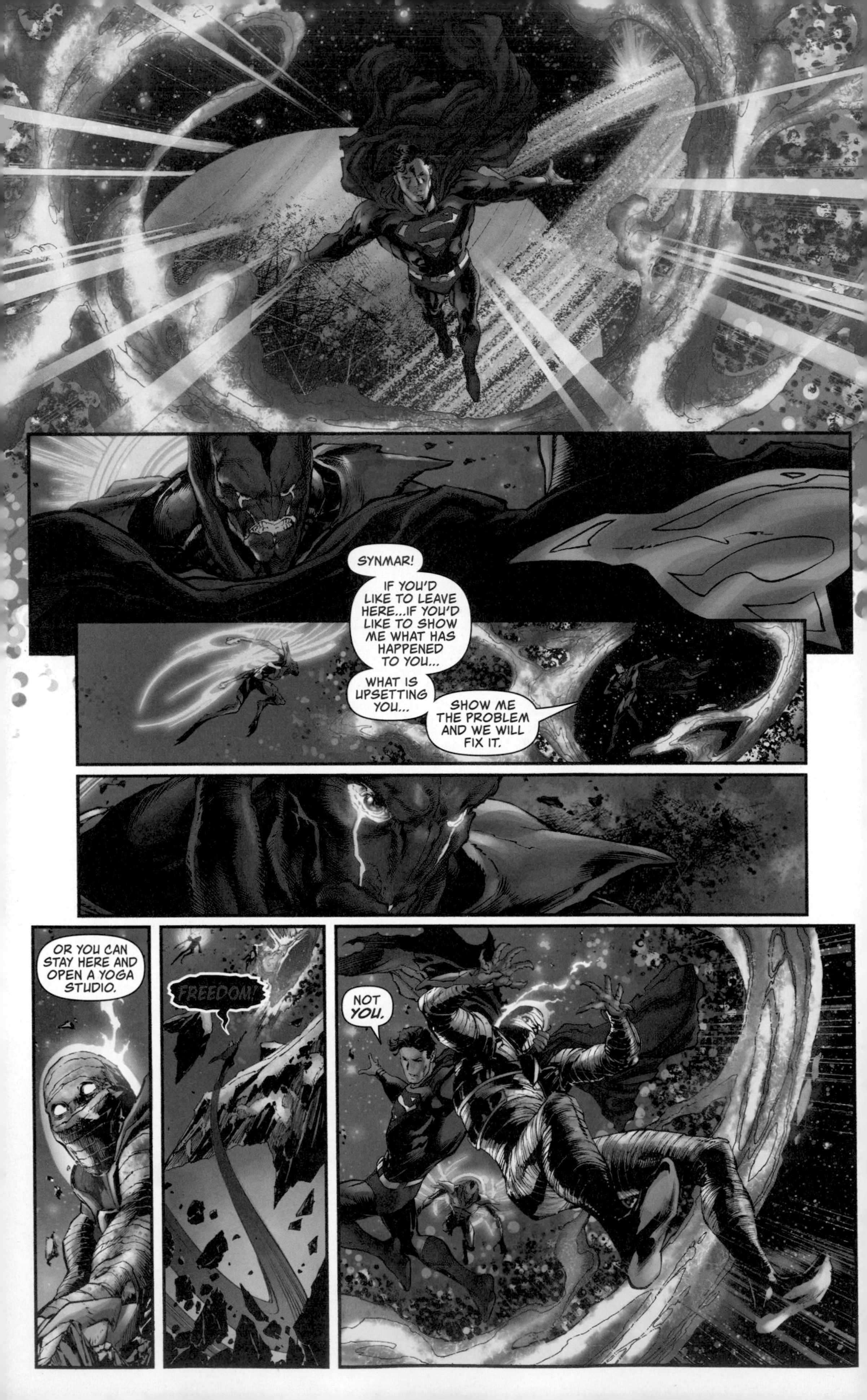
SYNMAR!
IF YOU'D LIKE TO LEAVE HERE...IF YOU'D LIKE TO SHOW ME WHAT HAS HAPPENED TO YOU...
WHAT IS UPSETTING YOU...
SHOW ME THE PROBLEM AND WE WILL FIX IT.
OR YOU CAN STAY HERE AND OPEN A YOGA STUDIO.
FREEDOM!
NOT YOU.

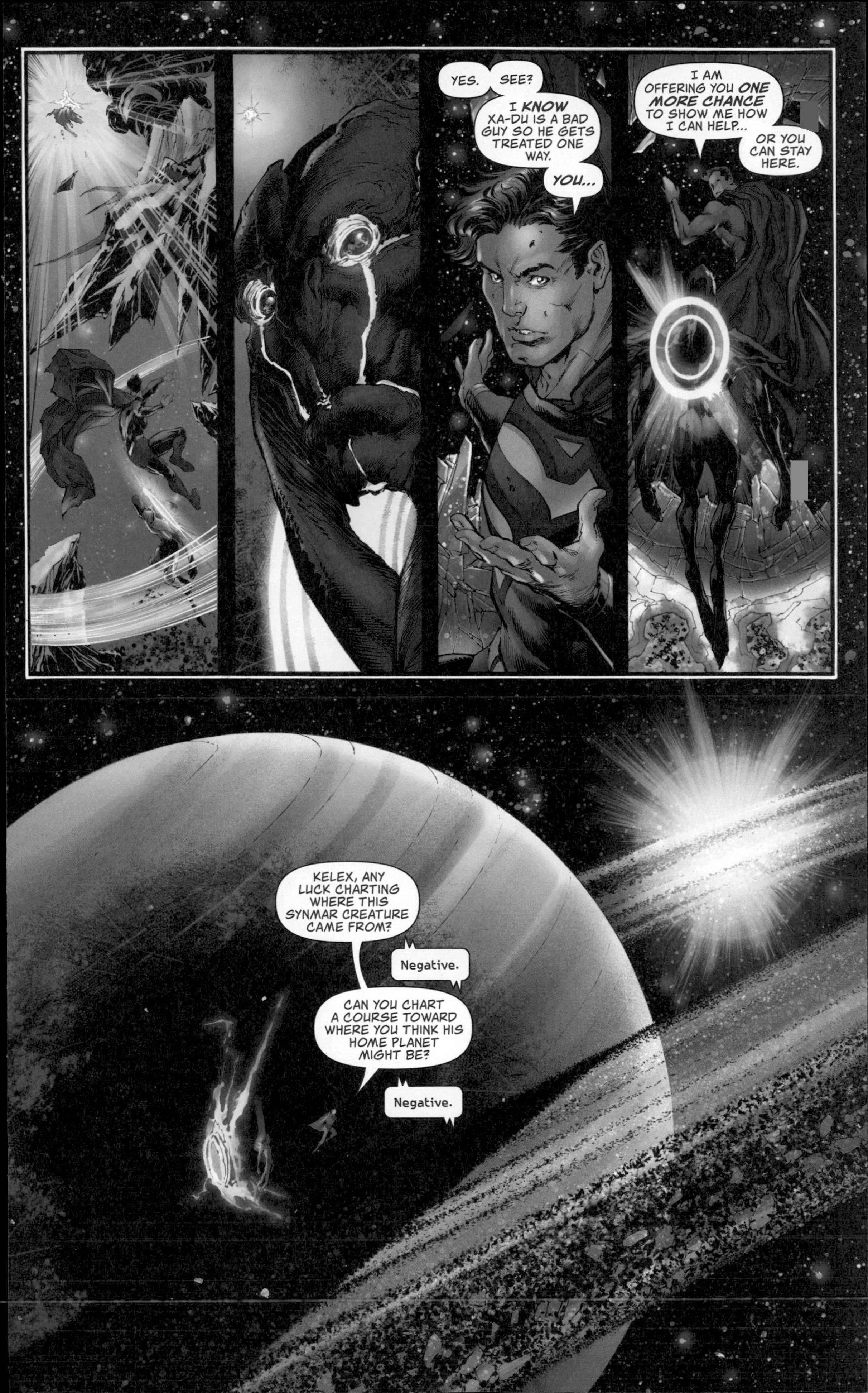
YES.
SEE?
I KNOW XA-DU IS A BAD GUY SO HE GETS TREATED ONE WAY.
YOU...
I AM OFFERING YOU ONE MORE CHANCE TO SHOW ME HOW I CAN HELP...
OR YOU CAN STAY HERE.
KELEX, ANY LUCK CHARTING WHERE THIS SYNMAR CREATURE CAME FROM?
Negative.
CAN YOU CHART A COURSE TOWARD WHERE YOU THINK HIS HOME PLANET MIGHT BE?
Negative.

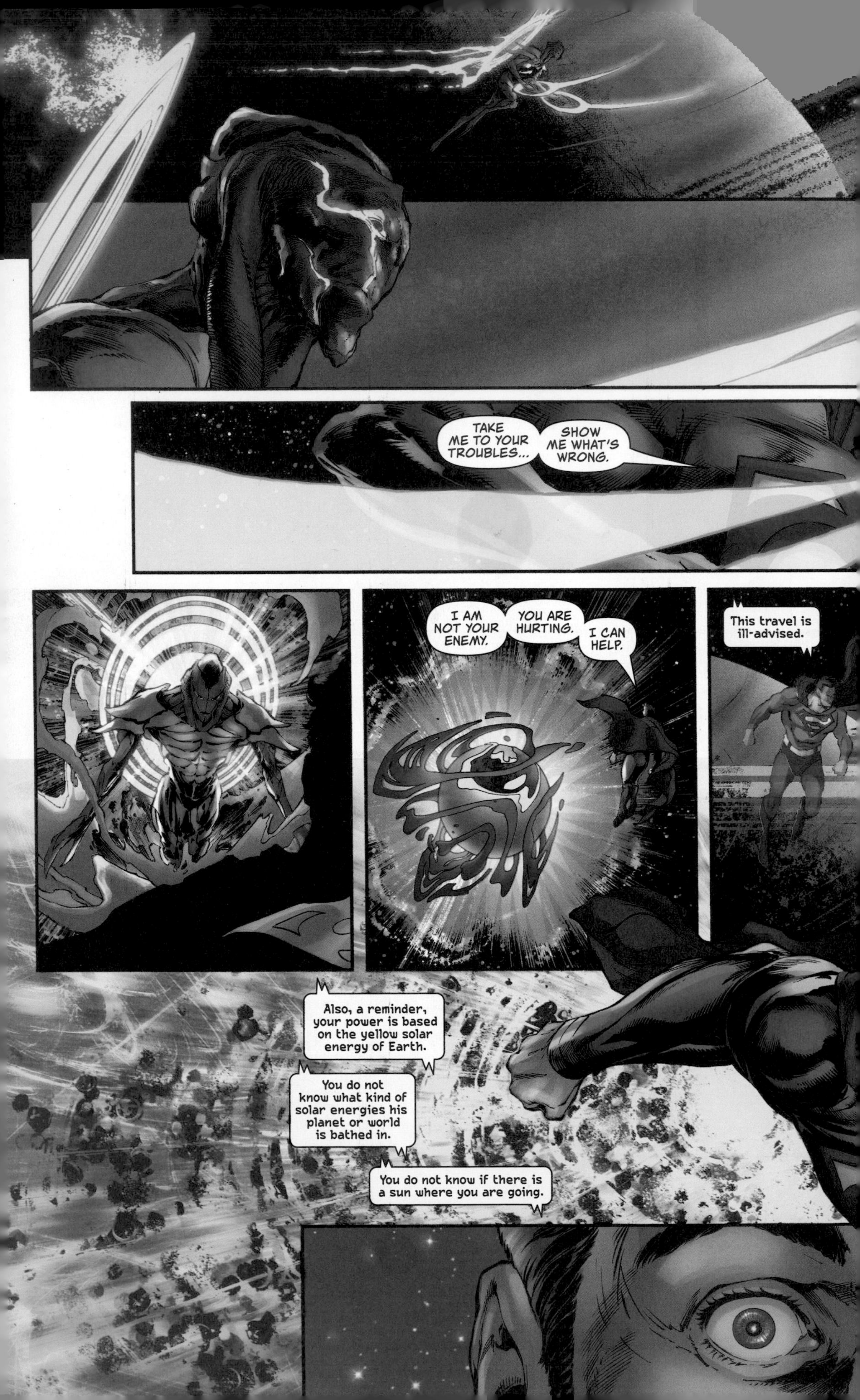
TAKE ME TO YOUR TROUBLES...
SHOW ME WHAT'S WRONG.
I AM NOT YOUR ENEMY.
YOU ARE HURTING.
I CAN HELP.
This travel is ill-advised.
Also, a reminder, your power is based on the yellow solar energy of Earth.
You do not know what kind of solar energies his planet or world is bathed in.
You do not know if there is a sun where you are going.

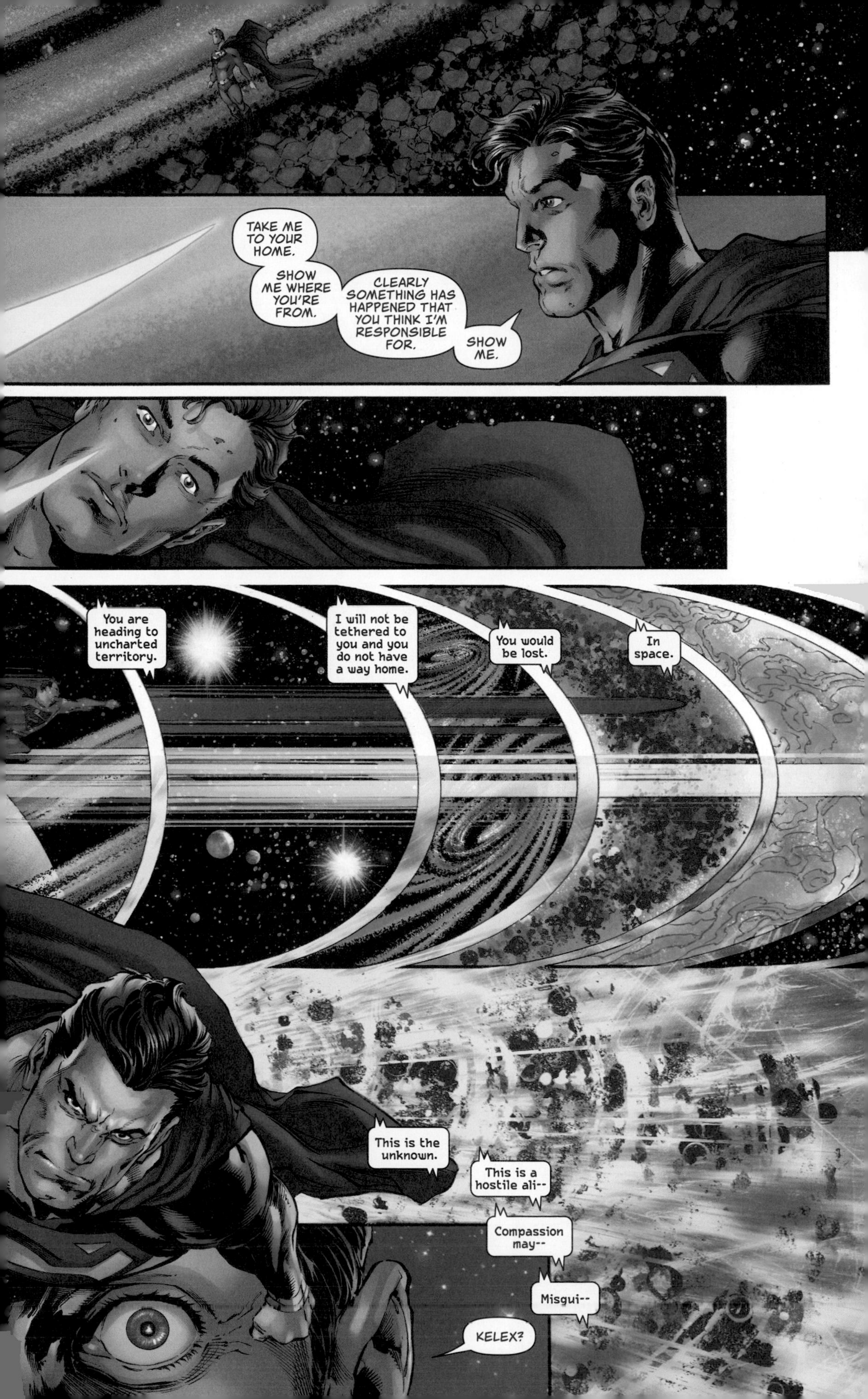

TAKE ME TO YOUR HOME.
SHOW ME WHERE YOU'RE FROM.
CLEARLY SOMETHING HAS HAPPENED THAT YOU THINK I'M RESPONSIBLE FOR.
SHOW ME.
You are heading to uncharted territory.
I will not be tethered to you and you do not have a way home.
You would be lost.
In space.
This is the unknown.
This is a hostile ali--
Compassion may--
Misgui--
KELEX?

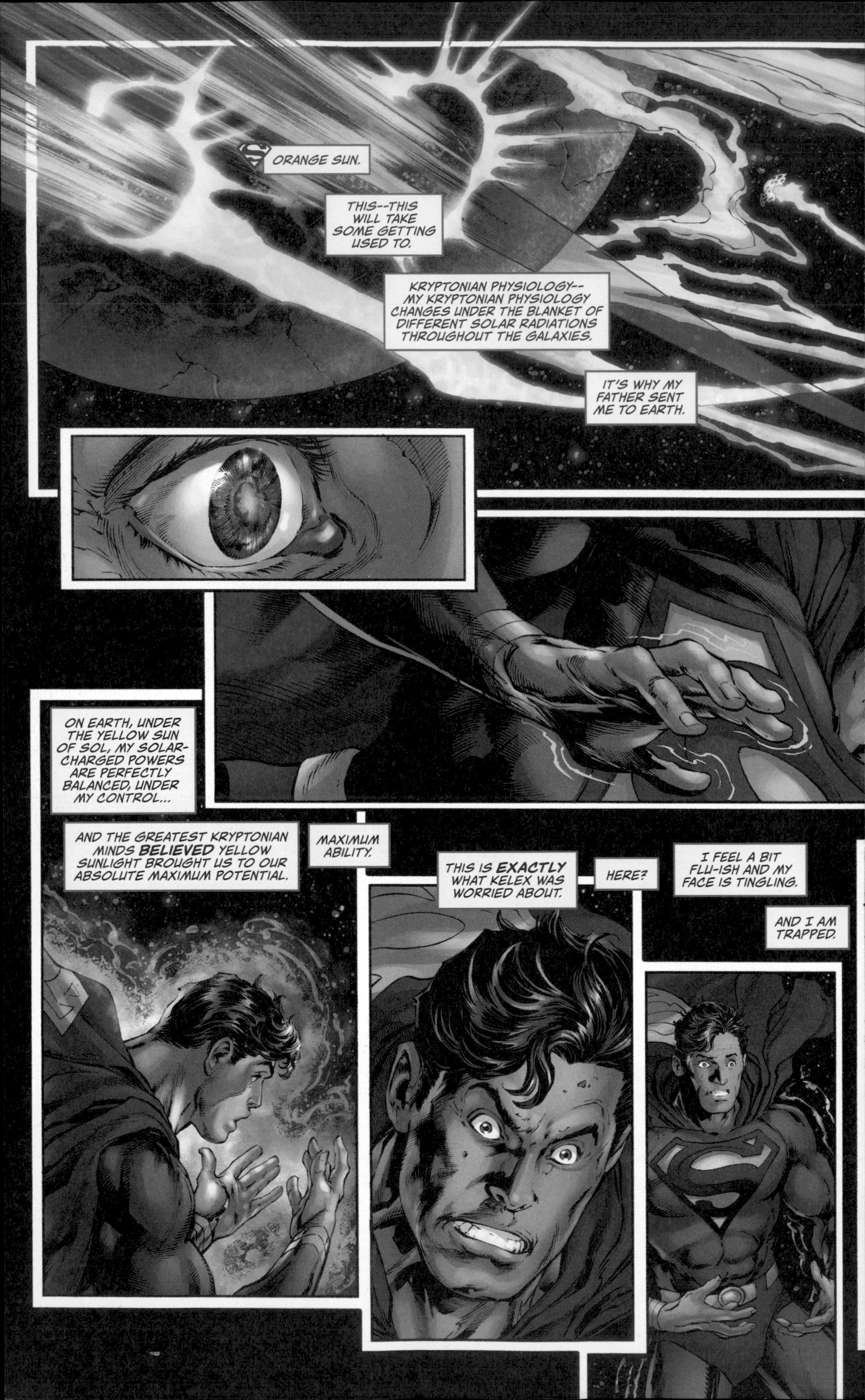
ORANGE SUN.
THIS--THIS WILL TAKE SOME GETTING USED TO.
KRYPTONIAN PHYSIOLOGY--MY KRYPTONIAN PHYSIOLOGY CHANGES UNDER THE BLANKET OF DIFFERENT SOLAR RADIATIONS THROUGHOUT THE GALAXIES.
IT'S WHY MY FATHER SENT ME TO EARTH.
ON EARTH, UNDER THE YELLOW SUN OF SOL, MY SOLAR-CHARGED POWERS ARE PERFECTLY BALANCED, UNDER MY CONTROL...
AND THE GREATEST KRYPTONIAN MINDS **BELIEVED** YELLOW SUNLIGHT BROUGHT US TO OUR ABSOLUTE MAXIMUM POTENTIAL.
MAXIMUM ABILITY.
THIS IS **EXACTLY** WHAT KELEX WAS WORRIED ABOUT.
HERE?
I FEEL A BIT FLU-ISH AND MY FACE IS TINGLING.
AND I AM TRAPPED.

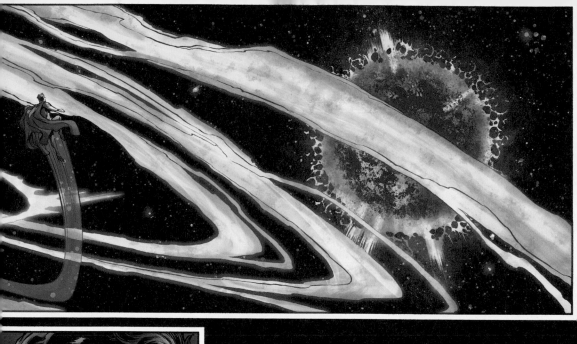

KELEX?

MMHH!

I AM BEING CONTAINED BY A FORCE I CANNOT SEE OR EVEN FEEL WHEN I PUSH BACK ON IT.

I'D BE FASCINATED IF I WASN'T UNDER THE CONTROL OF THIS.

THIS MIGHT BE, MAYBE, THE MOST ALIEN ENVIRONMENT I HAVE EVER ENCOUNTERED.

I JUST WANTED TO UNDER-STAND--

SYNMAR!

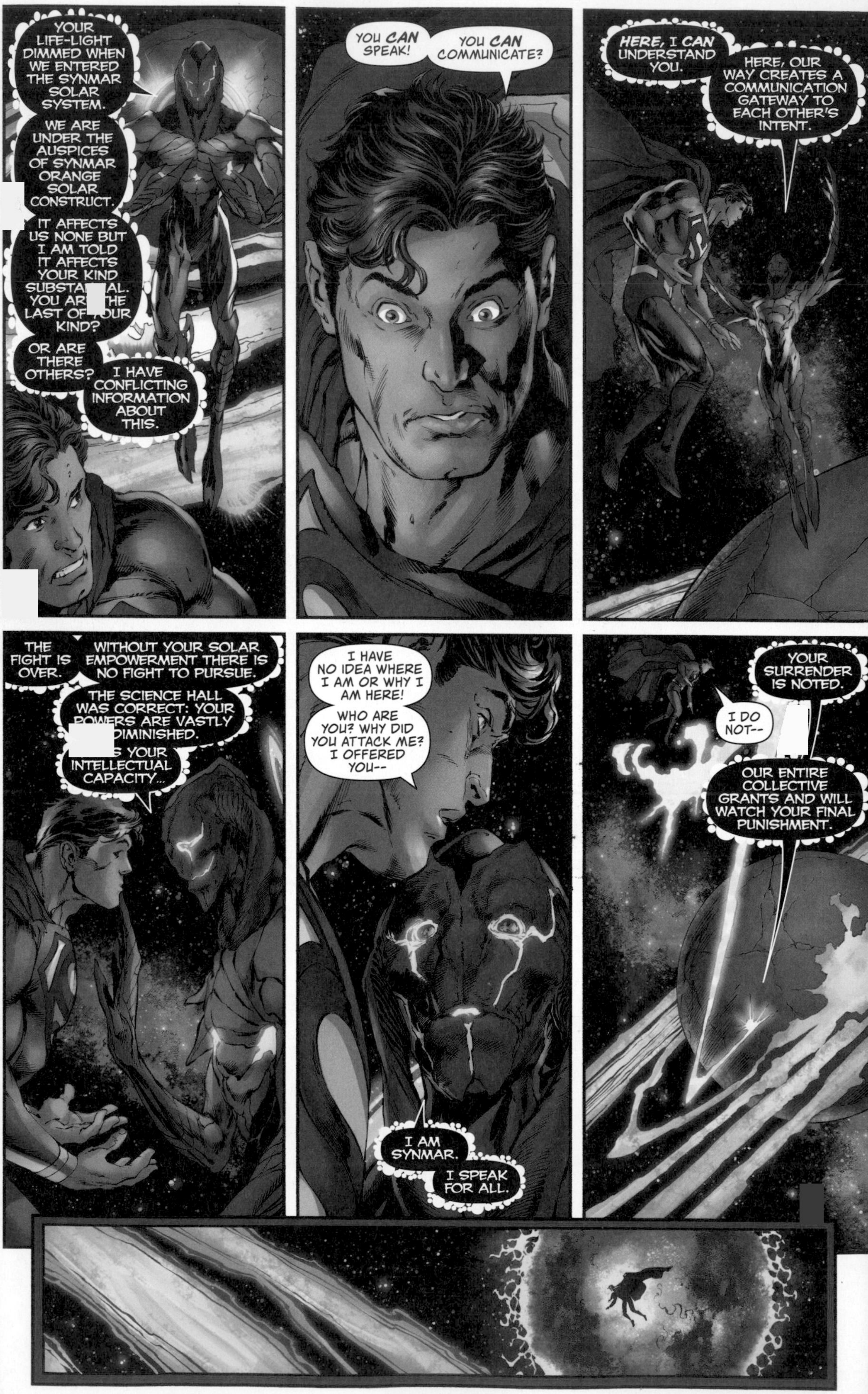
YOUR LIFE-LIGHT DIMMED WHEN WE ENTERED THE SYNMAR SOLAR SYSTEM.
WE ARE UNDER THE AUSPICES OF SYNMAR ORANGE SOLAR CONSTRUCT.
IT AFFECTS US NONE BUT I AM TOLD IT AFFECTS YOUR KIND SUBSTA AL. YOU AR THE LAST OF OUR KIND?
OR ARE THERE OTHERS?
I HAVE CONFLICTING INFORMATION ABOUT THIS.
YOU CAN SPEAK!
YOU CAN COMMUNICATE?
HERE, I CAN UNDERSTAND YOU.
HERE, OUR WAY CREATES A COMMUNICATION GATEWAY TO EACH OTHER'S INTENT.
THE FIGHT IS OVER.
WITHOUT YOUR SOLAR EMPOWERMENT THERE IS NO FIGHT TO PURSUE.
THE SCIENCE HALL WAS CORRECT: YOUR POWERS ARE VASTLY DIMINISHED.
S YOUR INTELLECTUAL CAPACITY...
I HAVE NO IDEA WHERE I AM OR WHY I AM HERE!
WHO ARE YOU? WHY DID YOU ATTACK ME? I OFFERED YOU--
I AM SYNMAR.
I SPEAK FOR ALL.
YOUR SURRENDER IS NOTED.
I DO NOT--
OUR ENTIRE COLLECTIVE GRANTS AND WILL WATCH YOUR FINAL PUNISHMENT.

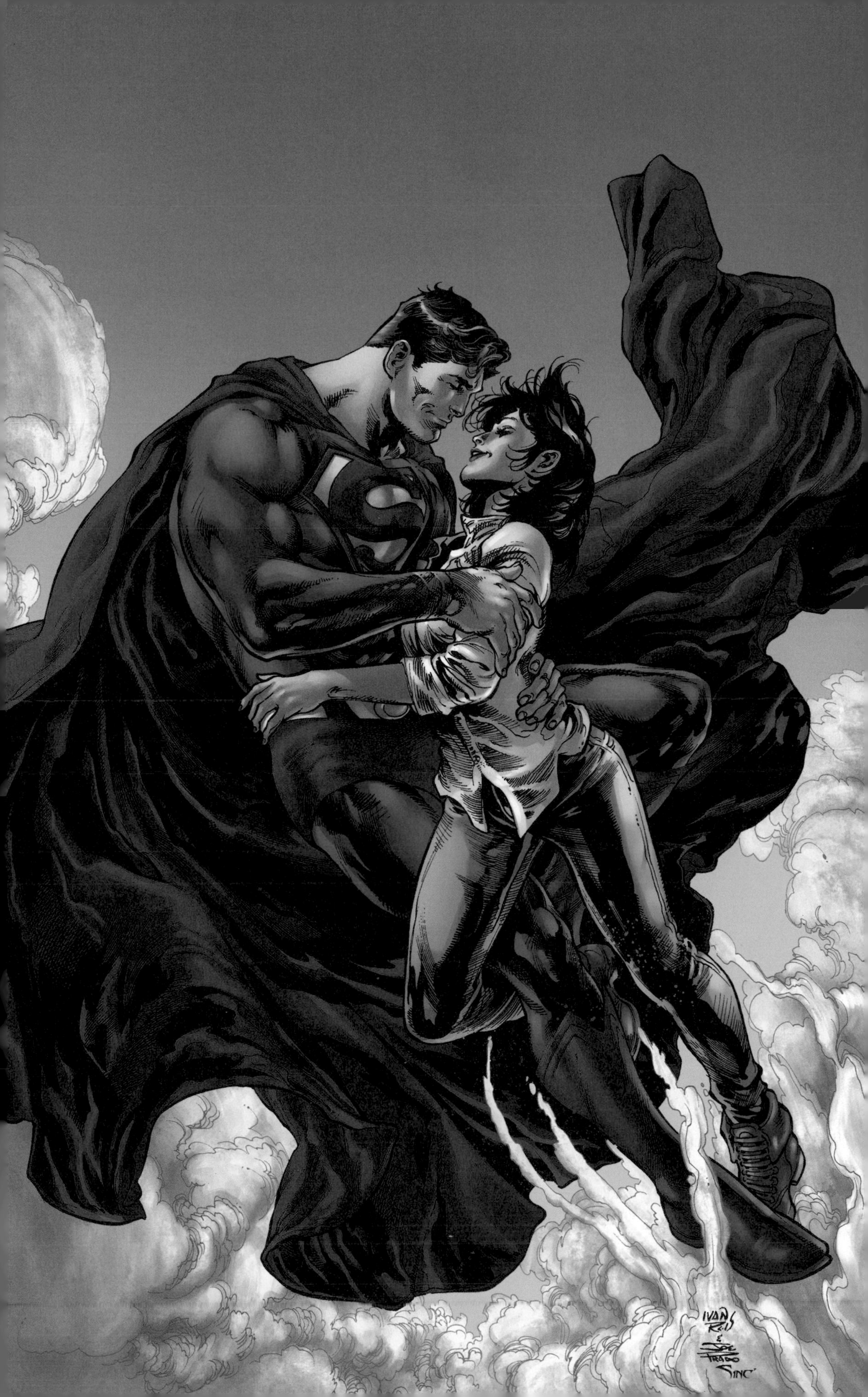

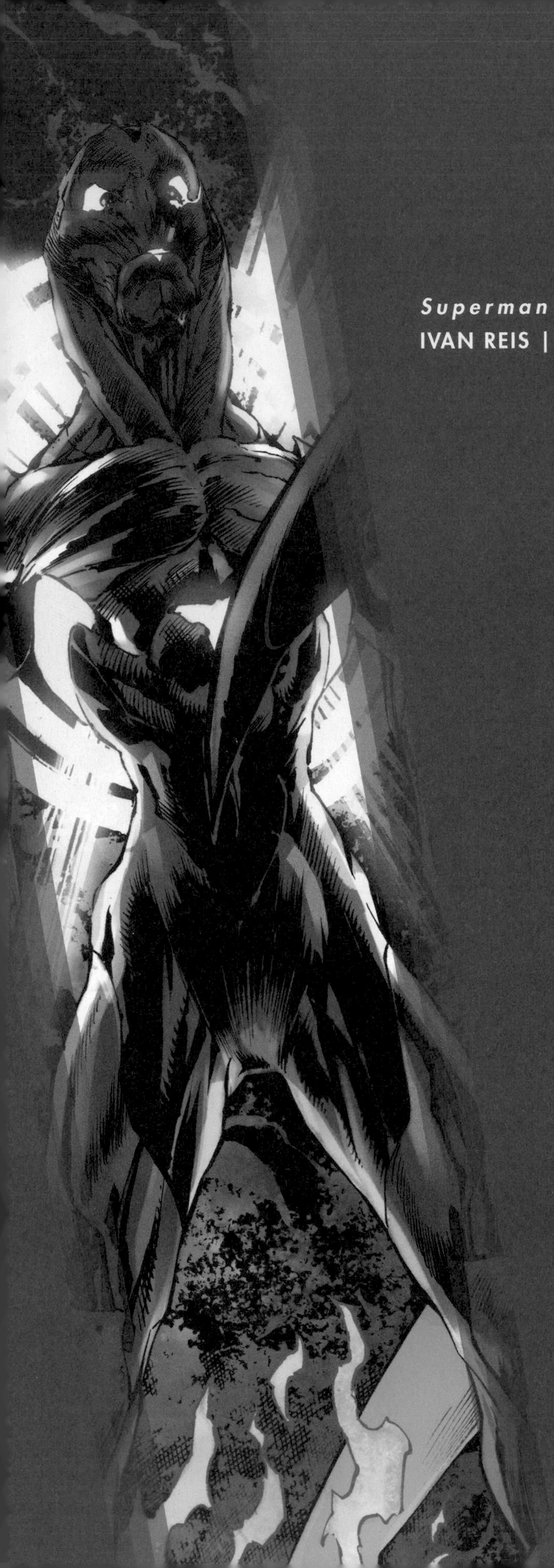

Superman #28 main cover by
IVAN REIS | JOE PRADO | ALEX SINCLAIR

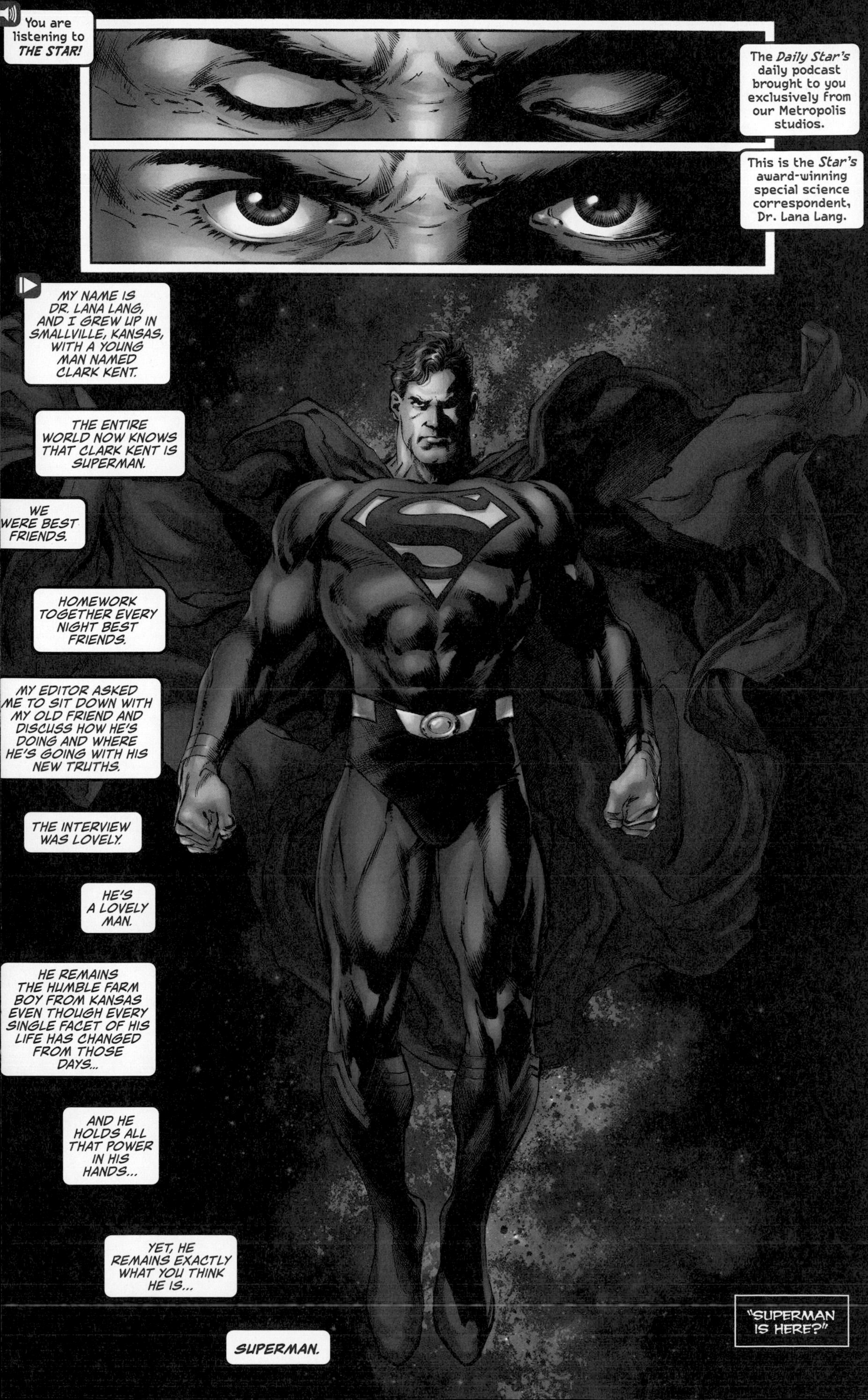
You are listening to THE STAR!
The Daily Star's daily podcast brought to you exclusively from our Metropolis studios.
This is the Star's award-winning special science correspondent, Dr. Lana Lang.
MY NAME IS DR. LANA LANG, AND I GREW UP IN SMALLVILLE, KANSAS, WITH A YOUNG MAN NAMED CLARK KENT.
THE ENTIRE WORLD NOW KNOWS THAT CLARK KENT IS SUPERMAN.
WE WERE BEST FRIENDS.
HOMEWORK TOGETHER EVERY NIGHT BEST FRIENDS.
MY EDITOR ASKED ME TO SIT DOWN WITH MY OLD FRIEND AND DISCUSS HOW HE'S DOING AND WHERE HE'S GOING WITH HIS NEW TRUTHS.
THE INTERVIEW WAS LOVELY.
HE'S A LOVELY MAN.
HE REMAINS THE HUMBLE FARM BOY FROM KANSAS EVEN THOUGH EVERY SINGLE FACET OF HIS LIFE HAS CHANGED FROM THOSE DAYS...
AND HE HOLDS ALL THAT POWER IN HIS HANDS...
YET, HE REMAINS EXACTLY WHAT YOU THINK HE IS...
SUPERMAN.
"SUPERMAN IS HERE?"

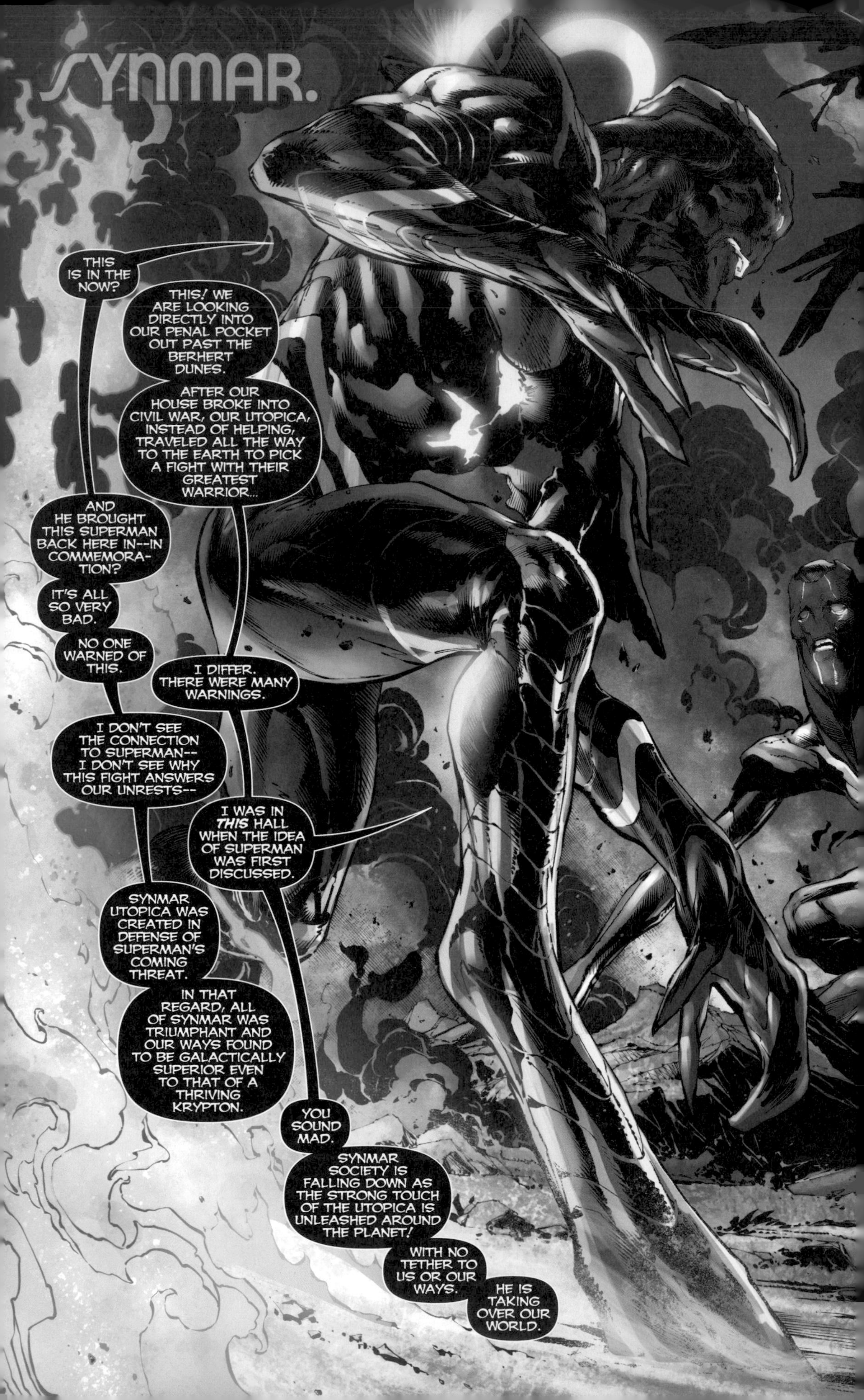
SYNMAR.
THIS IS IN THE NOW?
THIS! WE ARE LOOKING DIRECTLY INTO OUR PENAL POCKET OUT PAST THE BERHERT DUNES.
AFTER OUR HOUSE BROKE INTO CIVIL WAR, OUR UTOPICA, INSTEAD OF HELPING, TRAVELED ALL THE WAY TO THE EARTH TO PICK A FIGHT WITH THEIR GREATEST WARRIOR...
AND HE BROUGHT THIS SUPERMAN BACK HERE IN--IN COMMEMORATION?
IT'S ALL SO VERY BAD.
NO ONE WARNED OF THIS.
I DIFFER. THERE WERE MANY WARNINGS.
I DON'T SEE THE CONNECTION TO SUPERMAN-- I DON'T SEE WHY THIS FIGHT ANSWERS OUR UNRESTS--
I WAS IN *THIS* HALL WHEN THE IDEA OF SUPERMAN WAS FIRST DISCUSSED.
SYNMAR UTOPICA WAS CREATED IN DEFENSE OF SUPERMAN'S COMING THREAT.
IN THAT REGARD, ALL OF SYNMAR WAS TRIUMPHANT AND OUR WAYS FOUND TO BE GALACTICALLY SUPERIOR EVEN TO THAT OF A THRIVING KRYPTON.
YOU SOUND MAD.
SYNMAR SOCIETY IS FALLING DOWN AS THE STRONG TOUCH OF THE UTOPICA IS UNLEASHED AROUND THE PLANET!
WITH NO TETHER TO US OR OUR WAYS.
HE IS TAKING OVER OUR WORLD.

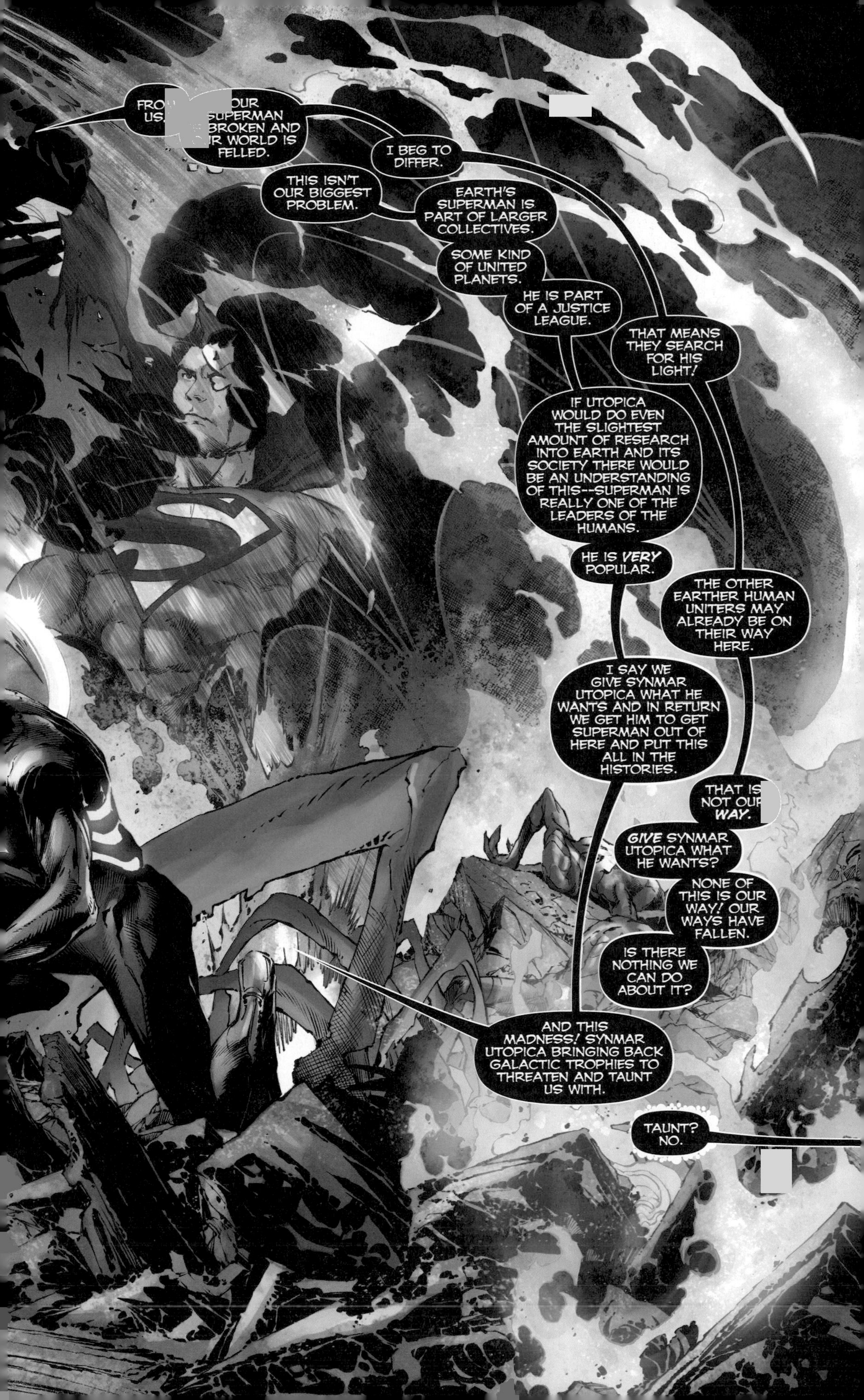

FRO OUR US SUPERMAN BROKEN AND UR WORLD IS FELLED.
I BEG TO DIFFER.
THIS ISN'T OUR BIGGEST PROBLEM.
EARTH'S SUPERMAN IS PART OF LARGER COLLECTIVES.
SOME KIND OF UNITED PLANETS.
HE IS PART OF A JUSTICE LEAGUE.
THAT MEANS THEY SEARCH FOR HIS LIGHT!
IF UTOPICA WOULD DO EVEN THE SLIGHTEST AMOUNT OF RESEARCH INTO EARTH AND ITS SOCIETY THERE WOULD BE AN UNDERSTANDING OF THIS--SUPERMAN IS REALLY ONE OF THE LEADERS OF THE HUMANS.
HE IS *VERY* POPULAR.
THE OTHER EARTHER HUMAN UNITERS MAY ALREADY BE ON THEIR WAY HERE.
I SAY WE GIVE SYNMAR UTOPICA WHAT HE WANTS AND IN RETURN WE GET HIM TO GET SUPERMAN OUT OF HERE AND PUT THIS ALL IN THE HISTORIES.
THAT IS NOT OUR *WAY.*
GIVE SYNMAR UTOPICA WHAT HE WANTS?
NONE OF THIS IS OUR WAY! OUR WAYS HAVE FALLEN.
IS THERE NOTHING WE CAN DO ABOUT IT?
AND THIS MADNESS! SYNMAR UTOPICA BRINGING BACK GALACTIC TROPHIES TO THREATEN AND TAUNT US WITH.
TAUNT? NO.

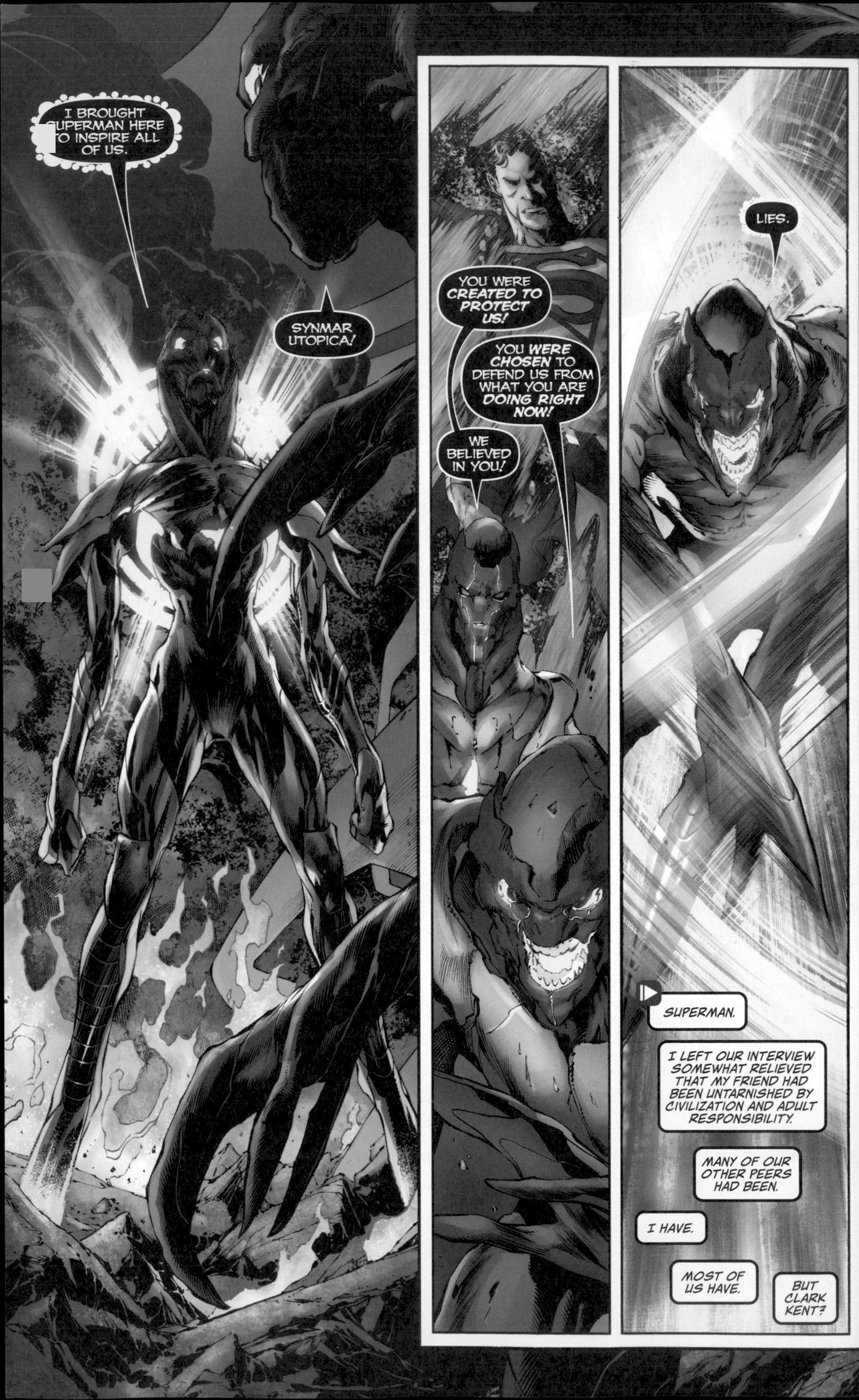
I BROUGHT SUPERMAN HERE TO INSPIRE ALL OF US.
SYNMAR UTOPICA!
YOU WERE CREATED TO PROTECT US!
YOU WERE CHOSEN TO DEFEND US FROM WHAT YOU ARE DOING RIGHT NOW!
WE BELIEVED IN YOU!
LIES.
SUPERMAN.
I LEFT OUR INTERVIEW SOMEWHAT RELIEVED THAT MY FRIEND HAD BEEN UNTARNISHED BY CIVILIZATION AND ADULT RESPONSIBILITY.
MANY OF OUR OTHER PEERS HAD BEEN.
I HAVE.
MOST OF US HAVE.
BUT CLARK KENT?

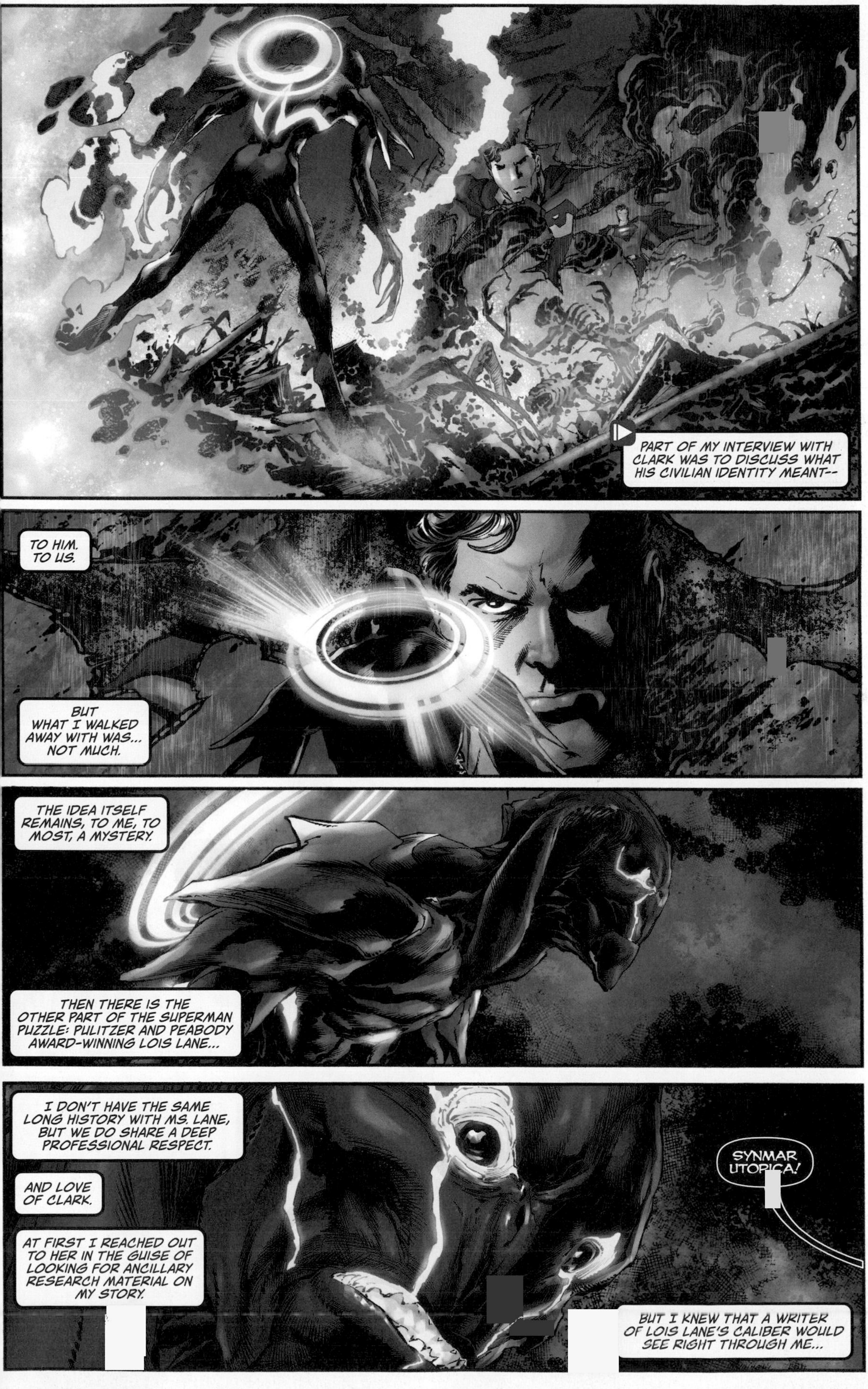
PART OF MY INTERVIEW WITH CLARK WAS TO DISCUSS WHAT HIS CIVILIAN IDENTITY MEANT--
TO HIM. TO US.
BUT WHAT I WALKED AWAY WITH WAS... NOT MUCH.
THE IDEA ITSELF REMAINS, TO ME, TO MOST, A MYSTERY.
THEN THERE IS THE OTHER PART OF THE SUPERMAN PUZZLE: PULITZER AND PEABODY AWARD-WINNING LOIS LANE...
I DON'T HAVE THE SAME LONG HISTORY WITH MS. LANE, BUT WE DO SHARE A DEEP PROFESSIONAL RESPECT.
AND LOVE OF CLARK.
AT FIRST I REACHED OUT TO HER IN THE GUISE OF LOOKING FOR ANCILLARY RESEARCH MATERIAL ON MY STORY.
SYNMAR UTOPICA!
BUT I KNEW THAT A WRITER OF LOIS LANE'S CALIBER WOULD SEE RIGHT THROUGH ME...

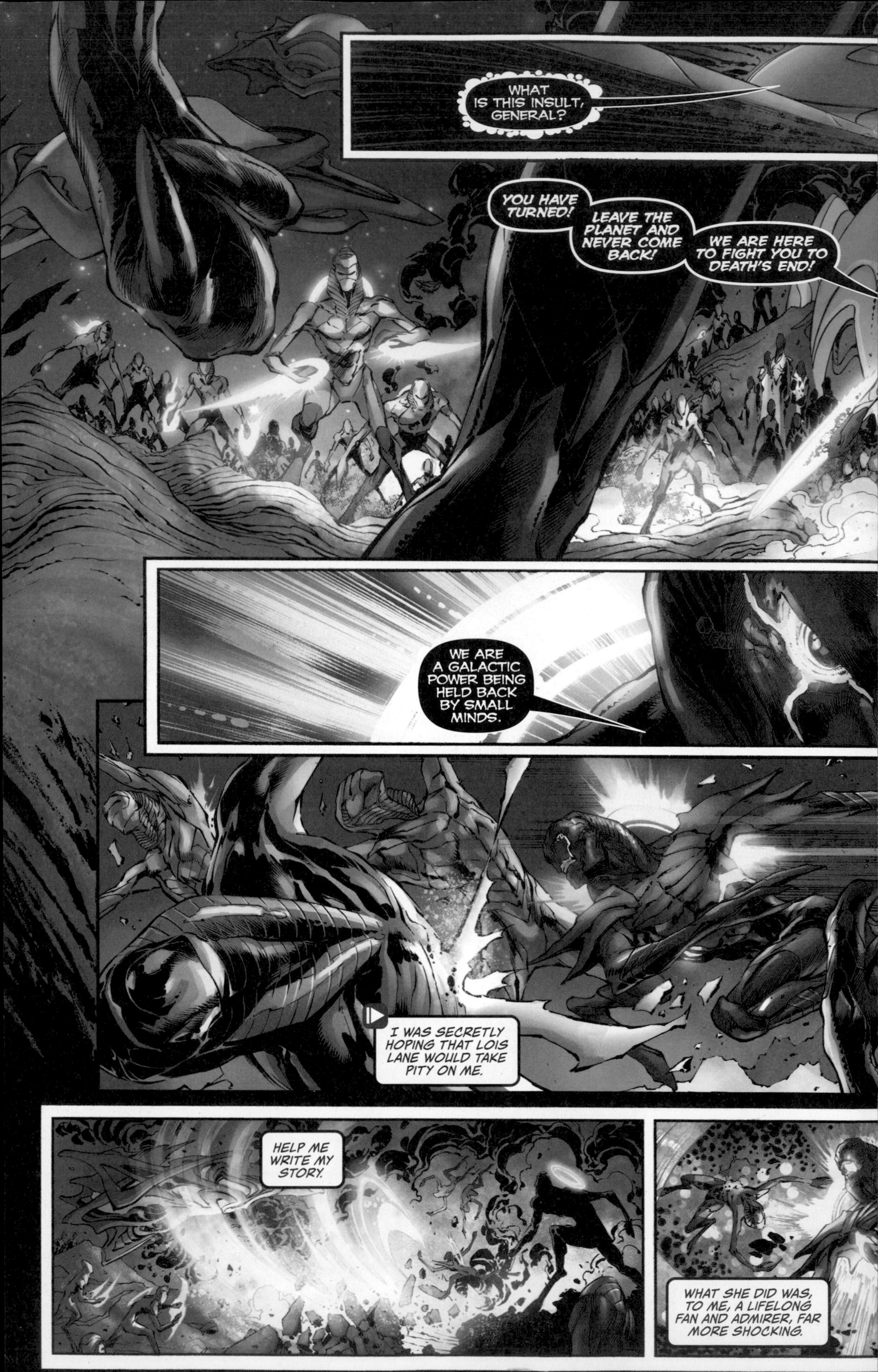
WHAT IS THIS INSULT, GENERAL?
YOU HAVE TURNED!
LEAVE THE PLANET AND NEVER COME BACK!
WE ARE HERE TO FIGHT YOU TO DEATH'S END!
WE ARE A GALACTIC POWER BEING HELD BACK BY SMALL MINDS.
I WAS SECRETLY HOPING THAT LOIS LANE WOULD TAKE PITY ON ME.
HELP ME WRITE MY STORY.
WHAT SHE DID WAS, TO ME, A LIFELONG FAN AND ADMIRER, FAR MORE SHOCKING.

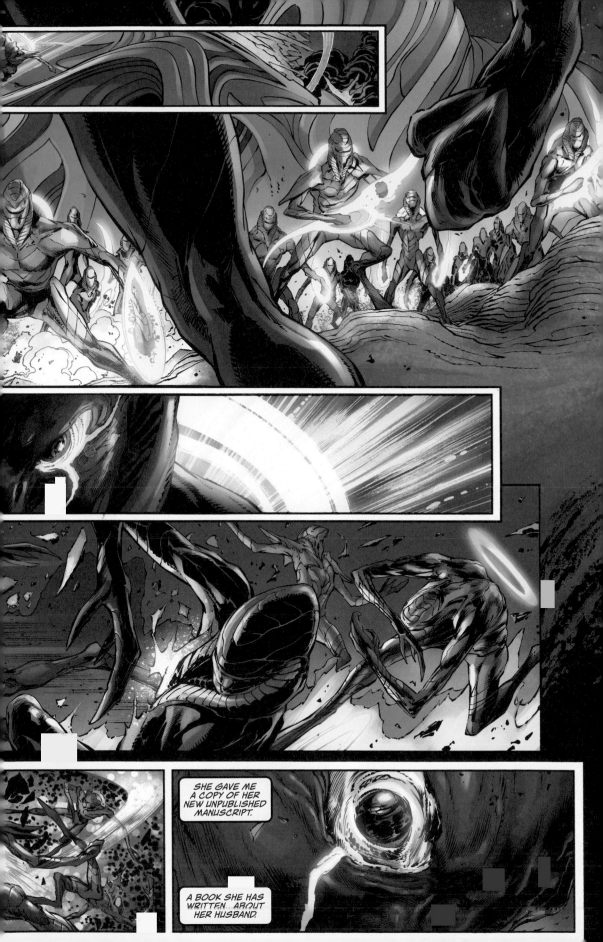

SHE GAVE ME A COPY OF HER NEW UNPUBLISHED MANUSCRIPT.

A BOOK SHE HAS WRITTEN...ABOUT HER HUSBAND.

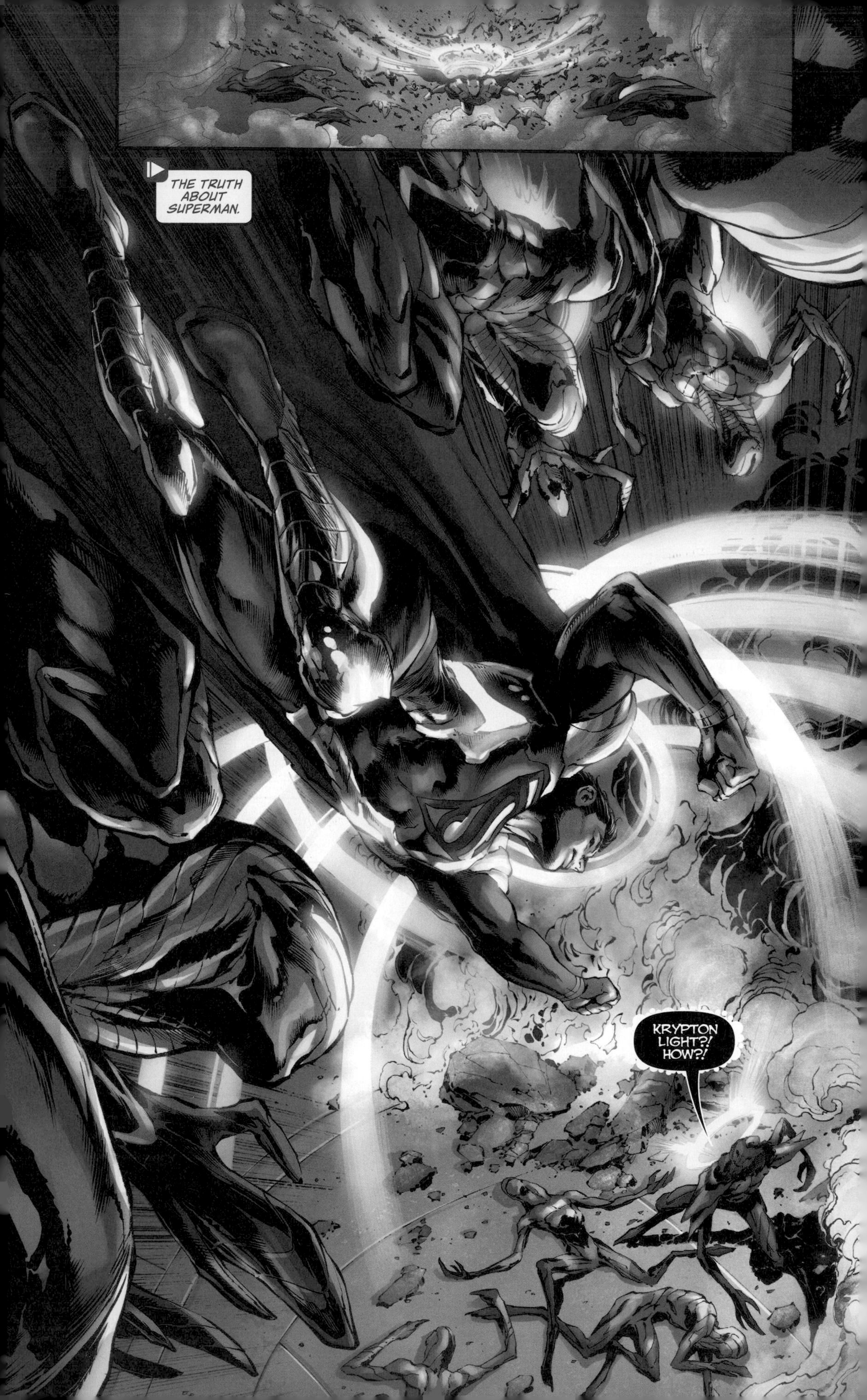
THE TRUTH ABOUT SUPERMAN.
KRYPTON LIGHT?! HOW?!

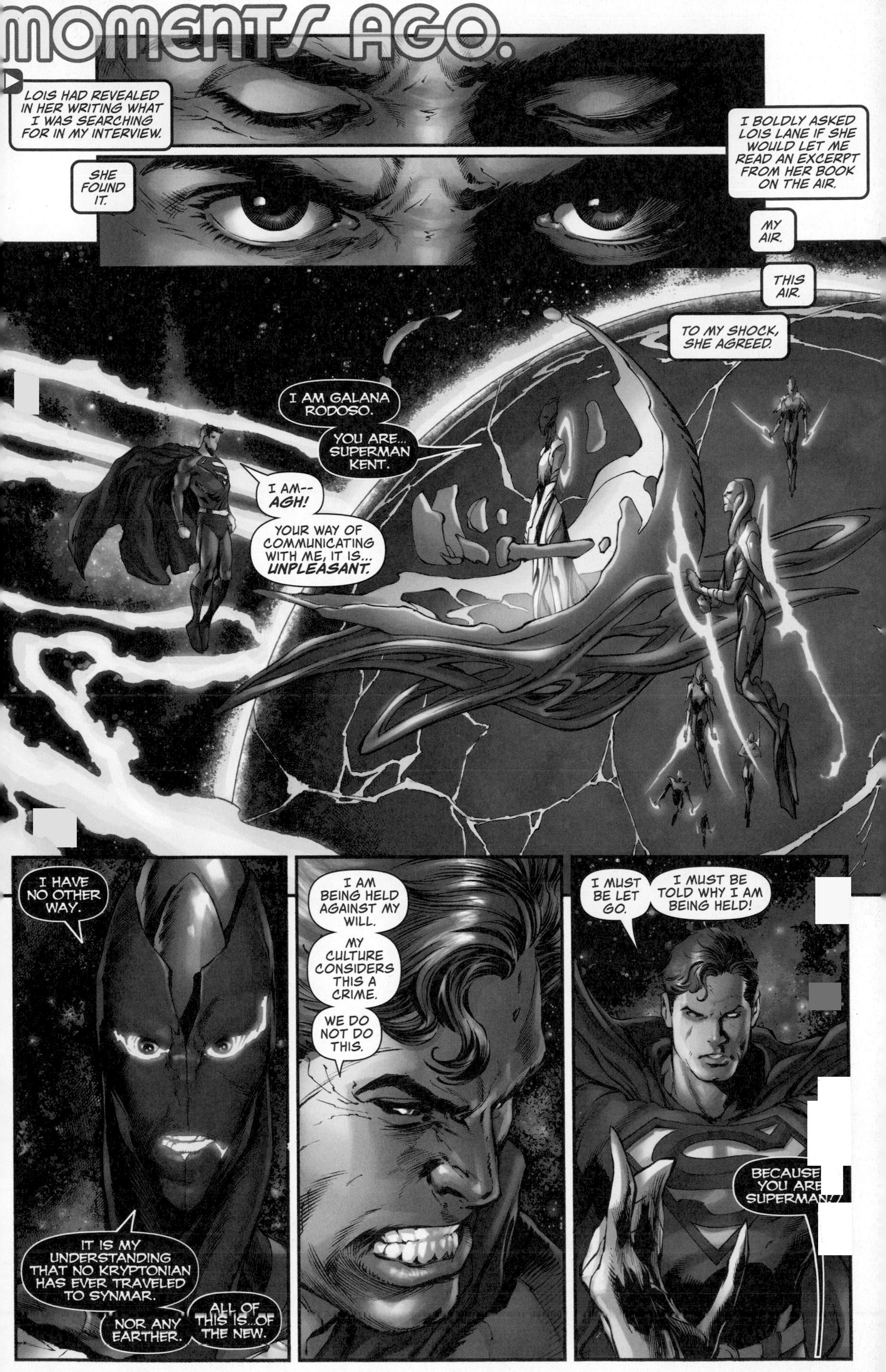
MOMENTS AGO.
LOIS HAD REVEALED IN HER WRITING WHAT I WAS SEARCHING FOR IN MY INTERVIEW.
SHE FOUND IT.
I BOLDLY ASKED LOIS LANE IF SHE WOULD LET ME READ AN EXCERPT FROM HER BOOK ON THE AIR.
MY AIR.
THIS AIR.
TO MY SHOCK, SHE AGREED.
I AM GALANA RODOSO.
YOU ARE... SUPERMAN KENT.
I AM-- AGH!
YOUR WAY OF COMMUNICATING WITH ME, IT IS... UNPLEASANT.
I HAVE NO OTHER WAY.
IT IS MY UNDERSTANDING THAT NO KRYPTONIAN HAS EVER TRAVELED TO SYNMAR.
NOR ANY EARTHER.
ALL OF THIS IS...OF THE NEW.
I AM BEING HELD AGAINST MY WILL.
MY CULTURE CONSIDERS THIS A CRIME.
WE DO NOT DO THIS.
I MUST BE LET GO.
I MUST BE TOLD WHY I AM BEING HELD!
BECAUSE YOU ARE SUPERMAN

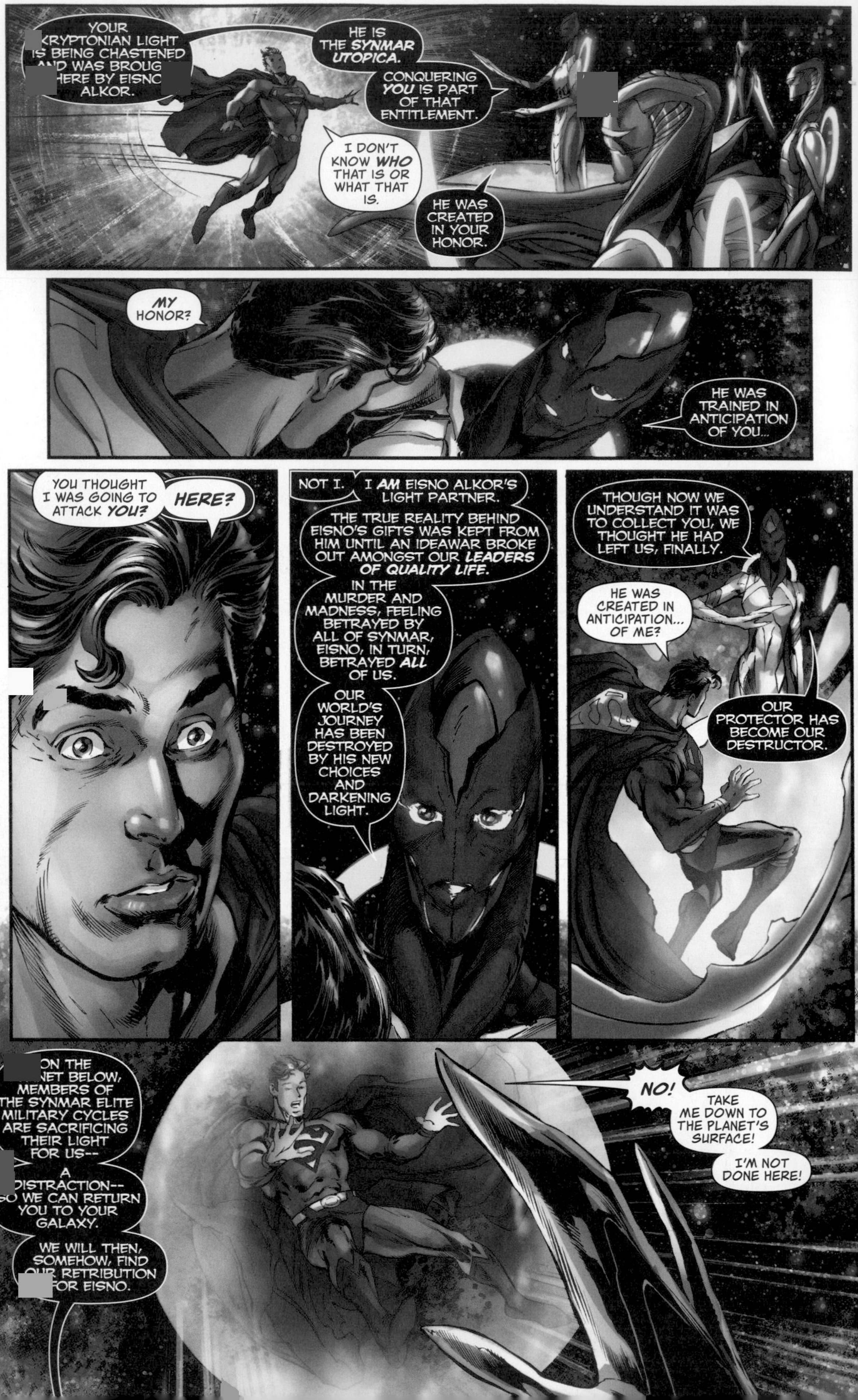

YOUR KRYPTONIAN LIGHT IS BEING CHASTENED AND WAS BROUG HERE BY EISNO ALKOR.
HE IS THE SYNMAR UTOPICA.
CONQUERING YOU IS PART OF THAT ENTITLEMENT.
I DON'T KNOW WHO THAT IS OR WHAT THAT IS.
HE WAS CREATED IN YOUR HONOR.
MY HONOR?
HE WAS TRAINED IN ANTICIPATION OF YOU...
YOU THOUGHT I WAS GOING TO ATTACK YOU?
HERE?
NOT I.
I AM EISNO ALKOR'S LIGHT PARTNER.
THE TRUE REALITY BEHIND EISNO'S GIFTS WAS KEPT FROM HIM UNTIL AN IDEAWAR BROKE OUT AMONGST OUR LEADERS OF QUALITY LIFE.
IN THE MURDER AND MADNESS, FEELING BETRAYED BY ALL OF SYNMAR, EISNO, IN TURN, BETRAYED ALL OF US.
OUR WORLD'S JOURNEY HAS BEEN DESTROYED BY HIS NEW CHOICES AND DARKENING LIGHT.
THOUGH NOW WE UNDERSTAND IT WAS TO COLLECT YOU, WE THOUGHT HE HAD LEFT US, FINALLY.
HE WAS CREATED IN ANTICIPATION... OF ME?
OUR PROTECTOR HAS BECOME OUR DESTRUCTOR.
ON THE NET BELOW, MEMBERS OF THE SYNMAR ELITE MILITARY CYCLES ARE SACRIFICING THEIR LIGHT FOR US--
A DISTRACTION-- SO WE CAN RETURN YOU TO YOUR GALAXY.
WE WILL THEN, SOMEHOW, FIND OUR RETRIBUTION FOR EISNO.
NO!
TAKE ME DOWN TO THE PLANET'S SURFACE!
I'M NOT DONE HERE!

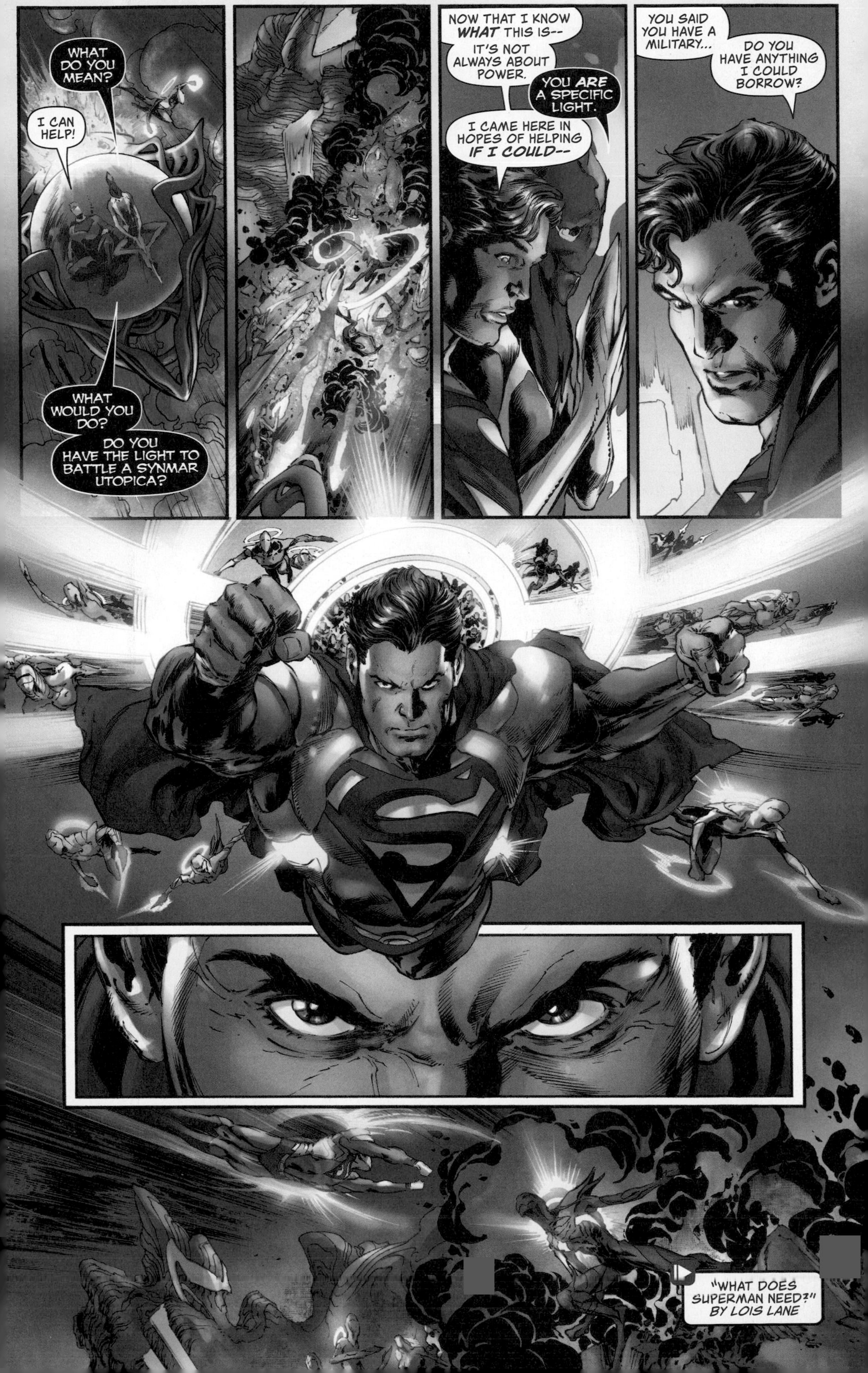
WHAT DO YOU MEAN?
I CAN HELP!
WHAT WOULD YOU DO?
DO YOU HAVE THE LIGHT TO BATTLE A SYNMAR UTOPICA?
NOW THAT I KNOW WHAT THIS IS--
IT'S NOT ALWAYS ABOUT POWER.
YOU ARE A SPECIFIC LIGHT.
I CAME HERE IN HOPES OF HELPING IF I COULD--
YOU SAID YOU HAVE A MILITARY...
DO YOU HAVE ANYTHING I COULD BORROW?
"WHAT DOES SUPERMAN NEED?" BY LOIS LANE

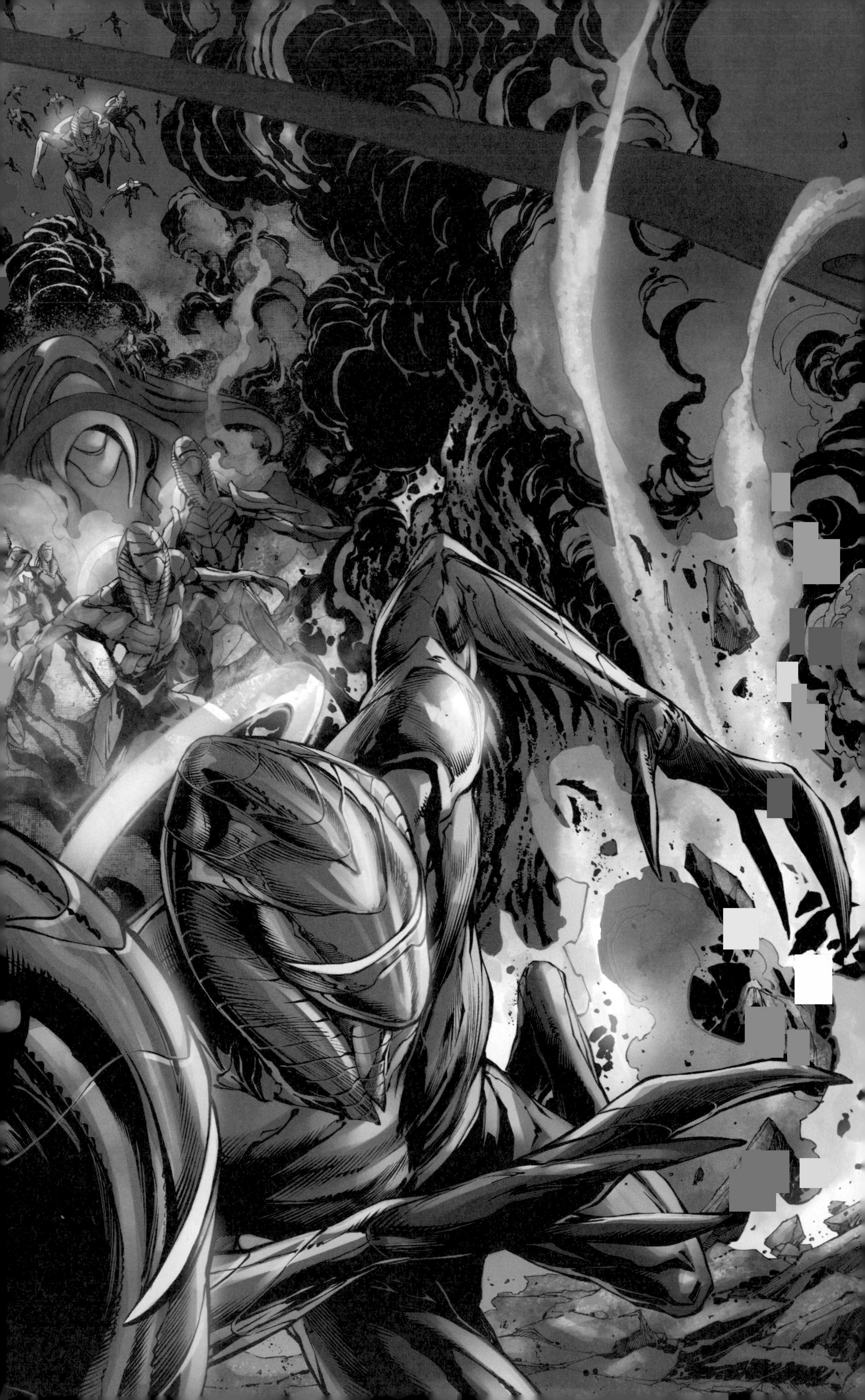

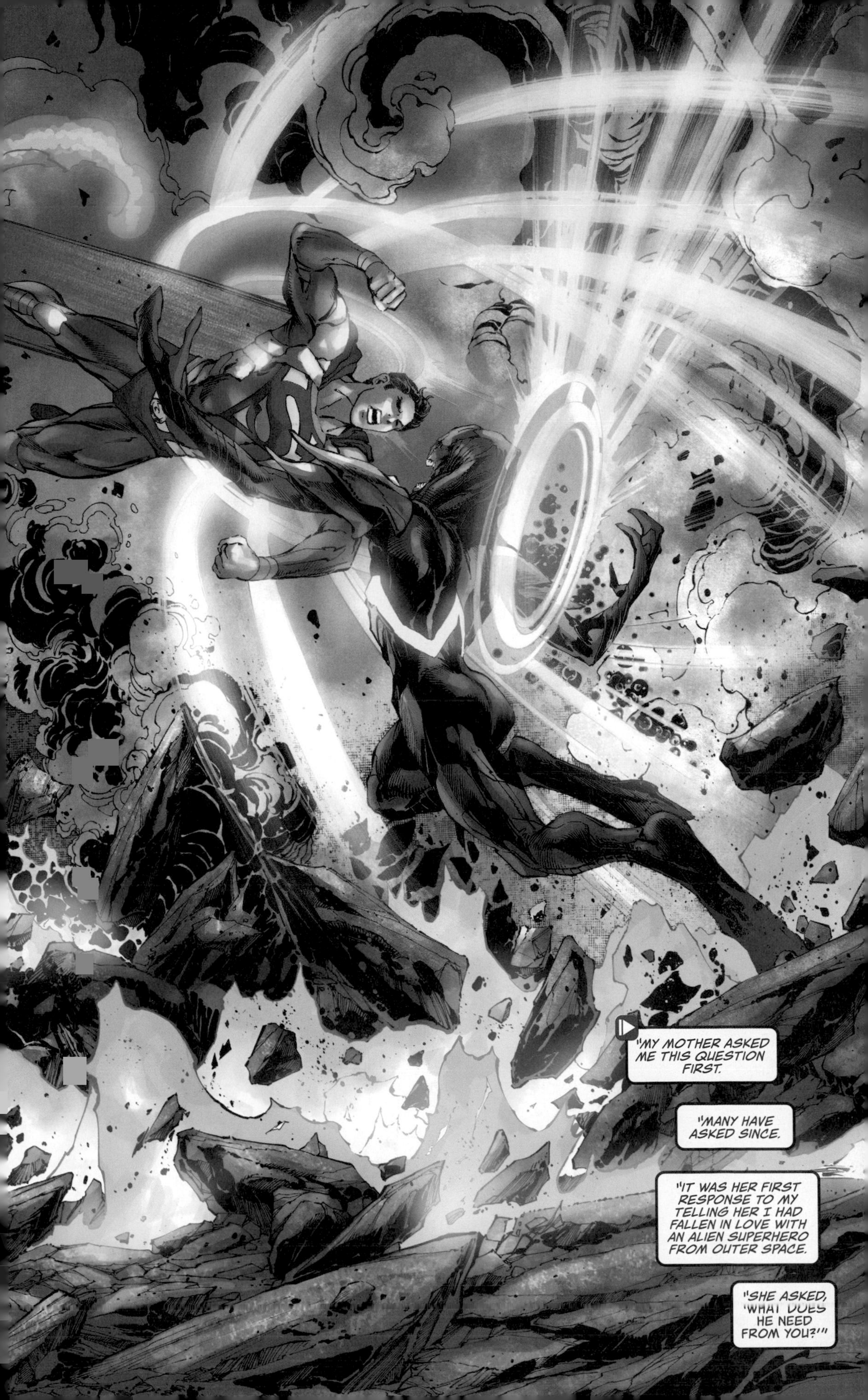
"MY MOTHER ASKED ME THIS QUESTION FIRST.
"MANY HAVE ASKED SINCE.
"IT WAS HER FIRST RESPONSE TO MY TELLING HER I HAD FALLEN IN LOVE WITH AN ALIEN SUPERHERO FROM OUTER SPACE.
"SHE ASKED, 'WHAT DOES HE NEED FROM YOU?'"

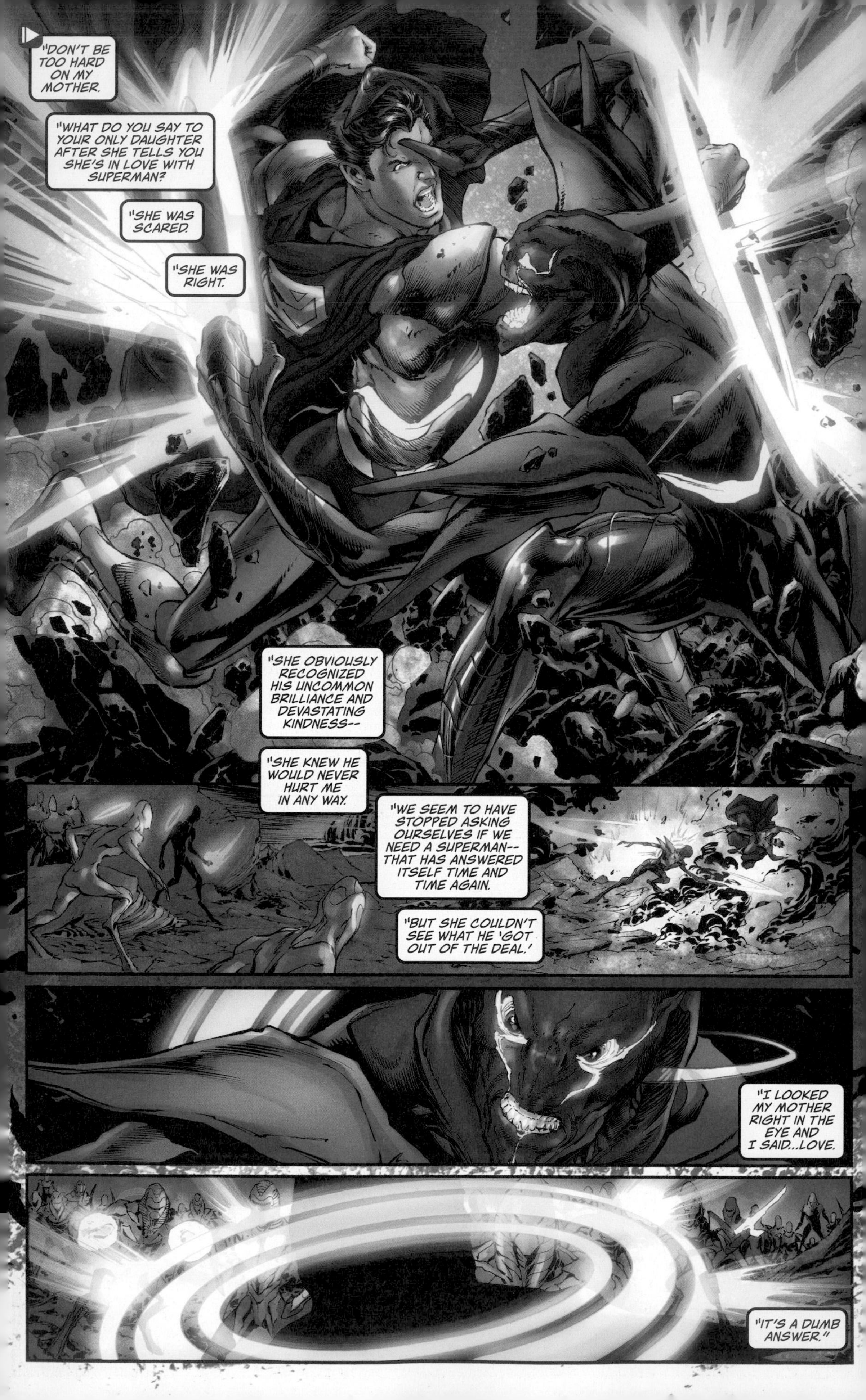
"DON'T BE TOO HARD ON MY MOTHER.
"WHAT DO YOU SAY TO YOUR ONLY DAUGHTER AFTER SHE TELLS YOU SHE'S IN LOVE WITH SUPERMAN?
"SHE WAS SCARED.
"SHE WAS RIGHT.
"SHE OBVIOUSLY RECOGNIZED HIS UNCOMMON BRILLIANCE AND DEVASTATING KINDNESS--
"SHE KNEW HE WOULD NEVER HURT ME IN ANY WAY.
"WE SEEM TO HAVE STOPPED ASKING OURSELVES IF WE NEED A SUPERMAN--THAT HAS ANSWERED ITSELF TIME AND TIME AGAIN.
"BUT SHE COULDN'T SEE WHAT HE 'GOT OUT OF THE DEAL.'
"I LOOKED MY MOTHER RIGHT IN THE EYE AND I SAID...LOVE.
"IT'S A DUMB ANSWER."

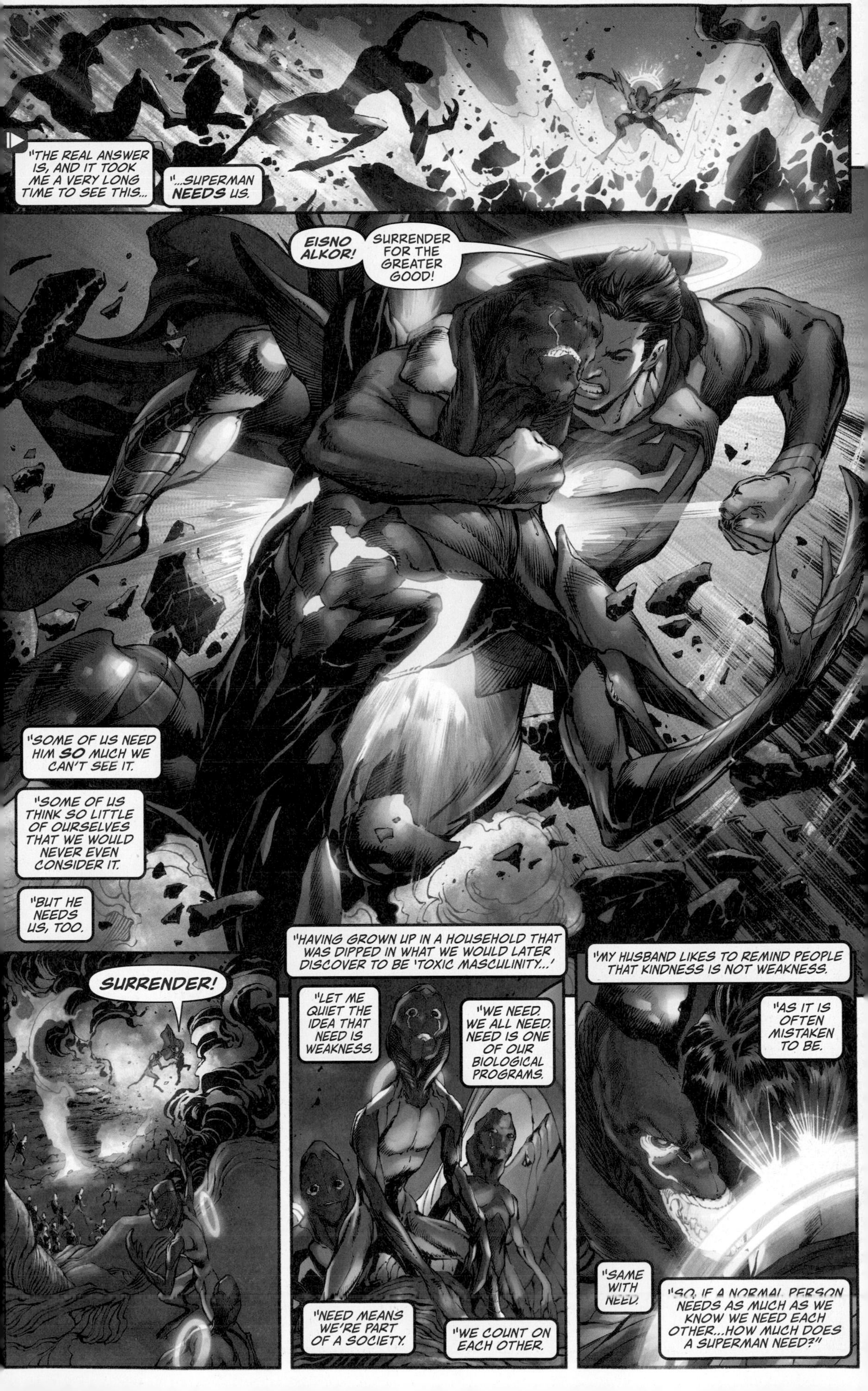
"THE REAL ANSWER IS, AND IT TOOK ME A VERY LONG TIME TO SEE THIS...
"...SUPERMAN NEEDS US.
EISNO ALKOR!
SURRENDER FOR THE GREATER GOOD!
"SOME OF US NEED HIM SO MUCH WE CAN'T SEE IT.
"SOME OF US THINK SO LITTLE OF OURSELVES THAT WE WOULD NEVER EVEN CONSIDER IT.
"BUT HE NEEDS US, TOO.
SURRENDER!
"HAVING GROWN UP IN A HOUSEHOLD THAT WAS DIPPED IN WHAT WE WOULD LATER DISCOVER TO BE 'TOXIC MASCULINITY...'
"LET ME QUIET THE IDEA THAT NEED IS WEAKNESS.
"WE NEED. WE ALL NEED. NEED IS ONE OF OUR BIOLOGICAL PROGRAMS.
"NEED MEANS WE'RE PART OF A SOCIETY.
"WE COUNT ON EACH OTHER.
"MY HUSBAND LIKES TO REMIND PEOPLE THAT KINDNESS IS NOT WEAKNESS.
"AS IT IS OFTEN MISTAKEN TO BE.
"SAME WITH NEED.
"SO, IF A NORMAL PERSON NEEDS AS MUCH AS WE KNOW WE NEED EACH OTHER...HOW MUCH DOES A SUPERMAN NEED?"

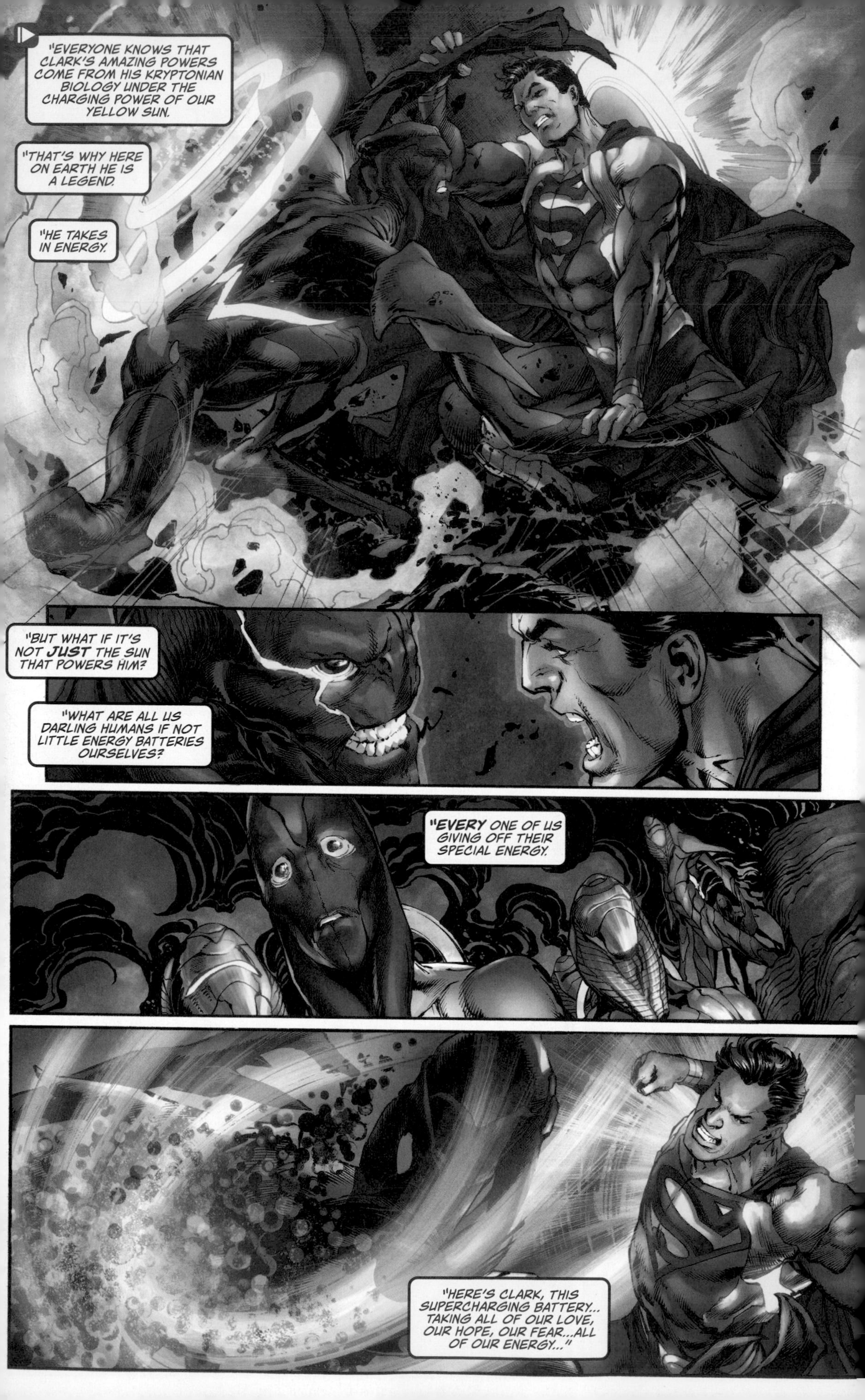
"EVERYONE KNOWS THAT CLARK'S AMAZING POWERS COME FROM HIS KRYPTONIAN BIOLOGY UNDER THE CHARGING POWER OF OUR YELLOW SUN.
"THAT'S WHY HERE ON EARTH HE IS A LEGEND.
"HE TAKES IN ENERGY.
"BUT WHAT IF IT'S NOT JUST THE SUN THAT POWERS HIM?
"WHAT ARE ALL US DARLING HUMANS IF NOT LITTLE ENERGY BATTERIES OURSELVES?
"EVERY ONE OF US GIVING OFF THEIR SPECIAL ENERGY.
"HERE'S CLARK, THIS SUPERCHARGING BATTERY... TAKING ALL OF OUR LOVE, OUR HOPE, OUR FEAR...ALL OF OUR ENERGY..."

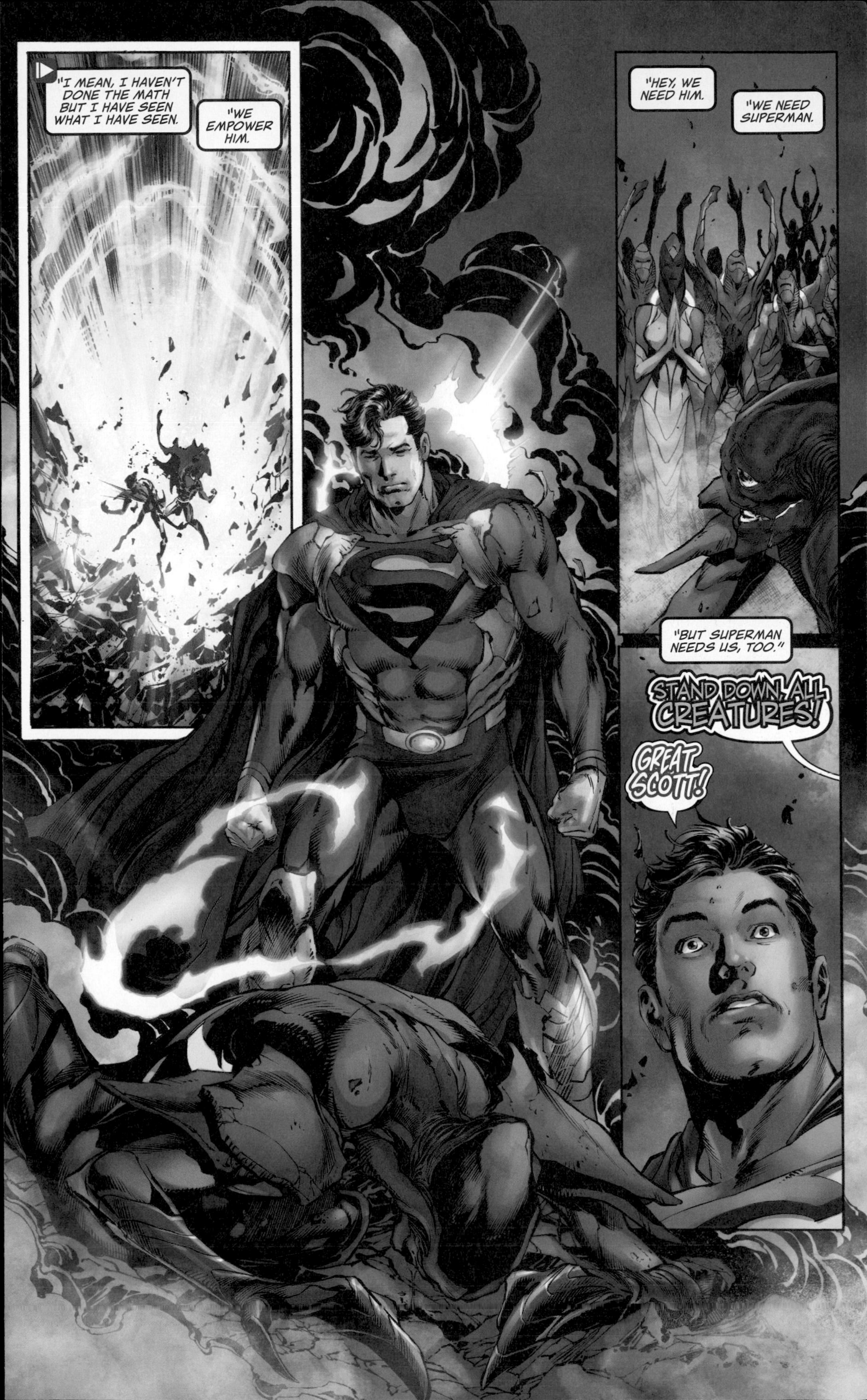
"I MEAN, I HAVEN'T DONE THE MATH BUT I HAVE SEEN WHAT I HAVE SEEN.
"WE EMPOWER HIM.
"HEY, WE NEED HIM.
"WE NEED SUPERMAN.
"BUT SUPERMAN NEEDS US, TOO."
STAND DOWN, ALL CREATURES!
GREAT SCOTT!

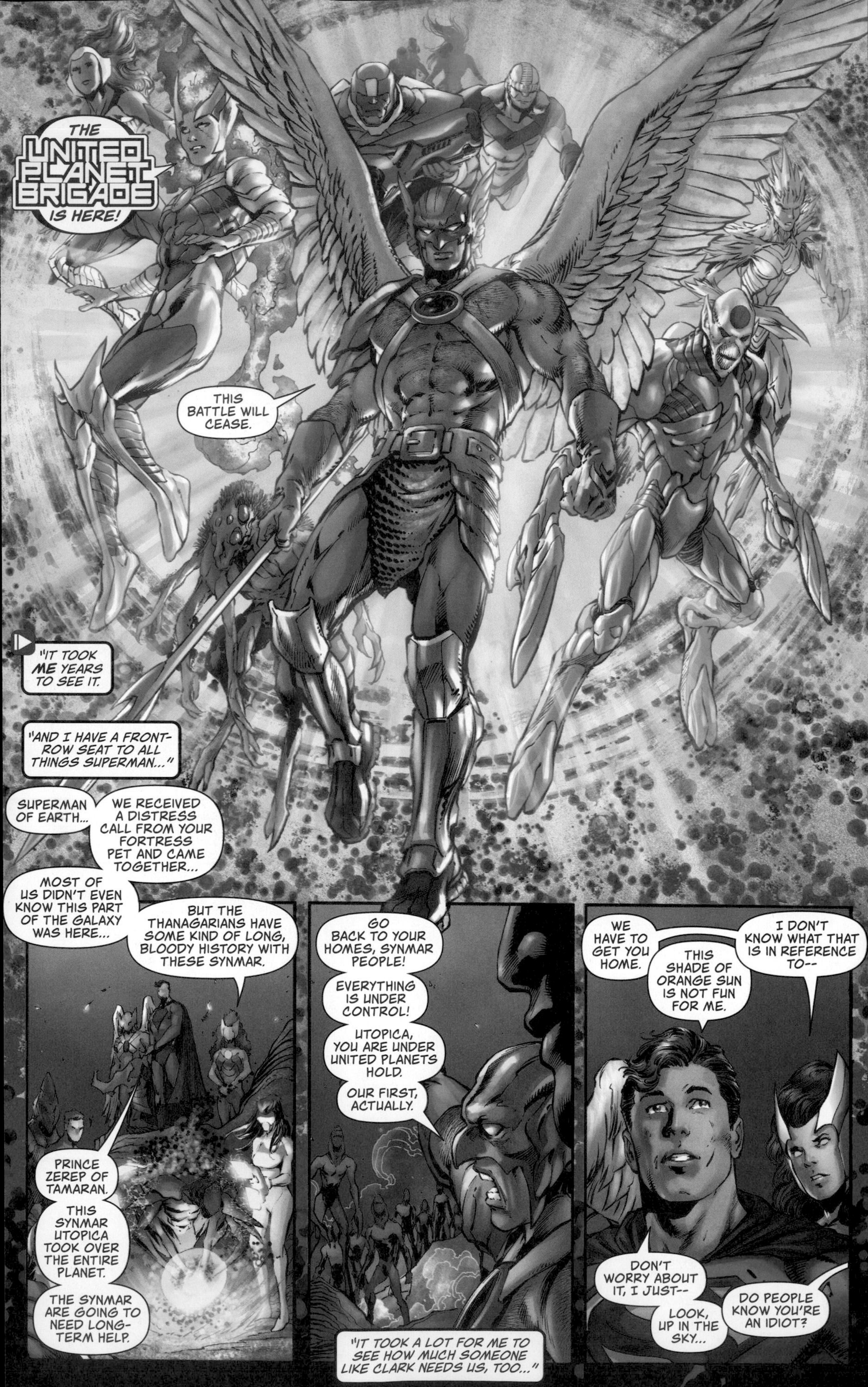
THE UNITED PLANET BRIGADE IS HERE!
THIS BATTLE WILL CEASE.
"IT TOOK ME YEARS TO SEE IT.
"AND I HAVE A FRONT-ROW SEAT TO ALL THINGS SUPERMAN..."
SUPERMAN OF EARTH...
WE RECEIVED A DISTRESS CALL FROM YOUR FORTRESS PET AND CAME TOGETHER...
MOST OF US DIDN'T EVEN KNOW THIS PART OF THE GALAXY WAS HERE...
BUT THE THANAGARIANS HAVE SOME KIND OF LONG, BLOODY HISTORY WITH THESE SYNMAR.
PRINCE ZEREP OF TAMARAN.
THIS SYNMAR UTOPICA TOOK OVER THE ENTIRE PLANET.
THE SYNMAR ARE GOING TO NEED LONG-TERM HELP.
GO BACK TO YOUR HOMES, SYNMAR PEOPLE!
EVERYTHING IS UNDER CONTROL!
UTOPICA, YOU ARE UNDER UNITED PLANETS HOLD.
OUR FIRST, ACTUALLY.
"IT TOOK A LOT FOR ME TO SEE HOW MUCH SOMEONE LIKE CLARK NEEDS US, TOO..."
WE HAVE TO GET YOU HOME.
I DON'T KNOW WHAT THAT IS IN REFERENCE TO--
THIS SHADE OF ORANGE SUN IS NOT FUN FOR ME.
DON'T WORRY ABOUT IT, I JUST--
LOOK, UP IN THE SKY...
DO PEOPLE KNOW YOU'RE AN IDIOT?

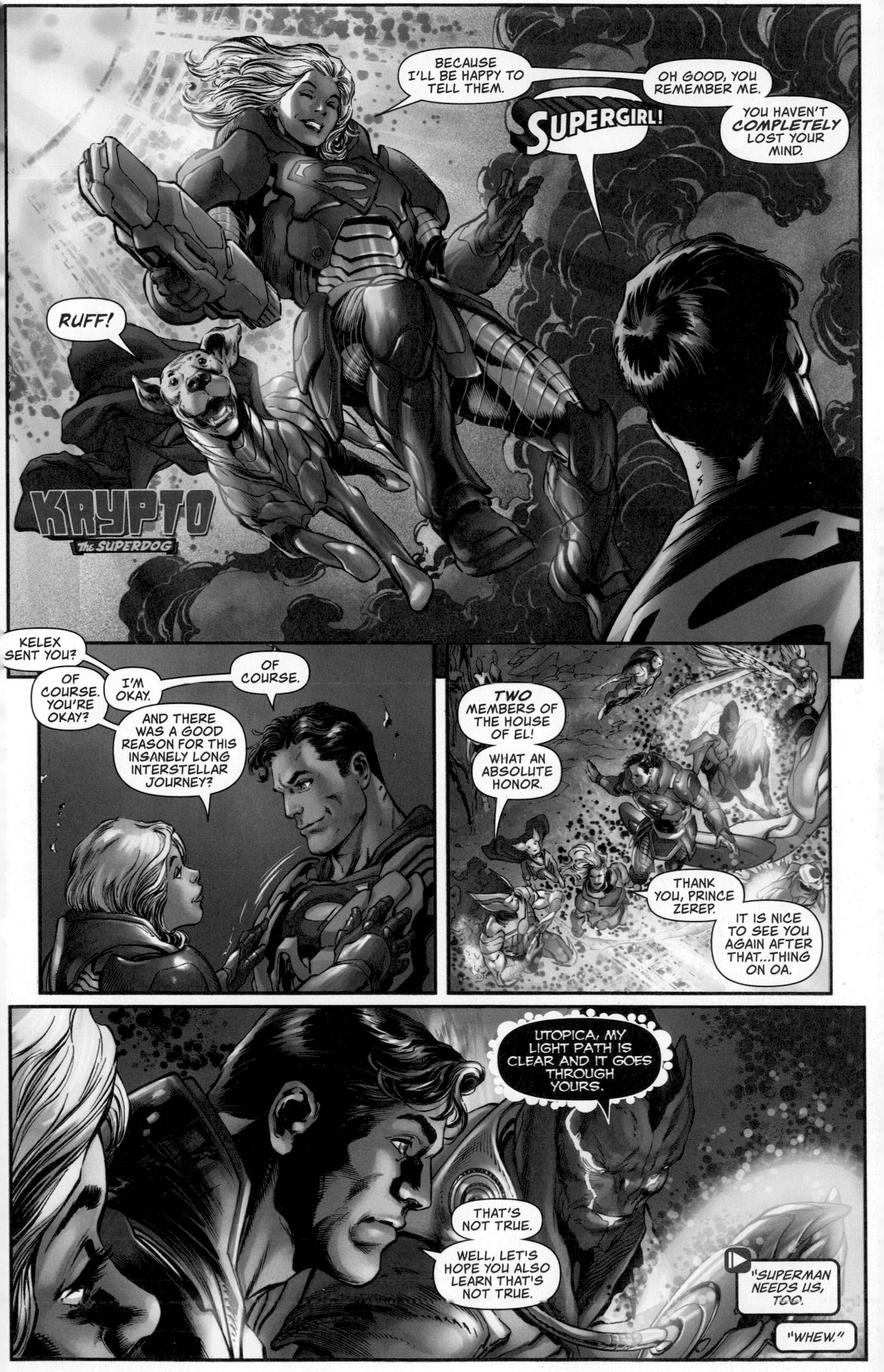
BECAUSE I'LL BE HAPPY TO TELL THEM.
OH GOOD, YOU REMEMBER ME.
YOU HAVEN'T COMPLETELY LOST YOUR MIND.
SUPERGIRL!
RUFF!
KRYPTO The SUPERDOG
KELEX SENT YOU?
OF COURSE. YOU'RE OKAY?
I'M OKAY.
OF COURSE.
AND THERE WAS A GOOD REASON FOR THIS INSANELY LONG INTERSTELLAR JOURNEY?
TWO MEMBERS OF THE HOUSE OF EL!
WHAT AN ABSOLUTE HONOR.
THANK YOU, PRINCE ZEREP.
IT IS NICE TO SEE YOU AGAIN AFTER THAT...THING ON OA.
UTOPICA, MY LIGHT PATH IS CLEAR AND IT GOES THROUGH YOURS.
THAT'S NOT TRUE.
WELL, LET'S HOPE YOU ALSO LEARN THAT'S NOT TRUE.
"SUPERMAN NEEDS US, TOO.
"WHEW."

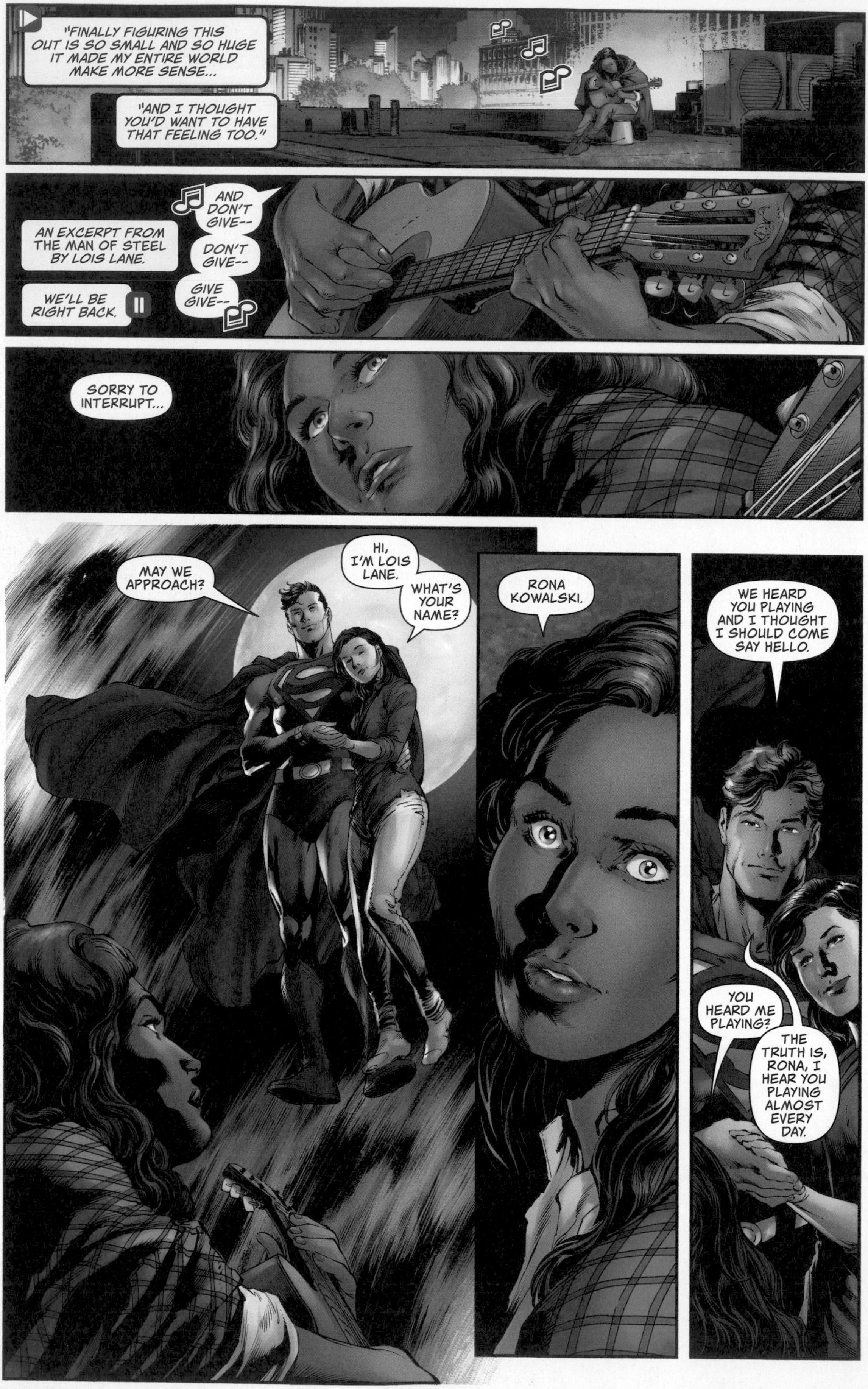
"FINALLY FIGURING THIS OUT IS SO SMALL AND SO HUGE IT MADE MY ENTIRE WORLD MAKE MORE SENSE...
"AND I THOUGHT YOU'D WANT TO HAVE THAT FEELING TOO."
AN EXCERPT FROM THE MAN OF STEEL BY LOIS LANE.
WE'LL BE RIGHT BACK.
AND DON'T GIVE--
DON'T GIVE--
GIVE GIVE--
SORRY TO INTERRUPT...
MAY WE APPROACH?
HI, I'M LOIS LANE.
WHAT'S YOUR NAME?
RONA KOWALSKI.
WE HEARD YOU PLAYING AND I THOUGHT I SHOULD COME SAY HELLO.
YOU HEARD ME PLAYING?
THE TRUTH IS, RONA, I HEAR YOU PLAYING ALMOST EVERY DAY.

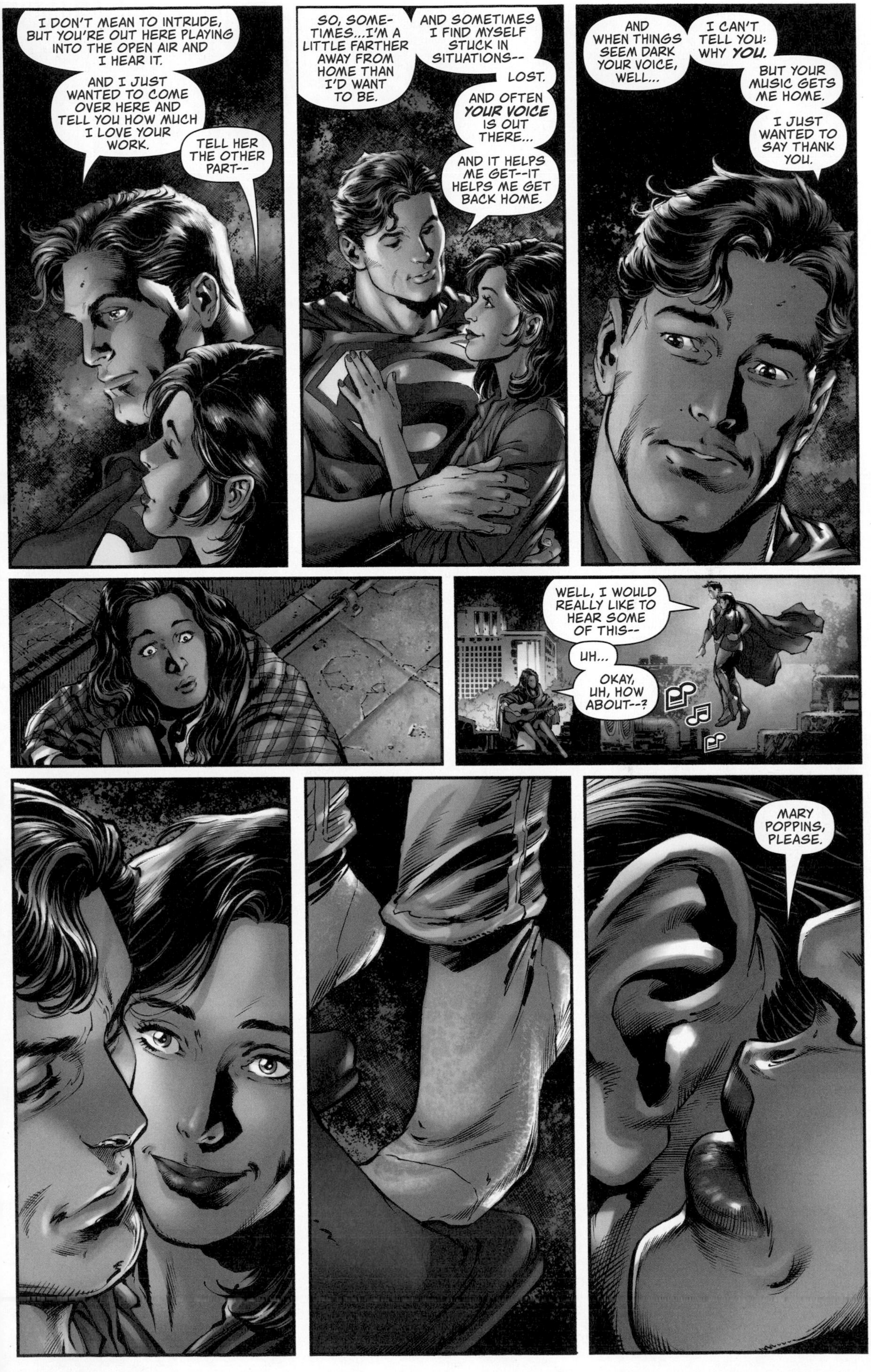
I DON'T MEAN TO INTRUDE, BUT YOU'RE OUT HERE PLAYING INTO THE OPEN AIR AND I HEAR IT.
AND I JUST WANTED TO COME OVER HERE AND TELL YOU HOW MUCH I LOVE YOUR WORK.
TELL HER THE OTHER PART--
SO, SOMETIMES...I'M A LITTLE FARTHER AWAY FROM HOME THAN I'D WANT TO BE.
AND SOMETIMES I FIND MYSELF STUCK IN SITUATIONS--
LOST.
AND OFTEN YOUR VOICE IS OUT THERE...
AND IT HELPS ME GET--IT HELPS ME GET BACK HOME.
AND WHEN THINGS SEEM DARK YOUR VOICE, WELL...
I CAN'T TELL YOU: WHY YOU.
BUT YOUR MUSIC GETS ME HOME.
I JUST WANTED TO SAY THANK YOU.
WELL, I WOULD REALLY LIKE TO HEAR SOME OF THIS--
UH...
OKAY, UH, HOW ABOUT--?
MARY POPPINS, PLEASE.

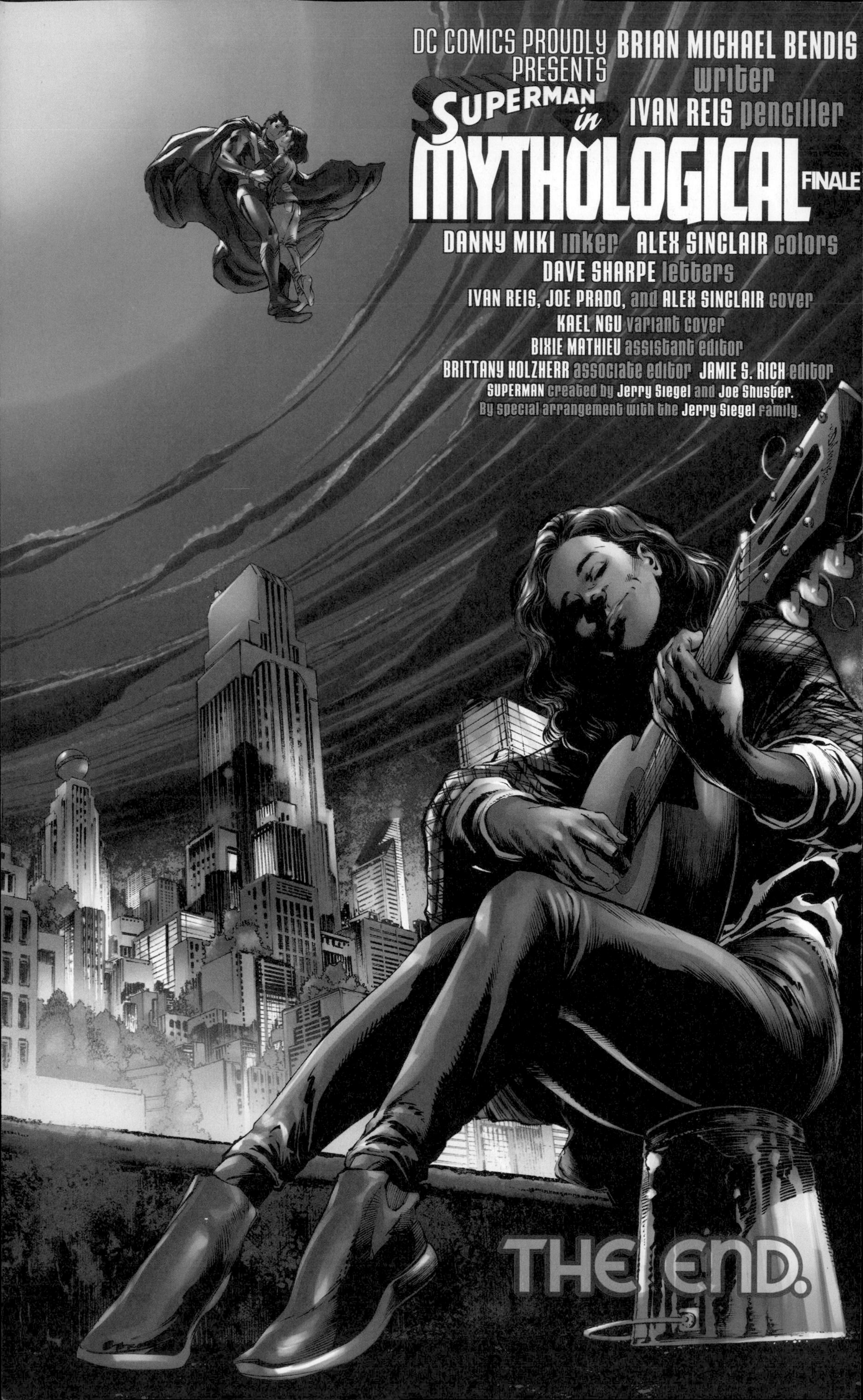

DC COMICS PROUDLY PRESENTS
SUPERMAN in MYTHOLOGICAL FINALE
BRIAN MICHAEL BENDIS writer
IVAN REIS penciller
DANNY MIKI inker ALEX SINCLAIR colors
DAVE SHARPE letters
IVAN REIS, JOE PRADO, and ALEX SINCLAIR cover
KAEL NGU variant cover
BIXIE MATHIEU assistant editor
BRITTANY HOLZHERR associate editor JAMIE S. RICH editor
SUPERMAN created by Jerry Siegel and Joe Shuster.
By special arrangement with the Jerry Siegel family.
THE END.

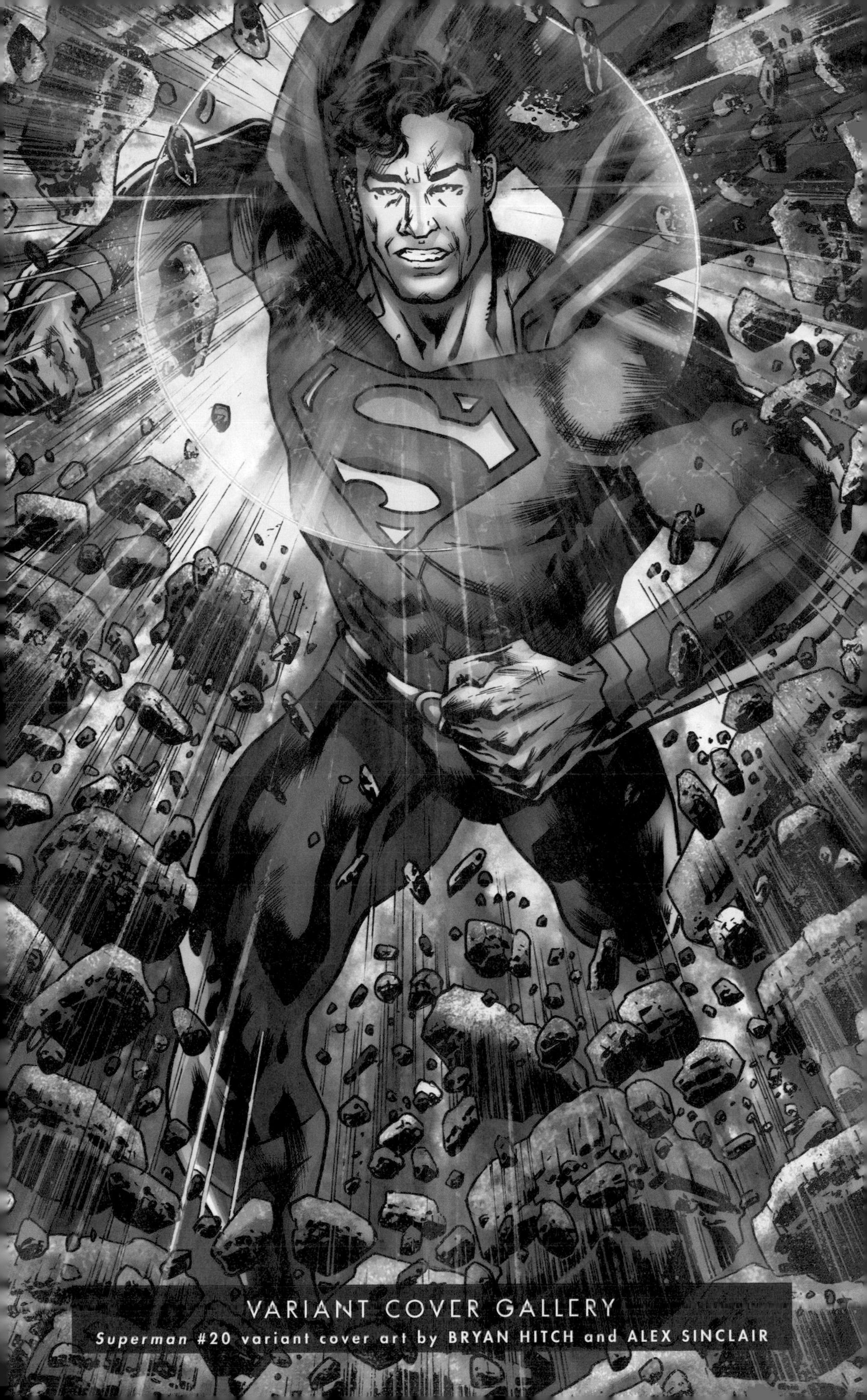

VARIANT COVER GALLERY

Superman #20 variant cover art by **BRYAN HITCH** and **ALEX SINCLAIR**

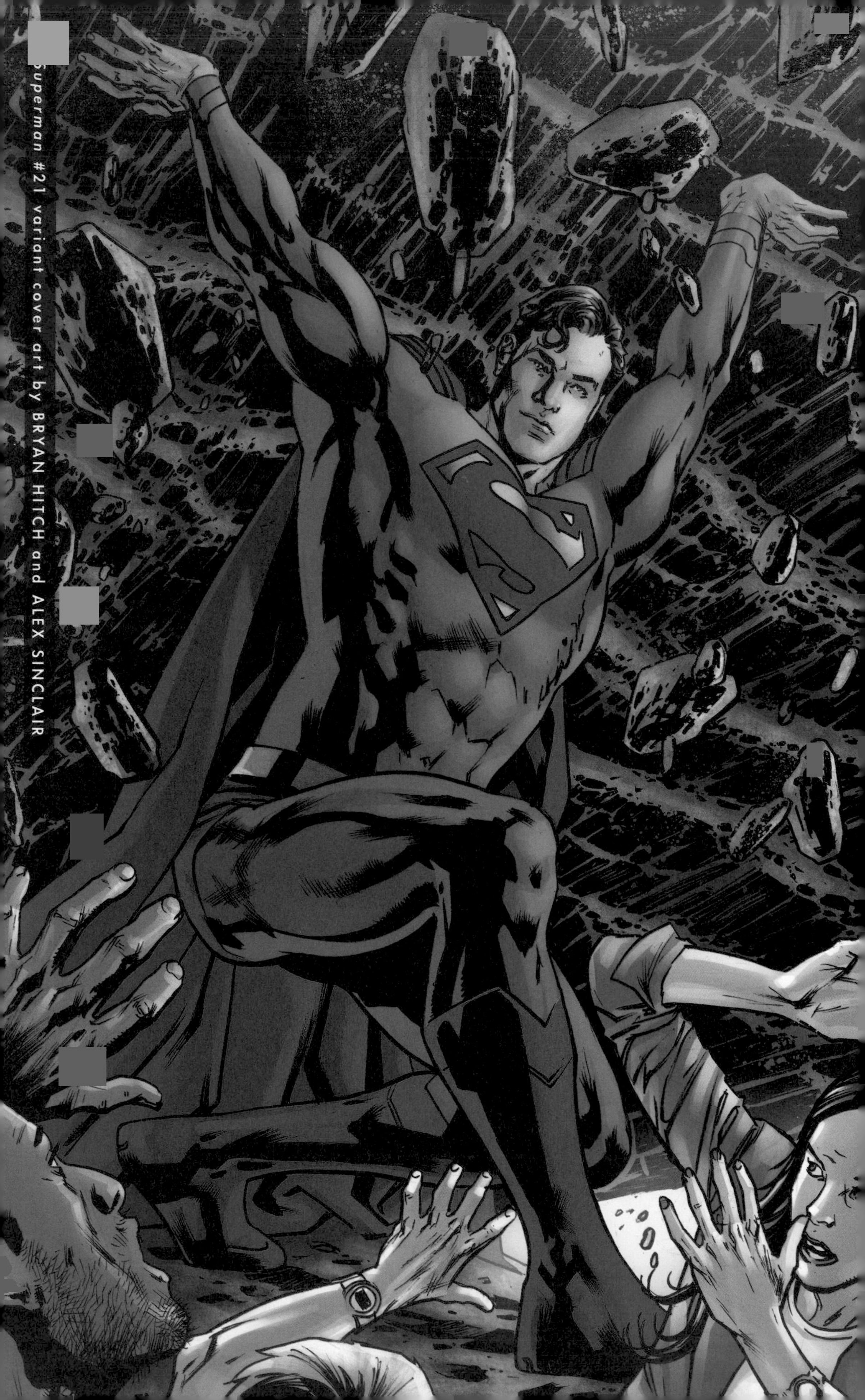

Superman #21 variant cover art by BRYAN HITCH and ALEX SINCLAIR

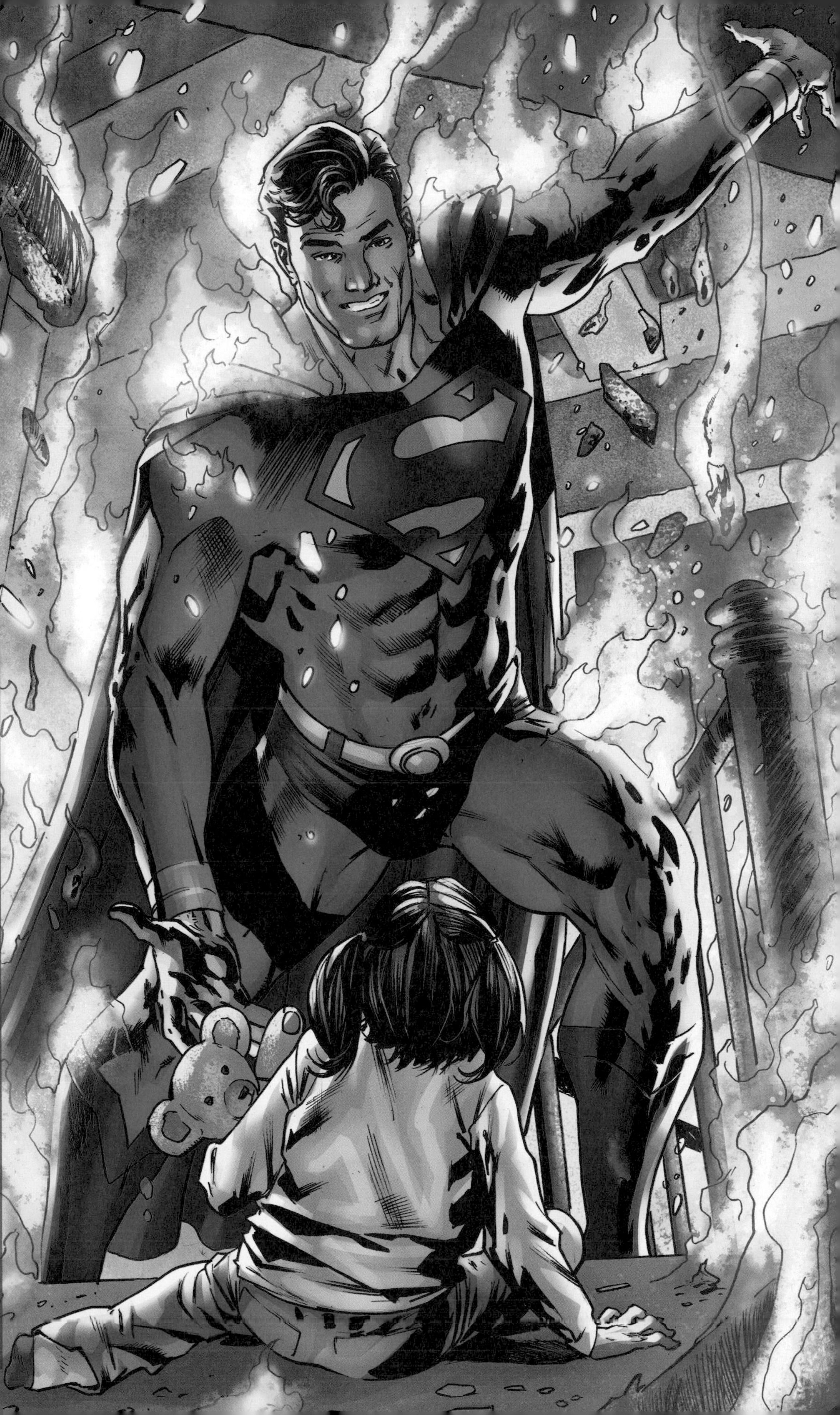

Superman #22 variant cover art by BRYAN HITCH and ALEX SINCLAIR

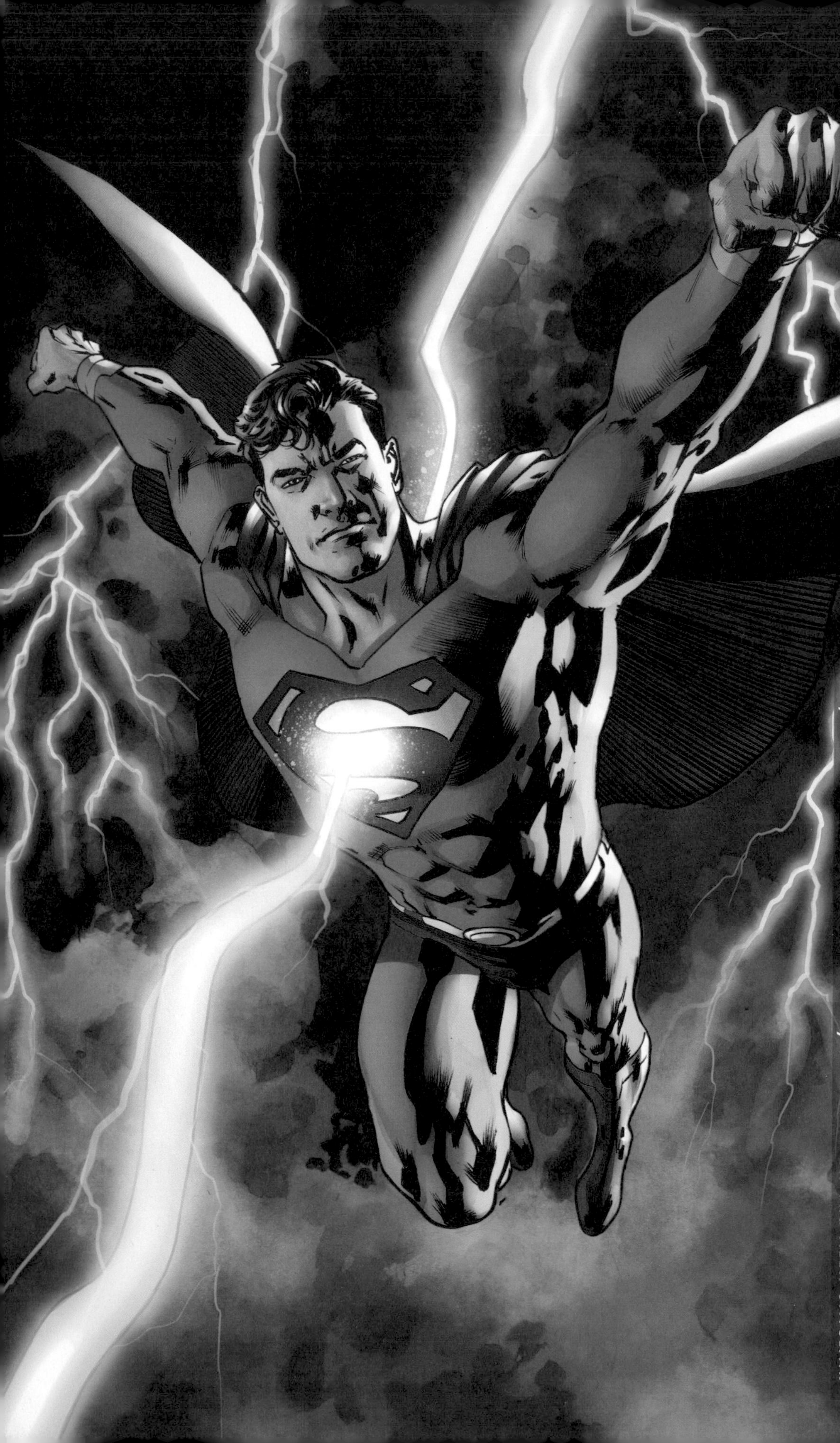

Superman #23 variant cover art by BRYAN HITCH and ALEX SINCLAIR

Superman #24 variant cover art by BRYAN HITCH and ALEX SINCLAIR

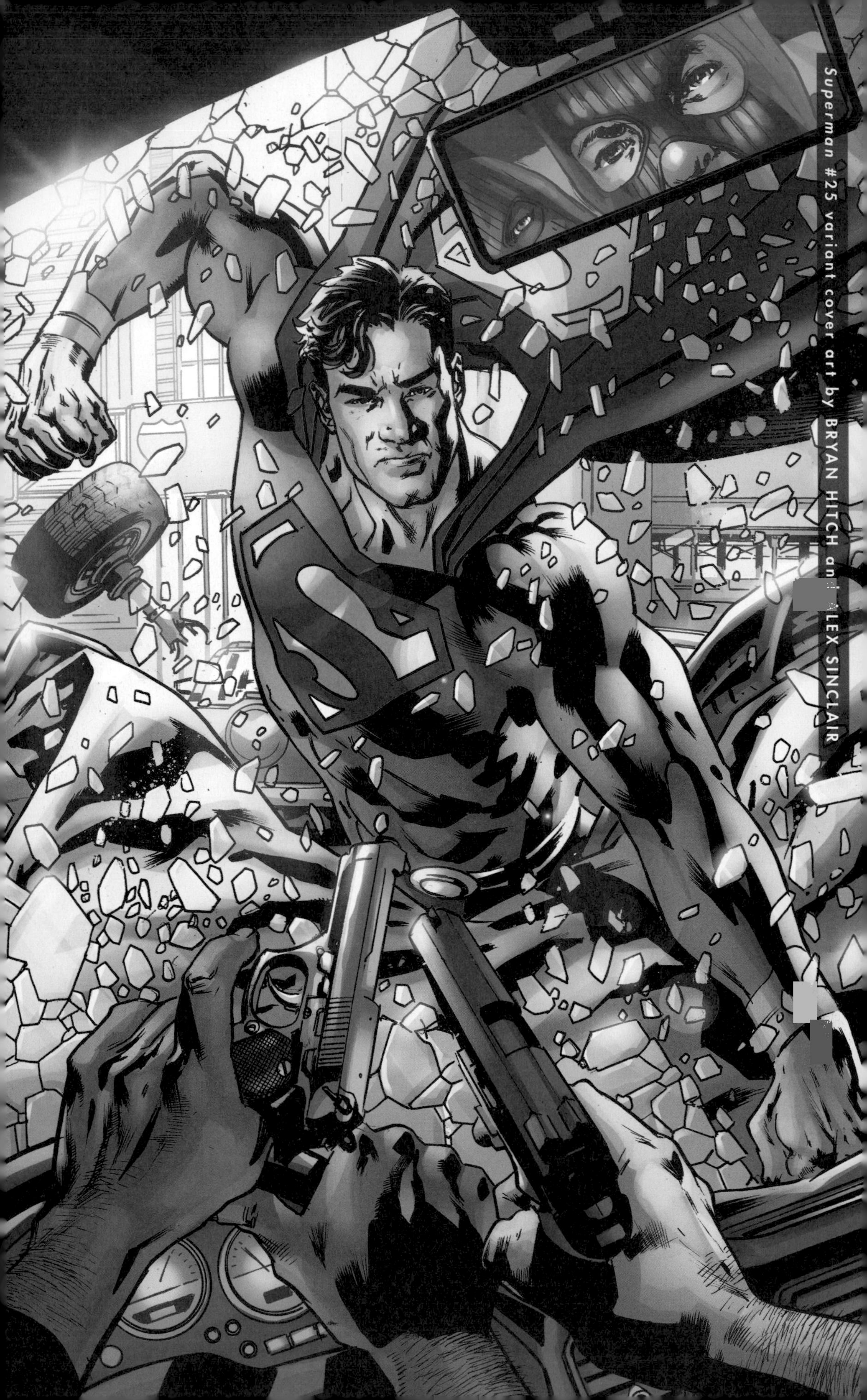

Superman #25 variant cover art by BRYAN HITCH and ALEX SINCLAIR

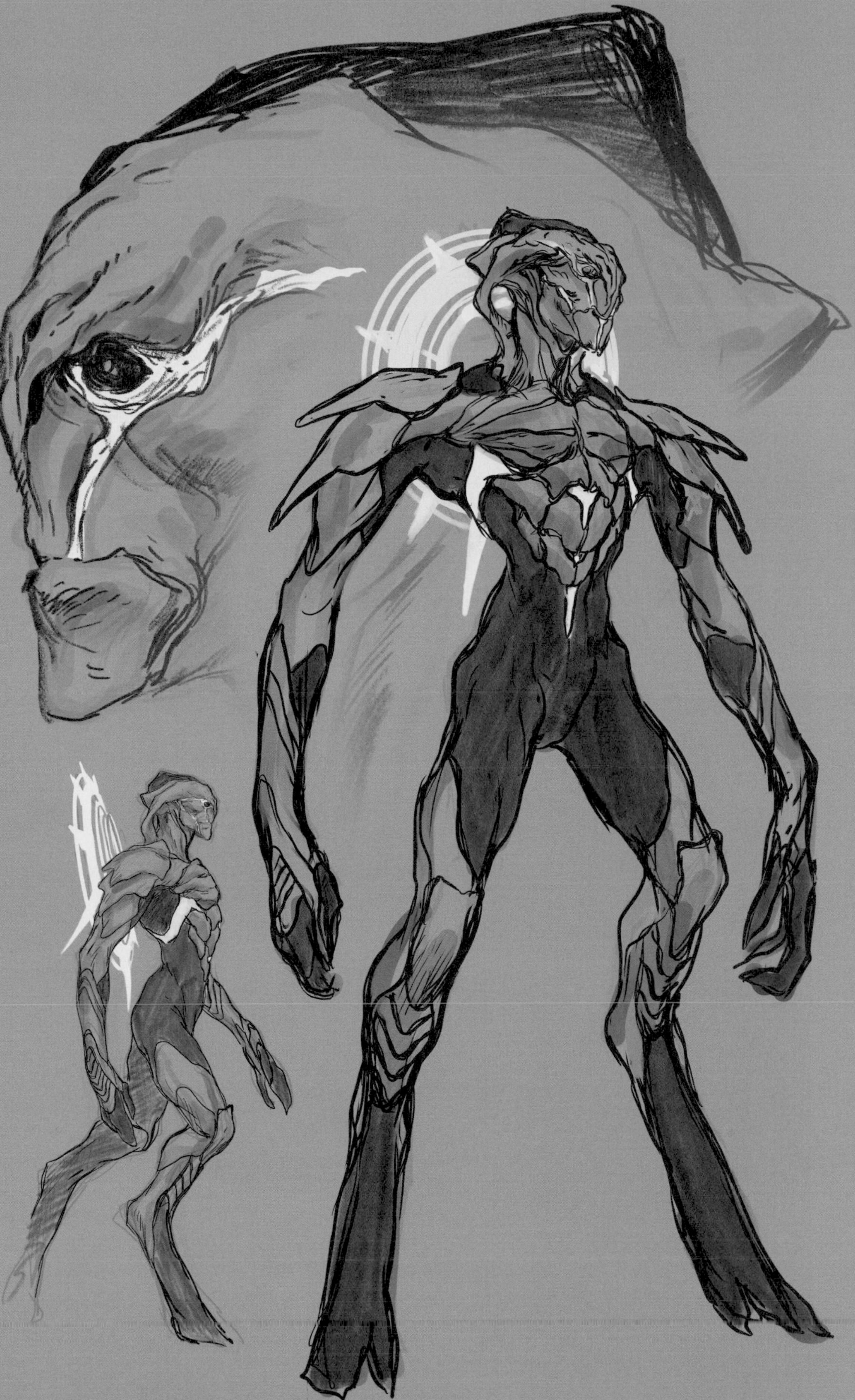

Superman #25 design variant cover art by IVAN REIS

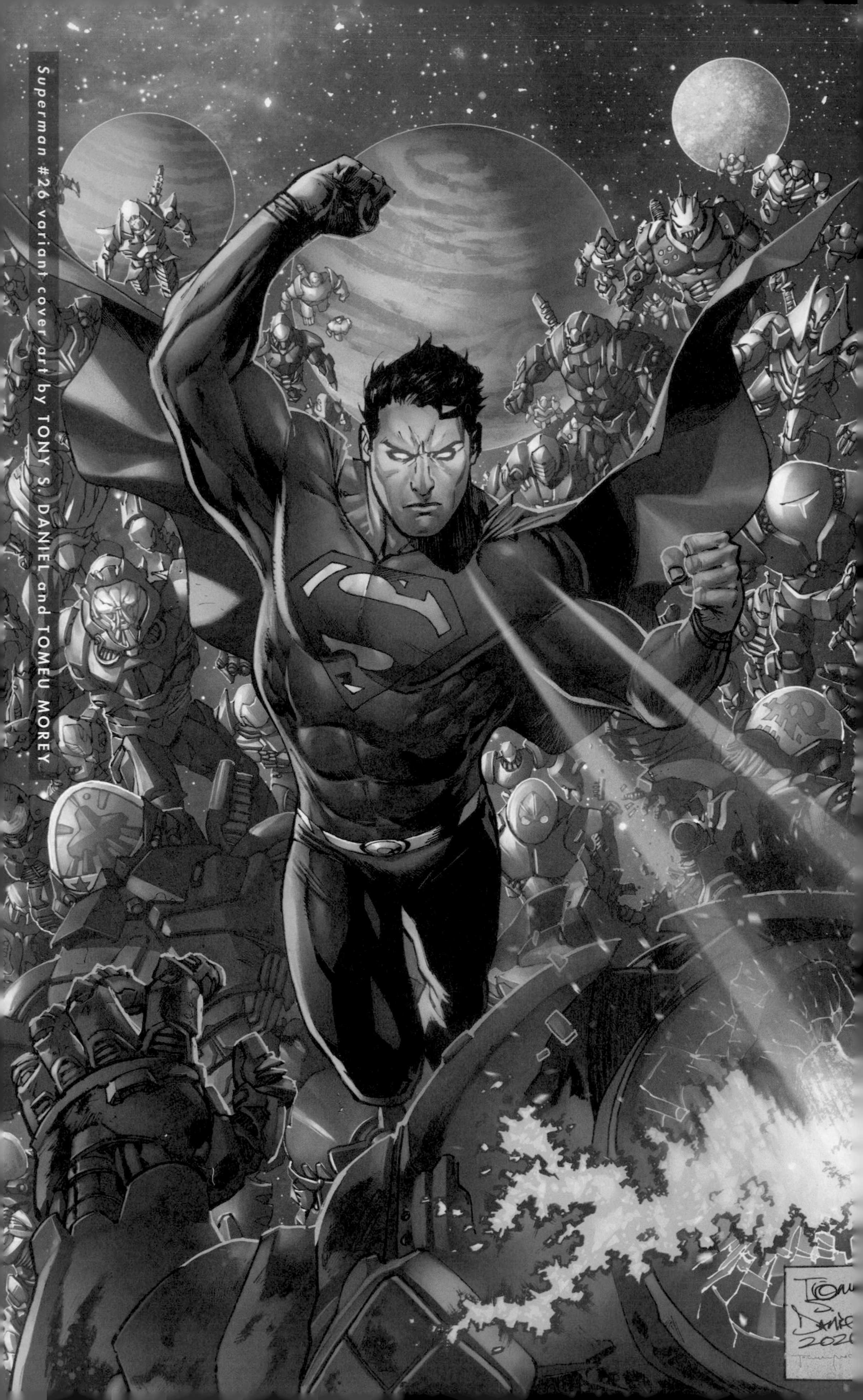

Superman #26 variant cover art by TONY S. DANIEL and TOMEU MOREY

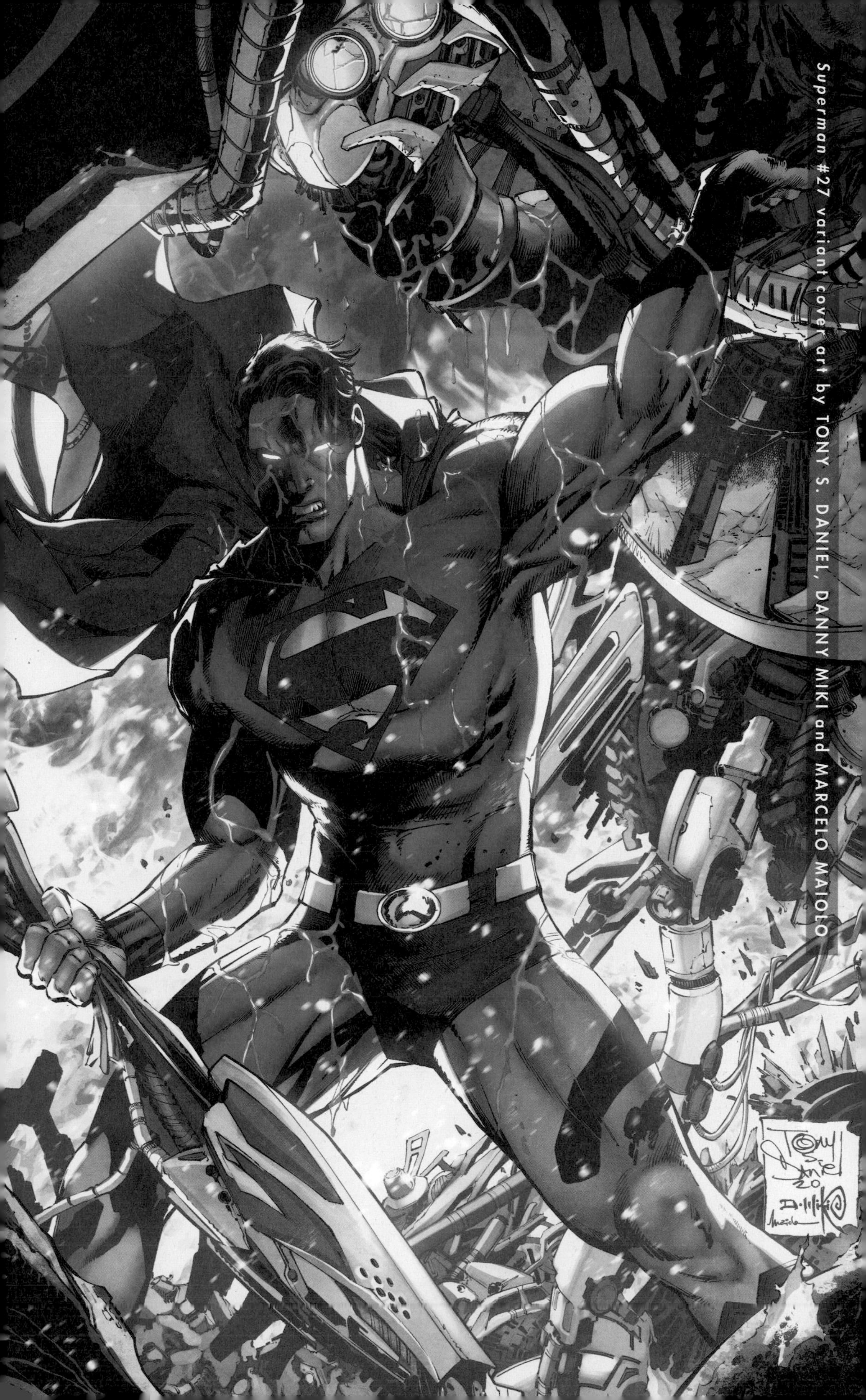

Superman #27 variant cover art by TONY S. DANIEL, DANNY MIKI and MARCELO MAIOLO

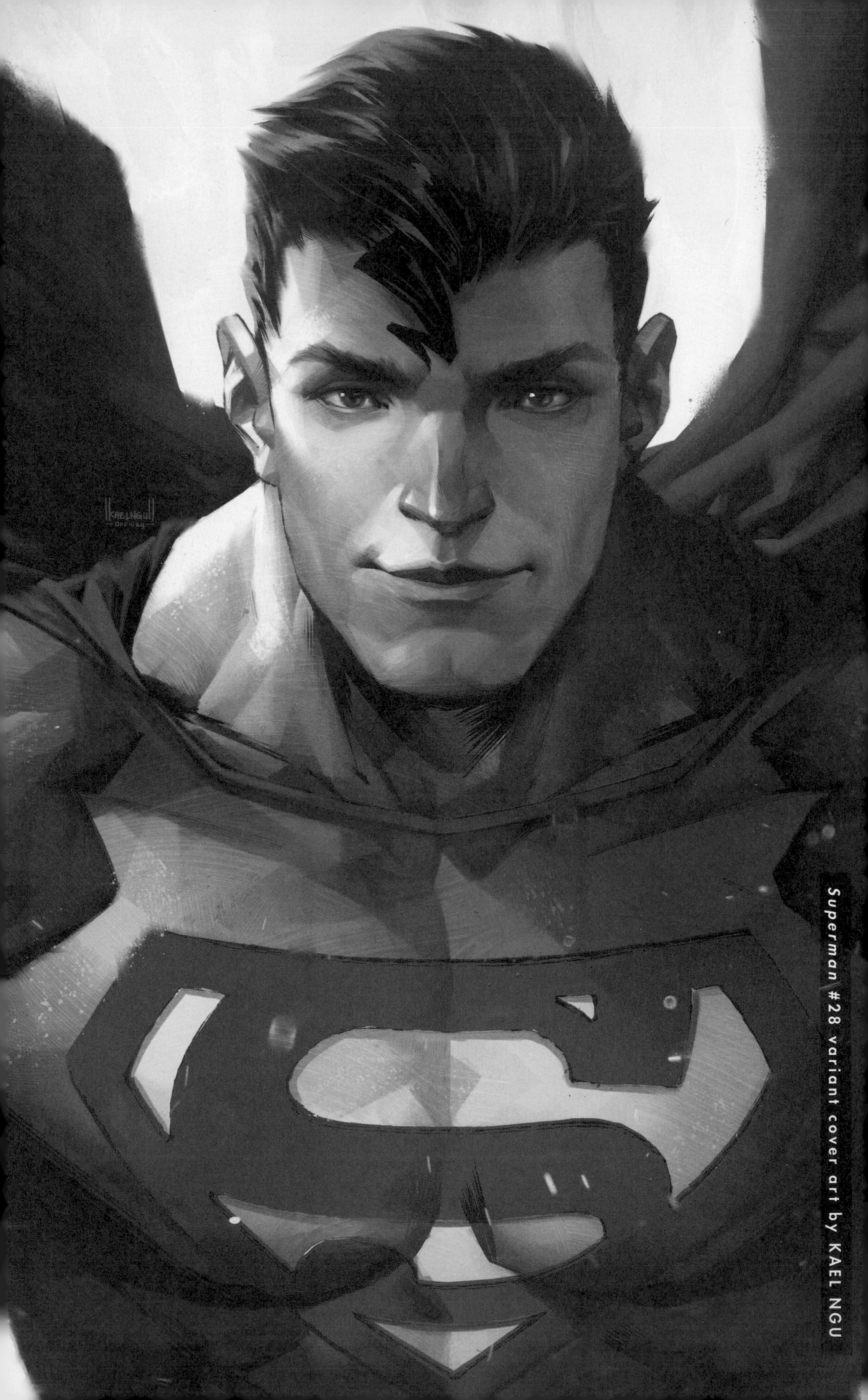

Superman #28 variant cover art by KAEL NGU

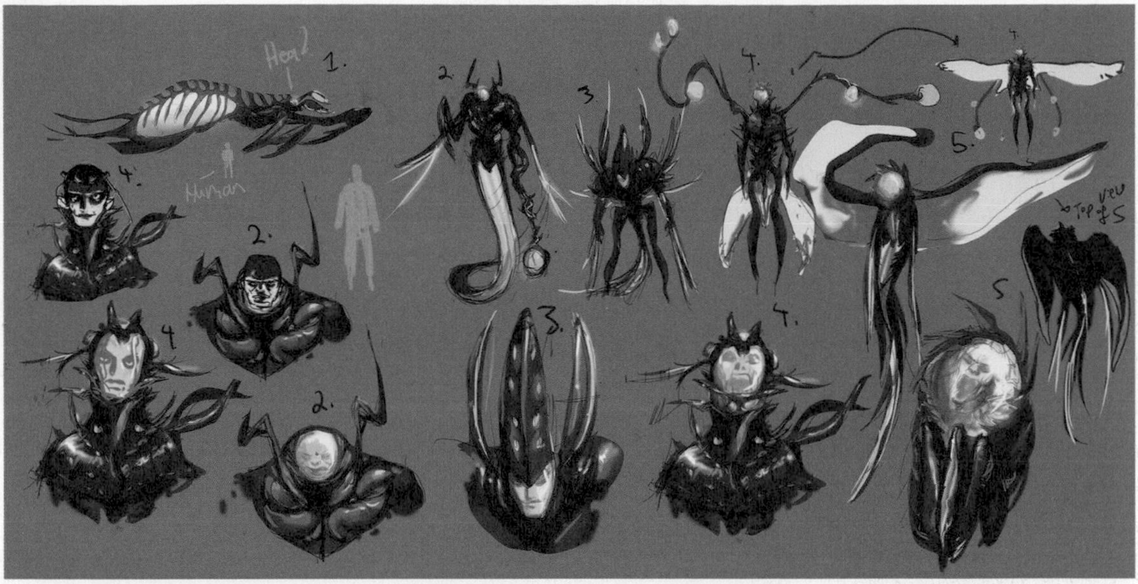
Head
Human

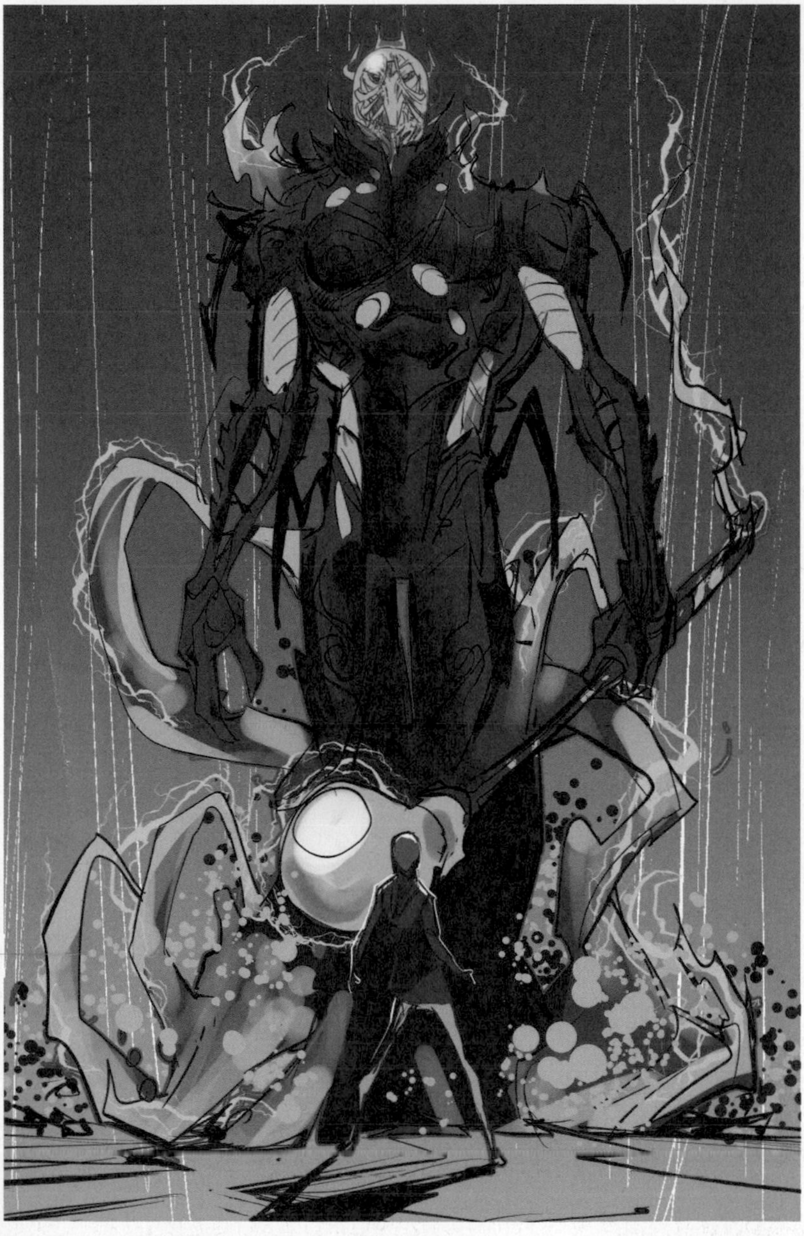

VILLAIN DESIGN GALLERY: **XANADOTH**

Initial Designs by RILEY ROSSMO

Final Look by JOHN TIMMS

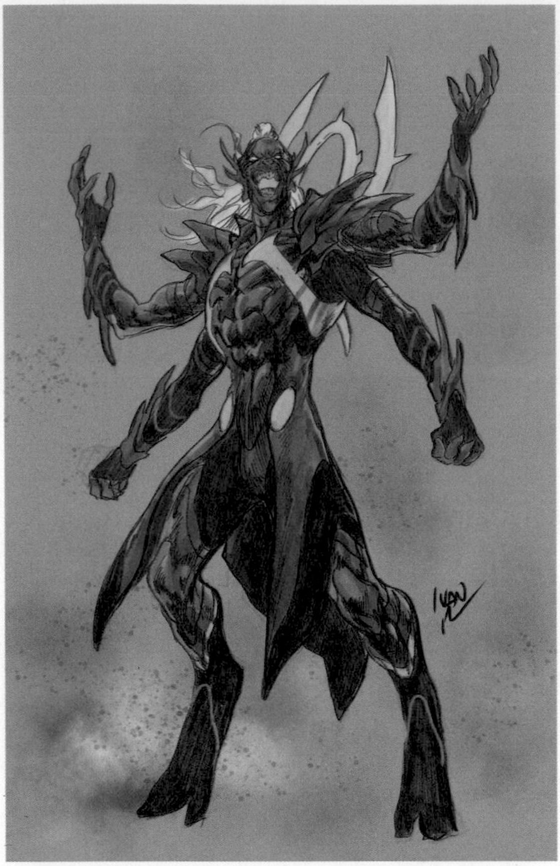
IVAN

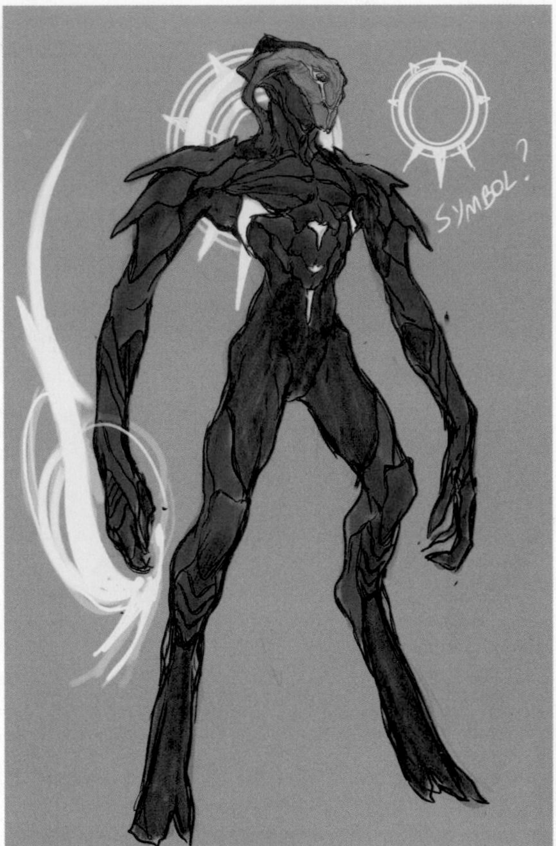
SYMBOL?

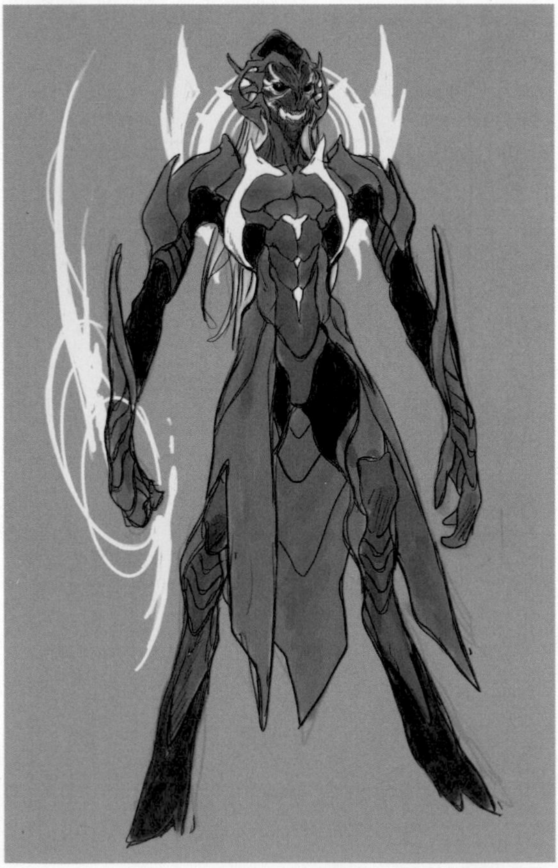

VILLAIN DESIGN GALLERY: **SYNMAR**

Designs by IVAN REIS